The United Nations and
Changing World Politics

THE UNITED NATIONS

AND CHANGING

WORLD POLITICS

FOURTH EDITION

Thomas G. Weiss
The CUNY Graduate Center

David P. Forsythe
University of Nebraska

Roger A. Coate
University of South Carolina

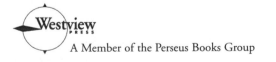

Westview
PRESS
A Member of the Perseus Books Group

Copyright © 2004 by Westview Press, A Member of the Perseus Books Group

Published in 2004 in the United States of America by Westview Press, 5500 Central Avenue, Boulder, Colorado 80301–2877, and in the United Kingdom by Westview Press, 12 Hid's Copse Road, Cumnor Hill, Oxford OX2 9JJ

Visit us on the World Wide Web at www.westviewpress.com

Library of Congress Cataloging-in-Publication Data

Weiss, Thomas George.
    The United Nations and changing world politics / Thomas G. Weiss, David P. Forsythe, and Roger A. Coate.—4th ed.
        p. cm.
    Includes bibliographical references and index.
    ISBN 0–8133–4207–4 (hardcover: alk. paper)
    ISBN 0–8133–4206–6 (paperback: alk. paper)
    1. United Nations. 2. World politics—1989– . I. Forsythe, David P., 1941– .
II. Coate, Roger A. III. Title.
JZ4984.5 .W45 2004
341.23'1—dc22

                                                                                2003025193

The paper used in this publication meets the requirements of the American National Standard for Permanence of Paper for Printed Library Materials Z39.48–1984.

10   9   8   7   6   5   4   3   2   1

Contents

Tables and Illustrations

Foreword to the Second Edition

Inis L. Claude Jr.
Professor Emeritus, University of Virginia

Since the end of the Cold War, the United Nations has enjoyed—and suffered—a burst of unaccustomed prominence. The organization initially gained attention as sponsor of the successful effort to roll back Iraq's conquest of Kuwait. Euphoric expectations of a global collective security apparatus soon gave way to disillusionment as the United Nations became conspicuously involved in disasters in Somalia and Bosnia. In any case, the United Nations is no longer ignored and neglected; whether it is regarded with utopian idealism or with cynical disdain, it has achieved notable visibility.

The organization's revived prominence has continued largely because of the role it has undertaken in dealing with many of the crises that have erupted within states. We no longer hear the United Nations praised or scorned as a talkshop. Rather, evaluations of the organization now relate mainly to what it does, tries to do, or should do or to what it should be equipped to do as an operating agency in the field. The focus of international relations is no longer exclusively interstate but has become predominantly intrastate, and the most significant activity of the United Nations is no longer that occurring at headquarters but that taking place in trouble spots around the globe.

These changes intensify the need for serious study of the United Nations with a view to development of realistic and sophisticated understanding of the nature of the organization, its possibilities and limitations, its merits and defects, the promise that it holds, and the dangers that it poses. Above all, we need to examine the United Nations in its political context, regarding it as essentially an institutional framework within which states make decisions and allocate resources, arranging to do a variety of things with, to, for, and against each other. Americans, in particular, need to escape the illusion that the world organization is some gigantic "it," beneficent or sinister, and to realize that the United Nations is instead a "we"—ourselves and other states. States acting jointly as well as singly are primary members of the cast in the drama of international politics.

The authors of this volume are keenly aware of this reality. Whether they are writing about the use of the United Nations in operations relating to peace and security or its role in protecting human rights and responding to humanitarian needs or its programs in economic and environmental fields, they emphasize its political character. Wisely forgoing the effort to present a comprehensive history of the United Nations and related agencies, they concentrate on the areas in which the United Nations has recently been most actively engaged. In so doing, they illuminate the changes that are sweeping the world in the post–Cold War era and the responding changes in the character of the United Nations and in its agenda. Students who seek a thoughtful analysis of the multilateral aspects of today's international relations will find it here. The book effectively conveys the thoughts of three well-qualified scholars; even better, it informs and stimulates the reader to develop his or her own thinking on the subject. I stand by the proposition that I enunciated a generation ago: The United Nations has too many supporters and opponents and too few students. May their tribe increase!

Foreword to the Third Edition

Leon Gordenker

Professor Emeritus, Princeton University,
Center of International Studies

As this is written, soldiers wearing patches indicating participation in a mission for the United Nations have been taken captive in Sierra Leone. From Lebanon, where the Israeli military has just withdrawn from its so-called security zone, voices call for a strengthened presence by the United Nations to ensure tranquillity. Ironically, for more than forty years, spokesmen on both sides of that border have often vilified UN activities, and on many occasions actions rendered peacekeeping ineffective. In New York, the five main nuclear powers complemented an existing nonproliferation treaty, worked out thirty years ago by the United Nations, by pledging to eliminate nuclear weapons. In Washington, renewed obstacles in the U.S. Senate to paying a financial obligation for UN membership ensure continuing penury for the organization to which almost every country of every conceivable size and capacity belongs. In Geneva, in meeting rooms that date back to the League of Nations, a gathering of experts on human rights pores over reports to the United Nations. The intrusiveness of their discussion into national domains would have made the nationalistic hair of old-school diplomats stand up in shock. A covey of representatives from nongovernmental organizations intensely follows the proceedings for which they provide information. In East Timor, a UN mission offers help with the construction of a government.

On many a day during the last fifty-five years such a paragraph about UN activities could have been written. And, as now, it would have ignored more than it disclosed.

The United Nations, then, is a fact of our global life. To say so is not a defense of the organization, a claim about its worthiness, or a denunciation. It rather signals a need to understand this fact, to explain its boundaries, to fit it with other facts of contemporary life. This book, by three authors who have been close observers and students of, and participants in, several UN activities, fills that need.

The authors do not pretend to relate everything that could be known about the UN system. To begin with, UN history, spanning more than half a century, has been anything but fully compiled. And it is as complex as the world around it. Other parts of the story remain cloistered in inaccessible governmental and organizational archives.

The UN decisionmaking process includes some of the best and worst practices of international diplomacy and parliamentary procedure. Much of it consists of painstaking searches for agreement on texts on which representatives of many governments can agree. This effort involves speech-making that can be incomprehensible to the untutored onlooker. Some of the keys to understanding can be found in the usually bland published documents prepared by international civil servants in the name of the UN Secretary-General. Outside the meeting rooms, guarded informal encounters, instructions from national capitals that remain secret, and sometimes flamboyant nationalistic demands complement the public proceedings.

The words that set out what is agreed, encoded in diplomatic language and the catch phrases of international law, themselves guarantee little. They have to be applied by governments, most of which, it is sad to admit, either routinely avoid giving the words the fullest execution or do not have the means to do so. But words, as the Universal Declaration of Human Rights illustrates, can have lasting and even profound effects on what governments and their subjects do.

As the book suggests, no single theory provides a shortcut to understanding all of this. Some of the simpler theoretical approaches, much loved by muscle flexers, simply fail to explain much. Nor do analytical frameworks that concentrate on claims of national interests as seen from the perspectives of national capitals. Beyond the UN institutions, moreover, lies an increasingly complex, intertwined set of extragovernmental practices, organizations, and communications channels that help shape the UN agenda.

Instead of an encyclopedic approach or an abstract sketch, this book highlights three of the most important sectors of UN concern—peace and security, human rights, and sustainable development and environmental protection. As a result of digging deeply in those sectors, some of the main historical developments also emerge. Policy issues are clearly posed, the nature of the UN process comes into view. Some nuanced judgments about success and failure are drawn.

At the same time, the demand for a third edition of this book makes clear that as a totality the book admirably introduces its subject. Moreover, it opens doors to more inquiry. Why is the UN system so complex? How does it match and diverge from the actual world around it? Is it paralyzed by its own diplomatic culture? Can it be counted on to continue to develop? Can it, and should it, have a greater influence on international relations generally? What encourages that development and what holds it back? For that matter, is the institution's form, built around the concept of national sovereignty and parliamentary and diplomatic procedures, increasingly obsolete in a world that each day less resembles that of 1945, when the United Nations was created?

If the responses to such questions remain uncertain, cause controversy, and seem beyond terse summaries, avoiding them will not make them disappear. They challenge imagination, bedevil statesmen, intrigue scholars, and ultimately condition our future as they have affected our past. In providing an analytical and historical framework for understanding where the United Nations has been, Weiss, Forsythe, and Coate provide the foundation for understanding where its future may lie.

Foreword to the Fourth Edition

James O. C. Jonah

Senior Fellow, Ralph Bunche Institute for International Studies
UN Under-Secretary-General (ret.)

Supporters and defenders of the United Nations system have often bemoaned the fact that despite the commendable contribution that it continues to make in the alleviation of human suffering and the promotion of social and economic developments and human rights, the UN is often dismissed as a failure or irrelevant due to its perceived shortcomings in maintaining international peace and security. Although this concern is unfortunate, it is understandable that the general public should measure the success or relevance of the world organization in terms of its political and security preoccupation. After all, the UN Charter proclaims loudly that its central goal is to prevent succeeding generations from the scourge of war. The gloom surrounding the UN's future is particularly noticeable in the aftermath of the War in Iraq as this book goes to press in January 2004.

The fact that this is the fourth edition of *The United Nations and Changing World Politics* speaks volumes about why the book has been so successful. It presents an unusually well-informed and comprehensive analysis of what the UN has undertaken and achieved in the past fifty-seven years. They also have not shied away from the failures by both parts of what they label "the two United Nations," the arena where states make decisions and the secretariat that executes many of them. The three authors— Thomas G. Weiss, David P. Forsythe, and Roger A. Coate—include a former UN staff member, and they are all keen observers of the UN system. Their title is apt, for they have presented a clear and thoughtful analysis of the manner in which changing world politics has had an impact on the performance, problems, and prospects of the world organization. The publication of this new edition provides a wealth of knowledge to enable scholars, students, and commentators to better understand the factors that account for the present dilemma with which the United Nations is confronted.

While the end of the Cold War has resulted in the emergence of a sole superpower with a predisposition to project military power, preemptively or otherwise, the fundamentals for understanding the UN have not changed. No matter what one's ideological views, the willingness and determination of major powers to change regimes that they do not like is nothing new. The U.S. and the then Soviet Union, with varying justifications, successfully conducted regime changes without much concern for the UN Charter. The only difference is that what was once done covertly is now pronounced publicly. Students of history know that the implication of the Yalta Agreements, as reflected in the Charter, placed the five permanent members (P-5) virtually above the provisions of the organization's constitution. Accordingly, only a naïve observer could believe that the Security Council could prevent one of the permanent members from pursuing what it considered to be of supreme importance to its national interests. You do not have to be the hyperpower to ignore the Security Council, you only have to be one of the five.

Inis Claude, in justifying the useful role of the veto in the Security Council, observed that its use is an indication of a deadlock in the council that requires serious negotiations among the permanent members.[1] What has been hoped for over the years was that the P-5 would exercise maximum restraint, refrain from excessive use of the veto, and respect the decent and clearly expressed opinion of humankind. Even though Charter principles limit the use of force, they do permit it under certain circumstances, especially as set out in Article 51. But as was evident in the case of the first Gulf War of 1991, the council authorized the use of force by the so-called "coalition of the willing" to remove Iraqi forces from Kuwait. The Security Council took this action not because of the overwhelming influence of the only superpower—at the time, U.S. primacy had already become clear—but because of the unprecedented behavior of Iraq. For the first time since the Charter was agreed to in San Francisco in 1945, a sovereign member of the organization (Kuwait) was wiped off the map. Therefore, even the natural allies of Iraq were critical of its action and called for intervention by the Security Council. It was this unanimous international revulsion against Baghdad's behavior that may have led President George H. W. Bush to declare, somewhat prematurely, the existence of the "new world order."

The painful debate in the Security Council in the winter of 2003 over the use of force in Iraq, or more precisely over the issue of preemption and regime change, should draw our attention to the reality that nothing fundamentally has changed. Despite its status as the only superpower, the United States could not override concerns of the other members of the Security Council over its policy in Iraq. Apart from the UK and Spain, which were the other co-sponsors of the draft resolution, other members of the council were prepared to give more time to the UN inspectors to determine the existence of weapons of mass destruction (WMD) in Iraq. It is unrealistic to argue that the only superpower could compel the United Nations to do what the majority of the member states did not wish to undertake. Even the way and manner in which Washington projects its power should be placed in context. Would the United States have succeeded in changing the regime in Afghanistan without full cooperation of Pakistan and other states in the periphery of Afghanistan? Or would the U.S.-UK coalition have succeeded in Iraq without the cooperation of states in the area that allowed the deployment of coalition forces in their countries in preparation for the commencement of the campaign?

With the view of implementing their policy on oil-for-food as well as the modalities of their administration of postwar Iraq, both Washington and London understood that they had to bring along other members of the Security Council in order to obtain its blessing. [2] This is a good illustration that the Security Council is not dead.[3]

The obituaries have been premature. It has always been the case that member states, particularly the P-5, will willingly resort to the Security Council or other organs of the United Nations if they believe that they can obtain support for their policies.

The disagreement in the council over Iraq further raises three issues that are discussed in the book and need further emphasis here. The first is the nature of international politics. Whether one likes it or not, balance of power still functions in international politics. U.S. preponderance of power will certainly provoke the creation of a coalition to balance that superpower. It should, therefore, come as no surprise that three permanent members, France, Russia, China, together with Germany, have made serious attempts to restrain U.S. power by using the Security Council. This should only surprise those who have argued that the concept of balance of power is dead. This natural tendency could not be stopped by threats or insults—it is inevitable. For Washington to win support for its position and policy, it should be mindful of what the prominent historian Louis J. Halle once referred to as the "economy of power." The United States has to come to grips with the reality that "the consent enjoyed by a great power tends to diminish when its force is used in ways that are regarded as illegitimate whether against a small or another great power."[4]

The second issue that needs further elucidation is the role of the secretariat and its head, the Secretary-General. Too often, commentators of the United Nations have played down the role of the secretariat, forgetting that it is one of the six main organs of the United Nations. Although the Secretary-General is its head, the secretariat has its own esprit de corps and is grounded in the concept of an international civil service. What was clear in the Security Council debate over the implementation of Resolution 1441 in November 2002, which created a legal-diplomatic framework for dealing with Iraq, was the role of the inspectors. Under the new dispensation of the UN Monitoring, Verification and Inspection Commission (UNMOVIC), they were bona fide international civil servants. They stood in stark contrast to the earlier inspection units, the UN Special Commission (UNSCOM), which was based on the concept of "loaned officers."[5] The majority of the council's members displayed confidence in UNMOVIC inspectors and were prepared to rely on their judgment before deciding whether the use of force was necessary. Here was a case where war and peace were to be determined by the independence of the world organization's civil servants. And it is to the credit of UNMOVIC that despite threats and browbeating, the inspectors stood their ground and informed the council that while they had not obtained full cooperation of the Iraqi officials, they were not prepared to make a definitive judgment that there existed material breach that justified war.

Moreover, the leadership of the Secretary-General is crucial. Regrettably, we have reached a stage where some commentators and officials are saying that because of the existence of one superpower, the Secretary-General should accommodate himself to that new reality. Such comments take little cognizance of the history of the United Nations. At the most acute stage of the Cold War, within the halls of the General Assembly, Secretary-General Dag Hammarskjöld was publicly challenged by Soviet Premier Nikita Khrushchev, the leader of the era's second superpower. Hammarskjöld did not bend to the threat and insults but rose in defense of his office and the necessary independence of the international civil service. Accordingly, at that crucial stage of the UN's history, Moscow was promoting the concept of a three-headed monster, a troika, instead of a single leader. This would have definitely destroyed the United Nations. It was the courageous leadership of Hammarskjöld in his opposition to that proposal that ensured the United Nations' survival.

During the conflict in Iraq, it was unusual that the Secretary-General, although he had indicated his opposition to the war, kept quiet during the period of intense bombing when civilian lives were lost. While the Archbishop of Canterbury and the Pope were outspoken, nothing was heard from the thirty-eighth floor of UN headquarters. When the Secretary-General did finally speak, it was too late. Is it too much to expect to have a truly independent Secretary-General? One major obstacle is the practice of campaigning for the office. Undoubtedly, this has changed the nature of the position and has made it vulnerable to great-power control and influence. To prevent such an outcome, the proposal has often been made to limit an individual to hold a one term of seven years.

The third issue that is not explicitly discussed in the book but is implied in many of its sections is the availability of accurate and independent information for the Security Council to make wise decisions. Mention has already been made of the council's reliance on UNMOVIC inspectors. Within the Secretariat there were attempts to obtain reliable and timely information by independent channels by establishing the Office for Research and the Collection of Information (ORCI) in 1987, but there was no linkage with the Security Council except for the responsibility of the Secretary-General under Article 99 of the Charter. The topic that has now resurfaced is the prominence and accuracy of information provided by member states.

The art of "spinning" has developed to such an extent that it is becoming increasingly difficult to discern facts from fiction, and the council has become victim to this. It is in this sense that members were reluctant to take at face value U.S. Secretary of State Colin Powell's presentation to the council in February 2003. In this context one must not forget what UK Prime Minister Winston Churchill said during World War II: "In war time, truth is so precious that she should always be attended by a bodyguard of lies."[6]

The authors of this volume have done a commendable service by providing the crucial ingredients for a better appreciation of the United Nations in all its diverse aspects and phases. Unlike most textbooks, this collaboration by Weiss, Forsythe, and Coate provides a theoretically and conceptually rich text that is also readable and informed by concrete activities by the world organization. This is "must" reading for anyone interested in the United Nations.

Among other things, and I stress this in concluding, the United Nations has gone through several phases when it was alternatively warmly embraced, viewed with profound skepticism and disenchantment, and viewed as the convenient punching bag by ill-informed critics. There is, therefore, no need for panic or despair concerning the travail of the world body after the U.S.-led invasion of Iraq. Nevertheless, the process of realistic reforms of the institution should proceed, particularly with respect to the Security Council. We now know that there is urgent need to revisit the use of the veto and the expansion of the Security Council to bring in Japan, Germany, and representatives of Africa, Asia, and Latin America. The financing of the organization should be on firmer ground, aimed at making the assessment of contribution more fair and equitable. For a greater part of the history of the United Nations, there was a struggle for universality; now we have obtained universality of membership. The difficult task ahead is to convince the general membership that this valuable institution belongs to all of its members and not just those that are powerful and affluent.

Notes

1. Inis L. Claude Jr., *Power and International Relations* (New York: Random House, 1962), pp. 158–165.

2. UN document S/PV.4644, 2002.

3. See, for example, Michael Glennon, "Why the Security Council Failed," *Foreign Affairs* 82, no. 3 (May–June 2003), pp. 16–35.

4. Louis J. Halle, *Civilization and Foreign Policy* (New York: Harper Brothers Publishers, 1955), p. 81.

5. For a discussion, see Jean E. Krasno and James S. Sutterlin, *The United Nations and Iraq: Defanging the Viper* (Westport, Conn. Praeger, 2003).

6. Quoted by Anthony Cave Brown, *Bodyguard of Lies*, Volume I (New York: Harper & Row, 1975), p. 11.

Preface to the Fourth Edition

As the name implies, *The United Nations and Changing World Politics* is about the United Nations (UN) system and the role of the UN and its associated family of specialized agencies in global governance. Writing a preface for this fourth edition is both encouraging and discouraging. As authors we are delighted that so many colleagues and students have found it to be a useful book. In an age with ever-decreasing shelf lives for examinations of contemporary events, we also have been gratified to verify that our original analyses and structure held up well to subsequent events from 1994 through 2003. The three organizing themes in this volume—international peace and security, human rights and humanitarian action, and sustainable human development—continue to provide plenty of grist for analytical and policy mills of the post–post–Cold War world. It was of course necessary to update information and correct minor errors, but readers of the fourth edition will recognize much of its predecessors here.

At the same time, we can hardly be encouraged by the fortunes in the interim of the world organization itself and of multilateralism more generally. As discussed in the pages that follow, the United Nations has in many ways been on a roller-coaster ride since the end of the Cold War, especially in the area of peace and security. Moreover, by 2003 it continued to teeter on the brink of financial insolvency. The UN's chronic financial difficulties were only partially improved by the U.S.'s payment of past dues in the wake of the attacks in New York and Washington on September 11, 2001, by Al Qaeda. Washington, wanting UN endorsement for its security concerns, quickly showed what had been true all along regarding its payments to the UN—namely that the issue was less about money and more about symbolic politics. In general the United States had withheld UN payments because it objected to UN independent policies that deviated from Washington's preferences and challenged its unfettered sovereignty.

We are not card-carrying members of the UN fan club, but we remain persuaded that something like the world organization would have to be created if the present one ceased to exist. In spite of dire predictions, this remains true after the decision by Washington and London to pursue the war in Iraq without Security Council approval. Hence, we have endeavored first and foremost to capture the essence of the United Nations as a political organization caught in the struggle to make public policy through the exercise of power. We stress how representatives of member states and other actors seek to use UN symbols and procedures to shape policy. Those actors do not approach the UN only or even primarily in terms of peace and justice. They may give some attention to these abstract values, but they are primarily driven by their own values, needs, and interests. Indeed, a classic study of the UN and the great powers concluded that conceptions of immediate interests, not long-term and abstract concerns for peace and justice, have been the most important factors in shaping UN activities.[1]

Policymaking always involves power, understood as a synonym for influence. We also observe how UN structure and processes constrain the exercise of power. Hard power is coercion through manipulation of economic resources and through military force. Soft power is persuasion and pressure through words and symbolic acts. The central question for those interested in the United Nations is: Who seeks what policy objective, using what power, and with what outcome? What occurs at the UN, to paraphrase Harold Lasswell, is about who governs across national boundaries and who gets what, when, how.[2]

From another view the United Nations is about global governance without a world government, or about how transnational problems can be collectively managed in the absence of the "normal" attributes of government. These attributes include a true legislature, a single executive branch, an integrated court system, and, above all, a legitimate monopoly on the exercise of force. Our primary objective is to get students to understand the UN as part of the fabric of world politics.

We also wanted to capture the essence of public international law as an institution that exerts real influence on real political struggles. We emphasize that, like all public law, international law is not a technical subject independent of politics but rather part and parcel of world politics. International law is formulated through a political process, frequently centering on the United Nations. Consequently, international law interacts with world politics, sometimes shaping it greatly and sometimes only slightly or not at all.

Whatever its ultimate impact on a given policy or situation, international law is influential in UN proceedings. Indeed, the world organization is a construction of international law because the UN Charter is a multilateral treaty. The ever-present, often subtle, influence of international law is perhaps better understood by those who practice politics at the UN than by many academics observing the process from the outside. We want readers to understand how international law interacts with "pure" politics; how attention to international legal rules (reflecting formalized policy) interacts with subsequent considerations of policy and power.

Moreover, we want to stress the importance of history. The present and the future have a history. When seemingly new issues arise, there is almost always a background to the issue that affects its management or disposition. When U.S. Secretary of State Colin Powell spoke at the UN Security Council in early 2003 about whether Iraq had complied with previous council resolutions demanding a certain disarmament, many commentators referred to the council in 1962. Then, U.S. Representative Adlai Stevenson dramatically confronted the Soviet Union over the issue of Soviet missiles in Cuba. It turned out that in 2003 the United States did not have the kind of compelling evidence—the "smoking gun"—of denied weapons activity presented some forty years earlier. Still, UN history was part of the drama for Powell's presentation. History does not necessarily determine the future, but history often affects the future. The history of such issues as using force, coordinating humanitarian assistance, or promoting sustainable development affects new policy decisions. We want readers to know the political and legal history of the UN so that present and future choices can be analyzed and debated against that background.

The notion of change has long bedeviled social scientists. We have found it easier to chart the past than to understand the full implications of current issues, or where policy decisions on those issues may take us in the future. Nevertheless, we want to try to say as much as we can about change in world politics and what this might mean for the future of the United Nations. We do not pretend to possess privileged knowledge of the future, but we do want to encourage and guide readers to look at several ways of understanding the political changes that drive events in the UN system.

We have intentionally kept discussion of social science theories to a minimum. One can certainly use UN affairs to test some of the major schools of thought that seek a shortcut to, or a parsimonious understanding of, the essentials of international relations. For a different audience we could discuss whether realism, liberalism, constructivism, Marxism, or some other theory helped explain developments at the UN. But to test the validity of each of those theories, and others, one needs a detailed knowledge of UN debates, resolutions, and field operations. We wanted to present an analytical summary of the detailed UN record here, unencumbered by devotion to one theoretical preference or a survey of all.

Moreover, the number of theoretical options is great, encompassing, in addition to the above, others such as feminism and functionalism. Still further, we know that major schools of thought have numerous subschools. Scholars have shown that there are many varieties of realists, liberals, and Marxists. Furthermore, there is much debate about the boundary between realism and liberalism. Some users of our third edition thought that we showed great sensitivity to power politics, which would seem to make us some type of realist. But other users saw our work as reflecting some type of institutional and state-centered liberalism. When the United States utilized the UN in 2002 regarding Afghanistan, was this an example of realism—because the UN was used to maximize state power? Or did Washington's policy reflect liberalism—because there was attention to international law? We consciously chose to avoid much of this theoretical debate with our eclectic and a-theoretical approach. At the same time, we would be only too happy to participate in theoretical discussions at another time and place. Already we use some "middle range" theories in this book—for example, how knowledge affects power and policy, whether one can get to peace by the "back door" of functional cooperation, whether democracies comprise a peaceful security community.

We have endeavored to design this book so that it can be used in at least two ways. First, we want it to serve as a core text in college courses on international organization and the United Nations. Second, we want it to be useful as supplemental reading in other courses, such as international relations and international law. Thus we have sought to present the essentials of politics at the UN in three central arenas: security, human rights, and sustainable human development.

We selected these areas not only because of their intrinsic importance in world politics but also because the United Nations has had significant normative and operational impacts in all three. But we have not tried to write everything we know about the UN. For example in this new edition, we have not discussed the history of disarmament in the security section because, Iraq and North Korea aside, the UN has had few operational responsibilities in the area; such a discussion would dilute the emphasis on the concrete illustrations of significant military activities over the past half century. At the same time, we have included a new section on terrorism, which obviously has increased importance since September 11, 2001.

Each of us drafted a section of the book in 1994. Each of us then rewrote all sections. After four editions, pride of authorship definitely yielded to collective judgment. Our collaboration has, we hope, not only discouraged ill-informed and parochial points of view but produced a synergy and a better text than any one of us could have written on our own. Each of us had conducted original research and taught about the three crucial areas of UN activity that provide the central framework for this book. We have also spent considerable time working within, or consulting with, international organizations. The numerous endnotes to each chapter also contain, we believe, sensible suggestions for additional research by even advanced students.

Four outside reviewers read the original manuscript of the first edition in 1993. Craig Murphy of Wellesley College and Lawrence Finkelstein, then at Northern Illinois University, are both recognized scholars of international organization and world politics; they provided comments through the cooperation of the International Organization Section of the International Studies Association. Two other readers, unknown to us, were provided by Westview Press. A discussion group focused on this manuscript at the annual meeting of the Academic Council on the United Nations System (ACUNS) held in Montreal during June 1993. Another ISA panel focused on the book at the 2002 conference in New Orleans. Thus this book is in some ways a product of the International Studies Association and ACUNS. Although only the authors are responsible for the final version, we acknowledge with gratitude the time and effort that others put into improving our work.

We would like to express our special gratitude to those staff members of our respective academic institutions who—with good humor and professionalism—assisted in the preparation of the various versions of the manuscript: Susan Costa, Mary Lhowe, Melissa Phillips, Fred Fullerton, Laura Sadovnikoff, and Elisa Athonvarangkul. Without their help final texts would have been considerably slower in appearing and certainly less well presented. Another word of appreciation goes to those younger researchers who have helped at one stage or another in framing arguments, checking facts and endnotes, and prodding their mentors: Peter Breil, Christopher Brodhead, Cindy Collins, Paula L'Ecuyer, Jean Garrison, Mutuma Ruteere, Barbara Ann Rieffer, Kekesha Harris, Peter Söderholm, and Corinne Jiminez. We also would like to thank the photographers whose work enhances these pages; photos from the UN archives have appropriate credits, but we would like to highlight those by Jae M. Kim, a Korean photojournalist and former student of Tom Weiss.

The three authors are sympathetic to multilateral organizations in general, and to the United Nations in particular. We believe that the UN fits into a complicated world situation that does not often yield to unilateral undertakings. We believe that the first Clinton administration recognized this reality when initially describing its foreign policy as one that pursued "assertive multilateralism." Although it retreated from this rhetoric, it was reluctant to act without collective approval and support. Madeleine Albright, Secretary of State for the second Clinton administration, stated clearly in 1993, when she was U.S. Permanent Representative to the United Nations, what remains valid today: "There will be many occasions when we need to bring pressure to bear on the belligerents of the post–Cold War period and use our influence to prevent ethnic and other regional conflicts from erupting. But usually we will not want to act alone—our stake will be limited and direct U.S. intervention unwise."[3] This orientation was much in evidence in 1999 when the Clinton administration led the bombing of Serbia over the issue of Kosovo, even when its multilateralism was to be found in NATO rather than the UN.

Even more to the point, when the Republican administration of George W. Bush responded to world affairs after the attacks of September 11, 2001, Washington found that multilateralism was important to the success of its policies in the war on terrorism. It then went to the Security Council in November 2002 to put pressure on Iraq, but subsequently abandoned the council when it could not obtain its primary objective, nine votes of support. It was striking that after the major combat in Iraq in 2003, the United States went back to the council to get collective approval for its plans for occupation and postconflict policies. Whether state foreign policy was embedded in the Security Council or some regional organization or some "coalition of the willing," multilateralism remained a key element of legitimacy and support. In all societies, what is legal or legitimate is, most often, collectively approved. So it is in modern world politics. This central fact mandates attention to the role of the United Nations and other international organizations.

We do not believe that our views are accurately described as "Wilsonian idealism" or that we reflect uncritical support for various international organizations. A preference for multilateral diplomacy is not idealistic at the start of the twenty-first century. On the contrary, unilateralists promoting an image of unbridled state control over events are the real utopians of the twenty-first century.

In principle we believe that collectively endorsed policies within the confines of the UN Charter stand a better chance of being successful than others. We usually are suspicious of unilateral actions; we believe in the beneficial effects of channeling perceptions of national interests through the process of collective evaluation. Thus we do not endorse the view that states should use the UN framework only as a last resort. We believe that much damage has been done to world affairs by states that disregard the UN Charter and shun serious multilateral consultation, whether during the Cold War or after. Multilateral diplomacy can be complicated and messy, but much unilateral action can be dangerous and destructive.

Nevertheless, we point out the weaknesses of the UN system. We do not hesitate to discuss places where the organization has not measured up to reasonable expectations. After all, the UN is not a religion. It is something not to be worshipped but to be critically analyzed. It is basically a political organization, even if it is affected by international law. And it is primarily affected by the foreign policies of member states, even if independent international civil servants like Secretary-General Kofi Annan have important roles to play. We believe that constructive criticism of the United Nations is essential for a more peaceful, just, and prosperous world. Parts of the UN are clearly badly designed. We do not shy away from this reality. Officials representing the UN have made some terrible decisions. We do not shrink from recognizing this either.

If we can get students to better understand the United Nations as a political organization, affected by international law, with its own history; if we can accurately portray the UN as greatly affected by basic changes in its political milieu; and if we can provide insights about what the UN has done and how these efforts might be improved in the future, we will have succeeded in this endeavor.

Each of the three substantive parts starts with an overview of basic ideas about the UN and that issue area (security, human rights, and sustainable human development). Each follows with a historical overview of how the UN has been involved and a discussion on changes that might lead to improved UN performance. Current events until June 2003 have been incorporated into the text. Each part situates the broader political changes driving events at the UN; the nature of these political changes appears prominently in both the introduction and the conclusion.

THOMAS G. WEISS
DAVID P. FORSYTHE
ROGER A. COATE
July 2003

Notes

1. John G. Stoessinger, *The United Nations and the Superpowers* (New York: Random House, 1966), p. 178.

2. Harold D. Lasswell, *Politics: Who Gets What, When, How* (New York: McGraw-Hill, 1936).

3. Quoted in the *Washington Post, National Weekly Edition*, June 21–27, 1993, p. 16.

Acronyms

ACC	Administrative Committee on Coordination [now the United Nations System Chief Executives Board for Coordination (CEB)]
ACP	African, Caribbean, and Pacific states
ACUNS	Academic Council on the United Nations System
ASCEND	Agenda of Science for Environment and Development into the Twenty-first Century
ASEAN	Association of Southeast Asian Nations
CAT	Committee Against Torture
CCMS	Committee on the Challenges of Modern Society
CCSQ	Consultative Committee on Substantive Questions
CEB	United Nations System Chief Executives Board for Coordination
CEDAW	Committee on the Elimination of Discrimination Against Women
CERD	Committee on the Elimination of Racial Discrimination
CESCR	Committee on Economic, Social, and Cultural Rights
CIDIE	Committee of International Development Institutions on the Environment
CIS	Commonwealth of Independent States
CONGO	Conference on Non-Governmental Organizations in Consultative Status with ECOSOC
CRC	Committee on the Rights of the Child
CSCE	Conference on Security and Cooperation in Europe
CSD	Commission on Sustainable Development
CSO	Civil Society Organization
CTC	Counter-Terrorism Committee
DESA	United Nations Department for Economic and Social Affairs
DHA	Department of Humanitarian Affairs
DOEM	Designated Officials for Environmental Matters
DOMREP	Mission of the Representative of the Secretary-General in the Dominican Republic

DPA	Department of Political Affairs
DPKO	Department of Peace-keeping Operations
DSR	Deputy special representative
EC	European Community
EC-ESA	Economic and Social Affairs Executive Committee
ECA	Economic Commission for Africa
ECAFE	Economic Commission for Asia and the Far East
ECE	Economic Commission for Europe
ECHA	Executive Committee for Humanitarian Affairs
ECLAC	Economic Commission for Latin America and the Caribbean
ECOMOG	Military Observer Group of the Economic Community of West African States
ECOSOC	Economic and Social Council
ECOWAS	Economic Community of West African States
EEC	European Economic Community
ELCI	Environment Liaison Centre International
EPTA	Expanded Program of Technical Assistance
ERC	Emergency Relief Coordinator
ESCAP	Economic and Social Commission for Asia and the Pacific
ESCWA	Economic and Social Commission for Western Asia
EU	European Union
FAO	Food and Agriculture Organization
FMLN	Frente Farabundo Martí para la Liberación Nacional (Farabundo Martí National Liberation Front)
G-7	Group of Seven
G-77	Group of 77
GA	General Assembly
GATT	General Agreement on Tariffs and Trade
GCC	Gulf Cooperation Council
GDP	Gross Domestic Product
GEF	Global Environmental Facility
GPA	Global Programme on AIDS
GSDF	Global Sustainable Development Facility
HABITAT	UN Conference on Human Settlements

HDI	Human Development Index
HIPC	Heavily Indebted Poor Countries Initiative
HIV/AIDS	Human Immunodeficiency Virus/Acquired Immunodeficiency Syndrome
HRC	Human Rights Committee
HRFOR	Human Rights Field Operation in Rwanda
IADB	Inter-American Defense Board
IAEA	International Atomic Energy Agency
IASC	Interagency standing committee
IBP	International Biological Programme
IBRD	International Bank for Reconstruction and Development (the World Bank)
ICAO	International Civil Aviation Organization
ICC	International Criminal Court
ICCAT	International Convention for the Conservation of Atlantic Tunas
ICISS	International Commission on Intervention and State Sovereignty
ICJ	International Court of Justice
ICPD	International Conference on Population and Development
ICRC	International Committee of the Red Cross
ICSU	International Council of Scientific Unions
ICT	Information and Communications Technology
ICTFY	International Criminal Tribunal for the Former Yugoslavia
ICTR	International Criminal Tribunal for Rwanda
IDA	International Development Association
IDB	Inter-American Development Bank
IDP	Internally Displaced Person
IFAD	International Fund for Agricultural Development
IFC	International Facilitating Committee
IFC	International Finance Corporation
IFIs	International Financial Institutions
IFOR	Implementation Force (in the former Yugoslavia)
IGBP	International Geosphere-Biosphere Programme
IGO	Intergovernmental Organization
ILO	International Labor Organization

IMF	International Monetary Fund
IMO	International Maritime Organization
INSTRAW	International Research and Training Institute for the Advancement of Women
INTERFET	International Force in East Timor
IOC	International Oceanographic Commission
IPDC	International Programme for the Development of Communication
ISSC	International Social Science Council
ITO	International Trade Organization
ITU	International Telecommunications Union
IUCN	International Union for the Conservation of Nature and National Resources
JCGP	Joint Consultative Group on Policy
KFOR	Kosovo Force
KLA	Kosovo Liberation Army
LDCs	Lesser-Developed Countries
LLDCs	Landlocked least developing countries
MAB	Man and the Biosphere Project
MDGs	Millennium Development Goals
MDGR	Millennium Development Goal Report
MFN	Most Favored Nation
MIGA	Multilateral Investment Guarantee Agency
MINURSO	UN Mission for the Referendum in Western Sahara
MMI	Money Matters Initiative
MNF	Multinational Force
MONUA	United Nations Observer Mission in Angola
MONUC	United Nations Observer Mission in the Democratic Republic of the Congo
MSC	Military Staff Committee
NAFTA	North American Free Trade Agreement
NAM	Non-Aligned Movement
NATO	North Atlantic Treaty Organization
NGO	Nongovernmental organization
NIEO	New International Economic Order

NSA	Nonstate Actor
NWICO	New World Information and Communication Order
OAS	Organization of American States
OAU	Organization of African Unity
OCHA	Office for the Coordination of Humanitarian Affairs
ODA	Official Development Assistance
ODC	Overseas Development Council
OECD	Organization for Economic Cooperation and Development
OHRLLS	Office of the High Representative for the Least Developed Countries, Landlocked Developing Countries, and Small Island Developing States
OILPOL	International Convention for the Prevention of Pollution at Sea by Oil
OMS	Operational Manual Statement
ONUC	United Nations Operation in the Congo
ONUCA	United Nations Observer Group in Central America
ONUMOZ	United Nations Operation in Mozambique
ONUSAL	United Nations Observer Mission in El Salvador
ONUVEH	United Nations Observer Mission to Verify the Electoral Process in Haiti
ONUVEN	United Nations Observer Mission to Verify the Electoral Process in Nicaragua
OPEC	Organization of Petroleum Exporting Countries
OPPRC	International Convention on Oil Pollution Preparedness Response and Cooperation
ORCI	Office for Research and Collection of Information
OSCE	Organization on Security and Cooperation in Europe
PDD	Presidential Decision Directive
PLO	Palestine Liberation Organization
PrepCom	UNCHE Preparatory Committee
PRGF	Proverty reduction growth facility
PRSP	Poverty reduction strategy paper
PVOs	Private Voluntary Organizations
RPG	Refugee Policy Group
RUF	Revolutionary United Front

SAARC   South Asian Association for Regional Cooperation

SADCC   Southern African Development Coordination Conference

SARS   Severe Acute Respiratory Syndrome

SCOPE   Scientific Committee on Problems of the Environment

SHD   Sustainable Human Development

SIDS   Small Island Developing States

SMG   Senior Management Group

SRSG   Special Representative of the Secretary-General

STABEX   Stabilization of Export Earnings

SUM   Special Unit for Microfinance

SUNFED   Special United Nations Fund for Economic Development

SU/TCDC   United Nations Special Unit for Technical Cooperation Among
               Developing Countries

SWAPO   South-West Africa People's Organization

TAC   Technical Assistance Committee

TDB   Trade and Development Board

TNC   Transnational Corporation

TRIPS   Trade-Related Aspects of Intellectual Property Rights

UDI   Unilateral Declaration of Independence

UNAIDS   Joint United Nations Programme on HIV/AIDS

UNAMET   United Nations Mission in East Timor

UNAMIR   United Nations Assistance Mission in Rwanda

UNAMSIL   United Nations Mission for Sierra Leone

UNASOG   United Nations Aouzou Strip Observer Group

UNAVEM   United Nations Angola Verification Mission

UNCAST   United Nations Conference on Applications of Science and
               Technology for the Benefit of Less Developed Areas

UNCDF   United Nations Capital Development Fund

UNCED   United Nations Conference on Environment and Development

UNCHE   United Nations Conference on the Human Environment

UNCHS   United Nations Center for Human Settlements (HABITAT)

UNCITRAL   United Nations Commission on International Trade Law

UNCLOS   United Nations Conference on the Law of the Sea

UNCRO   United Nations Confidence Restoration Operation

UNCTAD	United Nations Conference on Trade and Development
UNDAF	United Nations Development Assistance Framework
UNDCP	United Nations International Drug Control Programme
UNDG	United Nations Development Group
UNDOF	United Nations Disengagement Observer Force
UNDP	United Nations Development Programme
UNDRO	United Nations Disaster Relief Office
UNEF	United Nations Emergency Force
UNEP	United Nations Environment Programme
UNESCO	United Nations Educational, Scientific, and Cultural Organization
UNFCCC	United Nations Framework Convention on Climate Change
UNFDA	United Nations Development Assistance Framework
UNFICYP	United Nations Peace-keeping Force in Cyprus
UNFPA	United Nations Population Fund (formerly Fund for Population Activities)
UNGA	United Nations General Assembly
UNGOMAP	United Nations Good Offices Mission in Afghanistan and Pakistan
UNHCHR	United Nations High Commissioner for Human Rights
UNHCR	United Nations High Commissioner for Refugees
UNICEF	United Nations International Children's Emergency Fund
UNIDO	United Nations Industrial Development Organization
UNIFEM	United Nations Development Fund for Women
UNIFIL	United Nations Interim Force in Lebanon
UNIIMOG	United Nations Iran-Iraq Military Observer Group
UNIKOM	United Nations Iraq-Kuwait Observation Mission
UNIPOM	United Nations India-Pakistan Observation Mission
UNITA	National Union for the Total Independence of Angola
UNITAF	Unified Task Force (in Somalia)
UNITAR	United Nations Institute for Training and Research
UNITS	United Nations Information Technology Service
UNMIBH	United Nations Mission in Bosnia and Herzegovina
UNMIG	United Nations Observer Mission in Georgia
UNMIH	United Nations Mission in Haiti
UNMIK	United Nations Interim Administration Mission in Kosovo

UNMOGIP	United Nations Military Observer Group in India and Pakistan
UNMOP	United Nations Mission of Observers in Prevlaka
UNMOT	United Nations Mission of Observers in Tajikistan
UNMOVIC	United Nations Monitoring, Verification and Inspection Commission
UNO	United Nations Organization
UNOGIL	United Nations Observer Group in Lebanon
UNOMIG	United Nations Observer Mission in Georgia
UNOMIL	United Nations Observer Mission in Liberia
UNOMSIL	United Nations Observer Mission in Sierra Leone
UNOMUR	United Nations Observer Mission in Uganda and Rwanda
UNOPS	United Nations Office for Project Services
UNOSOM	United Nations Operation in Somalia
UNPREDEP	United Nations Preventive Deployment Force
UNPROFOR	United Nations Protection Force (in the former Yugoslavia)
UNPSG	United Nations Civilian Police Support Group
UNRRA	United Nations Relief and Rehabilitation Administration
UNRWA	United Nations Relief and Works Agency
UNSCOM	United Nations Special Commission
UNSF	United Nations Security Force
UNSMIH	United Nations Support Mission in Haiti
UNTAC	United Nations Transitional Authority in Cambodia
UNTAES	United Nations Transitional Administration for Eastern Slavonia, Baranja and Western Sirmium
UNTAET	United Nations Transitional Administration in East Timor
UNTAG	United Nations Transition Assistance Group in Namibia
UNTEA	United Nations Temporary Executive Authority
UNTSO	United Nations Truce Supervision Organization
UNU	United Nations University
UNV	United Nations Volunteers
UNYOM	United Nations Yemen Observation Mission
UPU	Universal Postal Union
USSR	Union of Soviet Socialist Republics
VOLAGS	Volunteer agencies

WACAP	World Alliance of Cities Against Poverty
WCED	World Commission on Environment and Development
WCRP	World Climate Research Programme
WEU	Western European Union
WFP	World Food Programme
WHO	World Health Organization
WIPO	World Intellectual Property Organization
WMO	World Meteorological Organization
WRI	World Resources Institute
WSSD	World Summit on Sustainable Development
WTO	World Trade Organization
WWF	World Wide Fund for Nature

Introduction

The most casual observer of the international scene can see that
the problem of world order has not been solved.
—INIS L. CLAUDE JR.,
Swords into Plowshares

At the dawn of the twenty-first century even the most casual observer of international affairs is deeply affected by the notion of change. As the twentieth century began, global multilateral relations and universal international organizations were in their infancy. Experiments with international unions, conference diplomacy, and the expansion of multilateral relations beyond Europe remained fledgling. As the decades unfolded, so did universal multilateralism, albeit on the European state-system model. Challenged by the increasing lethality of warfare and the associated evolving norm of the illegality of aggressive war, the first great experiment with collective security—the League of Nations—was launched.

This experiment failed, but after the second great European war of the century became a global conflict, national governmental leaders once again began to search for a way to prevent global conflicts from happening anew. Under the leadership of officials from the United States and Great Britain, a second great experiment in universal international organization was launched. This time, however, the collective security agreement was seen as part of a more comprehensive global arrangement in which the guarantees of collective security were linked to a series of international institutions aimed at promoting and fostering the social and economic conditions necessary for peace to prevail. Many of the social and economic elements of the postwar world order were, in fact, agreed on before the formal adoption of the UN Charter. The UN system was born plural and decentralized and was never intended to approximate a centralized unitary system. At the same time, the UN system was born from pragmatism and not utopianism, as some would have us believe. A great war against fascism and irrationalism had just been fought and won; the price of a third great war during the twentieth century was simply viewed as too great—the nuclear era had begun. The UN founding fathers saw the UN as the harnassing of state power for the management of pressing problems. This is hardly wild-eyed idealism run amuck.

In this first decade of the current millennium, it is difficult to conceive of a world without multilateralism. The national rulers of today began their attentiveness to world events when the United Nations was in the headlines and on the front pages of even local newspapers. UN officials were managing more than 20,000 troops in the old Belgian Congo in the 1960s (later Zaire and more recently once again the Congo). Secretary-General Dag Hammarskjöld died while coping with that crisis, which almost caused the collapse of the world organization. UN diplomatic and military personnel have been deeply involved in Middle Eastern politics since the late 1940s in Palestine but especially in the 1956 Suez crisis and the 1967 Arab-Israeli War.

These officials then watched as their predecessors placed the United Nations on a back burner. For much of the 1970s and even more in the 1980s, major states often seemed to bypass the world organization. Some developing countries continued to look upon the UN as central to world politics, but both Washington and Moscow seemed to favor action outside it. Circles of opinion in the U.S. capital, both public and private, were particularly harsh in their criticisms of the organization in the 1980s. The first Reagan administration, and related think tanks like the Heritage Foundation, manifested a deep distrust of multilateral diplomacy. One Reagan official, Charles Lichenstein, assigned to the UN, spoke publicly of "waving . . . a fond farewell as [the UN] sailed into the sunset."[1] Several U.S. allies also shied away from an organization whose "automatic" voting majorities had shifted over the decades from being controlled by the United States to being dominated by developing countries. Even some of these developing countries, however, appeared at times to despair of an organization whose resolutions were not followed by commitment to action.

All parties then watched again, and some participated, as a marked change came over the organization in the wake of the collapse of European communism from 1985 to 1991. Mikhail Gorbachev, then the first secretary of the Communist Party of the Soviet Union, called upon the UN in a September 1987 article in *Pravda* to play a more central role in world politics as a cornerstone of global security. Then boldly, more boldly than any previous leader of a superpower, Gorbachev embraced the UN and its collective security mechanism as a cornerstone of Soviet security policy. The Reagan administration, the most unilateralist in modern American political history until that point, responded cautiously. Nonetheless, by the end of the George H. W. Bush administration in 1993, the United States had used the UN to a great extent in dealing with such major issues as the Iraqi invasion of Kuwait in 1990, although earlier it had bypassed the UN on other matters such as the invasion of Panama in 1989. By the mid 1990s, the UN was back again on the front pages and in the headlines—and on CNN as well.

Many in the global South were cautious as the "two elephants," to paraphrase a popularly used analogy during that period, and their three Security Council permanent-member counterparts began to dance the dance of consensus, which led to an unprecedented use of the Security Council as a global security mechanism. In the years immediately following the end of the Cold War, there was a tremendous surge in UN peacekeeping and enforcement activities. In the period from 1988 to 1993, there were substantially more UN military operations—over twenty new operations were launched—than during the entire first four decades of the world organization. Great euphoria reigned in pro-internationalist circles in the United States just as great concern reigned in many smaller member states of the world organization.

The roller-coaster ride continued as the UN's peacekeeping and peace enforcement profile once again changed. The scope of the UN Security Council's business slowed greatly after the 1988–1993 period. In the next five years, until December 1998, sixteen peacekeeping operations were authorized. However, that number is misleading because seven were offshoots of previous missions. Of the remaining new operations, only the third UN Angola Verification Mission (UNAVEM III) was of significant size (with 6,500 troops) and duration. Both the total number of UN blue helmets and the peacekeeping budget fell by two-thirds from 1994 to 1998, reflecting disillusionment with the results from involvement in Somalia, Rwanda, and the Balkans.

In 1999, change set in again, effectively more than doubling the number of personnel involved in UN security operations. Major new missions were launched in Sierra Leone (6,260 military troops and observers), East Timor (9,150 troops and observers), and Kosovo (approximately 4,500 UN and partner organization personnel and civilian police). But the numbers of operations and personnel tell only part of the story. The missions in Kosovo, East Timor, and another smaller new operation, the UN Observer Mission in the Democratic Republic of the Congo (MONUC), represented a qualitatively different kind of operation. These operations are exceedingly complex and multidimensional. They are mandated the tasks of creating viable political and social institutions, rebuilding basic social and economic infrastructures, strengthening the rule of law as well as protecting human rights, and demobilizing former combatants and reintegrating them into society. Greatly expanding on earlier multidimensional operations, especially in El Salvador and Cambodia, the new efforts aimed to reconstitute viable states, an ambitious effort that critics referred to as "neocolonialism" but that one observer, Jarat Chopra, has dubbed "peace-maintenance."[2]

This intense involvement in post-conflict peacebuilding took a new form following the attacks on the United States on September 11, 2001. The overthrow of the Taliban regime in Afghanistan led to a new type of UN involvement, a so-called light footprint by the UN so that Afghans played a prominent role, rather than foreigners. In post-combat Iraq in 2003, the UN made almost no footprint. The UN Security Council approved control by the United States and the United Kingdom. These two states had led the combat to remove the government of Saddam Hussein, even without UN approval. They were therefore determined to remain in charge of post-combat occupation, at least for a time.

At the same time, as discussed in Parts Two and Three of this book, the UN's roles in promoting humanitarian affairs and human rights—and also sustainable human development—have continued to evolve. The *Human Development Reports* of the UN Development Programme (UNDP) indicate that the world may be losing, not gaining, ground toward the objective of promoting sustainable human development. The 1996 report, for example, highlighted two "disturbing" findings:

- Economic growth has been failing over much of the past fifteen years in about 100 countries, with almost a third of the world's people. And the links between growth and human development are failing for people in many countries with lopsided development—with either good growth but little human development, or good human development but little or no growth.[3]
- In seventy of those countries, average incomes in 1993 were less than they were in 1980. In forty-three of those countries, average incomes were less than they had

been in 1970. If the communications revolution is an engine of growth, the fact that the poorest 20 percent of the globe's countries contain only 0.2 percent of Internet users is startling. Clearly, the four development decades of the United Nations have not met with complete successes. Many poor countries have become ever more marginalized in the world economy, and global inequality continues to increase substantially.[4]

But these statistics tell only part of the story. Even in the peacekeeping arena, the character of UN operations has been changing. Fewer than 20 percent of the UN missions launched since 1988, for example, have been in response to interstate conflict, the type for which the founders of the world organization had planned. The majority of UN operations has been primarily intrastate. Antiquated notions of the inviolability and absolute character of state sovereignty have been called into question by new types of threats to international peace and security—as well as the sanctity of the notion of noninterference in the internal affairs of states. After all, once human rights became an international subject, it is difficult to understand what could remain a matter of purely domestic jurisdiction protected by state sovereignty. If the state's relation to "its" citizens was now a matter of extensive international law, what was left in the core of domestic jurisdiction that would be unaffected by international developments?

So, in sum to this point, there was constant change in world politics; this led to ups and downs in UN responses to major issues, but overall the UN continued to be centrally involved in many if not most important situations—certain critical circles of opinion in the U.S. notwithstanding.

The Legal Foundations of Sovereignty

Since about the middle of the seventeenth century, when the Peace of Westphalia (1648) essentially ended European religious wars, powerful political circles have accepted that the world should be divided into territorial states. Before that time there were dynastic empires, city-states, feudalistic orders, clans and tribes, churches, and a variety of other arrangements for organizing persons into broader groupings for personal identity and problem solving. From about the middle of the fifteenth century to the middle of the seventeenth, the territorial state emerged, first in Europe and then elsewhere, as the basic unit of social organization that presumably commanded primary loyalty and was responsible at least for order, and eventually for justice and prosperity, within a state's boundaries. European rulers found the institution of the state useful and perpetuated its image; then politically aware persons outside the West adopted the notion of the state to resist domination by European states.

Even after 1648, however, many other groupings persisted. In Europe, Napoleon sought to substitute a French empire for several states as late as the nineteenth century, and European colonialism persisted in Africa until the 1970s (the Portuguese were the last Europeans to abandon their African colonies, in 1974, although South Africa controlled Namibia until 1992). Despite these exceptions and the persistence of clan, ethnic, and religious identities, most of those exercising power increasingly promoted the perception that the basic political-legal unit of world affairs was the state: a governing system within a specific geographical area, with a stable (nonnomadic) population and a functioning and presumably independent government. The territorial state may have extraterritorial jurisdiction, such as control of maritime areas not technically owned by the state, but we leave that subject matter to advanced students of international law.

Frequently the territorial state is referred to as the "nation-state." This label is not totally false, but it can be misleading because nations and states are not the same. A nation is a people (a group of persons professing solidarity on the basis of language, religion, history, or some other bonding element) linked to a state. Legally speaking, where there is a state there is a nation, but there may be several peoples within a state. For example, in Switzerland (officially the Helvetian Confederation), by legal definition there is the Swiss nation, but in reality there are four peoples linked to that state: the Swiss-Germans, the Swiss-French, the Swiss-Italians, and the Swiss-Romanisch. The confusing notion of a multinational state also has arisen along with a divided nation (East and West Germany between 1945 and 1989 and North and South Korea today) and states with irredentist claims (Serbia). From one point of view the word "nation" refers to any self-proclaimed national people as well as to the totality of persons governed by a state. There is the state of Belgium; there is the nation of Belgians; and within Belgium there are the Flemish people (the Dutch speakers) and the Walloons (the French speakers), some of whom discuss making claims to be an independent nation. Whether the French-speaking and Dutch-speaking Belgians see themselves as a sub-national or national people, with a right to some autonomy or independence, depends on social psychology and politics, not on objective science.

State Sovereignty

The emergence of the territorial state (a governing system for a specific territory with a stable population and a functioning government) was accompanied by the notion that the state was sovereign. Accordingly, the sovereignty of all other social groupings was legally subordinated to the sovereignty of the state. Political and legal theorists argued that sovereignty resided in territorial states' rulers; they had ultimate authority to make policy within a state's borders. Those who negotiated the two treaties making up the Peace of Westphalia wanted to stop the religious wars that had brought such destruction to Europe; they specified that whoever ruled a certain territory could determine the religion of that territory. Europeans further developed the ideas about state sovereignty. For example, Jean Bodin, a sixteenth-century French economics writer, thought the notion of sovereignty a useful argument on behalf of the monarchs of new states who were trying to suppress the power of feudal officials contesting the power of the emerging state rulers.

State sovereignty was thus an idea that arose in a particular place at a particular time. But it came to be widely accepted as European political influence spread around the world. It was an argument about legal rights, but it was intended to affect power. All states were said to be sovereign equals, regardless of their actual "power"—meaning capability to control outcomes. They had the right to control policy within their jurisdictions even if they did not have the power to do it. Framed in the language of the abstract state, sovereignty enhanced the power of those persons making up the government that represented the state.

But if the territorial state, and the government that spoke for it, was sovereign within its boundaries, were there no outside rules and organizations with some authority over the state? Sovereignty arose as an idea designed to produce order, to stop violence between and within states over religious questions. But did state sovereignty become, on balance, an idea that guaranteed international disorder? Was it necessary to think of relations between and among states as anarchical—not in the sense of chaos but in the sense of interactions among equal sovereigns recognizing no higher rules and organizations?

The original versions of state sovereignty, coming as they did out of a Europe that was nominally Christian, emphasized external limits on monarchs by virtue of the "higher" norms of natural law. These monarchs were said to be the highest secular authorities, but they still were inferior to an external set of rules—at least from the viewpoint of political and religious theorists. But as Europe became more and more secular—which is to say, as the Catholic Church in Rome gave up its pretenses at territorial empire and increasingly emphasized the spiritual domain, at least in church dogma—the presumed restraints of natural law theory fell away. Thus the notion of state sovereignty came to represent absolute secular authority.

There was always some political duplicity in all of this. The more powerful states, while agreeing that all states were equally sovereign, repeatedly violated the national jurisdiction of the weaker states. As Stephen Krasner argues, the evolution and entrenchment of state sovereignty in international relations reflected "organized hypocrisy."[5]

State sovereignty, originally designed to produce order and to buttress central authority within the state, led to negative external consequences, the main one being that central authority over global society and interstate relations was undermined. All territorial states came to be seen as equal in the sense of having ultimate authority to prescribe what "should be" in their jurisdictions. No outside rules and organizations were held to be superior to the state. Only those rules consented to, and only those organizations voluntarily accepted, could exist in interstate relations. This was the Westphalian system of world politics. Thus states were legally free to make war, violate human rights, neglect the welfare of citizens, and damage the ecology.

So interstate relations came to be conceived of as part of what political scientists often characterize as an "anarchical society." Individuals existed and were grouped into nations. Nations were governed by states. States had governments. Sovereignty was an attribute of states, but it was exercised by governments. What was frequently called national sovereignty was actually state sovereignty. Whether the persons of a nation were sovereign referred to whether the state derived its legitimacy ultimately from popular will. This latter issue was, presumably, an interior or domestic question for the state; foreign actors had no authority to pronounce on it. Once a state's sovereignty was established in world politics, external actors were not supposed to comment on national or popular sovereignty, since that was an internal matter for the sovereign state.

This notion of state sovereignty is a political-legal prism. It is a fact only in the sense that if it is accepted, it becomes part of the dominant psychology of an era—the same way slavery was accepted as part of the natural order of things in a previous era. The notion is not physical fact, like energy or a doorknob. Since state sovereignty is not a material fact or necessity but an intellectual or social construct about who should have ultimate authority to make policy, there can be reasonable differences of opinion about it.

Indeed, there are differences—reasonable and otherwise—about who should govern in international society and world politics. Should the state, through its government, have the ultimate and absolute right to govern—regardless of all other considerations? Should regional intergovernmental organizations like the European Union (EU) have the ultimate say about proper policy within a state? Should local communities? Should the United Nations? Does the answer depend on what policy question one is addressing? Does the answer depend on how much suffering or destruction is occurring? Should state entities be given the first chance at managing a problem, but not ultimate authority if they fail to resolve it?

These are the very questions that are being raised at the United Nations at the beginning of the twenty-first century. For example, by 1992 the state had disintegrated in the geographical area known as Somalia, which is to say that the governing system for the territory did not function. If there is no effective government to represent the state, should the UN be the organization ultimately responsible for ending disorder and starvation and helping to reestablish the state? If disputes within a state, such as was the case in Bosnia and Herzegovina and between Bosnia and Herzegovina and a smaller Yugoslavia (Serbia and Montenegro), lead to mass murder, mass migration, and mass misery, should the UN be ultimately responsible? Or, as was the controversial case in Kosovo, should another multilateral organization—to wit, NATO (North Atlantic Treaty Organization)—override claims to sovereignty by Serbia? If states fail to take proper action in relation to major violations of international criminal law (genocide, major war crimes, crimes against humanity), should the new International Criminal Court (ICC) have the right to prosecute and convict the individuals responsible?

Governments act in the name of states to determine how to manage certain transnational problems. On occasion they have agreed to let an international organization have the ultimate say as to what should be done. For example, more than forty states in Europe, forming the Council of Europe, have created the European Convention on Human Rights. Under this treaty, the European Court of Human Rights has the ultimate say as to the correct interpretation of the convention, and the court regularly issues judgments to states concerning the legality of their policies. If one starts, as do European governments, with the notion that their states are sovereign, then one should say that these states have used their sovereignty to create international bodies that restrict the authority of the state. Among these states, the protection of human rights on a transnational basis is valued more highly than state independence. States have used their freedom to make policies that reduce their freedom. Initial sovereignty, linked to territory, has been used to restrict that sovereignty by means of an international body acting primarily on the basis of nonterritorial considerations.

This situation was not typical of interstate relations in the 1990s, and that is not likely to change in the foreseeable future. There are relatively few other examples of what is called "supranational" authority in world politics at the beginning of the new century. Although much noise arises in Washington about the powers of the World Trade Organization's (WTO) dispute panels to dictate policy to states, the WTO authority is modest. It is states that make the ultimate decision whether to apply sanctions for violations of WTO rules.

In any case most states, especially the newer ones that have achieved formal independence as a result of rapid decolonization since the 1950s, value state sovereignty more than supranational cooperation to improve security, protect human rights, or pursue sustainable development. Indeed, several older states also highly value state sovereignty. Edward Luck has pointed to American "exceptionalism" and traditional skepticism about inroads on its authority as every bit as ferocious as any Third World state.[6] China, too, argues that only the state, not outside parties, can determine what is best for the Chinese people, whether in the realm of security, human rights, or sustainable human development. There may be considerable international cooperation. But it usually falls short of being supranational and of giving an international organization the legal right to override state independence. The United States, for example, has neither ratified the InterAmerican Convention on Human Rights nor accepted the jurisdiction and authority of the InterAmerican Court of Human Rights.

Nevertheless, as the peoples and states of the world become more interconnected materially and morally, demands increase for effective international management. As persons become not just interconnected but interdependent (meaning that their relations become sensitive), demands increase for international management at the expense of state sovereignty. That is to say, Americans are interconnected with Hondurans concerning trade in bananas; but Americans can do without Honduran bananas and not become very upset. At the same time, Americans were interdependent with Kuwaitis concerning trade in oil; this relationship was sensitive because its alteration would have caused a major disruption in American society. Because of interdependence involving sensitive relations, some issues that were formerly considered domestic or inconsequential have come to be redefined as international or significant because of the strength of transnational concern—of either a material or a moral nature.

The UN Security Council determined that human rights repression in Iraq in 1991 threatened international peace and security, that the breakdown of order within Somalia in 1992 was a proper area for UN enforcement action, and that the humanitarian situation in Bosnia from 1992 was such that all states and other actors were entitled to use "all measures necessary" to provide humanitarian assistance. Situations similar to these used to be considered within the domestic jurisdiction of states. But the situations inside Iraq, Somalia, and Bosnia—and more recently in Rwanda, Haiti, Albania, Kosovo, and East Timor—came to be redefined as proper international concerns, subject to action by the United Nations and other external actors. In all these cases the principle of state sovereignty yielded to a transnational demand for the effective treatment of pressing problems. Indeed, the "responsibility to protect" civilians emerged as a mainstream concern.[7] Hence there is a growing demand for global governance, not in the sense of a unified world government, but in the sense of effective transnational management of pressing problems.

It is certainly true that in many parts of the world existing states are under pressure from within because a variety of groups—usually loosely called "ethnic," although they often are based on religious, linguistic, or other cultural characteristics—demand some form of sovereignty and self-determination. Many demands cause problems, but conflict is particularly pronounced when self-determination takes the form of a demand for a people's right to construct a new state. But in these cases the idea of accepting the territorial state as the basic unit of world politics is not at issue, at least in principle. What is at issue, and unfortunately fought over frequently, is which states and nations should be recognized. At one point, for example, Georgia was an internal province of the state known as the Union of Soviet Socialist Republics (USSR); at another time it became a national state. Since Georgian independence, some Ossetians have not been content to be a people within Georgia but wish to be a nation with their own state. Not far away, another former Soviet province, Chechnya, became part of another successor state, Russia, and began a bloody war to be recognized as more than autonomous after making a declaration of independent statehood without consultations; a reluctant Russia decided to destroy Chechnya in order to save it from itself and for the Russian state. The issue is not whether to have territorial states but whether the state that is sovereign over a particular population or geographical area should be the former USSR, Georgia, or Ossetia in the first case and the former USSR, Russia, or Chechnya in the second.

The state may be simultaneously under attack from several quarters. Some believe that the managers of transnational corporations have a global vision, doing what is best for the company without much thought about state boundaries. Some observers write of the globalization of finance capital and the meshing of the perspectives of corporate executives, regardless of nationality. Some moralists may also give scant regard to national boundaries. Thus for either material or moral reasons, some observers may endorse a supranational approach to problem solving, but state sovereignty persists as a nonmaterial fact in the perceptions of most political elites. It is reaffirmed in principle at each annual meeting of the UN General Assembly. But state sovereignty, linked to the power and independence of those who govern in the name of the state, is not the only value in world politics. Other values include enhanced security, human rights, and sustainable human development. And there is, in fact, considerable debate about the precise meaning of all these social constructs.

Much of world politics consists of managing the contradictions between conceptions of state sovereignty, on the one hand, and the desire for improved security, human rights, and sustainable human development, on the other hand. These contradictions are not the only ones in world politics, and managing them is not the only pressing need, but they constitute a fault line that permeates much debate at the United Nations. Sovereignty versus other considerations is one of the leading issues— if not the leading issue—in changing world politics at the beginning of the twenty-first century. One scholar had earlier observed that "although the picture is blurred and in many places hard to decipher, there has been movement away from the decentralized system of respect for sovereignty and toward a more centralized system of decision that in some respects approaches being international governance."[8]

Changing *Raisons d'État*

Those who rule in the name of the state, basing their views on the principle of state sovereignty, have claimed the right to determine what norms and actions are needed in the national interest. What English speakers call "national interests" is perhaps better captured by what French speakers call *raisons d'état:* "reasons of state." It is fair to ask whether those who rule are primarily concerned about the interests of the nation, meaning the people, or the interests of the state, meaning the government of the state, or their own interests.

Nomenclature aside, individuals acting in the name of a state display a variety of interests. Some scholars assume that state interests must of necessity come down on the side of state power and independence. This is frequently true. From a self-interested point of view, this may be rational. If we assume an anarchical international society without effective governing arrangements, it may seem rational to protect the independent power of the state. That power can then be used to secure "good things" for the nation.

It is provocative to inquire whether states—at least some of them, some of the time—may be coming to see their interests in fundamentally different ways. There is a question whether the growing interconnectedness and interdependence among governments and peoples is causing at least some states sometimes to seek more effective management of transnational problems at the expense of state separateness. The belief that democratic states have a long-run interest in multilateralism was christened "good international citizenship" by Gareth Evans, Australia's foreign minister in the early 1990s.[9] A similarly broad vision often underpins Canada's human security agenda.[10] No single national government, for example, is able unilaterally to solve the problem of the thinning ozone layer. In regard to this issue, states can secure their long-term interests in a healthy environment only through multilateral action. Such situations can lead to the adoption of shared norms, such as the Montreal Protocol, or to concrete action by an international organization such as the United Nations Environment Programme (UNEP). The result can create important legal and organizational restrictions on states.

States remain sovereign as an abstract principle, at least in the eyes of those who rule. But the operational application of sovereignty is another matter. Perceptions of *raisons d'état* cause state actors sometimes to subordinate state authority and independence to multilateral norms and procedures.

In order to manage problems, state officials may increasingly agree to important principles, rules, and decisionmaking procedures featuring a cluster of different actors. The notion of an international regime has come into vogue as a way of describing this reality. An international regime is a set of principles, rules, and procedures for "governing," or managing, an issue. The norms (principles and rules) can be legal, diplomatic, informal, or even tacit. The procedures frequently include non-governmental and intergovernmental organizations as well as states. World politics is frequently characterized by a network of different actors, all focusing on the same problem. Not infrequently, several parts of the UN system are involved in this network approach to problem solving.

There is, for example, an international refugee regime. The norms of managing refugee problems derive both from international law and from UN General Assembly resolutions, which are not immediately binding in international law, as well as from daily practice. The various actors involved in trying to apply these norms in concrete situations are states, non-governmental organizations (NGOs) such as the American Refugee Committee, and different parts of the UN system such as the office of the UN High Commissioner for Refugees (UNHCR).

States have determined that it is in their interest to coordinate policies to manage refugee problems. And they have constructed norms and organizations to pursue this goal. This application of *raisons d'état* may stem from moral or practical concerns—and most likely from some combination of the two. U.S. officials may want to help Cuban refugees because they are human beings victimized by communism, and because the United States wants to keep Fidel Castro from dumping mental patients and other undesirables on U.S. shores. Both viewpoints lead to use of the UNHCR to screen and interview Cuban immigrants to determine if individuals have either a well-founded fear of persecution or mental health problems and a criminal background.

Many states appear to be "learning" a new concept of *raisons d'état*—one that is conducive to an expansion in the authority, resources, and tasks of the United Nations. Given the impact of communications and other technologies, states may be in the process of learning that their own interests would be best served by greater international cooperation. Many state leaders learned from World War I that there was a need for the League of Nations to institute a cooling-off period so that states would not rush blindly into hugely destructive wars. State actors learned from World War II that a stronger world organization was needed, one with a security council that had the authority to make binding decisions to oppose calculated aggression and cope with other threats to the peace. Some state leaders subsequently learned and promoted the notion that peacekeeping was needed to respond to security crises during the Cold War so that armed disputes could be managed without triggering another world war.

States progressively adjusted their policies on security affairs, based on perceptions of interests, in ways that increased the importance of international organizations. The process was not a zero-sum game in which the state lost and the United Nations won. Rather, states won in the sense of obtaining greater barriers against armed attacks on them, and the UN won in the sense of being given more authority and tasks than the League of Nations once had.

Traditional international law considered resort to war to be within the sovereign competence of states. If state officials perceived that their interests justified force, it was used. But increasingly state authorities, not ivory-tower academics or pacifists, have agreed that changing patterns of warfare require international attempts to avoid or constrain force. Interest in peace and security has been combined with an interest in state authority, power, and independence. The result is international norms and organizations that continue to depend on state authority and power even as those norms and organizations try to restrain unwise, and eventually illegal, uses or threats of force.

State actors originally thought that their best interests were served by absolute sovereignty and complete freedom in the choice of policy. They learned that this was a dangerous and frequently destructive situation. From the viewpoint of their own interests, limiting the recourse to and the process of force was highly desirable. That led to the part of international law called *jus ad bellum* (law regulating recourse to war) and also *jus in bello* (law regulating the process of war). International laws and organizations were developed to contribute to state welfare even as they limited state freedom.

Central questions now are: How far are state actors willing to go in this process of international cooperation? How far can they be nudged by intergovernmental organizations (IGOs), NGOs, and public opinion? Are state actors willing to do more than create modern versions of the League of Nations—international organizations without the authority and resources to play decisive roles in world politics? Are they willing to cede significant authority and resources, as in the European Union, so that international organizations can act somewhat apart from state control in ways that really make a difference across borders? Can the UN be more than a debating society and a set of passive procedures?

The United Nations: Actor or Institutional Framework?

Many journalists and not a few other observers use phrases like "the UN failed" (to stop ethnic cleansing in the Balkans), or "the UN was successful" (in checking Iraqi aggression against Kuwait). This phraseology obscures a complex reality. The UN is most fundamentally an intergovernmental organization in which key decisions are made by governments representing states. The UN Charter may say initially, "We the peoples," but the members of the UN are states. The UN is also a broad and complex system of policymaking and administration in which some decisions are made by individuals who are not instructed by states. Non-governmental organizations are also active—and sometimes influential—in this system.

When it is said that the Security Council decided to authorize force in Somalia or the Balkans, in reality representatives of fifteen states made the decision, acting as the Security Council according to the UN Charter. They may have been influenced by reports from the UN Secretary-General, who in theory and often in practice is independent from state control and is responsible only to the Charter. Nevertheless, state representatives decide. Moreover, to the extent that UN decisions involve force or economic resources, or considerable diplomatic pressure, these elements of UN action are, in effect, borrowed from member states. The same point is true for the General Assembly and all other UN bodies made up of states. States make most of the important decisions taken in the name of the United Nations, however much they may be influenced, pressured, or educated by independent UN personnel or NGOs.

But authority—and influence flowing from it—may be delegated by IGO bodies to independent UN personnel. And the Charter confers some independent authority

A view of the United Nations headquarters in Manhattan as seen from the southwest. The headquarters site covers approximately 16 acres, from 42nd to 48th Streets between First Avenue and the East River. (UN Photo 165054/L)

on the Secretary-General. For example, he may address the Security Council and indeed call it into session. He makes an annual report on the work of the organization to the General Assembly in which he can try to focus attention on certain problems and solutions. Moreover, certain UN organs are made up of independent persons, not state officials—for example, the UN Sub-Commission on Protection of

Minorities, now the UN Sub-Commission on Human Rights. UN agencies have independent secretariats. Within the broad system, UN personnel may come to exercise some influence as independent actors not controlled by states. Their authority is not supranational, but their influence may be significant. Hence, they cannot tell states how to act, but they may be able to induce states to behave in certain ways.

Once member states created the UN Refugee Office (UNHCR), funded it, and authorized it to deliver humanitarian assistance in the Balkans, the High Commissioner for Refugees—in the 1993 crisis and throughout the 1990s, Sadako Ogata—was able to direct great attention to the situation in Bosnia by ordering a suspension of that humanitarian assistance on her own authority. She succeeded in altering priorities, at least temporarily. She compelled the UN Secretary-General, state officials, and other policymakers to address the problem of interference with humanitarian assistance.

The United Nations is primarily an institutional funnel through which member states may channel their foreign policies. The UN Charter is the closest thing that we have to a global constitution. When state actors comply with the Charter and use UN procedures, their policies acquire the legitimacy that stems from international law. They also acquire the legitimacy that stems from collective political approval. Normally, policies that are seen as legal and collectively approved are more likely than not to be successful. The weight of collective political approval may induce recalcitrant political authorities to accept a UN policy or program. It is better to have UN approval than otherwise.

The question of legitimacy in world politics is a complicated matter. In Iraq in 2003, as in Kosovo in 1999, or for that matter in Grenada in 1982, the United States used military force in another state without Security Council approval. It sought to create legitimacy for its action by obtaining collective support. Regarding Kosovo, for example, some thought legitimacy was enhanced by the fact that NATO was made up of nineteen liberal democracies who were responding to gross violations of human rights, and that the threatened vetoes by Russia and China in the Security Council were not well considered. Thus legitimacy in the first use of force is a subjective matter. In the view of some, what may not be fully legal in international law may still be legitimate in moral or political terms. Still, the safest ground on which to rest military action is prior approval by the UN Security Council.

In the pages that follow we speak mostly of decisions at the United Nations. We write of politics at or through the UN. We are careful to distinguish the UN as framework from the UN as actor. Most of the time the former rather than the latter situation obtains. Nevertheless, at times "the UN" is phraseology that refers to important behavior by independent persons representing the world organization. For example, in El Salvador in the early 1990s, UN Secretary-General Javier Pérez de Cuéllar and his representatives, especially his personal representative, Alvaro de Soto, played crucial roles in ameliorating the civil war. In places like El Salvador, the world organization's staff members have greatly affected decisions in the field and at headquarters concerning UN peacekeeping, mediation, and observation. It is also true that state foreign policy was important in El Salvador, both within the UN framework (for instance, via U.S. votes in the Security Council in favor of human rights and peace) and outside the UN system (for instance, U.S. unilateral commitments regarding foreign assistance). National reconciliation in El Salvador was advanced by states acting outside the UN, by state-controlled decisions within the UN, and by the independent actions of UN personnel. Moreover, the role of nongovernmental actors in El Salvador should not be minimized, including the decisions by the armed opposition (the Frente Farabundo Martí para la Liberación Nacional, or the FMLN), by local NGOs (churches and people's groups), and by external human rights and aid agencies. This tapestry of decisionmaking both circumscribes and energizes the United Nations, a theme that permeates this book.

One of the more interesting questions in the new millennium is whether the growing demand for UN management of transnational problems will lead to greater or reduced willingness by member states to confer authority on the world organization's personnel and to transfer the resources necessary to resolve problems effectively. The options and processes are complex.

In Somalia in mid 1992, UN Secretary-General Boutros Boutros-Ghali publicly pressured states to demonstrate the same concern for suffering there as they were showing for the "white-man's war" in the Balkans. Key states responded by using the Security Council to authorize all necessary means (including force) for the creation of a secure environment for the delivery of humanitarian assistance in Somalia. That use of force was effectively controlled first by the United States—which was more-or-less deputized to represent the Security Council. But the Unified Task Force (UNITAF) of soldiers in Somalia progressively became a more international force. Then, it was transformed into the first enforcement action truly controlled by UN personnel. To understand accurately "the UN" in Somalia, it is necessary over time to distinguish independent UN personnel, decisions made by states in the name of the UN, and decisions made by states outside the UN.

By and large, state decisions outside the United Nations affect what "the UN" is allowed to do, or how UN procedures and symbols are employed. President George Bush's decision in late 1992 to commit U.S. ground troops in Somalia was the key to what followed. Only when that decision had been made in the White House could the Security Council proceed to authorize force and then actually facilitate the delivery of humanitarian assistance. However much the U.S. president may have been influenced by the Secretary-General or by reports from the communications media, it was a state decision outside the UN that constituted, for a given time span, the independent variable explaining what happened. In this sense the UN became the dependent variable—that is, the factor that came into play once President Bush decided to move forward.

In terms of a fundamental generalization, political factors outside the UN are primary and factors inside the UN are secondary. The end of the Cold War, indeed the end of the Soviet Union, primarily explained the renaissance of UN security activities that began in the late 1980s. It was not the Security Council that ended the Cold War. It was the end of the Cold War that allowed the Security Council to act with renewed consensus and commitment and vigor.

Once allowed to act, UN personnel and organs may independently influence states and other actors. What was once a secondary factor, dependent on state approval, may come to be a primary factor in the ongoing process to make and implement policies. Once member states decided to create an environmental program, UNEP came to exert some relatively independent influence—both in cleaning up the Mediterranean Sea and in coordinating scientific evidence about the need to protect the ozone layer.

In any event, state decisions about power and policy constitute the primary force driving events at the UN. When important states show a convergence in policy, "the UN" may be allowed to act. Without that political agreement, all parts of the UN system will be severely restricted in what they can accomplish. This has been true since 1945. The end of the Cold War has not altered this fundamental fact.

UN Politics

In the exercise of power needed to make and implement policies through the United Nations, states naturally seek allies. Academic and diplomatic observers have been prone to adopt generalizations about different political alliances, coalitions, or blocs within the United Nations. The countries of the West—that is, the Western industrialized democracies that are members of the Organization for Economic Cooperation and Development (OECD), sometimes joined by Israel—frequently have been grouped as the First World. The "developing countries," basically all of the countries of Asia, Africa, and Latin America, have been examined under the rubric of the Third World, the South, the Non-Aligned Movement (NAM), or the Group of 77 (or G-77, for the original constellation of seventy-seven states, which has now grown to some 130 members). The "socialist countries," when the Soviet Union and its European allies existed, were also called the East and the Second World. The West and the East, in a curious bit of mathematical geography, were added together to constitute the North, or the developed countries, in juxtaposition to the South, or the developing countries.

Although these distinctions roughly correspond to the bulk of voting patterns during the Cold War, they have become less useful over time. Not only has the bloc of European socialist states and the Soviet Union ceased to exist, but also some of this terminology was in fact never accurate: Cuba was hardly nonaligned, and the socialist countries were developed in few ways beyond weaponry.

The end of the Cold War has allowed scholars, and especially diplomats, to begin to look more objectively at alliances within the United Nations, although many of the labels from the former era remain. For example, it is now quite common to point out that developing countries consist of a series of crosscutting alignments reflecting the heterogeneous character of their economies and ideologies.[11] In the past, it was politically more correct to speak of the Third World as if it were homogeneous, with little hesitation in grouping Singapore's and Chad's economies or Costa Rica's and North Korea's ideologies.

Only on a few issues—like emphasizing the importance of the General Assembly, where each state has one vote—do developing countries show common interests. In such instances, and in some other international forums, the North-South divide continues to be salient. Frequently developing countries subdivide according to the issue before the UN: between radicals and moderates, between Islamic and non-Islamic, between those in the region and outside, between maritime and landlocked, between those achieving significant economic growth and otherwise. Even within the Western group, there have always been numerous differences, which have come more to the fore with the abrupt disappearance of East-West tensions. Divisions among and within all groups over the pursuit of war against Iraq in 2003 was a clear example of this phenomenon.

Given the changing nature of world politics and ongoing learning processes that can shape views toward state sovereignty and *raisons d'état*, new alignments and coalitions should be anticipated. Indeed, as world politics change, so does the United Nations. In 1991 the General Assembly, whose majority of developing countries normally reflects concern for traditional notions of state sovereignty, voted by consensus to condemn the military coup in (briefly) democratic Haiti. Subsequently, many of these same countries supported the imposition of economic sanctions—first at the regional level through the Organization of American States (OAS) and afterward through the UN—and eventually military enforcement action authorized by the Security Council to restore the elected government. The nature of government as democratic or authoritarian, a subject that had mostly been considered a domestic affair protected by the principle of state sovereignty, came to be seen by all states as a legitimate subject for diplomatic action through the UN.

In the following pages we inquire more systematically into changing world politics, and what they portend for the United Nations as the world organization gropes with security, human rights, and sustainable human development. These three issues encompass the central challenges to improving the human condition and hence the central tests for international organization in the present era.

Part One of this book introduces the evolving efforts of the United Nations to combat threats to international peace and security. Because it is impossible to understand the nature of international cooperation without a grasp of the Charter's provisions for pacific settlement of disputes, enforcement, and regional arrangements, we first cover the theory of collective security in Chapter 1. Chapter 2 deals with UN security efforts during the Cold War and then turns to economic sanctions and the creation of the peacekeeping function. Although not mentioned in the Charter, peacekeeping is a distinctive contribution of the UN and has been its main activity in the security field for some forty years. In Chapter 3, "UN Security Operations After the Cold War," we explain the renaissance in UN activities, including peacekeeping, enforcement, and a series of other actions in such troubled regions as Cambodia, the former Yugoslavia, Somalia, Rwanda, and Haiti. Chapter 4, "Groping into the Twenty-First Century," contains a discussion of the political dynamics at work and suggestions about changes in the UN to make it better able to address security challenges in the twenty-first century, including terrorism.

Part Two introduces UN efforts to protect human rights and humanitarian values in conflicts. Chapter 5 briefly traces the origins of international action on human rights, indicating what the UN contributed to principles on human rights. Chapter 6 focuses on UN activity to help implement the human rights principles that member states have formally accepted. Finally, there is a balance sheet in Chapter 7 on UN developments in the field of human rights, exploring some of the dynamics that drive events and what they portend for the future.

Part Three introduces efforts by the United Nations to build sustainable human development. Chapter 8 examines the evolution of international attempts to build a humane capitalist world order and explores the progression of various theoretical frameworks for promoting development. Chapter 9 focuses on UN institutions and activity to build sustainable human security and presents some information about how the UN is structured for economic and environmental policymaking. In Chapter 10, we explore the role of the United Nations in promoting development and human security in the context of the forces and tensions of globalization. We conclude with a short summary.

Notes

1. Quoted in Robert Gregg, *About Face? The United States and the United Nations* (Boulder: Lynne Rienner, 1993), p. 68.

2. Jarat Chopra, *Peace-Maintenance: The Evolution of International Political Authority* (London: Routledge, 1999).

3. United Nations Development Programme, *Human Development Report 1996* (New York: Oxford University Press, 1996), p. 1.

4. United Nations Development Programme, *Human Development Report 2002* (New York: Oxford University Press, 2002), pp. 10–11.

5. Stephen Krasner, *Sovereignty: Organized Hypocrisy* (Princeton: Princeton University Press, 1999). See also Thomas J. Biersteker and Cynthia Weber, eds., *State Sovereignty as Social Construct* (Cambridge: Cambridge University Press, 1996).

6. Edward Luck, *Mixed Messages: American Politics and International Organization 1919–1999* (Washington, D.C.: Brookings Institution, 1999).

7. International Commission on Intervention and State Sovereignty, *The Responsibility to Protect* (Ottawa: ICISS, 2001). See also J. L. Holzgrefe and Robert O. Keohane, eds., *Humanitarian Intervention: Ethical, Legal, and Political Dilemmas* (Cambridge: Cambridge University Press, 2003).

8. Lawrence S. Finkelstein, ed., *Politics in the United Nations System* (Durham, N.C.: Duke University Press, 1988), p. 30.

9. See Nicholas J. Wheeler and Tim Dunne, "Good International Citizenship: A Third Way for British Foreign Policy," *International Affairs* 74, no. 4 (1998), pp.847–870.

10. Lloyd Axworthy, "Human Security and Global Governance," *Global Governance* 7, no.1 (2001), pp.19–23. See further Edward Newman and Oliver P. Richmond, eds., *The United Nations and Human Security* (New York: Palgrave, 2001).

11. Soo Yeon Kim and Bruce Russett, "The New Politics of Voting Alignments in the United Nations General Assembly," *International Organization* 50, no. 4 (Autumn 1996), pp. 629–652. [See also Evan Luard, *A History of the United Nations: The Years of Western Domination* (London: Macmillan, 1982).

Part ONE

International Peace and Security

1   The Theory of UN Collective Security

The fall of the Berlin Wall in November 1989 and the disappearance of the Soviet Union in late 1991 ushered in a period of rapid change in world politics. These political events outside the United Nations caused fundamental change within the world organization. In the wake of the Cold War, many citizens and diplomats expressed optimism about the role of UN multilateralism in a "new world order." Although the UN has always been dependent for its functioning on the nature of the world political system in which it operates, institutions still matter. How the United Nations organizes itself, what it seeks to do, and how it does it are important. Even if the UN remains largely dependent on the nature and quality of state foreign policy, UN officials have some room to maneuver in carrying out tasks. This is certainly true for security issues, the focus of this first part.

There were other changes involving the UN in the wake of the attacks on the United States by Al Qaeda on September 11, 2001. Washington, wanting to obtain multilateral endorsement of its security policies, quickly paid off the arrears that had accumulated in its assessed dues to the UN. It then sought and received the Security Council's blessing for several of its security objectives, such as approving military attacks on the Taliban government in Afghanistan that was sheltering Al Qaeda and approving plans that were intended to shut down financing for "terrorism." Only a year later, in returning to the UN for legitimacy in expanding a war in Iraq, Washington was successful in securing a renewed inspections regime but was subsequently rebuffed in seeking a specific authorization to use military force. Change outside the UN drives developments inside; the world organization, principally the Security Council, was thrust into important roles.

Security, traditionally defined, was supposed to be the primary task of the United Nations Organization (UNO) in the larger family of international organizations—the UN system—that was created during World War II. With the signing of the UN Charter on June 26, 1945, the world undertook a new experiment in organizing states to control war. Two world wars within two decades, the Holocaust, and the advent of the nuclear age produced the political will to improve on the League of Nations. The international community rejected isolationism and committed itself to trying to safeguard the peace that had been won at great cost. In the inspiring words of the Charter's preamble, the UN's role was to save "succeeding generations from the scourge of war, which twice in our lifetime has brought untold sorrow to mankind."

The League of Nations, although technically not outlawing war, had established a set of procedures constituting a cooling-off period for states contemplating the use of force. This approach to peace was conditioned by the judgment that the advent of World War I had been caused by emotionalism and mistaken perceptions. Time was needed for rationality to prevail. This approach to peace had clearly been inadequate to stop Hitler's premeditated aggressions, which in some ways were not only rational but astute (for example, his anticipation of appeasement on the part of the Western democracies).

Equally deficient was the legalistic approach to peace reflected in the Kellogg-Briand Pact, which outlawed war as an instrument of foreign policy. It did nothing to change the nature of world politics. It did not provide peaceful means of conflict resolution. It just made war illegal.

At the San Francisco conference where the Charter was drafted, diplomats first made the threat or use of force illegal except in self-defense. Then, unlike during the League period, they gave the United Nations the authority to enforce the peace through diplomatic, economic, and even military action in response to "threats to the peace, . . . acts of aggression or . . . breaches of the peace." State power, or perhaps even independent UN power, was to be put at the service of the Security Council to protect the peace.

Even a novice of world politics is aware that the reality of the past half century has diverged dramatically from these ideals. In the 1990s, usually thirty-five "major" wars—that is, with at least 1,000 deaths in a year—were occurring. At the same time, newspaper headlines and media presentations daily indicate the presence of the United Nations in conflicts around the world.

Pioneering Cooperation: The Nineteenth Century and the League of Nations

However unrepresentational in terms of population and geography, the "global" system was initially centered upon Europe after the Peace of Westphalia, which ended the Thirty Years' War in 1648. The equality of states was the purported foundation of the global system, but in practice, inequalities abounded. A variety of institutions gradually grew up in pursuit of order and stability in what remained an "anarchical society."[1] There was no central authority or world government even though there were transnational efforts to manage problems. The four principal institutions were "balance-of-power" diplomacy to prevent the emergence of a dominant power; international law; international diplomatic conferences to settle major problems; and diplomatic practices through which states remained in contact, preferring negotiations to conflict. Individual states were supposedly sovereign, having ultimate legal authority in their jurisdictions—which were mainly territorial. But they recognized that the predictability and stability that resulted from norms and obligations would be in their own self-interest. International organizations, which helped to codify these rules and monitor their implementation, were important elements in what observers now commonly call "international society."[2]

The Congress of Vienna in 1815 represents the first modern attempt at organizing states to preserve the peace. It is the precursor to contemporary international organizations. After the defeat of the French emperor Napoleon Bonaparte by Russia,

Prussia, Great Britain, and Austria, the victors sponsored a conference to determine the shape of the new Europe. Working with weaker states, they sought to achieve an ongoing distribution of power that would deter future aggression and prevent the rise of another conqueror of Napoleonic magnitude. By raising the stakes of aggression through coordinated foreign policies, the Congress of Vienna wished to ensure against aggression's recurrence. The interests of victorious states became those of the international system.

The sponsors of the conference agreed to meet periodically, but the congress system was too visionary for the realpolitik world in which states sought to protect their power. It was replaced by the Concert of Europe, a less organized but more durable forum for deliberations by major powers. The Concert limited its attention to problems of international significance as they arose (as opposed to the more prevention-oriented Congress) and met seventeen times from 1830 to 1884. For instance, during an 1884 meeting that continues to have repercussions, the Concert met to divide colonial rights to Africa among vying European imperialist powers after the race to acquire territories threatened to get out of hand. The Congress and Concert opened up diplomatic channels among states and established the beginnings of an executive council somewhat akin to the UN Security Council.

The Hague conferences in 1899 and 1907 sought to regulate the laws of war. Their deliberations were more inclusive than the Concert's and included some states from other continents. Delegates representing twenty-six states, of which five were non-European, attended the first conference. In 1907 this number increased to forty-four states, including twenty-four non-European ones. The Hague conferences represent the first example of gathering diverse countries into an international security system aspiring to universal membership, as the United Nations was to do decades later. The Hague conferences spelled out the framework for the Permanent Court of Arbitration as well as rules governing the conduct of war.[3] They also served as a step to universalize debates on international issues. In so doing, they provided an antecedent for the UN General Assembly.

In addition to these efforts to address security problems directly, several agencies designed to facilitate trade and financial transfers among nations were established in the nineteenth century and became precursors of the types of functional organizations that have grown significantly since World War II.[4] Some see these agencies as contributing to security indirectly by entangling states in a web of social and economic cooperation strong enough to make war irrational. These agencies arose after states recognized the commercial benefits of interstate cooperation. The International Telegraphic Union, which was created in 1865 using the same acronym as the present International Telecommunications Union (ITU), was the first to be established to help provide interstate communication links. Technological advances encouraged the development of new international organizations and led to greater interstate cooperation in such institutions as the Universal Postal Union (UPU), the International Bureau for Weights and Measures, and the International Institute of Agriculture.

But once again, armed conflict on a massive scale led to a significant push to increase the authority and power of international organizations.[5] In 1919 in the aftermath of the first "war to end all wars," it was apparent that a better means was needed to prevent widespread interstate violence. From the Versailles Peace Conference arose the League of Nations Covenant (or "constitution") on January 20, 1920, but the League ultimately proved unsuccessful in its quest to preserve the peace. However, its experiences provided lessons later about how to structure a collective-security system. Under Article 10 of the League's Covenant, members pledged "to respect and preserve as against external aggression the territorial integrity and existing political independence of all Members of the League." This language was the main target of critics in the U.S. Senate, which ultimately refused to consent to the Covenant in spite of the fact that President Woodrow Wilson had championed the League.

Articles 11 through 17 contained the germ of a collective-security system. The two main organs of the League were the assembly, which contained all member states and met annually, and the less universal council, which was supposed to contain the more powerful states as members, met more frequently, and could be convened in a crisis. The council normally dealt with matters that threatened the peace, although some of these matters came before the assembly. The lack of clarity about the roles of the assembly and the council was a weakness; all problems regularly came before both bodies.

Voting mechanisms reflected the traditional practices of multilateral diplomacy. Although majority voting existed in principle for some issues, a sovereign state could not be compelled to submit to the will of the majority when, in its own interpretation, its national interests were threatened. Hence, unanimity came to be the standard operating procedure except for inconsequential issues. The League relied on commitments by states not to use force except in self-defense until a process of pacific settlement had been completed. That process was to begin with a complaint by a disputant or by another member of the League. In essence, members undertook a legal obligation to use the organization if they themselves could not end a dispute. At least on paper, the League's Covenant embodied a working system of security.

Several flaws in the League's composition and constitution ultimately contributed to its failure. The Covenant restricted the right to go to war but did not outlaw it, which was the focus of the Kellogg-Briand Pact, also not implemented; recourse to warfare remained an option for states. The assumption of universal membership proved flawed: The United States never joined the League, depriving the collective-security apparatus of a much-needed member; the Soviet Union joined only in 1934; Japan left in 1931, and Italy in 1937; Germany joined in 1926 but left in 1933. Unanimity among all members was required for action, but members could refuse to take part in League-sponsored activities and leave if they chose. Moreover, the provisions for establishing the League were an integral part of the Treaty of Versailles, from which Axis powers were initially excluded, an exclusion leading ultimately to resentment and sabotage.

As time wore on, other problems aggravated these obvious weaknesses. Members reestablished alliance systems and refused to take the necessary institutional actions to check aggression. The League was unable to reverse Japan's takeover of Manchuria; the Italian invasion of Abyssinia; the German remilitarization of the Rhineland and subsequent takeover of the Sudetenland; or the intervention by Italy, Germany, and the Soviet Union in the Spanish civil war. The gradual buildup of war machines proceeded apace, and the collapse of the fledgling collective-security system was complete with the German invasion of Poland in 1939. The League, intended to prevent accidental war as had occurred in 1914, broke down under the premeditated expansion of particularly Germany and Japan in the 1930s. So the international community headed down the road to World War II, although the formal dissolution of the League did not occur until 1946.

Collective Security in General

The idea of collective security can be traced through a long history of proposals to deal with war and peace.[6] The central thread has remained the same: All states would join forces to prevent one of their number from using coercion to gain advantage. Under such a system, no government could conquer another or otherwise disturb the peace for fear of retribution from all other governments. Any attack would be treated as if it were an attack on each of them. The notion of self-defense, universally agreed on as a right of sovereign states, was expanded to include the international community's right to prevent war.

The apparent common sense and appealing simplicity of the logic of collective security can be contrasted with the difficulties of its application. Indeed, some have come to question whether collective security can be relied upon with confidence to protect or restore the peace. Skeptics ask: In a world with a large number of states (more than 190 UN members in 2003), will not states defect from the collective enterprise, in pursuit of their own narrow national interests, and thereby undermine the collective effort? This is the old problem of the hunters and the stag. As the hunters encircle the stag, one hunter defects to chase a rabbit he will not have to share with others. Another does the same. Soon the stag escapes through the gaps in the collective effort.[7]

Experience with collective security indicates considerable "gaps" when this collective effort has been contemplated, whether during the League or the UN era. First, some states have refused to join a collective-sanctioning effort because they have already defined their friends and enemies. It was inconceivable that the United States would have joined in a UN effort at collective security against one of its North Atlantic Treaty Organization (NATO) allies or that the Soviet Union would have done so against its Warsaw Pact allies. Not only is a pre-established alliance system not a form of collective security, but such alliances also are incompatible with global collective security. In an exceptional move, the United States did indeed oppose the British, French, and Israeli invasion of Egypt in 1956 and eventually helped to roll it back by diplomacy. But the United States never seriously considered UN sanctions against its allies in 1956, precisely because it wanted to maintain their cooperation in the Cold War. Under true collective security, all aggressors have to be treated the same. All threats to and breaches of the peace have to be firmly opposed. This requirement seems beyond the realm of most great powers in history, which have always had their cultural and strategic friends.

Second, there is the problem of power. It has been quite clear since 1945 that the international community of states would have major and probably insurmountable problems in applying collective security against a nuclear state, especially the United States, the USSR, Britain, France, or China. How could one justify the massive destruction that could result from trying to apply forcible collective security against such a state, even if clear-cut aggression had occurred?

But the problem of regulating powerful aggressors goes beyond the nuclear question. Many states control such conventional forces, or biological and chemical weapons of mass destruction, or economic resources, that collective security against them would be highly disruptive to international society. For this reason, the international community has had to content itself with diplomatic opposition to such acts as the U.S. invasions of Grenada and Panama in the 1980s, knowing full well that any attempt at military or economic sanctioning would be disruptive and ineffectual. It is not only the great powers that are difficult to manage. South Africa, Saudi Arabia, Israel, Vietnam, and other lesser powers also have considerable economic and military strength that can make them important actors depending upon issues and timing. Even a small and poor state like North Korea is difficult to sanction, because of the assumption that it possesses a few nuclear weapons and other troublesome arms.

Third, collective security can be costly to those supporting it. Sanctions cut both ways, affecting not only the aggressor but the defenders. When it was a member of the League of Nations, Switzerland did not want to put effective economic sanctions on Mussolini's Italy after the invasion of Ethiopia because this would have hurt the part of Switzerland's economy that was interdependent with Italy's. The memory of this situation helped keep Switzerland from joining the United Nations until 2002. Although communist Bulgaria voted in the UN for sanctions against white-ruled South Africa, it then sold arms to South Africa under the table. Bulgaria did not want to miss out on profits from the arms trade despite its formal support for economic collective security against the white-minority government in Pretoria. It was one thing for states to accept that apartheid constituted a threat to the peace. It was another for states to engage collectively against apartheid at a cost to their own narrow national interests.

Fourth, the concept of collective security is based on the assumption that all victims are equally important—that the international community of states will respond in the same way to an attack on Bosnia or Armenia as to an attack on Kuwait or Germany. Even aside from the issue of standing alliances, this, too, is a very high standard. Historical evidence shows that most states have differentiated between states worth defending and otherwise. In the 1990s the United States was willing to disrupt its home front by putting almost half a million military personnel into the liberation of Kuwait, but it dithered about taking decisive action to liberate Bosnia, which was progressively carved up by ethnic Serbians and Croatians until the Dayton accords of late 1995. The fact that Kuwait possessed much oil sold in the United States and to U.S. allies, and that Bosnia seemed to lack both economic resources and strategic value, was surely not irrelevant to Washington's policy toward the two situations. As a result, decisive and forcible collective security occurred through Desert Storm in 1991. But indecisive and mostly nonforcible collective-security efforts were tried in Bosnia until a Croatian-Bosnian offensive finally goaded the West to act in autumn 1995.

Despite increased interconnectedness among states as a general rule, some states still do not matter very much. This was true of Rwanda in 1994 when it was wracked by social conflict that reached genocidal proportions. The UN Security Council refused to intervene to stop the slaughter that left perhaps 800,000 dead. On the other hand, the U.S. led NATO in a bombing campaign against Serbia in 1999 over the primary issue of human rights violations in the small province of Kosovo. It is very difficult to get UN member states to apply collective security in a consistent way, irrespective of size and geo-strategic value.

Collective security has been viewed sometimes as a halfway house between world government and the pure state system. It has been seen by some as a process that could make the state system more humane by making it more secure. Forms of collective security have worked at times. Iraqi aggression against Kuwait was rolled back in 1991 through collective force authorized by the UN, as was a military coup in Haiti after UN-sponsored economic sanctions fell short. But these tend to be the exceptional examples proving the general rule that collective security, either military or economic, is exceedingly difficult to organize and enforce. After all, despite an overwhelming global consensus that white-minority rule in Africa was wrong, UN economic sanctions against Rhodesia lasted from 1966 until 1979 and probably were not decisive in achieving black self-determination and majority rule in the country, which became known as Zimbabwe. States have numerous narrow national interests that they are reluctant to see overridden in the name of peace or justice. They therefore tend to defect from inconvenient collective-security efforts. There is also the problem that state members of the Security Council may genuinely disagree as to when economic and military enforcement measures are in order. Such was the case in 2002 and 2003 when the council was divided over how to enforce disarmament measures in Iraq. If the situation were otherwise, which is to say that if international agreement on enforcement issues were easier, one could probably achieve world government, not just collective security.[8]

The United Nations and Security: Some Basics

The foundations of the United Nations were laid in the midst of World War II. In August 1941, four months before the United States entered the war, President Franklin D. Roosevelt agreed on the Atlantic Charter with Britain's prime minister, Winston Churchill. The latter's strong preference for a clear statement about a collective security organization in the postwar world was diluted by Roosevelt, who feared a negative reaction from Congress. Nevertheless, on New Year's Day 1942, less than a month after the American entry into the war, twenty-six governments signed the Declaration of the United Nations, which called for mutual support among the allied signatories and a "more permanent system of general security."

The leaders of the Allied forces (the United States, the Soviet Union, Great Britain, France, and China) proceeded over time to negotiate the guidelines for the world organization. At the Teheran, Dumbarton Oaks, and Yalta conferences, these countries mapped out their plans for the postwar era. At the same time, academics and practitioners studied previous experiences in order to guide the international admin-istration of the future.[9]

Later, the Allies invited other countries to join the deliberations that eventually led to the establishment of the United Nations in June 1945 at the San Francisco con-ference. Tensions began to appear as early as the Dumbarton Oaks conference in August 1944, but a fundamental spirit of cooperation existed among the major pow-ers during the process of designing the world organization. The fifty-one countries invited to San Francisco included all governments that had declared war on the Axis before March 1945 or signed the Declaration of the United Nations. The Allies were fighting a common enemy and supporting one another. The East-West split that came to be the dominant tension in world politics had not yet taken place.

In this environment, Allied leaders drew up plans for an organization based on existing goodwill to prevent the recurrence of another world war. Although the dele-gates used rhetoric about "the peoples of the United Nations," participants repre-sented governments that in turn represented states that were supposed to be sovereign and independent. The new organization was not intended to be a supranational entity (or world government), and the UN Charter enshrines the doctrine of state sover-eignty.

There was only one exception to the rule of seeking a consensus among govern-ments and respecting the narrow calculations of *raisons d'état*, and this exception became the focus of Chapter VII of the UN Charter. Using lessons from the failed League of Nations, the founders designed the United Nations to actively maintain peace around the world, to mobilize military might if necessary to enforce interna-tional decisions, and to shift from unanimous to majority voting (exclusive of the veto, to be discussed shortly).

Let us now examine both the institutional and legal bases for UN action in the security arena.

The Organizational Basics

The two central bodies to directly safeguard the peace are the Security Council and the General Assembly. Chapter V of the UN Charter designates the Security Council as the organ primarily responsible for maintaining international peace and security. It now has fifteen members. It was increased in 1965 from eleven as originally specified in the Charter to reflect the rapid increase in membership after decolonization. Many observers argue that it should change again to reflect altered power relations (for example, in order to make room for such countries as Japan, Germany, Brazil, South Africa, Egypt and India). In the communications age, both the Secretary-General and other observers have quipped that CNN is already the sixteenth member.

The most powerful states assumed special roles. The lack of participation by sev-eral great powers clearly had been a shortcoming at various junctures for the League of Nations. The United States and the Soviet Union insisted on the veto. In the end, these two great powers, along with France, China, and Great Britain, became perma-nent members, each with a veto over decisions. The remaining ten members are elected to two-year terms by the General Assembly. When electing the nonpermanent

Edward R. Stettinius Jr., chairman of the U.S. delegation, signs the UN Charter in San Francisco on June 26, 1945. President Harry S Truman stands by. (UNCIO Photo 2463)

members, the assembly tries to maintain a geographical balance by including representatives of the four major regions of the world: usually three from Africa, two from Asia, three from Europe, and two from Latin America.

The Security Council, whose permanent members were supposedly the most powerful military states in 1945, is vested with the duty of maintaining international peace and security. Unlike in the League of Nations, UN member states are legally required to abide by "decisions." The logic is that since permanent members possess the military capability to act quickly and decisively, no potential aggressor will challenge organizational strictures.

The permanent members are accorded special responsibilities and privileges in the collective-security schema. They pay more of the bills, and no decision can be made on nonprocedural questions unless they agree. The permanent members' veto powers ensure that on important questions they assent, or at least abstain. It was recognized that no enforcement action could take place against one of the great powers of the international system without creating a major war—the very thing that the United

Nations had been established to forestall By preventing action against a permanent member, the veto saved the organization from wrecking itself in operations against its most powerful members. Enforcement actions can be undertaken only with great-power cooperation.

After expanding in 1965, the Security Council altered its decisionmaking process. Enlargement of the council has reduced the mathematical weight that the permanent members hold in the voting. Nine affirmative votes are now needed to pass a resolution. Barring permanent member vetoes, all permanent members and one nonpermanent member could theoretically abstain from a vote without jeopardizing the passage of a resolution, although some unity among the five permanent members is practically indispensable. Also, the unity of the Non-Aligned Movement on most issues has essentially introduced a type of "sixth veto" when developing countries coalesce against a particular action.

Disagreement during the formal voting process has been reduced by efforts to gain a consensus during informal consultations before any vote. Two hundred seventy-nine vetoes were cast during the Cold War, but not one was cast from May 1990 until May 1993, and only a few have been used since. With or without vetoes, the need for more flexibility for multilateral diplomacy remained. So instead of the formal sessions riddled with vetoes that characterized the early years, crucial discussions now occur informally under the aegis of the president until the Security Council is ready either to make a decision or to vote formally. The presidency of the council revolves monthly and plays a critical role in this process of smoothing the way to a vote. The president meets with the Secretary-General to identify the parties to a dispute, negotiates with the permanent members to ensure that the veto will not be used, and consults with the nonaligned members of the Security Council and other relevant groups or actors. Accordingly, unified decisionmaking is facilitated and disunity in the council can be reduced.[10]

The General Assembly, where every member state is represented, serves as a more open forum for discussion. Duties include election of heads of other UN organs, budgetary and administrative decisions, and joint control of decisions on Charter amendments and admission of new members to the organization.

The General Assembly's role in relation to international peace and security increased for a time with the passage of the Uniting for Peace Resolution in 1950. In circumstances where the Security Council is unable to act, the General Assembly, acting in accordance with the provisions of the Uniting for Peace Resolution, can take measures in accordance with the purpose and spirit of the world organization. When used, this resolution obscured the distinctions between the Security Council and the General Assembly. There is disagreement whether this procedure is illegal, represents a de facto alteration of the Charter, or constitutes a new legal rule in spite of provisions for formal amendment in Articles 108 and 109. Supporters of the resolution argued that the Security Council's formal responsibility for maintaining peace was "primary" but not "exclusive." The importance of the resolution was political, symbolic, and psychological, if not legal.

This resolution, which can be initiated either by the General Assembly or Security Council, was first enacted in 1950 to allow the assembly to address North Korean aggression in South Korea amidst Security Council inaction after its initial condemnation of aggression and approval of assistance to South Korea. The absence of the Soviet Union (protesting Taiwan's occupation of the "Chinese seat" on the council in spite of the victory by the Chinese communists under Mao Zedong) had permitted the initial call for assistance and the subsequent military action against North Korea and its allies. But once Moscow ended its boycott and entered the fray, the Security Council was paralyzed by the Soviet veto.

The Uniting for Peace Resolution was not used again until 1956, when permanent members were involved in two crises. The General Assembly approved UN actions in the Suez crisis because effective action in the Security Council had been blocked by France and Britain; earlier that year, the assembly had censured the use of armed force by Moscow in Hungary.[11] Another use was in 1960, after the Security Council became deadlocked over the Congo operation because the Soviet Union and the United States supported different sides in the conflict. These situations are discussed in greater detail in Chapter 2.

The Charter spells out other important actors in this domain: the executive head of the organization (the Secretary-General); the professional staff (the secretariat); and the UN's judicial organ (the International Court of Justice, or ICJ). Selected by the General Assembly upon the recommendation of the Security Council, the Secretary-General is the chief executive officer. The secretariat of the United Nations consists of some 8,700 regular civilian staff members in New York and around the world working directly for the Secretary-General. Their number rises to about 50,000 if the specialized agencies and the Washington-based financial institutions are included. In matters of peace and security, several departments are involved. At the outset of the term of the sixth Secretary-General, Boutros Boutros-Ghali, the central work of the organization in matters of peace and security became the focus of an administrative reform of the inner cabinet under the direction of Under-Secretaries-General for political affairs, humanitarian affairs, and peacekeeping operations. Depending on the number of security operations at any moment over the past two decades, somewhere between 10,000 and 80,000 UN soldiers, police, and other special personnel also have served under the Secretary-General.

Beyond organizing and directing staff, the Secretary-General plays an instrumental role in the mediation of disputes, negotiations between or among warring parties, and deployment of UN-sponsored forces. This role reaches beyond that assigned to any other international official. An important mechanism in this regard is the appointment of special and personal representatives or envoys of the Secretary-General, who undertake missions in conflict areas. As of June 2003, there were no fewer than fifty such special envoys.

Although Article 99 of the UN Charter has not been used much, it makes it possible for the Secretary-General to "bring to the attention of the Security Council any matter which in his opinion may threaten the maintenance of international peace and security." Without formally invoking Article 99, the Secretary-General can still press his views behind the scenes with the great powers. His personal judgment and readiness to run risks and take initiatives is crucial to the accomplishment of his duties.

Article 99 was used only by Secretaries-General Dag Hammarskjöld in the Congo and, arguably, Trygve Lie in Korea and Kurt Waldheim in Iran. But the role of the Secretary-General and the possible resort to Article 99 provide the basis for less dramatic but potentially very useful activities.[12] "Quiet diplomacy" was Hammarskjöld's description, although sometimes the displeasure of governments became noisy.[13]

Whether Article 99 is invoked or not, the Secretary-General's actions are closely scrutinized by governments. Depending upon the political climate, criticism can be scathing, and it certainly affects the UN secretariat. Secretary-General U Thant was stridently criticized by the West for pulling UN troops from the Sinai in 1967, just as Lie and Hammarskjöld had been criticized by the Soviet bloc for their respective actions in Korea and the Congo. More recently, Secretaries-General Pérez de Cuéllar, Boutros-Ghali, and Kofi Annan have been criticized for their actions in the Persian Gulf, Bosnia, Somalia, and Iraq. As with all visible policy positions, criticism goes with this job. However, since the time of Trygve Lie and the Korean War, the Secretary-General has rarely issued a harsh public judgment concerning armed conflict for the very good reason that he is not effective if he loses the confidence of important states.

The International Court of Justice can have an impact on conflict. Modeled upon the Permanent Court of International Justice, which was also based in the Hague, the ICJ is a main organ of the United Nations, whereas its predecessor had functioned outside the League of Nations. Hence, all members of the UN are automatically parties to the ICJ's statute, although they are not bound by its jurisdiction without a voluntary acceptance. Composed of fifteen independent justices serving staggered nine-year terms and elected by a majority of both the General Assembly and the Security Council, the ICJ has jurisdiction over all matters referred to it. Its judgments are binding, but it has almost no means to enforce its judgments.

States refer cases to the court through agreements, either general (for example, via treaty), or ad hoc. As specified in Article 36 of its statute, the ICJ has jurisdiction between or among states that have accepted the same obligation. The court may also provide nonbinding but useful judgments through advisory opinions when requested to do so by a major UN organ or certain specialized bodies. The court's potential for helping to prevent breaches of the peace results from its independent judgments about treaty interpretations, questions of international law, the existence of facts, or the nature of reparations in situations that might otherwise result in the resort to armed force. In reality, the ICJ has had little effect on international peace and security. It generally hands down only a few decisions per year (about two or three during the Cold War and some ten to twelve thereafter), and rarely have they concerned an international conflict involving serious violence.

The Legal Basics

The core of the UN Charter concerning security questions is Article 2, paragraph 4: All states shall refrain from the threat or use of force in their international relations. On the one hand, Article 2(4) is visionary, even idealistic. States have engaged in the threat or use of force repeatedly in the history of world politics. How could it be otherwise when there are few procedures to guarantee peaceful change? That being so, it is quite remarkable that Article 2(4) has not completely withered away under the pressures of a violent world.

On the other hand, a world without the threat or use of force continues to be the primary objective of the United Nations. When Iraq invaded Kuwait, the international community started its response by labeling such action impermissible under the UN Charter. The same process has occurred in numerous other situations, although the language and form of international responses vary. The UN General Assembly opposed not only Iraq's invasion of Kuwait but also the U.S. invasions of Grenada and Panama, Vietnam's invasion of Cambodia, the Soviet Union's invasion of Afghanistan, India's invasion of East Pakistan, and so on.

In fact, Article 2(4) is not a dead letter. After the Cold War, a state contemplating the use of force to resolve a dispute, especially if not a great power, cannot be sure that its action will not result in some type of condemnation and punishment. To be sure, the process is not automatic; UN resolutions may be worded in a soft way, and actual sanctions can vary. As we noted earlier, the functioning of collective security frequently shows one political bias or another. Nevertheless, Article 2(4) is alive and reasonably well as a general standard of achievement.

According to the General Assembly in the 1970s, if a state engages in the first use of force, it has probably committed aggression. That is, the first use of force will normally be regarded as aggressive and nondefensive unless the Security Council holds otherwise. Individual or collective self-defense under Article 51 remains the only clearly legal use of force. Anticipatory self-defense, in which the purported defender state uses force first, in the face of an imminent armed attack, is not completely ruled out, but it is not explicitly endorsed either. The UN Security Council never did fully and clearly evaluate the Israeli first use of force in 1967 in the face of various Arab threats. The Bush Doctrine of preemption, articulated in 2002, reawakened debate over the legitimate first use of force. Given the dangerous nature of the logic of striking first on the basis of a purely national judgment, especially when the alleged threat is not imminent, great controversy greeted this aspect of U.S. security policy. The Bush Doctrine was the main reason France and others would not support first use of force against Iraq in 2003. In the past, similar claims had met a similar response, as when Israel claimed the right to strike first to take out an Iraqi nuclear reactor in 1981, a strike that was unanimously condemned by the council.

Inherent in this discussion is that force means military action. A number of developing countries wanted force to include economic coercion, but this view has not prevailed in General Assembly debates. Analytical clarity requires keeping in mind the continuum from outside military intervention through the everyday exercise of political influence through the unconscious impact of such "soft power" as culture and language.[14] International relations frequently involve states' affecting the internal affairs of other countries, although most diplomats prefer to avoid "intervention," which implies the forceful action by outsiders, in favor of "involvement" or "intrusion" or "interference."[15]

In addition to dealing with aggression entailing first use of force, Article 42 states that there can be threats to and breaches of the peace. Neither the Security Council nor the World Court has ever clarified the difference between "aggression" and a "breach of the peace." But it is clear that a situation can create a threat to the peace without necessarily consisting of armed attack by one state on another. In the spring of 1991, for example, the Security Council declared that the consequences of the human rights situation in Iraq constituted a threat to the peace. At that time the government of Saddam Hussein was engaged in such repression that hundreds of thousands of persons were being displaced within Iraq or were fleeing into Turkey or Iran.

Thus, not only interstate force but also other actions constituting a threat to the peace can violate the UN law of peaceful international relations. In the mid-1960s the UN authorized economic sanctions on Rhodesia. That territory was characterized by a unilateral declaration of independence from the United Kingdom, denial of many internationally recognized human rights, and growing violence between the white-minority government and the Patriotic Front. The Organization of African Unity (OAU) and eventually the UN General Assembly called the Patriotic Front a national liberation movement. There was no armed attack by one state on another, yet the Security Council said that there was no peace and that binding economic sanctions were in order.

This brings us to the crucial point that when the Security Council finds a situation of aggression, or threat to or breach of the peace, it can impose binding sanctions. In effect, the council can make international law. Chapter VII of the Charter, containing Articles 39 to 51, gives far more legal authority than the council of the League of Nations ever had. During the Cold War, the Security Council imposed binding sanctions on only two targets: the Ian Smith government in Rhodesia and the makers of apartheid in South Africa. Since the end of the Cold War, the Security Council has levied mandatory economic sanctions on a variety of parties in Iraq, Haiti, Yugoslavia, and elsewhere. It imposed a binding arms embargo on all parties fighting in the Balkans. It did not impose but did authorize military action for the liberation of Kuwait. Likewise, it did not require but did authorize all necessary means for the delivery of humanitarian assistance in both Somalia and Bosnia. All this occurred under Chapter VII of the Charter, leading to legally binding decisions by the Security Council. These decisions were not recommendations; they were mandatory from the viewpoint of international law.

It is still true that most Security Council resolutions, and all General Assembly resolutions except for those setting the budget, constitute recommendations, legally speaking. When dealing with peace and security issues, the council usually acts under Chapter VI, not Chapter VII. Chapter VI deals with the pacific settlement of disputes. Under this part of the Charter the council suggests to parties how they might resolve their disputes. Traditional peacekeeping, even though UN personnel may be lightly armed, takes place under Chapter VI. UN peacekeepers do not shoot their way into situations; they proceed with the consent of the parties, usually to supervise some cease-fire or other agreement. But the theory of the Charter's operation always entailed the notion that persuasion under Chapter VI should be seen against the more coercive possibilities under Chapter VII. If the parties cannot agree, upon pacific urging of the Security Council under the purview of Chapter VI, they might face sanctions under Chapter VII.

One of the great complexities facing the world organization in the twenty-first century is that although the Charter was written for states, much political instability and violence arise today either from violence within states or from violence across state boundaries by nonstate actors (NSAs). The problems in Somalia and Liberia, to name just two, arose from the absence of a functioning state and a government capable of speaking in the name of the state. In the legal vacuum, various armed factions exercise as much power as they can. In Bosnia, the problems stemmed not just from Yugoslavian and Croatian foreign policies but from the actions of Bosnian Serbs and Bosnian Croats who were, in effect, unrecognized or quasi-recognized rebels in an internationalized internal armed conflict. In Cambodia, four groups vied for power. In Sri Lanka, armed Tamils have long sought to violently carve a new state out of that island. We have already mentioned the prominence of Al Qaeda and other "terrorist" groups. Particularly after September 11, 2001, the importance of transnational NSAs seems obvious.

In these and other situations it is not clear what Article 2(7) means, namely, whether the UN, and presumably also a member state, can intervene in matters previously considered to be part of domestic jurisdiction. If the consequences of repression by the Iraqi government against Iraqis, including those who remain physically within Iraq, constitute a threat to international peace and security—as the council said in 1991—then what is left to constitute domestic jurisdiction? If the UN and its member states are entitled to use all necessary means to provide a secure environment for humanitarian assistance inside Somalia—as the council stated in 1992—in a situation in which the external material consequences for any other state were slight, then domestic jurisdiction means very little. If the restoration of a deposed but duly elected government is the basis for a Chapter VII intervention in Haiti—as the council stated in 1994—then what is the difference between domestic and international affairs? If the bombing of Belgrade over its repressive actions in its former province of Kosovo is condoned, what actions can be considered purely domestic?

The Permanent Court of International Justice was surely correct when it said in the 1920s that the dividing line between domestic and international jurisdictions was a changing one, depending on the nature of international relations. It is surely true that the realm of international action has been expanding. The political fact is that the Security Council, driven by the foreign policies of its members, is attempting to deal more with the causes of violence even if they arise from conditions within states than just with conditions between states. Legal notions follow from these political facts. Human security inside states may be as important at times to the Security Council as traditional notions of security between states.

As usual, power matters. If the United Kingdom says that the situation in Northern Ireland is a domestic matter, this view may carry the day because of the power of the UK and its friends. Surely some matters clearly remain a part of domestic jurisdiction. Elections to the legislature in Nebraska, Rhode Island, and South Carolina, said to be internal or domestic by the powerful United States, are not going to be supervised by the United Nations—although national elections in El Salvador, Nicaragua, Haiti, Angola, and Cambodia have been. (And perhaps it is not unreasonable to say that elections in Florida should be supervised by the UN in the future!)

Increasingly the United Nations, especially through Security Council action, has undertaken all sorts of deeply intrusive actions pertaining to human rights and economic affairs inside states in an effort to resolve security problems. Security issues do not separate so easily from these other concerns in many contemporary conflicts. In Cambodia, in theory if not fully in practice, UN personnel were in charge of governmental ministries. In theory at least, the UN governed Cambodia on an interim basis. The limits to UN action, respecting Article 2(7) and domestic jurisdiction, are first and foremost political. If the international community of states wants to act in Somalia or Cambodia or Iraq, via the UN, Article 2(7) will be redefined to fit the situation. States have ratified the UN Charter, which conveys powers of autointerpretation on the Security Council. What the international political traffic will bear determines the meaning of this article.

The precise boundaries of state sovereignty are elusive. If sovereignty means that a national government sets policy in its domestic jurisdiction, evolving international standards suggest that this remains true only as long as a national government adheres to international law. Perhaps the best example was Saddam Hussein's government following the conclusion of the 1991 Gulf War. He set policy in Iraq only as long as his government did not engage in aggression and did not engage in gross violations of internationally recognized human rights. When his government engaged in aggression, as against Kuwait, the United Nations put Iraq into a type of "receivership" in which it forfeited many attributes of a sovereign state—for example, it was no longer free to fashion its national security policy as it thought best, and it had to forgo using certain weapons. When it engaged in gross human rights violations, it had to tolerate UN protection of some threatened groups on Iraqi soil—for example, the Iraqi Kurds. When inspections for weapons of mass destruction resumed in November 2002, the extent of the outside intrusion was unprecedented.

The UN Secretary-General was referring to such trends when he wrote in 1992 that the time of absolute sovereignty had passed. Boutros-Ghali wrote in *Foreign Affairs*, "The centuries-old doctrine of absolute and exclusive sovereignty no longer stands, and was in fact never so absolute as it was conceived to be in theory. A major intellectual requirement of our time is to rethink the question of sovereignty."[16]

His successor, Kofi Annan, has been even more outspoken on the subject:

> State sovereignty, in its most basic sense, is being redefined—not least by the forces of globalization and international cooperation. States are now widely understood to be instruments at the service of their peoples, and not vice versa. At the same time individual sovereignty—by which I mean the fundamental freedom of each individual, enshrined in the charter of the UN and subsequent international treaties—has been enhanced by a renewed and spreading consciousness of individual rights. . . . This developing international norm in favour of intervention to protect civilians from wholesale slaughter will no doubt continue to pose profound challenges to the international community. In some quarters it will arouse distrust, scepticism, even hostility. But I believe on balance we should welcome it.[17]

Much remains to be done concerning the United Nations and security issues. Under Article 43 of the Charter, all states are obligated to conclude an agreement with the Military Staff Committee, a subsidiary of the Security Council, whereby military forces are made available to the UN. No state has ever concluded such an agreement, leaving the council and Secretary-General with the task of constructing military forces mostly de novo for each security crisis in which UN force is contemplated.

In the past the great powers could not agree among themselves about how to construct Article 43 agreements—for example, covering large as opposed to small forces. Some observers thought that during the Cold War neither Washington nor Moscow was seriously interested in these agreements. And in the United States, the question of Article 43 agreements got entangled in the controversy over "war powers," and whether the president alone was entitled to use various types of force pursuant to a Security Council resolution under Chapter VII. So this important matter remains unfinished over half a century after the Charter was signed.[18]

Partly because of this situation, the UN has resorted to the "sheriff's posse"[19] approach to a number of security crises—as in Korea, Iraq, Somalia, Haiti, and East Timor. In effect, the UN enters into a "contract" with the United States or other major powers to enforce UN policy in countering either aggression or threats to the peace. In the former Yugoslavia following the Dayton accords, NATO became the UN's agent. This is not so different from the Rhodesian situation in the 1960s and 1970s, when the Security Council authorized the British navy to enforce the mandatory embargo in Mozambique territory. This approach has the advantage of efficiency, which is no small matter when lives are on the line. But it has the drawback of the loss of UN control over its own policies, entailing loss of accountability for precisely what is done in the name of the UN.

Chapter VIII of the Charter lays out a theory for UN linkage with regional organizations. This subject is important enough for extended analysis, particularly in light of calls to expand regional organizations' roles in the international security arena.

Regional Arrangements

One question is whether it is more appropriate to deal with local conflict through multilateral organizations whose scope is regional (for instance, the European Union or NATO) or universal (for instance, the United Nations).[20] The preference for regional management of regional conflict was enshrined in Chapter VIII of the UN Charter at the urging of Washington, based on the insistence of its Latin American allies. The Persian Gulf War produced a strong sense that the original security provisions of the Charter, including a renewed interest in regional organizations, could sometimes be implemented. Secretary-General Boutros-Ghali's *An Agenda for Peace* contains a chapter on these organizations. A group of eminent persons called together by the Swedish prime minister in 1991 also called upon world leaders to "act determinedly to build a new system for peace and security, at both a global and regional scale."[21] Virtually all policy analyses of multilateralism in the last decade emphasize a division of labor between the United Nations and regional organizations.

There is some reason to believe that regional organizations are an appropriate locus for action because local instability poses a greater threat to regional actors. At the outset of the present Charter regime, the preference for peaceful settlement was clearly articulated. Even Article 21 of the Covenant of the League of Nations noted the validity of regional understandings as a basis for maintaining peace. However, many observers tend to overlook the fact that the relative balance between regionalism and universalism was one of the most controversial aspects at the San Francisco conference.[22]

One of the major themes running throughout this text is the importance of networks of institutions linked to the work of the United Nations. The field of security is quite distinct from the other issue areas—human rights and sustainable development—that are treated later. In the area of security, non-governmental organizations have been relatively inconsequential, but regional institutions play a central role. This generalization is almost the opposite for the issues of human rights and development, which are discussed in Parts Two and Three of this volume, because non-governmental actors have come to play such crucial roles.

The creation of the Security Council, with its enforcement power, gave globalism a significant edge over regionalism; Chapter VIII, "Regional Arrangements," was considered essential. The basic idea was that an effort would be made to settle local disputes regionally before referring them to the United Nations and that the Security Council would remain an option mainly if regional efforts failed. Chapter VIII was designed to limit Security Council deliberations to the most severe and intractable disputes.

Article 52 of Chapter VIII declares, "Nothing in the present Charter precludes the existence of regional arrangements or agencies dealing with matters relating to the maintenance of international peace and security" under the condition that "their activities are consistent with the Purposes and Principles of the United Nations." This article encourages states to use regional organizations before directing their conflicts to the Security Council and also recommends that the council make use of regional arrangements. Articles 53 and 54 define relations between the UN and regional organizations by prohibiting the latter from taking peace and security measures without Security Council authorization and by insisting that regional organizations inform the council.

The active use of the veto throughout the Cold War not only prevented the use of the Security Council but also meant that regional organizations sometimes provided Washington and Moscow with convenient pretexts for containing disputes within organizations that were themselves under superpower control. In what was then Washington's backyard, crises in Guatemala, Cuba, Panama, and the Dominican Republic were relegated to the Organization of American States, dominated by the United States. In what was then Moscow's backyard, Hungary and Czechoslovakia were in the jurisdiction of the "socialist community" of the Warsaw Pact, dominated by the Soviet Union.

The supposed deficiencies of universal international organizations and the resulting apparent strengths of regional ones should be examined in light of the ambiguity of region as a concept, the overstretched capacities of the UN in international peace and security, and the purported better familiarity with local crises by the member states of regional organizations. There is a lack of specificity in Chapter VIII; in the opening paragraph the framers deliberately avoided precision, thereby allowing governments the flexibility to fashion instruments to foster international peace and security. Although the commonsensical notion of region is related to geography, the ambiguity of the Charter means that a region can also be conceived of geopolitically, culturally, ideologically, and economically. Such groups could include treaty-based organizations that pre- or postdate the United Nations or ad hoc mechanisms created to deal with a specific concern.

In addition to including such geographic entities as the OAU or the OAS, the Charter's definition of a regional organization might also include NATO, the Islamic Conference, the Warsaw Treaty Organization, the OECD, and the Contadora Group. Recent research points to the emergence of such "subregional" units as the Gulf Cooperation Council (GCC) and the Southern African Development Coordination Conference (SADCC) as potentially significant.[23] The concept of regionalism remains a conundrum.

A second issue concerns institutional resources. The United Nations continues to experience grave financial difficulties and sorely lacks sufficient and qualified staff. The steady, skyrocketing growth of the UN peacekeeping budget until 1996 to meet needs in the former Yugoslavia, Cambodia, and Somalia—while payments remained unacceptably slow and arrears approached $3.5 billion in the mid–1990s—meant the organization was seriously overstretched and groping for help from regional institutions.[24]

The great powers appear reluctant to pay for any substantial expansion of UN conflict management. The end of East-West tensions diminishes the perceived Western interests in many regional conflicts. Moreover, the war on terrorism introduced other priorities, not just in the United States but throughout the Western world. And greatpower resources seem limited by, among other things, the nature of a globalized economy and an economic downturn that is a recession in reality if not in statistical terms. Governing elites and publics sought to divert expenditure from foreign policy to postponed domestic economic and social needs during the first decade after the Cold War. Smaller powers traditionally active in peacekeeping are unlikely to continue to pick up more of the tab. They share the economic problems of the larger states.

In this context, regional approaches to crisis management and conflict resolution may seem attractive. States near to a country in conflict suffer most from the destabilizing consequences of war in their area. They receive the refugees and bear the political, social, and economic consequences, willingly or unwillingly, of combatants from neighboring countries seeking sanctuary. They face the choice of pacifying and repatriating combatant and noncombatant aliens on their territory or of resisting hot pursuit by those from whom these refugees have fled. Local conflict and the consequent perceptions of regional instability dampen investment flows and retard growth. They divert public resources into defense expenditures.

States from a region at war appear to be well suited to mediating local conflicts. They understand the dynamics of the strife and of the cultures involved more intimately than outsiders do. Leaders are far more likely to have personal connections to protagonists, and these connections may be used as a basis for mediation. Involvement by other regional powers or organizations is less likely to be perceived as illegitimate interference than would involvement by extraregional organizations. Finally, issues of local conflict are far more likely to be given full and urgent consideration in regional gatherings than in global ones; the latter have much broader agendas and many more distractions.

The apparent advantages of regional institutions exist more in theory than in practice. In reality, these organizations are far less capable than the United Nations. The concept of regionalism is inchoate and not useful as a policy tool to guide decisions under Chapter VIII of the UN Charter. The institutional capacities of non-Western regional organizations are so feeble that they have not been able to carry out mandates in peace and security. The so-called comparative superiority of organizations in the actual region in conflict is more than offset by such practical disadvantages as partisanship, resource shortages, and local rivalries. Apart from very unusual circumstances (the exception being NATO forces, and NATO has been careful not to call itself regional in order to avoid implying any subservience to the Security Council), regional organizations have neither sufficient military capacity nor diplomatic leverage.

Many of the factors ostensibly favoring regional organizations are questionable. Regional actors do tend to suffer most from the destructive consequences of conflict among their neighbors. At the same time, they frequently have stakes in these conflicts, are committed to one side or another, and stand to benefit by influencing the outcome. Sometimes they even are active participants. In this sense, their structure of interests is more complex than many proponents of regional organizations suggest. Their shared interest in the public good of regional stability is often accompanied by unilateral interest in obtaining specific favorable outcomes.

Since a favorable result for one regional power is likely to enhance its regional position at the expense of others, those others are likely to oppose such initiatives. In the terminology of international relations theory, we have simultaneous considerations of absolute gain (stability) and relative gain (power). There is no certainty that stability will predominate. Indeed, the recent literature provides compelling arguments to the effect that cooperation and regime maintenance are particularly difficult where questions of power are prominent, as in national security.[25] Such issues are far more likely to be prominent in regional international relations than they are at the global level.

Situating crises in their regional historical and political contexts enhances the overall argument considerably. In Africa, the paralysis and bankruptcy of the OAU—now renamed the African Union—in curbing intervention and in managing the civil war in Angola reflected deep disagreement among its own members about the desirable outcome of the process of liberation. With its headquarters in Addis Ababa, the OAU appeared particularly inept in helping to end the Ethiopian civil war. The lack of any substantial OAU initiative also arose from the fact that other African states were deeply implicated in the conflict in pursuit of diverging national interests. Similar difficulties were evident in efforts to cope with crises in Chad and the Western Sahara. In Somalia, the OAU was critically handicapped by the initial reluctance of members to sanction outside involvement in an internal conflict. In Liberia and Sierra Leone, OAU inaction led to Nigeria's use of the Economic Community of West African States (ECOWAS) to contain the violence of a civil war. The modern African Union proved irrelevant to the bloodletting in the Congo circa 2003; many member states were deeply and directly involved on different sides on different issues.

In South Asia, it is hard to see how any regionally based initiative to settle the Afghan civil war might have succeeded, not only because of the presence of Soviet forces but also because India had no interest in seeing a pro-Pakistani or Islamic fundamentalist regime in Kabul. To take a more extreme case, the capacity of the South Asian Association for Regional Cooperation (SAARC) to act as a neutral mediator of conflict between India and Pakistan over Kashmir is extremely problematic; the two principal members of the organization are the very states involved. Elsewhere on the continent, efforts by the Association of Southeast Asian Nations (ASEAN) to resolve the Cambodian conflict were handicapped by differing conceptions of Chinese and Vietnamese threats to the region. More recently, the UN Security Council authorized an Australian-led multinational force (INTERFET) to restore peace and security in East Timor, an action taken with the acquiescence of the Indonesian government.

In Central America, the ability of the OAS to deal effectively with civil wars in Nicaragua and El Salvador was inhibited greatly by the U.S. failure to abide by the essential norm of nonintervention in its pursuit of a unilateral agenda to prevent revolution in El Salvador and reverse it in Nicaragua. The capacity of the European Community to come up with an effective response to the civil war in Croatia was significantly constrained by deep differences of opinion between France and Germany, and a number of disagreements among NATO members hampered military humanitarianism in Bosnia and Herzegovina.

Regional organizations replicate regional power imbalances. They may be used by the more powerful to expand their influence at the expense of the weak. Nigeria's manipulation of ECOWAS in Liberia is perhaps a most obvious case. Another is the Arab League's efforts to establish order in the Lebanese civil conflict, largely a fig leaf for one member's pursuing a long-standing desire to form a "greater Syria." Efforts to seek a UN blessing for Russian arbitration of disputes in the former Soviet Union amount to dressing up traditional Russian hegemony in the cloak of Commonwealth of Independent States (CIS) peacekeeping. This problem has appeared, or is likely to appear, in regions where power imbalances are so substantial that it is not possible for weaker states in coalition to balance against the strong. Cases in point include South Africa in southern Africa, Nigeria in West Africa, India in South Asia, Indonesia in Southeast Asia, and the United States in the Americas.

A further concrete problem with regional organizations as managers of conflict is that frequently their membership is not inclusive and their coverage is partial. OAU conflict management in southern Africa was inhibited by the organization's exclusion of the region's major military and economic power—South Africa. The same might be said of ASEAN's role, given the historical exclusion of Vietnam, Laos, and Cambodia. In light of the vast differences in their levels of economic development, this situation is unlikely to change once these anomalous exclusions are rectified. The Arab League excludes one of the three major regional powers (Iran). The Gulf Cooperation Council excludes two of three (Iraq and Iran). In a number of these instances (the OAU in southern Africa, the GCC in the Gulf, and ASEAN), the consciousness of the organization is defined in large part by its members' opposition to the threat posed by the excluded parties. The premise of these organizations has been partiality, hardly a capacity for neutral intervention and security management.

Moreover, these organizations have traditionally demonstrated their greatest structural weaknesses in dealing with civil war, the main growth industry for international conflict managers. This shortcoming follows in part from the international legal impediments associated with the doctrine of noninterference in internal affairs. These impediments have proven even more acute for many countries in the Third World, preoccupied with exerting control over their own tenuous bases of power.[26]

Perhaps most important in many instances, the reluctance to become involved in civil conflict reflects the sensitivity of regional powers to creating precedents that might later be used to justify intervention in their own countries. In Africa, for example, many governments are themselves threatened by the possibility of civil conflict, which leads to caution about fostering norms that would legitimize regional involvement in such conflicts. Curiously, the challenge to the sovereignty of colonial powers facilitated decolonization. But newly independent countries immediately became staunch defenders of state sovereignty, a sentiment that is also prevalent in central Europe and the former Soviet republics. Respect for conventional definitions of sovereignty has verged on slavishness. This weakness was shared during the Cold War by the United Nations; it is likely to play out more strongly at the regional level.

For all of these reasons, the general case for reliance on regional organizations is weak. If they were in theory the appropriate instrument for conflict management, their organizational, financial, and military capacities, as well as their fund of peace-keeping and conflict management experience, would be superior to those of the United Nations. The opposite is true. For example, it is illustrative to compare the frequency of regional conflict in Africa with the paucity of substantive attempts by the OAU—or now the African Union—to manage such conflict and the persistent reliance on external assistance for regional security. Although the OAS has a staff and even enjoys the professionalism of officers in the Inter-American Defense Board (IADB), its domination by the United States has largely discredited the institution in the peace and security arena. During the Nicaraguan and El Salvadoran mediation efforts, the OAS had to take a clear secondary position to the United Nations. Other regional organizations that have been active in regional conflicts, including ASEAN and the Organization on Security and Cooperation in Europe (OSCE), exist more on paper and during intergovernmental sessions than in fact; they have little institutional infrastructure. The OSCE's capacities have, however, begun to develop in response to requests for help in the former Soviet Union and especially in the former Yugoslavia to implement the Dayton agreements and follow-up to the war in Kosovo.

At the same time, the United Nations is overstretched. Given the demands that threaten to outstrip its resources, it would appear desirable to shift some of the burden to regional institutions. The question arises whether member states should determine on a case-by-case basis the comparative advantages of specific regional institutions. How could such institutions, either constituted by treaty or formed on an ad hoc basis to meet a crisis, work best in tandem with the UN?

The pursuit of the Gulf War in 1991 and the creation of safe havens for Iraqi Kurds were clear and successful illustrations of what we might call military "subcontracting" to the Allied Coalition, as is NATO's ongoing presence in the former Yugoslavia. A more controversial and less successful example was Somalia, where a U.S.-led effort was mounted to break the back of warlord-induced famine. Moreover, three Security Council decisions between late June and late July 1994 indicated the relevance of military intervention by major powers in regions of their traditional interests: a Russian plan to deploy its troops in Georgia to end the three-year-old civil war; the French intervention in Rwanda, supposedly to cope with genocidal conflict; and the U.S. plan to spearhead a military invasion to reverse the military coup in Haiti. The decision in Budapest in December 1994 by the then Conference (now Organization) on Security and Cooperation in Europe to authorize troops from the Commonwealth of Independent States and other OSCE member states after a definitive agreement in Nagorno-Karabakh is another illustration of subcontracting. So was the earlier effort by Nigeria and other countries of the Economic Community of West African States in Liberia and Sierra Leone, along with Australia's leadership in East Timor.

The results from these arrangements have not been consistently superior to the UN's record. Yet the evident gap between the UN's capacities and persistent demands for help could be filled by regional powers, or even hegemons, operating under the scrutiny of a wider community of states.[27] The argument has become stronger in light of the experience in Kosovo and more especially the smooth handover in Timor from the Australian-led force to the UN one in February 2000.

In attempting to determine a possible division of labor between global and regional organizations to meet the exigencies of particular conflicts, distinctions should be made between Europe and developing countries as well as between the use of outside military forces to keep the peace and diplomatic measures for negotiations. In Europe, UN diplomacy could well be combined with the use of NATO forces under a UN flag in regional disputes, as throughout the former Yugoslavia. Also, by 2003 there were steps to create a military capacity for the EU. In developing countries, the division of labor could be different. In crises of manageable size (for example, in Guatemala), the UN could deploy its troops and work closely with regional partners in diplomatic arm-twisting. In more dangerous conflicts like the ones in Somalia and the Congo, UN diplomacy could be teamed with the troops of countries willing to run risks in a coalition.

In short, there is good reason to doubt not just the will but also the capacity of regional organizations to perform well in the management of conflict within their areas. The end of the Cold War has done little to change this conclusion. Widespread euphoria about the potential of regional organizations needs to be tempered with the results of recent efforts. We revisit these themes in Chapters 3 and 4.

Straying from the Course

Since 1945, untold numbers of wars have broken out and tens of millions of people have perished as a result.[28] According to the logic of the Charter, the leadership for the UN's peace and security duties rests on the shoulders of a small segment of the international community, notably the great powers. Conflict between Washington and

Moscow poisoned the atmosphere and prevented their working together on most issues of security during the Cold War. World politics often made it impossible to act collectively, and states often chose to disobey or ignore the prohibitions and restrictions on the use of force to pursue *raisons d'état*.

In place of the ideal collective-security system, the UN developed alternate means to mitigate certain conflicts under the term "peacekeeping." Familiarity with this particular creation of the UN is necessary to understand the Cold War period and beyond. It is to this story that we now turn.

Notes

1. See Hedley Bull, *The Anarchical Society* (New York: Oxford University Press, 1977).

2. See Adam Watson, "European International Society and Its Expansion," in Hedley Bull and Adam Watson, eds., *The Expansion of International Society* (Oxford: Oxford University Press, 1986), pp. 23–25. For a discussion of historical developments since 1880 in relation to building functional international institutions, see Craig N. Murphy, *International Organization and Industrial Change: Global Governance Since 1850* (Cambridge, U.K.: Polity Press, 1994).

3. The codification of these rules began and has continued under the auspices of the International Committee of the Red Cross. See David P. Forsythe, *Humanitarian Politics: The International Committee of the Red Cross* (Baltimore: Johns Hopkins University Press, 1977); and *The Geneva Conventions of August 12, 1949*, and *Protocols Additional to the Geneva Conventions of 12 August 1949* (Geneva: ICRC, 1989).

4. For a discussion, see Inis L. Claude Jr., *Swords into Plowshares* (New York: Random House, 1964), pp. 3–34; Harold Jacobson, *Networks of Interdependence* (New York: Knopf, 1984), chap. 2; and Thomas G. Weiss, *International Bureaucracy* (Lexington, Mass.: D. C. Heath, 1975), pp. 3–47.

5. For a quantification of this dynamic, see Robert S. Jordan with Clive Archer, Gregory P. Granger, and Kerry Ordes, *International Organizations: A Comparative Approach to the Management of Cooperation*, fourth edition (New York: Praeger, 2001).

6. For a discussion, see F. H. Hinsley, *Power and the Pursuit of Peace* (Cambridge, U.K.: Cambridge University Press, 1963), pp. 1–238; S. J. Hambleben, *Plans for World Peace Through Six Centuries* (Chicago: University of Chicago Press, 1943); F. P. Walters, *A History of the League of Nations,* 2 vols. (London: Oxford University Press, 1952).

7. Lynn H. Miller, *Global Order: Values and Power in International Politics,* second edition (Boulder: Westview Press, 1990), pp. 46–50.

8. Chapter 12 of Claude, *Swords into Plowshares,* is still the best single treatment of collective security. The interested reader is also referred to Inis L. Claude Jr., *Power and International Relations* (New York: Random House, 1962); Ernst B. Haas, "Types of Collective Security: An Examination of Operational Concepts," *American Political Science Review* 49, no. 1 (1955), pp. 40–62; Thomas G. Weiss, ed., *Collective Security in a Changing World* (Boulder: Lynne Rienner, 1993); and George W. Downs, ed., *Collective Security Beyond the Cold War* (Ann Arbor: University of Michigan Press, 1994). For a statistical view, see John Mearsheimer, "The False Promise of International Institutions," *International Security* 19, no. 3 (Winter 1994–1995), pp. 5–49.

9. See, for example, Egon Ranshofen-Wertheimer, *The International Secretariat: A Great Experiment in International Administration* (Washington, D.C.: Carnegie Endowment, 1945).

10. Johan Kaufmann, *United Nations Decision-Making* (Rockville, Md.: Sijthoff and Noordhoff, 1980), pp. 43–52. See also Sydney D. Bailey and Sam Daws, *The Procedure of the UN*

Security Council, Third Edition (Oxford: Oxford University Press, 1998); and James P. Muldoon et al., *Multilateral Diplomacy and the United Nations Today* (Boulder: Westview Press, 1999).

11. See M. J. Peterson, *The General Assembly in World Politics* (Boston: Allen and Unwin, 1986). This book is the single best treatment of the General Assembly. For a discussion of formal and informal processes, see Johan Kaufmann, *Conference Diplomacy: An Introductory Analysis*, rev. ed. (Dordrecht: Martinus Nijhoff, 1988).

12. The best sources for the Charter are Leland Goodrich, Edvard Hambro, and Anne Patricia Simons, *Charter of the United Nations* (New York: Columbia University Press, 1969); and Bruno Simma, *The Charter of the United Nations: A Commentary* (Oxford University, 2002).

13. See Benjamin Rivlin and Leon Gordenker, eds., *The Challenging Role of the UN Secretary-General* (Westport, Conn.: Praeger, 1993). For recent autobiographies see Javier Pérez de Cuéllar, *Pilgrimage for Peace: A Secretary-General's Memoirs* (New York: St. Martin's Press, 1997); and Boutos Boutros-Ghali, *Unvanquished: A U.S.-U.N. Saga* (Mississauga, Ontario: Random House of Canada, Limited, 1999).

14. For discussion see Joseph P. Nye Jr., *Bound to Lead: The Changing Nature of American Power* (New York: Basic Books, 1990), and *The Paradox of American Power: Why the World's Only Superpower Can't Go It Alone* (Oxford: Oxford University, 2002).

15. See Stanley Hoffmann, "The Problem of Intervention," in Hedley Bull, ed., *Intervention in World Politics* (New York: Oxford University Press, 1984), pp. 7–28.

16. Boutros Boutros-Ghali, "Empowering the United Nations," *Foreign Affairs* 72, no. 5 (Winter 1992–1993), pp. 98–99.

17. Kofi Annan, "Two Concepts of Sovereignty," *The Economist* (September 18, 1999).

18. See Eric Grove, "UN Armed Forces and the Military Staff Committee: A Look Back," *International Security* 17, no. 4 (Spring 1993), pp. 172–181.

19. See Brian Urquhart, "Beyond the 'Sheriff's Posse,'" *Survival* 32, no. 3 (May–June 1990), pp. 196–205.

20. For a lengthier discussion, see S. Neil MacFarlane and Thomas G. Weiss, "Regional Organizations and Regional Security," *Security Studies* 2, no. 1 (Autumn 1992), pp. 6–37.

21. See *The Stockholm Initiative on Global Security and Governance* (Stockholm: Prime Minister's Office, 1991), p. 5.

22. See Francis O. Wilcox, "Regionalism and the United Nations," *International Organization* 19, no. 3 (Summer 1965), pp. 789–811; and Tom J. Farer, "The Role of Regional Collective Security Arrangements," in Weiss, *Collective Security*, pp. 153–189.

23. See William T. Tow, *Subregional Security Cooperation in the Third World* (Boulder: Lynne Rienner, 1990).

24. For a discussion of the resulting dangers, see Charles W. Maynes, "Containing Ethnic Conflict," *Foreign Policy* no. 90 (Spring 1993), pp. 3–21; and Stephen John Stedman, "The New Interventionists," *Foreign Affairs* 72, no. 1 (1993), pp. 1–16.

25. On this point, see Joseph Grieco, "Anarchy and the Limits of Cooperation: A Realist Critique of the Newest Liberal Institutionalism," *International Organization* 62, no. 3 (Summer 1988), pp. 488–507; and John Mearsheimer, "Instability in Europe After the Cold War," *International Security* 15, no. 1 (Summer 1990), p. 44.

26. See Mohammed Ayoob, *The Third World Security Predicament: State Making, Regional Conflict, and the International System* (Boulder: Lynne Rienner, 1995); and Brian Job, ed., *The Insecurity Dilemma: National Security of Third World States* (Boulder: Lynne Rienner, 1992).

27. The discussion about the components of accountability was first made in relationship to Russia by Jarat Chopra and Thomas G. Weiss, "Prospects for Containing Conflict in the Former Second World," *Security Studies* 4, no. 3 (Spring 1995), pp. 552–583; see also Lena Jonson and Clive Archer, eds., *Peacekeeping and the Role of Russia in Eurasia* (Boulder: Westview

Press, 1996). For an extended argument about a "partnership" between the UN and regional organizations, see Alan K. Henrikson, "The Growth of Regional Organizations and the Role of the United Nations," in Louise Fawcett and Andrew Hurrell, eds., *Regionalism in World Politics: Regional Organizations and World Order* (Oxford: Oxford University Press, 1995), pp. 122–168.

28. For a discussion of the unsettling numbers, see the annual publications of the International Institute for Strategic Studies, *Strategic Survey 2002/2003* and the *Military Balance 2002–2003* (Oxford: Oxford University Press, 2002).

2 The Reality of UN Security Efforts During the Cold War

The Early Years: Palestine, Korea, Suez, the Congo

Even before World War II officially ended, fifty-five countries signed the UN Charter on June 26, 1945. The Charter's requirement for unanimity among the permanent members of the Security Council indicated the realities of power politics at the time. The Security Council was created less out of naïve idealism and more out of a hardheaded effort to mesh state power with international law, a link that is necessary for effective enforcement actions. However, the underlying assumption that members could often agree—unrealistic with hindsight and even to astute observers then—was not borne out with any frequency until after the Cold War. But for a brief time after World War II, an improved international order with greater reason, law, assumption of unity, and collective security seemed feasible.

The onset of the Cold War in the late 1940s quickly ended the big-power cooperation on which the postwar order had been predicated. Nonetheless, in the early years the UN became involved in four major security crises that influenced subsequent developments and possibilities: in Palestine, Korea, Suez, and the Congo. Directly after Israel declared its independence in 1948, war broke out between it and its four neighbors—Egypt, Jordan, Lebanon, and Syria. Soon thereafter, the Security Council ordered a cease-fire under Chapter VII and created an observer team under Chapter VI to supervise it. This group grew into the United Nations Truce Supervision Organization (UNTSO) in 1949 and assumed the role of sentry.

Observer groups deployed along the borders of Israel and of its neighbors were unarmed and operated with the consent of the parties involved. Close to 600 observers were eventually deployed, including army units from Belgium, France, the United States, and Sweden. The presence of soldiers from France and the United States was afterward considered by some to be an aberration. However, the United Kingdom was involved in the UN operation in Cyprus from the very beginning in 1960 and France, in the operation in Lebanon almost from the outset in 1978. Although the United States normally provided logistics to begin operations, participation by permanent members with ground troops in UN forces normally was avoided.

Troops were unarmed and had no enforcement capability, but their presence sometimes deterred truce violations. They represented the international community, which often enabled them to exercise their mandates without relying upon military might.

Also, warring parties knew that their truce violations would be objectively reported to UN headquarters in New York for possible further action. Although observers wore the uniforms of their respective national armies, their first allegiance theoretically was to the world organization, symbolized by UN armbands. Later, blue helmets and berets became the trademark of UN peacekeepers. The observers were paid by their national armies and granted a stipend by the organization. UNTSO's activities continue to be financed from the UN's regular operating budget.

UNTSO has performed a variety of important tasks. UNTSO observers set up demilitarized zones along the Israeli-Egyptian and Israeli-Syrian borders, established Mixed Armistice Commissions along each border to investigate complaints and allegations of truce violations, and verified compliance with the General Armistice Agreements. If a truce violation occurred, the chief of staff of UNTSO attempted to deal with the matter locally, negotiating cease-fires when necessary. Finding means of deescalating crises before they blossom into significant threats to the peace has been a chief function of the operation.

UNTSO also became a training ground and resource center for other peacekeeping operations; its observers and administrators were consistently redeployed in other parts of the world. UNTSO's experience over the years has been integrated into other operations to improve their functioning.

UNTSO did, unfortunately, contribute to a freezing of the conflict. From 1949 to 1956 and then to 1967 the main parties to the conflict were unwilling to use major force to break apart the stalemate. UNTSO was there to police the status quo. Being freed from major military violence, the parties lacked the necessary motivation to make concessions for a more genuine peace. This problem of successful UN peacekeeping contributing to the freezing but not solution of conflict was to reappear in Cyprus and other places.

The first coercive action taken in the name of the United Nations concerned the Korean peninsula.[1] UN involvement in this crisis merits careful attention because some observers consider the UN to have engaged in a type of collective security there between 1950 and 1953. Others call UN involvement in Korea a police action. Still others consider the UN role in Korea a unique experience defying standard terminology.

Labels aside for the moment, some history bears recalling. World War II left Korea divided, with Soviet forces occupying the North and U.S. forces the South. A UN call for withdrawal of foreign troops and elections throughout a unified Korea was opposed by communist governments, leading to elections only in the South and the withdrawal of most U.S. troops. In June 1950, forces from North Korea (the Democratic Republic of Korea) attacked South Korea (the Republic of Korea). The Soviet Union conspired with the North and China, initially unprepared for the attack, eventually became a major belligerent on the side of the North.

Even though U.S. Secretary of State Dean Acheson had previously given a speech indicating that South Korea was not within an extensive U.S. defensive perimeter, President Harry S. Truman and Acheson agreed immediately that this attack on a noncommunist small state must be resisted. At the time, the USSR was boycotting the Security Council to protest the presence of a representative from the exiled government on Taiwan in the permanent seat reserved for China, thus excluding from the council the communist government on the mainland. Therefore, the United States knew that the Security Council would not be stymied by a communist veto and would adopt some type of resolution on Korea. So the United States did not hesitate to refer the Korean situation to the council.

Even so, the Truman administration began to order U.S. military forces to Korea even before the Security Council adopted a resolution under Chapter VII declaring that North Korea had committed a breach of the peace, and before the council recommended, but did not require, that UN members furnish all appropriate assistance (including military assistance) to South Korea. When Moscow returned to its council seat late in 1950, the General Assembly improvised, through the Uniting for Peace Resolution, to continue support for the South in the name of the United Nations.

In essence, Security Council resolutions on Korea provided international legitimacy to U.S. decisions, in the eyes of many states and Western public opinion. The Truman administration was determined to stop communist expansion in East Asia, and it claimed that it had the legal right to do so under the U.S. Constitution. It proceeded without a congressional declaration of war or any other specific authorizing measure, and it was prepared to proceed without UN authorization—although once this was obtained, the Truman administration emphasized UN approval in its search for support both at home and abroad.

The UN's symbol and reputation were therefore thrust into a security dilemma of major proportions, even though the permanent members of the council, and the communist government of China outside the council, were definitely not in agreement. Once the USSR returned to deliberations, it became impossible for the council to direct military actions being taken in its name. During the Soviet absence, a unified UN command had been established. In reality, it deputized the United States to lead the defense of South Korea in the name of the United Nations. When the early tide of the contest turned in favor of the South, Truman decided to carry the war all the way to the Chinese border. This was a fateful decision that prolonged the war by bringing Chinese forces into the fight in major proportions—and thus continued the war until 1953, when stalemate restored the status quo ante. All important strategic and tactical decisions pertaining to Korea that carried the UN's name were in fact made in the White House or the Pentagon. A number of other states fought for the defense of South Korea, but that military operation was, in fact, a U.S. operation behind a blue international fig leaf.

The defense of South Korea was not a classic example of collective security. True, a truncated Security Council clearly labeled the situation a breach of the peace, something that was not to occur again during the Cold War. True, the council in effect authorized military support for the South, but it did not mandate it, a form of council action that was to be repeated in the 1990s concerning Iraq, Somalia, and Bosnia. But neither the council nor its Military Staff Committee really controlled the use of UN symbols. No Article 43 agreements transferring national military units to the UN were concluded. And the Secretary-General, Trygve Lie of Norway, played almost no role in the situation once he came out clearly against the North Korean invasion. The USSR stopped treating him as Secretary-General. Given that power play, he was eventually forced to resign because of his ineffectiveness. He was legally correct to take a

Prisoners guarded by a South Korean soldier wait to be taken to a POW camp near Inchon in October 1950. (UN Photo 32240)

public stand against aggression, but such a stand left him without the necessary political support of a major power during the Cold War. Subsequent Secretaries-General tried to learn from his difficulties, representing Charter values but, they hoped, without antagonizing the permanent members whose support was necessary for successful UN action.

The 1956 Suez Canal crisis was quite distinct from the Korean crisis. It resulted in the first use of what became known as "peacekeepers" to separate warring parties. France, Britain, and Israel had attacked Soviet-backed Egypt against the wishes of the United States, claiming a right to use force to keep the Suez Canal open after Egyptian president Gamel Abdel Nasser had closed it. Britain and France used their vetoes, and action by the Security Council was blocked. The General Assembly resorted to the Uniting for Peace Resolution—this time for peacekeeping, not enforcement—and directed Secretary-General Dag Hammarskjöld to create a force to supervise the ceasefire between Israel and Egypt once it had been arranged. The first UN Emergency

Congolese refugees uprooted from their homes by fighting in Katanga Province wait for water at a refugee camp in September 1961. (UN Photo 71906)

Force (UNEF I) oversaw the disengagement of forces and served as a buffer between Israel and Egypt. In this instance, Washington and Moscow were not so far apart. In fact, President Dwight D. Eisenhower acted in the spirit of collective security by preventing traditional U.S. allies from proceeding with what he regarded as aggression. UN peacekeeping in 1956 and for a decade thereafter was hailed as a great success.

At the same time, the efforts by the world organization to deal with one of the most traumatic decolonizations, in the former Belgian Congo (then Zaire and more recently once again the Congo), illustrated the limits of peacekeeping. (The tradition of acronyms in English was set aside as operations in Spanish- and French-speaking countries became more widespread beginning in the late 1980s.) The ONUC (or United Nations Operation in the Congo) almost bankrupted the world organization and also threatened its political life; and Secretary-General Hammarskjöld lost his own life in a suspicious plane crash in the country.

The conflict was both international (caused by the intervention of Belgium in its former colony) and domestic (caused by the secession of a province within the new state). The nearly total absence of a government infrastructure entailed a massive involvement of UN civilian administrators in addition to 20,000 UN soldiers. After having used his Article 99 powers to get the world organization involved, the Secretary-General became embroiled in a situation in which the Soviet Union, its allies, and many nonaligned countries supported the national prime minister, who was subsequently murdered while under arrest; the Western powers and the UN organization supported the president. At one point the president fired the prime minister, and the

UN Secretary-General Dag Hammarskjöld visits children of a village composed of Yemeni immigrants in the Jerusalem hills in May 1956. (UN Photo 50052)

prime minister fired the president, leaving no clear central authority in place. As in Somalia later, this type of political vacuum created enormous problems for the United Nations as well as the opening for action.

Instead of neutral peacekeepers, UN forces became an enforcement army for the central government, which the UN created with Western support. In this process the world organization could not count on cooperation from the warring parties within the Congo. Some troop contributors resisted UN command and control; others removed their soldiers to register their objections. The Soviet Union, and later France, refused to pay assessments. This phase of the dispute almost destroyed the UN, and the General Assembly had to suspend voting for a time in order to dodge the question of who was in arrears on payments and thus who could vote. Moscow went further in trying to destroy Hammarskjöld's independence by suggesting the replacement of the Secretary-General with a troika (or a three-person administrative structure at the top of the organization).

Four years later, the UN departed a unified Congo, and some observers viewed this as an important achievement. Many African states were threatened by secessionist movements (for example, the one in Biafra that erupted into a Nigerian civil war in 1967). The UN thus helped to keep alive the possibility of the policy adopted by the Organization of African Unity (OAU) at its first meeting in Addis Ababa in 1963, namely, that no colonial border could be called into question. Yet the world organization also had acquired an operational black eye in Africa as a result of its clearly partisan stance. No UN troops were sent again until the end of the Cold War (to Namibia). The UN also had a large budgetary deficit and a hesitancy to become involved in internal wars.

At the end of the 1973 Arab-Israeli War, the second United Nations Emergency Force (UNEF II) provided another and largely successful example of separation of forces. The rules developed to govern its operation as an armed interpositional force became the blueprint for other traditional peacekeeping operations. UNEF II was composed of troops from Austria, Finland, Ireland, Sweden, Canada, Ghana, Indonesia, Nepal, Panama, Peru, Poland, and Senegal—nations representing each of the world's four major regions. The operation consisted of over 7,000 persons at its peak. UNEF II's original mandate was for six months, but the Security Council renewed it continually until 1979, when the U.S.-brokered Israeli-Egyptian peace accord was signed. Essentially, UNEF II functioned as an impartial force designed to establish a demilitarized zone, supervise it, and safeguard other provisions of the truce. Small-scale force was used to stop those who tried to breach international lines. The presence of UNEF II had a calming influence on the region through its ensuring that Israel and Egypt were kept apart.

The success of both UNEF I and II, and the problems with the operation in the Congo, catalyzed traditional peacekeeping, the subject to which we now turn.

Understanding Peacekeeping

As mentioned earlier, the effective projection of military power under international control to enforce international decisions against aggressors was supposed to distinguish the United Nations from the League of Nations. The onset of East-West tensions made this impossible on a systematic basis. The United States sought to keep the Soviet Union at arm's length from UN security efforts. A new means of peace maintenance was necessary, one that would permit the world organization to act within carefully defined limits when the major powers agreed or at least acquiesced.

UN peacekeeping proved mostly capable of navigating the turbulent waters of the Cold War through its mostly neutral stance and limited range of activities. Again, global politics determined the nature of UN activities. Although peacekeeping is not specifically mentioned in the Charter, it became the organization's primary function in the domain of peace and security. The use of troop contingents for this purpose is widely recognized as having begun during the 1956 crisis in Suez. Contemporary

TABLE 2.1   UN Peacekeeping Operations During the Cold War and
During the Initial Thaw

Years Active	Operation
1948–present	United Nations Truce Supervision Organization (UNTSO, based in Jerusalem)
1949–present	United Nations Military Observer Group in India and Pakistan (UNMOGIP)
1956–1967	United Nations Emergency Force (UNEF I, Suez Canal)
1958	United Nations Observation Group in Lebanon (UNOGIL)
1960–1964	United Nations Operation in the Congo (ONUC)
1962–1963	United Nations Force in New West Guinea (UNSF, in West Iran)
1963–1964	United Nations Yemen Observation Mission (UNYOM)
1964–present	United Nations Peace-keeping Force in Cyprus (UNFICYP)
1965–1966	United Nations India-Pakistan Observation Mission (UNIPOM)
1965–1966	Mission of the Representative of the Secretary-General in the Dominican Republic (DOMREP)
1973–1979	Second United Nations Emergency Force (UNEF II, Suez Canal and later the Sinai Peninsula)
1974–present	United Nations Disengagement Observer Force (UNDOF, Golan Heights)
1978–present	United Nations Interim Force in Lebanon (UNIFL)
1988–1990	United Nations Good Offices Mission in Afghanistan and Pakistan (UNGOMAP)
1988–1991	United Nations Iran-Iraq Military Observer Group (UNIIMOG)
1989–1990	United Nations Transition Assistance Group (UNTAG, in Namibia)
1989–1991	United Nations Angola Verification Mission (UNAVEM I)
1989–1992	United Nations Observer Group in Central America (ONUCA)

accounts credit Lester B. Pearson, then Canada's secretary of state for external affairs, with proposing to the General Assembly that Secretary-General Hammarskjöld organize an "international police force that would step in until a political settlement could be reached."[2]

Close to 500,000 military, police, and civilian personnel—distinguished from national soldiers by their trademark powder-blue helmets and berets—served in UN peacekeeping forces during the Cold War, and some 700 lost their lives in UN service during this period. Alfred Nobel hardly intended to honor soldiers when he created the peace prize that bears his name, and no military organization had received the prize throughout its eighty-seven-year history until December 1988, when UN peacekeepers received the prestigious award. This date serves as the turning point in the following discussion to distinguish UN security activities during and after the Cold War.

The Cold War and the Birth of Peacekeeping, 1948–1988

The lack of any specific reference to peacekeeping in the Charter led Hammarskjöld to coin the poetic and apt expression "Chapter six and a half," which referred to stretching the original meaning of Chapter VI. And certainly peacekeeping "can rightly be called the invention of the United Nations," as Secretary-General Boutros Boutros-Ghali claims in *An Agenda for Peace*.[3] The lack of a clear international constitutional basis makes a consensus definition of peacekeeping difficult, particularly because peacekeeping operations have been improvised in response to the specific requirements of individual conflicts. Despite the lack of consensus and the multiplicity of sources,[4] Under-Secretary-General Marrack Goulding provided a sensible definition of peacekeeping: "United Nations field operations in which international personnel, civilian and/or military, are deployed with the consent of the parties and under United Nations command to help control and resolve actual or potential international conflicts or internal conflicts which have a clear international dimension."[5]

The first thirteen UN peacekeeping and military observer operations deployed during the Cold War are listed in Table 2.1.[6] Five were still in the field in mid-2003. From 1948 to 1988, peacekeepers typically served two functions: observing the peace (that is, monitoring and reporting on the maintenance of cease-fires) and keeping the peace (that is, providing an interpositional buffer between belligerents and establishing zones of disengagement). The forces were normally composed of troops from small or nonaligned states, with permanent members of the Security Council and other major powers making troop contributions only under exceptional circumstances. Lightly armed, these neutral troops were symbolically deployed between belligerents who had agreed to stop fighting; they rarely used force and then only in self-defense and as a last resort. Rather than being based on any military prowess, the influence of UN peacekeepers in this period resulted from the cooperation of belligerents mixed with the moral weight of the international community of states.[7]

Peacekeeping operations essentially defended the status quo. They helped suspend a conflict and gain time so that belligerents could be brought closer to the negotiating table. However, these operations do not by themselves guarantee the successful pursuit of negotiations. They are often easier to institute than to dismantle, as the case of thirty years of this activity in Cyprus demonstrates. The termination of peacekeeping operations creates a vacuum and has serious consequences for the stability of a region, as happened in 1967 at the outbreak of the Arab-Israeli War following the withdrawal of UNEF I at Egypt's request.

Detailed histories of the first decades of peacekeeping are readily available. One illustration of the UN's handling of conflict in this period of East-West tensions helps to set the stage for a discussion of general principles that will bring in other UN operations. The UN Disengagement Observer Force (UNDOF) represents a classic example of international compromise during the Cold War. This operation was designed as a microcosm of geopolitics, with a NATO member and a neutral on the pro-Western Israeli side of the line of separation and a member of the Warsaw Pact and a neutral on the pro-Soviet Syrian side. UNDOF was established on May 31, 1974, upon the conclusion of disengagement agreements between Israel and Syria that called for an Israeli withdrawal from all areas it occupied within Syria, the establishment of a buffer zone to separate the Syrian and Israeli armies, and the creation of areas of restricted armaments on either side of the buffer zone. UNDOF was charged with verifying Israel's withdrawal, establishing the buffer zones, and monitoring levels of militarization in the restricted zones.

UNDOF employed 1,250 armed soldiers, including ninety military observers. Troop deployment emphasized equal contributions by countries that were either politically neutral or sympathetic to the West or East. Originally, Peru, Canada, Poland, and Austria provided troops for the operation. (The Peruvian troops were replaced by Iranians in 1975 and by Finns in 1979.) Canadian and Peruvian forces operate along the Israeli side; Polish and Austrian troops operate in Syrian territory.

Despite the declared hostility between Israel and Syria, UNDOF proved instrumental in maintaining peace on the Golan Heights between the two longtime foes. From 1977 through 2002, no major incidents have occurred in areas under UNDOF's jurisdiction. Success is attributable to several factors: The details of the operation were thoroughly defined before its implementation, leaving little room for disagreement; Israel and Syria cooperated with UNDOF; and the Security Council supported the operation fully.

Principles of Traditional Peacekeeping

The man who helped give operational meaning to "peacekeeping," Sir Brian Urquhart, has summarized the characteristics of UN operations—which can be gleaned inductively from the case of UNDOF—during the Cold War as follows: consent of the parties, continuing strong support of the Security Council, a clear and practicable mandate, nonuse of force except in the last resort and in self-defense, the willingness of troop contributors to furnish military forces, and the willingness of member states to make available requisite financing.[8] It is worth developing each of the points as a bridge to our subsequent discussion of future efforts that go beyond traditional limitations.

Consent Is Imperative Before Operations Begin. In many ways, consent is the keystone of traditional peacekeeping, for two reasons. First, it helps to insulate the UN decisionmaking process against great-power dissent. For example, in Cyprus and Lebanon the Soviet Union's desire to obstruct was overcome because the parties themselves had asked for UN help.

Second, consent greatly reduces the likelihood that peacekeepers will encounter resistance while carrying out their duties. Peacekeepers are physically in no position to challenge the authority of belligerents (either states or opposition groups), and so they assume a nonconfrontational stance toward local authorities. Traditional peacekeepers do not impinge on sovereignty. In fact, it is imperative to achieve consent re operations begin.

e emphasis that traditional missions place on consent does have drawbacks, as ervers have noted: "Peacekeeping forces cannot often create conditions for success."[9] For example, belligerents will normally consent to a peacekeeping mission once wartime goals have been achieved or losses have made belligerents war-weary. In instances where neither of these conditions has been met, it becomes necessary to find alternate ways to induce warring parties to achieve and maintain consent. Moreover, major powers need to pressure their clients not only to consent but also to negotiate. When the political will is lacking, wars either continue unaddressed by the organization or UN peacekeepers become inextricably tied down in conflict, neither able to bring peace to the area nor able to withdraw from it. For example, the United Nations Peace-keeping Force in Cyprus (UNFICYP), originally deployed in 1964 to separate warring Turkish and Greek Cypriot communities, remains in the field because consent for deployment has not been matched by a willingness to negotiate the peace. Likewise, the United Nations Military Observer Group in India and Pakistan (UNMOGIP), established in 1949; UNDOF, created in 1974; and the United Nations Interim Force in Lebanon (UNIFIL), deployed in 1978—all continued to operate as of the time of writing because of the absence of political conditions allowing for their removal.

Peacekeeping Operations Need Full Support from the Security Council. Security Council support is necessary not only in the beginning stages of the mission, when decisions regarding budgets, troop allotments, and other strategic priorities are made, but also in its later stages, when mandates come up for renewal. The host of problems in the Congo illustrates the dangers of proceeding without the support of the major powers in the Security Council. Backing by both the United States and the Soviet Union of UNEF I in the General Assembly was the only case in which the United States and the USSR abandoned the Security Council and then resorted to the General Assembly to get around a veto in the Security Council. A practice has developed for the Security Council to renew the mandate of missions several times—frequently semiannually for years on end—in order to keep pressure on parties who may be threatened with the possible withdrawal of peacekeepers. Full Security Council support also enhances the symbolic power of an operation.

Participating Nations Need to Provide Troops and to Accept Risks. Successful peacekeeping missions require the self-sustained presence of individual peacekeeping battalions, each of which must be independent but also must function under UN command. Frequently they will be deploying in areas of heavy militarization. Mortal danger exists for peacekeepers. Democratic governments in particular that provide troops must be willing to accept the risks inherent in a given mission, and they also must be able to defend such expenditures and losses before their parliaments.

Permanent members do not normally contribute troops except for logistical support, a specialty of the United States, which during the Cold War essentially airlifted most start-up troops and provisions for UN operations. Keeping major powers from an active role in peacekeeping was imperative for the neutrality that successful peacekeeping strives to attain. Washington and Moscow were thought to be especially tainted by the causes that they supported worldwide.

The experience with exceptions to this rule has been mixed. Because of the special circumstances involved in Britain's possession of extraterritorial bases on the island of

Cyprus, the United Kingdom was involved in the UN's operations there from the outset; that effort has been worthwhile. The experience of French peacekeepers deployed in UNIFIL in Lebanon has been a source of problems because of France's perceived involvement as an ex-colonial power on the Christian side of the conflict. Consequently, French troops came under attack by local factions and were forced to withdraw from the zone of operations and to remain in the UN compound in Naqoura. This experience was a smaller-scale indication of the problems that would be incurred later by both the United States and France in the non-UN operation in Beirut in 1984, when some 300 soldiers were killed.[10]

A Clear and Precise Mandate Is Desirable. The goals of the mission should be clear, obtainable, and known to all parties involved. Enunciation of the mission's objectives reduces local suspicion. Yet a certain degree of flexibility is desirable so that the peacekeepers may adapt their operating strategies to better fit changing circumstances. The goals of the operation may be expanded or reduced as the situation warrants. In fact, diplomatic vagueness may at times be necessary in Security Council voting to secure support or to keep future options open.

Force Is Used Only in Self-Defense and as a Last Resort. Peacekeepers derive their influence from the diplomatic support of the international community, and therefore they use force only as a last resort and in self-defense. The *Peacekeeper's Handbook* states this wisdom: "The degree of force (used) must only be sufficient to achieve the mission on hand and to prevent, as far as possible, loss of human life and/or serious injury. Force should *not* be initiated, except possibly after continuous harassment when it becomes necessary to restore a situation so that the United Nations can fulfill its responsibilities."[11]

Peacekeeping techniques differ greatly from those taught to most soldiers and officers by their national training authorities. However, in the past only the Scandinavian states and Canada have trained large numbers of their recruits and officers specifically for the peacekeeping method. Soldiers from other countries have often found themselves unprepared for peacekeeping situations where the prohibition against the use of force contradicts their standard military training.

Using minimal force affords several advantages.[12] With limited military capability, peacekeepers are not threatening to belligerents. So belligerents are apt to treat peacekeepers, who are unable to take part in the conflict militarily, with less suspicion than they direct toward regular forces. Peacekeepers are often able to mediate and forestall local flare-ups of violence.

Traditionally, peacekeeping forces have had the luxury of operating without enemies. The need to operate at peak military efficiency has not been as great as it would have been if "enemies," in the normal sense of the term, had existed. As a result, the administrative, technological, and strategic structures that sustain peacekeeping have reflected the need for professional diplomatic and political expertise more than the need for professional soldiers.

Brian E. Urquhart, Under-Secretary-General for special political affairs, answers questions in June 1985 about his mission to the Middle East to free soldiers of the UN Interim Force in Lebanon. (UN Photo 165579/Y. Nagata)

"Chapter Six and a Half" on Hold, 1978–1988

As mentioned earlier, from 1948 to 1978 thirteen UN peacekeeping operations took place. In the ten years after 1978, however, no new operations materialized, even as a rash of regional conflicts involving the superpowers or their proxies sprang up around the globe.[13]

The last operation approved before the hiatus of a decade highlights the difficulties encountered by the United Nations during this period. UNIFIL in Lebanon was beset with problems similar to those experienced in the Congo during the 1960s, where domestic conflict and an absence of government structures had given the world organization an operational black eye.[14] UNIFIL's difficulties illustrate the dangers inherent in operations that lack both clear mandates and the effective cooperation of belligerents and that operate amidst political chaos and great-power disagreement.

UNIFIL was established at the Security Council's request on March 19, 1978, following Israel's military incursion into southern Lebanon. Israel claimed that military raids and shellings by members of the Palestine Liberation Organization (PLO), who were based in southern Lebanon, threatened Israeli peace and security. Israel's response embarrassed its primary ally, the United States. Washington used its influence in the Security Council to create UNIFIL as a face-saving means for Israel to withdraw. The operation's duties included confirmation of the Israeli withdrawal; establishment and maintenance of an area of operations; prevention of renewed fighting among the PLO, the Southern Lebanese Army (Christian militia backed by Israel and led by Major Saad Haddad), and Israel; and the restoration of Lebanese sovereignty over southern Lebanon

At UNIFIL's maximum strength, over 7,000 soldiers were deployed, including contingents from Fiji, France, Ghana, Iran, Ireland, Nepal, the Netherlands, Nigeria, Norway, Senegal, and Canada. UNIFIL encountered significant problems due to the conflicting interests of the major parties involved in southern Lebanon. Israel refused to cede control of the South to UNIFIL, choosing instead to rely upon Major Haddad's Southern Lebanese Army, which resisted UNIFIL's efforts to gain control in the area. The PLO demanded that it be allowed to operate freely in the South to continue its resistance against Israel. The Lebanese government insisted that UNIFIL assume control of the entire region, including areas controlled by Haddad. Consequently, UNIFIL found itself sandwiched between the PLO and Haddad's forces; its contingents routinely came under fire. The PLO continued its military maneuverings against Israel, and Haddad's forces continued their attacks on the PLO. In 1982, as Israel reinvaded Lebanon and marched to Beirut, UNIFIL stood by, powerless, in the face of Israel's superior firepower and the unwillingness of troop contributors or the UN membership to resist. UNIFIL's refusal to stand its ground echoed Egypt's 1967 request to withdraw UNEF I; once UN troops were pulled out, war ensued.

The lack of political will among the regional participants and troop contributors was matched by the incapacity of the Lebanese government's army and police. Yet, UNIFIL has become part of the local infrastructure,[15] and its withdrawal would be very disruptive. It would have resulted in greater instances of fighting between the PLO, Israel, and Haddad's army, and a probable third Israeli intervention would almost certainly have been countered by direct Syrian opposition. Despite its limitations, UNIFIL continues to operate.

Much of the impetus for the increased tension between East and West and for the end of new UN deployments came from Washington after the Reagan administration assumed power in 1981. Elected on a platform of anticommunism, the rebuilding of the national defense system, and fiscal conservatism, the administration was determined to roll back Soviet gains in the Third World. Washington scorned the UN and cast it aside as a bastion of Third World nationalism and procommunism. The UN's peacekeeping operations were tarred with the same brush.

Noncooperation with the UN reached a new nadir from 1985 to 1987, when Washington also refused to pay its assessed dues (including a portion of the assessment for UNIFIL, which the United States had originally insisted upon).[16] The organization was in near bankruptcy at the same time that traditional respect for international law seemed to evaporate and unilateral action gained favor.[17] Intervening in Grenada, bombing Libya, and supporting insurgencies in Nicaragua, Angola, Afghanistan, and Cambodia attested to Washington's preferences. The Soviet Union countered these initiatives. Central America, the Horn of Africa, much of southern Africa, and parts of Asia became battlegrounds for the superpowers or their proxies. This situation

Israeli troops withdraw in accordance with UNDOF disengagement agreement.
(UN/DPI Photo/N. Nagata)

changed only with the Gorbachev regime in the Soviet Union and the advent of glasnost and perestroika, which figure in the next chapter.

Economic Sanctions

Short of sending international forces, a group of states may attempt to isolate an aggressor by cutting off diplomatic or economic relations with a view toward altering offensive behavior. These are coercive, albeit nonforcible, actions. Diplomatic and economic sanctions are significantly more emphatic than the political influence that makes up the everyday stuff of foreign policy, even if less emphatic than the dispatch of troops.

It is useful to imagine a spectrum ranging from political influence to outside military intervention. Economic sanctions are a form of nonforcible enforcement. For the same reasons that military coercion was not possible during the Cold War, these milder forms of enforcement were also largely underused. The exceptions were the cases of two pariahs, Rhodesia and South Africa, whose domestic racist policies were considered abhorrent. These earlier experiences are worth discussing, however, as a prelude to actions after the end of the Cold War because the Security Council continues to redefine other types of apparently domestic policies of states as threatening enough to international peace and security to justify Chapter VII action.

As a reaction to Rhodesia's Unilateral Declaration of Independence (UDI) from the United Kingdom in 1965, the Security Council in 1966 ordered limited economic sanctions under Chapter VII of the Charter for the first time in UN history.[18] Whether the trigger was more due to the UDI or the human rights situation for Africans is debatable, but the result was that the council characterized the situation as a "threat to the peace." The council toughened the stance against the white-minority government by including all exports and imports (except for some foodstuffs, educational materials, and medicines). These sanctions became "comprehensive" in 1968.

The sanctions initially extracted some costs from the government of Rhodesian prime minister Ian Smith. But, ironically, they eventually helped immunize the country against outside pressure in the form of nonforcible sanctions because they prompted a successful program of import substitution. Although most members of the UN complied, those who counted did not. The United States, for example, openly violated sanctions after the Byrd amendment by Congress allowed trade with Rhodesia even though the U.S. had voted for sanctions in the Security Council. According to U.S. judicial doctrine, if Congress uses its statutory authority to violate international law intentionally, domestic courts will defer to congressional action in U.S. jurisdiction. Many private traders as well as some other African countries also traded with Rhodesia, including the neighboring countries of Mozambique (a Portuguese colony) and the Republic of South Africa.

Although the Security Council authorized a forceful blockade to interrupt supplies of oil and the British navy did halt a few tankers, there was insufficient political will to effectively blockade the ports and coastlines of Mozambique and South Africa. Hence, the Security Council can hardly be credited with the establishment of an independent Zimbabwe in 1979. The costs of the protracted guerrilla warfare ultimately led to the decolonization of Rhodesia through the negotiations at Lancaster House in England under the mediation of Lord Carrington, the British foreign minister. At a key point, South Africa indicated its support for a negotiated solution, thus depriving Ian Smith of his most important sanctions-breaker.

UN-imposed sanctions against South Africa reflected the judgment that racial discrimination (apartheid) was considered a threat to the peace. Limited economic sanctions, an embargo on arms sales to South Africa, embargoes against South African athletic teams, and selective divestment were all part of a visible campaign to isolate South Africa. These acts exerted pressure whose impact is difficult to quantify, although observers usually assert that they have played an important role. Initially, South Africa's high-cost industry thrived by trying to replace missing imports (as had Rhodesia's), and it even managed to produce a variety of sophisticated arms that eventually became a major export. The changes that have occurred in South Africa since 1990 have certainly been dramatic, but they probably result more from the dynamics of the internal struggle by the black majority and the end of the Cold War than from nonforcible sanctions. Sanctions no doubt contributed to altering the domestic balance by demonstrating the risks and the costs of being isolated, but measuring their precise impact requires greater empirical work. Private "sanctions" should also be noted, as a number of Western businesses progressively pulled out of this violence-prone area.

Security Council sanctions are enforcement tools to address a breach of the peace or a threat to international peace and security. They should be analyzed as distinct from bilateral economic sanctions (for example, those used by Washington against Moscow during the Cold War) or those imposed by treaty (for example, the Montreal Protocol to protect the ozone). The UN Charter never uses the word "sanctions" in Chapter VII, but Article 41 speaks of "what measures not involving the use of armed force are to be employed to give effect to its decisions." The use of partial or comprehensive sanctions, particularly at early stages in armed conflicts, is a subject to which we return at the end of Chapter 3.

Notes

1. See Leon Gordenker, *The UN Secretary-General and the Maintenance of Peace* (New York: Columbia University Press, 1967); and Leland M. Goodrich, *Korea: A Study of U.S. Policy* (New York: Council on Foreign Relations, 1956).

2. Max Harrelson, *Fires All Around the Horizon: The UN's Uphill Battle to Preserve the Peace* (New York: Praeger, 1989), p. 89.

3. Boutros Boutros-Ghali, *An Agenda for Peace: Preventive Diplomacy, Peacemaking and Peace-keeping* (New York: UN, 1992), para. 46.

4. Other definitions can be found in United Nations, *The Blue Helmets: A Review of United Nations Peace-keeping* (New York: UNDPI, 1990), p. 4; Alan James, *Peacekeeping in International Politics* (London: Macmillan, 1990), p. 1; and Boutros-Ghali, *An Agenda for Peace,* para. 20.

5. Marrack Goulding, "The Changing Role of the United Nations in Conflict Resolution and Peace-keeping," speech given at the Singapore Institute of Policy Studies, March 13, 1991, p. 9. See also Marrack Goulding, "The Evolution of Peacekeeping," *International Affairs* 69, no.3 (May 1993), pp. 451–464.

6. For further analyses of peacekeeping during the Cold War, see Thomas G. Weiss and Jarat Chopra, *Peacekeeping: An ACUNS Teaching Text* (Hanover: Academic Council on the United Nations System, 1992), pp. 1–20. For a discussion of operations during the Cold War but with an emphasis on transferring lessons to the present, see Sally Morphet, "UN Peacekeeping and Election-Monitoring," in Adam Roberts and Benedict Kingsbury, eds., *United Nations, Divided World: The UN's Roles in International Relations* (Oxford: Clarendon Press, 1993), pp. 183–239. The United Nations published its own volume, *The Blue Helmets* (New York: UN, 1985), which was revised in 1990 and 1996. Updates are now on the United Nations website at www.un.org. See also Rosalyn Higgins, *United Nations Peacekeeping, Documents and Commentary*, Vols. 1–4 (Oxford: Oxford University Press, 1969, 1970, 1980, 1981).

7. For a discussion of UN and non-UN operations in a comparative military perspective in this period, see John Mackinlay, *The Peacekeepers* (London: Unwin Hyman, 1989). See also Augustus Richard Norton and Thomas G. Weiss, *UN Peacekeepers, Soldiers with a Difference* (New York: Foreign Policy Association, 1990); William J. Durch, ed., *The Evolution of UN Peacekeeping* (New York: St. Martin's Press, 1993); and Paul Diehl, *International Peacekeeping* (Baltimore: Johns Hopkins University Press, 1993).

8. Brian Urquhart, "Beyond the 'Sheriff's Posse," *Survival* 32, no. 3 (May–June 1990), p. 198; see also his autobiography, *A Life in Peace and War* (New York: Harper and Row, 1987).

9. John Mackinlay and Jarat Chopra, "Second Generation Multinational Operations," *Washington Quarterly* 15, no. 3 (Summer 1992), p. 114.

10. For a discussion of these issues, see Mackinlay, *The Peacekeepers;* and Pierre Le Peillet, *Les berets blues de l'ONU* (Paris: Editions France-Empire, 1988).

11. International Peace Academy, *Peacekeeper's Handbook* (New York: Pergamon, 1984), p. 56.

12. See F. T. Liu, *United Nations Peacekeeping and the Non-Use of Force* (Boulder: Lynne Rienner, 1992).

13. For a discussion of this period, see S. Neil MacFarlane, *Superpower Rivalry and Third World Radicalism* (Baltimore: Johns Hopkins University Press, 1985); Elizabeth Valkenier, *The Soviet Union and the Third World* (New York: Praeger, 1985); and Jerry Hough, *The Struggle for the Third World* (Washington, D.C.: Brookings Institution, 1986).

14. For a discussion, see Bjorn Skogmo, *UNIFIL: International Peacekeeping in Lebanon* (Boulder: Lynne Rienner, 1989); and E. A. Erskine, *Mission with UNIFIL* (London: Hurst, 1989).

15. See Marianne Heiberg, "Peacekeepers and Local Populations: Some Comments on UNIFIL," in Indar Jit Rikhye and Kjell Skjelsback, eds., *The United Nations and Peacekeeping* (London: Macmillan, 1990), pp. 147–169.

16. See Jeffrey Harrod and Nico Shrijver, eds., *The UN Under Attack* (London: Gower, 1988).

17. See David P. Forsythe, *The Politics of International Law: U.S. Foreign Policy Reconsidered* (Boulder: Lynne Rienner, 1990).

18. See Henry Wiseman and Alistair M. Taylor, *From Rhodesia to Zimbabwe* (New York: Pergamon, 1981); and Stephen John Stedman, *Peacemaking in Civil War: International Mediation in Zimbabwe, 1974–1980* (Boulder: Lynne Rienner, 1991). The League of Nations had previously tried limited sanctions against Franco's Spain.

3   UN Security Operations After the Cold War

A Changing World: New Goals, New Roles

Vowing to reform his country politically and economically, Soviet leader Mikhail Gorbachev prescribed programs aimed at integrating the Soviet economy into the world economy and reducing East-West tensions. In so doing, he helped reinvigorate multilateralism generally and UN peacekeeping more particularly.[1] Signs became clear in 1987. Moscow vowed to pay its debt of over $200 million to the UN shortly after the Soviet leader's September article in *Pravda* that clearly enunciated, at least to keen observers, the possibility of renewed interest in the United Nations and collective security.

Gorbachev officially redefined the Soviet Union's relationship with the UN in 1988 at the General Assembly, calling for an extension of his domestic "new thinking" to apply to the management of international conflicts. The shift in Soviet policy resulted from that country's need to withdraw support from numerous conflicts and concentrate on economic reform. A decade of military buildup and wars by proxy had drained its treasury, and the USSR had to retract its overstretched foreign policy. Decisions to withdraw from Cam Ranh Bay in Vietnam and from Cuba, Ethiopia, and Yemen indicated how necessary drastic retrenchment had become in Moscow's priorities. UN peacekeeping provided a face-saving means to withdraw from what Gorbachev described as the "bleeding wound" of Afghanistan. Here we have a classic case of "imperial overstretch" in which a great power finds that its foreign commitments exceed its ability to support them over time, repeatedly the cause of decline for such powers.[2]

Changes in Moscow's attitudes toward the UN influenced the international climate and more particularly Washington's approach to the world organization. In 1988, President Ronald Reagan abruptly altered his public stance and praised the work of the organization, the Secretary-General, and UN peacekeepers. After helping to spearhead attacks that had led to almost a decade of UN-bashing, he declared at the General Assembly that "the United Nations has the opportunity to live and breathe and work as never before" and vowed to repay U.S. debts to the organization. This orientation was continued by President George H. W. Bush, a former U.S. permanent representative to the UN. Big-power cooperation grew, allowing the Security Council to resume part of its role as a guarantor of international peace and security, including the dramatic efforts to reverse Iraqi aggression against Kuwait. At the same time, an emphasis on the UN was a convenient way for France, Great Britain, and

Russia[3] to maintain international preeminence despite their declining economic, political, and military significance. Even for the United States, it is better—less costly and contentious—to proceed as a hegemonic rather than dominant power. That is, even for the U.S. it is better to proceed through the UN on the basis of cooperation rather than having to coerce other states into compliance.

The First UN Military Operations After the End of the Cold War, 1988–1993

In 1988 and 1989, the collegiality and regular collaboration among great powers in the Security Council, which had been foreseen in 1945, finally seemed possible. After a ten-year gap in deploying new UN security operations, five post–Cold War operations (listed at the bottom of Table 2.1) were launched—in Afghanistan, astride the Iran-Iraq border, and in Angola, Namibia, and Central America (for Nicaragua).

These operations were finished by 1993 and were similar to those of the past. It is true that they incorporated some new elements in the improvisation that is so characteristic of peacekeeping. For example, there were large numbers of civilians in tandem with soldiers in Namibia and Central America; the first supervision of domestic elections as well as the collection of weapons from insurgents took place in Nicaragua. These precedents illustrated clearly the UN's capacity for evolution and growth in the new era, although improvisation and task expansion had been present in earlier UN activities. However, these new operations were extensions of the time-tested recipe for UN peacekeeping. In particular, these initial post–Cold War operations all enjoyed the consent of fighting parties and relied upon defensive concepts of force employed by modestly equipped UN soldiers, few of whom came from armies of the major powers. (Peace operations began since 1991 are listed in Table 3.1; those that continue as of 2003 are found in Table 3.2; and those that have been completed since the first ones are listed in Table 3.3.) Two of the operations also fall into the traditional peacekeeping category—the follow-up operation in Angola and the one in the Western Sahara.

However, this table also contains operations that are so different in scope and mandate that they could be characterized as "peacekeeping" only by stretching analytical categories almost to the breaking point. Three of them (in Cambodia, the former Yugoslavia, and Somalia) indicate the new challenges for UN operations that are providing the basis for the military departures, as suggested in Boutros-Ghali's *An Agenda for Peace*. The evolution of these and two other subsequent operations (Rwanda and Haiti) illustrate the limits of UN military operations, which is where we conclude this chapter. One operation in Iraq-Kuwait merits discussion because its deployment followed the first controversial enforcement action of the post–Cold War era, Operation Desert Storm, which figures prominently in our discussion of moving toward the future.

These operations are quite distinct from traditional peacekeeping. The distinction between the former and latter, with Somalia as the turning point, will become clear by the end of this chapter. Before we analyze precisely how the new field operations illustrate challenges for the future, it is useful to examine in more detail a few cases of post–Cold War cooperation that cemented big-power collaboration and made possi-

TABLE 3.1   UN Peace and Security Operations from End of Cold War to the Present

Years Active	*Operation*
1991–1992	United Nations Advance Mission in Cambodia (UNAMIC)
1991–1995	United Nations Observer Mission in El Salvador (ONUSAL)
1991–1995	United Nations Angola Verification Mission II (UNAVEM I)
1991–Present	United Nations Mission for the Referendum in Western Sahara (MINURSO)
1991–Present	United Nations Iraq-Kuwait Observer Mission (UNIKOM)
1992–1993	United Nations Transitional Authority in Cambodia (UNTAC)
1992–1993	United Nations Operation in Somalia I (UNOSOM I)
1992–1993	United Nations Operation in Mozambique (ONUMOZ)
1992–1995	United Nations Protection Force, former Yugoslavia (UNPROFOR)
1993–1994	United Nations Mission Uganda-Rwanda (ONOMUR)
1993–1995	United Nations Operation in Somalia II (UNOSOM II)
1993–1996	United Nations Mission in Haiti (UNMIH)
1993–1996	United Nations Assistance Mission for Rwanda (UNAMIR)
1993–1997	United Nations Observer Mission in Liberia (UNOMIL)
1993–Present	United Nations Observer Mission in Georgia (UNOMIG)
1994	United Nations Auzou Strip Observer Group (UNOSOG, Chad/Libya)
1994–2000	United Nations Mission in Tajikistan (UNMOT)
1995–1996	United Nations Confidence Restoration Operation, Croatia (UNCRO)
1995–1997	United Nations Angola Verification Mission III (UNAVEM III)
1995–1999	United Nations Preventive Deployment Force, former Yugoslav Republic of Macedonia (UNPREDEP)
1995–2002	United Nations Mission in Bosnia and Herzegovina (UNMIBH)
1996–1997	United Nations Support Mission in Haiti (UNSMIH)

ble the movement toward, at a minimum, bolder UN operations. At a maximum, these cases suggest the revival of collective security as a possible policy option for governments in the new era.

The Rebirth of Peacekeeping

The UN Good Offices Mission in Afghanistan and Pakistan (UNGOMAP), the UN Iran-Iraq Military Observer Group (UNIIMOG), the first UN Angola Verification Mission (UNAVEM I), and the UN Transition Assistance Group in Namibia (UNTAG) were missions that renewed peacekeeping's visibility and perceived workability in the international arena of conflict resolution. UNGOMAP, UNIIMOG, and UNTAG are also significant because they afforded the UN the opportunity to demonstrate its usefulness in war zones, a capacity that had been frozen from 1978 to 1988. Successes built confidence and allowed the UN to move back toward center stage, and the operations provided the space to experiment with innovations beyond the scope of previous deployments.

These operations are examples of "observation," a diverse set of tasks that occupies the least controversial part of peacekeeping activities. The oldest UN operation of this type, the United Nations Truce Supervision Organization (UNTSO), has been observing the Middle East since 1948 as we already noted. Traditionally, observation has meant investigation, armistice supervision, maintenance of a cease-fire, supervision of plebiscites, oversight of the cessation of fighting, and reports to headquarters. It has been expanded to include the verification of troop withdrawal, the organization and observation of elections, the voluntary surrender of weapons, and human rights verification. These operations are distinct from the other traditional task: interposition (for example, on the Golan Heights), which was discussed earlier.

UNGOMAP verified the withdrawal of Soviet troops from Afghanistan after 1988. The USSR had entered the country in 1979 to ensure a friendly Afghan government in Kabul. By the early 1980s Afghanistan had become the Soviet Union's Vietnam. The Soviets had become inextricably tied down in an unwinnable conflict against the Mujahideen, armed local groups backed by Pakistan and the United States. Soviet withdrawal became an economic and political imperative.

The Gorbachev administration sought a face-saving device to extricate itself. The 1988 Geneva Accords provided the means to achieve Soviet withdrawal, mutual noninterference and nonintervention pledges between Pakistan and Afghanistan, the return of refugees, and noninterference pledges from Washington and Moscow. These accords had been brokered by the United Nations and the indefatigable efforts of Under-Secretary-General Diego Cordovez beginning in 1982.

The deployment of UNGOMAP was not accompanied by the political will needed to implement the international agreements concerning peace, elections, and disarmament. The symbolic size of the operation—fifty officers divided between Islamabad and Kabul—attested to its inability to independently perform tasks other than reporting on the Soviet withdrawal after the fact. However, the operation provided an appropriate face-saving device for Moscow, which helped pave the way to a potential peace by reducing the direct East-West character of the conflict.

Just south of Afghanistan, the Iran-Iraq War finally drew to a close. Eight years after the war began, one year after the Security Council ordered a cease-fire with the compulsory intent provided for under Chapter VII, and after about 1 million lives had been lost, UNIIMOG was set up by the Security Council in August 1988 to ensure the maintenance of the cease-fire astride the international border. It established cease-fire lines between Iranian and Iraqi troops, observed the maintenance of the cease-fire, and investigated complaints to defuse minor truce violations before they escalated into peace-threatening situations.

Composed of 350 unarmed observers from over twenty-five states, UNIIMOG played a useful role in preserving the cease-fire between Iran and Iraq, two nations whose mutual antagonism continued after the cessation of hostilities. In its first five months alone, UNIIMOG investigated some 2,000 complaints of truce infractions. Although UNIIMOG was instrumental in stopping a deterioration, it was more Iraq's diminished position after the 1991 Persian Gulf War that kept the peace than any diplomatic effort.

Much farther south in Africa, Angola, Cuba, and South Africa signed a trilateral agreement on December 22, 1988. This provided for the simultaneous withdrawal of Cuban troops from Angola and of South African troops and administrators from Namibia. This diplomatic breakthrough was monitored successfully by the first United Nations Angola Verification Mission, which led the way for the UN-sponsored peace process that brought Namibian independence on March 21, 1990, from South Africa's illegal colonial rule. The second UNAVEM was more problematic because civil war returned in spite of UN-supervised elections at the end of 1992; the difficulties faced by this group are discussed with other more problematic operations later in this chapter.

Also on the African continent, UNTAG was established to facilitate and monitor South Africa's withdrawal from Namibia and to set up free and fair elections to determine the future government and constitution of Namibia. It was the last major decolonization effort under UN auspices. To achieve these ends, UNTAG was tasked with monitoring and facilitating the departure of South Africa's army and the withdrawal and confinement of the South-West Africa People's Organization's (SWAPO) fighters to base camps in Angola, monitor the southwest African police force controlled by South Africa to prevent meddling in elections, oversee the repeal of discriminatory laws that threatened the fairness of the election, help ensure the respect for amnesty to political prisoners, and provide for the return of all Namibian refugees. UNTAG also registered voters and facilitated information about the election process.

At its maximum deployment, nearly 8,000 persons were involved in UNTAG—about 4,500 military personnel, 2,000 civilian personnel, and 1,000 police officers. It was the first sizable operation in Africa since the contested one in the Congo almost three decades earlier. The operation was rushed into the field in order to respect an April deadline. Hundreds of SWAPO fighters crossed the border on the first day after the UN's deployment in violation of the letter of the agreement, although they claimed that they had interpreted the text otherwise. In any event, South Africa–supported defense forces killed several hundred SWAPO guerrillas, the heaviest casualties in two decades of armed conflict.

But the parties to the conflict, in particular South Africa, were committed to making the operation work. UNTAG is generally considered a success. Virtually the entire population was registered to vote. SWAPO won forty-one of seventy-two seats in the Constitutional Constituents Assembly and was duly empowered to lead the formation of the Namibian government. On March 21, 1990—ahead of schedule and under budget—UN Secretary-General Javier Pérez de Cuéllar swore in Sam Nujoma as president of Namibia.

UNTAG provides a helpful analytical hinge between the old and new types of UN security operations. It went smoothly because traditional rules were followed—especially consent and minimal use of force. At the same time, it undertook several new tasks related to civil administration, elections, and police activities. These tasks foreshadowed new UN activities that would intrude more into the affairs of "sovereign" states rather than being part of a decolonization effort.

Moving Toward the Next Generation

The work of the United Nations in Central America during the late 1980s and early 1990s provides a transition in our discussion of the progressive movement toward a new generation of peacekeeping and peace-enforcement operations.[4] World politics was changing and so were the possibilities for action by the UN. Governments removed political obstacles that had previously blocked or impeded activities by the world organization. Although not at all comparable in most ways, the UN's efforts in Central America were similar to the Afghanistan operation in one way: The world organization was helping a superpower move beyond an unwinnable confrontation in its own backyard. An analysis of the United Nations Observer Group in Central America (ONUCA), the United Nations Observer Mission to Verify the Electoral Process in Nicaragua (ONUVEN), and the United Nations Observer Mission in El Salvador (ONUSAL) illustrates the complex transition process that the UN's peace and security functions began to undergo. These also set the stage for the analysis of the UN-sponsored Chapter VII enforcement action against Iraq. ONUSAL in particular shows the independent nature of UN action when states give the world organization some political room to maneuver.

In the late 1980s, the conclusion of the so-called Esquipulas II agreements between the countries of Central America—Nicaragua, Costa Rica, El Salvador, Guatemala, and Honduras—began the peace process that ended a decade of civil war and instability in the region. The cornerstone of the agreements involved setting up free and fair elections in Nicaragua once border raids had stopped and demobilization had begun. Irregular forces had operated along the borders of nearly every country in the region. It was hoped that these measures would bring lasting peace to the region.

In addition to calling for elections in Nicaragua, the Esquipulas II agreements prohibited aid to rebel groups and the use of the territory of one state for guerrilla activity in another. ONUCA (1989–1992) was established to ensure that these provisions were respected. Although ONUCA was officially an "observer" mission, duties were far-reaching. They included verifying that all forms of military assistance to insurgent forces had ceased and preventing states from sponsoring such activity for infiltration into neighboring countries. ONUCA observers made spot checks and random investigations of areas prone to guerrilla activity along the borders of Nicaragua, El Salvador, Guatemala, Honduras, and Costa Rica. Although the signatories to Esquipulas II were expected to cooperate with ONUCA, the participation of the Nicaraguan resistance movement, the contras, was not ensured until after the electoral defeat of the Sandinista government in February 1990. ONUCA military observers operated in a tense, potentially dangerous situation where armed attacks were possible.

ONUCA's mandate expanded after the Nicaraguan election to include demobilizing the contras. Bases were set up inside the borders of Nicaragua, where many rebel soldiers came and handed over some of their weapons and military equipment to ONUCA soldiers, who destroyed them and helped to advance demilitarization. In spite of the continued existence of arms among disgruntled partisans of both the contra and Sandinista causes, this was the first instance of UN involvement in demilitarization through the physical collection and destruction of armaments. This task is important for conflict resolution in areas where heavily armed regular as well as irregular forces need to be drastically reduced before any meaningful consultative process can occur. The collection of arms has been integrated into numerous subsequent UN peacekeeping operations and has been made even more rigorous.[5] The importance of such a task was recognized by the United Kingdom as part of its efforts to end direct rule over Northern Ireland in 1999–2000.

ONUVEN was created to ensure the fairness of elections in Nicaragua. It was the first example of UN observation of elections inside a recognized state, an extraordinary intrusion according to conventional notions of domestic jurisdiction. It operated in tandem with ONUCA's soldiers, but ONUVEN consisted of some 120 civilian observers who monitored the election process, from start to finish, to ensure that it was free and fair. They verified that political parties were equitably represented in the Supreme Electoral Council; that there was political, organizational, and operational freedom for all political parties; that all political parties had equal access to state television and radio broadcasts; and that the electoral rolls were drawn up fairly. It also reported any perceived unfairness to the Supreme Electoral Council, made recommendations about possible remedial action, and reported to the Secretary-General.

One unusual development was the extent to which the UN operations were linked to supporting efforts from regional and non-governmental organizations. The Organization of American States (OAS)—in particular the secretaries-general of the UN and the OAS—cooperated closely in diplomatic efforts and in civilian observation. During the Nicaraguan elections, a host of such non-governmental groups as former U.S. president Jimmy Carter's (the Council of Freely Elected Heads of Government) provided additional outside observers as part of a large international network.

The operation began in August 1989 and ended in February 1990 with the surprising electoral defeat of the Sandinista government. ONUVEN's success—which was fortified by its linkages to the OAS and private groups—has enhanced the prospects of UN election-monitoring teams working within the boundaries of states. This practice has gained wider international acceptance even when no armed conflict has taken place. For instance, from June 1990 to January 1991, the United Nations Observer Mission to Verify the Electoral Process in Haiti (ONUVEH) performed tasks similar to the missions in Nicaragua, which set the stage for subsequent UN action when the duly elected government of Jean-Bertrand Aristide was overthrown. ONUVEN's civilian composition has changed the content of peacekeeping's definition by blurring the distinction between civilian and military operations and between security and human rights.

In neighboring El Salvador, ONUSAL was an essential element in helping to move beyond a decade of brutal civil war in which over 75,000 persons had been killed and numerous human rights abuses had taken place. The government and rebel sides, and their foreign backers, came to a stalemate. This created the conditions for successful UN mediation, although much creativity was required to make it work. Negotiations under the good offices of the UN Secretary-General led to a detailed agreement on January 1, 1992, which was actually initialed a few hours after Javier Pérez de Cuéllar had completed his second five-year term.

An essential component of moving beyond the war was the use of UN civilian and military personnel in what, by historical standards, would have been seen as unacceptable outside interference in purely domestic affairs. Ongoing human rights violations were to be prevented through an elaborate observation and monitoring system that began before an official cease-fire. Previous violations by both the army and the government as well as by the armed opposition, the FMLN, were to be investigated by a truth commission. The highly controversial findings—including the documentation of a former president's approval of the assassination of a dissident archbishop and the incrimination of a sitting defense minister in other murders—served to clear the air, although the exact impact of the political processes within the country took time to have effects. There was also a second commission to identify those military personnel who had committed major human rights violations.

In addition, ONUSAL personnel collected and destroyed many insurgents' weapons and helped oversee the creation of a new national army staff college, where students included former members of the armed opposition in addition to new recruits and members of the national army. Some of the early UN involvement on the ground in El Salvador took place even before the cease-fire was signed, thus putting UN observers at some risk.

Whatever the ultimate value of these experiences for making future UN security operations possible, the renaissance in the world organization can certainly be dated from the 1991 Persian Gulf War. The consequences not only influenced governments trying to deal with Central America but also continue to be felt in the international arena.

Moving Toward Enforcement

As indicated at the outset, comprehensive visions and long-term plans for international organizations have limited value. Vastly more important are creative adaptations by the UN's member states and civil servants. Political changes and crises occur, and then governments and the United Nations react. Precedents are created that circumscribe what is possible later. Given the importance of the actions surrounding events in the Persian Gulf beginning in 1990, it is worthwhile to discuss here the war, subsequent humanitarian actions, and sanctions. We turn to these topics in Part Two.

Strengths and Weaknesses of UN Involvement in the 1991 Gulf War

On August 2, 1990, Iraqi armed forces swept past the border of neighboring Kuwait and quickly gained control of the tiny, oil-rich country. The invasion met with uniform condemnation in the United Nations, including the Security Council's first unequivocal statement about a breach of the peace since 1950 and the Korean War. From early August until the end of the year, the Security Council passed twelve resolutions directed at securing Iraq's withdrawal from Kuwait. The council invoked Chapter VII, Articles 39 through 41, to lay the guidelines for the first post–Cold War enforcement action. Resolutions 661 of August 6 and 665 of August 25 called upon member states to establish economic sanctions against Iraq and to use force to police them. Resolution 678 of November 29 authorized member states to use "all necessary means" to expel Iraq from Kuwait and thus represented a major shift in strategy. The organization's experience during the Persian Gulf War contains valuable lessons about the needs of a workable collective-security system for the future.

At Washington's insistence, January 15, 1991, was negotiated as the deadline for the use of military force. Iraq remained in Kuwait past this date, and the U.S.-led coalition of twenty-eight states began military operations two days later.[6] A bombing campaign against Iraq and its troops commenced, followed by a ground war one month later in which about half a million U.S. military personnel were involved. The coalition's victory reversed the Iraqi invasion and occupation. It placed the United Nations at the center of the international security stage.

Members of the Allied Coalition lost relatively few lives, but tens of thousands of Iraqi civilians and perhaps many more soldiers were killed, so questions were raised about the proportionality of UN-sponsored actions.[7] The Security Council's process of decisionmaking and the conduct of the war have led some critics to be skeptical about the precise value of the Gulf War as a precedent for subsequent Chapter VII enforcement action.[8] Dominance by the United States, the decision to replace non-forcible sanctions with force as the dominant means of ensuring Iraq's compliance with the organization's wishes, the extensive use of force that ensued, and the UN's inability to command and control the operation all became concerns for thoughtful observers. Each of these criticisms raises important questions about the ability of the UN's collective-security apparatus to function properly. The criticisms remained pertinent in 2003 when primarily the U.S. and the UK made the decision to go to war with Iraq after failing to receive a Security Council blessing.

The first criticism of the Persian Gulf War—that the United States too easily used the United Nations to rubber-stamp its own agenda—was a more general criticism of geopolitics after the disappearance of the Soviet Union as a superpower. Washington used its influence to foster perceived national interests, creating and maintaining a diverse coalition against Iraq. In the view of such critics, the process by which the coalition was created illustrated the extent to which the UN had become a blatant reflection of U.S. influence. The UN had never been a completely neutral forum— Western dominance in the early years had been partially replaced beginning in the 1960s by the Third World's "automatic majority" in the General Assembly, but not in the Security Council. This Third World majority had contributed to the UN-bashing by two Republican administrations. Yet the United States was able to use its considerable political and economic clout in the Security Council to ensure that its Persian Gulf agenda was approved. Political concessions were provided to the USSR to gain its approval for enforcement and to China for its abstentions (instead of vetoes). Washington promised financial aid and debt relief to a number of developing countries for their votes and withdrew aid commitments to Yemen in retribution for its opposing the use of force. This is precisely the way a hegemonic power is supposed to operate, making the "side payments" necessary to get many other states to consent to what the hegemon desires.[9]

Nonforcible sanctions were overtaken by forcible ones after only three months, since nonviolent means of securing an Iraqi withdrawal also troubled many critics. According to Article 42, the Security Council may authorize force after all other means of settlement, and economic sanctions in particular, have proven inadequate. Yet the Security Council chose to use military force before the sanctions leveled against Iraq had had a chance to take full effect. Critics pointed out that in South Africa, by contrast, partial sanctions had not been discarded in favor of military force even though that country's racist policy had been condemned for decades. They also noted that Israel's expansion and continued occupation of territories from 1967 had not been met with either economic or military sanctions. At the same time, sanctions take a long time to take effect, and in the meantime violence occurs under occupation. When economic sanctions were applied later to Haiti, some observers said military force should have been used earlier and would have caused less suffering.[10]

The third criticism of the handling of the 1991 Persian Gulf War is that no limits on the use of force were enacted and that the organization exerted no control over the U.S. military operation. According to the Charter, military enforcement operations are to be directed and controlled by the Military Staff Committee (MSC) so that the UN can exercise control and military forces can be held accountable to the international community for their actions. As in Korea forty years earlier, command and control of the Gulf War was in the hands of the U.S.-led coalition forces. Only this time, in the Persian Gulf, there was no blue flag and no decision specifically authorizing the preponderant U.S. role. The Security Council was essentially a spectator, but U.S. control appeared necessary for reasons of efficiency as well as political support.

Resolution 678 authorized "all necessary means" and made no restrictions on what kind of, how much, and how long force could be used. According to critics, Washington was therefore left with a blank check to pursue the expulsion of Iraq. Some argue that authorizations of this kind run contrary to the spirit of the world organization, especially in this case because there was extensive civilian injury and damage inside Iraq.

These doubts and criticisms about the handling of the Persian Gulf War are pertinent to the UN's future security operations not because they are necessarily accurate but because they are widespread. The Persian Gulf War provides the first example of the existing security apparatus in an enforcement action in the post–Cold War era. Although the organization proved successful in achieving its stated objective—the expulsion of Iraq from Kuwait—the way that this goal was achieved continues to be debated by diplomats and scholars. Continuous UN decisionmaking was conducted through the Security Council, but the Article 42 variety of collective security was impossible because the UN troops and command structures foreseen in Article 43 had not been previously agreed upon. Actually, at least in the view of the United States in 1945, Article 43 agreements were to be for UN peacekeeping, not enforcement actions entailing significant combat. There was simply no alternative to the "subcontract" given to the twenty-eight members of the U.S.-led coalition. In view of the UN's limited capacities, such a procedure for enforcement operations seems inevitable for the foreseeable future.

Medical personnel from the multinational forces carry an Iraqi refugee into a camp near Safwan, Iraq, in March 1991. (UN Photo 158302/J. Isaac)

In spite of recommendations, the creation of a UN standing force would be prohibitively expensive. Moreover, it would remove the need to obtain approval from potential troop-contributing governments before sending troops into combat as long as the Permanent Five agreed. Even in the unlikely event that soldiers were made readily available to the UN on a standing basis, Secretary-General Boutros-Ghali himself points out that the UN will "perhaps never be sufficiently large or well enough equipped to deal with a threat from a major army equipped with sophisticated weapons."[11] The organization was ill prepared to handle the test posed by the 1991 Persian Gulf War. Finding ways to provide the organization with the logistic, military, and oversight capacities for future operations remains a high priority for the international community, but not one that is likely to be met in the near future. Thus the role of the council regarding military enforcement remains that of collective legitimization, rather than operational control of combat forces. And if the council fails to agree, and here we fast forward to the war to oust Saddam Hussein in 2003, major powers will proceed with what they perceive as legitimate use of military force.

Forceful Action in Northern Iraq on Behalf of Humanitarian Values

On April 5, 1991, the Security Council passed Resolution 688. It declared that the international repercussions of Saddam Hussein's repression of Kurdish and Shiite populations constituted a threat to international peace and security. It insisted that Iraq allow access to international relief organizations so that they could care for the belea-guered groups. Elite troops from the United States, the United Kingdom, France, and the Netherlands moved into Iraq—without explicit approval from the Security Coun-cil—and carved out a safe haven above the thirty-sixth parallel, which they guarded to ensure the security of UN relief operations. The council had already taken a broad view of its duty to protect human rights in Rhodesia and South Africa, but this reso-lution was a dramatic and straightforward linkage between human rights and inter-national peace and security. The notion of human security inside states was much dis-cussed in the corridors of the UN. In Iraq, the Hussein government agreed eventually to the presence of UN guards providing security to agencies working with Iraqi Kurds, but obviously under Western military pressure.

Many in the West applauded Resolution 688 as a vigorous step toward enforcing human rights protection,[12] but others feared the precedent. "Who decides?" became a rallying cry for those, particularly in the global South, who opposed granting the Security Council, dominated by Western foreign policy interests, the authority of Chapter VII to intervene for humanitarian reasons. Later humanitarian responses—in Somalia, Bosnia and Herzegovina, Rwanda, Haiti, Kosovo, and East Timor—served to keep the debate alive about the weight to be given state sovereignty relative to the international community's duty to protect human rights. This theme reappears in later humanitarian crises in this chapter, as does the reformulation of the "respon-sibility to protect."[13]

The effort under UN auspices in northern Iraq actually continued the efforts of outside actors to help persons in dire straits that had been attempted in the late 1960s in the Nigerian civil war, and which had led two scholars to write about "an extraor-dinary remedy, an exception to the postulates of State sovereignty and territorial invi-olability that are fundamental to the traditional theory if not actual practice of inter-national law."[14] These events suggest a double standard. Certain humanitarian crises and widespread media coverage create a domestic and international political climate that fosters action by Washington and the United Nations. Similar if not greater humanitarian emergencies in other parts of the world (for example, in Liberia, Angola, the Sudan, or Democratic Congo) are ignored for long periods. Moreover, events in the spring of 1991 created a controversial reference point for later decisions also pertaining to Iraq. In 2003 Washington, London, and some allies decided to use force pursuant to earlier council resolutions demanding widespread disarmament by the Saddam Hussein government. Once again, the council had not explicitly author-ized military force, but the United States and its allies claimed a right to interpret pre-vious resolutions as they saw fit.

Nonforcible Sanctions in the Post–Cold War Era: Humani-tarian Dilemmas

Economic sanctions have long been seen as a policy option to give teeth to certain international decisions. As with many other policy tools available in theory to the international community, their use was impeded in practice during the Cold War.

After using nonforcible sanctions only twice during the Cold War, the Security Council resorted to them more than a dozen times during the decade of the 1990s. Partial or comprehensive sanctions were decided on by the Security Council against various countries: Iraq, the states of the former Yugoslavia, Libya, Liberia, Somalia, Haiti, and Rwanda. Moreover, the council also imposed them on several nonstate actors, including the Khmer Rouge in Cambodia (when it was called Kampuchea), and the National Union for the Total Independence of Angola (UNITA), and the Afghan faction known as the Taliban, which also called itself the Islamic Emirate of Afghanistan. More needs to be known about their precise impact, in particular about their negative and sometimes dire humanitarian consequences.[15]

Research reveals three pertinent challenges. The first results from the nature of modern warfare as exemplified by the 1991 Persian Gulf War.[16] The Gulf crisis dramatizes the extent to which the international responses in modern armed conflicts can themselves do serious harm to innocent and powerless civilians. The political strategies adopted, the economic sanctions imposed, and the military force authorized by the Security Council not only created additional hardships but also complicated the ability of the UN's own humanitarian agencies to help civilians caught in the throes of conflict. OAS and UN economic sanctions harmed as many as 100,000 people in Haiti in 1993, most of whom were children.

Since the international community has available only a limited range of sanctions when a state refuses to respect a decision made by the Security Council, the question arises as to what better approach might be employed. Before the Security Council decides on enforcement action with potentially major humanitarian consequences, organizations with humanitarian competence and responsibilities could be consulted. Whether the impact is upon citizens in the pariah country or elsewhere, the staff of the United Nations Children's Fund (UNICEF), the United Nations High Commissioner for Refugees (UNHCR), the World Health Organization (WHO), and the World Food Programme (WFP) are well situated to warn against, anticipate, and monitor such consequences. There are also private humanitarian agencies that consult regularly with UN bodies and can provide informed information on the humane impact of sanctions. Or if the Security Council decides to proceed, governments could provide resources to the UN system so that it could respond fully to the immediate and longer-term human consequences of sanctions.[17] These options were not explored during the 1991 Persian Gulf crisis. UN planning in 2003 in anticipation of a coalition attack on Iraq, while improved, was also insufficient.

The second challenge is an eminently practical one. It concerns how to provide humanitarian sustenance after the initial outpouring of international concern has subsided and humanitarian interests are left to vie with other causes for the international spotlight. Resolution 688 insisted that Iraq provide the United Nations with humanitarian access to its people. As indicated earlier and as will be pursued in the next part of this book, this resolution was a watershed,[18] but the exact impact of sanctions on the behavior of the Iraqi government is not well understood. There was an obvious backlash in Baghdad against UN assertive humanitarianism. It would be easy to dismiss out of hand the government's actions, which created havoc for some months with UN and NGO efforts, because this was a regime whose human rights abuses against its own population and brinkmanship tactics were well documented; but behind Iraq's machinations were understandable reactions against the Security Council's treatment of Iraq. International assistance flowed more easily to minority populations in revolt against Baghdad than to civilians in equal need in parts of the country under the central government's control.

The third challenge relates to timing the deployment of UN military forces in conjunction with economic sanctions. Enshrined in the UN Charter is the assumption that nonforcible sanctions should be tried first; only when they fail should collective military action ensue. The suffering civilian populations of the former Yugoslavia and Haiti provided compelling reasons to rethink the conventional wisdom. In the former Yugoslavia, the case could be made that a vigorous and earlier preventive deployment of UN soldiers to Bosnia and Herzegovina (rather than just to Croatia, with a symbolic administrative presence in Sarajevo) might have obviated the later need for sanctions to pressure Belgrade and Serbian irregulars and might have prevented the grisly war that ensued. In fact, this was part of the justification for the preventive positioning of UN observers as part of the United Nations Protection Force (UNPROFOR) in Macedonia in December 1992. In Haiti, some observers, with considerable reason, queried whether an earlier military enforcement action to restore an elected government would have entailed far less civilian suffering than extended economic sanctions did, particularly because the willingness to use such overwhelming force was visible in September 1994. In short, the reluctance to use force may not always be a good thing, if delay means that civilians suffer and aid agencies are projected into conflict as a substitute for needed military intervention.

Operational Quandaries: Cambodia, the Former Yugoslavia, Somalia, Rwanda, and Haiti

The United Nations encountered conditions in several operations during the 1990s that highlight the inadequacy of the traditional principles of peacekeeping. In order to deal with the kinds of challenges faced by the United Nations in operations such as the UN Transitional Authority in Cambodia (UNTAC), the second and third UN Angola Verification Missions (UNAVEM II and UNAVEM III), the UN Protection Force (UNPROFOR) in the former Yugoslavia, the first and second UN Operations in Somalia (UNOSOM), the UN Assistance Mission in Rwanda (UNAMIR), and the UN Mission in Haiti (UNMIH), the world organization sought new ways of responding to conflict.

These operations were qualitatively and quantitatively different from UN operations during the Cold War. They indicated that the formal consent of the parties cannot be assumed to mean very much on the ground. Also, the military effectiveness required from, and the dangers faced by, UN military forces go far beyond the parameters of traditional lightly armed peacekeepers. Moreover, these operations suggest the magnitude of the new demands on the UN for services that threatened to overwhelm troop contributors and to break the bank. After stable levels of about 10,000 troops and a budget of a few hundred million dollars in the early post–Cold War period, the

Participants in an UNTAC demining course learn to cope with tripwires near Siem Reap Town, Cambodia, 1993. (UNHCR Photo/I. Guest)

numbers jumped rapidly. In the mid-1990s, 70,000 to 80,000 blue-helmeted soldiers were authorized by the UN's annualized peacekeeping budget, which approached $4 billion in 1995. Accumulated total arrears in these years hovered around $3.5 billion—that is, almost equal to this budget and approaching three times the regular UN budget. The roller-coaster ride continued between 1996 and 1998, when both the number of soldiers and the budget dropped precipitously by two-thirds, at least partially reflecting the world organization's overextension and administrative indigestion. It changed again in the new millennium as police efforts in Kosovo and military ones in Timor and the Congo began. Throughout, arrears remained at a critical level, and the world organization's cash reserves often covered barely one month's expenditures. (Table 3.2 depicts ongoing UN security operations as of December 2002, and Table 3.3, those previously completed.)

As the 1990s came to a close, significant cash-flow problems continued—former Under-Secretary-General for administration Dick Thornburg earlier had referred to the situation as a "financial bungee jump"—even if the money appeared almost trivial or a "bargain" according to a prominent group of bankers.[19] Any UN spending can be compared with the U.S. Defense Department budget, which was, for example, some $375 billion in 2003, before the costs of the war with Iraq and subsequent peace-building expenditures. The UN's annual budget for security operations during that same period would represent only a few days of Operation Desert Storm in 1991 or about the annual budget of the New York City police and fire departments. The assessed U.S. contribution to these operations, about 30 percent of the total bill, was only about .05 percent of the U.S. defense budget. The cost of a few weeks of fighting in Iraq in 2003, estimated at some $60–80 billion, dwarfs either the annual UN administrative budget of about $1.25 billion or the annual total spending of the UN system of some $10 billion.

What exactly were the operational quandaries? The Cambodian operation amounted to the UN's taking over, at least in theory, all the important civilian administration of the country while simultaneously disarming guerrillas and governmental armed forces. The United Nations registered most of the nation for the first democratic election in the country's history. In size and complexity, UNTAC rivaled the contested operation from 1960 to 1964 in the Congo. The UNTAC deployment was based—as are most UN undertakings—on national budgetary projections out of touch with real military requirements. These estimates were based on best-case scenarios; the situation on the ground was closer to worst-case ones.

Japan's desire—sustained in part by U.S. and other pressures—to make a large contribution to this operation in "its own region" was important—especially given the later U.S. desire to "pick and choose" among complicated field operations. Despite many problems and despite sometimes fatal attacks on its personnel, Japan stayed the course in Cambodia—in part because it was urged to stay by Yasushi Akashi, a Japanese national who was head of the UN operation in that country.

Years of internal conflict had left Cambodia's infrastructure devastated and its population displaced. In response, the United Nations invested over $1.6 billion and over 22,000 military and civilian personnel. Yet UNTAC's success was hardly a foregone conclusion, particularly in light of the Khmer Rouge's unwillingness to respect key elements of agreements and Prince Norodom Sihanouk's stated position that the peace process and elections should continue with or without the Khmer Rouge. Failure here could have seriously undermined the confidence of member states attempting an undertaking of this scale or complexity elsewhere.

The elections in May 1993 were a turning point. A Khmer Rouge attack on a UN fuel and ammunition dump three weeks before the elections in May 1993 exposed how inadequately prepared UN soldiers were to resist even symbolic military maneuvers, let alone a return to full-scale civil war. However, the elections were held and returned Prince Sihanouk to power as the head of a coalition that included the former government and part of the opposition—but excluded the Khmer Rouge. The UN's achievement was that the Khmer people struggled for power for the first time by means of a secret ballot. The relative lack of violence—the Khmer Rouge had demonstrated that it could attack with impunity—happened in spite of UNTAC, not because of it. However, since the United Nations began to pull out its personnel as quickly as possible after the elections, some wondered whether the withdrawal was not premature and what, if anything, the UN would do if civil war erupted. The uneasy internal peace managed to hold, the Khmer Rouge continued to weaken, and the UN stayed heavily involved in diplomacy—mainly trying to liberalize the Heng Sen government, as in discussions about what to do about past and present violations of human rights.[20]

In the former Yugoslavia, the UN became involved in a military operation on European soil after many years in which regional conflicts were assumed to be a

UNPROFOR soldiers in Stari Vitez, Yugoslavia. (UN Photo 186716/J. Isaac)

monopoly of developing countries. Although the prospect of a UN field operation in Europe seemed almost surrealistic before the collapse of the Soviet Union, the Balkans and some republics of the former Soviet Union emerged as the possible scene of growth in future demand for UN security operations.[21]

The dissolution of the former Yugoslavia entailed violence and displacement of a magnitude not seen in Europe since World War II. The UN's initial involvement in Croatia, with close to 14,000 peacekeepers, achieved some objectives, but there was massive disregard for law and human welfare. These troops did not prevent ethnic cleansing, detention camps, refugees, killing, and atrocities, particularly in neighboring Bosnia and Herzegovina. Europeans and the Western alliance were unable to get the parties to halt their internecine fighting during 1992. The UN was sucked into a conflict that it had sought to avoid. It was the last resort in trying to ensure the delivery of humanitarian assistance to Muslims and Croats under siege from Serbia and Serbian irregulars.

The 1,500 UN soldiers initially assigned to the Sarajevo area quickly proved to be inadequate. The Security Council later authorized adding 8,000 more soldiers to protect humanitarian convoys and to escort detainees in Bosnia and Herzegovina. The United Nations also asked NATO to enforce a no-fly zone for Serbian aircraft. In an approach reminiscent of the voluntary financing of the United Nations Peace-keeping Force in Cyprus (UNFICYP), the Secretary-General insisted that these additional humanitarian soldiers be provided at no cost to the world organization, and NATO countries responded. Later, U.S. airdrops of food to isolated and ravaged Muslim communities were seen mostly as a symbolic gesture by the Clinton administration, but they helped save lives. These efforts were insufficient to halt the bloodshed or inhibit the carving up of Bosnia and Herzegovina by the Serbs and Croats.

After months of efforts by the UN special envoy, former U.S. secretary of state Cyrus Vance, and the European Community's mediator, former British foreign minister David Owen, a tenuous plan to create a "Swiss-like" set of ten semiautonomous ethnic enclaves within Bosnia and Herzegovina was finally agreed upon by the belligerents. NATO was approached to help make sure that the agreement—however unacceptable to critics who argued that the arrangements rewarded Serbian aggression—would stick.

This operation would have been the most costly and dangerous UN undertaking to date. NATO plans at the time included contingencies from 50,000 to 150,000 troops, on top of the NATO enforcement of the no-fly zone over Bosnia. But these plans were overtaken almost immediately by renewed Serbian and Croatian military offensives. When former Norwegian foreign minister Thorvald Stoltenberg took over from Cyrus Vance in May 1993, it was clear that Bosnia would be partitioned. Serbian war efforts had left Serbia in control of 70 percent of the territory, and Croatia held another 20 percent. The Bosnian Muslims were left with what were euphemistically called UN safe areas, a series of European Gaza Strips, only worse, since they were subjected to repeated military attacks.

Preventive deployment also was initiated at this time in what everyone except the Greeks wished to call Macedonia. In an effort to forestall the type of carnage that had struck elsewhere in the former Yugoslavia, the UN began to deploy 1,000 observers in December 1992. This group reached its full strength half a year later.

The need to interdict overflights by Serbian aircraft was yet another advance in efforts to expand UN-approved security operations. The initial calls by the Security Council for a halt to overflights began in autumn 1992, but it was not until summer 1993 that the United States began to press its allies and NATO began to bomb Serbian positions. But by that time, Serbia and Croatia were already in control of most of the Bosnian territory that they sought. Finger-pointing and rhetorical attacks continued in the West throughout 1993, as did violence against civilians.

The situation in the Balkans demonstrated that the United Nations also can provide the means for governments to pretend to do something without really doing very much. There was a shift from Chapter VI to Chapter VII operations, but without the necessary political will to make the shift work. It can even be argued that, ironically, the half measures in Bosnia were worse than no action at all. Given their traditional operating procedures and constraints, UN soldiers were not strong enough to deter the Serbs. But they deterred the international community from the possibility of more assertive intervention under Chapter VII because the troops, along with humanitarian workers, were vulnerable targets. Although assistance to refugees saved lives, it also helped foster ethnic cleansing by cooperating in the movement of unwanted populations. Airdrops of food made it seem as if people salved consciences while massive and unspeakable human rights abuses continued unabated. Thus, even inadequate UN military and humanitarian action constituted a powerful palliative.[22]

The initial feebleness was followed by a steadily growing number of additional UN troops that, although mainly from NATO countries, were equally feeble. This contingent ultimately reached about 50,000 (including a rapid-reaction force mounted by NATO in summer 1995) but in fact never acted as a war-fighting force until it was goaded into action by a Croatian-Bosnian offensive in August and September that pushed the Serbs out of Krajina. No-fly zones were imposed but not fully enforced; other forms of saber rattling, including low-altitude sorties over Serbian positions and warnings about possible retaliatory air strikes, were tried; and the Security Council passed what the *Economist* called "the confetti of paper resolutions."[23] As Lawrence Freedman observed, the Security Council "experimented with almost every available form of coercion short of war."[24]

But the West's token half measures under UN auspices did little to halt Serbian irredentism and consolidation of territory in either Croatia or Bosnia; nor did these measures prevent the initial expansion of Croatian claims in Bosnia. The UN mandatory arms embargo instituted in September 1991 had benefited primarily the Serbs, who controlled the bulk of the military hardware of the former Yugoslav army. Given their traditional operating procedures and constraints—not to mention their small numbers and inadequate equipment—UN soldiers were powerless to deter the Serbs. The vulnerability of UN "protectors" was regularly invoked by Europeans as a rationale against more forceful military measures.

The idea of "safe areas" brought derision because the least safe places in the Balkans were under UN control. The ultimate ignominy arrived in summer 1995 when two of these enclaves in eastern Bosnia were overrun by Bosnian Serbs whose tactics included mass executions of Muslims. Srebrenica became the largest massacre in Europe since 1945, and a synonym for UN impotence as the outmanned Dutch peacekeeping unit withdrew rather than act. Shortly before this, Serbs had chained UN blue helmets to strategic targets and thereby prevented NATO air raids.[25]

UN peacekeepers in Croatia were unable to implement their mandate because they received no cooperation from the Croats or Krajina Serbs. In Bosnia, UN forces were under Chapter VII but lacked the capability to apply coercive force across a wide front. Shortly before resigning in January 1994 from a soldier's nightmare as UN commander in Bosnia, Lt. Gen. Francis Briquemont lamented the disparity between rhetoric and reality: "There is a fantastic gap between the resolutions of the Security Council, the will to execute those resolutions, and the means available to commanders in the field."[26]

The international community's unwillingness to react militarily in the former Yugoslavia until August 1995 provides a case study of what not to do. This inaction left many of the inhabitants of the region mistrustful of the United Nations and lent a new and disgraceful connotation to the word "peacekeeping." Bound by the traditional rules of engagement (fire only in self-defense and only after being fired upon), UN troops never fought a single battle with any of the factions in Bosnia that routinely disrupted relief convoys. The rules of engagement led to the appeasement of local forces rather than to the enforcement of UN mandates. The provisions for economic and military sanctions in the UN Charter were designed to back up international decisions to counteract aggression and to halt atrocities in just such situations as the one in Bosnia. Yet with apt gallows humor, many in Zagreb and Sarajevo referred repeatedly to the UN soldiers as "eunuchs at the orgy."

In fact, a much heavier dose of NATO bombing and U.S. arm-twisting proved necessary to compel the belligerents, sequestered at Ohio's Wright-Patterson Air Force Base in November 1995, to attempt to reach a political settlement. The Dayton peace agreements laid the groundwork for military deployment by almost 60,000 NATO soldiers (one-third from the United States). Although the numbers of soldiers in the successive NATO operations diminished over time, still many observers wondered why UN peacekeepers—poorly equipped and without a mandate—were deployed when there was no peace to keep and why NATO war-fighters appeared when there was. Observers usually point to the "Somalia syndrome" as the turning point in soured public attitudes toward the world organization (a case that we will come to next). But Richard Holbrooke, the former U.S. Assistant Secretary of State who became UN Ambassador in 1999 and is generally credited with having engineered the Dayton accords, suggests, "The damage that Bosnia did to the U.N. was incalculable."[27]

The Dayton peace agreement called on the Security Council to establish a transitional administration to govern the region of Eastern Slavonia, Baranja, and Western Sirmium and on January 15, 1996, the Security Council responded by creating UNTAES (United Nations Transitional Administration for Eastern Slavonia, Baranja and Western Sirmium), which comprised both military and civilian components. The 5,000 troops were tasked with supervising and facilitating demilitarization of the region, monitoring the return of refugees and displaced persons, and assisting in implementing other aspects of the Dayton agreement. The civilian component, comprising primarily civilian police, focused on restoring law and order, organizing and conducting elections, and assisting in the coordination of plans for the development and economic reconstruction of the region. The UNTAES mandate terminated on January 15, 1998, having accomplished those tasks within the power of its limited mandate, yet without the Dayton agreement being fully implemented. The UN presence was continued in the area, but only by a small civilian United Nations Police Support Group (UNPSG) of 180 officers charged with monitoring the performance of Croatian police mainly in connection with the return of displaced persons.

The situation in the Balkans was terrible; but Somalia provided another complicated challenge for UN involvement in internal wars and a breakdown in governance, or "complex emergencies." The Middle East had previously provided analysts with the specter of Lebanonization, meaning the fragmentation of a country along sectarian lines, as one of the worst epithets in politics. Somalia became another example of violent fragmentation, but one without an ethnic logic. A single ethnic group sharing the same religion, history, and language split into heavily armed clans. Somalia had no government in any meaningful sense, and one-third of the population risked death from starvation because humanitarians could not reach the needy.

The Security Council at the end of August 1992 authorized 3,000 to 4,000 UN soldiers to help, applying Chapter VII to yet another situation by authorizing the reinforcement of the United Nations Operation in Somalia (UNOSOM I). The goal

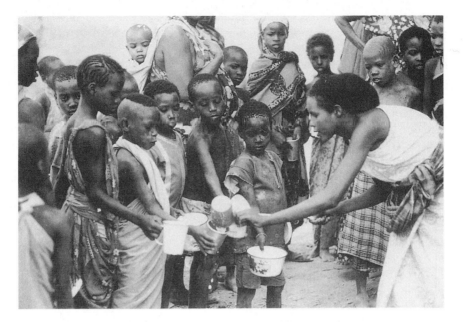

Somalian children receiving food in 1992. (UN Photo 146504/J. Isaac)

was to help protect the delivery of humanitarian succor throughout that hapless country. While the council made formal reference to Chapter VII, quiet diplomacy obtained the consent of the leading clans for deployment of UN force. That force was directed initially not against clan leaders but against bandits interfering with relief. The most important delivery point for relief was not a UN agency, but rather the private International Committee of the Red Cross (ICRC).

In December 1992 President George H. W. Bush, perhaps because of his lame-duck status, which freed him from any concern besides doing good in the world, moved vigorously to propose a U.S.-led humanitarian intervention. Within days of the passage of Security Council Resolution 794, the first of what would become over 27,000 U.S. troops arrived to provide a modicum of security to help sustain civilians. They were augmented by 10,000 soldiers from twenty-two other countries. This effort was labeled Operation Restore Hope from the American side, or the Unified Task Force (UNITAF), an acronym that reflected the authorization from the Security Council to use force to ensure the delivery of humanitarian relief. UNITAF was always under U.S. operational command. With virtually no casualties, humanitarian space was created and modest disarming of local bandits began.

UNITAF ceased operations in April 1993, when the second phase of the UN Operation in Somalia began as authorized by Security Council Resolution 814. For the second time, in the wake of UNPROFOR in Bosnia which was also given a coercive mandate from time to time, the Secretary-General directly commanded a military force deployed under Chapter VII. The Security Council authorized UNOSOM II under Chapter VII to use whatever force was necessary to disarm Somali warlords who might refuse to surrender their arms and to ensure access to suffering civilians. At its maximum strength, some 20,000 soldiers and 8,000 logistical troops from thirty-three countries were deployed.

As in Cambodia, almost 3,000 civilian officials were expected to take over the administration of a country, only this time a country that was totally without a functioning government. Significantly, the United States initially remained on the ground with logistics troops for the first time under the command of a UN general—who was an officer from a NATO country, Turkey. Another 1,300 soldiers, including 400 Army Rangers, were held in reserve as a "rapid-reaction force" in boats offshore. These latter U.S. units were under strictly U.S. command.

In retaliation against attacks on UN peacekeepers and aid personnel, U.S. Cobra helicopter gunships were called in by the UN command in June and July 1993 against the armed supporters of one of the main belligerents, General Mohammed Aideed. These attacks were followed by the arrival of U.S. Army Rangers later in the summer. These violent flare-ups got the United Nations into the awkward business of retaliation, which elicited more violence and the assassination of foreign journalists and aid workers and further attacks on U.S. troops, including the ugly scene in October 1993 when the bodies of dead Marines were dragged by crowds through the streets of Mogadishu in front of television cameras.

The shift from Chapter VI to Chapter VII, and along with it a significant expansion of objectives from humanitarian relief to nation- and state-building, constituted one set of problems. The absence of political commitment and staying power was yet another. In Washington, the approval of Presidential Decision Directive 25 (PDD 25) in May 1994 marked the official end to the Clinton administration's attitude of assertive multilateralism. This phrase had become a liability to the Democrats in American domestic politics, as Republicans attacked a supposed U.S. subservience to the United Nations. The Clinton administration had left itself open to this attack by misrepresenting the situation in Somalia, trying to blame UN officials for what had been, in fact, decisions by U.S. military personnel. Given the virtual necessity for Washington's participation in major multilateral military operations, the unseemly images of eighteen dead troops in October 1993 were considerably more costly than the tragic loss of these individuals. Military multilateralism was put in abeyance. The "Somalia syndrome" was linked to its predecessor, the "Vietnam syndrome."

Observers have criticized the military's involvement in the Horn of Africa on numerous grounds. Figuring prominently in such observations have been the obsession with Mogadishu and the "Wild West" hunt, complete with a wanted poster, for Aideed. Then there was the slowness to engage in behalf of disarmament and nation-building. In addition, there was a striking disequilibrium between the military and humanitarian components. The costs of Operation Restore Hope alone, at $1 billion, amounted to three times Washington's total aid contributions to Somalia since independence. Seven months of UNOSOM II in 1993 were estimated to cost $1.5 billion, of which the lowest estimate for humanitarian aid was 0.7 percent of the total and the highest 10 percent.[28] Also, as UN objectives expanded, resources were actually reduced.

When the last UN soldiers pulled out of Somalia in March 1995, the ultimate result of military and humanitarian help was unclear. Three years and some $4 billion had left the warring parties better armed, rested, and poised to resume civil war. But the worst of starvation had been brought under control. In 2003 Somalia still remained without a viable national government, although concerted diplomatic efforts continued outside the UN to improve the situation.

Another horror had developed simultaneously in East Africa, where long-standing social tensions in Rwanda led to the genocide of perhaps 800,000 of Rwanda's Tutsi minority by the Hutu majority. Relatedly, about 2 million persons were displaced within Rwanda, with another 2 million refugees fleeing into neighboring states.

International military forces had actually been on the scene during this time. UNAMIR had been present in Kigali for about eight months, to facilitate the Arusha Peace Accords between Rwandan Hutu and Tutsi elements when the genocide commenced on April 6, 1994. The Security Council actually reduced these UN military forces a few days later, after a small number of Belgian peacekeepers had been abused and killed, despite the previous request of the Canadian commander of the blue helmets for an augmented force. Later the council authorized two stand-alone initiatives. There was a two-month effort through the French-led Opération Turquoise from June to August, supposedly in order to stabilize the southwestern part of the country on the basis of Security Council Resolution 929, although the French used their presence to protect some of their Hutu allies despite their participation in genocide. There was also the massive two-month logistics effort through the U.S. Operation Support Hope in July and August to provide relief to the Goma region in Zaire. Numerous national contingents also deployed to this region in support of the assistance efforts by the UNHCR.

Ironically, fostering a secure environment—a task in which the military has the clear, comparative advantage—was the least visible operation. The military's cautious standard operating procedures accompanied by the widespread concerns among governments about a possible quagmire paralyzed international military responses for two months while as many as 10 percent of Rwanda's population were murdered. Arguably, Opération Turquoise prevented another refugee crisis of the record-setting magnitude of the one in May in Goma, Zaire, where almost 1 million Rwandan refugees appeared virtually overnight. The first crisis was accompanied by a cholera epidemic that is variously estimated to have killed between 50,000 and 80,000 people.[29]

Massive amounts of food, clothing, medicine, shelter, and water were delivered. Outside armed forces thus made essential contributions by using their unexcelled logistical and organizational resources, but only *after* the genocide had occurred. Rapid military action in April proved totally unfeasible, but the costs of the genocide, massive displacement, and a ruined economy (including decades of wasted development assistance and outside investment) were borne almost immediately afterward by the same governments that had refused to respond militarily a few weeks earlier.

The role of the media in provoking international responses continues to be controversial.[30] Rwanda illustrates probably better than the other cases that such coverage may be necessary for humanitarian assistance even if it is insufficient for timely and robust military action. When enough gruesome images appear in the media, the daily legislative preoccupation with cost-cutting is momentarily suspended. There is evidence that many wealthier societies, in particular those of the West, are viscerally and ethically unable to ignore certain massive tragedies even though the initial reaction is to do nothing. Rwanda shows, however, that if governments are determined not to send troops, even media coverage of sudden and massive genocide may not change that governmental view. Reactions in the face of some 150,000 deaths in the three-year period beginning in October 1993 in neighboring Burundi indicate that changes in international practices lag substantially behind changes in international rhetoric. There are fewer political risks in costly humanitarian assistance than in preventive action with possible casualties—or the potential for protracted involvement in a civil war.

The UN's role in response to the Rwandan crisis stands as one of its greatest acknowledged failures, just as previous development efforts are now acknowledged to have exacerbated tensions.[31] Several years later, Secretary-General Kofi Annan, who had been in charge of the UN's peacekeeping department in New York during the crisis, felt compelled during a visit to Kigali to confess, "We must and we do acknowledge that the world failed Rwanda at that time of evil. The international community and the United Nations could not muster the political will to confront it."[32] In a later statement he continued, "There was a United Nations force in the country at the time, but it was neither mandated nor equipped for the kind of forceful action which would have been needed to prevent or halt the genocide. On behalf of the United Nations, I acknowledge this failure and express my deep remorse."[33] It was Kofi Annan who had "buried" the cable from the Canadian commander, General Romeo Dallaire, asking for a proactive role to head off the 1994 genocide.[34]

As discussed earlier, the evolving situation in Angola posed serious problems for UNAVEM II. The results of the UN-supervised election in September 1997 were contested by the National Union for the Total Independence of Angola (UNITA), and renewed fighting ensued. Accordingly, the Security Council revised the UNAVEM II mandate to include a larger peacemaking role. On November 20, 1994, a peace agreement, the Lusaka Protocol, was signed between the government and UNITA, and in February 1995 the Security Council set up a new mission, UNAVEM III, to monitor and verify the protocol. Plagued by criticisms that UNAVEM II had been understaffed and underfinanced, the new mission was mandated a force of up to 7,000 military troops and another 1,000 civilian personnel and military observers. However, the council kept UNAVEM on a short leash and kept the respective mandates to short time periods. Not surprisingly this strategy led to "donor fatigue" and frustration regarding "staying the course." In June 1997, the Security Council transformed UNAVEM III into the UN Observer Mission in Angola (MONUA), which was to assist the conflicting parties in consolidating peace while slowly withdrawing UN military personnel. A civilian police component would continue to verify the fulfillment of the peace agreement. Like the mandate of UNAVEM, MONUA's mandate was kept short and was renewed several times, but no real peace was won.

During the week of December 27, 1998–January 2, 1999, two UN-chartered planes were shot down over UNITA-held territory. A month later the Secretary-General recommended and the Security Council endorsed the removal of all MONUA personnel. The situation continued to deteriorate. Thus ten years and $1.5 billion later the UN had failed to establish enduring peace.

Meanwhile in the Caribbean, nine months after the United Nations had overseen the first democratic elections in Haiti, the populist priest Jean-Bertrand Aristide was overthrown by a military junta led by General Raoul Cédras. The inclusion of Haiti in our discussion is of interest for a number of reasons. Although Haiti had not really endured a civil war, it had all the attributes of a failed state—in particular, political instability, widespread poverty, massive migration, and human rights abuses. It also became the target of international coercive actions—that is, both nonforcible and forcible sanctions under Chapter VII of the UN Charter similar to those in the other war-torn countries analyzed earlier. Moreover, the basis for outside intervention was the restoration of a democratically elected government; this precedent has potential implications because of its widespread relevance for other countries in crisis.

Multilateral military forces were essential to the solution that ultimately resulted in late 1994. First, however, came the embarrassing performance of the UN Mission in Haiti (UNMIH I), including the ignominious retreat by the USS *Harlan County,* which carried unarmed American and Canadian military observers, in September 1993 following a rowdy demonstration on the docks in Port-au-Prince. In September 1994, the first soldiers of the UN-authorized and U.S.-led Multinational Force (MNF) landed in Haiti on the basis of Security Council Resolution 940. What Pentagon wordsmiths labeled Operation Uphold Democracy grew quickly to 21,000 troops—almost all American except for 1,000 police and soldiers from twenty-nine countries, mostly from the eastern Caribbean. This operation ensured the departure of the illegal military regime and the restoration of the elected government.

Most important for this analysis, the MNF used overwhelming military force— although there was only a single military person killed in action and the local population was almost universally supportive—to accomplish two important tasks with clear humanitarian impacts. First and most immediately, the MNF brought an end to the punishing economic sanctions that had crippled the local economy and penalized Haiti's most vulnerable groups because the programs of humanitarian and development agencies were paralyzed. Second, the MNF established a secure and stable environment that stemmed the tide of refugees, facilitated the rather expeditious repatriation of some 370,000 refugees, and immediately stopped the worst human rights abuses.

Washington expended about $1 billion for troops—of which only one-fifth was over and above what normal Department of Defense expenditures would have been had the troops been at their home base in the United States—and another $325 million on assistance in the first half year, only a small part of which was administered by American soldiers directly. Once the MNF achieved its goals, it was entrusted at the end of March 1995 with the next UN Mission in Haiti (UNMIH II). The 6,000 soldiers from over a dozen countries had an annual budget of about $350 million. The continued involvement of a substantial number of U.S. Special Forces (2,500) and an American force commander for the UN follow-on operation demonstrated concretely Washington's commitment through the end of February 1996. UNMIH was extended for four additional months at about half its former size (without American soldiers) before it was replaced by the even smaller UN Support Mission in Haiti (UNSMIH) in July for a period of twelve months. A small UN presence was continued for the remainder of the decade, working with the government of Haiti to professionalize the Haitian National Police. These latter periods of UN involvement were characterized by Canadian financial, political, and military leadership.

Haiti provides a relatively straightforward and positive balance sheet—at least in the short term. By 2003 Haiti was still characterized by political instability and widespread poverty. There were few complications or casualties from the UN-authorized military deployment, given the weakness of the Haitian military, although the intervention did too little to improve the police and judiciary and absolutely nothing to alter the fundamental economic situation. The disparity in the distribution of wealth and power between a tiny elite and the vast majority of the population made Haiti one of the world's most polarized societies; this inequality had led to the rise and fall of Aristide. Ironically, the most important humanitarian impact of the Chapter VII military intervention was probably the end of the Chapter VII economic sanctions, which had devastated the local economy and the poor.

As in other military interventions, the perception that the interests of key states were threatened spurred leadership and risk-taking. The geography of the crisis brought into prominence not just Washington but also Ottawa and several Caribbean countries. Washington was particularly anxious to end the perceived "flood" of boat people upsetting the demographics and politics of places like south Florida and Louisiana. The success of the military deployment was dramatic, notwithstanding that it was authorized to restore democracy rather than respond to a complex emergency. (It is noteworthy that both the U.S. Congress and the Pentagon were initially lukewarm about what turned out to be a considerably successful operation.) The effective use of military force and the resulting humanitarian benefits have led some observers to question the chronology and logic of the UN Charter's calling for nonforcible economic sanctions before forcible military action.

A swifter military intervention undoubtedly would have proved more humanitarian than a tightening of the screws through economic sanctions. It would have accomplished the major goal of replacing the de facto regime with the constitutional authorities but would have avoided the massive suffering and dislocations from sanctions. "Sanctions, as is generally recognized, are a blunt instrument," wrote Boutros-Ghali. "They raise the ethical question of whether suffering inflicted on vulnerable groups in the target country is a legitimate means of exerting pressure on political leaders whose behaviour is unlikely to be affected by the plight of their subjects."[35]

The most significant feature of the international responses just discussed has been the growing willingness to address, rather than ignore, fundamental problems within the borders of war-torn states. As the UN Development Programme (UNDP) calculated at the time, eighty-two armed conflicts broke out in the first half-decade following the collapse of the Berlin Wall, and seventy-nine were intrastate wars; in fact, two of the three remaining ones (Nagorno-Karabakh and Bosnia) also could legitimately have been categorized as civil wars.[36]

Having gone from famine to feast in the mid-1990s, the United Nations had a bad case of institutional indigestion. The climate had changed so much that Secretary-General Boutros Boutros-Ghali was obliged to write a follow-up, *Supplement to An Agenda for Peace,* to his earlier document. In this January 1995 report he noted, "This increased volume of activity would have strained the Organization even if the nature of the activity had remained unchanged."[37]

Ever-Evolving Security Operations: Kosovo, East Timor, and Sierra Leone

The UN's security activities, however, did not remain unchanged. In the face of new challenges the approaches of the past were found lacking if not totally inadequate. Yet the demand for action was as great as ever. The Balkans erupted once again into full-scale war and ethnic turmoil in Kosovo. What was hoped to be the beginning of a UN-supervised peaceful transition to independence from Indonesia for the people in East Timor turned into a bloody campaign of violence. In addition to renewed war in Angola, internal conflicts raged in numerous countries across Africa. Among the most serious of these were the civil wars in Sierra Leone and in the Democratic Republic of the Congo, where the horrors in Rwanda had spilled over into open civil war involving more than a half dozen external actors. In addition, for example, the Security Council held sessions in 1999 on the situations in Western Sahara, Ethiopia/Eritrea, Somalia, Guinea-Bissau, Burundi, the former Yugoslav Republic of Macedonia, Croatia, Bosnia and Herzegovina, Central African Republic, Georgia, Tajikistan, Afghanistan, Iraq and Kuwait, Haiti, Cyprus, Lebanon, Syria, Israel, and Libya.

In the face of these crises the critical question confronting the UN was how to respond effectively. The answer to this question emerged on a case-by-case basis, yet with each new response seemingly informed by and building on the last. The following discussion illustrates the evolution in "traditional" UN peacekeeping in these cases.

The Continuing Crisis in the Balkans

The pursuit of the 1991 Gulf War and the creation of safe havens for Kurds are illustrations of what we referred to in Chapter 1 as military "subcontracting," as was IFOR and SFOR (the Implementation Force and the Stabilization Force, respectively, in the former Yugoslavia); a more controversial example is Somalia. As mentioned earlier, the growing relevance of military intervention by major powers in regions of their traditional interests had become obvious in mid-1994. However controversial the results, the gap between UN capacities and demands for action led almost inevitably to calls for action by various states with the blessing of the larger community of states through either the explicit or the implicit approval of the Security Council.[38]

The actions of NATO in Kosovo in spring 1999 is a dramatic case in point. Depending on how one reads the script of diplomatic code embedded in Security Council resolutions, the action by NATO could be argued to represent a breach of

TABLE 3.2   Ongoing UN Peace and Security Operations as of 31 December 2002 [with starting dates] (annualized cost about $2.2 billion)

1. United Nations Truce Supervision Organization (UNTSO), Middle East, June 1948-
    Appropriation for 12 months $25.9 million
    Current strength (military) 154
2. United Nations Military Observer Group in India and Pakistan (UNMOGIP),
    January 1949-
    Appropriation for 12 months $9.2 million
    Current strength (military) 44
3. United Nations Peacekeeping Force in Cyprus (UNFICYP), March 1964-
    Appropriation for 12 months $45.6 million (gross), including voluntary
    contributions by Cyprus $15.2 million and Greece $6.5 million
    Current strength (military and police personnel) 1,245
4. United Nations Disengagement Observer Force (UNDOF), Golan Heights, June 1974-
    Appropriation for 12 months $40.8 million
    Current strength (military) 1, 043
5. United Nations Interim Force in Lebanon (UNIFIL), March 1978-
    Appropriation for 12 months $117.1 million
    Current strength (military) 2,077
6. United Nations Mission for the Referendum in Western Sahara (MINURSO) April1991-
    Appropriation for 12 months $43.4 million
    Current strength (military) 217
7. United Nations Iraq-Kuwait Observer Mission (UNIKOM), April 1991-
    Appropriation for 12 months $52.9 million (gross) with voluntary contribution of
    $35.2 million or two thirds, from Kuwait
    Current strength (military) 1,105
8. United Nations Observer Mission in Georgia (UNOMIG), August 1993-
    Appropriation for 12 months $33.1 million
    Current strength (military) 117
9. United Nations Organization Mission in the Democratic Republic ofthe Congo
    (MONUC), November 1999-
    Appropriation for 12 months $608.3 million
    Current strength (military) 4,420
10. United Nations Interim Administration in Kosovo (UNMIK), June 1999-
    Cost estimate not available
    Current strength (police) 4,468
11. United Nations Mission in Sierra Leone (UNAMSIL), October 1999-
    Appropriation for 12 months $699.8 million
    Current strength (military) 15,483
12. United Nations Mission in Ethiopia and Eritrea (UNMEE), July 2000-
    Appropriation for 12 months $230.9 million
    Current strength (military) 4,034
13. United Nations Mission of Support in East Timor (UNMISET), May 2002-
    Appropriation for 12 months $305.2 million
    Current strength (military and police personnel) 4,583
14. United Nations Assistance Mission in Afghanistan (UNAMA), May 2002-
    Data unavailable

SOURCE: United Nations Department of Peacekeeping Operations

international law or to have been launched with the implicit approval of the council. The Independent Commission on Kosovo, composed largely of human rights proponents, called it "illegal but legitimate"—that is, without the Security Council's blessing but justified in human terms.[39] The Secretary-General of NATO, Javier Solana, of course, chose the latter interpretation of Security Council Resolution 1199. On the other hand, both Russia and China condemned the action as illegal.[40] Russia weakened its own position by introducing a resolution criticizing the NATO bombing and asking that it be halted. The resolution's defeat by a wide (12-3) margin enhanced the status of NATO's action. In any case, Secretary-General Annan drew considerable criticism for his speech at the opening of the General Assembly in September 1999. Although he wished the Security Council had been able to give explicit approval to the bombing, he nonetheless could not condone idleness in the face of Serb atrocities.[41]

Diplomacy had failed to change Serbian policy. Time and again Yugoslav president Slobodan Milosevic demonstrated his blatant disregard for negotiated agreements. In late January 1999, U.S. officials shifted away from a diplomatic approach and threatened military action. The UN Secretary-General had apparently arrived at a similar conclusion. In a statement before NATO leaders in Brussels he indicated that indeed force might be necessary. In doing so, he praised past UN-NATO collaboration in Bosnia and suggested that a NATO-led mission under UN auspices might well be what was needed. He concluded:

> The bloody wars of the last decade have left us with no illusions about the difficulty of halting internal conflicts by reason or by force particularly against the wishes of the government of a sovereign state. But nor have they left us with any illusions about the need to use force, when all other means have failed. We may be reaching that limit, once again, in the former Yugoslavia.[42]

But neither NATO nor the UN was willing to give up totally the diplomatic approach. Hosting a peace conference in Rambouillet, France, in February, the United States, France, Germany, Italy, Russia, and the United Kingdom—the so-called contact group—endeavored to broker a solution between Yugoslavia and an Albanian Kosovar delegation. But especially Belgrade was unwilling to yield on key points and the talks floundered. The situation in Kosovo deteriorated even further.

On March 24, NATO began a seventy-seven-day aerial bombardment of Serbian targets. Soon after the bombing began, Serbian security forces launched an all-out campaign to exorcise Kosovo of its predominant ethnic-Albanian population. Within weeks a huge segment of Kosovo's 1.8 million ethnic Albanians had been displaced from their houses and villages. That is, initially the intervention accelerated flight and humanitarian suffering, However, as the NATO intervention progressed, air strikes intensified until finally, in the context of a Russian mediated settlement, Milosevic agreed on June 3 to an immediate and verifiable end to the violence and repression and to the withdrawal of all Serbian security forces.

Other aspects of the agreement included the deployment under UN auspices of an effective international civilian and security presence with substantial NATO participation, the establishment of an interim administration, safe return of all refugees and displaced persons, demilitarization of the KLA, and a substantially self-governing Kosovo.

On June 10, 1999, the council, in a 14–0–1 vote (China abstained), adopted Resolution 1244 (1999) authorizing an international civil and security presence in Kosovo under UN auspices. NATO's "humanitarian war" had been unusual to say the least, and many aid agencies had trouble pronouncing two words together, "humanitarian bombing."[43] But this new UN peace mission, the UN Interim Administration Mission in Kosovo (UNMIK), was unprecedented in its nature and scope. NATO authorized 49,000 troops to maintain security, but UNMIK was to assume authority over all the territory and people of Kosovo, including judicial, legislative, and executive powers. It was to move the region toward self-governance; perform all normal civilian administrative functions; provide humanitarian relief, including the safe return of refugees and displaced persons; maintain law and order and establish the rule of law; promote human rights; assist in reconstructing basic social and economic infrastructure; and facilitate the development of a democratic political order.

The mission was path-breaking in integrating several non-UN international organizations under a unified UN leadership. It was organized around four substantive pillars: civil administration (UN-led); humanitarian affairs (UNHCR-led); reconstruction (European Union-led); and democratic institution-building (OSCE-led). The scope was mind-boggling. Civil administration, for example, was to be comprehensive, including health, education, energy and public utilities, post and telecommunications, judicial, legal, public finance, trade, science, agriculture, environment, and democratization. Over 800,000 people had to be repatriated. Over 120,000 houses had been damaged or destroyed. Schools needed to be reestablished; food, medical aid, and other humanitarian assistance provided; electrical power, sanitation, and clean water restored; land mines cleared and security ensured; and so on. Although the initial UNMIK mandate was twelve months, the return of life in Kosovo to any semblance of normality will be a long time in coming. The notion of helping to create a liberal democracy in an area that had never known it seemed particularly optimistic. The jury is still out in 2003, but military forces have been reduced, elections held, and the rebuilding of a society begun.

Turmoil in East Timor

After over a decade and a half of UN-mediated efforts to resolve the issue of the status of East Timor, an agreement was reached on May 5, 1999, between Indonesia and Portugal (the last colonial power) regarding a process to determine the future of that long-troubled territory. The two states agreed that the UN Secretary-General would be responsible for organizing and conducting a popular consultation to determine whether the people of East Timor would accept or reject a special autonomous status within the unitary Republic of Indonesia. A rejection of such special status would mean that the UN would be responsible for administering the territory during the transition to independence. The June Security Council Resolution 1246 established the UN Mission in East Timor (UNAMET) with the mandate of conducting such a

A few among the estimated 230,000 displaced East Timorese sought shelter in Assunta Church in Kupang, West Timor, in September 1999. (UN/UNHCR Photo/F. Pagetti)

consultation. After several postponements the popular vote was held on August 30, and the special autonomy status option was overwhelmingly rejected in favor of independence.

News of the outcome stirred pro-integration forces backed by armed militias to violent action. Within a matter of weeks nearly a half million East Timorese were displaced from their homes and villages. Indonesian military troops and police were either unwilling or unable to restore order, and the security situation deteriorated. On September 15 the Security Council, in Resolution 1264, authorized the creation of a multilateral force to restore order and protect and support UNAMET and welcomed member states to lead, organize, and contribute troops to such a force. Sitting in the wings ready to act, an Australian-led force began arriving in East Timor less than a week later. Numerous arms had been twisted in Jakarta so that Indonesia "requested" the coalition force. In less than a month general order was restored, and the Indonesian People's Consultative Assembly voted on October 19 to formally recognize the results of the popular consultation. The following week the Security Council unanimously approved Resolution 1272, establishing the UN Transitional Administration in East Timor (UNTAET).

As in the case of UNMIK, the nature and scope of the UNTAET mission was exceedingly ambitious and wide-ranging.[44] As in the case in Kosovo and elsewhere, a country with substantial interests and motivation (in this case, Australia) took the military lead. It was empowered to exercise all legislative and executive powers and judicial authority; establish an effective civil administration; assist in the development of civil and social services; provide security and maintain law and order; ensure the coordination and delivery of humanitarian assistance, rehabilitation, and development assistance; promote sustainable development; and build the foundation for a stable liberal democracy. To carry out this mandate, authorization was given for a military component of 8,950 troops and 200 observers and a civilian police component of up to 1,640 personnel. As 1999 drew to a close, the security situation in East Timor was stable, and by spring 2000 the peacekeeping transition from INTERFET to UNTAET had been completed and the processes of reconstruction and state-building were under way. Any evaluation of such an effort at UN "trusteeship" must await the passage of time. However, it is worth noting that the UN's role involved, as in Kosovo, a heavy reliance on other IGOs and NGOs.

Reestablishing Stability in Sierra Leone

The year 1999 brought both great sorrow and hope to the people of Sierra Leone, who were reeling from over eight years of civil war. The bloody civil conflict that had intensified during 1998 turned even bloodier in January 1999, when rebel forces once again captured the capital, Freetown, and launched on a four-day spree of killing and destruction. Judges, journalists, human rights workers, government officials, civil servants, churches, hospitals, prisons, UN offices, and others were targets of the rebel alliance, comprising forces of the former junta and the Revolutionary United Front (RUF). Over 6,000 were killed and about 20 percent of the total stock of dwellings was destroyed. The UN Observer Mission in Sierra Leone (UNOMSIL), which had been established in June 1998, was evacuated.

Fighting continued throughout the spring and early summer, uprooting more than a million people, about 450,000 of whom fled to neighboring Guinea. The issue remained on the Security Council agenda, and the council kept extending UNOMSIL's mandate several months at a time. Finally, on July 7, 1999, a peace agreement, called the Lomé Peace Agreement, was negotiated between the government and the RUF. The Security Council responded positively to this move and on August 20 adopted unanimously Resolution 1260, extending and expanding the UNOMSIL mandate. The UN presence was further expanded in October when the council adopted Resolution 1270, creating a new mission, the UN Mission for Sierra Leone (UNAMSIL), which was mandated the tasks of: establishing a presence at key locations throughout the territory of Sierra Leone in order to assist the government of Sierra Leone in implementing the disarmament, demobilization, and reintegration of rebel troops; ensuring the security and freedom of movement of UN personnel; monitoring adherence to the cease-fire agreement of May 18; encouraging the parties to create confidence-building mechanisms and support their functioning; facilitating the delivery of humanitarian assistance; supporting the operations of UN civilian officials, including the special representative of the Secretary-General and his staff, human rights officers, and civil affairs officers; and providing support, as requested, for the

TABLE 3.3   UN Peace and Security Operations: Completed as of February 2003

Location	Acronym/Name	Duration
Middle East	UNEF I/First United Nations Emergency Force	November 1956– June 1967
Lebanon	UNOGIL/United Nations Observation Group in Lebanon	June 1958– December 1958
Congo	ONUC/United Nations Operation in the Congo	July 1960–June 1964
West New Guinea	UNSF/United Nations Security Force in West Guinea (West Irian)	October 1962– April 1963
Yemen	UNYOM/United Nations Yemen Observation Mission	July 1963– September 1964
Dominican Republic	DOMREP/Mission of the Representative of the Secretary-General in the Dominican Republic	May 1965– October 1966
India and Pakistan	UNIPOM/United Nations India-Pakistan Observation Mission	September 1965– March 1966
Middle East	UNEFII/Second United Nations Emergency Force	October 1973– July 1979
Afghanistan and Pakistan	UNGOMAP/United Nations Good Offices Mission in Afghanistan and Pakistan	April 1988– March 1990
Iran and Iraq	UNIIMOG/United Nations Iran-Iraq Military Observer Group	August 1988– February 1991
Angola	UNAVEM I/United Nations Angola Verification Mission I	January 1989– June 1991
Namibia	UNTAG/United Nations Transition Assistance Group	April 1989– March 1990
Central America	ONUCA/United Nations Observer Group in Central America	November 1989– January 1992
Angola	UNAVEM II/ Angola Verification Mission II	June 1991– February 1995
El Salvador	ONUSAL/United Nations Observer Mission in El Salvador	July 1991– April 1995
Cambodia	UNAMIC/United Nations Advance Mission in Cambodia	October 1991– March 1992
Cambodia	UNTAC/United Nations Transitional Authority in Cambodia	March 1992– September 1993
Former Yugoslavia	UNPROFOR/United Nations Protection Force	March 1992– December 1995
Somalia	UNOSOM I/United Nations Operation in Somalia I	April 1992– March 1993
Mozambique	ONUMOZ/United Nations Operation in Mozambique	December 1992– December 1994

Location	Acronym/Name	Duration
Somalia	United Nations Operation in Somalia	March 1993–March 1995
Rwanda and Uganda	UNOMUR/United Nations Observer Mission Uganda-Rwanda	June 1993–September 1994
Haiti	UNMIH/United Nations Mission in Haiti	September 1993–June 1996
Liberia	UNOMIL/United Nations Observer Mission in Liberia	September 1993–September 1997
Rwanda	UNAMIR/United Nations Assistance Mission for Rwanda	October 1993–March 1996
Chad and Libya	UNASOG/United Nations Aousou Strip Observer Group	May 1994–June 1994
Rwanda	Operation Turquoise	June 1994
Angola	UNAVEM III/United Nations Angola Verification Mission III	February 1995–June 1997
Croatia	UNCRO/United Nations Confidence Restoration Organization	March 1995–January 1996
Former Yugoslav Republic of Macedonia	UNPREDEP/United Nations Preventive Deployment Force	March 1995–February 1999
Croatia	UNTAES/United Nations Transitional Administration for Eastern Slavonia, Balanja and Western Sirmium	January 1996–January 1998
Haiti	UNSMIH/United Nations Support Mission in Haiti	July 1996–July 1997
Guatemala	MINUGUA/United Nations Verification Mission in Guatemala	January 1997–May 1997
Angola	MONUA/United Nations Observer Mission in Angola	July 1997–February 1999
Haiti	UNTMIH/United Nations Transition Mission in Haiti	August 1997–November 1997
Croatia	United Nations Civilian Police Support Group	January 1998–October 1998
Sierra Leone	UNOMSIL/United Nations Mission of Observers in Sierra Leone	July 1988–October 1999
Central African Republic	MINURCA/United Nations Mission in Central African Republic	April 1998–February 2000
Haiti	MIPONUH/United Nations Civilian Police Mission in Haiti	December 1997–March 2000
East Timor	UNTAET/United Nations Transitional Administration in East Timor	October 1999–May 2002
Tajikistan	UNMOT/United Nations Mission in Tajikistan	December 1994–May 2000

Location	Acronym/Name	Duration
Bosnia and Herzegovina	UNMIBH/ United Nations Mission in Bosnia and Herzegovina	December 1995– December 2002
Prevlaka Province, Croatia/Federal Republic of Yugoslavia	UNMOP/United Nations Mission of Observers in Prevlaka	February 1996– December 2002

Note: Although authorised by the UN Security Council, Operation Turquoise was commanded and financed by France.

elections, which are to be held in accordance with the present constitution of Sierra Leone.

Although not as broad ranging or complex as the new missions in Kosovo and East Timor, a new mandate for a force of 6,000 soldiers (from Nigeria, Kenya, and Guinea) was authorized under Chapter VII with the authority to use force if necessary to protect UN personnel and civilians under imminent threat of physical violence. The situation in Sierra Leone became generally stable but tense as 45,000 former combatants remained armed and in control of the diamond mines.

Conclusion

What are the lessons for the United Nations that emerge from security operations after the Cold War?

These three new operations represent a qualitatively different kind of UN peace mission. Although earlier efforts in Cambodia and El Salvador were ambitious, these are of a different magnitude. They are exceedingly complex and multidisciplinary. They represent attempts to create or re-create civil order and respect for the rule of law where governance and stability has either broken down or been nonexistent. They entail reconstructing the social and economic infrastructure, building democratic political institutions, providing humanitarian assistance, and much more. As stated above, "learning by doing" seems the order of the day. Not to act seems to many unthinkable, but how precisely to act remains uncertain. These kinds of challenges are what lie ahead for UN peacekeepers in the twenty-first century. Hence we can conceive of traditional peacekeeping and complex peacekeeping, both operating under Chapter VI of the Charter. The former involves primarily neutral interposition to supervise cease-fire lines and other military demarcations. The latter involves a complex range of tasks mostly intended to move post-conflict or failed states toward a liberal democratic order.[45]

Observers continue to debate the extent to which the present world disorder is new or old,[46] but the two dominant norms of world politics during the Cold War— namely, that borders were sacrosanct and that secession was unthinkable—no longer generate the enthusiasm that they once did, even among states. At the same time, an

Secretary-General Kofi Annan holds the Nobel Peace Prize awarded in December 2000 to the United Nations and to him, as the organization's Secretary-General.
(UN/DPI Photo by S. Bermeniev)

almost visceral respect for nonintervention in the internal affairs of states has made way for a more subtle interpretation, according to which on occasion the rights of individuals take precedence over the rights of repressive governments and the sovereign states that they represent.

Until early in 1993, the dominant perception of outside intervention under UN auspices was largely positive. Rolling back Baghdad's aggression against Kuwait along with the dramatic life-saving activities by the U.S.-led coalitions in northern Iraq and initially in Somalia had led to high hopes. In spite of the lack of resolve in Bosnia, it seemed possible that we were entering an era when governments and insurgents would no longer be allowed to abuse their citizens with impunity. Some analysts even worried then about "the new interventionists."[47] The new emphasis on protecting persons inside states led to a focus on human security. This new focus co-existed alongside the older notion of traditional inter-state military security.[48]

An interesting lens through which to examine normative and operational change emerges from the International Commission on Intervention and State Sovereignty (ICISS). The commission's report, *The Responsibility To Protect*, and an accompanying volume of supporting research with the same title were presented in mid-December 2001 to UN Secretary-General Kofi Annan.[49]

The report provides a snapshot of issues surrounding non-consensual international military action to foster values, and the commission responded to two sets of events.

The first were several moral pleas in 1999 from the future (in 2001) Nobel Laureate, UN Secretary-General Annan. As hinted earlier, he argued that human rights concerns transcended claims of sovereignty, a theme that he put forward more delicately a year later at the Millennium Summit.[50] The reaction was loud, bitter, and predictable, especially from China, Russia, and much of the Third World. "Intervention"—for whatever reasons, including humanitarian—was a taboo.[51]

The second set of events concerned the divergent reactions—or rather, the non-reactions—by the Security Council to Rwanda and Kosovo. In 1994 intervention was too little and too late to halt or even slow the murder of what may have been as many as 800,000 people in the Great Lakes region of Africa. In 1999 the formidable North Atlantic Treaty Organization (NATO) finessed the council and waged war for the first time in Kosovo. But many observers saw the seventy-seven-day bombing effort as being too much and too early, perhaps creating as much human suffering as it relieved. In both cases, the UN Security Council was not in a position to act expeditiously and authorize the use of deadly force to protect vulnerable populations.

The essential results of *The Responsibility to Protect* report are twofold. First, it reformulates the conceptual basis for humanitarian intervention. It calls for moving away from the rights of interveners toward the rights of victims and the obligations of outsiders to act. The responsibility to protect includes action not only to intervene when large-scale loss of life occurs but also to prevent armed conflicts and to help mend societies.

Second, the ICISS proposes a new international default setting—a modified just-war doctrine for future interventions to sustain humanitarian values or human rights. As a result of the Cold War, the Security Council was largely missing in action regarding humanitarian matters. There was a *tabula rasa*—no resolution mentioned the humanitarian aspects of any conflict from 1945 until the Six-Day War of 1967.[52] The first mention of the ICRC was not until 1978. And in the 1970s and 1980s, "the Security Council gave humanitarian aspects of armed conflict limited priority . . . but the early nineteen-nineties can be seen as a watershed."[53] During the first half of the decade, twice as many resolutions were passed as during the first forty-five years of UN history. They contained repeated references, in the context of Chapter VII, to humanitarian crises amounting to have threats to international peace and security, and repeated demands for parties to have respect for the principles of international humanitarian law, a subject to which we return in Part Two.

The ICISS, like the authors of this text, reiterates the central role of the Security Council, reformed and enlarged or not, and urges it to act. But if it does not, humanitarians and victims are left where the Secretary-General himself was in September 1999 when he queried his diplomatic audience about their reactions had there been a state or a group of states willing to act in April 1994 even without a Security Council imprimatur. "Should such a coalition have stood aside," he asked rhetorically, "and allowed the horror to unfold?"[54] The answer by any of the 800,000 dead Rwandans would be clear even if in UN circles it remains cloudy.

In short, enthusiasm for UN helping hands must be tempered with the realities of UN operations. There certainly is no evidence of a diminishing number of complex emergencies within which the military might help quell ethnic violence, create humanitarian space, and protect fundamental human rights. One is not obliged to agree with Robert Kaplan's apocalyptic visions[55] to recognize a distressing fragmentation of societies that may require outside military intervention if minorities are not to be subjugated or annihilated—which of course is also an option, although states are loath to admit as much publicly. And as long as these threats to human security exist, a role for the United Nations will be debated, given the weaknesses of regional options and the reluctance of any one state to become the world's policeman.

However, it is essential to keep in mind that coercive military intervention necessitates a revision of conventional wisdom regarding the lack of consent for Chapter VII operations. By definition, intervention does not require "consent" from the warring parties, but it does from the domestic constituencies of troop-contributing countries and from affected local populations.

Thus there is a progression of three steps underlying this lesson. First, intervention must be preceded by establishing and maintaining the consent of the publics that send their sons and daughters into hostile environments. For example, Americans were prepared for possible casualties prior to Washington's involvement on the ground in Kuwait and Iraq, but they were not prepared, nor was their consent sought, in the Somalia case. Second, although consent by definition is not forthcoming from local belligerents for Chapter VII, the consent of local populations must be sought and nurtured. Again, Somalia illustrates the neglect by third-party intervenors of local populations manipulated easily by belligerents into believing that those who come to assist them are contributing to their pain. Third and finally, with legitimacy established for possible deaths in action of soldiers and for the presence of "outsiders," there should be no compromises made in robustly making all requisite military efforts to establish quickly a secure environment.

If there is no commitment to satisfying all three steps, then there should be no intervention. The "messiness" of intervention comes from both lack of legitimacy and lack of efficiency, which the first lesson addresses. A well-planned, systematic response is required, but only after consent has been garnered from local populations in both troop-contributing states and the area of conflict. It is necessary for outsiders to reestablish security quickly and credibly in part of a disputed territory even if subsequently additional reinforcements are sent or another strategy evolves. This is the opposite of a slowly-turning-the-screws approach in the hopes that either political will or a meaningful strategy will appear over time. If there is no clarity about mission and little commitment to equipping the UN to act responsibly, "then the U.N. and the world at large," in John Ruggie's words, "are better off by lowering the organization's military profile and not muddling in the strategic calculus of states."[56]

And what about the UN as something of an independent variable, the semi-independent actor staffed with a semiautonomous civil service? Without putting too fine a point on it, we maintain that the history of security operations after the Cold War indicates that the United Nations is incapable of exercising command and control over combat operations. The capacity to plan, support, and command peacekeeping, let alone peace-enforcement, missions is scarcely greater now than during the Cold War. And this situation will not change in the foreseeable future.

Burning Kuwait oil wells with a destroyed Iraqi tank in the foreground.
(UN Photo 158181/J. Isaac)

States have made modest improvements to augment the UN secretariat's anemic military expertise and intelligence capacities—for example, a round-the-clock situation room and satellite telephones—and still others are feasible and desirable. The Canadians and Dutch were joined by twenty-two other countries as "the friends of rapid reaction," and they proposed in 1996 a mobile military headquarters capable of fielding command teams within hours of a Security Council decision. Seven states (Austria, Canada, Denmark, the Netherlands, Norway, Poland, and Sweden) signed an agreement to set up a 4,000-member UN Standby High Readiness Brigade, which could be used by the Security Council for peacekeeping or preventive operations. Although its existence would perhaps be helpful in exercising a restraining effect on combatants, the real problem is the reluctance of states to move quickly and to authorize forces large enough to do the job. This reality became perfectly clear when

Canada offered to lead a UN effort in eastern Zaire in autumn 1995, and no one volunteered. In short there is no chance that states will empower the world organization with the wherewithal to contradict Michael Mandelbaum's harsh judgment that "the U.N. itself can no more conduct military operations on a large scale on its own than a trade association of hospitals can conduct heart surgery."[57]

Taking advantage of experience over the 1990s and the demonstrated need for change, Secretary-General Annan appointed a high-level international panel to examine critically the UN's handling of peace operations. Led by Lakhdar Brahimi, a former Algerian foreign minister and experienced UN troubleshooter who ended up afterward as the Special Representative in Afghanistan, the panel found a great deal to criticize, as shown in its August 2000 report.[58] The blunt language focused on getting states to take their responsibilities seriously, on creating clear mandates and reasonable goals, and providing well-trained and equipped troops. None of the prescriptions offered would surprise the readers of these pages, nor would the absence of consensus that has followed and the accompanying lack of implementation.

There are two reasons for arguing that the United Nations as actor should distance itself from actually exercising coercion. First, states are unwilling to provide the Secretary-General with the necessary tools for Chapter VII. Standby troops and funds, independent intelligence, and appropriate systems for command and control along with professional personnel are simply not forthcoming. There is simply no question of independent action.

Second, and perhaps more important, the strength of the office of the Secretary-General lies in its neutrality, which is derived from the lack of vested interests. Giandomenico Picco, a former senior official who negotiated the release of hostages in Lebanon, has argued persuasively that "transforming the institution of the Secretary-General into a pale imitation of a state" in order "to mange the use of force may well be a suicidal embrace."[59] When the security situation has somewhat stabilized, the Secretary-General must be prepared to facilitate the administration of collapsed states, but *after* the warring parties themselves are exhausted or cleansed from a territory or following a humanitarian intervention. Proceeding in these ways requires separating military intervention from civilian administration in order to break a cycle of violence and to create both a respite and the preconditions for a return of an interim government. Moreover, in order to maintain credibility as a third party, the United Nations—insofar as it is separate from states—should refrain from taking sides. Fen Hampson concluded his comprehensive study on the UN's negotiating the end to five ethnic conflicts with the suggestion, "Enforcement is therefore best left to others."[60] The UN Security Council should still authorize enforcement on selected occasions, but such efforts should be subcontracted to regional arrangements or coalitions of the willing.

The failure to distinguish between the military operations that the United Nations secretariat can manage (traditional and even slightly muscular peacekeeping) and those that it cannot and should not (enforcement) has led to obfuscation. The latter are problematic under any circumstances, but they have given governments that are unable and unwilling to act decisively the opportunity to treat the United Nations as scapegoat. One is reminded of the third UN Secretary-General, U Thant, who commented wryly, "It is not surprising that the organization should often be blamed for failing to solve problems that have already been found to be insoluble by governments."[61]

With Richard Holbrooke of the United States presiding in the Security Council in January 2000, the focus was on Africa's woes. Everyone agreed that a peacekeeping force in the Democratic Republic of the Congo was desirable. Yet, with what is somewhat hyperbolically called "Africa's World War," the force of some 5,000 soldiers was way too small when there was no peace to keep. Subsequent chaos in the Congo only confirmed the accuracy of the original skepticism. By early 2003, more people had died in that huge country, many of them innocent civilians, than in any other conflict situation in the world at that time, although one would never know it from coverage by the Western communications media. The UN field presence remained symbolic, because of lack of political will in New York to make a greater practical impact. Later in 2003, discussion of a new UN force, led by the French, was still a matter of tokenism. The force would have a limited mandate for a limited area. Comprehensive solutions were out of reach.

At the same time, a positive development within the UN has been the ability, on occasion, to call a spade a shovel. The UN Secretary-General's 1999 report on Srebrenica and the Ingmar Carlsson report on Rwanda contained plenty of blame to go around and were followed by two other remarkably frank documents—about the failings of sanctions against Angola—by a group under Robert Fowler.[62] To conclude on a central theme, it is important to hold states accountable for a lack of political will but also important to hold senior UN officials' feet to the fire because they are relatively independent actors in crises who are capable of choices, of doing the right or the wrong thing. State political will, or the lack thereof, matters. But UN officials matter as well.

Notes

1. For a discussion of this historical period, see Thomas G. Weiss and Meryl A. Kessler, "Moscow's U.N. Policy," *Foreign Policy* no. 79 (Summer 1990), pp. 94–112. For a series of essays about the initial impact of these changes, see Thomas G. Weiss and Meryl A. Kessler, eds., *Third World Security in the Post–Cold War Era* (Boulder: Lynne Rienner, 1991); Thomas G. Weiss and James G. Blight, eds., *The Suffering Grass: Superpowers and Regional Conflict in Southern Africa and the Caribbean* (Boulder: Lynne Rienner, 1992); and G. R. Berridge, *Return to the UN* (London: Macmillan, 1991).

2. Paul Kennedy, *The Rise and Fall of the Great Powers: Economic Change and Military Conflict from 1500 to 2000* (New York: Random House, 1987).

3. When the Soviet Union dissolved, Russia was its successor state. As such, it assumed the permanent seat on the Security Council beginning in 1991.

4. See Tom J. Farer, ed., *Beyond Sovereignty: Collectively Defending Democracy in the Americas* (Baltimore: Johns Hopkins University Press, 1996).

5. See Mats R. Berdal, *Disarmament and Demobilisation After Civil Wars* (Oxford: Oxford University Press, 1996).

6. Washington's shift to forcible liberation occurred just after U.S. congressional elections. The Senate approved of the new strategy by only five votes, which almost led to a constitutional crisis in the United States over "war powers."

7. For a discussion of the legitimacy of the Persian Gulf War, see Oscar Schachter, "United Nations Law in the Gulf Conflict," and Burns H. Weston, "Security Council Resolution 678 and Persian Gulf Decision Making: Precarious Legitimacy," both in *American Journal of International Law* 85, no. 3 (July 1991).

8. For a series of skeptical views, see essays by Stephen Lewis, Clovis Maksoud, and Robert C. Johansen, "The United Nations After the Gulf War," *World Policy Journal* 8, no. 3 (Summer 1991), pp. 539–574.

9. For discussions of the Gramscian notion of hegemonic power compared to dominant power see Joseph S. Nye Jr., *The Paradox of American Power: Why the World's Only Superpower Can't Go It Alone* (Oxford: Oxford University Press, 2002); and Robert J. Lieber, ed., *Eagle Rules: Foreign Policy and American Primary in the Twenty-First Century)* Upper Saddle River, N.J.: Prentice-Hall, 2002, ch. 1.]

10. See David Cortright and George A. Lopez, *The Sanctions Decade: Assessing UN Strategies in the 1990s* (Boulder: Lynne Rienner, 2000).

11. Boutros Boutros-Ghali, *An Agenda for Peace: Preventive Diplomacy, Peacemaking and Peace-keeping* (New York: UN, 1992), para. 43.

12. This controversial subject was launched by the French government, especially by Mario Bettati and Bernard Kouchner, *Le devoir d'ingérence* (Paris: DeNoël, 1987); Bernard Kouchner, *Le malheur des autres* (Paris: Odile Jacob, 1991); and Mario Bettati, *Le droit d'ingérence* (Paris: Odile Jacob, 1996).

13. International Commission on Intervention and State Sovereignty, *The Responsibility to Protect* (Ottawa: ICISS, 2001). For a view about the dangers from such an approach, see Robert Jackson, *The Global Covenant: Human Conduct in a World of States* (Oxford: Oxford University Press, 1998).

14. Michael Reisman and Myres S. McDougal, "Humanitarian Intervention to Protect the Ibos," in Richard Lillich, ed., *Humanitarian Intervention and the United Nations* (Charlottesville: University of Virginia Press, 1973), p. 168.

15. See David Cortright and George A. Lopez, eds., *Economic Sanctions: Panacea or Peacebuilding in a Post–Cold War World?* (Boulder: Westview Press, 1995); *The Sanctions Decade;* and *Sanctions and the Search for Security* (Boulder: Lynne Rienner, 2002). Previous research had concentrated largely upon the utility of sanctions as a foreign policy tool of the United States. See Gary Clyde Hufbauer, Jeffrey J. Schott, and Kimberly Ann Elliott, *Economic Sanctions Reconsidered: History and Current Policy*, and *Economic Sanctions Reconsidered: Supplemental Case Histories* (Washington, D.C.: Institute for International Economics, 1990), which updated *Economic Sanctions in Pursuit of Foreign Policy Goals* (Washington, D.C.: Institute for International Economics, 1983). See also David A. Baldwin, *Economic Statecraft* (Princeton: Princeton University Press, 1985); Theodore Goldi and Robert Shuey, *U.S. Economic Sanctions Imposed Against Specific Countries: 1979 to the Present* (Washington, D.C.: Congressional Research Service, 1992); and Lisa Martin, *Coercive Cooperation: Explaining Multilateral Economic Sanctions* (Princeton: Princeton University Press, 1992). For a discussion of the humanitarian consequences, see David Cortright, George A. Lopez, Larry Minear, and Thomas G. Weiss, *Political Gain and Civilian Pain: The Humanitarian Impact of Economic Sanctions* (Boulder: Westview Press, 1997).

16. For a discussion of these issues, see Larry Minear and Thomas G. Weiss, "Groping and Coping in the Gulf Crisis: Discerning the Shape of a New Humanitarian Order," *World Policy Journal* 9, no. 4 (Fall–Winter 1992), pp. 755–777.

17. In many ways, the call to make provisions for vulnerable populations in the wake of sanctions is analogous to efforts to mitigate structural adjustment policies. For a discussion, see Richard Jolly and Ralph van der Hoeven, eds., *Adjustment with a Human Face—Record and*

Relevance, World Development (special issue) 19, no. 12 (1991). For general discussions of this issue, see Lori Fisler Damrosch, "The Civilian Impact of Economic Sanctions," in Damrosch, ed., *Enforcing Restraint: Collective Intervention in Internal Conflicts* (New York: Council on Foreign Relations, 1993), pp. 274–315; and Patrick Clawson, "Sanctions as Punishment, Enforcement, and Prelude to Further Action," *Ethics and International Affairs 7* (1993), pp. 17–37.

18. See Jarat Chopra and Thomas G. Weiss, "Sovereignty Is No Longer Sacrosanct: Codifying Humanitarian Intervention," *Ethics and International Affairs* 6 (1992), pp. 95–117; and David J. Scheffer, "Toward a Modern Doctrine of Humanitarian Intervention," *University of Toledo Law Review* 23, no. 2 (Winter 1992), pp. 253–293.

19. See *Financing an Effective United Nations* (New York: Ford Foundation, 1993), a report of an expert group chaired by Paul Volker and Shijuro Ogata.

20. See Stephen R. Rather, *The New UN Peacekeeping* (New York: St. Martin's Press, 1995); and Michael W. Doyle, Ian Johnstone, and Robert C. Orr, eds., *Keeping the Peace: Multidimensional UN Operations in Cambodia and El Salvador* (Cambridge: Cambridge University Press, 1997).

21. For a discussion of these possibilities before the UN's involvement in the former Soviet bloc, see Thomas G. Weiss and Kurt M. Campbell, "The United Nations and Eastern Europe," *World Policy Journal* 7, no. 3 (Summer 1990), pp. 575–592. For another treatment, see Jarat Chopra and Thomas G. Weiss, "Prospects for Containing Conflict in the Former Second World," *Security Studies* 4, no. 3 (Spring 1995), pp. 552–583.

22. This argument is made in greater depth in Thomas G. Weiss, "Collective Spinelessness: U.N. Actions in the Former Yugoslavia," in Richard H. Ullman, ed., *The World and Yugoslavia's Wars* (New York: Council on Foreign Relations, 1996), pp. 59–96. For a comparative look at this period, see William J. Durch, *UN Peacekeeping, American Policy, and the Uncivil Wars of the 1990s* (New York: St. Martin's Press, 1997). See also James S. Sutterlin, *The United Nations and the Maintenance of International Security: A Challenge to be Met* (Westport, Conn.: Praeger, 1995); Muthia Alagappa and Takashi Inoguchi, eds., *International Security Management and the United Nations* (Tokyo: United Nations University Press, 1998); Donald C. F. Daniel and Bradd C. Hayes, eds., *Beyond Traditional Peacekeeping* (London: Macmillan, 1995); and Olara A. Otunnu and Michael W. Doyle, eds., Forword by Nelson Mandela, *Peacemaking and Peacekeeping for the New Century* (Lanham: Rowman & Littlefield, 1998).

23. "In Bosnia's Fog," *Economist*, April 23, 1994, p. 16.

24. Lawrence Freedman, "Why the West Failed," *Foreign Policy* 97 (Winter 1994–1995), p. 59.

25. For a report from an official inquiry, see Netherlands Institute for War Documentation, *Srebenica, a 'Safe' Area: Reconstruction, Background, Consequences, and Analyses of the Fall of a Safe Area* (Amsterdam: Boom Publishers, 2002), http://www.screbenica.nl/en/.

26. "U.N. Bosnia Commander Wants More Troops, Fewer Resolutions," *New York Times*, December 31, 1993.

27. Quoted by Alison Mitchell, "Clinton's About-Face," *New York Times*, September 24, 1996, p. A8. For a discussion of the impact of Somalia, see Tom J. Farer, "Intervention in Unnatural Humanitarian Emergencies: Lessons of the First Phase," *Human Rights Quarterly* 18, no. 1 (February 1996), pp. 1–22; and Thomas G. Weiss, "Overcoming the Somalia Syndrome—'Operation Rekindle Hope'?" *Global Governance* 1, no. 2 (May–August 1995), pp. 171–187.

28. See Debarati G. Sapir and Hedwig Deconinck, "The Paradox of Humanitarian Assistance and Military Intervention in Somalia," in Thomas G. Weiss, ed., *The United Nations and Civil Wars* (Boulder: Lynne Rienner, 1995), p. 168.

29. See Larry Minear and Philippe Guillot, *Soldiers to the Rescue: Humanitarian Lessons from Rwanda* (Paris: OECD, 1996); Gérard Prunier, *The Rwanda Crisis: History of a Genocide* (New York: Columbia University Press, 1995); Joint Evaluation of Emergency Assistance to Rwanda, *The International Response to Conflict and Genocide: Lessons from the Rwandan Experience,* 5 vols. (Copenhagen: Joint Evaluation of Emergency Assistance to Rwanda, March 1995).

30. For discussions of this phenomenon in relationship to this crisis, see Robert I. Rotberg and Thomas G. Weiss, eds., *From Massacres to Genocide: The Media, Public Policy, and Humanitarian Crises* (Washington, D.C.: Brookings Institution, 1996); Larry Minear, Colin Scott, and Thomas G. Weiss, *The News Media, Civil War, and Humanitarian Action* (Boulder: Lynne Rienner, 1996); Charles C. Moskos and Thomas E. Ricks, *Reporting War When There Is No War* (Chicago: McCormick Tribune Foundation, 1996); Edward Girardet, ed., *Somalia, Rwanda, and Beyond: The Role of the International Media in Wars and Humanitarian Crises* (Dublin: Crosslines Communications, 1995); Johanna Newman, *Lights, Camera, War* (New York: St. Martin's Press, 1996); and Nik Gowing, *Real-Time Television Coverage of Armed Conflicts and Diplomatic Crises* (Cambridge, UK: Harvard Shorenstein Center, 1994).

31. See Peter Uvin, *Aiding Violence: The Development Enterprise in Rwanda* (West Hartford, Conn.: Kumarian, 1998).

32. Kofi Annan, Address to the Parliament of Rwanda, Kigali, May 7, 1998, document SG/SM/6552.

33. Kofi Annan, "Statement on Receiving the Report of the Independent Inquiry into the Actions of the United Nations during the 1994 Genocide in Rwanda," United Nations, New York, December 16, 1999.

34. See further Michael N. Barnett, *Eyewitness to a Genocide: The United Nations and Rwanda,* (Ithaca, N.Y.: Cornell University Press, 2002). Barnett faults the culture of the UN bureaucracy in New York for not responding better to the clear signs of genocide evident for a long time in Rwanda. For the UN's own hard-hitting report, see http://www.un.org/News/ossg/rwanda_report.htm.

35. Boutros Boutros-Ghali, *Supplement to An Agenda for Peace,* document A/50/60-S/1995, January 5, 1995, para. 70, reprinted in *An Agenda for Peace 1995* (New York: United Nations, 1995) along with the 1992 *An Agenda for Peace.* Paragraph numbers are the same in the original.

36. United Nations Development Programme, *Human Development Report 1994* (New York: Oxford University Press, 1994), p. 47.

37. Boutros-Ghali, *Supplement,* para. 77.

38. See Thomas G. Weiss, ed., *Beyond UN Subcontracting: Task-Sharing with Regional Security Arrangements and Service-Providing NGOs* (London: Macmillan, 1998); and William B. Tow, *Subregional Security Cooperation in the Third World* (Boulder: Lynne Rienner, 1990).

39. Independent Commission on Kosovo, *Kosovo Report: Conflict, International Response, Lessons Learned* (Oxford: Oxford University Press, 2000).

40. *Financial Times,* October 8, 1998.

41. Kofi A. Annan, "Secretary-General's Speech to the 54th Session of the General Assembly," September 20, 1999. This and other speeches on humanitarian intervention are published in the *Question of Intervention: Statements by the Secretary-General* (New York: UN, 1999).

42. UN Press Release SG/SM/6878, January 28, 1999.

43. Adam Roberts, "NATO's 'Humanitarian War' in Kosovo," *Survival* 41, no. 3 (Autumn 1999), pp. 102–123.

44. See Michael G. Smith with Moreen Dee, *Peacekeeping in East Timor: The Path to Independence* (Boulder: Lynne Rienner, 2003).

45. David P. Forsythe, "Human Rights and International Security: United Nations Field Operations Redux," in Monique Castermans-Holleman, et al., eds., *The Role of the Nation-State in the 21ˢᵗ Century* (The Hague: Kluwer, 1998), pp. 265–276.

46. See Mohammed Ayoob, "The New-Old Disorder in the Third World," in Thomas G. Weiss, ed., *Collective Security in a Changing World* (Boulder: Lynne Rienner, 1993), pp. 13–30.

47. Stephen John Stedman, "The New Interventionists," *Foreign Affairs* 72, no. 1 (1993), pp. 1–16. For an exhaustive review of the literature, see Oliver Ramsbotham and Tom Woodhouse, *Humanitarian Intervention in Contemporary Conflict* (Oxford: Polity Press, 1996). See also John Harriss, ed., *The Politics of Humanitarian Intervention* (London: Pinter, 1995); James Mayall, ed., *The New Interventionism: United Nations Experience in Cambodia, Former Yugoslavia, and Somalia* (New York: Cambridge University Press, 1996); and Jan Neederveen Pieterse, ed., *World Orders in the Making: Humanitarian Intervention and Beyond* (London: Macmillan, 1998).

48. See Rob McRac and Don Hubert, eds., *Human Security and the New Diplomacy: Protecting People, Promoting Peace* (Montreal & Kingston: McGill-Queen's University Press, 2001).

49. International Commission on Intervention and State Sovereignty, *The Responsibility to Protect: Report* (Ottawa: ICISS, 2001). See also *The Responsibility To Protect: Research, Bibliography, and Background* (Ottawa: ICISS, 2001), primary authors Thomas G. Weiss and Don Hubert. For a scholarly review of the implications, see Adam Roberts, "The Price of Protection," *Survival* 44, no. 4 (Winter 2002–2003), pp. 157–161; and Joelle Tanguy, "Redefining Sovereignty and Intervention," *Ethics & International Affairs* 17, no. 1 (2003), pp. 141–148.

50. Annan, *The Question of Intervention*, and *"We, the Peoples": The United Nations in the 21ˢᵗ Century* (New York: UN, 2000). For a discussion of the controversy surrounding the speech in September 1999, see Thomas G. Weiss, "The Politics of Humanitarian Ideas," *Security Dialogue* 31, no. 1 (March 2000), pp. 11–23.

51. For an overview, see Mohammed Ayoob, "Humanitarian Intervention and International Society," *Global Governance* 7, no. 3 (July–September. 2001), pp. 225–230; and Jackson, *The Global Covenant*.

52. Christine Bourloyannis, "The Security Council of the United Nations and the Implementation of International Humanitarian Law," *Denver Journal of International Law and Policy* 20, no. 3 (1993), p. 43.

53. Th. A. van Baarda, "The Involvement of the Security Council in Maintaining International Law," *Netherlands Quarterly of Human Rights* 12, no. 1 (1994), p. 140.

54. Annan, *The Question of Intervention—Statements by the Secretary-General*, p. 39.

55. Robert D. Kaplan, "The Coming Anarchy," *Atlantic Monthly* 273, no. 2 (February 1994), pp. 44–76, and *The Ends of the Earth: A Journey at the Dawn of the 21st Century* (New York: Random House, 1996).

56. John Gerard Ruggie, *The United Nations and the Collective Use of Force: Whither? or Whether?* (New York: United Nations Association of the USA, 1996), p. 1.

57. Michael Mandelbaum, "The Reluctance to Intervene," *Foreign Policy* no. 95 (Summer 1994), p. 11.

58. United Nations, *Report of the Panel on United Nations Peace Operations*, document A/55/305-S/2000/809, August 21, 2000. For a discussion, see David M. Malone and Ramesh Thakur, "UN Peacekeeping: Lessons Learned?" *Global Governance* 7, no. 1 (January–March 2001), pp. 11–17.

59. Giandomenico Picco, "The U.N. and the Use of Force," *Foreign Affairs* 73, no. 5 (September–October 1994), p. 15.

60. Fen Osler Hampson, *Nurturing Peace: Why Peace Settlements Succeed or Fail* (Washington, D.C.: U.S. Institute of Peace Press, 1996), p. 226. See also William I. Zartman, *Elusive Peace: Negotiating an End to Civil Wars* (Washington, D.C.: Brookings Institution, 1995).

61. U Thant, *View from the U.N.* (Garden City, N.Y.: Doubleday, 1978), p. 32.

62. Annan, *Report on the Fall of Srebrenica*, document A54/549, November 15, 1999; *Report of the Independent Inquiry into the Actions of the United Nations During the 1994 Genocide in Rwanda*, document S/1999/1257, December 15, 1999; and *Report of the Panel of Experts on Violations of Security Council Sanctions Against UNITA*, document S/2000/203, March 10, 2000.

4   Groping into the Twenty-First Century

In looking ahead to future security operations, we should retain our focus on the political dynamics that will propel UN activities. The political landscape, which reappears in the next two parts of this volume as well, helps us situate whether and how the world organization can respond to contemporary security challenges—which confront both member states and the secretariat, or what we called at the outset "the two United Nations." Before analyzing the overall dynamics, we begin with a lengthy look at September 11 and the war against Iraq, crucial events for the UN as well as for the United States.

After September 11, What's New?

It is difficult to begin a future-oriented chapter about the UN and security without examining the events since September 11, 2001, and the so-called War on Terrorism.[1] A few days after the tragic attacks on New York and Washington, which killed some 3,000 civilians, twice the number of combatants who died in the Japanese attack on Pearl Harbor in 1941, Secretary-General Kofi Annan outlined the relevance of the topic: "Terrorism is a global menace. It calls for a united, global response. To defeat it, all nations must take counsel together, and act in unison. That is why we have the United Nations."[2]

As the organization with the primary responsibility for the maintenance of international peace and security, the UN should be at the forefront of the international response to terrorism.[3] The fact that it has not been deserves attention and explanation. Until the 1990s, terrorism was dealt with almost entirely by the General Assembly, which approached the issue as a general problem of international law, rather than one relating to specific events or conflicts. There are twelve existing UN conventions related to terrorism, which identify particular forms of outlawed action but contain no definition of terrorism per se.[4] The lack of consensus among member states about the definitional issue exposes a rift in the world organization. It also explains at least in part why the UN has not been central to this problem. The UN can only act when its members allow it to act, on the basis of agreed ends and means.

At the very time that the United States was invading Iraq in 2003 partially because of Iraq's alleged links to terrorism, the United States was itself organizing certain Iraqis into a private fighting force, because of future plans for Iraq. In the 1980s the U.S. organized another fighting force, the contras, to pressure and/or overthrow the Sandinista government of Nicaragua. In the 1950s Washington organized a private force to overthrow the government of Guatemala. Naturally the United States did not see itself as engaging in state-supported terrorism, but certain other governments disagreed.

The struggle over how to define terrorism is affected by many concerns by various states, such as their wanting to protect the option of small-scale and supposedly nongovernmental violent resistance to foreign occupation, like the French resistance against Nazi Germany in the 1940s. Other states want to protect the option of using small scale and supposedly non-governmental force to harass what they see as unjust domination, as the American colonists did early on against their British masters. Reaching broad transnational agreement on the definition of terrorism is no easy matter. Some states may find it useful to oppose the terrorism du jour, but they usually want to preserve their freedom in choosing use of force in the future.

Nevertheless, several points are clear. Attacks on civilians who take no active part in hostilities are prohibited by international humanitarian law, specifically the 1949 Geneva Conventions and additional Protocols of 1977. Various other treaties prohibit such things as attacks on diplomats, the interference with civilian aircraft, and so forth. Thus, as mentioned above, the international community of states can and has reached agreement on prohibited targets of violence, thereby bypassing disagreement on an all-encompassing definition of terrorism.

Beginning in the early 1990s the Security Council began to examine terrorism more, primarily at Washington's instigation and in response to several events: the downing of a Pan American flight over Lockerbie, Scotland, and other aerial incidents in the late 1980s; the attempted assassination of Egyptian president Hosni Mubarak in 1995; and the bombings of U.S. embassies in East Africa in 1998. In each case, the Security Council responded by imposing sanctions against certain states: against Libya and the Sudan for refusing to extradite suspects, and against the Taliban regime in Afghanistan for supporting terrorist groups and refusing to extradite Osama bin Laden.

This approach changed in the aftermath of September 11. Whereas states like Israel, Spain, Germany, and others had experienced terrorism in the past, this time it was the one hyperpower that had been attacked. The Security Council acted immediately and endorsed measures ranging from approval of the use of force in self-defense to requiring member states to undertake wide-ranging and comprehensive measures against terrorism. Previously an issue drawing inconsistent attention from both the General Assembly and the Security Council, terrorism quickly became a persistent and systematic focus at the UN.

The council's responses are noteworthy. Resolution 1368, passed the day after the attacks on U.S. territory, recognized "the inherent right of individual or collective self-defense," the first time that it was formally recognized as a legitimate response to non-state violence. A few weeks later, the Security Council passed a comprehensive resolution that outlined a series of wide-ranging measures to be undertaken by states to "prevent and suppress" terrorist acts. Resolution 1373 details the requirements to be taken by member states, including changes to national legislation. The resolution established the Counter-Terrorism Committee (CTC) to monitor member state implementation of these measures. Once again the council shrunk the domain of purely domestic affairs, in that national legislation including tax laws for contributions to charities was subjected to international monitoring and mandates.

The General Assembly's work in developing international conventions on terrorism, while subsequently overshadowed by the Security Council, remains important and may increase. The codification of emerging norms can perhaps best take place in a forum that is able to take a comprehensive, politically informed, and longer-term view. The most significant advantage of the assembly is that it is an inclusive forum involving all member states. It is also the place where decisions about the allocation of organizational resources are made, thus giving it a direct impact on determining the administrative capability of the world organization to deal with terrorism. Still, this organizational capacity is greatly affected by member states' political will.

The UN Secretary-General and the secretariat also have a role to play. Like the General Assembly, the Secretary-General has the ability to take less reactive, more comprehensive approaches. After September 11, Kofi Annan established a Policy Working Group on terrorism to examine how the UN should deal with terrorism.[5] He also remained poised to play a role in dealing with specific situations and responding to events through the use of his good offices.

In spite of much discourse to the contrary, how the United Nations might have dealt with Iraq was only partially connected with the U.S. "War on Terrorism." The U.S. decision to go to war with Iraq in March 2003 related more to the issue of compliance with Security Council resolutions, the question of Iraq's possible possession of weapons of mass destruction prohibited by the UN, and the U.S.'s demonstration of its military might than to Iraqi terrorism against the United States. The government of Saddam Hussein had clearly supported violence against the state of Israel via groups like Hamas. But at the time of writing no evidence has surfaced linking Iraq to the attacks on New York and Washington, or indicating any substantial links to Al Qaeda. Nevertheless, the debate at the UN about how to appropriately deal with Iraq is important for a discussion about the nature of the UN and world politics. The struggle over resolutions in the Security Council, the publication of a new doctrine of a very broad anticipatory self-defense, or preemption, in the U.S. National Security Strategy of September 2002, Washington's and London's taking forceful action without UN authorization, and the U.S. declaration of a goal of "regime change" in Iraq, however, are relevant to an argument about the role of international law and the UN in a world of one military giant having been attacked by a non-state actor.[6]

The U.S. invocation of self-defense against terrorism in response to September 11, approved by the council; its military campaign in Afghanistan to dislodge a government that was intertwined with a terrorist network, also approved by the council; and its focus on weapons of mass destruction in Iraq that might be put at the disposal of terrorists, within the framework of previous UN resolutions, are indications of a continuation of traditional concerns about state security that are by no means incompatible with international law and organization. To this point basic U.S. foreign policy was largely consistent with and supportive of international law and the UN. Moreover, President George W. Bush was persuaded by Secretary of State Colin Powell to return to the council in the fall of 2002, even after the United States had started its military buildup in the Persian Gulf during that previous summer. These actions represent an indication that the United Nations still matters. Obtaining international legitimacy through UN endorsement still counts for something, even to the United States, with its primacy of military might.

The rest of the story about Iraq and the UN in 2003 is not so encouraging for the future role of the UN in world politics. Events demonstrated a fundamental point that had not changed since 1945, the same point demonstrated by Kosovo in 1999, namely that the members of the Security Council needed to be in agreement for that body to be effective even in a diplomatic rather than military sense. The council was in agreement up to a point, demanding Iraqi compliance with a long list of previous disarmament resolutions, and stating that serious consequences would follow upon further non-compliance (Resolution 1441). As the year 2002 turned into 2003, the Bush administration tried to get the council to state that the time for diplomacy had ended and that military operations were appropriate. But Washington was unable to muster the nine votes for its draft resolution (co-sponsored by Britain and Spain), much less counter an expected veto of its proposal by France, Russia, and/or China. In fact, in addition to the United States, Britain, Spain, and perhaps Bulgaria, votes for war were hard to find in the council. This was a remarkable development, because in the fall of 2001 the council had endorsed U.S. military strikes on the Taliban government in Afghanistan, which had supported the Al Qaeda network, and in fall 2002, the council had unanimously called for rapid disarmament or "serious consequences."

Hence the end of the Cold War did not mean the end of profound disagreement in the council on issues of peace and war, as already evident in the Kosovo crisis of 1999. States like France and Russia did not believe that the United States had demonstrated a substantial link between Iraq and past or future terroristic attacks on the United States. The Bush administration's argument that in the future Saddam Hussein *might* cooperate with terrorists in some type of attack on the United States seemed too amorphous for many states to justify an invasion of Iraq. These dissenting states were troubled by what had come to be called the Bush Doctrine, namely that the United States championed a broad notion of preemptive or anticipatory self-defense. One can understand this hesitation by many states. Washington argued essentially that it alone would determine what government, because of its own actions or through state-supported terrorism, would be targeted by the extremely powerful U.S. military machine. It did not promote consensus that the United States was departing from the notion in international law of a limited preemption doctrine that might be appropriate when threats were immediate and overwhelming, leaving no time for further diplomacy. This approach, articulated in the nineteenth century in the Caroline affair, was replaced by Washington with the much broader standard of a possible and distant threat. This latter standard was not a doctrine that many states wanted the council to endorse in the Iraqi case.[7]

There were other complications. The council had created a new weapons inspection regime centered on an ad hoc monitoring, verification, and inspection commission (UNMOVIC) for chemical and biological weapons, and on the IAEA for nuclear weapons. These two UN agencies, one ad hoc and one permanent, had elicited some cooperation from Saddam Hussein—in the context of a basically Anglo-Saxon military buildup in the Persian Gulf that eventually reached about 300,000 soldiers. Many states wanted to avoid war by giving these inspection units more time to work, whereas Washington and its allies, especially Britain, felt that Iraq could always evade at least the more important inspection efforts. Moreover, Washington was concerned about protracted diplomacy that would undercut its military pressure. Still further hesitation lay in the fact that whereas the Bush administration talked of disarmament, other states thought the United States had always been interested in the removal of the Saddam Hussein regime. Indeed, it was noted by several observers that administration officials had talked of removing that regime even before the attacks of September 11, 2001.

It is possible that many subplots were at work to fracture the Security Council over what to do about Iraq. Some observers thought that France was again demonstrating a persistent effort to play the role of global power even when its economic and military might no longer easily led in that direction, an effort that had repeatedly caused it to differ with the United States on any number of issues. Some thought that Russia was only too happy to make difficulties for a United States that had seemed disdainful of a major Russian role after the Cold War, as for example on issues pertaining to missile defense. Moreover, Russia had economic interests both in Iraq and in a continued high price for oil, one of Russia's chief exports. Still other observers thought that certain council members, like the German government, opposed U.S. policy in order to appeal to domestic public opinion and win elections. Some thought the Bush administration was never interested in the type of multilateral diplomacy that sometimes constrained unilateral decisionmaking in Washington and that the Bush team simply wanted to use its power superiority to take out a "rogue state" and part of "the axis of evil"—even absent any substantial connection to Al Qaeda or any other group interested in attacks on the United States.

Be all of that as it may, similar to the debate about Kosovo in 1999, the Security Council could not present a united front regarding Iraq in 2003. Unlike Kosovo, Washington could not fall back on the collective approval of the liberal democratic states making up NATO, because NATO was also divided over Iraq—as was the European Union. The United States could only seek legitimization through a coalition of willing states that was less impressive than for the Gulf War in 1991.

The importance of the Iraqi question in 2003 raised the issue of the continued viability of the UN system for the maintenance or restoration of international peace and security, such was the media coverage of the split within the Security Council. U.S. officials sometimes said that the council had been irresponsible in not maintaining a tough line in keeping with the terms of Resolution 1441 on the consequences of the failure of Iraq to disarm. French officials sometimes said that a council that only rubber-stamped the dubious arguments of Washington would have no credibility in the eyes of the world. These views overstated the crisis, because both with regard to Kosovo in 1999 and earlier with regard to northern Iraq in the spring of 1991, the United States and its allies had used military force without explicit council approval— and the UN had not collapsed.

As we suggested earlier in this book, the question of the collective authorization of force was a perennial one in international relations, especially when an armed attack against a state had not occurred. In the future the council would exist and be seized of similar questions. Moreover, various UN agencies would certainly be involved in post-conflict Iraq, and the Security Council had demonstrated that some of this humanitarian work could have a security dimension. It remains true, however, that the Bush Doctrine of anticipatory self-defense even when the alleged threat did not constitute a clear and present danger was difficult to square with the Charter paradigm for regulating force. There is no doubt but that in the final analysis, U.S. policy toward Iraq in 2003, supposedly linked to a "war" against terrorism, did great damage to the UN and international law. It was so perceived by much of the world.[8]

Political Dynamics

Throughout the preceding chapters, we focused on certain political factors that drive the UN's security operations. Chief among these was the end of the East-West struggle that has placed the United States and its allies in an unusual leadership position. With their consent and political support, the United Nations is theoretically able to play a growing role in maintaining international peace and security. Developing countries—still referred to as the "Third World" or the "Global South"—no longer can block Security Council resolutions that lead to deep involvement in what used to be considered domestic affairs. Indeed, in a number of cases, states from the Global South are part of the U.S.-led coalition that acts in the name of the UN. Such was the case, for example, when Syria and other developing countries supported council Resolution 1441 demanding extensive disarmament from Saddam Hussein's Iraqi government in late 2002.

The end of the East-West struggle, however, has also removed the lid and permitted the explosion of violence and civil wars. States continue to be the main forces in international politics, but they are increasingly subject to pressures from nonstate actors. A more comprehensive view of security characterizes international debates. This view of security reflects a complex reality, not just of the military arena but also of human rights and sustainable development, which we analyze later. A vague sense of moral obligation to those outside one's own borders has always spurred philanthropists and humanitarians; technology now makes awareness of the plight of others instantaneous and more poignant. Interdependence, stemming from technological and communications innovations and also from economic linkages and environmental deterioration, has lessened the control that states exercise over their economies, cultures, and political structures.

What does this all mean for the future of the United Nations? After coping with fifty years of limitations on its activity, can it perform a far more ambitious role as orchestrator of the peace, or will it simply face new limitations? The answer is complex. The peace and security mechanisms of the United Nations need reform; the world organization is woefully overstretched; and the UN can and must adapt to the needs of the next generation of operations.

The complexity of the answer partially reflects the turmoil of our times. Chapter 3 began with a discussion of the rebirth of the United Nations in the late 1980s and early 1990s and ended with hopeful uncertainty tinged with some disillusionment.

Today, the hopefulness of that earlier period seems like ancient history. The almost giddy euphoria surrounding the end of the Cold War was remarkably short-lived; policy and scholarly communities awakened with a hangover and more sober appreciations of the UN role pertaining to international peace and security. The Iraqi crisis of 2003 made some earlier considerations of the UN's security role seem tame. But a brief look back still merits our attention.

Two key documents written by the sixth UN Secretary-General, Boutros Boutros-Ghali, remind us of pressing issues, beyond the key issue of council cohesion, inherited by the seventh UN Secretary-General, Kofi Annan.[9] In June 1992, *An Agenda for Peace* was published. No other international public policy document of that time generated so much discussion by practitioners and scholars. Boutros-Ghali's report framed debate and contained many intriguing suggestions, but it became best known for its ambitious view of the UN's potential for multilateral conflict management. Barely two and a half years later—and with the problems in Bosnia, Somalia, and Rwanda very much in the news—Boutros-Ghali recognized how much his proposals had exceeded the expectations of governments and the abilities of the United Nations. In a progress report issued in January 1995 to mark the UN's fiftieth anniversary, *Supplement to An Agenda for Peace*, the Secretary-General trimmed his sails and recommended caution about the UN's security role. Kofi Annan continued the theme of modest expectations beginning with his acceptance speech in mid-December 1996. Readers may recall that the Brahimi report on UN security operations continued the same theme, stressing the limits of UN capability in security operations and stressing the need for the UN to say no to certain roles until it had upgraded its capabilities— which, as ever, depended on the willingness of member states to transfer authority and power to the organization.[10]

There is virtually no UN track record and even less consensus among governments and experts for the several military initiatives outlined by Secretary-General Boutros-Ghali. World politics is increasingly characterized by levels of violence in micronationalist struggles that were not imagined by the framers of the Charter or even by pundits a few years ago.[11] The search for order is likely to be no simpler in the near future than it was in the recent past, as decolonization and self-determination take new forms and as ethnic particularism pushes its way onto the local and global agenda. Already the Soviet Union and Yugoslavia have given birth to almost twenty countries; Somalia and Haiti ceased in 1993 to have anything resembling organized governance, earning the appellation of "failed states." The Al Qaeda attacks on the United States threw the diplomatic and military spotlight on "terrorism." In the face of this new world disorder, major political and operational dilemmas result for the UN.

For example, preventive deployment of UN forces is the centerpiece of preventive diplomacy to forestall strife. If only one country or party to a civil conflict requests troops, the United Nations could become a party to the conflict by taking sides, thereby hindering mediation by the world organization, which needs a sterling reputation for neutrality in order to mediate. Or even if parties to a conflict agree initially to a preventive buffer, one of them could change its position and ask the UN to leave. The disastrous pullout of forces from UNEF I in 1967 based on an Egyptian request

Rwandan refugees returning to Gisenyi from Goma, Zaire, in July 1994.
(UN Photo 186788/J. Isaac)

led to war. This serves as a pertinent reminder of what happens when states change policy about the desirability of a cease-fire. The departure of UNEF I inevitably contributed to another Mideast conflagration; now pressures can be exerted on the United Nations to remain when parties change their minds and return to armed conflict. But UN forces cannot be easy targets. If they stay, they have to become combat forces with the chance to prevail.

It is even possible that the early presence of UN forces could foster moves toward violent secession. Preventive deployment still may be desirable in these circumstances, as illustrated by the operation in Macedonia that began in December 1992. Yet governments that provide troops on the basis of consent and the likelihood of low or no casualties may not wish to continue under altered conditions. When a preventive force is deployed, the contingencies that could require various types of escalation must be agreed in advance. This requirement may discourage responses from troop-contributing countries.

The protection of UN administrative and humanitarian personnel is an obvious and growing challenge stressed in *An Agenda for Peace*. But citing peacekeeping and the UN guards' contingent in Iraq is not useful. As described earlier, the strength of peacekeepers arose more from the moral backing of the international community than from any military wherewithal. Furthermore, UN guards were helpful in Iraq for a time not because of their own military capabilities, which consisted mainly of security officers armed with pistols and clad in blue baseball caps. The successful performance of duties was related to three realities: The UN guards were based in a country whose population and military had been bombed into submission by the allied war effort; Iraq initially found them less odious than Western soldiers; and the physical presence and backup firepower of the allied coalition remained in the area as insurance against Iraqi hostility.

The most significant departures in the report are organized, somewhat surprisingly and confusingly, under the rubric of peacemaking. The usual notion concerns such peaceful measures as mediation and good offices, outlined in Chapter VI of the UN Charter and discussed earlier. In an unusual stylistic presentation, one that confuses readers and decisionmakers, peacemaking in *An Agenda for Peace* includes even such Chapter VII actions as economic and military sanctions. Although it is not well formulated, this is a key idea. The creation of "peace enforcement units" would be a major departure in the sense that cease-fires would be guaranteed by UN soldiers when parties no longer agreed to respect a negotiated halt to carnage.

Conceptual issues in *An Agenda for Peace* should be clarified because they obscure practical insights. Diplomats, international civil servants, and scholars need to squarely face a series of conceptual issues. Although there is a different Secretary-General, the issues have not been resolved, and Kofi Annan's tenure has done little to alter the fundamental ambiguities.

First, what type of prominence should be accorded to state sovereignty? Several times Secretary-General Boutros Boutros-Ghali affirmed the importance of conventional notions of sovereignty. These notions are also reiterated in many debates and international forums. At the same time, he presented a host of arguments about the erosion of state sovereignty. Unlike his successor, Kofi Annan (who as we have seen sees a distinct limit to claims of sovereignty when gross violations of human rights are concerned), Boutros-Ghali appeared hesitant to emphasize enforcement actions—for example, in humanitarian emergencies or in gross violations of human rights—where sovereignty is being superseded.

Many countries, not just in the West but also in the Third World, are reevaluating their positions. During the 1990s conventional notions of state sovereignty in countries like Somalia and Yugoslavia made little legal or operational sense. In Somalia there was no effective sovereign; in Yugoslavia genocidal actions meant that sovereignty was being exercised irresponsibly or not at all. The U.S. "war" on terrorism led to such actions as a fatal military strike inside Yemen against alleged terrorists. The silence of the Yemeni government could be read as de facto consent to this action, but respect for traditional notions of sovereignty was not high on Washington's agenda in this case.

Second, the nature and dynamics of peaceful relationships require that we pay more attention to nonstate actors (NSAs) and to differentiating among them based on their importance to the issue at hand. *An Agenda for Peace* approaches peace almost exclusively as involving relations among constituted political authorities, especially states. This is an inaccurate view of how peace is negotiated and sustained. It fails to provide insights about how to control what is widely called "terrorism" or to address the "greed and grievance" motivating many NSAs.[12]

Conflicts have deeper roots than governments or armed opposition groups hoping to assume power. The origins of armed conflicts as well as their mitigation and management must be conceived broadly enough to include a host of such non-governmental actors as clans, "terrorist groups," and the International Committee of the Red Cross (ICRC). People make war and people respond to it. Experience in the Sudan,[13] for example, suggests that the UN as an intergovernmental organization is frequently at a disadvantage in dealing with irregular forces and insurgents. Private relief agencies may be better placed than intergovernmental ones for delivery of goods in war zones. The role of nonstate intermediaries in internal armed conflicts may be heightened in the post–Cold War era. Non-governmental organizations (NGOs) and other nonstate actors are less important in the security arena than in human rights and sustainable development, as we see later in this book. Nonetheless, the United Nations must take them more adequately into account in a working international security system. When it came to post-conflict operations in places like East Timor, Bosnia, Kosovo, and Afghanistan, many NGOs and IGOs were essential to developments, even if Special Representatives of the UN Secretary-General like Lakhdar Brahimi in Afghanistan was officially in charge of everything, and even if states still provided resources and basic authorization.

The third conceptual clarification, with the most direct impact on UN military operations, concerns the changing nature of what John Mackinlay and Jarat Chopra originally labeled "second generation multinational operations."[14] In its newest and most dangerous operations the United Nations needs in some cases to move beyond the consent of warring parties and to resort to military capabilities that were not available to UN soldiers in the past. But it has to be stated that gaining consensus in New York for such enforcement actions is often not easy.

It is more accurate to speak of a departure from peacekeeping rather than a mere extension of the traditional operations, which are at the opposite end of a continuum from Chapter VII enforcement. The most interesting proposals in *An Agenda for Peace* fall between these extremes: preventive deployment, military assistance to civil authorities, protection of humanitarian relief efforts, guaranteed rights of passage, and enforcement of cease-fires.

These proposals constitute at least a "Chapter six-and-three-quarters" because they are even closer to Chapter VII. They require a level of military professionalism and discipline not commonly found in earlier UN operations. They require routine participation from the armies of major powers. Accomplishing the tasks in these operations goes far beyond both the expectations and the capacities of most countries that have contributed troops to UN peacekeeping operations during the Cold War. The UN's resourcefulness as a mediator has outstripped its capability as a military organizer.

The United Nations has virtually no professional military expertise, and the secretariat in New York is unable to increase its capacities in this area. A temporary increase in military personnel lent by Western governments was ended in the late 1990s when the G-77 countries complained about the imbalance. As new operations were being initiated in Timor, Kosovo, and the Congo, the Department of Peacekeeping Operations (DPKO) could draw upon fewer staff than the Department of Public Information.

A mother and child seeking security at the Morini border
crossing between Kosovo and Albania in April 1999.
(UN/UNHCR Photo/R. Chalasani)

The literal position of UN troops is dangerous and awkward. Many analysts,
diplomats, and UN staff stumble more figuratively when they fail to distinguish
clearly old-style "peacekeeping"—the interposition of neutral forces when warring
parties have agreed to a cease-fire, or at least to putting one in place. They employ the
same term—even if qualified by such adjectives as "wider" peacekeeping by Whitehall
or "aggravated" peacekeeping by the Pentagon—for a variety of situations where consent is absent or problematic and where military capacity outranks moral authority.
The confusion is even greater when an operation shifts from Chapter VI to VII
(Somalia and Rwanda) or combines the two (the former Yugoslavia).

The United Nations has demonstrated for several decades that it can manage
Chapter VI military operations of the more classical or traditional variety. We should
recall that peacekeeping is often called "Chapter six-and-a-half," former Secretary-
General Dag Hammarskjöld's clever indication that this UN invention was not fore-

seen by the Charter's framers. But peacekeeping is really an extension of Chapter VI rather than a would-be Chapter VII. At the same time, the United Nations also has demonstrated its inability to handle Chapter VII, which the Secretary-General clearly recognized in his 1995 *Supplement*: "Neither the Security Council nor the Secretary-General at present has the capacity to deploy, direct, command and control operations for this purpose."[15] The inability to manage full-scale or even selective enforcement cannot be wished away; nor can it be overcome by tinkering. The world organization's diplomatic and bureaucratic structures are inimical to initiating and overseeing military efforts when serious fighting rages, where coercion rather than consent is the norm.

Part of the problem has been that until very recently the United Nations has relied too heavily on the experience of past operations when coping with post–Cold War crises instead of delineating distinct new characteristics. Peacekeeping should be reserved for consensual missions, which is where the UN secretariat has a comparative advantage. Otherwise, peacekeeping becomes an infinitely elastic concept without operational significance. It is not a cure-all for the chaos of ethnonationalism but a discrete tool for conflict management when consent is present, and political rather than military expertise is required.

In his first press conference of 1995, as he was about to introduce the new conventional wisdom, Secretary-General Boutros-Ghali straightforwardly recognized "that the United Nations does not have the capacity to carry out huge peace enforcement operations, and that when the Security Council decides on a peace enforcement operation, our advice is that the Security Council mandate a group of Member States, [those which] have the capability."[16] The lack of UN operational capacities remains an acute challenge in the twenty-first century.

Operational Changes: Adapting to New Conflicts

As has been argued throughout preceding sections, the nature of much conflict is changing. And the United Nations is being called on to deal with kinds of armed conflict not imagined when the UN Charter was drafted. The world organization and its member states probably will not often face the classic interstate confrontation that precipitated the collective response in the 1991 Persian Gulf War. The 2003 war on Iraq was, however, what international lawyers call a classic international armed conflict. It remains true that instances of cross-border attacks from national armies aimed at annexation of another state's territory are becoming rarer. *Intra*state conflict is replacing *inter*state conflict as the dominant menace to international peace and security. Fueled by ethnic, economic, and nationalist desires for autonomy inside the borders of existing geographic states, civil war is becoming the most common form of armed conflict. Insurgent groups fight existing governments or sometimes other insurgents either for control or for secession.

The UN's security mechanism was not designed to deal with violence and wars of this kind, and the blue helmets have encountered their most significant problems in attempting to quell internal wars. More than 1,500 blue-helmeted soldiers have died while serving in the United Nations since 1948, more than half since the Cold War's end. Although the ideal of collective security could be applied to intrastate activity, the UN Charter was designed to prevent recurrences of World War II—characterized by the invasion of one state by another. The world organization is ill equipped to deal with conflicts existing within internationally recognized borders. Improving its capabilities in this area requires changes in the approach to sovereignty and the operational components of international forces in order to safeguard peace and security.

The extent to which the principle of state sovereignty has been the foundation of the international system should be clear to readers by now. Despite the presence of numerous challenges to their supremacy, states are unwilling as a matter of principle in most instances to cede daily sovereignty to improve the functioning of the UN. However, changes in world politics in the past half-century have steadily chipped away at the foundation, and changes since the mid-1980s have created a new potential for multilateral action.[17] Sovereignty, of course, has never been a fixed notion.[18] Notwithstanding the observers who see national interests and military power as the only answer to an anarchical international system, recent political changes—the immediate ones after the Cold War and the deeper ones resulting from interdependence—have on occasion and for some countries shifted the balance between the authority of states and the authority of international society.[19]

The United Nations itself reflects an institutional structure created in one historical period that is trying to cope with the challenges of a different era. A conceptual and operational leap must be made, striking a new balance between state sovereignty and the need for effective UN security operations in the post–Cold War era. A Westphalian vocabulary is of doubtful utility for Somalias, Rwandas, Liberias, Burundis, Timors, and Yugoslavias. A first step would be a straightforward confrontation with the meaning of "consent" when there is no sovereign or when a sovereign acts in an opprobrious way and pursues genocide as a policy. If the international community of states is willing through the Security Council to apply, instead of to talk about, the use of overwhelming force, then consent is unnecessary. If not, then the consent of powerful local actors remains the sine qua non of successful UN operations.

In particular, readers should recall an earlier discussion about the implications of many Chapter VII operations that had humanitarian motivations or dimensions. The opening sentence of the report by the International Commission on Intervention and State Sovereignty (ICISS)[20] essentially endorses what Francis M. Deng, the UN Secretary-General's Special Representative for Internally Displaced Persons, calls "sovereignty as responsibility."[21] It is primarily state authorities whose citizens are threatened that have "the responsibility to protect." Yet, a residual responsibility rests with the larger community of states when an aberrant member of their club misbehaves egregiously or simply implodes. The status of state sovereignty is not challenged per se but rather reinforced. However, if a state is unwilling or unable to exercise its protective responsibilities for the rights of its own citizens, it temporarily forfeits its moral claim to be treated as legitimate. Its sovereignty, as well as its right to non-intervention, is suspended; and the residual responsibility necessitates vigorous action by outsiders to protect populations at risk. In brief, the four traditional characteristics of a state in the

Westphalian system (territory, authority, population, independent government) are supplemented by a fifth (respect for human rights).

Conceptual and practical alterations to the UN's military operations need to parallel those made in the domain of sovereignty. How is the United Nations to operate effectively in intrastate conflicts where the consent of warring parties is likely to be less than that found in traditional operations or where consent evaporates after the parties have agreed to stop fighting but find that elections or other events no longer go their way? The world organization requires military teeth when it runs the risk of encountering active and perilous opposition. Future UN security operations need to be better armed and more able to operate like professional armies. But if political will is not present, it is better to negotiate with powerful parties. Otherwise, the Security Council discredits itself.

In particular, two types of military operations merit and have been receiving more routine implementation. First, there is the growing and obvious need for military support for humanitarian activities.[22] In spite of the UN's efforts in Bosnia and Herzegovina, Somalia, and northern Iraq, former Secretary-General Boutros-Ghali's two reports were remarkably reticent about ensuring that truly opprobrious behavior against civilians by governments or insurgents is no longer tolerated. Such actions amount to "intervention," a term that does not figure in the reports. To enforce new standards of behavior, Boutros-Ghali chose to sidestep this issue, mainly, one suspects, to avoid sensitivities in developing countries toward outside interference in what many governments still argue are their domestic affairs. As discussed earlier, his successor, Kofi Annan, has been less hesitant in this regard.

On the one hand, it is understandable that Boutros-Ghali wished to avoid the controversy and bitterness of the General Assembly's annual discussions of humanitarian matters. On the other hand, his approach was difficult to fathom because his report responded to a request from the January 1992 summit of the Security Council, which cited the need to respond to nonmilitary threats to the peace, including humanitarian crises. Among the major powers in the South, China and India continued to maintain fervent postcolonial interpretations of nonintervention even as they were willing to intervene unilaterally in Tibet or Sri Lanka. The paradox—Article 2(7) was originally overruled to permit decolonization—has not yet dawned on their diplomats. Militaries around the world have assets that could be used effectively in humanitarian crises; recruitment literature has begun to feature soldiers performing humanitarian duties. A further discussion of this capacity occurs in the next part of this book.

The second type of operation, peace-enforcement units, represents the crossover point after traditional peacekeeping. Unlike many proposals—for example, for factfinding or preventive diplomacy—this one is controversial and worrisome. The exact nature of the commitment of governments to the next generation of UN forces will quickly become clear when peace enforcement is debated. The fault line will become obvious with answers to such questions as, What happens when there is a dramatic change in the basis on which contributors have originally supplied troops? What kind of reserve firepower will the Security Council make available? How will the Permanent Five and other major powers participate? Who needs to agree to a cease-fire—all warring parties or just some of these parties or the Security Council? When will the

President George W. Bush and Secretary-General Kofi Annan at Ground Zero. (UN/DPI photo)

Security Council make the decision to "enforce" the peace—before a breakdown occurs or only after a new crisis has arisen?

Several proposals have been put forth by secretaries-general and scholars in regard to ways in which the UN can effectively upgrade its military capacity. In addition to supporting the establishment of peace-enforcement units, they have called for the conclusion of some Article 43 agreements with governments concerning their troop contributions; these negotiations have been stalled since the late 1940s. Standing forces would appear prohibitively expensive, but troops on reserve or standby status (that is, on call for UN service but maintained in their country of origin until duty calls and a government agrees) appear more feasible than in the past.

The world organization would then have a reserve body of trained forces immediately deployable. The existence of standby forces could allow for preventive peace-keeping where conflict seems imminent. Preventive deployment could take place when requested by two states seeking to discourage hostilities from taking place between themselves or by a single country threatened by military attack. Peace-enforcement units, which are outside the framework of Article 43 according to the Secretary-General, would probably never deter aggression by a big power but "would be useful . . . in meeting any threat posed by a military force of a lesser order."[23] Moreover, such forces could serve as a tripwire that when crossed or engaged could unleash Chapter VII proceedings and act, in the words of a group of parliamentarians, "as a

Members of UNTAET's Portuguese contingent are accompanied by a group of local children as they conduct a security patrol in the Becora district of Dili. (UN/DPI Photo/E. Debede)

deterrent to possible aggression by another state and as a signal of the resolve of the international community."[24]

The Cold War stopped the Military Staff Committee (MSC) from becoming an operational reality for directing enforcement operations. Although enforcement operations under the command of the MSC are quite unlikely, the body could serve as a useful, informal source of military expertise for the Secretary-General and his staff. The Security Council would continue to decide, on a case-by-case basis, what type of command-and-central arrangement would be used.

The organization searches for ways and money to upgrade its military capability to meet future needs. The financing for peacekeeping lags far behind demand. Both Boutros Boutros-Ghali and Kofi Annan, like their predecessors, have been categorical in this regard. Boutros-Ghali, for example, lamented, "A chasm has developed between the tasks entrusted to this Organization and the financial means provided to it. The truth of the matter is that our vision cannot really extend to the prospects opening before us as long as our financing remains myopic."[25] In spite of increased demand and praise, peacekeeping arrears have grown steadily since the Nobel Peace Prize was awarded to UN peacekeeping forces in 1988.

An absolute priority should be given to placing ongoing and future UN military operations on more solid financial bases. Implementation of some of the Secretary-General's suggestions could bring relief, particularly those for accelerating payments, reducing arrears through more discipline in payments schedules, and levying interest on arrears. One noncontroversial item, the creation of a $50-million revolving fund to help the United Nations move more swiftly, was implemented in 1993; this fund should be enlarged to reflect UN operations. Budgeting UN military operations as a national defense allocation, as is the case in some countries, rather than as an expenditure of the foreign ministries, would go a long way toward better fact-finding, preventive diplomacy, and peacekeeping. UN operations should be recognized as a specific contribution to a country's national security.

As mentioned earlier, the amount contributed by member states should be contrasted with the sums spent on defense worldwide. Annual global defense expenditures were over $1 trillion at the moment that the UN's peacekeeping coffers were over $1 billion in arrears. Ten billion dollars would be available if every country devoted 1 percent of its defense budget to UN military efforts. Other measures, such as surcharges on the sale of weaponry and on the use of UN-provided services—for example, ensuring the right of passage for ships—could help provide more income, although these options are politically dubious. There is no real alternative to governments' respecting their international treaty obligations to pay the bills for UN security operations, the solution supported by an independent group of bankers and politicians.[26]

Representational Changes: Adapting the Organization's Structure to the Interstate System

In the aftermath of the Cold War, and not withstanding splits in the council over northern Iraq in 1991, Kosovo in 1999, and Iraq in 2003, the Security Council has begun—at least more so than during the Cold War—to fulfill its duties as a guarantor of international peace and security. In this book we have charted the numerous field missions deployed by the council after 1989 for security reasons. Permanent-member goodwill manifested itself in the shelving of the veto for three years beginning in May 1990, and there has been only scarce resort to it since. The clear threat of a veto, however, greatly affected matters both in 1999 and 2003. Changes in the international climate could render the Security Council less able to provide for peace and security. Neither the United States nor France showed much sensitivity to the damage that they were doing to collective security structures during their open disagreement over how to deal with Iraq in 2003, whether ones speaks of the UN Security Council, NATO, or the European Union. A particular problem resides in what the French call the "hyperpower" (*hyperpuissance)* of the United States—Washington has always had great trouble in accepting a multilateralism that constrains its national power.[27] Being the world's only remaining superpower accentuates the problem. Two possibilities for dealing with this situation are reform in the council and greater use of improved regional organizations.[28]

The collapse of the Soviet Union has left the Security Council with a composition that generally is sympathetic to the interests of the West.[29] With the Soviet Union no longer acting as a counterbalance to the United States, states such as India, Brazil, Nigeria, and Egypt believe that they deserve greater say in the council's decisionmaking. The continuing permanent membership of France and Great Britain, whose international influence has declined significantly since 1945, offends Japan and Germany, whose influence in decisionmaking is in no way commensurate with their funding of the organization's activities. Countries like Canada that contribute troops routinely to all UN operations complain of being left out of decisions that affect their soldiers.

Reform of the Security Council's permanent membership is permanently discussed in both the corridors and the plenaries of intergovernmental forums.[30] Possibilities for long-term reform involve changes in the Security Council's permanent membership; shorter-term changes involve longer and more frequent terms on the council for influential countries such as Japan, Germany, Nigeria, India, Egypt, and Brazil.

In spite of unequivocal rhetorical support from Washington and the fact that many other governments have declared themselves in favor of changing the composition of the Security Council, each major structural reform opens another Pandora's box: Which developing countries should be added? Should they be the most powerful or populous? After a civil war, should a splintered state retain its seat? Why should economic powers whose constitutions impede overseas military involvement be given a seat? Should there be three permanent European members? What about the European Union (EU)? Which countries should wield vetoes?

The introduction of changes could create additional decisionmaking problems that could result in stalemates like those faced by the Security Council during the Cold War. Assuming the continuation of at least some North-South ideological, political, and economic tensions that reflect growing disparities in wealth, decisionmaking in the council could become as paralyzed in the future as it was in the past. Instead of an automatic Soviet veto, other effective vetoes from dissenters or foot-draggers could thwart the Security Council.

To enhance the decisionmaking power of the council under these circumstances, reform of the veto system also has been proposed. This system has always been controversial because the interests or even the whims of a single permanent member can impede effective action when the rest of the international community is prepared to act. Although it is unlikely that the veto could be eliminated altogether, proposals have been made to lessen its impact. These include limiting the range of areas in which the veto can be used, allowing its use only when an item affects a permanent member's "supreme national interests," instituting a system of weighted voting that would allow the council to override a veto, and increasing the total number of negative votes needed to veto a resolution.

Finally, on the subject of reform of the council, we note that the founding fathers in 1945 made the Charter extremely difficult to amend. Such amendments require a two-thirds vote of the General Assembly, then ratification by two-thirds of the parliaments of member states, including affirmative action by all of the Permanent Five. Hence, given the controversy surrounding all proposals for reform, formal council restructuring is, at best, a long shot.

As demonstrated in the case of UNMIK in Kosovo, using regional organizations as a means to supplement the UN's collective-security system has now moved beyond the talking stage. Secretary-General Boutros-Ghali proposed that "regional action as matter of decentralization, delegation, and cooperation with UN efforts could not

Kosovo: Italian KFOR tank guarding the destroyed Serbian church in Gjakova in June 1999. Soon after this photo was taken, unidentified Albanian extremists succeeded in demolishing this church by bombs. (JAE/M. Kim)

only lighten the burden of the Council but also contribute to a deeper sense of participation, consensus and democratization in international affairs."[31] Yet, as we argued earlier, even the world's most highly developed regional organizations usually lack the capacity to serve as effective alternatives to UN military operations.

These organizations can play a helpful role in diplomatic arm-twisting, as was witnessed by the Association of Southeast Asian Nations (ASEAN) in Cambodia and by the Contadora Group in Central America. With the exception of the North Atlantic Treaty Organization—which possesses the most authoritative joint force in the world and has advanced cooperative procedures used in northern Iraq, the Balkans, and Afghanistan—regional organizations are and will remain poor sources for supplying international military forces to help quell interstate and local conflicts. The rhetoric about regional organizations flourishes in developing countries, but the hopes placed on them for their contribution to international peace and security seem unduly optimistic, if not altogether misplaced.

Regional organizations' military and financial capacities are lacking; and they inevitably contain states that are so embroiled in conflicts as to make community decisions impossible. The European Community's dithering in the former Yugoslavia illustrates the incapacity of even well-endowed organizations to effectively manage conflicts in their locale. The results reflected the lack of political will; nonetheless observers point to the "indispensability" of the United Nations.[32] NATO, the Western European Union (WEU), and the Conference on Security and Cooperation in Europe (CSCE) discussed helping with humanitarian relief in the former Yugoslavia, but political considerations prevented effective action. The NATO troops in Bosnia and Herzegovina were deployed from 1992 until 1995 under a UN flag. The coalitions in the Persian Gulf and Somalia made use of Security Council authorizations.

Although the United Nations is the most logical and important convener for future international military operations, the use of coercion poses almost insuperable problems for the world organization.[33] Thus, if coercion occurs at all, interventions in the near future will have to compensate for the military inadequacies of the United Nations. Experience suggests that UN decisions should trigger interventions to be subcontracted to coalitions of major states that are willing and able to act. Regional powers (for instance, Nigeria within West Africa and Russia within the erstwhile Soviet republics) could take the lead combined with larger regional (that is, the Economic Community of West African States and the Commonwealth of Independent States) or global coalitions. Perhaps only when regional powers cannot or will not take such a lead should more global powers (for example, France in Rwanda or the United States in Somalia) be expected to do so. However, blocking humanitarian intervention, which some powers are willing to conduct when others are reluctant to get involved (for example, the United States vis-à-vis Rwanda between early April and late June 1994), should be ruled out.

The multilateral capacity for coercion will no doubt depend in the future upon ad hoc coalitions, regional powers, and even hegemons. For the United States, former U.S. Assistant Secretary of State William Maynes dubbed this "benign realpolitik," which amounts to a revival of spheres of influence with UN oversight.[34] The Security Council is experimenting with a type of great-power politics, which the United Nations had originally been founded to end but which is pertinent in light of some of the inherent difficulties of multilateral mobilization and management of military force.

Boutros-Ghali recognized this reality when calling for "a new division of labour between the United Nations and regional organizations, under which the regional organization carries the main burden but a small United Nations operation supports it and verifies that it is functioning in a manner consistent with positions adopted by the Security Council."[35] Elsewhere, in justifying UN monitoring of Nigeria and ECOWAS in Liberia as well as Russia and the CIS in Tajikistan and Georgia, he had this to say: "Finding the right division of labour between the United Nations and regional organizations is not easy. But such cooperation brings greater legitimacy and support to international efforts. It eases the material and financial burden of the United Nations. It allows for comparative advantage."[36]

An observer might ask, "What's new about rationalization? Is the Secretary-General not grasping at straws in justifying a contemporary gunboat diplomacy? Is this not simply realpolitik?" Boutros-Ghali was aware of the dangers: "Authorization to serve as a surrogate might strengthen a particular power's sphere of influence and damage the United Nations' standing as an organization intended to coordinate security across regional blocs."[37]

The difference could be that major powers or their coalitions act on their own behalf as well as legitimately on behalf of the Security Council—thus they should be held accountable for their actions by the wider community of states authorizing outside interventions. Although major powers inevitably flex their military muscles when it is in their perceived interests to do so, they do not necessarily agree in advance to subject themselves to international law and outside monitoring of their behavior. The political and economic advantages attached to an imprimatur from the Security Council provide some leverage for the community of states to foster accountability in would-be subcontractors. In light of the incapacity of the United Nations, there is no alternative to making better use of regional organizations, without naïveté and with accountability.

Another conceptual movement has been the evolution of the notion "postconflict peacebuilding." The UN's experiences in this regard have been growing, as evidenced most clearly by the operations in Bosnia, Kosovo, East Timor, Afghanistan and, undoubtedly, Iraq. In this regard, peacebuilding is a work in progress, and Secretary-General Kofi Annan has been cautious to clarify in his 1997 *Reform Report* that, although peacebuilding must be supported by humanitarian and development activities, it also needs to reorient them in such a way that they become politically relevant in that they can serve to reduce the risk of resumed conflict and promote reconciliation and recovery.[38]

Relevant here is the combination of actors at work in Afghanistan. Enforcement action against the Taliban and Al Qaeda was carried out by a U.S.-led coalition acting with the green light of the Security Council. The UN then sponsored a peace conference that led to the emergence of an interim government under Hamid Karzai. Various NATO member states then took the lead in organizing an international military force that at least maintained some security in Kabul. Granted that, as feared by many observers, all post-conflict operations in Afghanistan suffered from lack of political commitment and resources from UN member states, at least there was a division of labor among outside agencies. UN major organs contented themselves with diplomatic and legitimating functions, leaving the heavy lifting of coercive action to states and military organizations like NATO. Not by coincidence, the Special Representative of the Secretary-General in Afghanistan was Lakhdar Brahimi, who had chaired a panel that in 2000 had recommended such an approach to security operations.[39]

Professional Changes: Strengthening the Secretariat

Paradoxically, the 1991 Persian Gulf War represented the first military enforcement action of the post–Cold War era, but the UN Secretary-General and the secretariat remained virtual outsiders to the process by which the war was waged. This pattern has been repeated, most recently in Afghanistan in 2001. Kosovo in 1999 and Iraq in 2003 are not entirely relevant, since the Security Council did not authorize force in either case. Although the initial Security Council authorizations were politically useful in 1991 and 2001, the coalition forces were not accountable to the world organization. Increasing the ability of the secretariat and thereby of the Security Council to

Afghanistan: American soldiers in Bahgram air base, a former Soviet military base in the 1980s. (JAE/M. Kim)

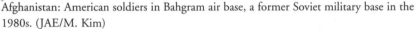

monitor enforcement operations has become a subject of heated discussions.[40] The enormous difficulties surrounding the deployment of the first UN troops with Chapter VII provisions under the command and control of the Secretary-General in Somalia serve to highlight the critical nature of this issue. Observers of UNPROFOR in the Balkans, which was sometimes given a Chapter VII mandate by the council, were struck by the muddled nature of UN command and control over that mostly unhappy experience.

Several proposals have been put forth to increase the Secretary-General's influence over Security Council decisionmaking and subsequent UN military operations. Article 99 of the Charter already empowers the Secretary-General to bring the Security Council's attention to matters that he believes could threaten international peace and security. Greater use of this article could allow the Secretary-General to place issues on the council's agenda that otherwise might be avoided due to their sensitivity. The double standard with which the council has addressed past threats to the peace could be mitigated if the Secretary-General were to use the powers of his office to try to ensure a more consistent consideration of issues even when powerful states might prefer to ignore them. Experience shows, however, from Trygve Lie in the 1950s to Boutros-Ghali in the 1990s, that the Secretary-General who completely offends a Permanent Five member cannot be an effective leader of the UN.

The Office of the Secretary-General has asked for a mandate to request advisory opinions from the International Court of Justice under Article 96 of the Charter. Such a course of action could allow the organization's head to help refine the legitimate definitions of those situations that present threats to the peace as well as to provide more concrete policy options that are both politically and legally acceptable. The key to advisory opinions is in the asking of the question to get a specific enough response. Time is also a problem because the ICJ never acts quickly. Moreover, given that the United States has made clear that it does not want the new International Criminal Court second-guessing its decisions about choice of weapons and targets in armed conflict, it is highly doubtful that Washington—or Moscow or Beijing—would welcome the Secretary-General's raising similar questions.

Agreement on standards may be increasingly necessary, however. Resolutions are often kept vague in order to secure intergovernmental assent ("all necessary means" in the war against Iraq created a host of questions about proportionality, and "all measures necessary" was quintessential UN doublespeak that did not permit sufficient action to help Bosnia's Muslims). The language of international decisions is sometimes too elliptical to allow a determination of which concrete actions and procedures would constitute legitimate follow-up. The Secretary-General—and not just the General Assembly, the Security Council, and other UN organs—should be authorized to request advisory opinions from the World Court to help reduce the criticism of selective application by the Security Council of the principles guiding decisionmaking. Although seeking the court's opinion would be harmful in the midst of a crisis, it could be useful in anticipating future contingencies.

As part of the reform process, steps have been taken to enhance the secretariat's means of fact-finding so that the Secretary-General can improve his access to timely, unbiased, and impartial accounts of dangerous situations. Special units have proliferated that focus exclusively on early warning and prevention. The mandate of these units is to provide greater access to information about potential threats to the peace, thus enhancing the secretariat's ability to launch preventive diplomacy and possibly to recommend preventive deployment. Of course, much more could be done, and the Secretary-General's office could and should be equipped and staffed to act as an effective crisis-monitoring center for events that threaten the peace.

Useful suggestions have been made to establish a "national security council" within the secretariat, complete with independent sources of intelligence and a means for autonomous interpretation of data supplied by governments, in order to provide early warning about crises. A fledgling effort to establish this type of unit, the Office for Research and Collection of Information (ORCI), was dismantled in 1992 as one of the first changes by newly elected Secretary-General Boutros-Ghali. A recommendation along the same lines by the Pakistani panel has been met with silence. But the need for a policy-planning unit has become more and more obvious; too few persons are looking toward the future. Considerable intelligence could be gleaned from public sources, including leading "think tanks", dealing with international relations.

Finally, the end of the Cold War has permitted the world organization to move toward reviving old-fashioned ideals of an objective and competent international civil service, upon which the organization was supposedly founded.[41] The success of the organization's activities begins and ends with the people in its employ. A long-ignored reality is the need to overhaul the international civil service, for which qualifications have long been secondary to geographic and political considerations.

After 1997, when Kofi Annan unveiled his strategy of a "quiet revolution" to reform the world organization, meaningful steps began to be taken to make the UN a more effective mechanism for administering and managing peacekeeping operations.[42] The creation and effective implementation of a rationalized cabinet system, consisting of the senior management group (SMG) comprising division heads and an executive committee system, introduced a much greater degree of horizontal cooperation than had been the case before. Senior officials throughout the organization (including those based in Geneva and Vienna through teleconferencing) meet weekly with the Secretary-General to review and discuss important issues. In addition, the executive committee on peace and security, which brings together those senior officials whose units deal with peacekeeping, holds biweekly discussions. This process is supplemented with a number of issue-specific task forces, including special task forces for each multidisciplinary peace operation, as well as special meetings involving a much wider set of actors who serve as operational partners in the field, including development and humanitarian agencies and international financial institutions.

In regard to headquarters operations, a division of authority has been worked out between the Department of Political Affairs (DPA), the Office for the Coordination of Humanitarian Affairs (OCHA), and the Department of Peace-keeping Operations (DPKO). The former has primary responsibility for preventive diplomacy and peacemaking, the middle one coordinates assistance, and the latter takes the lead in peacekeeping. Although these changes represent important steps in enhancing interdepartmental cooperation and improving the effectiveness of peace operations, the continued splitting of peacemaking and peacekeeping across separate administrative units serves to limit the overall effectiveness of such activities.

In the field, on the contrary, coordination has been centralized under the Special Representative of the Secretary-General, who assumes authority over all UN entities in the mission area. In cases where department expertise is especially crucial, such as in the Central African Republic and Liberia, for example, a UNDP resident coordinator (who in peacetime is the UN's point person) may also be appointed to serve as deputy head of mission. Within this structure special emphasis is placed on working in close cooperation with relevant parties, including NGOs.

As mentioned earlier, the scale of the administrative trusteeship operation in Kosovo was in many ways unprecedented. Among its most innovative features was its administrative structure. For the first time non-UN multilateral agencies were integrated directly into the governance structure of a multidimensional peacekeeping operation. Moreover several of the individuals selected for the team had extensive experience with NGOs and other elements of civil society. The Secretary-General originally selected Bernard Kouchner (founder of Médecins sans Frontières and former minister of health of France) to lead the UNMIK operation as his special representative. He then supplemented the administrative structure with four deputy special representatives (DSRs). Tom Koenigs, head of the environmental protection department of the City of Frankfurt and deputy-president of the NGO the Alliance for the Climate, was selected to represent the United Nations as the DSR for interim civil administration. A long-time UNHCR staff member, Dennis McNamara, was selected as DSR for humanitarian affairs. The head of the OSCE mission to Kosovo, Daan Everts, joined the team as DSR for institution-building. And Joly Dixon, director of international affairs of the European Commission, was appointed as DSR for economic reconstruction. The representatives of both the OSCE and the EU worked under the direct authority of the SRSG (Special Representative of the Secretary-General) and ultimately the Secretary-General.

This administrative arrangement reflects a deeper transformation that has been occurring in peace operations over the past decade. Peacekeeping personnel and contributing partners are being drawn from an ever-expanding range of institutions—international, national, and local. In addition to UN departments, programs, funds, and other bodies, peacekeepers are now being tapped from specialized agencies, international financial institutions, national bureaucracies, military and civilian police forces, regional organizations, NGOs, academia, and the private sector. Each peace mission brings with it a new context with a particular set of historical, cultural, social, and economic conditions, political constraints and requirements, and thus the need for a unique blend of partners and cooperative arrangements.

As the pool of potential partners grows, so does the necessity for developing systematic criteria for determining partnership acceptability. Of course, not all NGOs and other entities from civil society are necessarily constructive forces for building and sustaining peace. Neither may be all regional security organizations, as demonstrated by the numerous allegations of serious human rights violations by members of the Military Observer Group of the Economic Community of West African States (ECOMOG) force in Liberia and Sierra Leone. At the same time, however, a broad conception of partnerships is likely to be even more important in the future than it is now. Given the increasing importance placed on creating the requisite social and economic infrastructures for sustaining peace in conflict-torn regions, it seems that new and innovative types of partnerships with the private sector, religious groups, local governmental bodies, labor, and others will most likely be needed.

Determining whether to get involved or not in political-humanitarian crises requires familiarity with a host of actors besides states. Humanitarian action has made possible new coalitions—the media and the public can demand that something be done, the military can respond, and relief agencies can ask for help because on occasion they recognize both the war-fighting and logistic capacities of the armed forces. Commitments by major powers are greatly affected by their leaders' calculations of domestic costs, benefits, and risks. The arithmetic in part reflects the success of domestic and transnational constituencies in mobilizing support for humanitarian action, and in altering conceptions of interests and rewards.

One example is Washington's change of tack on Haiti in 1994 after effective lobbying by Jean-Bertrand Aristide and the Congressional Black Caucus.[43] American leadership in Haiti beginning in September 1994 and in Bosnia after the Dayton accords in November 1995 (a year and two years, respectively, after the October 1993 fiasco in Somalia) suggests that when interests are perceived to be sufficiently involved and foreign policy is framed accordingly, minds can be concentrated and changed. In Kosovo in 1999, humanitarian arguments managed to carry the day even when aerial bombing entailed deterioration in Washington's relations with Moscow and Beijing. As was the case in northern Iraq, and despite the Vietnam and Somalia syndromes, American interests were framed in Haiti, Bosnia, and ultimately Kosovo to merit use of the military with significant humanitarian motivations and certainly significant humanitarian consequences.

The use of force aside, an equally good example of the importance of numerous actors was the "Ottawa process" on antipersonnel land mines. This case is worth examining because of what its dynamics portend for the future, even if the mindset in Washington on this issue remains for the moment impervious to the humanitarian values that have penetrated the foreign policies of other countries. A transnational coalition successfully imbued the domestic politics of a sufficient number of states with enough humanitarian concern to redefine state interests in a way that led to the treaty.[44] Unlike many cases of transnationalism, this one touches directly on the high politics of military security.

This example suggests the importance of substate and transnational actors in influencing, framing, and ultimately redefining state interests.[45] The initial impetus in the anti-land-mines campaign was provided by a formidable coalition of civil society organizations. The International Campaign to Ban Land Mines grew out of private advocacy organizations whose main orientation was domestic and public (that is, oriented toward change in *state* behavior). Its success depended on coopting *states* (and notably Canada, the Scandinavian countries, and South Africa), in "determin[ing] what states want."[46] Their support depended not only on the moral appeal of the cause but also on the consideration of domestic and international political interests and risks.

State involvement was necessary to translate social pressure into international law. The key to the outcome was to move states and alter definitions of perceived interests by persuading politicians. A basic aspect of the process was to remove land mines from the rarefied realm of technical military strategy and to place the issue firmly in the political realm of domestic constituencies.[47]

Humanitarian values are in the forefront of concerns motivating many societal forces that may inform leaders' perceptions of interest. In commenting on the intervention in Kosovo, the journalist Max Frankel concluded, "It's those pictures of almost unfathomable atrocity that once again drive our politics."[48] This is not the place to discuss in depth the so-called CNN effect, which influences both the perception of tragedy and the pace of decisionmaking.[49] However, the increasing reach and efficiency of international communications, along with the related growing influence of transnational and non-governmental actors, point toward a changing domestic environment and decisionmaking context. Armed with graphic images of suffering, these nonstate actors help shape definitions of state interest. We are witnessing a phenomenon not of receding state authority, but of states' being influenced by coalitions of actors with humanitarian values. Their agendas to some extent and in some circumstances become those of their governments.[50] The advances in technology that permitted real-time coverage of the war in Iraq may have changed the equation yet again.

Depending on perspectives, 1999 was the *annus mirabilis* or *horibilis* for humanitarian action. Kosovo constituted a "humanitarian war." Coercion took place against the Milosevic government to stop persecution. In the West, and Washington particularly, intervention for humanitarian purposes was crucial enough to risk worsened relations with both Russia and China. And in some ways, the international reaction to East Timor was even more remarkable because only area specialists and stamp collectors could have located it on a map a few years earlier. But in spite of official and initially strong objections from the world's fourth most populous country, enough international pressure was exerted that Jakarta "requested" the deployment of the Australian-led coalition in Timor, which was followed by UN trusteeship and a UN peacekeeping force. Pressured or induced consent given by the targeted government is the "first cousin" to humanitarian intervention. Comparable actions are out of the question in Chechnya, Tibet, or Kashmir; but efforts in Indonesia suggest that humanitarian action is an option in more than powerless or failed states, even without formally overriding sovereignty.[51]

Member states and peoples across the world are looking toward the United Nations to muster multilateral responses for international and civil strife. In 2003, most states and expressions of public opinion, where the latter could be measured, indicated a preference for military action against Iraq only with the approval of the Security Council. This was true of public opinion even in the United States, where about 60 percent of the public favored the military option. Collective security in its most rigorous form, as directed by UN organs, has yet to be tested, but changing world politics indicate that the United Nations has been given another chance after the Cold War to implement the peace and security provisions of its Charter. It was striking that particularly after the Security Council could not agree on Kosovo in 1999, so much diplomacy and public interest focused on the council regarding Iraq in 2003. In the next big security crisis, the same phenomenon is again likely to be true, despite the widespread disappointment that the Permanent Five had not been able to agree on how to handle Saddam Hussein.

Human rights and sustainable development play a much less significant role in the Charter than military security. But these "softer" sides of the UN moved forward during the Cold War while collective-security mechanisms stalled. The end of the Cold War has had a decided impact on international efforts to constitute working regimes in these areas, too. Moreover, the meaning of "security" has come into question as issues of human rights, democratization, and sustainable human development have worked their way into global discourse about security matters.

Explaining Change

For the security domain, as will be the case in subsequent chapters for human rights and development, it is not easy to deal with matters of presumed knowledge and learning. What are the proper lessons to be drawn from decades of UN peacekeeping, from various efforts at enforcement, from failures to reach a common approach to Kosovo in 1999 and Iraq in 2003? Do different actors learn different things based on their existing ideologies or mindsets, indicating an absence of scientific certainty on these matters and the persistent presence of ever-changing policy debates?

It is truly remarkable in a disappointing way that so much UN peacekeeping, even of the traditional type, is still so unsystematic, still so ad hoc in composition and deployment. It is certainly the case that many states have not learned that international peace and security could be improved by concluding Article 43 agreements with the UN, which would provide the Secretary-General advance notice of what military units would be available for armed interposition under UN aegis. It may be that certain states like Canada "know" that a UN rapid reaction force could be a significant contribution to stability and humanitarian advance in a world of failed states and small wars. But it seems that many states—including the important ones with the most military wherewithal like the United States, China, and Russia—do not want to transfer much hard power to the UN even if under the ultimate authority of the Security Council, where they have a veto.

Thus, it is still the case, as of 2003, that the Secretary-General has to go begging and start from scratch if he advocates a multilateral force for places like Liberia or Congo. Even for the armed observation of cease-fires, which the UN has been doing on a fairly large scale since 1956, if not the late 1940s, there is no UN system that can be activated on short notice, ready for rapid deployment. Indeed, deployments were done more quickly in the 1950s and 1960s than now, because of the absence of political will in nastier conflicts. The problem is not intellectual. The problem is the absence of national and international political will. Important states simply do not wish to commit in advance even small, voluntary parts of their armed forces for deployments determined by the council and managed by the secretariat. Even for traditional peacekeeping, not to mention the more ambitious complex peacekeeping, there has not been much "learning lessons" but "spurning lessons." In short, policy changes to make the whole enterprise more streamlined and effective make good sense, just not political sense to key states.

Recent events regarding enforcement indicate the same lack of decisive change, the same lack of policy transformation, which would indicate not much learning in behalf of new knowledge. Iraq in 2003 demonstrated starkly what Kosovo had already shown in 1999, namely that the permanent members of the Security Council could be as deeply divided after the Cold War as during it. In both of those cases, one saw a determined hyperpower ready to employ its military superiority, even in the face of opposition within the council. Regarding Iraq in 2003, one could say in all honesty that much of the opposition was well considered and well argued, even if some of it stemmed from historic ambitions (for example, France) or domestic political calculation (for example, Germany). Iraq did not have substantial links with Al Qaeda, did not have large amounts of chemical or biological weapons in operational mode, did not have an active nuclear weapons program, and did not present a clear and present danger to U.S. security. It is fair to say that for the George W. Bush administration, being determined to exploit its power advantage over the Saddam Hussein regime, what it "learned" was that the members of the council could not be relied upon to endorse decisive preventive action. Kosovo had already demonstrated that war by multilateral committee was a bad idea. At the same time, what a majority of the council members "learned" about Saddam's Iraq was that diplomacy still had a chance of containing and deterring that regime. So "knowledge" in this case was not a scientific matter but a debatable proposition greatly affected by perceptions of power and relevant norms.

It may yet be the case that state members of the UN Security Council, ten of whom of course are not permanent members, may "learn" the benefits of involving the UN in post-combat security measures of occupation, state-building, and nation-building. On the one hand, it was evident at the time of writing that the U.S. was meeting many difficulties in trying to transform an occupied Iraq. On the other hand, the UN had demonstrated a certain messy success in administering Bosnia, Kosovo, and East Timor. Afghanistan was a separate case in which the UN was involved immediately after combat in a diplomatic way, but did not have major responsibility for security and other measures on the ground for the Hamid Karzai government. Post-combat Afghanistan was a fractured, dangerous, and deadly place. A UN-led transition effort could hardly have done worse, although a UN-led effort would still require the cooperation of the United States and NATO especially in the security domain.

Almost all actors, whether state participants or non-state observers and experts, had "learned the knowledge" that the UN was not good at the heavy lifting of combat, and that the UN lacked the independent power and management skills to move beyond collective legitimization and the less muscular forms of peacekeeping. There also seemed to be widespread learning in behalf of "smart" sanctions that targeted elites rather than the rank and file citizen who often had little control over events.

Notes

1. This discussion draws on Jane Boulden and Thomas G. Weiss, "Whither Terrorism and the United Nations?" in Jane Boulden and Thomas G. Weiss, eds., *Terrorism and the United Nations* (Bloomington, Ind.: Indiana University Press, 2004). See further Thomas G. Weiss, Margaret E.Chabon, and John Aoering, eds., *War on Terrorism and Iraq* (London: Routledge, 2004).

2. UN Press Release, SG/SM/7962/Rev.1, September 18, 2001.

3. Many studies of international relations, including our previous edition, gave insufficient attention to terrorism. For example, a well-known anthology about American priorities ignored the topic; see Michael E. Brown, ed., *America's Strategic Choices* (Cambridge: MIT Press, 2000). Daniel Philpott points out that religion, certainly one of the factors motivating the terrorist attacks, also was largely ignored by international relations scholars—yet another shortcoming because Al Qaeda's political theology challenges "the Westphalian synthesis, the fundamental authority structure of the international order": "The Challenge of September 11 to Secularism in International Relations," *World Politics* 55, no. 1 (October 2002), p. 92. He analyzed four prominent journals from 1980–1999 (*International Security, International Organization, International Studies Quarterly, and World Politics*) and found that only six or so of about 1,600 articles featured religion as an important influence in international relations. See Daniel Philpott, *Revolutions in Sovereignty: How Ideas Shaped Modern International Relations* (Princeton: Princeton University Press, 2001), p. 9.

4. See Adam Roberts, "Terrorism and International Order," in Lawrence Freedman, Christopher Hill, Adam Roberts, R. J. Vincent, Paul Wilkinson, and Philip Windsor, eds., *Ter-

rorism and International Order (London: Routledge and Kegan Paul/Royal Institute of International Affairs, 1986), pp. 9–10.

5. United Nations, *Report of the Policy Working Group on the United Nations and Terrorism*, document A/57/273/S/2002/875.

6. See further Rosemary Foot, S. Neil MacFarlane, and Michael Mastanduno, eds., *The United States and Multilateral Organizations* (Oxford: Oxford University Press, 2003).

7. Regarding the Caroline case and anticipatory self-defense in international law, see Anthony Clark Arend and Robert J. Beck, *International Law and the Use of Force* (London: Routledge, 1993). On the Bush Doctrine as a violation of the UN Charter, see Tom J. Farer, "Beyond the Charter Frame: Unilateralism or Condominium," *American Journal of International Law* 96, 2 (April 2002), pp.359–364. Israeli scholars, like Yoram Dienstein, in *War, Aggression and Self Defense,* second edition (Cambridge: Cambridge University Press, 1994), who endorse the notion of anticipatory self-defense as found in Israel's first use of force in 1967, still say that the threat of imminent attack is necessary in exercises of this form of self-defense.

8. On the great damage that the Bush policy toward Iraq did to the long effort to restrict the first use of force, see especially Michael J. Glennon, "Why the Security Council Failed," *Foreign Affairs,* 82, 3 (May–June 2003), pp. 16–35. On the broad perception that the Iraqi war in 2003 weakened the United Nations, see Meg Bortin, "Poll Shows U.S. Isolation," *International Herald Tribune,* June 4, 2003, www.iht.com/articles/98482.html.

9. Boutros Boutros-Ghali, *An Agenda for Peace 1995* (New York: U.N. 1995), contains both the original 1992 *An Agenda for Peace* and the 1995 *Supplement.* Paragraph numbers remain the same.

10. For a review of the Brahimi report, S/2000/809, see among many sources *A Global Agenda 2001–2002,* (Lanham, Md.: Rowman & Littlefied, 2002).

11. See James N. Rosenau, *Turbulence in World Politics: A Theory of Change and Continuity* (Princeton: Princeton University Press, 1990); Thomas G. Weiss and Meryl A. Kessler, eds., *Third World Security in the Post–Cold War Era* (Boulder: Lynne Rienner, 1991); Morton H. Halperin and David J. Scheffer, *Self-Determination in the New World Order* (Washington, D.C.: Carnegie Endowment, 1992); Daniel Patrick Moynihan, *Pandemonium: Ethnicity in International Politics* (New York: Oxford University Press, 1993); Joel Kotkin, *Tribes: How Race, Religion, and Identity Determine Success in the New Global Economy* (New York: Random House, 1993); Michael E. Brown, ed., *The International Dimension of Internal Conflict* (Cambridge, Mass.: MIT Press, 1996); Ted Robert Gurr and Barbara Harff, *Ethnic Conflict in World Politics* (Boulder: Westview Press, 1994); and Gidon Gottlieb, *Nation Against State* (New York: Council on Foreign Relations, 1993). For discussions on the difficulties of negotiating the end to such wars, see I. William Zartman, ed., *Elusive Peace: Negotiating an End to Civil Wars* (Washington, D.C.: Brookings Institution, 1995); Fen Osler Hampson, *Nurturing Peace: Why Peace Settlements Succeed or Fail* (Washington, D.C.: U.S. Institute of Peace Press, 1996); and Stephen John Stedman, Donald Rothchild, and Elizabeth M. Cousens, eds., *Ending Civil Wars: The Implementation of Peace Agreements* (Boulder: Lynne Rienner, 2002).

12. See Mats Berdal and David M. Mallone, eds., *Greed and Grievance: Economic Agenda in Civil Wars* (Boulder: Lynne Rienner, 2000); David Keen, *The Economic Functions of Violence in Civil Wars* (Oxford: Oxford University Press, 1997), Adelphi Paper 320; and Mark Duffield, *Global Governance and the New Wars: The Merging of Development and Security* (London: Zed, 2001).

13. See Larry Minear et al., *Humanitarianism Under Siege: A Critical Review of Operation Lifeline Sudan* (Trenton, N.J.: Red Sea Press, 1991); and Francis M. Deng and Larry Minear, *The Challenge of Famine Relief* (Washington, D.C.: Brookings Institution, 1993).

14. John Mackinlay and Jarat Chopra, "Second Generation Multinational Operations," *Washington Quarterly* 15, no. 3 (Summer 1992), pp. 113–134.

15. Boutros-Ghali, *Supplement*, para. 77.

16. Boutros Boutros-Ghali, "Transcript of Press Conference," January 5, 1995, press release SG/SM/5518, p. 5.

17. See James Rosenau, *The United Nations in a Turbulent World* (Boulder: Lynne Rienner, 1992).

18. See, for example, Stephen J. Krasner, *Sovereignty: Organized Hypocrisy* (Princeton: Princeton University Press, 1999); and Philpott, *Revolutions in Sovereignty*.

19. See the classic treatment by Kenneth Waltz, *Man, the State and War* (New York: Columbia University Press, 1968), in contrast with Philip Allott, *Eunomia: New Order for a New World* (New York: Oxford University Press, 1990).

20. International Commission on Intervention and State Sovereignty, *The Responsibility to Protect* (Ottawa: ICISS, 2001).

21. Francis M. Deng, *Protecting the Dispossessed: A Challenge for the International Community* (Washington, D.C.: Brookings Institution, 1993); Francis M. Deng et al., *Sovereignty as Responsibility* (Washington, D.C.: Brookings Institution, 1995); and Francis M. Deng, "Frontiers of Sovereignty," *Leiden Journal of International Law* 8, no. 2 (1995), pp. 249–286.

22. See Thomas G. Weiss and Cindy Collins, *Humanitarian Challenges and Intervention: World Politics and the Dilemmas of Help*, second edition (Boulder: Westview Press, 2000); Thomas G. Weiss, *Military-Civilian Interactions: Intervening in Humanitarian Crises* (Lanham, Md.: Rowman & Littlefield, 1999); and Thomas G. Weiss and Don Hubert, *The Responsibility to Protect: Research, Bibliography, and Background* (Ottawa: ICISS, 2001), chapter 8.

23. Boutros-Ghali, *An Agenda for Peace*, para. 43.

24. From the "Ottawa Declaration on UN Collective Security" adopted by the inaugural meeting of Global Action's Parliamentary Commission on Peacekeeping and Collective Security, May 22, 1991.

25. Boutros-Ghali, *An Agenda for Peace*, para. 69.

26. For other ideas about financing, see the thoughts of a group of experts under the chairmanship of Paul Volker and Shijuro Ogata, *Financing an Effective United Nations* (New York: Ford Foundation, 1993).

27. Edward C. Luck, *Mixed Messages: American Politics and International Organization 1919–1999* (Washington, D.C.: Brookings Institution, 1999). See also John Gerard Ruggie, *Winning the Peace: America and World Order in the New Era* (New York: Columbia University Press, 1996).

28. For a discussion, see David M. Malone, ed., *The Future of the Security Council* (Boulder: Lynne Rienner, forthcoming); and Thomas A. Weiss, "The Illusion of Security Council Reform," *Washington Quarterly* 26, 4 (Autumn 2003), pp. 147–161.

29. For a quantitative and qualitative discussion, see Ernest B. Haas, "Collective Conflict Management: Evidence for a New World Order?" in Thomas G. Weiss, ed., *Collective Security in a Changing World* (Boulder: Lynne Rienner, 1993), pp. 63–117.

30. See Edward C. Luck, *Reforming the United Nations: Lessons from a History in Progress* (New Haven, Conn.: ACUNS, 2003), Occasional Paper No. 1, pp. 7–16. See also Brian Urquhart and Erskine Childers, *A World in Need of Leadership: Tomorrow's United Nations—A Fresh Appraisal* (Uppsala, Sweden: Dag Hammarskjöld Foundation, 1996); Commission on Global Governance, *Our Global Neighborhood* (Oxford: Oxford University Press, 1995); South Centre, *For a Strong and Democratic United Nations: A South Perspective on UN Reform* (Geneva: South Centre, 1995); and Erskine Childers and Brian Urquhart, *Renewing the United Nations System* (Upland, Pa.: DIANE Publishing Company, 1999).

31. Boutros-Ghali, *An Agenda for Peace*, para. 64.

32. John Zametica, *The Yugoslav Conflict, Adelphi Paper 270* (London: International Institute for Strategic Studies, 1992), p. 67.

33. For an outspoken and skeptical realist view, see John J. Mearsheimer, "The False Promise of International Institutions," *International Security* 19, no. 3 (Winter 1994–1995), pp. 5–49.

34. Charles William Maynes, "A Workable Clinton Doctrine," *Foreign Policy* 93 (Winter 1993–1994), pp. 3–20.

35. Boutros-Ghali, *Supplement*, para. 86. For a skeptical view, see Benjamin Rivlin, "Prospects for a Division of Labour Between the UN and Regional Bodies in Peace-keeping," in Klaus Hüfner, ed., *Agenda for Change* (Opladen: Leske and Budrich, 1995), pp. 137–149.

36. Press release SG/SM/5804, November 1, 1995, p. 2. For an extended argument about a "partnership" between the UN and regional organizations, see Alan K. Henrikson, "The Growth of Regionalism and the Role of the United Nations," in Louise Fawcett and Andrew Hurrell, eds., *Regionalism in World Politics: Regional Organizations and World Order* (Oxford: Oxford University Press, 1996), pp. 122–168.

37. Boutros Boutros-Ghali, "Global Leadership After the Cold War," *Foreign Affairs* 75, no. 2 (March–April 1996), p. 95.

38. Kofi Annan, *Renewing the United Nations: A Programme for Reform* (New York: U.N., 1997).

39. United Nations, *Report of the Panel on United Nations Peace Operations*, document A/55/305–S/2000/809, August 21, 2000.

40. See John Mackinlay, "The Requirement for a Multinational Enforcement Capability," in Weiss, *Collective Security*, pp. 139–152.

41. The classic treatment of this subject is by Dag Hammarskjöld, "The International Civil Servant in Law and in Fact," lecture of May 30, 1961 (Oxford: Clarendon Press, 1961). For further information, see Thomas G. Weiss, *International Bureaucracy* (Lexington, Mass.: Heath, 1975); and Robert S. Jordan, ed., *International Administration: Its Evolution and Contemporary Applications* (New York: Oxford University Press, 1971).

42. Kofi Annan, "The Quiet Revolution," *Global Governance* 4, no. 2 (April–June 1998), pp. 123–138.

43. David Malone, *Decision-Taking in the UN Security Council: The Case of Haiti, 1990–97* (Oxford: Oxford University Press, 1998).

44. See Stephen Biddle et al., *The Military Utility of Landmines Implications for Arms Control* (Alexandria, Va.: Institute for Defense Analyses, 1994).

45. See Thomas Risse, Stephen C. Ropp, and Kathryn Sikkink, eds., *The Power of Human Rights: International Norms and Domestic Change* (Cambridge, UK: Cambridge University Press, 1999).

46. Richard Price, "Reversing the Gun Sights: Transnational Civil Society Targets Land Mines," *International Organization* LII, no. 3 (Summer 1998), p. 617.

47. For a comparison across cases of NGO, IGO, and governmental partnerships, see Don Hubert, *The Landmine Ban: A Case Study in Humanitarian Advocacy*, Occasional Paper #42 (Providence, R.I.: Watson Institute, 2000).

48. Max Frankel, "Our Humanity Vs. Their Sovereignty," *New York Times Magazine*, May 2, 1999, p. 36.

49. See Nik Gowing, *Media Coverage: Help or Hindrance in Conflict Prevention* (New York: Carnegie Commission on Preventing Deadly Conflict, 1997); Warren P. Stroble, *Late-Breaking Foreign Policy: The News Media's Influence on Peace Operations* (Washington, DC.: U.S. Institute of Peace Press, 1997); Edward R. Girardet, ed., *Somalia, Rwanda, and Beyond: The Role of the*

International Media in Wars and Humanitarian Crises (Dublin: Crosslines Publications, 1995); Johanna Neuman, *Lights, Camera, War: Is Media Technology Driving International Politics?* (New York: St. Martin's Press, 1996); Colin Scott, Larry Minear, and Thomas G. Weiss, *The News Media, Humanitarian Action, and Civil War* (Boulder: Lynne Rienner, 1996); and Robert I. Rotberg and Thomas G. Weiss, eds., *From Massacres to Genocide: The Media, Public Policy, and Humanitarian Crises* (Washington, DC.: Brookings Institution, 1996).

50. See S. Neil MacFarlane and Thomas G. Weiss, "Political Interest and Humanitarian Action," *Security Studies* 10, no. 1 (Autumn 2000), pp. 166–198.

51. Donald K. Emmerson, "Moralpolitik: The Timor Test," *National Interest* no. 58 (Winter 1999–2000), pp. 57–62.

Part TWO

Human Rights and Humanitarian Affairs

5 The United Nations, Human Rights, and Humanitarian Affairs

The Theory

The celebration in 1998 of the fiftieth anniversary of the Universal Declaration of Human Rights served to focus world attention on the important role the UN has played in promulgating and promoting international human rights norms and principles. It served to remind that the principles espoused in the declaration, an elaboration of the UN Charter, placed limits on governments' claims to unbridled sovereignty. According to those principles, there exist certain established standards of civilized conduct that apply to all states and that govern the relationship between governments and those over whom they rule.

Yet, in January 2003, the respected British magazine *The Economist* ran a cover story under the title, "Is torture ever justified?" This focus was a follow-up to a story in *The Washington Post* reporting that in its war on terrorism, the United States was using "stress and duress" interrogation techniques on prisoners detained in Afghanistan and at its detention facility in Guantanamo Bay, Cuba. At Guantanamo, by early 2003 there had been some twenty suicide attempts by prisoners. Moreover, according to these media sources, the United States had transferred certain prisoners to friendly states like Egypt, Morocco, and Jordan where interrogation procedures were, euphemistically speaking, harsh. Such was the effect of feelings of insecurity on internationally recognized human rights, like the total prohibition of torture in all situations. Social scientists could show that there was an inverse correlation between war and protection of many human rights, like the prohibition of torture. Indeed, after the attacks by Al Qaeda in the United States on September 11, 2001, a lawyer at Harvard University openly advocated torture as a legitimate security measure.[1]

As far as the theory of human rights is concerned, since 1945, states have used their sovereignty to create international human rights obligations that in turn have restricted their operational sovereignty. The international law of human rights, developed on a global scale at the United Nations, clearly regulates what legal policies states can adopt even within their own territorial jurisdictions. International agreements on human rights norms have been followed at least occasionally by concrete, noteworthy developments showing that international organizations have begun to reach deeply into matters that were once considered the core of national domestic affairs.

Moreover, the process by which the assumed sovereignty of the territorial state has given way to shared authority and power between the state and international organizations is not a recent phenomenon. Although there have been some dramatic recent events, movement toward promoting and protecting human rights across borders has been going on for a century and a half. These changes accelerated with the start of the United Nations in 1945, became remarkable from about 1970, and became spasmodically dramatic from about 1991. The role of the UN in human rights figures to remain one of the more provocative subjects of the twenty-first century.

Noting these historical changes concerning the United Nations and human rights is not the same as being overly optimistic about these developments. Indeed, some UN proceedings on human rights would "depress Dr. Pangloss," a fictional character from Voltaire who believed all was for the best in this ideal world.[2] Although noteworthy in historical perspective, UN activity concerning human rights often displays an enormous gap between the law on the books and the law in action. At any given time or on any given issue, state expediency may supersede the application of UN human rights standards. Revolutionary change in a given context may not be institutionalized; similar situations can give rise to different UN roles and different outcomes for human rights. Any number of states, some of them with democratic governments, have opposed progressive action for human rights at the United Nations. If the international movement for human rights means separating the individual from full state control, then this movement has not always been well received by those who rule in the name of the state and who may be primarily interested in power, wealth, and independence.

The territorial state remains the most important legal-political entity in the modern world despite the obvious importance of ethnic, religious, and cultural identifications and an increasing number of actors in civil society everywhere. Thus many ethnic and religious groups try to capture control of the government so that they can speak officially for the state. The state constitutes the basic building block of the United Nations. State actors primarily shape the UN agenda and action on human rights, although states are pushed and pulled by other actors, such as private human rights groups and UN secretariat officials. In sum, although there are striking new developments at the UN concerning human rights, in general state authorities still control the most important final decisions. Not to be too crude in our generalization, nonetheless, traditional national interests still trump individual human rights much of the time in international relations.

Accelerating and decelerating developments concerning the United Nations and human rights were in evidence in 1993 at the World Conference on Human Rights, held in Vienna. Many states reaffirmed universal human rights, but a small minority of delegations, especially from Asia and the Middle East, argued for cultural relativism in an extreme form—namely, that there were few or no universal human rights, only rights specific to various countries, regions, or cultures. Some of the delegates making arguments in favor of extreme cultural relativism were representing states that were party to numerous human rights treaties, without reservations. A large number of NGOs attended the conference and tried to focus on concrete rights violations in specific countries, but most governments wanted to deal with abstract principles, not specific violations. At the same time that the U.S. delegation took a strong stand in favor of internationally recognized human rights in general, the Clinton administration refused to provide military specialists and protective troops to conduct an investigation into war crimes, that is, into the possible mass murder of hospital patients in Serbian-controlled territory in the Balkans. These examples show that a certain diplomatic progress concerning international human rights was accompanied by much controversy and reluctance to act decisively.

Some may wish to draw a distinction between human rights and humanitarian affairs. It is true that in international law, there are two legislative histories and bodies of law: one for human rights and one for international humanitarian law—the latter pertaining to situations of armed conflict. Increasingly human rights' groups like Amnesty International and Human Rights Watch concern themselves with the part of the laws of war pertaining to civilians and detained fighters in war, not just with human rights standards in peace. So, often human rights law and humanitarian law become part of one general focus on concern for the plight of individuals.

A distinction can sometimes be made between actions supposedly undertaken because persons have a legal right to them and actions undertaken because they are humane—whether persons are fundamentally entitled to the actions or not. For example, in the diplomacy of the Conference on Security and Cooperation in Europe (CSCE) during the Cold War, some families divided by the Iron Curtain were reunited in the name of humanitarianism. The objective was to achieve a humane outcome, sidestepping debates about a right to emigrate. Likewise, some foreign assistance is provided for victims of earthquakes and other natural disasters at least in part because of humane considerations, whether or not persons have a legal right to that international assistance.

The more compelling point, however, is that a great many international actions are undertaken for mixed motives with various justifications. The UN Security Council authorized the use of force, in effect, to curtail starvation in Somalia. To some, this was a response to the codified human rights to life, adequate nutrition, and health care. To others, this was acting humanely to alleviate suffering. To more than one lawyer, this was expanding the concept of international security to include humanitarian threats so that the Security Council could respond with a binding decision. But the reality was that the United Nations was used by the international community to try to improve order and reduce starvation and malnutrition. Whether outside troops went into Somalia for reasons of human rights or humanitarian affairs was a theoretical distinction without operational significance.

In this section we refer mostly to "human rights." Sometimes we note that UN involvement in a situation is oriented toward humane outcomes, whether or not the language of human rights is employed. Internationally recognized human rights have been defined so broadly that one can rationalize almost any action designed to improve the human condition in terms of fundamental rights, if one wishes to do so. Given the extent of violence in the world, those concerned about individuals in dire straits need to be aware of international humanitarian law for armed conflicts, and the long effort to create humanitarian space in the midst of what belligerents call "military necessity."

Understanding Rights

Human rights are fundamental entitlements of persons, constituting means to the end of minimal human dignity or social justice. If persons have human rights, they are entitled to a fundamental claim that others must do, or refrain from doing, something. Since governments speaking for states are primarily responsible for order and social justice in their jurisdictions, governments are the primary targets of these personal and fundamental claims. If an individual has a right to freedom from torture, governments are obligated to respond by seeing to it that torture does not occur. If an individual has a right to adequate health care, governments are obligated to respond by seeing to it that such health care is provided, especially to those who cannot afford to purchase it in private markets.

The legal system codifies what are recognized as human rights at any point in time. The legal system, of course, recognizes many legal rights. The ones seen as most fundamental to human dignity—that is, a life worthy of being lived—are called human rights. There is a difference between fundamental human rights and other legal rights that are perhaps important but not, relatively speaking, fundamental. This theoretical distinction between fundamental and important rights can and does give rise to debate. Is access to minimal health care fundamental, and thus a human right, as the Canadian legal system guarantees? Or is that access only something that people should have if they can afford it, as the U.S. system implies? Why does the U.S. legal system recognize the legal right of a patient to sue a doctor for negligence but not allow that same person access to adequate health care as a human right?

There is even more debate about the origin of human rights outside of codification in the legal system. Legal positivists are content to accept the identification of human rights as found in the legal system. But others, especially philosophers, wish to know what are the "true" or "moral" human rights that exist independently of legal codification. Natural law theorists, for example, believe that human rights exist in natural law as provided by a supreme being. Analytical theorists believe there are moral rights associated inherently with persons; the legal system only indicates a changing view of what these moral rights are.[3] According to Michael Ignatieff, we now have human rights at home and abroad not because of philosophy but because of history. If one reads history and notes the chronic abuse of individuals by public authorities, and if one notes that those societies that accept human rights do a better job of providing for the welfare of their citizens, that is sufficient justification for human rights.[4] The point to be stressed here is that despite this long-standing debate about the ultimate origin of human rights, many societies do come to some agreement about fundamental rights, writing them into national constitutions and other basic legal instruments. As we shall see, in international society there is formal agreement on what are universal human rights at the dawn of the twenty-first century.

International Origins

When territorial states arose and became consolidated in the middle of the seventeenth century, human rights were treated, if at all, as national rather than international issues. Indeed, the core of the 1648 Peace of Westphalia, designed to end the religious wars of Europe, indicated that the territorial ruler would henceforth determine the religion of the territory. In the modern language of rights, freedom of religion, or its absence, was left to the territorial ruler. The dominant international rule was what today we call state sovereignty. Any question of human rights was subsumed under that ordering principle. It was unfortunate that the ordering principle of state sovereignty led to considerable disorder.

Later, the Americans in 1776–1787 decided to recognize human rights, and the French in 1789 attempted to do so. These revolutions had no immediate legal effect, and sometimes no immediate political effect, on other nations. In fact, many non-Western peoples and their rulers were not immediately affected by these two national revolutions, oriented as they were to definitions of what were then called "the rights of man." Many non-Western societies, such as China, continued to rely primarily on supposedly enlightened leaders for human dignity and social justice. Such leaders might be seen as limited by social or religious principles, but they were not widely seen as limited by personal rights. No such rights could be found in constitutions, which often were nonexistent anyway. In sum, in the state system human rights were mostly seen and practiced as a national, not an international, matter. Some nations recognized the basic idea of human rights and devised laws accordingly; some did not.

During the middle of the nineteenth century, Western nations, which tended to dominate much of the world at that time, were swept by a wave of international sentiment.[5] It may be true that the notion of human rights was not particularly resurrected then.[6] But growing international concern for the plight of persons without regard to nationality laid the moral foundations for a later resurrection and expansion of the notion of personal rights. Moral concern led eventually to an explosion in human rights developments.

In some ways Marxism was part of this European-based transnational concern for the individual, since Marx focused on the plight of the industrialized worker under early and crude capitalism. Marx was not a persistent and consistent champion of all individual rights, being especially critical of unbridled property rights. But early Marxism had its moral dimensions about individual suffering. Two other moral or social movements occurred about the same time and are usually cited as the earliest manifestations of internationally recognized human rights. In the 1860s, about the time Marx wrote *Das Kapital*, a Swiss businessman named Henry Dunant started what is now called the International Red Cross and Red Crescent Movement. Dunant was appalled that in the battle of Solferino (1859) in what is now Italy, which was entangled in the war for the Austrian succession, wounded soldiers were simply left on the battlefield. Armies had no adequate medical corps. European armies of that time had more veterinarians to care for horses than doctors to care for soldiers.[7] He therefore foresaw what became national Red Cross societies, and these putatively private agencies not only geared up for practical action in war but also lobbied governments for new treaties to protect sick and wounded soldiers. In 1864 the first Geneva Convention for Victims of War was concluded, providing legal protection and assistance to fighters disabled in international war.

Any comparison between Marx and Dunant should not be pushed too far; Dunant was, after all, a Christian capitalist businessman, although not a very successful one. (For those interested in trivia, Friedrich Engels was much more successful.) Yet both Marx and Dunant saw a widespread or international problem, and both devised (in very different ways) an international solution. Dunant and his successors in the Red Cross and Red Crescent Movement did not immediately use the language of human rights. They spoke in terms of governmental obligation to provide protection and assistance to victims of war. They spoke of the neutrality of medical services. Victims came to be defined not only as sick and wounded combatants but also as civilians in a war zone or under military occupation. Eventually about twenty legal instruments came to be called international humanitarian law, or the law of human rights in armed conflict. Specific treaty language aside, here was another international development from the 1860s being used to enhance human dignity on an international basis.

Still another effort in the nineteenth century to identify and correct a problem of human dignity on an international basis was the antislavery movement. By 1890 in Brussels, all the major Western states had finally signed a multilateral treaty prohibiting the African slave trade. This capped a movement that had started about the turn of the century in Britain. Just as private Red Cross organizations had pushed for protection and assistance for victims of war, so the London-based Anti-Slavery Society and other private groups pushed the British government in particular to stop the slave trade. Britain outlawed the trade in the first decade of the nineteenth century; obtained a broader, similar international agreement at the Congress of Vienna in 1815; and thereafter used the British navy to try to enforce its ban on the slave trade.

But the early resistance by the United States and other major slave-trading states was overcome only toward the end of the century. Britain was pushed by private groups and had done much. Yet an international agreement on principles and applications, reaching deeply into the European colonies in Africa, was necessary to significantly reduce this long-accepted and lucrative practice. In the twentieth century freedom from slavery, the slave trade, and slavery-like practices came to be accepted as an internationally recognized human right. Its roots lay in the transnational morality of the nineteenth century.

This trend of focusing on human need across national borders increased during the League of Nations era, although most efforts met with less than full success. How could it be otherwise in an era of fascism, militarism, nationalism, racism, and isolationism? In retrospect it was amazing that much was attempted in the name of transnational moralism and international human rights.

Efforts were made at the Versailles Conference in 1919 to write into the League of Nations Covenant rights to religious freedom and racial equality. The British even proposed a right of outside intervention into states to protect religious freedom. These proposals failed largely because of Woodrow Wilson. Despite a Japanese push for the endorsement of racial equality, the U.S. president was so adamantly against any mention of race that U.S. and UK proposals on religious freedom were withdrawn.[8] During the 1930s the League's Assembly debated the merits of an international agreement on human rights in general, but French and Polish proposals to this effect failed. Some states were opposed in principle, and some did not want to antagonize Nazi Germany, given the prevailing policy of accommodation or appeasement. Nevertheless, the language of universal human rights was appearing more and more in diplomacy. European NGOs were especially active on the subject.

More successful were efforts to codify and institutionalize labor rights. Whether to undercut the appeals of Marxist revolution, to reflect Marxist concern for labor's plight, or for other reasons, the International Labor Organisation (ILO) was created and based in Geneva alongside the League. Its tripartite membership consisted of government, labor, and management delegations, one from each member state. This structure was conducive to the approval of a series of treaties and other agreements recognizing labor rights, as well as to the development of mechanisms to monitor state practice under the treaties. The ILO thus preceded the United Nations but continued after 1945 as technically a UN agency, although one highly independent of the principal UN organs. It was one of the first international organizations to monitor internationally recognized rights within states.[9]

Although the League Covenant failed to deal with human rights in general, its Article 23 did indicate that the League should be concerned with social justice. In addition to calling for international coordination of labor policy, Article 23 called on member states to take action on such matters as "native inhabitants," "traffic in women and children," "opium and other dangerous drugs," "freedom of communications," and "the prevention and control of disease."

The League of Nations was connected to the minority treaties designed for about a dozen states after World War I in an effort to curtail the ethnic passions that had contributed to the outbreak of the Great War in the Balkans. Only a few states were legally obligated to give special rights to minorities. The system of minority treaties did not function very well under the acute nationalist pressures of the 1930s. So dismal was the League record on minority rights that global efforts at minority protection per se were not renewed by the United Nations until the 1980s—a gap of about fifty years. One UN agency carried the name Subcommission on Protection of Minorities, but it did not in fact take up the question of minority protection for some four decades. The minority treaties provided some useful experience. For instance, under certain treaty provisions individuals could directly petition the League Council, the organization's most important body, for redress of alleged treaty violations. Ironically, in 1933 the Nazis paid some compensation for early anti-Semitism, responding to individual petitions under this system.[10]

Also, the League mandate system sought to protect the welfare of dependent peoples. The Permanent Mandates Commission supervised the European states that controlled certain territories taken from the losing side in World War I. Those European states were theoretically obligated to rule for the welfare of dependent peoples. Peoples in "A" mandates were supposed to be allowed to exercise their collective right to self-determination in the relatively near future. The Permanent Mandates Commission (PMC) was made up of experts named by the League Council, and it established a reputation for integrity—so much so that the controlling states regarded it as a nuisance. There was some exercise of the right of individual petition, and the PMC publicized some of the shortcomings from the policies of mandatory powers.[11]

In other ways, too, the League of Nations tried to promote humane values—a synonym for social justice. In some cases it sought to improve the situation of persons without actually codifying their rights. In so doing it laid the foundation for later rights developments. For example, the League of Nations Refugee Office sought to help refugees, which was useful in 1951 when the UN sponsored a treaty on refugee rights.

In retrospect it seems clear enough that increased interaction among peoples, no doubt produced by changes in travel and communications technology, led in time to an increased moral solidarity—or concern for human dignity across borders. War victims increasingly were seen as entitled to certain humane treatment regardless of nationality. Slavery and the slave trade were seen as wrong regardless of what nationalities were involved. Labor was seen as needing protective regulation regardless of where the factory or shop was located. Minorities in more than one state were seen as being victimized. Developed states accepted a vague obligation to the League to rule at least some dependent territories for the good of the inhabitants. Refugees came to be seen as presenting common needs, wherever they might be found.

As one scholar has noted, these and other developments in the late nineteenth and early twentieth centuries expressed "an epochal shift in moral sentiment."[12] Another scholar wrote of the growing "moral interdependence" that was to undergird the creation of human rights "regimes" in the UN era.[13] True, this moral solidarity was not cohesive enough to eradicate many of the ills addressed. How could it be otherwise in the 1930s, when some major states (Germany, Italy, and Japan) were glorifying brutal power at the service of particular races or nationalities? One major state (the Soviet Union) had an extensive record of brutal repression and exploitation within its borders. And one major state (the United States) refused to put its putative power at the service of systematic international cooperation. Moreover, at home the United States engaged in its own version of apartheid (namely, legally sanctioned racial discrimination) as well as blatantly racist immigration laws. Thus, there might have been some shift toward a cosmopolitan morality that tended to disregard national boundaries and citizenship. But "thick morality" still centered on national communities and was subject to the disease of chauvinistic nationalism. "Thin morality" was left for international society.

Legal and organizational developments were more important as historical stepping stones than as durable solutions in and of themselves. It might be said that international moral solidarity was strong enough to create certain laws, agreements, and organizations. But states lacked sufficient political will to make these legal and organizational arrangements function effectively. Compassion did not always fit well with traditional *raisons d'état*.[14]

Nevertheless, when the United Nations was created in 1945, there was a growing corpus of legal and organizational experience that the international community could draw on in trying to improve international order and justice. By 1948, without doubt, it became conventional wisdom that internationally recognized human rights would have to be reaffirmed and expanded, not erased. There was no turning back. The UN would have to devise better ways of improving human dignity, through both law and organization.

Basic Norms in the UN Era

By the time of the San Francisco Conference in 1945, at which the Charter of the United Nations was drafted and approved, several actors believed that the new world organization would deal with universal human rights. Despite all the difficulties faced by the international community during the League period in trying to deal with the violation of human rights, European fascism and Asian militarism had convinced important actors that renewed attention should be directed to the safeguarding of human rights.

This determination to write human rights into the UN Charter, which had not been done in the League Covenant, actually preceded widespread knowledge about the extent of the Holocaust in areas under Nazi control.[15] This renewed attention to fundamental individual rights, therefore, was less a reaction to specific knowledge about German (and Japanese) atrocities and more a culmination of changing opinion that had gained momentum in the 1940s. Intellectual opinion in Britain and the United States, as well as activity by non-governmental organizations in the latter, had been pushing for an endorsement of human rights as a statement about the rationale for World War II. Franklin D. Roosevelt had stressed the importance of four freedoms, including freedom from "want." A handful of Latin American states joined in this push to emphasize human rights as a statement about civilized nations. Eleanor Roosevelt became an outspoken champion of human rights in general and women's rights in particular. In the UN Human Rights Commission, however, which Eleanor Roosevelt chaired in the 1940s, the most outspoken advocate for women's rights was the Indian representative, Hansa Mehta.

The Truman administration, under pressure from both NGOs and concerned Latin American states, and unlike the Wilson administration in 1919, agreed to a series of statements on human rights in the Charter and successfully lobbied the other victorious great powers. This was not an easy decision for the Truman administration, particularly given the continuation of legally sanctioned and widely supported racial discrimination within the United States. Whether the Truman administration was genuinely and deeply committed to getting human rights into the Charter[16] or whether it was pushed in that direction by others[17] remains a point of historical debate. There is some evidence that Truman himself genuinely believed that protecting human rights was indeed linked to a more peaceful international order.

Why Stalin accepted these human rights statements is not clear, especially given the widespread political murder and persecution within the Soviet Union in the 1930s and 1940s. Perhaps Moscow saw this human rights language as useful in deflecting criticism of Soviet policies, particularly since the Charter language was vague and not immediately followed by specifics on application. Another view is that Stalin saw the language of rights as useful in his attempt to focus on socialism—that is, one might accept the general wording on rights if one intended to concentrate only on social and economic rights.[18] This would not be the last time the Soviet Union underestimated the influence of language written into international agreements. The 1975 Helsinki Accord, and especially its provisions on human rights and humanitarian affairs, generated pressures that helped weaken European communism. The Soviet Union indeed initially resisted human rights language in the Helsinki Accord, but it eventually accepted that language in the mistaken notion that the codification and dissemination of human rights would not upset totalitarian control.[19]

The 1945 Charter statements on human rights, although more than some had originally wanted, were vague. Nevertheless, they provided the legal cornerstone or foundation for a later legal and diplomatic revolution.

The Charter's preamble states in its second clause that a principal purpose of the UN is "to affirm faith in fundamental human rights." Again, in Article 1, the Charter says that one of the purposes of the organization is to promote and encourage "respect for human rights and for fundamental freedoms for all without distinction as to race, sex, language, or religion." In Article 55, the Charter imposes on states these legal obligations:

> With a view to the creation of conditions of stability and well-being which are necessary for peaceful and friendly relations among nations based on respect for the principle of equal rights and self-determination of peoples, the United Nations shall promote:
> A. higher standards of living, full employment, and conditions of economic and social progress and development;
> B. solutions of international economic, social, health, and related problems; and international cultural and educational cooperation; and
> C. universal respect for, and observance of, human rights and fundamental freedoms for all without distinction as to race, sex, language, or religion.

This was followed by Article 56, under which "all Members pledge themselves to take joint and separate action in cooperation with the Organization for the achievement of the purposes set forth in Article 55."

The language of Article 55 would have one believe that the Charter was endorsing the notion of human rights because they were linked to international peace and security. There was considerable belief in the Western democracies that states respecting human rights in the form of civil and political rights would not make war on others. In this view, brutal authoritarian states, those that denied civil and political rights, were inherently aggressive, whereas democracies were inherently peaceful. At the same time and as previously explained, many people have accepted the notion of human rights by seeing them as a means to human dignity, not necessarily or primarily as a means to social peace.

Which of these two motivations drove the diplomatic process in 1945? The answer undoubtedly is both. Some policymakers may have genuinely seen human rights as linked to peace, and others may have accepted that rationale as a useful justification while believing that one should promote and protect human rights for reasons of human dignity disconnected from questions of peace and war. Motivation and justification are not the same,[20] but in reality it can be difficult to separate the two.

Vietnamese refugees in a detention area of Phnom Penh, Cambodia, 1992. (UN Photo 125271/J. Robaton)

The relationship between human rights and peace merits additional discussion because of its intrinsic importance to world politics. If there is a clear correlation between at least some human rights and peace, then human rights have importance not only for a direct and "micro" contribution to human dignity. Human rights may also contribute to human dignity in a "macro" sense by enhancing international—and perhaps national—security and stability by eliminating major violence.

Much research has been directed to the question of the connection between various human rights and international and national peace—with peace being defined as the absence of widespread violence between or within nations. It would seem that the following five statements accurately summarize some of that voluminous research.

First, liberal democratic governments (those that emerge from, and thereafter respect, widespread civil and political rights) tend not to engage in international war with one other.[21] It is difficult to document international war between or among democracies, although some scholars believe that the absence of war is not because of democracy. The United Kingdom and the United States fought in 1812, but one scholar holds that because of the severely limited franchise, the United States did not become a democracy until the 1820s and Britain not until the 1830s.[22] There is great debate about threshold conditions for democracy. For instance, one view is that the United States did not become a democracy until women, 50 percent of the population, gained the franchise. In the American Civil War, the Union and the Confederacy both had elected presidents, but the Confederacy was not recognized as a separate state by many outsiders, and it also severely restricted the voting franchise. At the start of World War I, Germany manifested a very broad franchise, but its parliament lacked authority and its kaiser went unchecked in making much policy. Even though some scholars think the historical absence of war between democracies is either a statistical accident or explicable by security factors, other scholars continue to strongly insist that liberal democracies do not war on each other.

Second, liberal democratic governments have used covert force against other elected governments that are not perceived to be truly in the liberal democratic community. The United States during the Cold War used force to overthrow some elected governments in developing countries—for example, Iran in 1953 (Mohammed Mossadeq was elected by Iran's parliament), Guatemala in 1954 (Jacobo Arbenz Guzman was genuinely if imperfectly elected in a popular vote), Chile in 1973 (Salvador Allende won a plurality), and Nicaragua after 1984 (some international observers regarded Daniel Ortega as genuinely if imperfectly elected).[23] Several democracies used force to remove the Patrice Lumumba government in the Congo in the 1960s; those elections, too, were imperfect but reflected popular sentiment.[24]

Third, some industrialized liberal democratic governments seem to be war-prone and clearly have initiated force against authoritarian governments. Britain, France, and the United States are among the most war-prone states, owing perhaps to their power and geography. Liberal democratic governments initiated hostilities in the Spanish-American War of 1898 and the Suez crisis of 1956, not to mention U.S. use of force in Grenada and Panama in the 1980s, or in Iraq in 2003.

Fourth, human rights of various types do not correlate clearly and easily with major national violence such as civil wars and rebellions.[25] In some of these situations a particular human rights issue may be important—for example, slavery in the American Civil War, ethnic and religious persecution in the Romanian violence of 1989, and perceived ethnic discrimination in contemporary Sri Lanka. But in other civil wars and similar intranational violence, human rights factors seemed not to be a leading cause—for example, the Russian civil war of 1917 and the Chinese civil war in the 1930s. The Universal Declaration of Human Rights (discussed further on) presents itself, in part, as a barrier to national revolution against repression. This follows the Jeffersonian philosophy that if human rights are not respected, revolution may be justified. But this linkage between human rights violations and national violence is difficult to verify as a prominent and recurring pattern. Any number of repressive and exploitative governing arrangements have lasted for a relatively long time. And various rights-protective governments have yielded under violent pressure to more authoritarian elites. There does not seem to be one generalized reason, such as human

Eleanor Roosevelt holding a Universal Declaration of Human Rights poster. (UN/DPI Photo 23783)

rights violations, economic conditions, or other factors, for intranational rebellion and civil war.

Fifth, armed conflict seems clearly to lead to an increase in human rights violations.[26] If some uncertainty remains about whether liberal democracy at home leads to a certain peace abroad, a reverse pattern does not seem open to debate. When states participate in international and internal armed conflict, there is almost always a rise in violations of rights of personal integrity and an increase in forced disappearance, torture, arbitrary arrest, and other violations of important civil rights. Human rights may or may not lead to peace, but peace is conducive to enhanced human rights.

Whether one accepts as valid a linkage between various human rights and peace—and the broad subject is certainly complex—it remains a historical fact that the UN Charter ushered in an era of lofty rhetoric about universal human rights.

Core Norms Beyond the Charter

The UN Charter presented the interesting situation of codifying a commitment to human rights before there was an international definition or list of human rights. To answer the question of what internationally recognized human rights states are obligated to apply, the United Nations in its early years made an effort to specify Charter principles. On December 10, 1948—now recognized as International Human Rights

Day—the General Assembly adopted the Universal Declaration of Human Rights without a negative vote (but with eight abstentions: the USSR and its allies, Saudi Arabia, and South Africa). This resolution, not legally binding at the time of adoption, listed thirty human rights principles. They fell into three broad clusters.[27]

First-Generation Negative Rights

First-generation negative rights are the civil and political rights that are well-known in the West, called "first-generation" because they were the ones first endorsed in national constitutions and called "negative" because civil rights in particular blocked public authority from interfering with the private person in civil society. These were the rights to freedom of thought, speech, religion, privacy, and assembly–plus the right to participate in the making of public policy. In the view of some observers, these are the only true human rights. In the view of others, these are the most important human rights because if one has civil and political rights one can use them to obtain and apply the others. In the view of still others, these rights are not so important because if one lacks the material basics of life such as food, shelter, health care, and education, civil and political rights become meaningless.

Second-Generation Positive Rights

Second-generation positive rights are the socioeconomic rights emphasized, rhetorically at least, mostly outside the West.[28] They are called "second-generation" because they were associated with various twentieth-century revolutions emphasizing material benefits, and "positive" because they obligated public authority to take positive steps to ensure minimal food, shelter, and health care. As indicated previously, there is considerable debate as to how important they are. In the United States, the Democratic Carter and Clinton administrations accepted them in theory and gave them some rhetorical attention. Republican administrations from Ronald Reagan to George W. Bush rejected them as dangerous to individual responsibility and leading to big government.

Third-Generation Solidarity Rights

Third-generation solidarity rights are the group of rights emphasized at least rhetorically by some contemporary actors, called "third-generation" because they followed the other two clusters and called "solidarity" because they supposedly pertain to collections of persons rather than to individuals. Later formulations have included claims to a right to peace, development, and a healthy environment as the common heritage of humankind.

This tripartite breakdown, although perhaps useful to summarize developments, can be overdone. And the increasing trend, pushed especially by Mary Robinson, the former president of Ireland, who stepped down in September 2002 as the High

TABLE 5.1   UN Human Rights Conventions, December 2002

Convention (grouped by subject)	Year opened for ratification	Year entered into force	Number of ratifications, accessions, acceptances (December 2002)
General Human Rights			
International Covenant on Civil and Political Rights	1966	1976	149
Optional Protocol to the International Covenant on Civil and Political Rights (private petition)	1966	1976	104
Second Optional Protocol to the International Covenant on Civil and Political Rights (abolition of death penalty)	1989	1991	49
International Covenant on Economic, Social and Cultural Rights	1966	1976	146
Racial Discrimination			
International Convention on the Elimination of All Forms of Racial Discrimination	1966	1969	165
International Convention on the Suppression and Punishment of the Crime of Apartheid	1973	1976	110
International Convention Against Apartheid in Sports	1985	1988	58
Rights of Women			
Convention on the Political Rights of Women	1953	1954	115
Convention on the Nationality of Married Women	1957	1958	70
Convention on Consent to Marriage, Minimum Age for Marriage, and Registration of Marriages	1962	1964	49
Convention on the Elimination of All Forms of Discrimination Against Women	1979	1981	170
Optional Protocol to the Convention on the Elimination of All Forms of Discrimination Against Women (communication procedures)	1999	2000	47

Convention (grouped by subject)	Year opened for ratification	Year entered into force	Number of ratifications, accessions, acceptances (December 2002)
Slavery and Related Matters			
Slavery Convention of 1926, as amended in 1953	1953	1955	59
Protocol Amending the 1926 Slavery Convention	1953	1953	59
Supplementary Convention on the Abolition of Slavery, the Slave Trade, and Institutions and Practices Similar to Slavery	1956	1957	119
Convention for the Suppression of the Traffic in Persons and the Exploitation of the Prostitution of Others	1950	1951	74
Refugees and Stateless Persons			
Convention Relating to the Status of Refugees	1951	1954	140
Protocol Relating to the Status of Refugees (extends time of original convention)	1967	1967	138
Convention Relating to the Status of Stateless Persons	1954	1960	54
Convention on the Reduction of Statelessness	1961	1975	26
Other			
Convention on the Prevention and Punishment of the Crime of Genocide	1948	1951	133
Convention on the International Right of Correction	1952	1962	15
Convention on the Non-Applicability of Statutory Limitations of War Crimes and Crimes Against Humanity	1968	1970	45
Convention Against Torture and Other Cruel, Inhuman, or Degrading Treatment or Punishment	1984	1987	132
Convention on the Rights of the Child	1989	1989	191
Optional Protocol to the Convention on the Rights of the Child (on the Involvement of Children in Armed Conflict)	2000	2002	42
Optional protocol to the Convention on the Rights of the Child (on the Sale of Children, Child Prostitution, and Child Pornography)	2000	2002	42

Commissioner for Human Rights (UNHCHR), is that first-, second-, and third-generation rights should be viewed as a "package." [29] To apply negative rights, positive action must be taken. The U.S. Department of Justice spends billions each year to see that civil and political rights are respected. Second-generation socioeconomic rights were emphasized very early by the Catholic Church and relatively early by the state of Ireland and various Latin American states. Collective rights can also pertain to individuals. Moreover, they are not so new. The right to national self-determination is actually a right of peoples or nations that has been (a vague) part of international law for decades.

It is clear, however, that the United States is an outlier among states that traditionally support human rights. It has not ratified three of six core treaties—the ones protecting economic, cultural, and social rights, children's rights, and eliminating discrimination against women. Within the G-7, the United States is the only country that has not ratified any of these. This is especially problematic because the treaties create a common basis for a discussion between industrialized countries of the North and most developing countries in the Global South.

In any event, just three years after the UN Charter came into legal effect, the General Assembly agreed on a list of human rights principles as a statement of aspirations. No state voting for the Universal Declaration of Human Rights succeeded in meeting all its terms through national legislation and practice. This vote was the homage that vice paid to virtue. As readers are no doubt aware, this would not be the last time that state diplomacy presented a large measure of hypocrisy.

Since that time, the Universal Declaration of Human Rights has acquired a status beyond the normal or regular General Assembly recommendation. Some national courts have held that parts of the declaration have passed into customary international law and thus became legally binding. This seems to be the case, for example, with the declaration's Article 5, prohibiting torture. The overall legal status of the declaration is unclear. Some authorities and publicists believe the entire declaration is now legally binding, whereas others say this is true only of parts of it. The International Court of Justice in the Hague has not rendered an opinion on this question.[30]

The broad impact of the declaration has been considerable. Its principles have been endorsed in numerous national constitutions and other legal and quasi-legal documents. All the new or newly independent European states that once had communist governments accepted its principles in theory in the 1990s, which is not necessarily the same as applying those principles in fact. Of the eight states abstaining in 1948, seven had renounced their abstention by 1993. Only Saudi Arabia continued to object openly to the declaration. Even China, despite its repressive policies and government, issued statements accepting the abstract validity of the universal declaration.

Having adopted the declaration, parties in the United Nations then turned to an even more specific elaboration of internationally recognized human rights. The decision was made to negotiate two separate core human rights treaties, one on civil and political rights and one on social, economic, and cultural rights. This was not done only, or even primarily, because of theoretical or ideological differences among states. The different types of rights also were seen as requiring different types of follow-up. A widely held view was that civil-political rights could be implemented immediately,

The Palais des Nations, UN Office at Geneva. (UN/DPI Photo/P. Klee)

given sufficient political will, and were enforceable by judicial proceedings. By comparison, socioeconomic rights were seen as requiring certain policies over time, as greatly affected by economic and social factors, and hence as not subject to immediate enforcement by court order. As mentioned earlier, the more recent approach within the United Nations, especially in the General Assembly, is to blur distinctions and consider rights comprehensively.

By 1956 two UN covenants, or multilateral treaties, were essentially complete on the two clusters of rights. By 1966 they were formally approved by states voting in the General Assembly, the time lag indicating that not all states were enthusiastic about the emergence of human rights treaties limiting state sovereignty. By 1976 the sufficient number of state adherences had been obtained to bring the treaties into legal force by parties giving their formal consent. By 2003 almost 150 states were parties to the two covenants: the UN Covenant on Economic, Social, and Cultural Rights (146) and the UN Covenant on Civil and Political Rights (149). Few followed the example of the United States of accepting one but rejecting the other (the United States became a party to the civil-political covenant in 1992, with reservations, but not to the socioeconomic covenant). Most states accepted both covenants.

By 2003 more than fifty states (not including the United States) had agreed that their citizens had the right to petition the UN Human Rights Committee (after recourse to national efforts) alleging a violation of the civil-political covenant by a government. The Human Rights Committee was made up of individual experts, not governmental representatives. It was not a court but a mediation service that could direct negative publicity toward an offending and recalcitrant government. It worked to prod governments toward fulfilling their international commitments. All states that accepted the socioeconomic covenant were automatically supervised by a UN Committee of Experts. After a slow start, that committee, too, began a systematic effort to persuade states to honor their commitments. The mechanisms of both committees are treated below.

These three documents, the 1948 Universal Declaration of Human Rights and the two 1966 UN covenants, make up the International Bill of Rights, a core list of internationally recognized human rights. Most of the treaty provisions are clarifications of, and elaborations on, the thirty norms found in the declaration. There are a few discrepancies. The declaration notes a right to private property, but this right was not codified in the two covenants. After the fall of European communism, the General Assembly on several occasions returned to a recognition of property rights. As already noted, there was a broad and formal acceptance of this International Bill of Rights. At the same time, a number of governments were tardy in filing reports with both the Human Rights Committee under the civil-political covenant and the Committee of Experts under the socioeconomic covenant. But from either 1966 or 1976, depending on which date is emphasized, there was a core definition of universal human rights in legally binding form with a monitoring process designed to specify what the treaties meant.

Supplementing the Core

During most of the UN era, states were willing to endorse abstract human rights. But until the 1990s, they were not willing to create specialized human rights courts—or even to make the global treaties enforceable through national courts. In the next chapter we address ad hoc international criminal courts for former Yugoslavia and Rwanda and the movement toward a permanent international criminal court with broad jurisdiction, as well as the Pinochet case from Chile involving national action concerning torture and other crimes against humanity. Traditionally, in the absence of dependable adjudication, states tried to reinforce the International Bill of Rights, while protecting their legal independence, by negotiating more human rights treaties. This is a way to bring diplomatic emphasis to a problem, to raise awareness of a problem, or to further specify state obligation in the hopes that specificity will improve behavior. The process is similar to some aspects of national law. In the United States, if the Congress is dissatisfied with executive performance under a law, rather than seek adjudication in the courts, an action that frequently is unproductive, the Congress will pass a more specific follow-up law.[31]

As of 2003, about 100 international human rights instruments exist. These include conventions, protocols, declarations, codes of conduct, and formal statements of standards and basic principles. Table 5.1 summarizes the situation. Despite overlap, duplication, and sometimes inconsistency with the International Bill of Rights, the United Nations has seen the emergence of treaties on racial discrimination, apartheid, political rights of women, discrimination against women, slavery, the slave trade and slavery-like practices, genocide, hostages, torture, the nationality of married women, stateless persons, refugees, marriage, prostitution, children, and discrimination in education. The International Labor Organization has sponsored treaties on forced labor, the right to organize, and rights to collective bargaining, among others.

Some regional human rights treaties fall outside the domain of the UN, as do some treaties on human rights in armed conflict that are sponsored by the International Committee of the Red Cross (ICRC) and Switzerland, which is the official depository for what is called "international humanitarian law" (IHL). So diplomatic events, especially related to IHL, technically outside the UN, ran in the same direction of further specifying international standards on human rights and humanitarian affairs.

In 1949 the international community adopted four conventions for victims of war. Initially drafted by the ICRC, the Geneva Conventions of August 1949 sought to codify and improve on the humanitarian practices undertaken during World War II. For the first time in history, a treaty was directed to the rights of civilians in international armed conflict and in occupied territory resulting from armed conflict. Each of the four Geneva Conventions of 1949 contained an article (hence Common Article 3) that extended written humanitarian law into internal armed conflict. The ICRC, although technically a Swiss private association, was given the right in public international law to see detainees resulting from international armed conflict.[32] And for the first time in history, civilians in occupied territory were given a right to humanitarian assistance.

This body of humanitarian law, from one point of view the international law for human rights in armed conflict, was further developed in 1977 through two protocols (or additional treaties): Protocol I for international armed conflict and Protocol II for internal armed conflict. Normative standards continued to evolve. For example, for the first time in the history of warfare, Protocol I prohibited the starvation of civilians as a legal means of warfare. Protocol II represented the first separate treaty on victims in internal war.

There were also notable regional human rights developments. A regional human rights regime was created in Western Europe, and it served as an excellent model for the international protection of human rights. The European Convention on Human Rights and Fundamental Freedoms defined a set of civil and political rights. The European Commission on Human Rights served for a time as a collective conciliator, responding to state or private complaints to seek out-of-court settlements. The European Court of Human Rights eventually existed to give binding judgments about the legality of state policies under the European Convention on Human Rights.

All states in the Council of Europe bound themselves to abide by the convention. All governments allowed their citizens to have the right of individual petition to the commission, a body that could then—failing a negotiated agreement—take the petition to the European Court of Human Rights. All states eventually accepted the supranational authority of the court. Its judgments holding state policies illegal were voluntarily complied with by member states. Such was the political consensus in support of human rights within the Council of Europe. This regional international regime for human rights functioned through international agencies made up of unin-

UNICEF supplies the Zarghuna Girls School with educational supplies, teachers' training, and assists in repairing the infrastructure. (UN/DPI Photo/E. Debede)

structed individuals rather than state officials—although there was also a Committee of Ministers made up of state representatives.

In the mid-1990s, Council of Europe members progressively moved toward giving individuals standing to sue in the European Court of Human Rights without having the commission represent them. Thus an individual would have almost the same legal "personality" or status in the court as a state. Persons came to acquire both substantive and procedure rights of note, a distinctive feature, since formerly it was possible to present a case—or have full "personality," in the language of international lawyers—only as a state.

In fact, the European system for the international protection of civil and political rights under the European Human Rights Convention generated such a large number of cases that, to streamline procedure, the commission was done away with. Individuals were allowed to proceed directly to a lower chamber of the International Court for an initial review of the admissibility of their complaint. If the complaint met procedural requirements, the individual could then move on to the substantive phase, basically on an equal footing with state representatives. There were other regional human rights regimes in the Western Hemisphere and Africa, but they did not match the West European record in successfully protecting human rights.

A number of supplemental human rights treaties are in varying stages of negotiation at the United Nations at the time of writing, including those on indigenous peoples and minorities. A collective right to development has been declared by various

UN bodies, including the General Assembly, and may become the subject matter of a treaty.

There has been an explosion of diplomatic activity concerning setting human rights standards internationally. There is an already sizable, and still expanding, part of international law dealing with human rights. Human rights have been formally accepted as a legitimate part of international relations. Most states do not oppose these normative developments in the abstract—that is, they do not dispute that international law should regulate the rights of persons even when persons are within states in "normal" times. This generalization also pertains to international or internal armed conflict, and to public emergency—although some rights protections can be modified in these exceptional situations. The United Nations clearly is acting within accepted bounds in establishing human rights standards. For ease of reference, Table 5.1 contains a list of human rights that are generally accepted to be protected under international law.

One of the themes that appears in Part Three of this volume is globalization, but it is worth noting here that this phenomenon—which means many things to many people—represents a powerful challenge to integrate human rights more effectively into efforts to ensure a values-led globalization process. Upon her resignation from the UN, former High Commissioner for Human Rights Mary Robinson founded the Ethical Globalization Initiative to pursue her agenda.[33] The progressive integration of economies and societies, a helpful definition formed by the ILO's World Commission on the Social Dimensions of Globalization,[34] has generated uneven benefits. While an academic debate continues about whether globalization is new,[35] its costs are borne unevenly. Future human rights challenges include the need for global policies to address a host of problems, including human rights, that emerge from such global problems as transnational criminal and terrorist activities, human trafficking, and HIV/AIDS.

As noted in Part One, the Permanent Court of International Justice, the first embodiment of the World Court, said in the early 1920s that what is international and what is domestic changes with the changing nature of international relations.[36] The UN era has clearly seen the shrinking of the zone of exclusive or essential domestic jurisdiction. Article 2, paragraph 7, mandates that the UN shall not "intervene" in matters "essentially" within the domestic jurisdiction of states. The diplomatic record confirms, however, that most human rights matters are no longer viewed by most states as essentially within domestic jurisdiction. Certainly the establishment of international standards on human rights cannot logically be considered an unlawful intrusion into state internal affairs. And as noted in Part One and as will be confirmed in the next chapter, if the Security Council decides that international peace and security are threatened, even UN "intervention"—in the sense of forcible or coercive action—can be taken to rectify human rights violations.

As the extensive standard-setting activity of particularly the UN has made clear, at least in legal theory, human rights have been internationalized. Beyond standard setting, an answer is emerging to the ancient question: *Quis custodiet ipsos custodes?* (Who shall guard the guardians?) In the field of human rights, the United Nations will supervise governmental policy against the background of global norms.

Notes

1. Dana Priest and Barton Gellman, "For CIA Suspects Abroad, Brass-Knuckle Treatment," *Washington Post,* December 27, 2002, www.iht.com/articles/81546.html. This article generated virtually no reaction in official Washington. Compare "Is torture ever justified?" *The Economist,* January 11–17, 2003, www.econmist.com. The Harvard lawyer Alan Dershowitz defended some use of torture in a debate with Kenneth Roth of Human Rights Watch on NBC, "Today Show," March 4, 2003.

2. Tom J. Farer, "The UN and Human Rights: More than a Whimper, Less than a Roar," in Adam Roberts and Benedict Kingsbury, eds., *United Nations, Divided World* (New York: Oxford University Press, Clarendon Paperback, second edition, 1993), p. 129.

3. Jack Donnelly, *Universal Human Rights in Theory and Practice* (Ithaca, N.Y.: Cornell University Press, second edition, 2003), pp. 7–21.

4. Michael Ignatieff, *Human Rights as Politics and Idolatry* (Princeton: Princeton University Press, 2001).

5. John F. Hutchinson, "Rethinking the Origins of the Red Cross," *Bulletin of Historical Medicine* 63, pp. 557–578. See also his *Champions of Charity: War and the Rise of the Red Cross* (Boulder: Westview Press, 1996).

6. Jan Herman Burgers, "The Road to San Francisco: The Revival of the Human Rights Idea in the Twentieth Century," *Human Rights Quarterly* 14, no.2 (1992), pp. 447–478.

7. François Bugnion, *Le Comité International de la Croix-Rouge et la protection des victims de la guerre* (Geneva: ICRC, 1994). An English edition is forthcoming. For an overview, see Edwin M. Smith, "The Law of War and Humanitarian War: A Turbulent Vista," *Global Governance* 9, no.1 (January–March 2003), pp. 115-134. For documents with an introduction see Adam Roberts and Richard Guelff, eds., *Documents on the Laws of War* (Oxford: Oxford University Press, 2001).

8. Paul Gordon Lauren, *Power and Prejudice: The Politics and Diplomacy of Racial Discrimination* (Boulder: Westview Press, 1988), pp. 76–101; Burgers, "Road to San Francisco," p. 449.

9. Ernst Haas, *Human Rights and International Action* (Stanford: Stanford University Press, 1970). See further Hector G. Bartolomei de la Cruz, et al., *The International Labor Organization: The International Standards System and Basic Human Rights* (Boulder: Westview Press, 1996).

10. Burgers, "Road to San Francisco," p. 456.

11. Neta Crawford, *Argument and Change in World Politics: Ethics, Decolonization, and Humanitarian Intervention* (Cambridge: Cambridge University Press, 2002). She argues that the League PMC was important over time in the effort to delegitamize colonialism.

12. Farer, "UN and Human Rights," p. 97.

13. Jack Donnelly, "International Human Rights: A Regime Analysis," *International Organization* 40, no. 3 (Summer 1985), pp. 599–642.

14. Farer, "UN and Human Rights," p. 98.

15. See Burgers, "Road to San Francisco."

16. Cathal J. Nolan, *Principled Diplomacy: Security and Rights in U.S. Foreign Policy* (Westport, Conn.: Greenwood Press, 1993), pp. 181–202.

17. Burgers, "Road to San Francisco," p. 475.

18. See Nolan, *Principled Diplomacy.*

19. See further Daniel C. Thomas, *The Helsinki Effect: International Norms, Human Rights, and the Demise of Communism* (Princeton: Princeton University Press, 2001); and William

Korey, *The Promises We Keep: Human Rights, the Helsinki Process, and American Foreign Policy* (New York: St. Martin's Press, 1993).

20. Robert W. Tucker and David C. Hendrickson, *The Imperial Temptation: The New World Order and America's Purpose* (New York: Council on Foreign Relations Press, 1992), p. 86.

21. See, among others, Bruce Russett, "Politics and Alternative Security: Toward a More Democratic, Therefore More Peaceful World," in Burns Weston, ed., *Alternative Security: Living Without Nuclear Deterrence* (Boulder: Westview Press, 1990), pp. 107–136.

22. Samuel P. Huntington, *The Third Wave: Democratization in the Late Twentieth Century* (Norman: University of Oklahoma Press, 1991).

23. David P. Forsythe, "Democracy, War, and Covert Action," *Journal of Peace Research* 29 no. 4, pp. 385–396.

24. David N. Gibbs, *The Political Economy of Third World Intervention: Mines, Money, and US Policy in the Congo Crisis* (Chicago: University of Chicago Press, 1991).

25. David P. Forsythe, *Human Rights and Peace: International and National Dimensions* (Lincoln: University of Nebraska Press, 1993).

26. Steven C. Poe and C. Neal Tate, "Repression of Human Rights to Personal Integrity in the 1980s: A Global Analysis," *American Political Science Review* 88, no. 4 (December 1994), pp. 853–872.

27. See further Johannes Morsink, *The Universal Declaration of Human Rights: Origins, Drafting and Intent* (Philadelphia: University of Pennsylvania Press, 1999); and Mary Ann Glendon, *A World Made New: Eleanor Roosevelt and the Universal Declaration of Human Rights* (New York: Random House, 2001).

28. For recent discussions about taking these rights seriously, see William F. Felice, *The Global New Deal: Economic and Social Human Rights in World Politics* (Lanham, Md.: Rowman & Littlefield, 2003); and A Belden Fields, *Rethinking Human Rights for the New Millennium* (New York: Palgrave, 2003).

29. This is the theme of UNDP, *Human Development Report 2000* (New York: Oxford University Press, 2000).

30. See Hurst Hannum, "The Status of the Universal Declaration of Human Rights in National and International Law," *Georgia Journal of International and Comparative Law* 25 (1995–1996), pp. 287–397.

31. David P. Forsythe, *Human Rights and U.S. Foreign Policy: Congress Reconsidered* (Gainesville: University Press of Florida, 1988).

32. To better establish its independence, the ICRC and the government of Switzerland signed a headquarters agreement protecting its premises and personnel from review or intrusion by Swiss authorities, as if the ICRC were an intergovernmental organization. The ICRC seems neither fully public nor fully private, legally speaking; rather it is *sui generis* (or unique or in a category by itself). See David P. Forsythe, *The Humanitarians: The International Committee of the Red Cross,* forthcoming.

33. See http://www.eginitiative.org.

34. See http://www.ILO.org/public/english/wcsdg/index.htm.

35. See David Held and Anthony McGrew, David Goldblatt, and Jonathan Perraton, *Global Transformation: Politics, Economics and Culture* (Palo Alto, Calif.: Stanford University Press, 1999); James P. Muldoon et al., *Multilateral Diplomacy and the United Nations Today* (Boulder: Westview Press, 1999); and James Rosenau and Ernst-Otto Czempiel, eds., *Governance without Government* (Cambridge: Cambridge University Press, 1992).

36. Nationality Decrees in Tunis and Morocco, Permanent Court of International Justice, Series B, no. 4, *World Court Report*, p. 143.

6 The United Nations and Applying Human Rights Standards

A variety of offices and agencies within the UN system are active in trying to see that the norms of internationally recognized human rights are applied by states and other actors.[1] States that are members of the UN, through their governmental authorities, have primary responsibility in this regard. Individuals and private groups may have obligations in the field of human rights, and non-governmental actors may play a large role at the UN. But under international law governments are legally obligated to make national law and practice consistent with international agreements.

Where application of rights means protection, the function of the UN system is usually indirect. This means that UN organizations normally try to encourage, push, prod, and ultimately embarrass states into taking steps to guarantee the proper practice of rights. UN organizations normally begin to seek protection through positive steps of encouragement and then gradually shift to more critical stances. There also is a small human rights assistance program that takes a cooperative approach to improving rights protection. On occasion the Security Council authorizes outside parties to undertake direct protection, and it is possible for UN officials themselves to engage in direct protection. We return to these points in the conclusion to this section.

The overall UN process of helping to apply international human rights standards is exceedingly broad and complex. The structure of the main organizational components underpinning that process is illustrated in Figure 6.1. One fundamental point is that UN diplomacy for human rights may be considered to be a type of informal education or socialization, in which one hopes to "teach" new attitudes that benefit individuals. The desired attitude change may take a long time.[2] Another fundamental point is that the United Nations is extensively engaged in supervising state behavior under international standards on human rights. Actors concerned with other aspects of international relations—for example, sustainable development, as we see in the third part of this volume—are still trying to achieve the extent of international supervision (although not necessarily all its manifestations) already achieved in the field of human rights.

The Security Council

As explained in Part One of this book, the Security Council has the authority to declare a situation a threat to or a breach of the peace. When the council so declares,

154

FIGURE 6.1 UN Human Rights Organizational Structure

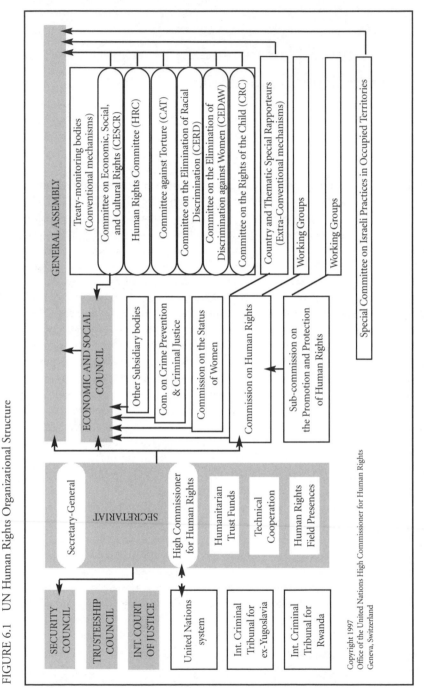

SOURCE: United Nations High Commissioner for Human Rights, website: http://www.unhchr.ch/hrostr.htm

it can invoke Chapter VII of the Charter and reach a "decision" binding on all states. Such decisions can entail economic or military action. On several occasions the Security Council has linked a human rights situation to a threat to or breach of the peace or it has otherwise reached a legally binding decision declaring that economic or military steps are needed to correct a human rights problem. As long as the council links human rights to security issues, it has a broad mandate to act under Chapter VII. Despite the initial concerns of several states, the council in 1993 referred to Chapter VII to create a war-crimes tribunal for the former Yugoslavia. Later it created a similar court for Rwanda and Sierra Leone. The war-crimes tribunals after World War II, in Germany and Japan, had been created by separate treaty and military executive order, respectively, not by the UN Security Council.

These binding council decisions under Chapter VII are in addition to the more usual advisory resolutions that, although not directly and legally binding on states, may generate some influence for human rights. As we noted in Part One, in 1989 the council created the UN Transition Assistance Group in Namibia (UNTAG) to oversee the transition to statehood. Among its other duties, UNTAG engaged in the verification of free and fair elections, and thus of the human right to participation in governing arrangements. From a legalistic view, the suggestive council resolutions were not legally binding on states, although they were binding on other UN organs and agencies.

Similarly, the Security Council created a UN commission to collect information about war crimes being committed in the Balkans. Once again, this resolution was not legally binding on states, although it was binding on the rest of the UN system. It has always been true that, in the theory of the Charter, the council would recommend actions, but these recommendations were to be seen against the background of possible further binding action under Chapter VII. Hence, theory has become operational in several situations pertaining to human rights.

Action by the Security Council under Chapter VII shows the maximum concern for human rights expressed through the United Nations. During the Cold War, only two situations led to the invocation of Chapter VII concerning human rights; both pertained to white-minority rule in southern Africa. We emphasized earlier the coercive aspects of sanctions; here we stress the rationale behind them, namely, the protection of basic human rights.

In 1966, followed by more comprehensive action in 1968, the Security Council voted mandatory economic sanctions on the Ian Smith government of what was then southern Rhodesia. The 1968 resolution mentioned the human rights situation as one justification for the sanctions. Another justification responded to illegal secession from the United Kingdom. These sanctions remained in effect until 1979, when majority rule was obtained in the new state of Zimbabwe. Although the sanctions were too gradual and porous to have been the only cause of the fall of white-minority rule in Rhodesia, they were the first attempt at UN collective economic measures—of a mandatory nature—at least partly in the name of human rights.

In 1977 the Security Council voted a mandatory arms embargo on the Republic of South Africa. Human rights were not explicitly mentioned, only "the situation in South Africa," but the basic issues of concern to the international community were apartheid, the denial of a people's right to self-determination, and majority rule—all defined as human rights issues in international law. The arms embargo, although perhaps manifesting some symbolic value, was too limited and again too porous to end apartheid by itself. It was one element among many that led to progressive change in South Africa by the 1990s.

After the end of the Cold War, the Security Council expanded the use of Chapter VII in relation to human rights, and the rest of this section provides a rights-focused summary of developments already discussed more generally. In the spring of 1991, after the Persian Gulf War, known as Operation Desert Storm, the council declared that the international repercussions of the human rights situation in Iraq, especially pertaining to the Iraqi Kurds, constituted a threat to international peace and security. Iraqi Kurds were fleeing into both Iran and Turkey to escape repression, although international armed conflict among states was not imminent over this migration. This was the first explicit declaration by the council that violating human rights created a security threat, since the resolutions on both Rhodesia and South Africa had been vague.

The Security Council did not expressly authorize the use of force to stop Iraqi repression of its citizens, but several states claimed that the council had implicitly authorized force for that purpose. Led by the United States, these states created a protected area for Iraqi Kurds in northern Iraq. Air power was later used in southern Iraq, arguably for the protection of Iraqi Shiites then being repressed by the government, again with the claim that the council had implicitly approved such force. These claims were never authoritatively evaluated.

Three "political" factors were crucial in the evolution of events: the overall weakness of the Iraqi government after its widely condemned and unsuccessful invasion of Kuwait in 1990, continuing U.S. commitment against the various policies of Saddam Hussein, and widespread deference to the United States as the only global military superpower. The United States in the Security Council was widely seen as being tough on Iraq, but not so tough on some other states, such as Israel, concerning implementation of equally demanding council resolutions linked to human rights and international humanitarian law.

In the Balkans following the breakup of greater Yugoslavia, the Security Council, apart from its other actions, authorized the use of "all necessary means" for the delivery of humanitarian assistance in Bosnia. The initial UN peacekeeping forces were deployed under Chapter VI; humanitarian assistance was treated under Chapter VII. Once again, the diplomatic language "all necessary means" was a euphemism for authorizing military force.

In spite of this authorizing language, the lengthy discussion in Chapter 3 made clear that UN member states remained more reluctant to use force in Bosnia than in the Persian Gulf without the expressed consent of the various fighting parties. Member states' officials, including those in the United States, feared a complex and open-ended involvement in the Balkans that might come to resemble the Vietnam War. The cases of Rhodesia, South Africa, and Iraq showed that the council could link human rights violations to international peace and security. Although the Security Council declared the same linkage in Bosnia's case, it was evident that the council might be extremely cautious about implementing what it had declared when the military costs were high. In other words, the costs of enforcement carried weight in considering whether to insist upon respect for agreed-upon standards of human rights.

Likewise, when the council adopted resolutions on the question of Balkan war crimes and related atrocities, the resolutions looked at least for a time more like diplomatic bluff than like strong political will to stop such gross violations of human rights as genocide, political murder, and the use of rape as a political weapon. Even systematic rape as a weapon of war and of ethnic cleansing did not motivate the Security Council to decisive action. Information was collected for possible war crimes prosecutions, but initially there was no permanent international criminal court to which that information could be submitted. In early 1993 the Security Council resolved to create such an international court strictly for the armed conflict in the Balkans, but a number of major hurdles remained. The number of suspects was great. The international community did not have physical custody of most of them. A paper trail proving violations of international law was needed that would stand up in court. Moreover, parties seeking a negotiated solution to the political and humanitarian problems of the area needed cooperation from some of the persons identified as potential war criminals.[3]

Political factors had encouraged the Security Council to break new ground concerning human rights in Iraq. But different political factors led to caution by the council in dealing with the Balkans. The council endorsed the Dayton agreements, after which NATO deployed some 60,000 troops, including approximately 20,000 Americans, to constitute IFOR—the Implementation Force. Although this military deployment helped end the fighting and secured the disengagement of fighting parties, IFOR was reluctant at first to use force to try to arrest indicted war criminals or to secure the safe return of refugees and displaced persons. Both of these human rights objectives were written into the Dayton accords but were not pursued rigorously.

Initially in Somalia in 1992, in the context of extensive coverage of the situation by the Western communications media, the council authorized "all necessary means" to create "a secure environment" for the delivery of humanitarian relief. In addition, the council declared that in that "unique" situation—referring to the chaos that constituted the absence of sovereignty—civilians had a right to humanitarian assistance. Anyone blocking delivery of that assistance would be committing a war crime for which there was individual responsibility. Under this path-breaking resolution, some 37,000 troops—mostly from the United States—were deployed in Somalia to maintain the order necessary to feed starving civilians. As a result of Security Council Resolution 814, the United Nations took control of this operation with 28,000 of its own blue helmets in May 1993. This was the first Chapter VII military operation under actual command and control of the United Nations.

The primary political factors encouraging these developments in Somalia were not only media coverage and exhortations from the UN Secretary-General but also the absence of a national government, which had disintegrated into a multi-sided civil war approaching anarchy. Moreover, the costs of the undertaking were judged by military establishments, perhaps mistakenly, to be reasonable. The international community, including developing countries prone to defend the traditional notion of state sovereignty, found it easier to act when there was no national government whose consent was being bypassed. And from the viewpoint of the developed countries, the local armed factions, unlike perhaps in the Balkans, were clearly no match for Western military forces.

From these events it was obvious that the Security Council might authorize direct protection for persons such as the Kurds in Iraq or millions of civilians in southern Somalia. International peace and security could mean not just the security of states from foreign attack but also the security of persons inside states. The International Court of Justice (ICJ) would seem to have the right to review such council determinations in the light of the wording of the Charter and other parts of international law.[4] The ICJ had not done so on human rights or humanitarian issues. So the linkage between human rights and a security question was whatever the council said it was. There existed no agreed-upon criteria in the 1990s for coercion to enforce human rights or humanitarian law; such actions reflected what the international political traffic would bear.

In Somalia, there was not much risk of international violence, or even much international disruption outside the country. Yet the Security Council still invoked Chapter VII and passed Resolution 794, which ordered fighting parties to resolve their differences and permit humanitarian assistance. In reality, the council was applying Chapter VII to an internal conflict with primary emphasis on humanitarian action. This application has led some observers to conclude that the Security Council was developing, after 1990 and especially in Somalia, a doctrine of truly humanitarian intervention apart from issues of international peace and security.[5] Formally, however, the council asserted not a right of forcible humanitarian intervention per se but a right to respond to situations that it said threatened international peace and security. Likewise, the council did not formally elevate the notion of human security inside states to a level equal with traditional interstate security. But thinking about human security, and especially the protection of civilians, informed council decisions.[6]

Likewise in Haiti in 1994, the council labeled the situation a threat to international peace. The situation clearly did not involve a threat of attack on any other state by the weak authoritarian government. Rather, the most pressing international issue was the flight of asylum seekers to the United States, which stemmed from an abusive national regime that also failed to promote sustainable development. Once the council authorized the use of all necessary means to restore democracy, the United States was in a strong position to threaten the use of force. The reactionary rulers eventually agreed to yield peacefully, and migration to the United States was greatly reduced. A bevy of UN and other agencies subsequently tried to consolidate the fragile democracy in Haiti. The situation by 2003 seemed an improvement over pre–1994, but many problems regarding human rights remained.

The actual external agents of outside protection for Iraq, Somalia, the Balkans, and Haiti, for example, were states, through their military establishments. The Security Council played an authorizing role, but a very minor operational role. The delivery of assistance under the aegis of the International Red Cross and Red Crescent Movement, which was a form of guaranteeing socioeconomic human rights, initially went well in Somalia. But the Balkans showed equally clearly that some situations did not

Haitians take to the streets of Port-au-Prince to celebrate the election of Jean-Bertrand Aristide in 1990. The United Nations Observer Mission to Verify the Electoral Process in Haiti (ONUVEH) and UN security observers assisted with the process of holding the first democratic elections in Haiti's history. (UN Photo 177258/M. Grant)

lend themselves easily to outside intervention, even for those with the purest of motives. People had internationally recognized human rights, in both peace and war. But guaranteeing those rights involved complex calculations about feasibility linked to power.

The Security Council can authorize a member state or regional organization to enforce human rights, or the council itself can manage direct enforcement. For the first time, UN personnel in Somalia, beginning in May 1993, directly managed a UN military operation to enforce human rights. What the UN had previously done, in addition to authorizing enforcement by others, was to provide armed observation and reporting elements, usually referred to as peacekeeping forces, in connection with human rights in a number of situations. In places such as Nicaragua, El Salvador, Namibia, and Cambodia, UN forces managed by UN personnel had mainly observed electoral and other agreements. But in these types of operations UN armed personnel had not tried to enforce human rights standards themselves. They had only observed the situation. They had the right—seldom used—to defend themselves with force. And they had reported back to New York on the theory that a UN organ would take steps with national parties to see that rights were protected. The more frequent UN role was not direct protection through enforcement of human rights norms but indirect protection by prodding others to take action.

Increasingly, traditional peacekeeping entailed a human rights element. As Secretary-General Boutros-Ghali wrote in his last annual report in 1996, "The United

Nations . . . has moved to integrate, to the extent possible, its human rights and humanitarian efforts with its peace efforts."[7] The first United Nations Angola Verification Mission (UNAVEM I) verified both troop movements and elections in Angola. The same was true of the United Nations Transition Assistance Group (UNTAG) in Namibia. The United Nations Protection Force (UNPROFOR) in the Balkans was intended to supervise a cease-fire and deliver humanitarian relief. In Cambodia, in an effort to achieve a national peace, the Khmer Rouge—killers of at least a million persons in the 1970s—were persuaded by UN personnel to sign the Geneva Conventions protecting human rights in armed conflict. In fact, all personnel of the United Nations Transitional Authority in Cambodia (UNTAC) were supposed to carry out human rights functions.

Throughout the 1990s it remained controversial whether the UN itself should enforce, rather than observe and mediate, human rights standards. In Somalia during 1993, in an effort to produce national reconciliation and an effective and democratic government, military forces under UN command fired on both civilian demonstrators and combatants and launched military operations against one of the major "warlords" of the country. There were scores of fatalities, and a chain reaction of violence led to declining enthusiasm for international involvement. These events greatly undermined risk-taking in Rwanda during 1994, when perhaps 800,000 persons were killed in ethnic violence. The Security Council did authorize Opération Turquois under Chapter VII during the later stages of massacres, but the limited military deployment by the French had little effect on political developments and actually led to the sheltering of some Hutus implicated in attacks, as they sought safe haven behind the UN shield.

Later the Secretary-General contacted a number of states with a view to a military deployment in Burundi, where similar ethnic violence was resulting in the "slow-motion genocide" of perhaps 150,000 persons during a five-year period. Of the fifty states approached, only twenty-one responded. Of these, eleven declined to be of help; of the remaining ten, only three offered ground troops.[8] The situation did not explode in a Rwanda-like fashion, but the country remained on the brink of a human rights disaster.[9]

The Security Council's response to the evolving humanitarian crisis in Kosovo in 1998–1999 added another twist to the story. Concerned with the increased violence and human rights violations in the territory, the council responded in September 1998 by condemning such acts and calling for an end to all such conflict and terrorism. Yet no concrete preventive or protection action was taken. And when NATO finally acted militarily to deal with the eroding human security situation in March 1999, it did so without explicit UN authorization. As discussed earlier, ironically this NATO action was met at first by a drastic increase in human rights violations against ethnic Albanians in Kosovo by Yugoslav security forces, creating a set of conditions that compelled the majority of the members of the Security Council to act. The resulting UNMIK operation can be viewed in large part as an attempt to design a post-conflict peacebuilding model that could bring about the conditions necessary to prevent the return of hostilities and provide the self-determination and future human security of the peoples of Kosovo.

The Security Council's complex and multidimensional operational responses to the crises in East Timor, Sierra Leone, and the Democratic Republic of the Congo similarly demonstrate a growing willingness to incorporate human rights elements, including special attention to children, directly into peacekeeping operations. They also reflect an increased commitment to the concept of comprehensive human security and peacebuilding.

As discussed in the previous chapter, the operational definition of security employed by the council has been evolving in recent years to include a much broader range of human security concerns, not the least of which are actions to stop genocide and other gross violations of human rights. In an extraordinary move, for example, in August 1999, the Security Council passed Resolution 1261 focusing on a thematic issue: children in armed conflict. The resolution strongly condemned "the targeting of children in situations of armed conflict, including killing and maiming, sexual violence, abduction and forced displacement, recruitment and use of children in armed conflict in violation of international law . . . and calls on all parties concerned to end such practices." How far council members are willing to go in meaningfully addressing such non-country-specific issues is yet to be seen.

The Security Council still had a long way to go to achieve a balanced and systematic record concerning the protection of human rights, especially under Chapter VII. Many more persons died in Rwanda during 1994 or in the Democratic Republic of the Congo in 2002 than died in Kosovo in 1999. Yet the council, pushed by Western states, had shown far more interest in the human rights violations of the Balkans than of Africa. Partly this double standard stemmed from the media coverage of Western-based reporting, partly from the interests of Western governments. A type of racism may also have been involved.

The General Assembly

Beyond standard-setting, the General Assembly practices indirect protection of human rights in two ways. It passes resolutions to condemn or otherwise draw attention to violations of human rights. It also creates and funds various agencies or meetings to deal with human rights.

About one-third of the General Assembly's resolutions each year deal with human rights. Many of these are adopted by consensus and constitute a rough barometer of which rights policies are judged most acceptable or egregious. For example, the fiftieth General Assembly responded to the execution of a Nigerian human rights and environmental activist, Ken Saro-Wiwa, with a resolution of condemnation of that military government. The vote was 101 to 14, with forty-seven abstentions (mostly by African states). This was one of forty-six human rights resolutions adopted during the 1995 session. The fifty-fourth session of the assembly in 1999 passed well over fifty such resolutions.

When a resolution targets a specific country or violation, it is difficult to evaluate the resolution's effect over time. It might be argued, for example, that the assembly's repeated condemnations of apartheid as practiced in South Africa had some impact on changing attitudes among South Africans. At the same time, many observers are not persuaded that words divorced from coercive power can have much effect in the short term.[10] In trying to account for change in South Africa, these observers would emphasize violence against apartheid, formal economic sanctions, and the shrinking of investments by the international business community.

Still, it would seem that General Assembly resolutions on human rights often send important signals, but this observation is difficult if not impossible to measure. The assembly supported the UN Secretary-General, for example, in his mediation of the civil war in El Salvador, which was tied to a human rights accord. Assembly action sent the signal to both the governmental and the rebel sides that the international community supported a negotiated end to that bloody conflict. This signaling role is shared with other UN agencies such as the Security Council, and the UN Human Rights Commission, covered below.[11]

There are times when a General Assembly resolution on human rights has worked against the protection of those rights. General Augusto Pinochet in Chile used assembly resolutions to rally nationalistic support for his rule despite the gross violations of basic rights that he was overseeing.[12] The assembly's 1975 declaration that Zionism was a form of racism not only antagonized Israel but alienated some of Israel's supporters from the assembly. The resolution did nothing for the practice of rights in either Israel proper or the occupied territories that Israel controlled militarily. The resolution was repealed in 1991.

The General Assembly, acting in its second role of structuring the UN system, has created a segment of the UN secretariat to deal with Palestinian rights and a committee to oversee Israeli practices pertaining to human rights in the territories militarily occupied since 1967. The assembly also voted to hold the World Conference on Human Rights during June 1993 in Vienna. Sometimes the assembly takes a half-step to help with rights. It created the Fund for Victims of Torture, but it refused to make the fund part of the regular UN budget. The fund relies on voluntary donations.

When decisions are not made by consensus, human rights policies reflect the majority controlling the General Assembly. From 1945 until about 1955, the Western majority was not very sensitive to issues of racial discrimination and tended to focus instead on issues like forced labor under communism. There followed a period in which the assembly tended to emphasize issues of national self-determination and an end to racial discrimination, reflecting the desires of the developing countries, which had recently become a different "automatic majority" through decolonization. After the end of the Cold War it remained to be seen whether an intensified North-South conflict would completely dominate human rights proceedings in the assembly.

There were certainly manifestations of this North-South conflict. For example, in the late 1980s and 1990s, developing countries successfully reaffirmed the principle of state sovereignty in the face of the industrialized countries' desires to emphasize a right of humanitarian assistance that would supersede state sovereignty. By the early twenty-first century little had changed in this debate. While the members of the International Commission on Intervention and State Sovereignty could assert "No More Rwanda's," states from the Global South like Algeria, despite the terrible violence occurring within it, stressed the supremacy of state sovereignty, as did Zimbabwe's President Robert Mugabe when criticism arose of his brutal internal crackdown. More stable states from the North, like Sweden, stressed the supremacy of the *droit d'ingérence* or the right of the international community to interfere inside states in the interests of the victims of violence or deprivation. There was no consensus in the assembly as to the proper limits of state sovereignty or when the UN was justified in approving action without state consent.

In other manifestations, the General Assembly was also characterized by fragmented views that shifted from issue to issue. On the question of human rights in Iraq during the 1990s, for example, a number of Islamic states thought that the Security Council, as led by the United States, had gone too far in restricting Iraqi sovereignty. On the question of human rights for Muslims in Bosnia, many Islamic states in the assembly wanted the Security Council to go further in challenging Yugoslav and Serbian policies toward Bosnia. Thus, Western states in the Security Council did not have a monopoly on double standards on human rights.

Although developing countries still controlled the majority of votes in the General Assembly, the West had predominant economic and military power. This situation provided the recipe for some accommodation between North and South, especially since the number of developing countries with governments prone to compromise rather than confrontation had grown substantially since the mid-1980s. Hence, in the assembly in the early 1990s, several resolutions endorsed democracy and the integration of civil and political rights into development decisions.[13] These resolutions of the 1990s were not a radical change from some earlier resolutions endorsing the equal value of all human rights, whether civil-political or socioeconomic. They did emphasize democracy more than other earlier resolutions. In fact, the General Assembly manifested more democracies by 2003 than at any other time in the organization's history.

It was historically important that after a decade of efforts by the assembly and certain of its subsidiary bodies, like the International Law Commission, 160 member states met in Rome in June–July 1998 to finalize a treaty on international criminal justice. Against some difficult odds, this United Nations Conference of Plenipotentiaries on the Establishment of an International Criminal Court was successful in doing just that. The resulting Rome Statute entered into force upon ratification by sixty states, which occurred on July 1, 2002. By early 2003 some ninety states had formally accepted the Rome Statute, and the first set of judges (who sit in their individual capacity rather than as state representatives) had been elected and took up their positions in the Hague. Canada's Philippe Kirsh was the court's first president, and Argentina's Luis Moreno Ocampo was its first chief prosecutor.

For the first time in world history, the UN had helped in the establishment of a global court to try individuals for certain egregious human rights violations, namely genocide, crimes against humanity, and the most serious of war crimes. The crime of aggression would join the subject matter jurisdiction of the court when it became properly specified in international law. The court's jurisdiction was complementary to states. This means that, unlike the two ad hoc criminal tribunals, for the former Yugoslavia and Rwanda, states retain the primary responsibility to respond to allegations of the stated abuses. The court, through the independent prosecutor, who, like the judges, is elected by states that have accepted the Rome Statute, only becomes active if a state is unwilling or unable to investigate such allegations and, if warranted, prosecute.

The future role of the court is unclear. The fact that some ninety states, including most NATO members that often deployed their military forces abroad, would accept the jurisdiction and authority of the court was encouraging for the protection of fundamental human rights. Yet, important states like the United States, Israel, Russia, China, India, and others rejected the court. The United States led an active opposition, threatening states that accepted the court with dire consequences, and concluding new agreements with as many states as possible in which the two states agreed not to turn over the other's citizens to the court. During 2002 the United States delayed extending deployments of UN blue helmets until the Security Council granted it a one-year extension, renewable, from the court's jurisdiction. Also in 2002, the U.S. Congress passed legislation, subsequently signed into law by President George W. Bush, dubbed "The Hague invasion act," that among other sections authorized the United States to use force to liberate any American citizen detained in relation to the ICC. The new court sits at The Hague, the Netherlands.

The United States claimed that it feared politically motivated and false charges against its citizens by other states, a rogue prosecutor who would engage in the same behavior, and legal exposure to its citizens that was unacceptable given the extensive security operations taken in the name of the UN or NATO. Many observers believed, however, that the strong U.S. opposition to the court was more ideological than pragmatic. Given that, for example, the prosecutor could not proceed with charges against a U.S. citizen unless such proceedings had been approved by a special panel of judges of the court, it seems that the United States was more interested in defending an absolute conception of state sovereignty and national independence than in resisting any probable dangers to its citizens. There could be a practical problem when and if the United States were to select targets and weapons that might contradict international humanitarian law, and thus constitute war crimes or crimes against humanity. The latter concept pertains to a systematic attack on civilians, whether in peace or war. Such charges about illegal U.S. policies had arisen in both Kosovo in 1999 and Afghanistan in 2001 with regard to such matters as military attacks on a TV station in Belgrade or the use of cluster bombs in civilian areas in Afghanistan. Such policy decisions pertaining to war were never independently investigated either by the U.S. Congress or the federal courts. In any event, while the court was accepted by the likes of Britain, France, Italy, and Canada, it was bitterly opposed by the United States as of 2003.[14] Indeed, two scholars warned of "international idealism run amuck."[15]

For the court to operate, in addition to conditions discussed above, either the state where the alleged crime took place, or the state of the defendant, would have to be a party to the Rome Statute. Ironically, therefore, when the United States engaged in armed conflict in Iraq in 2003, neither U.S. nor Iraqi citizens were subject to the court's jurisdiction since neither state had exercised the necessary consent. But British policymakers and military personnel were. Thus a state like France could file a complaint in the ICC about systematic policy in Iraq against a British national, but not against an American or an Iraqi.

The court marked a historical milestone in the evolution of efforts to improve the protection of important human rights. The ICC existed and could be "pulled off the shelf" if states did not exercise their primary responsibility to seriously follow up on allegations of certain major crimes. Whether it would actually play an active and important deterrent or enforcement role in international relations would be determined by future events.

The Office of the Secretary-General

It may sound surprising to some, but before the arrival in office of Kofi Annan, UN Secretaries-General did not display a major commitment to human rights.[16] Perhaps they had seen their primary role as producing progress on peace and security. This emphasis was understood until the recent past to mean that they could not speak out on specific human rights violations. Had Javier Pérez de Cuéllar, for example, made protection of individual human rights his primary concern, his office probably would have been unacceptable as mediator between Iran and Iraq, or between the Salvadoran armed forces and the FMLN, or in the Afghan situation after the Soviet invasion.

Virtually all Secretaries-General have engaged in good offices or quiet mediation for the advancement of human rights. But only Annan has systematically, though cautiously, thrown the full weight of his office into the quest for human rights protection. Whether one speaks of Dag Hammarskjöld or Kurt Waldheim, the point on human rights remains the same. Hammarskjöld, the Swedish economist, was personally not much interested in human rights at the United Nations and concentrated on finding a diplomatic role for the UN in the East-West conflict. Hammarskjöld did find time to take up the case of U.S. airmen detained in China after the Korean War. Waldheim, who served in the German army during World War II, was much less dynamic than Hammarskjöld. Yet he, too, took up human rights or humanitarian questions, such as the situation of refugees in Africa, somewhat ironically, in light of his own isolation following exposure of his Nazi past. Much the same could be said for U Thant from Burma, who was not as personally committed to individual rights as he was to the collective right of peoples to self-determination. But on occasion he, too, engaged in quiet diplomacy for human rights.

As human rights became more institutionalized in UN proceedings, however, Secretaries-General took a higher profile on rights issues. Pérez de Cuéllar is instructive in this regard. A cautious Peruvian diplomat, he entered office showing great deference to states, especially Latin ones. One of his first acts was to not renew the contract of his most senior human rights official, Theo van Boven of the Netherlands. Van Boven had irritated the Argentine junta, then in the process of murdering at least 9,000 Argentines, and its U.S. supporters. By the end of his term, Pérez de Cuéllar had projected the UN, by his own authority, deep into the affairs of both El Salvador and Nicaragua, including deep involvement on human rights issues.

In Nicaragua during Pérez's tenure, the UN came to oversee a regional peace accord, to supervise national elections for the first time in a sovereign state, and to collect weapons from a disbanding rebel force. He also oversaw human rights observers in Haiti in 1991, the first time UN election verification had taken place in a country not wracked at the time by civil conflict.

When human rights were linked to peace, Pérez de Cuéllar and his office came to be bold and innovative. And the two issues were indeed inseparable in places like El Salvador, Nicaragua, Namibia, Angola, Cambodia, Bosnia, East Timor, and Kosovo. The office of the Secretary-General took initiatives, then obtained the backing of both the General Assembly and the Security Council. Increasingly, the Secretary-General was drawn into rights questions that had previously been considered the domestic affairs of states.

Boutros Boutros-Ghali of Egypt followed in his predecessors' footsteps. Upon becoming Secretary-General in 1992, he seemed uninterested in human rights, even appointing an old friend without a human rights record as head of the UN Centre for Human Rights in Geneva. But within the year, Boutros-Ghali was as deeply involved in human rights issues as Pérez de Cuéllar had been. In El Salvador, for example, Boutros-Ghali was active in supporting President Alfredo Cristiani as he tried to purge the army of most of those who had committed gross violations of internationally recognized human rights. Boutros-Ghali was quite outspoken in promoting democratic or participatory values as part of the quest for economic development. This stand may not have been completely desired by some G–77 countries, but his speeches and reports in support of democratic development were backed by many donor countries. In the early 1990s the major donor countries pushed for more grassroots participation in the search for sustainable development, whether through bilateral programs, the World Bank, or agencies of the UN. The Secretary-General's position fit nicely within this paradigm shift in favor of the human right to participation in public affairs.

Moreover, he appointed the Swedish diplomat who had mediated the Iran-Iraq War, Jan Eliasson, to a new position for humanitarian assistance. This post evolved toward being a type of general troubleshooter for humanitarian affairs, which were difficult to insulate from wider human rights issues. By 2000 this position had evolved through several manifestations to become the Office for the Coordination of Humanitarian Affairs (OCHA). Its main role is to coordinate rapid and effective relief through the actions of mainly the UNHCR, UNICEF, the World Food Programme (WFP), and their NGO partners. Until 1993, the General Assembly had long been unwilling to formally create the post of a High Commissioner for Human Rights, largely because of opposition from developing and communist countries. But developing countries tolerated this new post.

There was a more-or-less straight-line progression: As human rights became more entrenched in UN proceedings, the UN Secretary-General became more openly active on the issue. This was especially true when the human rights issue was integrated with peace and security matters.

Below the highest levels of the office of the Secretary-General, parts of the secretariat have often actively tried to improve behavior under human rights norms.[17] Van Boven, who had annoyed the Argentine junta before his "non-renewal" by Pérez de Cuéllar, was the clearest example, but other UN officials also were active, frequently behind the scenes. Nevertheless, the Secretary-General sets the tone on human rights for the secretariat, and the fate of van Boven showed that these officials could do only so much without the support of the Secretary-General at the top.[18]

The UN's seventh Secretary-General, Kofi Annan, has been a much more activist human rights leader, including in his priority concerns the encouragement and advocacy of human rights, the rule of law, and the universal values of equality, tolerance, and human dignity as articulated in the UN Charter. One of his most eloquent statements in this regard was his address to the UNESCO (United Nations Educational, Scientific and Cultural Organization) ceremony marking the fiftieth anniversary of the Universal Declaration of Human Rights. In part he said:

> Our belief in the centrality of human rights to the work and life of the United Nations stems from a simple proposition: that States which respect human rights respect the rules of international society. States which respect human rights are more likely to seek cooperation and not confrontation, tolerance and not violence, moderation and not might, peace and not war. States which treat their own people with fundamental respect are more likely to treat their neighbours with the same respect. From this proposition, it is clear that human rights—in practice, as in principle—can have no walls and no boundaries.

One of Annan's pet projects was to try to galvanize the private for-profit sector into a greater interest in human rights, in partnership with the UN. Recognizing the economic power of transnational corporations (TNCs), the Secretary-General tried to get them to take a broad approach to their role in the world, one that reflected more social responsibility. In 1999 the Secretary-General launched the Global Compact, which projected certain universal principles relevant to business practices in the areas of human rights and the environment. The four main UN agencies that participated in this venture were the Office of the High Commissioner of Human Rights (UNHCHR), the International Labor Organization (ILO), the UN Development Programme (UNDP), and the UN Environmental Program (UNEP). Hoping to reduce especially what some called economic exploitation of labor (and damage to the environment), Annan worked hard to create this partnership—which had great implications for many human rights, even if much of the discourse was about social responsibility. By 2003 hundreds of corporations had signed on to this initiative.[19]

Secretary-General Annan also demonstrated the strength of his commitment to internationally recognized human rights by his nomination of a strong-willed High Commissioner for Human Rights: the former president of Ireland, Mary Robinson. It should also be said that such an appointment, which had its own merits, was initially much welcomed by the United States and certain other Western states, which after the Cold War seemed to want the United Nations to be more assertive in general on human rights issues. Robinson's departure in September 2002 came to a significant degree because Washington had become disillusioned with her.[20] Thus, Annan, in not reappointing Robinson, may have been bowing to the wishes of the one hyperpower. In any event, the third High Commissioner is a visible and dynamic, longtime UN official, Brazil's Sergio Vieira de Mello. He had such good relations with the George W. Bush administration that he was also appointed as the Secretary-General's representative in post-combat Iraq in 2003. Unfortunately he was killed when UN headquarters in Iraq was attacked by unknown actors in the second half of 2003.

The High Commissioner for Human Rights

Debate about the need for a UN High Commissioner for Human Rights had started in the 1940s. The 1993 UN Vienna conference on human rights recommended that the General Assembly create such a post. After a heavy lobbying campaign by a variety of actors, including many NGOs, the Carter Presidential Center, and the U.S. government, the General Assembly finally created the post that autumn. The office had a vague mandate with weak authority. Secretary-General Boutros-Ghali appointed as the first occupant José Ayala-Lasso of Ecuador, who had held several national posts, including foreign minister in a military government. He began his activities in 1994.

The first UN High Commissioner for Human Rights (UNHCHR) practiced quiet diplomacy rather than being a public advocate with an abrasive style. This approach helped alleviate some of the developing countries' fears that the post would be used exclusively to emphasize civil and political rights favored by the Western states, with the developing countries serving as "primary targets." The first High Commissioner had met with any number of developing countries with questionable human rights policies; during these visits, those policies had presumably been discussed. Among other activities, the first High Commissioner had tried to interject more attention to economic and social rights into the work of the UN regional commissions for economic development. This emphasis was continued by his successor.

Beyond making an annual report on international human rights at the UN, probably the most important work of the first High Commissioner was the establishment of human rights field missions inside countries either as part of, or as separate from, UN peacekeeping operations. The first of these missions was established in Rwanda, where the human rights field staff broke new ground in legal and diplomatic theory but achieved little in practical terms during its early deployment. The High Commissioner tried to turn Rwanda into a precedent by then creating field missions in other countries, the first of which were Abkhazia, Georgia, Colombia, and Zaire. By the end of the decade, a UN field presence for human rights had expanded to also include Cambodia, Central African Republic, Democratic Republic of the Congo, El Salvador, Gaza, Guatemala, Indonesia, Liberia, Malawi, Mongolia, Sierra Leone, South Africa, southern Africa, and southeast Europe. Once more, in the name of universal human rights, the UN was acting on matters that had once been considered fully part of domestic affairs. In addition to debates about human rights in New York and Geneva, the High Commissioner's office was trying to make a difference "on the ground."

The office of the High Commissioner also processed requests from states regarding electoral assistance. By the mid-1990s the High Commissioner's office was assisting seventeen states in the quest to hold free and fair elections that were internationally supervised. Regional IGOs and NGOs, along with state delegations, were also active in this regard.

The establishment of this post had created some confusion about the overall management and coordination of UN human rights work. Sometimes the High Commissioner, the office of the Secretary-General, and the UN Human Rights Commission did not seem to be playing from the same page of music; nor was it always clear who, if anyone, was the conductor. There was some increase in agreements on division of labor as the years progressed. And in 1997 the Center for Human Rights was merged with UNHCHR. But the office of the High Commissioner remained chronically short of staff and funds. And questions remained about the organization and effectiveness of the UN's human rights machinery.

Mary Robinson, the second High Commissioner, increasingly ran afoul of particularly the United States, and in 2002, as noted above, she resigned under pressure. Just as the United States had seen to it that Boutrous Boutros-Ghali did not continue as Secretary-General, so Washington made it clear that Robinson's high-profile discussion of human rights violations in places like China and Israeli-occupied territory did not please the United States. In China, the United States had adopted a bipartisan policy of engagement with authoritarian Beijing, in which human rights was relegated to quiet diplomacy, not public pressure. Regarding Israel, the United States had long declined to take up seriously Israel's repeated violations of the Fourth Geneva Convention of 1949 regulating occupied territory, as affirmed by various UN agencies as well as the guardian of international humanitarian law, the International Committee of the Red Cross. Because Robinson was more commited to raising the awareness of human rights, and also human rights violations, than to quiet diplomacy, she became an irritant not only to those states with serious human rights violations, but also to the United States, which had close relations with some of these same states. Washington also was not happy with the way Robinson ran the UN Conference on Racism and Xeonophobia in 2002, which featured many attacks on Israel. She was also a champion of socio-economic human rights, which Washington rejected.

Secretary-General Annan, whose diplomatic skills are normally commensurate with the demands of his position, then nominated, and the General Assembly approved, Sergio de Mello as UNHCHR, as noted above. De Mello, who had considerable UN experience in humanitarian and refugee matters, was from Brazil and known as much more of a polished diplomat than Robinson. Of course some private human rights groups thought he might be *too* polished, at the expense of defending human rights for the sake of getting along with the governments that violate them. The position of the UNHCHR—like that of the Secretary-General—was not an easy one.

The Human Rights Commission

If, when dealing with human rights, the broad and complex UN system is thought of as a wheel, the UN Human Rights Commission was traditionally the hub.[21] This commission is now made up of fifty-three states elected by the Economic and Social Council (ECOSOC); its history reflects in microcosm the legal and diplomatic revolution on human rights. Despite Western domination of the UN during its early years, the Human Rights Commission was content to promote rights by setting standards rather than by trying to protect them, even indirectly, through various forms of diplomatic pressure. The early commission adopted the position that it lacked the authority to inquire into rights behavior in specific states. When private complaints about rights violations came to the UN, the commission buried them in an elaborate proceeding leading nowhere, one of the most complicated trash baskets ever devised. The early commission, in the words of one careful observer, displayed a "fierce commitment to inoffensiveness."[22]

A North-South compromise, however, opened up new possibilities between 1967 and 1970. As a result, the Human Rights Commission began to deal with specific states and also began to examine private complaints more seriously. Developing states wanted to focus on Israel and South Africa, but developed states broadened the commission's mandate so that states like Greece under military rule (1967–1974) and Haiti under the Duvalier dynasty (1957–1986) also became targets of commission activity. Moreover, states at the commission agreed that private petitions could lead, after screening, to quiet diplomacy and even the publication of a "blacklist" of states with a pattern of gross violations of human rights. These private petitions, however, were treated in a confidential process that minimized the negative publicity that could be directed at an offending government. Ironically, a state could minimize public scrutiny of its rights record by responding somewhat to private petitions in the confidential process.

From the early 1970s to the early 1990s, the Human Rights Commission struggled to find ways of working for human rights in meaningful ways. Through a series of North-South coalitions, propelled partly by the efforts of human rights NGOs, the commission overcame persistent opposition and engaged in indirect protective activities. It created "thematic procedures" to deal with certain violations. That is, it created either working groups of states or special experts, called rapporteurs, to examine more than two dozen issues, such as forced disappearances, arbitrary detention, summary execution, torture, religious discrimination, mercenaries, and deprived or suffering children. Some working groups not only studied problems with reference to specific states but also sent official telegrams to political authorities and in other ways tried to help persons in the short term. In the mid-1990s the commission's rapporteur on racial discrimination spent considerable time focusing on conditions in the United States. The American media gave almost no coverage to the rapporteur's extended visit, and the resulting report had virtually no impact on American society.

The Human Rights Commission also dealt in various ways with a series of specific states, both publicly and privately. Over time that list of targeted states became balanced. During the waning days of the Cold War some of these targeted states were aligned with Washington (for example, El Salvador); others were aligned with Moscow (for example, Cuba). Communist China was extensively discussed after the Tiananmen Square massacre, proving that even permanent members of the Security Council are not immune to critical review. But in 1995 the commission refused, by a one-vote margin, to censure China for its repressive policies. In this same session, however, the commission adopted critical resolutions pertaining to a range of states in the global South, such as Zaire, Sudan, and Afghanistan, along with the former

Yugoslavia. This pattern continued into the early twenty-first century. Russia has been the only member of the Permanent Five to be officially censured by the UN Human Rights Commission. Russian brutal policies in dealing with secessioinist elements in Chechnya produced that outcome, which seemed to have virtually no effect in ameliorating the Russian policies under scrutiny.

The subject of human rights affects crucial questions of governmental power, and thus this intergovernmental commission was highly politicized. Various double standards and inconsistencies could be documented. Washington at times focused on rights violations in Cuba out of proportion to events there, especially compared to more serious rights violations in allied states like Guatemala and El Salvador.[23] Washington had long used human rights as a political weapon to dislodge the Castro government. During the Cold War, Moscow was openly opportunistic in the commission, using human rights as a weapon against Washington's allies, such as Pinochet's Chile from 1974 to about 1984, but remaining silent about major violations of human rights in communist states. Again, human rights language was put at the service of ideological and strategic calculations. Most of the developing states paid far more attention to rights violations by South Africa and Israel than to egregious ones in Idi Amin's Uganda or Indira Gandhi's India.

In 2002 Libya was put forward by the African caucus as president of the UN Human Rights Commission. Given Libya's poor record on many civil and political rights, it was obvious that the African caucus placed more emphasis on equitable geographical representation than on sterling performance in these human rights matters. Since, according to UN tradition, it was "Africa's turn" to hold the presidency of the commission, Libya was duly elected over the protests of the United States and certain other Western governments. Adding fuel to the fire, other prominently repressive governments like Cuba and Saudi Arabia were also elected to the commission. This episode showed clearly that for many states, especially in the Global South, human rights was still not taken seriously. After assuming the presidency, and contrary to promises of balance and integrity, the Libyan representative made polemical and biased speeches. Coming the year following the failure of the United States to be elected, for the first time, to the commission, these developments gave "the UN" a bad name in the field of human rights. But the source of the problem lay in the foreign policies of member states. While there was debate in the 1940s about whether the commission should be made up of state representatives or independent experts, there was never a formal movement to convert the commission from the former to the latter. The UN Human Rights Commision has never been made up of "a club of the clean." Some NGOs continued to argue that state members of the commission should have to meet certain standards, such as having ratified all the major human rights treaties. But the United States and others were opposed to this.

Interestingly, a number of elected governments, such as in India and the Philippines, opposed certain initiatives designed to help protect human rights.[24] They elevated either solidarity among developing countries or the principle of state sovereignty over rights protection. At times, regional or bloc voting prevailed. A number of Latin American states, including some that were democratic and sensitive to rights at home, tried to shield more repressive Latin American states from the Human Rights Commission's pressure. Again, emphasis on state sovereignty or cultural solidarity superseded UN efforts to protect rights.

For those with a historical perspective, the failure of democratic governments to rally to UN human rights issues should come as no surprise. At the end of World War II, Winston Churchill's government in London wanted to summarily execute high German officials rather than try them at Nuremberg,[25] and London was not enthusiastic about UN Charter's language on human rights because it might interfere with the smooth continuation of British colonialism.[26] Democratic states have probably displayed as many double standards in their foreign policies as other kinds of states.

Yet these double standards by states operated side by side with the principled work of human rights NGOs that participated heavily in commission proceedings. Overall the Human Rights Commission made fitful progress in monitoring rights. NGOs focused on the commission and increased in number.[27] By the 1990s large numbers of NGOs were active in all phases of the commission's proceedings.[28] Eventually the East-West conflict dissolved, and a number of former communist states became champions of human rights through the commission. The North-South conflict persisted, especially since more developing states had twice been added to the commission. Although this North-South conflict slowed the dynamism of the commission after the Cold War, the commission at the time of writing continued with its thematic procedures and country-specific measures.

Over time the commission dealt mostly with civil rights such as freedom from racial discrimination, torture, forced disappearances, summary execution, and arbitrary detention. This might be seen as a bias stemming from Western states and NGOs, and from developing countries aligned with the West. In defense of this orientation, one could argue that many of these civil rights protected fundamental personal integrity and were necessary to implement a right to life.

The commission did not, in fact, deal very frequently or specifically with socioeconomic rights. Developing states spent time debating a right to development, but most concrete efforts regarding socioeconomic rights in the UN system were handled by agencies like the United Nations Children's Fund (UNICEF) and the World Health Organization (WHO). The WHO, for example, passed resolutions on the human right to health care, then followed up with efforts to get states to adopt health policies consistent with those resolutions. Communist states during the Cold War might have talked about socioeconomic rights, but in their own countries shelter and health care were not treated as equal rights; they were subject to preferential disbursement based on political conformity and status. Apart from the work of the specialized agencies, socioeconomic rights in the UN system had always been, and remain, second-class rights receiving much less specific diplomatic attention than civil rights.[29] By 1996, there was some slightly renewed attention to socioeconomic rights, along with the much-debated right to development. For example, in 1996 the UN held a conference in Istanbul on human settlements. This "Habitat II" conference used the language of a human right to adequate housing. Increased attention has also been focused on the rights of indigenous peoples and other vulnerable groups within society, such as children, women, and ethnic minorities.

TABLE 6.1 Controversial Human Freedom Index

Countries Scoring High (perfect equals 40)	Countries Scoring Low
Sweden, 38	Iraq, 0
Denmark, 38	Libya, 1
Netherlands, 37	Romania, 1
Finland, 36	Ethiopia, 2
New Zealand, 36	China, 2
Austria, 36	South Africa, 3
Norway, 35	USSR, 3
France, 35	Bulgaria, 4
Germany, 35	Zaire, 5
Belgium, 35	Pakistan, 5
Canada, 34	Vietnam, 5
Switzerland, 34	Indonesia, 5
United States, 33	North Korea, 5
Australia, 33	Syria, 5
Japan, 32	Cuba, 5
United Kingdom, 32	Mozambique, 6
Greece, 31	Saudi Arabia, 6
Costa Rica, 31	Czechoslovakia, 6

SOURCE: UN Development Programme, *Human Development Report 1991* (New York: Oxford University Press, 1991), p. 20. Reprinted by permission of Oxford University Press, Inc.

The Human Rights Commission also had devoted little time and attention to political rights associated with democracy. As already noted, only about one-third of all states have stable liberal democratic governments. Most of the states represented in the commission were listed by Freedom House, a New York-based NGO, as either partly free or unfree.[30] Thus it was difficult to secure sustained attention to political rights. Additionally, some democratic governments did not want to emphasize democracy in their foreign policy because they had authoritarian allies or, like the Philippines in the 1990s, wanted favors from authoritarian states such as China. Moreover, many of the numerous authoritarian governments were engaged in brutal repression. These conditions caused the commission to focus on fundamental civil rights such as freedom from torture and summary execution. The emphasis had been liberalization, not democratization.

It was frequently difficult to prove that the Human Rights Commission had a specific and beneficial impact on a situation. It was one thing to chart changing commission procedures and activity; it was another to demonstrate that these changes inside the commission had led to changed behavior outside that body—namely, within nations. The commission wielded few resources besides diplomatic verbiage. The Security Council could authorize sanctions. The General Assembly commanded more publicity. States and regional organizations like the European Community disposed of economic resources. If a government believed that violation of human rights was necessary for the government's security or the broader national interest, words generated by the commission were unlikely to change the situation in the short term.

Moreover, as demonstrated further on, other organizations within the UN system were trying to use diplomacy to socialize or shame states into changing their record on human rights. The commission was central, but it was not a "super" agency. It did not supersede or even coordinate most of these other bodies. These latter organizations followed their own agendas and made their own reports without coordination by the UN Human Rights Commission.

Some observers were optimistic about the commission, particularly because its work is seen as most useful when it moves in tandem with other intergovernmental and non-governmental organizations. But when these observers used words like "significant" and "effective," they offered little evidence drawn from data or events outside commission meetings.[31]

During 1992, the commission held its first emergency session—on the subject of violations of rights in the former Yugoslavia. It appointed as special rapporteur on the subject a former prime minister of Poland, Tadeusz Mazowieki. But when his seventeen reports failed to lead to decisive action to stop atrocities, Mazowieki resigned in protest in July 1995. A second emergency session was held on the subject of Rwanda, but again no decisive intervention resulted and the genocide there continued.

On a somewhat brighter note, the commission has increasingly come to focus on providing states with advisory services and technical assistance for such activities as reforming national laws to incorporate international human rights norms and promote democratization, training criminal justice personnel, and promoting other related objectives. The commission also is making increased use of special rapporteurs, for both particular countries and general themes, and this holds some potential for long-term change.[32]

Supplemental Human Rights Bodies

The Sub-Commission

The UN Sub-Commission on Prevention of Discrimination and Protection of Minorities, now the UN Sub-Commission on Human Rights, is a second all-purpose human rights agency. It is composed of individual experts rather than state or governmental representatives. It screens private petitions before sending them to the Human Rights Commission. Many of these private petitions come from NGOs, not just from victimized individuals. After a dismal start to the petition process, as noted already, the sub-commission has begun to display increasing seriousness, but the process has generated only weak pressure. The process is confidential, with a minimum of vague publicity through the parent commission.

Much of the sub-commission's other work duplicates that of the Human Rights Commission. It has a predictable dynamic on a number of issues, so much so that its recommendations often have been rejected or ignored by government representatives in the commission. At one point during a financial crisis, the sub-commission's sessions were suspended. Many suggested that it be either drastically reformed or dissolved.[33] But at the time of writing it continues—if for no other reason than that its disappearance might send a signal of lessened commitment to human rights.

The Human Rights Committee

Not to be confused with the UN Human Rights Commission, which reports to the General Assembly through the Economic and Social Council (ECOSOC), the UN Human Rights Committee was created under the UN Covenant on Civil and Political Rights. Its membership of individual experts, elected by parties to that convention, functions only in relation to monitoring the implementation of the civil and political rights codified in that treaty. It reports to the General Assembly but is not part of the "regular" UN bureaucracy.

From the late 1970s the Human Rights Committee has processed state reports about implementation of the civil-political covenant and handled individual petitions when state parties have allowed their citizens that procedural right. Despite the Cold War, European communist states became parties to the covenant, and the committee managed to question many states in an objective way about their record on civil and political rights. In a few cases the committee clearly tried to pressure states like Uruguay to improve their records by using negative publicity. In a growing number of countries there is evidence to suggest that because of committee questions and observations a state has been led to change its national legislation to conform to the covenant's requirements. In some court cases judges have made explicit reference to the covenant or committee. One student of the process found matters "quietly encouraging."[34]

But many states are lax about reporting, and about fifty states that have adhered to the covenant have not consented to the right of individual petition. Some of the changes made by states after legal adherence have been small and technical. By the early 1990s only eight states had reported court cases that applied the covenant directly.[35] The committee seemed most influential when dealing with states committed to human rights but perhaps needing some prodding to conform to all international obligations. The United States, having ratified the covenant with significant and debatable reservations, understandings, and resolutions imposed by the Senate, found itself embroiled in an acrimonious exchange with the committee. The committee, among other things, questioned whether U.S. reservations were compatible with the spirit and purpose of the covenant, and the U.S. Senate, led by Jesse Helms (R-N.C.), then head of its foreign relations committee, questioned the right of the UN committee to review U.S. actions, then withheld certain appropriations to the UN. But even several U.S. allies questioned whether the United States could become a legal party to the covenant and still reserve the right not to make any changes in its incompatible national laws.[36] An ironic point was that during the Cold War, it was the communist states that took a highly restrictive view of the authority of the UN Human Rights Committee, arguing that it had no authority to make general comment on state reports. Yet after the Cold War, because of Helms and the Senate, the United States took the lead in challenging the authority of the committee.

About 36,000 Cambodians have been disabled by mines as a result of over a decade of bitter civil war. Handicap International runs this workshop for artificial limbs in Siem Reap Town. (UNHCR Photo/I. Guest)

Committee on Economic, Social, and Cultural Rights

The UN Covenant on Economic, Social and Cultural Rights authorized the ECOSOC to supervise the application of the treaty. State parties are obligated to submit a report periodically on state action to implement the covenant. This provision allows some members of ECOSOC to comment on state behavior under the treaty, even though the state making the comments is not a party to the treaty. The United States falls into this category.

In 1979, ECOSOC created a Committee of Governmental Experts to process these state reports. This committee, perhaps because it was drawn from governments, was unable to encourage serious attention to treaty obligations.[37] In 1985 ECOSOC replaced it with a Committee of Individual Experts. So, as we noted, whereas the UN Human Rights Commission has never had its membership changed from state representatives to individual experts, the monitoring mechanism under the Socio-Economic Covenant has been so changed.

This new socioeconomic committee has proved much more dynamic than its predecessors since 1987, when it first met. Initially taking a cooperative or positive approach toward reporting states, it has tried to get states to establish a national guideline for minimal standards of adequate food, shelter, health care, and the other rights found in the socioeconomic covenant. Thus the supervising committee did not seek at first to establish a global standard, or its standard, for socioeconomic rights. Rather, it prodded states to think seriously about what the covenant meant in their jurisdictions. The focus was on "the extent to which the most disadvantaged individuals in any given society are enjoying a basic minimum level of subsistence rights."[38] The committee sought to establish this not only by examination of legislation but also by socioeconomic statistics.

Alone among the UN monitoring mechanisms, the Committee of Individual Experts accepts written submissions from NGOs as well as from IGOs such as the International Labor Organization. But most human rights NGOs have not been active regarding these socioeconomic rights.[39] Most NGOs working for adequate food, clothing, shelter, and health care conducted humanitarian rather than human rights programs. This meant that NGOs such as Oxfam have been oriented more toward practical results in a country based on humanitarian concerns and oriented less toward lobbying for socioeconomic rights through the Committee of Individual Experts.

Over time this monitoring agency was drawing praise from many human rights advocates. According to one observer, by the committee's fifth session it showed independence, an effort to maximize its influence, effective procedures, specific and constructive recommendations to countries, and a willingness to say when a country was in violation of its commitments. The Committee of Individual Experts was particularly tough on the Dominican Republic, holding it in violation of the socioeconomic covenant concerning both Haitian workers cutting sugar cane and the right to adequate housing in general.

Several problems have plagued the committee, however. It has functioned in a political vacuum, since few powerful actors have wanted to devote diplomatic efforts to helping implement socioeconomic rights internationally. It has considered only a few state reports each year: In 1990, for example, reports were considered for only six out of ninety-seven state parties. Some reports have been late, and some have been delayed at the request of states. It is clear that this UN effort to monitor and improve state behavior pertaining to socioeconomic rights is to be a long-term project.

Other Supervising Committees

Four other human rights treaties create supervising committees of individual experts. There is the Committee on the Elimination of Racial Discrimination (CERD), the Committee on the Elimination of Discrimination Against Women (CEDAW), the Committee Against Torture (CAT), and the Committee on the Rights of the Child (CRC). They function in similar ways. They may have generated some slight influence on states that are parties to the treaties. None has had such remarkable influence as to merit detailed study.

A few words about CERD and its parent treaty against racial discrimination may help to outline the gap between normative theory and behavioral reality. There are more than 130 parties to this human rights treaty, and much rhetoric has been expended within the UN system about the evils of racial discrimination. Every four years state parties are required to submit comprehensive reports regarding compliance with treaty provisions, with briefer updating reports due every two years. Such reports serve as the primary input into the committee's work. Yet many states routinely fail to comply, thus making it difficult for the committee to fulfill its mandate. Also, in the

TABLE 6.2 Human Development Index, 1999

Top Ten	Bottom Ten
Canada	Sierra Leone
Norway	Niger
United States	Ethiopia
Japan	Burkina Faso
Belgium	Burundi
Sweden	Mozambique
Australia	Guinea-Bissau
Netherlands	Eritrea
Iceland	Mali
United Kingdom	Central African Republic

SOURCE: Based on information in UN Development Programme, *Human Development Report 1999* (New York: Oxford University Press, 1999), pp. 134–137. Reprinted by permission of Oxford University Press, Inc.

early 1990s only fourteen states had permitted their citizens to bring a private petition to CERD claiming violation of the treaty, as specified under the treaty's Article 14. Of these fourteen states, only two were African (Algeria and Senegal). No Asian state had agreed to this procedural right of private individuals or groups. The United States was not one of these fourteen. In 1991 there was only one such petition; and when a request went out to states to comment on the financing of CERD, only twenty states bothered to reply and only sixteen agreed to contribute more resources. Nothing was done to enhance the functioning of the monitoring committee.[40]

It is now widely recognized that there are serious problems in the overall monitoring of the various human rights treaties. State reports are filed late and are not always serious in substance. The monitoring committees now face a backlog of reports. Private petitions do not often lead to clear protection of rights within reasonable time. The media do not often cover proceedings or outcomes. Consequently, there have been various proposals to improve the fractured UN system of monitoring human rights treaties. Given the balkanization of the system, some have proposed merging the supervising committees. Others have proposed restricting membership on monitoring committees to individuals from only liberal democratic states. None of these proposals has led to significant change, although the committees do now meet to try to coordinate their efforts for greater impact.[41]

The UN High Commissioner for Refugees

Separate mention should be made of the office of the UN High Commissioner for Refugees (UNHCR).[42] Created by the General Assembly a year before the 1951 Refugee Convention, the UNHCR functions under that convention, and its 1967 Protocol, to provide protection and assistance to refugees and people in refugee-like situations. This latter terminology means that the General Assembly has authorized the UNHCR to deal, at least sometimes, with persons displaced within a state, with those fleeing war or breakdown in public order, and with those identified by the 1951 convention (and hence convention "refugees" who have crossed an international boundary because of a well-founded fear of persecution and who have broken normal relations with their government).

States themselves make the final determination of who is a convention refugee and therefore entitled to temporary asylum from persecution. The exact role of the UNHCR in protection can vary according to national law, but in general one primary role of the UNHCR is to help states determine who should not be returned to a situation of possible persecution. The agency calls this "legal" or "diplomatic" protection, and it can involve interviewing those who claim to be refugees, advising executive branches of government, and helping legislators with drafting or submitting legal papers in court cases.

By 2003 the number of persons of concern to UNHCR ranged between 15 million and 25 million. In 1998, for example, this target population included about 12 million refugees, 1 million asylum seekers, 3.5 million returnees, and 6 million internally displaced persons (IDPs) and others of concern.

Particularly when faced with an influx of unwanted persons, states may show a racial or ideological or other bias in their procedures that determine who is recognized as a legal refugee—and entitled not to be returned to a situation of danger. At times the UNHCR will publicly protest what a government is doing. For example, even though the United States is the largest contributor to the agency's voluntary budget, in 1992 the UNHCR officially protested the forced return of Haitians without a proper hearing about their refugee status. More recently, High Commissioner Rudd Lubbers publicly castigated European states for their restrictive immigration policies.

The agency also is involved in assistance. Rather than being an operating agency itself, the UNHCR normally supervises material and medical assistance to refugees, broadly defined, by contracting with NGOs to provide for the delivery of necessary goods and services to both refugees and internally displaced persons. In 1998 the agency had 244 offices in 118 countries with a staff of 5,528 and a total budget of $1.1 billion. About 425 NGOs were implementing partners. Most of the amounts raised through voluntary contributions were devoted to assistance, and most of this was spent in Africa and Asia. In the early 1990s the UNHCR was deeply involved in the Balkans, devoting about a third of its total resources there. From spring 1994 the agency was responsible for coordinating relief to some 2 million persons who had fled Rwanda. The growing emphasis on assistance has led some observers to criticize the diminishing role of traditional protection in the organization's priorities. A basis for this criticism is that many institutions can provide aid but only the UNHCR can protect refugees.

Convention refugees are the victims of human rights violations; those fleeing war and breakdowns in public authority may also be escaping human rights abuses. In general, however, other actors deal with fundamental human rights violations; the UNHCR is left with the intermediate task of coping with refugee flows.

Within this context, it is worth devoting attention to the evolution of the treatment of internally displaced persons.[43] The presence of these war victims in what

UNHCR calls "refugee-like situations" within their own war-torn countries is fundamentally a human rights issue. IDPs have become more numerous than refugees. At
the end of the last century, the number of refugees had shrunk to about 13.5 million
from earlier totals almost twice that high, but the number of IDPs had grown considerably larger (at least 17 million to 18 million, and conceivably twice that number). When IDPs were first counted in 1982, there were only a million, at which time
there were about 10.5 million refugees.[44]

In historical terms, the rapid evolution of measures on behalf of IDPs in the 1990s
and the embrace of their plight by IGOs and NGOs demonstrates the increasing
weight of human rights in state decisionmaking.[45] Efforts accelerated at the beginning
of the 1990s, when, as has so often been the case in the human rights arena, individuals and private institutions pushed governments and intergovernmental organizations to find a new way to deal with the growing problem of internal displacement.
Roberta Cohen documents that "as early as 1991, non-governmental organizations
(NGOs) began calling for the consolidation into a single document of the different
international standards that apply to IDPs."[46] As the numbers of internally displaced
victims rose, so did the decibel level within the UN Human Rights Commission of
the voices of such NGOs as the Quakers, the Refugee Policy Group, the World Council of Churches, and Caritas.

In 1992, Secretary-General Boutros-Ghali submitted the first analytical report on
IDPs to the UN Commission on Human Rights in Geneva.[47] In its Resolution
1992/73, and not without considerable controversy, the commission authorized the
Secretary-General to appoint a representative to explore "views and information from
all Governments on the human rights issues related to internally displaced persons,
including an examination of existing international human rights, humanitarian and
refugee law and standards and their applicability to the protection of and relief assistance to internally displaced persons."

Shortly thereafter the UN Secretary-General designated Francis M. Deng, a former Sudanese diplomat, as his representative on internally displaced persons. The
development of a comprehensive global approach for effective assistance and protection of IDPs was independently formulated and financed. In a number of publications, Deng assumed the continuing centrality of the Westphalian system and sought
to reconcile international involvement with the traditional prerogatives of the state
through "sovereignty as responsibility."[48] As noted in the earlier discussion of the evolution in humanitarian action, to the three characteristics usually considered attributes of a sovereign (territory, a people, and authority), Deng added a fourth (respect
for a minimal standard of human rights). The Secretary-General himself has not gone
as far as French personalities Bernard Kouchner (at one time head of the UN operation in Kosovo) and Mario Bettati would like, because he espouses no duty or obligation to override sovereignty.[49] But in his speech to the Fifty-fourth General Assembly, Kofi Annan approached Deng's notion of sovereignty as responsibility.[50] And the
International Commission on Intervention and State Sovereignty reiterated the crucial importance of this perspective in its 2001 report.[51]

The logic of this approach resides in underscoring a state's responsibilities and
accountabilities to domestic *and* international constituencies. Accordingly, a state

The UN High Commissioner for Refugees Sadako Ogata visits Sarajevo in July 1992. (UNHCR Photo/E. Dagnino, A. G. L. Ronchi)

would be unable to claim the prerogatives of sovereignty unless it meets internationally agreed-on responsibilities, which include respecting human rights and providing life sustenance to its citizens. Failure to meet such obligations would legitimize involvement and even military intervention by the society of responsible states.

Whether for IDPs or refugees, the UNHCR has always found it difficult to negotiate what it calls durable solutions. The preferred durable solution is repatriation, but this usually entails fundamental political change in the country of origin—something the UNHCR obviously cannot produce with the wave of a magic wand. The UNHCR does not deal with Palestinian refugees; they are serviced by the UN Relief and Works Agency (UNRWA).[52] But the fundamental problems remain the same. In the Middle East, at least two generations of refugees have been born in camps; "durable solutions" have proven elusive.

Both the UNHCR and UNRWA share other frustrations. Both are dependent on host-state cooperation for security and other policies in refugee camps. For Rwandan refugees in the Congo (formerly Zaire), as for Palestinian refugees in Lebanon or Syria, the host state makes decisions about what groups are allowed to have arms or engage in political activity. In both examples, refugee groups have been active, respectively, in preparation for launching armed attacks against the Tutsi government in Rwanda or any government in Israel. UN refugee agencies are caught in these types of political struggles without either the legal authority or the power to make a difference.[53] Because of such considerations in Zaire and Tanzania, some NGOs, or at least some of their national sections such as Doctors Without Borders, refused to service refugee needs, believing the NGO was contributing to a resumption of violence. The

TABLE 6.3   Top Financial Contributors to the International Committee of the Red Cross, 2001 (excluding services and in-kind donations)

Governments	National Red Cross/Crescent Societies
USA	German
United Kingdom	American
Switzerland	Norwegian
Netherlands	Japanese
(European Commission)	Spanish
Sweden	Swedish
Norway	British
Canada	Italian
Japan	Canadian
Italy	Dutch
Germany	Finnish
Denmark	Danish

SOURCE: ICRC Secretariat, *Annual Report 2001* at www.icrc.org

UNHCR decided to stay. It did not want to abandon genuine civilians who had been displaced and were really being held hostage by armed militias. In the view of the UNHCR, it was up to the UN Security Council to provide proper security in refugee camps.

Another durable solution entails resettlement. This option is made difficult because of the very large numbers of people involved in many migrations. In the early 1990s there were about 18 million refugees and persons in refugee-like situations and at least an equal number of internally displaced persons. Permanent resettlement for most refugees was out of the question as far as host states were concerned. For example, almost 5 million persons, or a third of the population, left Afghanistan during the fighting there in the 1980s. Iran and Pakistan hosted many of these persons. Resettlement was not a serious option given not only the numbers but also the lack of economic infrastructure of the two host states. And most refugees do not want to settle in a strange land if there is any hope of a sufficient change to make their home country safe.

Moreover, even smaller numbers of persons may seem too large. The United States tried to exclude as many Haitians as possible from coming to Florida during the 1980s. Many residents of Florida did not want more Haitian resettlement there. In the 1990s the German government decided it had too many foreigners of all nationalities applying for asylum there. The neo-Nazi right wing in Germany carried out a number of violent attacks. Further refugee resettlement, whether temporary or permanent, seemed out of the question to a German government struggling to maintain social peace. In fact, all countries of traditional resettlement for refugees, from Canada to Australia, decided to restrict as many refugees as possible during the 1980s and 1990s.

Rwandan children who lost their parents in a massacre rest at Ndosha Camp in Goma, Zaire, July 1994. (UN Photo 186797/J. Isaac)

It is relatively easy to restrict numbers when a country is one of second asylum, or resettlement. A state party to the 1951 treaty is not obligated to accept any refugees for resettlement. When dealing with refugees from Vietnam who are in Hong Kong, the United States can select whomever it wishes for entry into the United States.

Only a country of first asylum is legally obligated not to return those with a well-founded fear of persecution. Economic migrants can be returned legally, but for genuine refugees under the UN convention of 1951, there is no ceiling on the number permitted temporary safe haven in the form of asylum. This can be a problem from the point of view of *raisons d'état*. Thus the UNHCR can find itself trying to protect and assist refugees, but in a context in which the host government may have its own reasons for denying safe haven to as many as possible. The UNHCR does not have the legal authority to make the final determination, much less the power to get states to do what the UNHCR prefers.

In trying to manage large and politically sensitive problems, the UNHCR for a time developed a reputation for effectiveness. In 1981 it was awarded the Nobel Peace Prize. Afterward, however, criticisms increased about its internal management and external influence.[54] One High Commissioner, Jean-Pierre Hocké of Switzerland, resigned in the midst of controversy. In 1990 Sadako Ogata of Japan became the first woman to head the agency, and the dynamism and reputation of the agency seemed to regain some of the previous high ground. But by the end of the 1990s, however, questions continued to be raised about what had become a sizable bureaucracy. Ogata was replaced after two five-year terms by a former Dutch prime minister, Rudd Lubbers. Responding to the desires of the Western states that fund his budget, he instituted a series of cost cutting measures.

It should be emphasized that refugees and those in a refugee-like situations usually are fleeing human rights violations. It is only when the root causes of these human flows are addressed that the preferred durable solution, repatriation, can be achieved. This requires political commitment from the international community. For example, the large number of refugees from Afghanistan, who had taken refuge in neighboring countries like Pakistan and Iran, were only able to return in safety when the Taliban government was removed by international armed conflict in 2001, and the follow-on government of Hamid Karzai provided a more welcoming environment—although one that was not problem-free. In the meantime, the UNHCR is left to cope as best it can. This has been especially challenging in the context of the deteriorating humanitarian situation throughout much of Africa. Yet the approach to post-conflict peace-building employed under UN aegis in Bosnia, Kosovo, East Timor, and elsewhere in the late 1990s provided hope for some improved attention to these forcibly displaced.

Supervising Rights and Development

Despite vast amounts of words in the General Assembly and Human Rights Commission about socioeconomic rights and a claimed right of development, the first forty-five years of the United Nations witnessed few concrete efforts to translate this diplomatic rhetoric into policy. For much of the UN's history there was little serious effort among policymakers to devise programs that promoted economic growth in developing countries while integrating internationally recognized human rights. As a former head of the UN Centre for Human Rights documented, rhetoric about human rights and planning for economic growth was kept in separate compartments at the UN.[55] The United Nations Development Programme (UNDP), the World Bank, UNICEF, WHO, the World Food Programme (WFP), and other UN organizations went about their traditional business in developing countries without much regard for the language of rights. There was some programmatic rhetoric about "women in development," but this was not coordinated with legal instruments oriented to women's rights.

This situation began to change in the late 1980s and early 1990s. Important opinion leaders in developed countries became dissatisfied with the record of attempts to achieve economic growth through authoritarian governments. The record in Africa between 1955 and 1985 was especially poor. Political changes, particularly in Latin America but to a lesser extent elsewhere, gave rise to more democratic governments in developing countries. Seeking macronational economic growth without attention to human rights could lead to marginalization of sectors of society. Even the World Bank, which had long claimed that human rights factors were "political" and therefore not within the bank's mandate, began to reconsider its stance—albeit with considerable confusion. The bank, the largest lender to developing countries, began to emphasize what it called "good governance." This could and sometimes did entail attention to civil and political rights, even though competing interpretations abounded. Although the bank still sought to avoid taking a stand about democracy at the national level, it did endorse participatory development. Within the concept of social assessment, it made judgments about the extent of popular participation in development projects.[56]

As part of this broad shift by various actors toward incorporating human rights considerations into "development," the UNDP created indices trying to measure "human freedom" and "human development" in a socioeconomic context, which are suggested in Tables 6.1 and 6.2. Since the effort began in 1990 under the guidance of the late Pakistani economist Mahbub ul-Haq, the annual publication of the *Human Development Report*[57] has provoked a storm of controversy, often from developing countries.[58] Among other criticisms, publications from the UNDP were said to exceed the responsibilities of an international civil service. Developing countries had long been sensitive to secretariat officials' passing judgment about how states measured up to international standards. Contributing to the controversy was the undeniable fact that the methodology used to rank countries according to various human rights was debatable. UNDP abandoned its freedom index, but like the World Bank, the agency talked more about participatory development. It endorsed an active role for citizens' groups in development projects. This approach entailed defense of civil rights such as freedom of speech and freedom of association.

As noted, from 1987 the expert committee supervising the Covenant on Economic, Social, and Cultural Rights became more assertive than its predecessors. This increased activity, too, fed into the increased efforts at the United Nations to link human rights and development. And the UN Human Rights Commission began to study accurate indicators for social and economic rights. The basic logic of the claimed right to development, which had been accepted in resolution form by the General Assembly but not turned into a treaty right, was that economic development meant more than economic growth. Development meant economic growth with attention to civil-political and socioeconomic rights.

The logic of the International Bill of Rights is that economic growth is to be pursued primarily according to democratic state capitalism with a welfare state. There is to be political participation, which entails certain civil rights, in making public policy. The state is to exercise broad responsibility for the economy and society; private property is to be respected in principle; and the state is to guarantee minimal standards of material welfare, especially to those unable to purchase it. In hyperbolic synopsis, the International Bill of Rights calls for Sweden writ large.[59] Whether real life could be breathed into the right to development, especially over the opposition of conservatives in the United States, was not clear. Even if the Clinton administration proved more sympathetic than its predecessors to economic and social rights and to the right to development, it has been far from clear that the U.S. Senate would consent to treaties on these subjects or that Congress would provide much foreign assistance to fund projects abroad that were directed to minimum standards of food, clothing, shelter, and health care. Although the Bush administration pledged to add $5 billion at the International Conference on Financing for Development in March 2002, the United States ranked last among all OECD states in percentage of its GNP directed to official development assistance. For the United States, as for most other

Carla Del Ponte, Chief Prosecutor for the International Criminal Tribunal for the former Yugoslavia, meeting with Special Representative of the Secretary-General and UNMIK head, Hans Haekkerup, in Pristina. (UN/DPI Photo)

states, rhetoric in favor of human rights exceeded the reality of support for concrete UN human rights action.[60]

Emergency Assistance

But what happens when economic development (meaning economic growth accompanied by internationally recognized human rights) breaks down because of war, public emergency, or natural disaster (sometimes combined with corruption or incompetence)? The UN system has long been involved in trying to cope with natural disasters, whether those that evolve slowly (for example, drought) or suddenly (for example, earthquakes or volcanic eruption). The UN has increasingly become involved in responding to socioeconomic needs resulting from war and public emergencies.

In situations said to be peaceful or in the absence of acknowledged armed conflict, various UN organizations exist either to prepare for these disasters or to respond to them.[61] As mentioned earlier, in 1992 the Department of Humanitarian Affairs, incorporating the UN Disaster Relief Office (UNDRO), was created to coordinate international humanitarian relief. In January 1998, as part of the Secretary-General's reform initiative, the department was restructured and renamed the Office for the

Coordination of Humanitarian Affairs. OCHA is headed by an Under-Secretary-General who serves as emergency relief coordinator (ERC) responsible for coordinating disaster relief both within and outside the UN system. UNHCR and UNICEF usually play active, and sometimes lead, roles in coordinating international relief. The WFP is usually involved in logistics. WHO and the Food and Agriculture Organization (FAO) usually are not far behind. And the UNDP, which is supposed to coordinate all UN activities within a country, is also involved. The ERC has been mandated the responsibility of overseeing the rapid deployment of staff during crisis situations and ensuring that appropriate coordination mechanisms are set up.

Moreover, a galaxy of private relief organizations also is active. The International Federation of Red Cross and Red Crescent Societies, which loosely coordinates about 180 national units, sees natural disaster work as one of its primary reasons for being. Hundreds of other private agencies, such as Oxfam, Caritas, and Feed the Children, try to respond to natural disasters with emergency assistance.

A major problem with all of this international assistance, broadly conceived, is that no one really has been in charge. "Coordination" is an oft-used word to describe a loosely knit network of intergovernmental and non-governmental organizations as well as state agencies active in humanitarian relief. Every agency is in favor of coordination in principle, but few wish to be coordinated in practice. As has been accurately written, "There is no guarantee that emerging or existing situations of significant human suffering will be brought before the United Nations."[62]

There exists no system for triggering and delivering international disaster assistance; there is rather a hodgepodge of public and private agencies. And the independent role of the communications media in covering or ignoring a story is often important. Whether these actors are motivated to act because of a concern for the human rights to food, clothing, shelter, and health care (which has been rare) or because of humanitarian compassion (more prevalent), all of these actors have proceeded without central coordination—and thus with resulting overlap and confusion.

Various UN organizations have been protective of their decentralized independence. The private agencies have resisted coming under the full control of public authorities. Various agencies have competed among themselves for a slice of the action in a given situation and for credit for whatever accomplishments were achieved—said to be important for fund-raising.

To be sure, emergency assistance has been delivered and lives have been saved in a vast number of situations. Host governments have frequently welcomed international help for natural disasters, although some of the less savory governments have diverted sizable chunks of this aid to the pockets of the elite—for example, in Somoza's Nicaragua after a severe earthquake. The UN General Assembly, mostly reflecting the view of developing countries, has endorsed the idea of international assistance as long as state consent is obtained. Actors like the United States and the European Community have coordinated some of the assistance by providing public money to NGOs (sometimes called PVOs, private voluntary organizations, or VOLAGS, volunteer agencies). At times all of this activity is put under a UN umbrella, as in northern Iraq and the former Yugoslavia. But by and large, coordination in the form of an institutionalized response has been lacking. Coordinated effectiveness has to be constructed almost from scratch for each assistance operation by what Larry Minear has called the "humanitarian enterprise."[63]

Because of this long-recognized situation, the General Assembly in 1991 authorized in Resolution 46/182 a new position of Under-Secretary-General for emergency relief. But this official, however well intentioned and adept, still operates in a milieu in which public and private agencies resist central control over their independence of action and fund-raising. Donor states have expressed growing concern about this "nonsystem" and in the early 1990s issued a statement saying, "We commit ourselves to making the United Nations stronger, more efficient and more effective in order to protect human rights." At that time they also called for an "improvement in the UN system . . . to meet urgent humanitarian needs in time of crisis."[64] But decisive change for the better has not really materialized; in fact, the changes have been mainly cosmetic.[65]

With the creation of OCHA and the ERC a step was taken toward a more coherent coordination approach. The ERC chairs an interagency standing committee (IASC), which includes major UN and non-UN humanitarian actors. This body strives to facilitate interagency analysis and decisionmaking in response to humanitarian emergencies. Also, in his role as Under-Secretary-General, the head of OCHA serves as convenor of the Executive Committee for Humanitarian Affairs (ECHA), which is a cabinet-level forum for coordinating humanitarian policies within the UN. It is unclear how effective such coordination will be.

In armed conflicts and public emergencies stemming from so-called human-made disasters, the provision of emergency relief to civilians is only slightly more institutionalized. At least legal rights and duties have been clarified in international wars, and emergency relief in those situations has occurred—although not without problems. In relative terms, emergency assistance has usually fared worse in most internal wars—except for delayed assistance in Somalia.

By law and by tradition, the International Committee of the Red Cross (ICRC) coordinates international relief in international wars. The 1949 Geneva Conventions for victims of war, and the supplemental 1977 Protocol I, give the ICRC a preferred position for this task, especially since protecting powers (neutral states appointed by the fighting parties for humanitarian tasks) are rarely named anymore. As noted, the UN Security Council has affirmed the rights of civilians to international assistance in such wars, and belligerents have a legal duty to cooperate with neutral relief efforts. Protocol I from 1977 states clearly that starvation of civilians is not legally permitted in warfare and that belligerents are not legally permitted to attack objects vital to the survival of the civilian population.

The ICRC is a private agency whose sources of funds are summarized in Table 6.3 on page 182. The agency is specifically recognized in public international law and also by the General Assembly, which has accorded the ICRC observer status. (The Federation of Red Cross and Red Crescent Societies was also given observer status.) For large-scale relief the assembly prefers that UN organizations, along with NGOs, be the primary operational agents of humanitarian assistance and that the ICRC adopt a monitoring role.[66] In Somalia in the early 1990s, the ICRC remained to play a central role in relief, even after the Security Council authorized the use of force to deliver

Nelson Mandela speaks at a Cape Town rally the day before
his inauguration as President of South Africa. (UN/DPI
Photo/C. Sattleburger)

that relief. In other violent situations, as on the Indian subcontinent in 1971, the
ICRC worked closely with the UN system in monitoring the delivery of food and
other socioeconomic relief to East Pakistan/Bangladesh.

Here again the disorganization of the UN system regarding assistance comes into
play. There is no institutionalized lead agency for the UN in armed conflict, or in
peace. In the past, head agencies have been selected on an ad hoc basis by the UN Secretary-General. There is now the Under-Secretary-General for humanitarian affairs,
who must still negotiate operational details from a welter of options. What is now
called the Red Cross and Red Crescent Movement is either disorganized or decentralized; the ICRC does not fully control national Red Cross-Red Crescent units and
certainly not their international federation. There have been a number of suggestions
concerning how to improve the broad international response to civilian need in violent situations.[67]

The situation is even more complicated in internal armed conflict where one or more fighting parties does not represent a widely recognized state and where most of the fighting occurs primarily on the territory of one state. The laws of war (which also are called humanitarian law, the law of armed conflict, or the law for human rights in war) do not create a clear obligation to cooperate with the purveyors of humanitarian assistance. The ICRC is not given legal rights of leadership in internal war that are the same as in international war. Moreover, states and other fighting parties frequently disagree on whether an internal armed conflict exists as compared to a rebellion or insurrection falling under national rather than international law. The number of interstate wars has declined since 1945, but the number of violent situations seen by some as "internal wars" has risen, accompanied by great civilian loss of life and other suffering. A series of events since the end of the Cold War—within the former Yugoslavia and Soviet Union and within Somalia, Angola, Afghanistan, Burundi, Rwanda, Liberia, Mozambique, and Cambodia—suggests that atrocities and brutality seem a prevalent feature of what journalists call civil wars. In December 1996 in Chechnya, six Red Cross workers were murdered in their beds.

Neither the UN organization nor NGOs nor the ICRC has had consistent success in getting humanitarian assistance into places like the southern Sudan or, before that, parts of greater Ethiopia. The government of Indonesia may have been responsible for the deaths of 200,000 persons, mostly civilians, in fighting over East Timor in the 1970s, without any outside involvement to assist or protect civilians. The Khmer Rouge was unobstructed by anyone in the political murder of perhaps a million civilians in Cambodia in the 1970s. The Geneva Conventions and Protocols, supplemented by supportive UN Security Council resolutions, did not make much of an impact on Balkan parties motivated by expansion or revenge. Humanitarian assistance has no meaning to parties engaged in "ethnic cleansing," genocide, deliberate attacks on civilians and supposedly neutral personnel, and widespread rape and starvation as political weapons. Child soldiers and ragtag local militia make inculcation of humanitarian values difficult.

Given the difficulties encountered by both the United Nations and the ICRC in obtaining the consent of fighting parties in internal wars and public emergencies, some NGOs, like Médecins sans Frontières (Doctors Without Borders), have engaged in "cross-border" operations without consent. In the war in Afghanistan, fifty private agencies were reported to have acted on Afghan territory without the consent of Kabul.[68] Organizations like UNICEF and the WFP, not to mention the ICRC, are reluctant to proceed, although they have occasionally done so. Their policy guidance and funding come from states. Although they have relatively independent secretariats, they are part of an intergovernmental system whose officials must deal with governments in governing councils as well as in field programs. Executive heads of various UN organizations, and the office of the UN Secretary-General, have been creative in trying to cope with famine and disease in places like the southern Sudan and Somalia. But as a practical matter, trying to proceed without the consent of the warring parties can lead—and has led—to attacks on international and local relief personnel. Beyond legal niceties centering on sovereignty, there are practical concerns related to the safety of staff members. In the 1990s, more journalists and aid workers died than peacekeepers.

In general, international pressure is growing on warring parties in violent situations to permit access to civilians by humanitarian agencies. But UN organizations and the ICRC still have major difficulties in providing relief on neutral or balanced terms. Governmental consent was effectively overlooked by the international community in Somalia because there was no central government. Consent was bypassed to provide socioeconomic relief to Iraqi Kurds because the government in Baghdad was an international pariah after its invasion of Kuwait. "Consent" in East Timor from the Indonesian government was more a fiction than a fact because of the extreme pressure placed on Jakarta by Western donors. Situations in Bosnia and the Balkans, the Sudan, and old Ethiopia presented a different and more typical picture. The fighting parties regarded food relief as a political factor, and outside states saw very high costs in trying to coerce fighting parties into respecting the rights of civilians to adequate food, clothing, shelter, and health care. Many parties recoil at the paradox of "humanitarian war."[69] NATO's bombing of Kosovo and Serbia in 1999 brought this paradox into bold relief.

Addressing the nationalistic, ethnic, and communal wars and tensions of the 1990s was not only dramatic for states; it was traumatic as well for aid agencies. Until recently, the two most essential humanitarian principles (neutrality and impartiality) had been relatively uncontroversial, along with the key operating procedure of seeking consent from belligerents. These principles, too, became casualties in the 1990s.[70] A host of factors have challenged the classical posture: the complete disregard for international humanitarian law by war criminals and even by child soldiers; the direct targeting of civilians and relief personnel; the use of foreign aid to fuel conflicts and war economies; and the protracted nature of many so-called emergencies.[71] War has returned to Europe. In spite of the indictment and later arrest and trial of a sitting head of state (Slobodan Milosevic), whose head appeared on a "wanted" poster with a $5-million reward offered by Washington, genocide is alive and well.[72] In many ways, international humanitarian law seems to have been formulated to deal with a different world—one populated by governments and regular armies whose interests were often served by respecting the laws of war.[73] In writing of old-fashioned humanitarianism, David Rieff has gone so far as to suggest "the death of a good idea."[74]

In spite of these problems, and "identity crisis" is not too strong a term to describe the individual and collective soul-searching by civilian personnel, the preceding pages should have made clear that humanitarian values and expenditures on emergency assistance have expanded. "In the 1990s," summarized Adam Roberts, "humanitarian issues have played a historically unprecedented role in international politics."[75] In the dramatic example of the military campaign in Kosovo, Michael Ignatieff noted that "its legitimacy [depends] on what fifty years of human rights has done to our moral instincts, weakening the presumption in favor of state sovereignty, strengthening the presumption in favor of intervention when massacre and deportation become state policy."[76] The NATO bombing of Serbia over Kosovo may have been illegal in international law, in that NATO engaged in the first use of force without Security Council approval, but to many it was legitimate because of the moral argument suggested by Ignatieff.

Notes

1. In general, see Philip Alston, ed., *The United Nations and Human Rights* (Oxford: Clarendon Press, 1995); David P. Forsythe, "The UN and Human Rights at Fifty," *Global Governance* vol. 1 (1995), pp. 297–318, and *Human Rights in International Relations* (Cambridge: Cambridge University Press, 2000).

2. For an argument about the role of ideas and diplomacy in bringing about, over time, the end of slavery and formal colonialism, see Neta C. Crawford, *Argument and Change in World Politics: Ethics, Decolonization and Humanitarian Intervention* (Cambridge: Cambridge University Press, 2002).

3. Roger S. Clark and Madeleine Sann, eds., *The Prosecution of International Crimes: A Critical Study of the International Tribunal for the Former Yugoslavia* (New Brunswick, N.J.: Transaction, 1996).

4. Thomas M. Franck, "The 'Powers of Appreciation': Who Is the Ultimate Guardian of UN Legality?" *American Journal of International Law* 86, no. 519 (1992), pp. 519–523.

5. Fernando R. Tesón, "Changing Perceptions of Domestic Jurisdiction and Intervention," in Tom J. Farer, ed., *Beyond Sovereignty: Collectively Defending Democracy in the Americas* (Baltimore: Johns Hopkins University Press, 1996), pp. 29–51.

6. United Nations, *Report of the Secretary-General to the Security Council on the Protection of Civilians in Armed Conflicts*, March 30, 2001, UN document S/2001/331. The Security Council also adopted Resolution 1296 on protecting civilians on 19 April 2000; Resolution 1325 on protecting women's rights on October 31, 2000; and Resolution 1379 on protecting children's rights on November 20, 2001.

7. *Report of the Secretary on the Work of the Organization*, document A/51/1, para 1132.

8. *New York Times*, August 22, 1996, p. A9.

9. International Crisis Group, "A Framework for Responsible Aid to Burundi," http://www.intl-crisis-group.org/projects/showreport.cfm?reportid=901.

10. See, for example, Paul Gordon Lauren, *Power and Prejudice: The Politics and Diplomacy of Racial Discrimination* (Boulder: Westview Press, 1988), epilogue.

11. On the UN and El Salvador, and other human rights situations in the Western Hemisphere, see David P. Forsythe, "The United Nations, Democracy, and the Americas," in Tom J. Farer, ed., *Beyond Sovereignty: Collectively Defending Democracy in the Americas* (Baltimore: Johns Hopkins University Press, 1996), pp. 107–131; and WOLA, *Reluctant Reforms: The Cristiani Government and the International Community in the Process of Salvadoran Post-War Reconstruction* (Washington, D.C.: Washington Office on Latin America, 1993).

12. David P. Forsythe, *Human Rights and World Politics,* second revised edition (Lincoln: University of Nebraska Press, 1989), chapter 3.

13. John Tessitore and Susan Woolfson, eds., *A Global Agenda: Issues Before the 47th General Assembly of the United Nations* (Lanham, Md.: University Press of America, 1992), p. 240.

14. See further David P. Forsythe, "The United States and International Criminal Justice," *Human Rights Quarterly* 24, no. 4 (November 2002), pp. 974–991.

15. John Goldsmith and Stephen D. Krasner, "The Limits of Idealism," *Dædalus* 132, no.1 (Winter 2003), pp. 47–63.

16. David P. Forsythe, "The UN Secretary-General and Human Rights," in Benjamin Rivlin and Leon Gordenker, eds., *The Challenging Role of the UN Secretary-General* (Westport, Conn.: Greenwood Press, 1993), pp. 211–232.

17. Early influence by UN staff members in behalf of human rights can be seen in John P. Humphrey, *Human Rights and the United Nations* (New York: Transaction Books, 1984).

18. A joke circulating about the various recent heads of the UN Centre for Human Rights involved these characters: Van Boven was supposedly the most active and committed; his successor, Kurt Herndl, having seen what happened to van Boven, supposedly kept a low profile; his successor, Jan Martenson, was supposedly preoccupied with a public image for himself and his office; his successor, Antoine Blanca, was supposedly an old crony of the Secretary-General who had no interest in human rights. So the joke went like this: Van Boven (in fact) wrote the book *People Matter;* so Herndl supposedly wrote *States Matter;* Martenson, *I Matter;* Blanca, *It Doesn't Matter.*

19. http://www.unglobalcompact.org.

20. Brian Knowlton, "Rights Chief Talks of U.S. Role in Her Leaving," *International Herald Tribune,* July 31, 2002, p. 6.

21. Howard Tolley Jr., *The UN Commission on Human Rights* (Boulder: Westview Press, 1987).

22. Tom J. Farer, "The UN and Human Rights: More than a Whimper, Less than a Roar," in Adam Roberts and Benedict Kingsbury, eds., *United Nations, Divided World: The UN's Roles in International Relations* (Oxford: Clarendon Press, 1989), p. 123.

23. For an example of this American bias, see Morris B. Abram, "Human Rights and the United Nations: Past as Prologue," *Harvard Human Rights Law Journal* 4 (1991), pp. 69–83.

24. Tessitore and Woolfson, *A Global Agenda,* p. 236.

25. Telford Taylor, *The Anatomy of the Nuremberg Trials* (New York: Knopf, 1992), p. 29.

26. Cathal J. Nolan, *Principled Diplomacy: Security and Rights in U.S. Foreign Policy* (Westport, Conn.: Greenwood Press, 1993), chap. 7.

27. Tolley, *The UN Commission,* p. 179.

28. Joe W. Pitts III and David Weissbrodt, "Major Developments at the UN Commission on Human Rights in 1992," *Human Rights Quarterly* 15, no. 1 (February 1993), pp. 122–196.

29. Scott Leckie, "An Overview and Appraisal," *Human Rights Quarterly* 13, No. 3 (September 1991) p. 568. See also Paul Hunt, *Reclaiming Social Rights: International and Comparative Perspectives* (Aldershot,UK: Dartmouth, 1996).

30. Raymond Gastil, ed., *Freedom in the World, 1992* (New York: Freedom House, 1993).

31. See Pitts and Weissbrodt, "Major Developments," p. 17.

32. For a discussion, see Paulo Sérgio Pinheiro, "Musings of a Special Rapporteur on Human Rights," *Global Governance* 9, no.1 (January–March 2003), pp. 7–13.

33. Karen Reierson and David Weissbrodt, "The Forty-third Session of the UN Sub-Commission on Prevention of Discrimination and Protection of Minorities: The Sub-Commission Under Scrutiny," *Human Rights Quarterly* 14, no. 1 (February 1992), p. 271.

34. Cindy A. Cohn, "The Early Harvest: Domestic Legal Changes Related to the Human Rights Committee and the Covenant on Civil and Political Rights," *Human Rights Quarterly* 13 no. 2 (1991), pp. 320–321.

35. Cohn, "Early Harvest," p. 321.

36. William Schabas, "Spare the RUD or Spoil the Treaty: United States Challenges the Human Rights Committee on Reservations," in David P. Forsythe, ed., *The United States and Human Rights* (Lincoln: University of Nebraska Press, 2000), pp. 110–125.

37. David Harris, "Commentary by the Rapporteur on the Consideration of States Parties' Reports and International Cooperation" (paper presented at Symposium: The Implementation of the International Covenant on Economic, Social and Cultural Rights), *Human Rights Quarterly* 9, no. 1 (February 1997), p. 149.

38. Philip Alston and Bruno Simma, "First Session of the UN Committee on Economic, Social and Cultural Rights," *American Journal of International Law* 81 (1987), p. 750.

39. Leckie, "Overview and Appraisal," pp. 566–567.

40. UN, *UN Yearbook 1991* (New York: UN), p. 534.

41. See further Philip Alston and James Crawford, eds., *The Future of UN Human Rights Treaty Monitoring* (Cambridge: Cambridge University Press, 2000); and Anne Bayefsky, *The UN Human Rights Treaty System: Universality at the Crossroads* (Ardsley, N.Y.: Transnational Publishers, 2001).

42. See especially Gil Loescher, *The UNHCR and World Politics: A Perilous Path* (Oxford: Oxford University Press, 2001); Arthur C. Helton, *The Price of Indifference* (Oxford: Oxford University Press, 2002); Niclaus Steiner, Mark Gibney, and Gil Loescher, eds., *Problems of Protection: The UNHCR, Refugees, and Human Rights,* (New York: Routledge, 2003).

43. See Thomas G. Weiss, "Internal Exiles: What Next for Internally Displaced Persons?," *Third World Quarterly,* 24, no.3 (June 2003), and Kathleen Newland with Erin Patrick and Monette Zard, *No Refuge: The Challenge of Internal Displacements* (New York and Geneva: UNOCHA, 2003).

44. One can follow the changing numbers of "persons of concern" to the UNHCR by checking the different editions of *The Refugee Survey Quarterly,* published by the UNHCR, or by going to www.unhcr.org. For complete statistics on IDPs, see www.idpproject.org, maintained by the Norwegian Refugee Council.

45. See Thomas Risse, Stephen C. Rapp, and Kathryn Sikkink, *The Power of Human Rights: International Norms and Domestic Change* (New York: Cambridge University Press, 1999).

46. Michael Ignatieff, "Human Rights: The Midlife Crisis," *New York Review of Books* 46, no. 9 (May 20, 1999), p. 58.

47. Commission on Human Rights, *Analytical Report of the Secretary-General on Internally Displaced Persons*, UN document E/CN.4/1992/23.

48. Francis M. Deng, *Protecting the Dispossessed: A Challenge for the International Community* (Washington, D.C.: Brookings Institution, 1993); Francis M. Deng et al., *Sovereignty as Responsibility* (Washington, D.C.: Brookings Institution, 1995); and Francis M. Deng, "Frontiers of Sovereignty," *Leiden Journal of International Law* 8, no. 2 (1995), pp. 249–286. See also Roberta Cohen and Frances M. Deng, *Masses in Flight: The Global Crisis in Displacement* (Washington, D.C.: Brookings Institution, 1998); and Roberta Cohen and Frances M. Deng, eds., *The Forsaken People: Case Studies of the Internally Displaced* (Washington, D.C.: Brookings Institution, 1998).

49. Bernard Kouchner and Mario Bettati, *Le devoir d'ingérence* (Paris: Denoël, 1987); and Mario Bettati, *Le droit d'ingérence: Mutation de l'ordre international* (Paris: Odile Jacob, 1996).

50. Kofi Annan, "Secretary-General's Speech to the 54th Session of the General Assembly," September 20, 1999. Intervention was also a major theme in the annual *Report of the Secretary-General on the Work of the Organization,* Document A/54/1.

51. International Commission on Intervention and State Sovereignty, *The Responsibility to Protect* (Ottawa: ICISS, 2001).

52. Benjamin N. Schiff, *Refugees unto the Third Generation: UN Aid to Palestinians* (Syracuse, N.Y.: Syracuse University Press, 1995).

53. See further Fiona Terry, *Condemned to Repeat? The Paradox of Humanitarian Action* (Ithaca, N.Y.: Cornell University Press, 2002).

54. Tessitore and Woolfson, *A Global Agenda,* p. 260.

55. Theo van Boven, "Human Rights and Development: The UN Experience," in David P. Forsythe, ed., *Human Rights and Development* (London: Macmillan, 1989), pp. 121–135.

56. Internal World Bank documents increasingly dealt with human rights. See, for example, C. Mark Blackden, "Human Rights, Governance, and Development: Issues, Avenues, and Tasks," October 10, 1991, p. 17 plus attachments. For an overview, see David P. Forsythe,

"Human Rights, Development, and the United Nations," *Human Rights Quarterly* 19, no. 2 (May 1997), pp. 334–349.

57. This was published from 1990 to 2003 by Oxford University. The first ten (1990–1999) are available on CD-ROM.

58. Tessitore and Woolfson, *A Global Agenda*, p. 245.

59. Forsythe, *World Politics*, n. 5.

60. David P. Forsythe, "Human Rights and U.S. Foreign Policy: Two Levels, Two Worlds," *Political Studies* 43 (1995), pp. 111–130.

61. For a discussion of these organizations and the difficulties encountered in recent crises, see Thomas G. Weiss and Cindy Collins, *Humanitarian Challenges and Intervention,* second edition (Boulder: Westview Press, 2000); and Jonathan Moore, *The UN and Complex Emergencies* (Geneva: UN Research Institute for Social Development, 1996).

62. Francis M. Deng and Larry Minear, *The Challenges of Famine Relief: Emergency Operations in the Sudan* (Washington, D.C.: Brookings Institution, 1992), p. 125.

63. Larry Minear, *The Humanitarian Enterprise: Dilemmas and Discoveries* (West Bloomfield, Conn.: Kumarian, 2002).

64. David J. Scheffer, "Challenges Confronting Collective Security: Humanitarian Intervention," in U.S. Institute of Peace, *Three Views on the Issue of Humanitarian Intervention* (Washington, D.C.: U.S. Institute of Peace, 1992), p. 5.

65. Thomas G. Weiss, "Humanitarian Shell Games: Whither UN Reform?" *Security Dialogue* 29, no. 1 (March 1998), pp. 9–23.

66. David P. Forsythe, "Choices More Ethical than Legal: The International Committee of the Red Cross and Human Rights," *Ethics & International Affairs* 7 (1993), pp. 131–152.

67. For a discussion of future possibilities, see a series of essays from practitioners in Thomas G. Weiss and Larry Minear, eds., *Humanitarianism Across Borders: Sustaining Civilians in Times of War* (Boulder: Lynne Rienner, 1993).

68. Elizabeth Ferris, "Humanitarian Politics: Cross-Border Operations in the Horn of Africa," paper prepared for the International Studies Association annual meeting, Acapulco, Mexico, 1993, p. 3.

69. There is a vast literature on humanitarian intervention. Two scholarly treatments are Nicholas J. Wheeler, *Saving Strangers: Humanitarian Intervention in International Society* (Oxford: Oxford University Press, 2000); and Robert Keohane and J. L. Holzgrefe, eds., *Humanitarian Intervention,* (Cambridge, UK: Cambridge University Press, 2003). For an overview of the issue with key worded bibliography, see Thomas G. Weiss and Don Hubert, *The Responsibility to Protect: Research, Bibliography, Background* (Ottawa: ICISS, 2001).

70. See Thomas G. Weiss, "Principles, Politics, and Humanitarian Action," *Ethics and International Affairs* 13 (1999), pp. 1–22; as well as "Responses" by Cornelio Sommaruga, Joelle Tanguy, Fiona Terry, and David Rieff on pp. 23–42.

71. For more extensive discussions of this landscape, see Michael Maren, *The Road to Hell: The Ravaging Effects of Foreign Aid and International Charity* (New York: Free Press, 1997); and Alex de Waal, *Famine Crimes: Politics and the Disaster Relief Industry in Africa* (Oxford: James Currey, 1997). This debate was initiated by Alex de Waal and Rakiya Omaar, *Humanitarianism Unbound? Current Dilemmas Facing Multi-Mandate Relief Operations in Political Emergencies* (London: African Rights, 1994), Discussion Paper no. 5. For a discussion of the disarray among humanitarians, see, for example, John Borton, "The State of the International Humanitarian System," *Overseas Development Institute Briefing Paper* no. 1 (March 1998); Myron Wiener, "The Clash of Norms: Dilemmas in Refugee Policies," *Journal of Refugee Studies* 11, no. 4 (1998), pp. 1–21; and Mark Duffield, "NGO Relief in War Zones: Toward an Analysis of the New Aid Paradigm," in Thomas G. Weiss, ed., *Beyond UN Subcontracting: Task-Sharing*

with Regional Security Arrangements and Service-Providing NGOs (London: Macmillan, 1998), pp. 139–159. For a look at the political economy of conflict, see, for example, Mark Duffield, "The Political Economy of Internal War: Asset Transfer and the Internationalisation of Public Welfare in the Horn of Africa," in Joanna Macrae and Anthony Zwi, eds., *War and Hunger: Rethinking International Responses to Complex Emergencies* (London: Zed Books, 1994), pp. 5–69; David Keen, *The Economic Functions of Violence in Civil Wars* (Oxford: Oxford University Press, 1998), Adelphi Paper 320; and François Jean and Christophe Rufin, eds., *Economies des guerres civiles* (Paris: Hachette, 1996).

72. Samantha Power, in *A Problem from Hell: America and the Age of Genocide* (New York: Basic Books, 2002) finds that particularly the U.S. response to genocide has long been found wanting.

73. See Adam Roberts, "Implementation of the Laws of War in Late 20th Century Conflicts," Parts 1, 2, *Security Dialogue* 29, nos. 2 and 3 (June and September 1998), pp. 137–150 and 265–280; and a special issue on "Humanitarian Debate: Law, Policy, Action," *International Review of the Red Cross* 81, no. 833 (March 1999).

74. David Rieff, "The Death of a Good Idea," *Newsweek*, May 10, 1999, p. 65. However, Rieff seems to have changed his mind in several ways in *A Bed for the Night: Humanitarianism in Crisis* (New York: Simon and Schuster, 2002).

75. Adam Roberts, "The Role of Humanitarian Issues in International Politics in the 1990s," *International Review of the Red Cross* 81, no. 833 (March 1999), p. 19.

76. Michael Ignatieff, "Human Rights: The Midlife Crisis," *New York Review of Books* 46, no. 9 (May 20, 1999), p. 58.

7 Change, the United Nations, and Human Rights

It should be clear by now that the phrase "the United Nations" refers more to a framework, a stage, or an institutional setting than to an organization with the capacity for independent action. Although it is true that some persons, such as those in the office of the Secretary-General, can take relatively independent action, "the UN" mostly refers to a process in which the most important policy decisions are made by governments representing territorial states. Most fundamentally, "the UN" has become involved in changing policies toward human rights as states have changed their policies. But other actors have been important, too.

Overview of the United Nations and Rights

The promotion and protection of human rights has become one of the UN's more prominent activities. In the annual *United Nations Yearbook,* more pages are usually devoted to human rights, by far, than to any other subject matter. Those printed pages accurately reflect the attention given to UN diplomacy on human rights.

The United Nations has been crucial to the promotion of human rights, largely through the setting of standards through treaties. This role is logical, given that the UN is the only global intergovernmental organization to define universal human rights. Global rights treaties can be developed outside the UN, as shown by the development of international humanitarian law for armed conflict—with the ICRC serving as drafting secretariat and the Swiss government serving as convenor of diplomatic conferences. Yet the UN remains crucial for specifying human rights standards. The UN's other promotional work, such as its educational and technical assistance activities in the field of rights, has been less prominent. This does not mean that these activities are not important or should not be expanded.

There are now so many treaties on universal human rights that it can be asked whether the proliferation of norms has become counterproductive to advancing human rights. Internationally recognized human rights now include civil, political, social, economic, and cultural rights. There are demands for even more treaties covering solidarity rights, such as rights to development, peace, a healthy environment, and the fruits of the common heritage of humankind (for example, of Antarctica and the seabed). In fact, the General Assembly has dictated a lack of focus by voting that

The Peace Palace, seat of the International Court of Justice. (UN/DPI Photo/A. Brizzi)

all rights are of equal worth and are interdependent. But where does one begin serious work in the name of rights?

The UN's efforts at rights protection clearly have expanded, making a summary difficult to fashion. Once again, are there too many monitoring mechanisms and too many protective processes within the UN system?

Concern is growing about the cost of operating all the UN bodies working on rights issues. We noted in the previous chapter that questions had been raised about funding for the Committee on the Elimination of Racial Discrimination (CERD). The committee working for women's rights (CEDAW) had no budget in the early 1990s to pay word processors. At the same time the Centre for Human Rights had only six persons to process 300,000 private petitions alleging violations under the International Bill of Rights. Of the total UN regular (meaning administrative) budget, human rights protective activities have recently doubled but still account for less than 2 percent. This means that in the early twenty-first century the UN Human Rights Centre had about $25 million available for its global work in human rights. This is, in fact, a very small sum for the international public sector. The United States alone was spending about $500 million per year to promote democracy around the world.[1]

Moreover, there is an equally valid question about overlapping jurisdictions. On the subject of torture, the world now has the UN Sub-Commission on Human Rights, which takes up torture issues; the UN Human Rights Commission, which

Mary Robinson, former High Commissioner for Human Rights (UN/DPI photo/J. Bu)

does the same; the Economic and Social Council, which sometimes gets involved; the UN General Assembly, which sometimes tries to exert pressure against governments that torture; the UN Committee Against Torture, which functions under the 1986 Torture Convention; the European Committee Against Torture, which functions under a regional treaty; the ICRC, which functions either under the treaties of humanitarian law or according to its own traditions; and other NGOs such as Amnesty International that are active in this arena.

The fundamental problem for the UN in the issue-area of human rights is that states are willing to approve human rights standards and to allow diplomatic pressure short of effective enforcement, but they are still ambivalent about many measures of strong international enforcement. It was not until December 1993 that states voted in the General Assembly to create the post of UN High Commissioner for Human Rights; even then, as noted in Chapter 6, the mandate was vague and the office's authority was weak. To repeat the core problem, most states permit weak UN supervision of rights policies, but they do not systematically allow effective international enforcement.

So for those states whose authorities are genuinely interested in protecting human rights, the best course through the UN has been to adopt more treaties to emphasize the problems and to create more supervisory bodies for specialized diplomacy. But this strategy only compounds the problem of too many standards with too many overlapping bodies with too few resources. It is indeed a vicious circle, produced by state foreign policy at the UN.

It is true that in the 1990s there was a definite move in international relations to involve international courts more in enforcing at least some internationally recognized human rights. Earlier we noted the development of the two ad hoc tribunals established by the Security Council for the former Yugoslavia and for Rwanda. We also noted that the International Criminal Court had come into being in 2002. It remains to be seen whether these judicial developments can be consolidated and made to play an important role in international relations, given the opposition to especially the ICC by states like the United States, Russia, China, and Israel.

In the meantime several ideas have been put forward to improve the situation through diplomacy, at least in relative terms:

- The Secretary-General or his representative should present an annual human rights report, similar to his annual report on the work of the organization, to the General Assembly each September in which he draws attention to the most important rights problems. The UN High Commissioner for Human Rights already makes an annual report, but it does not receive the same attention as reports coming from the Secretary-General.
- Treaty-monitoring bodies should be allowed to participate in the work of other UN bodies—for example, the UN Human Rights Commission.
- The UN programs of technical assistance and education for human rights should be greatly expanded in order to strengthen national institutions for rights protection and thus to head off major rights problems before they become international crises.
- The office of the Secretary-General, in conjunction with the office of the UN High Commissioner for Refugees and the Office for the Coordination of Humanitarian Affairs, should further improve the UN early warning system to predict gross violations of internationally recognized human rights that are likely to lead to mass migration.
- A concerted effort should be made to integrate more extensively human rights considerations into development programs through the UNDP, World Bank, International Monetary Fund (IMF), and UN specialized agencies. Just as there is a new UN body on sustainable development, there should be a coordinating body on human rights in development. These efforts have been grouped under the rubric of "mainstreaming human rights," although to date there has been more rhetoric than real change.
- Greater use should be made of preventive diplomacy, such as the systematic dispatch of UN human rights observers in situations of tension, both to deter rights violations and to provide timely reporting to New York.

These are "doable" steps that could be taken without waiting for a radical alteration in state attitudes. Nevertheless a full revolution in UN action for human rights depends on further change in state foreign policies. But especially younger developing countries are very protective about any codification of norms encroaching on conventional notions of state sovereignty. And when it comes to its own sovereignty, the United States is as protective as states in the Global South like India or Mexico.

More on *Raisons d'État*

The meaning of national interest is not fixed.[2] "National interest," like "state sovereignty," is a social construct. Ideas about national interest are devised by humans in a process of change over time. For schools of thought like realism that emphasize the concept of national interest as a core component of international relations, the concept lacks precise and transcendent meaning. Whether human rights should be, or can be, linked to national interests is a matter of debate. Some say that ideas about human rights constitute intangible national interests. Many states increasingly have included human rights within the domain of state interests. This can be done for different reasons.

The delegations of some states have pursued human rights at the United Nations as a weapon in power struggles. The objective has been to delegitimize a certain government; the means has been to emphasize human rights violations. In the previous chapter we mentioned U.S. policy toward Cuba in the UN Human Rights Commission.[3]

Some states have adopted a broad definition of their own self-interests. They seek not just territorial integrity, political independence, and other goals directly related to the narrow and expedient interests of the state. They also define their interests in terms of an international society in which human dignity is advanced by serious attention to human rights. Just as governments have defined their domestic interests beyond physical security and economic welfare, so have governments used their foreign policy to advance human rights and humanitarian goals. The states making up NATO did this in Kosovo in 1999. The fact that this was outside the Charter resulted in an eminent group arguing for its "legitimacy" even if it was "illegal."[4]

Some states have adopted a variation on this theme by arguing that the practice of human rights not only advances human dignity but also advances security and national peace. They cite, for example, the lack of major international wars between stable democracies. Or they cite the need to deal with human rights violations to bring peace to countries like El Salvador or Bosnia.

Some states may even lend support to international action on human rights not because they believe any of the arguments above but simply because they feel pressured or obligated to support such action. For example, if Japan or Germany is to obtain a permanent seat in the Security Council, each will be expected to increase its attention to human rights in its foreign policies. That pressure may come from NGOs or from other states.

For all of these reasons, states have brought about a legal and diplomatic revolution with regard to the treatment of human rights at the United Nations. The same process has occurred in other multilateral fora such as the Council of Europe, the European Union, the Conference (now Organization) on Security and Cooperation in Europe (CSCE and OSCE), the Organization of American States (OAS), and to a lesser extent, the African Union and the Arab League. Clearly the Western-style liberal democracies especially have a human rights component to their foreign policies, and this affects the UN.

Any one state may pursue international action on human rights for different reasons at different times, or for many reasons at any given time. In the United States, the Franklin D. Roosevelt administration stressed the famous "Four Freedoms" in order to give meaning to the sacrifices of World War II. The Truman administration accepted human rights language in the UN Charter for the same reason and because it was pressured by NGOs and Latin American states to live up to its national self-image as a champion of human rights. The Eisenhower administration, like other U.S. governments, used human rights in the struggle with the Soviet Union, as when it used the General Assembly to discuss issues like forced labor. The Carter administration used human rights not only to try to rally domestic support but also because it genuinely wanted at least a Western Hemisphere sympathetic to fundamental personal rights. The second Reagan administration used human rights as part of an appeal to American greatness in the world, and as a way to undercut the radical left. The dictatorial Ferdinand Marcos was eased from power in the Philippines to undercut the New People's Army, and General Augusto Pinochet was eased out of the presidential palace in Chile to forestall a resurgence of radical opposition to his brutal rule.

It may be true, although difficult to prove, that the linkage of human rights to *raisons d'état* is at least sometimes a reflection of increasing moral solidarity in international society. That is, governmental authorities may speak in terms of their interests, but the deeper process may involve a moral stance on the dignity of persons without regard to nationality or borders. John Ruggie has shown that a concern to better the world is deeply ingrained in American culture and history and that this concern has often taken a multilateral form, including great attention to the United Nations, in the twentieth century.[5] Edward Luck, however, has correctly stressed the fundamental ambivalence in American attitudes toward multilateralism.[6] U.S. officials may speak of American strategic interests in a stable, democratic, and prosperous Europe; but the deeper driving force behind Washington's policy may be moral outrage at atrocities in the Balkans. In Bosnia and other parts of the former Yugoslavia, U.S. policy was intertwined with various multilateral efforts, including those of the United Nations.

Moral and practical components of state foreign policy may also be sufficiently entangled as to be inseparable. The United States may be morally outraged at atrocities in the Balkans and at the same time may believe that self-interest dictates opposition to Serbian atrocities of ethnic cleansing. Not to oppose those human rights violations would be to encourage more atrocities. Not to act against atrocities might be to encourage refugee flight that could destabilize friendly states.

Whether state foreign policies are driven by practical or moral wellsprings, or whether it is even possible to say what is expedience as compared to morality, the cumulative effect of this shifting and complex redefinition of the national interest has been to internationalize human rights. State authorities in general consider human rights, even if within a state's territorial boundaries, to be a proper subject for international discussion. They often are willing to engage in a wide range of diplomatic activity to promote and also indirectly to protect those rights. At times states are even willing to engage in economic coercion in the name of rights, and more rarely they at least agree to some type of military action to guarantee such fundamental rights as the access by suffering civilians to international help.

States have not abandoned the principle of state sovereignty. It is used as a defensive argument against UN action on human rights by different states on different issues at different times. The principle is especially favored by the authorities of weaker and younger developing countries that fear losing status and influence at the hands of more powerful states. Older, more powerful states like the United States are also not hesitant to trot out the tired slogans of state sovereignty when the international community of states, through some UN agency, questions American execution of minors or the mentally impaired. Yet over time, the appeal to restrictive notions of state sovereignty and their use have been weakened. As a result, UN organizations have expanded their diplomatic activity for human rights across and even within states; they also have occasionally resorted to economic and military sanctions in this area. The UN is now deeply involved on human rights issues to an extent completely unforeseen in 1945.

States have used their initial sovereignty to create UN standards and UN supervisory procedures that later have restricted their operational sovereignty in the field of human rights. In legal theory states are no longer free to treat even "their own" citizens as they wish. Internationally recognized human rights impose standards that are binding on governments. In political practice, governments may be pressured or coerced because of human rights violations. The process is far from consistent, systematic, reliable, and effective, but it is irreversible.

State Coalitions

In multilateral organizations like the United Nations, many key decisions are taken by voting, so coalitions among states become important. During the early years of the UN, the Western coalition controlled proceedings in the General Assembly and the Human Rights Commission. The International Bill of Rights was effectively negotiated between 1948 and 1956, and this was an important step in the promotion of internationally recognized human rights. Western states pushed for the Universal Declaration of Human Rights and at least the negotiation of the UN Covenant on Civil and Political Rights and the UN Covenant on Economic, Social, and Cultural Rights. The communist coalition played the game of negotiating the treaties and accepting human rights in theory while opposing the implementation of many internationally recognized rights in practice. Yet beyond setting standards there were few breakthroughs in UN diplomatic action for protecting human rights. This was a time when the Human Rights Commission issued its self-denying ordinance about investigations into specific problems and states.

Perhaps most important, the United States exercised little constructive leadership on human rights at the United Nations for several decades after about 1948.[7] The

United States was a dominant power and, to some states, a hegemonic power on security and economic issues. But it was neither dominant nor hegemonic on human rights. Human rights issues were a sensitive topic in the United States both because of legally sanctioned racial discrimination and because some members of Congress feared a more powerful executive through the treaty process. Many in the U.S. Senate in the 1950s feared that the president and his colleagues in the executive branch would expand their authority at the expense of both the Constitution and the Congress by concluding human rights treaties. The U.S. Supreme Court had held, in *Missouri vs. Holland,* that the federal government could acquire authority beyond the Constitution via the treaty-making power as long as a treaty did not contradict the Constitution. So the executive branch, with two-thirds of the Senate giving advice and consent, can expand on the fundamental rights mentioned in the U.S. Bill of Rights through the conclusion of human rights treaties.[8]

Many members of Congress tried to amend the U.S. Constitution to make all treaties non-self-executing. That is to say, if this approach were successful, no U.S. treaty could take legal effect within the United States without enabling or supplemental legislation by the entire Congress. This amendment would add a legislative step to the treaty process, similar to that in the United Kingdom, making it more difficult for the executive branch to change U.S. law via the treaty process, with only the Senate required to consent.

President Eisenhower, in order to keep the treaty process as simple as possible and to maintain the authority of the executive branch as much as possible, agreed not to press for U.S. ratification of human rights treaties if congressional forces would drop their effort to amend the Constitution through the so-called or generic Bricker amendment—named after the congressman who had led the fight for the constitutional amendment. There were several such efforts in the Congress, but no amendments were ever adopted. From Eisenhower's time until Jimmy Carter, no president asked the Senate for advice and consent on the two core UN human rights covenants.

Beyond the United States and the Western coalition of states, the admission of newly independent developing countries from 1955 and the acceleration of this pattern from 1960 drastically changed the voting on human rights issues at the United Nations. As indicated, the dynamics were fueled by a dialectical process resulting in a new synthesis. Developing countries sought to use the language of human rights to pressure Israel and South Africa, and the West countered with efforts to broaden those rights-oriented maneuvers. Human rights NGOs helped fashion this North-South compromise. The result was a new diplomatic dynamism in UN attempts to protect certain human rights in certain countries. The Soviet coalition added its own emphases, particularly focusing on rights violations in Pinochet's Chile after the overthrow of Marxist president Salvador Allende.

This North-South interchange on human rights, with the European communist states usually aligned with the South, accounted for many human rights developments at the United Nations during approximately 1970 to 1985. To take one example, much more rhetorical interest in a collective right to development was taken within the UN after the addition of many states from the Global South to the General Assembly's membership. This new alignment of states also helps to explain why some things did not happen at the UN on human rights. For instance, the UN was unable to put diplomatic pressure on Idi Amin's brutal government in Uganda because of the shield provided by the solidarity among developing countries and deferred to by communist countries. Discrimination by a black government against Asians and white Europeans was not of major concern in the General Assembly, a different type of double standard.

After the transition period of 1985–1991, during which European communism collapsed, the coalitions shifted. There were more democratic governments both in the General Assembly and on the Human Rights Commission, and there was more overall collaboration in the Security Council. Yet democratic governments, especially those in the Global South, like India, were not always enthusiastic about UN activities regarding protection of human rights. Several developing countries sought to block certain protective attempts by the Human Rights Commission. And cooperation in the Security Council was sometimes hampered by negative votes or abstentions.

Ambivalence on the part of developing countries about international action for human rights and humanitarian affairs was evident. They knew that their sovereignty was at issue. Most developing countries, for example, in the General Assembly refused to elevate a right to humanitarian assistance above the rights of state sovereignty. Resolutions on this subject that were adopted in the late 1980s and early 1990s were complex. Although reaffirming the principle of state sovereignty, Resolution 46/182 indicated that parties in a "country," but not necessarily only the government of a state, might request international assistance. It also suggested that the consent of a state to international humanitarian action might be tacit. In practice, developing countries went along with assertiveness by the international community in defeated Iraq after 1991 and in Somalia on behalf of outside action for human rights.

Beyond developing countries, some permanent members of the Security Council also were at times either ambivalent or reluctant about international action for human rights and humanitarian affairs. The Boris Yeltsin government of the Russian Federation, successor to the Soviet permanent seat in the council, expressed open reservations about some of the policies being pursued against rights violations by governments in Iraq and Serbia. The Chinese government did not support international action to protect human rights. But it chose to abstain on most council resolutions rather than veto them and thus to stimulate Western circles of opinion pushing for sanctions on China itself after the Tiananmen Square massacre of June 1989.

Observers will have to wait and see whether a predominant North-South conflict will continue significantly to limit UN efforts to protect human rights and whether Russia and China will regularly join developing countries in obstructing protective efforts.[9] We will also see whether UN protective action for human rights will be expanded because sufficient numbers of governments from the South and the former USSR join the West in pushing for enhanced protection. At the 1993 Vienna World Conference on Human Rights, most developing and formerly communist countries reaffirmed the idea of universal human rights. But since 1948 the central problem has not been the abstract codification of norms, but rather marshaling sufficient political will to deal with concrete violations of internationally recognized human rights.

Nonstate Actors

States may be the official building blocks of the United Nations, but nonstate actors have been active and sometimes influential in human rights and humanitarian matters. Three types of nonstate actors are discussed here: NGOs, individual experts, and secretariat personnel.

Precision is difficult when gauging the influence generated by NGOs on human rights matters. The most general problem is that their impact becomes intertwined with governmental and other influences, often making it impossible to say where NGO influence leaves off and governmental influence begins. If Amnesty International lobbies for new standards and monitoring mechanisms concerning torture, and if states in the General Assembly finally approve these ideas in treaty form, it is difficult to pinpoint what has occurred because of Amnesty International's efforts and what has occurred because of governmental policy.[10] The same analytical problem has been recognized in trying to chart the influence of interest groups in domestic politics by comparison to governmental officials.

Only a few genuine human rights NGOs are active on a transnational or international basis with a mandate linked to the International Bill of Rights: Amnesty International, the International Commission of Jurists, the International League for Human Rights, Human Rights Watch, Physicians for Human Rights, Doctors Without Borders, and a few others. The ICRC comes close to meeting this definitional test, although its historical mandate is linked more to the treaties on the laws of war than to the International Bill of Rights.

Other broadly oriented NGOs are active on human rights from time to time, but they are linked more to religion or some other normative standard than to the International Bill of Rights. An example is the World Council of Churches.

Moreover, some NGOs with narrower mandates take up particular human rights questions. They have more to do with a particular problem or nationality than with internationally recognized rights per se. Cultural Survival, for example, concentrates on indigenous peoples. Anti-Slavery International focuses on slavery, slave-like practices, and the slave trade. All sorts of nationally based or oriented groups take up particular causes while frequently ignoring the human rights situation in other nations.

The point to be stressed here, beyond these descriptive remarks, is that all of these NGOs have been active on human rights issues at the United Nations. And they certainly have generated some influence for the promotion and protection of human rights in the abstract. Their cumulative impact has been such that various states have opposed UN consultative status for some of the more assertive NGOs. In 1991 Cuba and some Arab states prevented Human Rights Watch, based in New York, from obtaining consultative status via ECOSOC. NGOs want to achieve that status because they gain the right to circulate documents and speak in UN meetings. During the Cold War several human rights NGOs were excluded from consultative status by communist and developing governments, a practice that continues. In 1995 Freedom House, based in New York, was temporarily denied consultative status by a coalition of states including democracies such as India and the Philippines. These states disliked the rating system and other reports authored by Freedom House. Had NGOs generated no influence, it is unlikely that certain governments would try so hard to keep them out of UN proceedings.

At the 1993 Vienna World Conference on Human Rights, this tension between governments and human rights NGOs was much in evidence. Some governments evidently feared the influence that might be generated by NGOs, perhaps by releasing damaging information to the world press. At a UN human rights conference in Teheran in 1968, NGOs had participated in the intergovernmental sessions. In Vienna in 1993, governments denied NGO participation in the official meetings but agreed to a separate NGO parallel conference. This formula was followed at the 1995 Beijing conference on women, and at the 2002 conference on racism in Durban, South Africa. On human rights as on many other subjects, states feel they cannot completely suppress NGOs, but many states try to limit NGO influence.

As a separate matter, the ICRC is the only nonstate actor working for human rights and humanitarian affairs that has been granted observer status in the General Assembly. This came about because of its close work with governments, especially in situations of armed conflict, and because of its reputation. The ICRC is a quasi-public actor, being explicitly recognized in international public law, such as the 1949 Geneva Conventions for armed conflict. But the ICRC follows a general policy of discretion and therefore does not normally reveal the details of what its delegates have observed inside states. Unlike Human Rights Watch and Amnesty International, for example, the ICRC does not normally rely on detailed public pressure to achieve its objectives. For all these reasons states were prepared to accord to the ICRC a status at the UN "higher" than other private or quasi-private agencies. (Later the International Federation of Red Cross and Red Crescent Societies, which focuses on development and natural disasters, was also accorded observer status; this is the federation of national Red Cross and Red Crescent aid societies.)

Large numbers of NGOs have consultative status and participate in meetings of the Human Rights Commission. They submit private complaints about a pattern of gross violations of human rights to the UN system. Their information is officially used in most of the monitoring agencies of the UN system such as the Human Rights Committee, the Committee on Economic and Social Rights, CERD, CEDAW, CAT, CRC, and others. Some NGOs have played influential roles behind the scenes in the adoption of General Assembly resolutions concerning human rights.

Just as private human rights groups have had an impact on national policies concerning human rights, so have NGOs had some influence on UN proceedings. A formal UN vote or document, reflecting the policy of a majority of governments, may have started or been advanced by one or more NGOs. Quite clearly the UN Declaration on Minorities and also the Declaration on Indigenous Peoples were advanced by the efforts of NGOs—although it was states that voted for the declarations. Some 1,000 NGOs attended the Vienna World Conference on Human Rights, conducting their own proceedings and engaging in the specific criticisms that state delegations at the conference agreed to avoid. Without doubt certain NGOs were influential in the negotiation and adoption of the treaties banning anti-personnel land mines and creating the International Criminal Court.

Just as it is certain that private groups have teamed with the U.S. Congress to improve human rights reporting by the Department of State,[11] so is it true that NGOs have teamed with interested governments to improve rights activity through the United Nations. If human rights NGOs had been absent at the UN during its first half-century, it is unlikely that the world organization's record would be as good as it is. The record is not good enough in the view of these same NGOs, but some positive steps have been taken.[12] It is useful here to recall the notion of international regimes, which combines international rules, public actors, and private actors, all in order to regulate or govern an issue area.[13]

Had those NGOs been absent, something would have been done on human rights nevertheless—not only because of states but because of secretariat personnel. John P. Humphrey of Canada, the first UN director-general of human rights, appears to have had some influence on the content of the Universal Declaration of Human Rights. Other secretariat personnel have advanced ideas or proposals that eventually were accepted by governments voting in UN bodies. Executive heads of UN agencies like UNICEF, WHO, and ILO have clearly taken action on their own for children's health care and for labor rights. All of this is apart from the human rights activity of the office of the Secretary-General itself, which we analyzed in the preceding chapter.

Moreover, the individual experts who have sat in the UN Sub-Commission on Protection of Minorities or who have been rapporteurs or other experts for the Human Rights Commission have often nudged the process along. Most of the monitoring agencies created by treaty have been staffed by individuals acting in their personal capacity. Many have been truly independent from their governments as well as serious about and dedicated to human rights.

Theories of Change

The sum total of state and nonstate input has caused the record of the United Nations regarding human rights to be what it is. Is there a summary statement that clarifies the dynamics of activity on human rights at the UN? Can we theorize why this activity has been what it has been, and can we project what directions this activity will take in the future?

Two related views are initially noteworthy in this regard. The first focuses on the notion of knowledge. Ernst Haas suggests that if private communities of knowledge come to an agreement on human rights, this agreement eventually will produce a policy consensus in the public sector.[14] When this public consensus emerges, the United Nations and other IGOs become empowered to take important action for human rights. There will be a complete change in the UN, not just partial change. For example, if most human rights groups could prove that civil and political rights were necessary for economic growth or that socioeconomic rights were necessary for stable democracy, that private agreement would eventually affect public policy through the United Nations and would lead to dramatic change.

The second and related view emphasizes learning. George Modelski returns to the ideas of Immanuel Kant to suggest that those who speak for states are in the process of learning a commitment to human rights, especially to the civil and political rights making up democracy.[15] In this view, historical evolution shows expanded learning of the benefits of democracy—whether in terms of human dignity or in terms of international peace.

Knowledge and Human Rights Change

If Haas's view is correct about the state of knowledge in epistemic communities, several generalizations emerge. First, if all or most private groups active on human rights agreed on particulars, this consensus of knowledge would eventually inform public policy in such a way that the United Nations would be mandated by governments to take more authoritative and effective action for human rights. We may be seeing a paradigm shift. Even the World Bank, which long sought to avoid the "political" matter of human rights, now says that economic growth should be pursued with attention to "good government," as noted in Chapter 6. The bank and its supporters have concluded—at least for now—that at least some authoritarian models of economic growth do not work very well. In fact, "good governance" has essentially been defined as the opposite of what authoritarian Third World and Soviet bloc countries did in the 1960s, 1970s, and 1980s. Clearly, the new approaches have positive human rights dimensions. Whether this new policy on "social assessment" by the bank stems from private agreement should be researched. Human rights NGOs certainly lobby the World Bank, but their impact on decisions is unclear.

It is important to observe, however, that knowledge about human rights is not so much scientific knowledge as moral judgment. It is even more difficult to achieve widespread agreement on morality than on scientific knowledge. Even within one nation with a dominant culture, private groups differ over such human rights issues as abortion, the death penalty, health care, and adequate nutrition.

It is one thing to get private groups to agree that children are better off if vaccinated. It is hard for anyone to disagree with a vaccination program or to advocate keeping WHO out of a poor country where it wants to conduct a vaccination program. Opinion is based on irrefutable scientific knowledge. It is another thing to get private circles of opinion to agree that internationally recognized human rights should be applied in all cultures and situations. Not all medical experts agree that health care should be treated as a human right. Not all medical personnel agree that abortion should be legal. There may be agreement on the technical process of how to perform an abortion, for that is based on science. But there clearly is not agreement on whether abortion should be legal, for that is based on moral judgment. Moral judgment is greatly affected by varieties of opinion because moral argument by definition is difficult to completely prove or disprove.

It cannot be shown scientifically that everyone will always, everywhere be better off if rights are applied. If repressive governments allow the practice of civil and political rights, many, if not most, will lose power. This may usher in a period of disorder and economic decline. The former Soviet Union is a clear example, at least in the short run. In repressive China, many persons have been advancing economically, since macroeconomic growth as stimulated by an expanding private sector was around 10 percent per year in the early 1990s. Many people in private circles of opinion do not believe that rights, especially political rights, would do anything but interrupt this beneficial process in China. Spectacular economic growth has been achieved in Singapore since the 1970s, but without full civil and political rights. Important religious circles in Islamic nations believe freedom of religion and gender equality would hurt society. Even actors that generally seek to protect rights do not insist on the application of rights in every situation. Many Western private groups do not press the issue of the practice of human rights in Saudi Arabia. They also defer to a military coup in Algeria that prevented the election of a fundamentalist Islamic party. Some of these groups believe on moral grounds that Western access to oil or blocking fundamentalist Islam justifies repressive governments. We know for sure that democratic rights in places such as Sri Lanka have led to illiberal governments that discriminate against minorities and commit other rights violations. So a commitment to human rights such as democratic political participation is less a matter of scientific proof of inherent progress and more a matter of moral and political choice in context.

Beyond the important distinction between scientific and moral knowledge in private networks, the public policy consensus across all governments at the United Nations concerning human rights is weak or incomplete. The formal consensus is broad, but the real consensus is weak. In other words, human rights treaties are widely accepted in law and widely violated in practice. Learning of "correct" policies has been more formal than substantive.

As long as this weak actual consensus exists, human rights activity will not lead to systematic and authoritative protection by the United Nations. New and potentially important steps may happen spasmodically, but these steps will fall short of full change leading to systematic and effective protection. The Security Council may authorize humanitarian intervention in Somalia, under the legal fiction of a response to a threat to international peace and security, but at roughly the same time it will fail to sponsor decisive action in similar situations in Liberia or the Sudan, much less Rwanda and Burundi. The council may set the stage for use of force in Iraq, at least partially in the name of persecuted civilians, but it will be lethargic about similarly appalling conditions in the Democratic Congo. Some observers speak of the "deepening" of "the UN human rights regime." But greater legal authority and financial resources have *not* been transferred to the UN High Commissioner for Human Rights or to the UN Human Rights Commission. (We analyze courts next.)

Knowledge, Learning, Courts

The issue of the UN and international courts provides a good test of the Haas theory of change, linked to knowledge, and the Modelski theory of change, linked to learning.[16] We already noted that the UN's International Law Commission, a technical body of individual legal experts not instructed by governments, discussed the creation of a standing international criminal court with jurisdiction over persons who are individually responsible under international law. And that the Security Council created a criminal court under Chapter VII of the Charter with jurisdiction over certain international crimes committed in the territory of the former Yugoslavia from 1993. And that the council created a second ad hoc criminal court with jurisdiction over various international crimes committed in Rwanda during 1994, when that country was the scene of genocide, political murder, war crimes, and other atrocities. Finally, we noted the emergence of a permanent International Criminal Court in 2002. By 2003, there was a further court operative in Sierra Leone, made up of national and international judges, using national and international law, and a similar hybrid was finally approved amid controversy in Cambodia. Regarding the latter, many human rights NGOs regarded it as too weak, while the Secretary-General said it was the only arrangement that would allow trials to occur.

Under the Modelski theory one can raise the question of whether states, acting through the UN, have shown a propensity to learn that international relations must be governed by a humane rule of law. Are states learning that they will be more secure, and their citizens better off, if there is either a permanent UN criminal court or a series of ad hoc criminal courts to deal with particular situations? To use semantics from the Haas theory, have private groups used their knowledge to push states into agreement on the demonstrable truth that just as all national societies have institutionalized procedures for criminal cases, so international relations should, too? Or are states just muddling through on this issue with incomplete agreement leading to the piling up of actions at the UN without any clear and firm overall position on authoritative and effective criminal courts?

Such learning—to the extent that it did occur—was clearly not universal. Some states, especially those that contemplate use of their militaries in armed conflict, are reluctant to create a judicial organ to which they might, as a last step under the principle of complementarity, have to turn over their citizens to face in the ICC, for example, charges of violations of the laws of war. Neither George W. Bush nor the Congress was supportive of the ICC. Indeed, there was active and vitriolic opposition. Clearly, the United States has not "learned" the advantages of having an ICC; nor is it clear that "knowledge" compels movement in this direction. Emotive or romantic nationalism may trump expert knowledge about the benefits of international criminal justice.

In general, state learning pertaining to international criminal law showed differences and inconsistencies. States tried ad hoc criminal courts now and then, but given the ninety ratifications of the ICC in 2003, about half of the UN membership was not all sure it wanted to be under the jurisdiction of a UN standing criminal court. States might feel the need to show a response to atrocities by creating ad hoc courts, but some of the same states might still eschew the costs of a decisive involvement that would curtail the atrocities and punish those responsible. States might agree in theory that individual punishment for atrocities is a good idea, but in particular situations they might like the freedom to negotiate and strike deals with war criminals and the like. In 2003, in the context of an impending war in Iraq, there was much discussion of the wisdom of offering Saddam Hussein amnesty and impunity for past atrocities, because such a process would avoid much destruction and bloodshed involved in his forceful removal and possible trial.

One can seek peace and justice through both diplomacy and criminal proceedings. In places like Yugoslavia in 1995 and immediately thereafter, it was not clear that one could pursue both avenues at once. If various political leaders had not been defeated and had retained power, and if one then had to include them in negotiations aimed at stopping the fighting and curtailing human rights violations, pursuing them as international criminals might not be the wisest course of action. This type of analysis pertained not just to leaders like Slobodan Milosevic in 1995 but also to Mohammed Farah Aideed in Somalia in 1993. In the Balkans, it might have been wise not to try to prosecute Milosevic in 1995–1996, but wise to put him in the dock by 2002. In writing the rules for the operation of international courts, one needed to allow also for humane progress through political choice and diplomacy. "Learning" on these matters is a precise and complicated matter.[17] Scientific evidence about the correct way to proceed is hard to come by. Many "experts" support different policies in different situations.

Then there was the equally complicated question of whether criminal proceedings contribute to or impede national reconciliation after armed conflict.[18] The theory behind criminal courts, national or international, is that license to commit atrocities has to end in order to "clear the air," provide catharsis to the victims and their families, and deter future violations of rights. But one could certainly question whether criminal trials of Hutus in Rwanda while a Tutsi-dominated government controlled the country would achieve the desired objectives. And in many places from South Africa to El Salvador, national and international officials concluded that the way to advance national reconciliation after brutal internal war was to avoid criminal proceedings as much as possible. One might utilize truth commissions to establish facts, but only in a few places, such as South Korea, Ethiopia and Germany, did trials proceed against former repressive rulers. It was not clear that such national trials were, on balance, a good thing. After dictatorship in Spain and Portugal, one moved toward stable liberal democracy by avoiding both trials and truth commissions.

Thus, acquiring human rights knowledge is a complicated affair about which reasonable persons can differ, and the UN's forays into international criminal justice have been carried out in the context of a lack of clear consensus and firm commitment about the "legalization" of the response to gross violations of human rights.[19]

Summary, with Reference to Democracy

The relation between knowledge, learning, and UN human rights activity can be summarized. It is difficult to achieve a broad consensus about human rights among private networks because one is dealing more with morality than with science. Without this NGO and "expert" agreement about human rights specifics, the consensus among governments on human rights and public policy will remain thin or incomplete. The situation is one of varied learning and incomplete change. There is more UN action for human rights now than before; but it still falls short of being fully systematic and institutionalized, as well as authoritative and effective.

For example, take the question of whether states are learning, on the basis of cumulative knowledge, a commitment to liberal democracy (meaning elected governments that are rights-protective). "The UN" certainly now advocates democratic development, as will become clear in Part Three of this book. Some evidence seems encouraging. Immanuel Kant suggested that over time liberal democracies would become more numerous. A wave of democratization from about the mid-1970s to the early 1990s seemed to verify that Kantian view from the eighteenth century. Francis Fukuyama argued in the early 1990s that right-thinking persons had to necessarily conclude that liberal democracy was the best way to respect individuals and limit governmental power. Thus the development of the norms of liberal democracy represented the end of history, at least in political theory, and a democrat became the last "political man."[20] Within the empirical democratic trend, however, there are illiberal democracies that are genuinely supported by majority opinion but are nevertheless not rights-protective. Yugoslavia under Milosevic and Croatia under Tudjman were clear examples. If it holds, this historical trend toward liberal democracy would suggest a growing acceptance not only of civil and political rights but of economic and social ones as well. Almost all democracies, except the United States, endorse the latter rights as well as the former.

But we should be wary. No more than about one-third of the states in the world have been truly stable or consolidated liberal democracies at any given time.[21] This was still true in the early twenty-first century. Moreover, earlier waves of democracy suffered setbacks or reverse waves, and this could happen again. Many states with democratic governments in the 1990s still manifested strong militaries not fully controlled by elected leaders. To take just one short era, democratic government was overthrown in Haiti in 1991, attacked in Venezuela in 1992, and suspended in Peru in 1992. After disappointing economic developments in many parts of the former Soviet Union, communist parties made a comeback through elections. Other democratic governments could easily suffer similar fates.

Over a rather long time, there has been an increase in recognition of the advantages of liberal democratic government. Respect for civil and political rights has grown, albeit in a zigzag rather than a linear progression. This learning had been enhanced, at least temporarily, by the various failures of authoritarian communism in Europe and authoritarian models among developing countries.

But in many countries ruled by newly democratic governments, there were major obstacles to the consolidation—meaning stabilization and maturation—of democracy. Perhaps most important, economic growth was slow or nonexistent, and the benefits of the economic system were widely perceived as inequitable. It was not self-evident that the new democratic governments, confronted with particularly daunting economic problems, could create the socioeconomic context that would sustain a new and fragile democracy. Particularly in Latin America, but elsewhere as well, democracy has been created but not necessarily consolidated. Consequently, authoritarianism has often returned. Were civil and political rights being learned systematically, or was democratic learning frequently followed by a re-learning of the advantages of authoritarianism in a vicious circle?

Moreover, not all democratic governments at the United Nations have fully supported its human rights program. U.S. authorities have at times tried to suppress diplomatic pressure on authoritarian friends. British officials have opposed all sorts of human rights initiatives.[22] The Indian government has at times elevated the principle of state sovereignty above UN pressure for human rights concerning itself and other developing countries.

A Web of Norms that Results in Change?

It has often been said that most situations in which human rights are respected are produced by national conditions—with only secondary influence from international factors.[23] This axiom contains considerable truth but can be overstated. The relaxation of the Soviet grip on Eastern Europe in the late 1980s was the key factor in unleashing local human rights forces. By 1996, there were more IGO, NGO, and state policies in operation in support of international human rights than ever before in world history. In some cases, as in Haiti in 1994, international factors were decisive—at least in the short run. The international context had definitely changed for the better.

A theory of transnational change and human rights is relevant to our discussion here. According to the book, *The Power of Human Rights*, a transnational advocacy network, made up of both private and public actors, can definitely bring about progressive change in behalf of rights of personal integrity, over time.[24] As argued in this theoretical work with case study examples, a merger of international and national actors can, over time, institutionalize human rights norms pertaining to summary execution, torture and mistreatment, and other fundamental civil rights referred to collectively as rights of personal integrity. Hence in this view, domestic private groups, acting in tandem with foreign actors of various sorts, can bring effective pressure for rights-protective change on repressive governments. In this theory, there is certainly an important place for both UN norms and UN actors. In fact, this theory allows for considerable variation in which actors in the transnational coalition exert the most influence in behalf of human rights—international NGOs, domestic private groups, officials of international organizations, officials of states. The sum total of the efforts of these various and shifting actors accounts for progressive change. It is the network or movement that counts, within which one or more UN actors may be found.

Furthermore, some research suggests that this hopeful theory of change in the domain of human rights can pertain not just to rights of personal integrity and to repressive non-Western governments. Some research suggests that the same "spiral model," originally developed to explain change regarding rights of personal integrity in repressive non-Western states, might also be helpful in understanding change on minority rights in emerging liberal democratic states in Eastern Europe.[25] In this view, the Czech Republic has come to better protect the rights of the Roma, and Romania has come to better protect the rights of its ethnic Hungarian minority, because of a transnational advocacy process that has grown steadily. In these two cases, it may have been the Council of Europe and the European Union, more than the United Nations, that largely accounted for pulling these governments into practicing what they had promised on minority rights. But in other cases, as in El Salvador in the late 1980s and early 1990s, one sees an important role for UN officials like the Secretary-General.

This theory about the importance of human rights norms and discourse over time, as linked to transnational pressure, which eventually traps states in their own stated commitments to human rights, can incorporate much incidental knowledge that we already knew about human rights and change. For example, UN sanctions against both Rhodesia and South Africa in the 1960s and 1970s did not create the resistance to white-minority rule. But these international actions helped to empower local citizens to confront the policies of governments based on racial discrimination. The Guatemalan ambassador to the United States had it exactly right when describing the democratic resistance to an authoritarian coup in 1993: It was the Guatemalan people, local human rights groups, national business elements, and even sectors of the military that demanded a return to democracy as a human right; the role of the international community was important but secondary.[26] The United Nations then accelerated its efforts in Guatemala, negotiating human rights agreements and mediating conflicts. The role of the world organization was to facilitate local trends toward liberal democracy, which by definition encompasses the protection of many human rights. A transnational focus remains necessary to encompass the totality of change pertaining to human rights.

Final Thoughts

None of the above denies the point that when UN efforts to protect human rights are tried, they must be pursued with determination. There is still much lip service to human rights at the UN that is not backed by serious commitment. For example, early innovations to meet the human rights challenges in the former Yugoslavia in the early 1990s received so little financial and political support that they were mere tokens. Innovative steps included the first emergency session convened by the UN Commission on Human Rights; the first deployment of field monitors by the UN Human Rights Centre (now UNHCHR); the appointment of a special rapporteur to report to the Security Council on human rights abuses and of a Commission of Experts to report on breaches of the Geneva Conventions; the assignment of human rights responsibilities to UNHCR protection officers in the field; and, most significant, the establishment of international war-crimes tribunals. But the credibility of these initiatives was undermined to the extent that they were not matched by the resources and leadership to make them work. Ineffectiveness is distressing enough for the victims in the former Yugoslavia. But perhaps even more important is the potential negative impact that weakness and failure will have for future violators of human rights, where effective international action will obviously be necessary.

Once again it is clear that frequently at the UN there is much disagreement about human rights protection. We are dealing with moral and political matters as much or more than with scientific knowledge; and particularly states have "learned" a variety of things from past experience. Given the legal starting point of state sovereignty, the international community has come a long way in generating respect for the idea of human rights. But "the UN" still has a long way to go before achieving the systematic observance of human rights as called for in the Charter "without distinction as to race or nationality, sex, language or religion."[27] Three analysts have recently put forward one image that may help readers understand the disconnect between rhetoric and reality in the human rights arena. There is a disparity between the normative and "operating" system.[28] The UN's operating system is not the basic equivalent of a computer operating system (for example, Microsoft Windows) that functions to allow the use of spreadsheets or word processing. Even when functioning well, the international human rights operating system requires consensus effort, intense diplomacy, and much luck to produce what are, at best, modest results.

Notes

1. *Funding Virtue: Civil Society Aid and Democracy Promotion* (Washington: Carnegie Endowment, 2000).

2. See further David P. Forsythe, ed., *Human Rights and Comparative Foreign Policy* (Tokyo: United Nations University Press, 2000).

3. On the use of human rights by governments that primarily has to do with their strategic or other expediential interests, see Kirsten Sellers, *The Rise and Rise of Human Rights* (Phoenix Mill, UK: Sutton Publishing, 2002).

4. Independent Commission on Kosovo, *Kosovo Report: Conflict, International Response, Lessons Learned* (Oxford: Oxford University Press, 2000).

5. John Ruggie, *Winning the Peace: America and World Order in the New Era* (New York: Columbia University Press, 1996).

6. Edward C. Luck, *Mixed Messages: American Politics and International Organization 1919–1999* (Washington: Brookings Institute, 1999).

7. Tony Evans, *US Hegemony and the Project of Universal Human Rights* (London: MacMillan, 1996).

8. Cathal J. Nolan, *Principled Diplomacy: Security* (Westport, Conn.: Greenwood Press, 1993).

9. On voting at the UN and the North-South conflict in particular, see Soo Yeon Kim and Bruce Russett, "New UN Voting Alignments," *International Organization* 50, no. 4 (Autumn 1996), pp. 629–652.

10. For a detailed case study of the role of Amnesty International in developing the UN treaty against torture, see Peter R. Baehr, "The General Assembly: Negotiating the Convention on Torture," in David P. Forsythe, ed., *The United Nations in the World Political Economy* (London: MacMillan, 1989), pp. 36–53.

11. David P. Forsythe, *Human Rights and U.S. Foreign Policy: Congress Reconsidered* (Gainesville: University Press of Florida, 1988).

12. Rodney Bruce Hall and Thomas J. Biersteker, *The Emergence of Private Authority in Global Governance* (Cambridge: Cambridge University Press, 2002).

13. See Stephen D. Krasner, ed., *International Regimes* (Ithaca, N.Y.: Cornell University Press, 1983).

14. Ernst B. Haas, *When Knowledge Is Power: Three Models of Change in International Organizations* (Berkeley: University of California Press, 1990).

15. George Modelski, "Is World Politics Evolutionary Learning?" *International Organization* 44 (Winter 1990), pp. 1–24.

16. On international courts and international criminal justice see Steven R. Ratner and Jason S. Abrams, *Accountability for Human Rights Atrocities in International Law: Beyond the Nuremberg Legacy* (Oxford: Clarendon Press, 1997); Aryeh Neier, *War Crimes: Brutality, Genocide, Terror, and the Struggle for Justice* (New York: Times Books, 1998); and Sarah B. Sewall and Carl Kaysen, eds., *The United States and the International Criminal Court: National Security and International Law* (Lanham, Md.: Rowman and Littlefield, 2000).

17. Martha Minow makes clear that there is no one response to atrocities that is always right in every situation; see *Between Vengeance and Forgiveness: Facing History After Genocide and Mass Violence* (Boston: Beacon Press, 1998).

18. See Rama Mani, *Beyond Retribution: Seeking Justice in the Shadows of War* (Cambridge: Polity, 2002).

19. For an overview of the "legalization" of international relations, see the special issue of *International Organization* (Summer 2000). This issue traces the growing demand for specific international law that is adjudicated.

20. Francis Fukuyama, *The End of History and the Last Man* (New York: Free Press, 1992).

21. Samuel P. Huntington, *The Third Wave: Democratization in the Late Twentieth Century* (Norman: University of Oklahoma Press, 1992).

22. Tom J. Farer, "The UN and Human Rights: More than a Whimper, Less than a Roar," in Adam Roberts and Benedict Kingsbury, eds., *United Nations, Divided World: The UN's Roles in International Relations* (Oxford: Clarendon Press, 1989), p. 126.

23. See, for example, Jack Donnelly, "Human Rights in the New World Order: Implications for Europe," in David P. Forsythe, ed., *Human Rights in the New Europe* (Lincoln: University of Nebraska Press, 1994).

24. Thomas Risse, Stephen C. Ropp, and Kathryn Sikkink, eds., *The Power of Human Rights: International Norms and Domestic Change* (Cambridge: Cambridge University Press, 1999).

25. Safia Swimmelar, "The Making of Minority Rights and the Return to Europe: International Norms and Transnational Actors in the Czech Republic and Romania," dissertation, University of Nebraska–Lincoln, 2003.

26. Edmond Mulet, "The Palace Coup That Failed," *New York Times*, June 22, 1993, p. A11.

27. See further David P. Forsythe, *Human Rights in International Relations* (Cambridge: Cambridge University Press, 2000), chapter 3.

28. See Paul E. Diehl, Charlotte Ku, and Daniel Zamora, "The Dynamics of International Law: The Intervention of Normative and Operating Systems," *International Organization* 57, no.3 (Winter 2003), pp. 43–75.

Part THREE

Sustainable Human Development

8   Theories of Development at the
United Nations

Introduction

"Development" has long dominated much of discourse and practice throughout the United Nations (UN) system.[1] About 800 million people in developing countries do not have enough food. Nearly 3 billion people struggle to survive on less than $2 a day, not to mention the 1.2 billion who have less than one dollar. That the numbers have not appreciably changed since the World Bank made the first calculations in 1990 seems appalling on the face of it.[2] Thus, the priority given to economic growth by many should be easy to understand on moral grounds alone, even though readers of this volume are presumably in advanced industrialized countries.[3] That the governments of countries in which so many citizens live in chronic poverty would emphasize development as a value in and of itself should also be obvious. At the same time, is there a broader importance to development? Why should readers of this volume or their governments care? Is there a pragmatic link between poverty in the Global South and important economic and security interests as defined by the Global North?[4]

Before the end of the Cold War, the linkage between the UN's work in economic and social domains and the world organization's peace mandate was usually made by emphasizing the argument that promoting social and economic development and protecting human rights are indirect approaches to "peace." That is to say, some observers believed that economic equity, the pursuit of economic growth, and the satisfaction of basic human needs could do more than just improve the material quality of life. They argued that at least some of the causes of violence between and within states could be decreased by reducing gross social and economic inequalities and deprivations. In *An Agenda for Peace*, for example, Secretary-General Boutros Boutros-Ghali highlighted this link between the UN's work in the social and economic realm and the promotion of international security. He placed economic despair, social injustice, and political oppression among the "deepest causes of conflict."[5] Some also believed international economic cooperation could lead to institutional structures to help regulate deadly violence.

Then, in the immediate post–Cold War period, the UN's peace and security mandate was increasingly viewed as involving much more than simply protecting people physically from military conflict. Promoting human security was seen to entail reducing perceived and real threats to individual and collective psychological and physical well-being. From this perspective, protecting people against agents and forces that could degrade their lives, values, and property is what the UN's development work is about. But, even then, other observers continued to manifest different views on the world organization's peace and security mandate and its development work. They suggested that much activity through the United Nations should focus on economic growth—and now also environmental protection—that is unrelated to questions of either political violence or human security. For them, the notion of acting through the United Nations for "development" has meant, and still means, primarily the pursuit of national macroeconomic growth. From this perspective, the goal of development was not to reduce violence among or within states. By the mid-1990s, official UN definitions of development were stated in "sustainable-human-development" terms and linked the pursuit of economic growth to the promotion of human security, not just national security. But this linkage was not always reflected in the policies of states—or even of UN agencies.

In the aftermath of the events of September 11, 2001, it is more widely acknowledged than ever that the traditional division of international issues into matters of "war and peace" on one hand, and questions of "economic and social" affairs on the other, no longer is sensible. Many of those participating in attacks on the United States, and in fighting for Al Qaeda in Afghanistan, came from countries with poor economic prospects for young males. These the *New York Times* foreign correspondent Thomas Friedman called "the standing around guys" who became the foot soldiers for terrorism and other radical causes. Thinking out of the traditional military security "box," however, is not easy for many diplomats and statesmen nurtured during the Cold War. Yet for the most part, the international community of states is coming to embrace the proposition that "[t]he concept of security must change—from an exclusive stress on national security to a much greater stress on people's security, from security through armaments to security through human development, from territorial security to food, employment, and environmental security."[6] Member states at the Millennium Summit in 2000 endorsed human security—the elimination of poverty and the promotion of sustainable development—as the world organization's highest priority. Creating the foundation for sustainable human security entails empowering individuals, groups, and communities to become engaged constructively and effectively in satisfying their own needs, values, and interests, thereby providing them with a genuine sense of control over their futures. This was given an additional boost with a report from an eminent group of persons headed by former UN High Commissioner for Refugees Sadako Ogata and Nobel Laureate Amartya Sen, which focuses on "shielding people from acute threats and empowering them to take charge of their own lives."[7]

In this context, the opening years of the twenty-first century have witnessed the emergence of a more or less coherent programmatic framework of development goals, objectives, and sectoral policy paradigms. As we make clear in the rest of this chapter, there was much anguish along the way, but at least a formal agreement emerged. This framework formed the foundation for the United Nations Millennium Declaration, adopted in September 2000 as General Assembly Resolution 55/2. Couched in the language of shared fundamental values—freedom, equality, solidarity, tolerance, respect for nature, and shared responsibility—the declaration focused on: eradicating extreme poverty; creating enabling environments at the national and international levels conducive to development; promoting good governance both domestically and internationally; mobilizing financial resources required for development; addressing the special needs of least-developed countries; dealing comprehensively and effectively with debt problems; and addressing the special needs of small island and land-locked developing countries. In line with the evolving global development framework, the assembled heads of state and government resolved to: promote gender equality and the empowerment of women; develop and implement strategies to increase employ-ment opportunities; encourage the pharmaceutical industry to make essential drugs more widely available in developing countries; develop strong partnerships with civil society; and ensure that the benefits of new technologies, especially information and communication technologies, are available to all.

Of course important differences persist. It is relevant to recall the formal consen-sus found in UN treaties on human rights. One should not conclude that UN mem-ber states are truly committed to what they have codified in those treaties, as Part Two has already demonstrated. Regarding development, rich countries generally place greater emphasis on promoting values such as good governance, the priority role of the market, the rule of law, and human rights at the domestic level. Developing coun-tries, on the other hand, tend to focus more on global economic inequalities, struc-tural barriers, resource mal-distribution and consumption, debt, and other develop-ment finance problems. All in all, however, consensus can be summed up in part as follows: "The primary resource for development is the great untapped reservoir of human creativity and talent of the people of the developing countries themselves; the release of this human potential requires investment in education, infrastructure, pub-lic health and other basic social services, as well as in production for the market . . . The central goal of public policy on financing for development must be to support equitable and sustainable growth in developing countries, reduce risks of systemic crises and make available the resources required for achieving key developmental goals."[8] Also, there appears to be genuine consensus that the eradication of extreme poverty and the promotion of sustainable development should be the major focus of development strategies. Good governance, the empowerment of stakeholders, popu-lar participation, and the rest of the litany of objectives represent means toward these ends. This new people-centered development agenda focuses on integrating and empowering relevant stakeholders, including especially women, youth, the poor, and other marginalized elements of society, in addition to civil society more generally and the private sector.

The discussion in this and the next two chapters suggests that the ideas promul-gated for the separate spheres of development and security in the United Nations might indeed be coming closer together. However, the synthesis does not at all seem to be the radically restructured one promoted during much of the 1970s and 1980s by the vast majority of UN member states under the rubric "New International Eco-nomic Order" (NIEO). To the contrary, since the end of the Cold War, the UN sys-tem has become increasingly free to function in the economic realm as it was designed to function—in the service of promoting a liberal capitalist order. Of course, from the beginning, many players and forces have opposed such an agenda and have moved to transform it. As these political discourses have played themselves out, numerous "worlds" became manifest under the same roof. To the extent that a consensual vision is being worked out, it must be understood in this context. As such, this chapter provides a brief overview of how development ideas have evolved over the UN's lifetime.

The Politics of Changing Theories

As discussed above, the notion of development has meant different things to different people. Unlike human rights and humanitarian affairs, there are no treaties specifying the exact and agreed goals of international action in this domain, although there are a host of resolutions (with specific targets that have rarely been met).

Like the notion of human rights, development can be pursued for its own sake as a worthy goal, or as a means to other desirable ends. If development means a quest for economic prosperity or personal fulfillment, then development can stand alone as a worthy cause. For example, one normally needs a certain degree of wealth to ensure proper health, education, and welfare. A certain amount of prosperity is inherently part of these other good things. But if it is seen as a pathway to international peace and security, development is instrumental in that wealthy states are economically intertwined, and the web of international economics makes war more difficult if not impossible to wage. For example, and building on the nineteenth-century philosophizing of Immanuel Kant's *Perpetual Peace*, Germany and France are now so closely integrated in trade and finance that the probability of war between these two historical antagonists has become zero. They both are stable liberal democracies, and they are highly integrated economically.[9] A closely related view is that economic development increases the probability of democratic governance at the national level, and democratic states tend not to wage war against each other, a topic discussed earlier in this volume.

Given the variety of perspectives on development, the United Nations system presents formidable problems of analysis. As the notion of development is a complex and controversial subject whose definition changes over time, UN approaches to development change as well. Moreover, the UN organs and agencies dealing in some way with development are so broad and numerous that sometimes the view of—and approach to—development in one part of the UN system is not necessarily shared in other parts. Nevertheless, it is essential to try to categorize the most important aspects of the UN and its development agenda. We do this in the remainder of this chapter by reviewing the historical evolution of the UN's development work in the context of changing theories of development. The following chapter examines the specific contributions to development of particular UN organs and agencies. Finally, we analyze the UN and development in the context of the debate about "globalization" in Chapter 10.

According to Kenneth Dadzie, a thoughtful observer with much practical experience in the UN system, the world organization has gone through four phases in dealing with the problem of development.[10] This is another way of saying the UN has tried four theories or general approaches to development that we elaborate for the reader below. These are helpful to keep in mind while examining later in this text the panoply of institutions and activities that have been initiated by the world organization over almost six decades.

Phase One: National State Capitalism (1945–1962)

The primary idea concerning the UN and development at first was pursuit of national economic growth by way of classical state capitalism. In other words, the UN endorsed state-centered economic liberalism. It was assumed that each country would adopt a large private for-profit sector based on extensive property rights, with minimal state regulation, to ensure the smooth functioning of the economic system. This approach reflected the initial dominance of Western capitalist states in the world organization; the weakness of communist states in voting and other UN arrangements; and the early absence of most of what is now called the "Global South," which over the period increasingly established national independence from colonialism.

Development was thus thought of primarily in national economic terms, although there was some attention within the UN to legal and governmental arrangements that were thought necessary to "proper" economics. Still, the emphasis was on lending through the World Bank and some foreign assistance (either through state bilateral policies or the UN Expanded Program of Technical Assistance, or EPTA) to create national infrastructures that would provide the basis for economic growth led by the private for-profit sector. Although the EPTA was symbolically important for establishing a role for the UN in the development area, its expenditures were nominal. Beginning with an initial operating fund of $20 million in 1951, the program grew only moderately over the next decade. The United States reduced its contribution from 60 percent downward over the years, and other rich countries failed to take up the slack.[11]

At the UN it was widely assumed—not withstanding the views of the minority of communist states—that the overall global situation was neutral or benign, and that if proper national decisions were taken, then national macro-economic growth would automatically occur over time. There was to be some *international* infrastructure, such as agreements on monetary exchange rates, communications, and the like.[12] But in general, the role of international organizations was to be slight, the World Bank and the IMF notwithstanding. States were obligated by the UN Charter to cooperate internationally on development matters and to report to the United Nations. But the principal UN organs, including the Economic and Social Council (ECOSOC), were not seen as having a major operational role in advancing development. ECOSOC and the General Assembly were seen as legitimating and coordinating mechanisms. In part this approach reflected the wariness of the rich Western capitalist states in affording too great a role to UN organizations characterized by broad membership and majority voting.

From the very beginning of the UN, the United States particularly and other important donor governments preferred to emphasize the role of the Bretton Woods institutions. The World Bank (or the Bank) and the International Monetary Fund (the Fund, or IMF), were created at a conference hotel by that name in New Hampshire. These agencies, although officially or technically part of the UN system, operated entirely independently from ECOSOC and the General Assembly, with proportional voting as determined by funding provided by member states. This arrangement gave the United States and other wealthy states not only control over decisions taken in the name of the World Bank and the Fund, but also significant influence in the selection of the executive heads of these two agencies. The president of the Bank has always been an American, and the president of the Fund has always been a European.[13]

Among many decisions at the Bank, the major donor countries agreed to create the International Development Association (IDA), the so-called soft loan window for developing countries. The dominance of the U.S. and Western approach can be seen in the history of an aborted UN idea. In the early 1950s developing countries used their growing numbers to vote into being the Special United Nations Fund for Economic Development (SUNFED) to augment technical assistance activities with long-term low-interest loans aimed at building infrastructure. The move to create such a fund was opposed by major donors. Washington first objected on grounds that the American people could not support such a capital fund while underwriting a war in Korea. But even after 1953 and the end of the Korean War, the United States continued its opposition. In the last analysis, SUNFED was still-born for lack of resources. Developing countries demonstrated that their increasing numbers at the UN could be translated into General Assembly and ECOSOC resolutions, but such developments amounted to little without financial resources. As was true on other matters, the United States did not trust international agencies that it did not control or heavily influence. Washington and other major donor governments hesitated or refused to contribute significantly to development programs guided by majority voting.

Even if the primary emphasis in early UN development approaches was on promoting macro national state-capitalism with minimal UN operational roles, numerous UN bodies helped in this process. This overall approach was not entirely consistent. If the name of the game most fundamentally was state-centered economic liberalism, why have so many international agencies dealing with development? Perhaps under the idea of "state-capitalism," meaning regulated capitalism, one needs considerable state or public regulation? Or perhaps, underdevelopment requires extra assistance? Two types of UN agencies were there almost from the beginning, the specialized agencies and regional economic commissions.

Thus the UN created regional development bodies to encourage economic growth and different approaches in the different geographical areas of the world.[14] And so one eventually found UN regional Economic Commissions for Europe (ECE in 1947), for Asia and the Far East (ECAFE in 1947, which later became ESCAP for "Asia and the Pacific"), for Latin America (ECLA, created in 1948, which later became ECLAC to include the "Caribbean"), for Africa (ECA in 1958), and for Western Asia (ESCWA, in 1973). Some of these came to be quite important in the evolution of ideas and norms, as was true of ECLA in the Western Hemisphere. On the other hand, some of these commissions never achieved their promise, and the one in Europe was eclipsed by other regional economic arrangements such as the Europe Economic Community (ECC), which evolved into the European Union (EU).

As for the specialized agencies, one has the International Labor Organization (ILO) carried over from the League of Nations, others like the World Meteorological Organization (WMO) carried over from the nineteenth century, and a host of new agencies such as the World Health Organization (WHO), the UN International Children's Emergency Fund (UNICEF), and the UN Educational, Scientific, and Cultural Organization (UNESCO). These and other specialized agencies each had their own chartering legal instrument, their own assessed dues system for funding, their own executive head, and often a separate headquarters location. States could join or withdraw from them independently of their membership in the United Nations itself. At one point, for example, the United States withdrew from both the ILO and UNESCO to protest certain policies. Such withdrawal did not affect membership in the UN narrowly defined or U.S. voting in the Security Council and General Assembly. Although ECOSOC was nominally the coordinator of all such UN organizations, their legal and financial arrangements ensured their independence. So from the beginning, the way the UN was set up ensured a "shotgun" approach to development. There might be a primary idea (national economic liberalism with minimal international involvement beyond basic infrastructure), but the application of this idea involved many agencies with different agendas. WHO may report to the General Assembly through ECOSOC, but the "major" UN organs do not tightly control the specialized agencies.[15]

Moreover, these numerous UN specialized agencies indicated that there was theory within theory. Beyond the UN's central idea of encouraging states to take the "right" decisions (comprising economic liberalism) and to achieve economic growth, there was the theory of functionalism that explained how to achieve international peace. If the classic theory of state-capitalism and economic liberalism was supposed to explain economic growth, the theory of functionalism was supposed to open the back door to world peace. Functionalism, as developed by David Mitrany, was purported to lead to world peace not by a frontal assault on aggression and other "political" questions, but by side-stepping these issues and concentrating on the separate elements of development.[16] A functional approach to development—that is, concentrating on labor issues, children's issues, science, education, culture, and so on—would not only advance economic and social development but also build functional networks so that states would learn cooperation in these functional areas. This functional cooperation would eventually spill over into "political" areas, allowing international agreement on aggression, self-defense, intervention, and the other subjects entailed in international peace and security.

So in this early UN approach to development, the classical theory of economic growth through state-capitalism and economic liberalism supposedly gave guidance on economic and social matters, while the theory of functionalism explained how *international* state-capitalism could contribute to peace. Actual attempts to apply the theory of functionalism, and its variant neo-functionalism, to development, particularly in Europe, led to reconsideration of functionalism as a path to peace.[17]

First of all, the various issues of development proved to be as political and contentious as any other issue. That is to say, matters of building infrastructure through specialized agencies involved both governmental decisions and controversy. Second, there could be "spillback" as well as "spillover." That is to say, the controversies over monetary policy and other technical issues could lead to such inter-governmental conflict that further advances of an "economic" nature could be halted or even set back for a time. Third, "political" issues beyond the immediate development process intruded on policy making. In Western Europe during the Cold War, considerations spawned by power struggles between the North Atlantic Treaty Organization (NATO) and Warsaw Pact countries affected decisions about building the European Community. These European policy decisions were not well explained by a functionalist theory that posited regional technical issues as dominant and able to be insulated. Global Great-Power struggles proved as important, or more important, than functionalist theory applied regionally.

Nevertheless, the early UN approach to poverty and economic backwardness in many countries was to reiterate for the globe the standard recipe of economic liberalism understood as national state-capitalism. The need for some international institutions did not detract from the central propositions of capitalist theory, namely that the role of public agencies was mainly to provide the infrastructure for, and other minor additions to, private national entrepreneurship.

Phase Two: International Affirmative Action (1962–1981)

Beginning about 1962 development activity that officially occurred under the UN principal organs focused on persistent income inequalities between the rich North and the poor South, between the developed and developing countries. After all, the 1960s were the first UN Development Decade.[18] Moreover, while many observers thought that seventy-five to a hundred years would be required for decolonization, the avalanche of newly independent states was almost completed by the middle of the 1960s. Indeed, an important element of the UN's liberal agenda was decolonizing the world. The idea of self-determination was one of the most powerful elements introduced into the UN Charter for the post-war era.[19] National liberation movements, international efforts orchestrated by the UN system, and fatigued colonial powers all contributed to putting out of business the Trusteeship Council, one of six principal UN organs. In fact, by 1994 with the independence of Palau, there were no more "trustees" to supervise. From the original fifty-one members in 1945, membership in the United Nations more than doubled to 104 in 1961.

One consequence was that the new majority of UN members preferred more transnational public regulation of private economic activity. This regulation was intended to benefit the poorer countries. Even at the World Bank, which did not completely share the new orientation to development by the General Assembly and ECOSOC and related development agencies, there was considerable rethinking about global underdevelopment. Thus both in the UN major organs and in the Bank, there was a willingness to reconsider the pursuit of development through traditional capitalist recipes. The automatic nature of development through national economic liber-

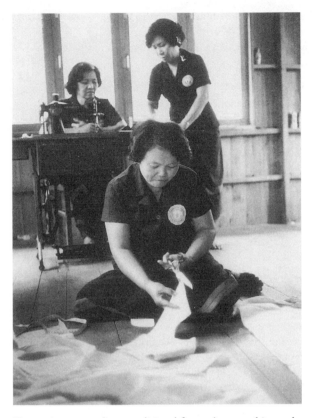

Housewives cut and sew traditional farmers' cotton shirts to be sold in local markets and the women's cooperative shop in Mung Mo, Thailand. The Voluntary Fund for the United Nations Decade for Women supports projects such as this in developing countries. (UN Photo 150947/C. Redenius)

alism was rethought in both circles of opinion. The turning point was the beginning of the preparations for the UN Conference on Trade and Development (UNC-TAD),[20] which we use as the beginning of the second period. The reader may wish to situate this and other UN development milestones for the first two periods that are summarized in Table 8.1.

The origins of this reorientation lay primarily in the thinking of Raúl Prebisch and his colleagues in ECLA. They argued that the international milieu was stacked against the poorer countries. On the basis of their experience mainly in the Western Hemisphere, Prebisch and his colleagues saw the countries of the "periphery" dominated and exploited by "the center"—namely, the wealthy developed countries at the center of world trade and finance. Since, for example, the price of finished goods exported by the rich continued to rise, while the price of natural goods exported by

TABLE 8.1   UN Development Milestones with a Strong Economic Flavor, 1943–1981

1943	United Nations Relief and Rehabilitation Administration (UNRRA)[a]
1947	Economic Commission for Asia and the Far East (ECAFE)[a]
1948	Economic Commission for Latin America (ECLA)[a]
1950	Expanded Program of Technical Assistance[a]
1955	Afro-Asian Conference in Bandung/Nonaligned Movement[a]
1956	International Finance Corporation[a]
1958	UN Special Fund[a] Economic Commission for Africa (ECA)[a]
1960	First UN Development Decade[a] Declaration on the Granting of Independence to Colonial Countries and Peoples International Development Association[a]
1964	United Nations Conference on Trade and Development (UNCTAD I)[a] Group of 77[a]
1965	United Nations Development Programme (UNDP)[a] United Nations Industrial Development Organisation (UNIDO)[a]
1973	OPEC Price Increase
1974	Sixth Special Session of UN General Assembly Declaration and Programme of Action on the Establishment of a New International Economic Order (NIEO) World Population Conference World Food Conference Economic and Social Commission for Western Asia (ESCWA)[a]
1975	Seventh Special Session of UN General Assembly UN World Conference of the International Women's Year UN Development Fund for Women (UNIFEM)[a]
1975– 1977	Conference on International Economic Co-operation
1976	UNCTAD IV UN Conference on Human Settlements (HABITAT) UN Decade for Womena
1979	OPEC Price Increase UN Conference on Science and Technology for Development
1980	Independent Commission on International Development Issues (Brandt Commission) Report UN World Conference of the Mid-Decade for Women

[a]Denotes the establishment of the body or commencement of the activity

the poor fluctuated greatly and tended to decline over time, the global terms of trade were inimical to the countries of the Global South. In this thinking, one found a ready-made explanation for the growing gap between the rich and poor countries. In this view, the General Agreement on Tariffs and Trade (GATT) governed an inherently discriminatory trading system that helped make the rich richer and the poor poorer.

Although there were many variants,[21] what was loosely grouped under the rubric of "dependency theory" proved attractive, not only to Latin Americans, but especially to the growing number of newly independent and former colonial territories eager to attribute their underdevelopment to factors entirely beyond their control. Those authorities that were socialist or had socialist leanings were also sympathetic to a view that found fault with transnational capitalism. In 1964 UNCTAD was voted into being—here, a "conference" refers to an organization. With Prebisch as its first Secretary-General, it advocated a restructuring of global economic relations to the advantage of the poorer countries. The views championed by UNCTAD were largely synonymous with the views of the Group of 77 (the major UN caucus of developing countries, which over time has grown to more than 103 members but maintains its original label).[22]

During a series of conferences in the mid–1970s, the Group of 77 formulated its agenda for restructuring the global political economy. The main thrust came during the Sixth Special Session of the General Assembly in late spring 1974, where the Declaration and Program of Action on the Establishment of a New International Economic Order was adopted, but with significant reservations by many Western countries and the United States in particular. The demands of the declaration were wide-ranging but can be classified into four broad themes: economic sovereignty, trade, aid, and participation.[23] These issues were raised time and again in various ways and in various settings during the remainder of the decade. The North-South battle lines quickly became unambiguously drawn and a very different version of "cold war" appeared. A number of "global ad hoc conferences"[24] focusing on specific issues, such as population and food, and the more broad-based Conference on International Economic Cooperation, which met in December 1975 and June 1977, provided additional forums for expanding at the global level what some called "dialogue" between North and South but would more accurately be labeled "invective."

Ten years later, the General Assembly itself presented a demand for a New International Economic Order intended to completely alter economic relations between the Global North and South.[25] The NIEO was supposed to be made up of a series of treaties that would greatly regulate transnational economics and redistribute power and wealth. There were to be specific measures on trade, investment, transnational corporations, official development assistance and the like.

The fate of the NIEO was to approximate the history of SUNFED. The majority of states at the UN might call special sessions of the General Assembly and have the votes to create revolutionary new schemes on paper to alter the distribution of economic power. But even with the newly found (and temporary) power of the Organization of Petroleum Exporting Countries (OPEC), the Global South was unable to persuade the Global North of the wisdom of such economic restructuring. In the wake of the 1973 war in the Middle East between Israel and principally Egypt, OPEC was able to implement for a time an oil embargo (to several countries) and a more general slow-down in oil deliveries (to the rest of the oil-importing countries). But in the last analysis OPEC was not able to force the United States and other Western countries to alter their support for Israel; and OPEC was not able to maintain its unity. More generally, OPEC was unable for long to use oil as a weapon in the larger struggle to compel rich countries to radically transform international economics so as to close the gap between the developed and developing countries. The United States and the rest of the West maintained the power to resist demands for a NIEO and adjusted to the new economic reality. Indeed in retrospect, many observers saw the growing debt problems of the 1980s as a more significant result of OPEC's temporary muscle-flexing than any alteration in global economic relations.

All the same, at the UN there was increased technical assistance to the poorer countries through the new UN Development Program (UNDP), created in 1965. UNDP reflected a merger of the earlier EPTA and the stillborn SUNFED. Still, there was great independence from UNDP by the specialized agencies, which refused to yield their independence. The so-called *Jackson Report* of 1969, named after its primary drafter, Sir Robert Jackson, calling for more centralization of development efforts in the UN system, fell mostly on deaf ears.[26] Funding for the new UNDP was an important factor in many countries but remained decidedly meager, as donor countries preferred the Bretton Woods institutions, and the World Bank in particular, as the main vehicle for multilateral development finance.

In a significant change, there was increasing activity in UN circles on behalf of ecology, which is suggested by Table 8.2. In 1972 the UN sponsored a major conference at Stockholm out of which came UNEP, the United Nations Environmental Programme. This was largely a new initiative from certain developed countries, mostly European, concerned that the pursuit of economic growth was causing fundamental harm to the environment. This "green movement" was not always welcomed by poorer countries. Many saw a focus on ecology as a way to retard their development. Seeing the environmental movement as a form of neo-colonialism, since the now developed states had grown rich without much attention to environmental destruction, some of the states of the Global South did not see environmental protection as an inherent part of development but rather as an impediment to a development defined in more strictly economic terms. Leaders of the G–77 like China and India did not lead on development issues, unless by "leadership" one means leading the opposition. These and other developing countries could be brought on board certain green treaties, such as the 1987 Montreal Protocol on protection of the ozone, but only with the carrots of compensatory financing.[27]

It is worth fast-forwarding for a moment to move beyond this chronology to indicate how complex the thinking about development was becoming. By the time of a second major UN conference on environment and development in 1992 in Rio, ecological concerns had been more securely fixed on the development agenda. Such precise subjects as deforestation, biodiversity, and climate change had all become regular—if still controversial—fixtures on the UN development agenda. So clearly during

TABLE 8.2   UN Development Milestones with a Strong Ecological Flavor, 1948–1982

1948	International Union for the Conservation of Nature and National Resources (IUCN)[a]
1964	International Biological Program[a]
1968	Intergovernmental Conference on Biosphere[a]
1970	Scientific Committee on Problems of the Environment (SCOPE)/ICSU[a]
1972	UN Conference on the Human Environment (UNCHE) Environmental Forum Limits to Growth published by the Club of Rome UN Environment Programme (UNEP)[a]
1973	Convention for the Prevention of Pollution by Ships (MARPOL)
1974–1981	UN Conference on the Law of the Sea
1976	UN Conference on Human Settlements (HABITAT)
1979	World Climate Conference Convention on Long-Range Transboundary Air Pollution
1980	Committee of International Development Institutions on the Environment (CIDIE)[a] World Conservation Strategy (ICSN/UNEP) Convention on Conservation of the Arctic Living Resources
1982	Convention on the Law of the Seas

[a]Denotes the establishment of the body or commencement of the activity

the second phase of UN approaches to development, the basic formula or recipe was becoming more varied and complicated.

Meanwhile, at the Bretton Woods institutions, there was also growing dissatisfaction with the lack of rapid economic progress in many parts of the Global South according to prevailing doctrines. But in these circles, there was an effort to counteract much of the statism preferred by many of the newly independent countries. The World Bank and the IMF began to implement structural adjustment programs, conditioning their loans on the willingness of developing states to prune back public spending and other public involvement in economic matters.[28] The Bank continued to emphasize export-led development, meaning precisely the emphasis on participation in the world economy that Prebisch and UNCTAD thought so detrimental to the developing countries under the rules of the game established by GATT. So the Bank in particular was not always playing on the same page of music as UNCTAD and the UN's other organizations.

Contrary to the predictions of the Prebisch group, a number of Asian states, dubbed the "East Asian Tigers," began to make rapid economic gains through, among other policies, emphasis on trade. Singapore, for example, in a period of about twenty

A slum in the city of São Paulo, Brazil, illustrates the shortage of adequate housing as rural settlements are being abandoned by people moving to the cities. (UN Photo 155212/C. Edinger)

years, surpassed Britain, its former colonial master, in per capita national income. But some of these "Tigers," such as South Korea, also continued various forms of "statism" through such measures as protecting key national industries from full global competition. In fact, countries like Japan had already proved successful at export-led economic growth through an industrial policy that amounted to state subsidies for, and other benefits to, selected national industries. There was extensive trade, but it was not free trade in the sense of pure economic competition. Clearly East Asia was not Latin America. Clearly Prebisch was not Lee Kuan Yew, the eminence grise of Singapore who believed that "Asian values," national discipline, and export-oriented capitalism could produce rapid development. A certain type of authoritarian development worked reasonably well in places like China, Singapore, Malaysia, South Korea, and Taiwan—at least in the short and intermediate term. In the latter two cases, authoritarian development gradually became liberal democratic development.

The Asian Tigers notwithstanding, the World Bank and IMF, given the low rates of economic growth in Africa and some other parts of the Global South, continued to press for certain policy changes in developing countries. Increasingly the World Bank was concerned about how non-economic factors like corruption and cronyism could affect rates of economic growth. According to its charter, the Bank was a non-political organization, but it came to adopt the policy that it should take into account factors that might not be strictly economic but that did affect economic growth. In Indonesia, for example, the Bank eventually issued a mea culpa, in effect apologizing for not addressing "crony capitalism" sooner.

At the same time, the World Bank, especially after Robert McNamara, the former U.S. secretary of defense and head of the Ford Motor Company, became its president in 1967, began to target poverty within developing countries. Convinced that national macro-economic growth, such as existed, was not trickling down to those living on less than $1 per day, the Bank began to make loans with a view to changing things at the grassroots level. The Bank began to pursue development loans not just from the top down, as it were, but also from the bottom up. With a focus especially on smaller loans to women, among other schemes, the Bank tried to undertake projects that would improve the lives of the most needy. It still undertook projects designed to promote macro national economic growth. Some of these projects, like funding for large hydroelectric dams, proved enormously controversial given the displacement of people and destruction of the environment that often occurred. But increasingly the Bank focused on pockets of poverty rather than macro national economic growth pure and simple. The Bank pursued its own version of international affirmative action, but not by focusing on terms of trade and other issues championed by UNCTAD. The Bank made loans at very low rates of interest to the poorest of the poor. It made loans, and even grants, for example, to poor families in South Asia so that their children could attend schools rather than work as child laborers.

Thus, the Bretton Woods institutions, no less than the General Assembly and ECOSOC, rethought much of the prevailing scheme for economic development— even if the former and latter agencies did not always adopt precisely the same revisions. The principal UN organs clearly focused on trying to change the overall economic environment, while the Bank and Fund focused mostly on various national reforms. All agreed that efforts during 1945–1962 that were intended to advance economic growth in the Global South needed reconsideration.

Phase Three: Return to Neo-Liberalism (1981–1989)

The economic thinking and political development in the West that contributed to the rise of Margaret Thatcher in Britain and Ronald Reagan in the United States led to changes in Western foreign economic policy. Given the power of these two states at the UN, they also led a return to classical economic thinking in the UN and related agencies. Many see the collapse of discussions at Cancún, Mexico, in 1981 as the end of an era—the last nail in the coffin of North-South dialogue about a radical restructuring of international economic relations and the beginning point for our discussion of a third major phase.

The end of this phase for us is marked by the fall of the Berlin Wall and the end of the Cold War in 1989. This not only discredited socialism as practiced by the Soviet Union and its allies, but also it reduced the tendency of the United States and other Western governments to acquiesce in rhetorical demands for changes in international economic relations. Instead, they articulated a new vision, what World Bank economist John Williamson called the "Washington consensus."[29] The Bretton Woods institutions and the U.S. government—hence, the "Washington" consensus although others dubbed it the "Maastricht consensus" because the European Union was also a firm supporter—stressed once again the role of private markets rather than governmental policies that intruded into those markets. Just as Ronald Reagan represented the dismantling of Franklin Roosevelt's New Deal in the American political economy, so the new orthodoxy in international economics represented a return to minimal regulation and maximum private entrepreneurship. This time around the Bretton Woods institutions and the UN system, at least for a while, were mostly in agreement.

Nothing better symbolized the new thinking, which in reality was the old thinking, about rigorous "economic freedom" than the Nestlé controversy of the early 1980s. Various resolutions were introduced in the World Health Organization (WHO) and also other UN bodies designed to protect lactating mothers and their infants from alleged marketing practices by the Nestlé Corporation of Switzerland. Supposedly that corporation was using sales personnel appearing as nurses and other medical personnel to advance sales of powered milk. Moreover, the product was being diluted, sometimes with unsafe water, to the detriment of children in the Global South. The Reagan administration initially opposed various UN non-binding resolutions designed to protect the health of the poor—all in the name of free enterprise and a general orientation that fought almost all additional public regulation. In the face of extensive public criticism, however, the Reagan administration shifted policies on the Nestlé affair.

Nevertheless, in the 1980s there was such a belief in the "magic of the market" that the Reagan team launched strong attacks even on the World Bank and International Monetary Fund, which previous U.S. administrations had found to be highly useful tools for U.S. foreign policy.[30] The Bank in the 1970s, for example, had shut off loans to Chile when the leftist Salvadore Allende was elected, thus backstopping a U.S. policy of covert intervention in Chilean politics designed to keep Allende from taking office. Given that the Bank was dominated by Western interests, it was hard to understand the Reagan initial critique that the Bank was detrimental to those same national interests. Be all that as it may, the Global South was in a weakened position both economically and politically, having already demonstrated its inability to realize the NIEO, and the Soviets and their allies were in the process of disintegration. So the return of neo-liberal developmental economics was complete, although most UN agencies never bought into the argument that the market alone could solve all problems. And toward the end of the period, some UN bodies began to criticize the impact on societies of economic liberalization—the most notable being UNICEF's concern with the impact on children.[31]

Phase Four: Sustainable Human Development (1989-present)

Kenneth Dadzie argues that international economic cooperation for development has entered a "mature phase" in which "Development itself is increasingly seen as a people-centered and equitable process whose ultimate goal must be the improvement of the human condition."[32] If true, this state of affairs has come about through a dialec-

Guatemalan refugees in class at Los Lirios camp in Quintana Roo, Mexico, 1984. (UNHCR Photo 14149/10.1984/D. Bregnard)

tical interchange between those Western governments stressing the role of markets and free trade, like Republican administrations in the United States, and other governments and international agencies stressing the role of public regulation and assistance for both social and economic reasons.

In May 1994 Secretary-General Boutros Boutros-Ghali presented the General Assembly with *An Agenda for Development.* Declaring development to be a fundamental human right, he presented a framework within which he highlighted the interdependent nature of peace, economy, civil society, democracy, social justice, and environment as indispensable components of the development process. In this regard, he pointed to the special position, role, and responsibility of the United Nations in promoting development in all its aspects but with specific regard to setting priorities and facilitating cooperation and coordination. This report did not cause the new consensus, but it did reflect it.

Over the decades, "development" thus has taken on various meanings as the global political context has shifted. As we have seen, in the early years, development was defined largely in terms of national economic growth as measured in aggregate and per capita income. It also meant national self-reliance for Third World countries. Slowly the added, and somewhat different, value of satisfying the basic needs of people crept onto the scene, but in a subordinated role. This definition slowly yielded ground to the incorporation of popular participation and local self-reliance in the satisfaction of basic needs. In this way, development discourse has come to embrace simultaneously four widely shared global values: peace (that is, nonviolence), human security (including human rights), sustainable human development, and ecological balance. Regardless of its precise character, the discourse was always framed in the context of the overall liberal capitalist world system.

It is hard to say exactly what caused this new synthesis in competing views. No doubt the election of George H. W. Bush and then Bill Clinton to the White House had much to do with the evolving state of affairs. Both were less ideological, in devotion to free market orthodoxy, than the Reagan administration. The demise of communism and increased pragmatism in the Global South also played their roles.

One might also be justified in thinking that half a century of discourse in and by the various UN agencies active on development matters made its own contribution to the present consensus. The combination of the needs to simultaneously foster economic development and ensure the availability of resources for future generations, "sustainable development," was framed by a commission headed by then Norwegian Prime Minister Gro Harlem Brundtland, who later headed the WHO.[33] In particular, a host of UN global conferences in the 1990s—on the human environment, women, population, human rights, and social development—articulated important elements of this consensus.[34]

From the intensive series of international conferences emerged a more or less coherent programmatic framework of liberal development goals, objectives, and sectoral policy paradigms. That framework formed the foundation for the United Nations Millennium Declaration and was couched in the language of shared fundamental values—freedom, equality, solidarity, tolerance, respect for nature, shared responsibility. For those who read it even casually, the UN Secretary-General's Millennium Report was reminiscent of U.S. President Franklin D. Roosevelt's "Four Freedoms" speech. The UN's foundations in liberal capitalist ideology appear not only to be still firmly in place but greatly strengthened by the absence of any potential significant challengers. Like Roosevelt's New Deal, the new international agreement contained elements of social democracy.

The new agreement on development may perhaps be well summarized not only by the UN Millennium Declaration, but also by the "Monterrey Consensus" of 2001. In the latter case, both the Global North and South agreed at a conference in Monterrey, Mexico, that governments of developing countries had an obligation to reform themselves for the purpose of economic efficiency, while those in developed countries had an obligation to provide meaningful assistance for that improved process of development. The administration of George W. Bush then followed with an announcement of a new Millennium Development Account of foreign assistance to the poorest countries. Recipient countries would have to meet certain criteria dealing both with economic effectiveness and good government. The Millennium Account would not be a multilateral arrangement, but rather would be administered by an independent corporation of the United States—if Congress approved what President Bush proposed. One of the points of criticism of the Millennium Account was that it would be more effective with broader results if it were an integral part of a multilateral process.

While recognizing that over time a certain synthesis had been achieved between advocates of rather pure capitalism and proponents of rather extensive public programming, one can still note that there are discontinuities in contemporary approaches to development through multilateral institutions. Chief among these is the lack of coordination between the World Trade Organization (WTO) and agencies representing ecological and human rights concerns. There is, to date, no link between the WTO, the ILO and other human rights agencies, and the UNEP and other environmental agencies.

In 1995 GATT was transformed into the WTO. Students of history will recall that John Maynard Keynes had proposed a three-legged stool for post-war economic management. And while the World Bank and the IMF were founded at Bretton Woods, the International Trade Organization (ITO) was never agreed to because of opposition from the U.S. Congress.

The rules of the WTO vigorously endorse capitalism, free trade, and minimal social regulation—whether that regulation is to protect the environment, human rights, or any other concern. There was a single-minded focus on strictly economic matters, so that, for example, U.S. national legislation to protect endangered sea turtles from certain fishing nets was struck down by a WTO dispute settlement panel as an inappropriate restraint on free trade.

Given the numbers of persons—in industrialized as well as developing countries—left behind by the forces of globalization, the unalloyed advantages of freer markets and technologically led specialization were less than obvious to many. Given such rules, decisions, and emphases within the WTO, it was not surprising that there was often a broad and intense reaction to WTO policies. The "battle of Seattle" was a highly visible reminder of this reaction, as violent street demonstrations and civil disobedience accompanied the WTO meeting in that city. It was as if the early days of the World Bank were being repeated. An important multilateral agency was approaching matters in an exceedingly narrow way, as if trade or development were only purely economic processes in which human rights and ecology and culture did not matter.

The creation of the WTO certainly did not mean that the UNEP went out of business, anymore than the emphasis on free trade meant that the ILO went out of business. But the continuing "Washington consensus" clearly left unresolved the relationship between trade and other strictly economic processes on the one hand, and matters like ecology and labor rights that had increasingly been considered part of a broader and legitimate conception of development, on the other hand.

In fact, at the World Bank no less than in UN circles, protecting the environment was increasingly seen as a legitimate part of development, the WTO policies notwithstanding. The World Bank joined with UNEP and UNDP to create the General Environmental Facility (GEF), through which Bank funding was combined with UNEP and UNDP programming. Moreover, in 1992 at the Rio Conference, states voted into being a new UN coordinating organ, the UN Commission on Sustainable Development (CSD) that clearly incorporated ecological concerns. This CSD was weak in legal authority, and hence weak in practical coordination, but even its name had symbolic importance.

As we saw earlier, basic theories or phases pertaining to the UN and development were complicated, if not to say convoluted, with different views coexisting in uneasy equilibrium. So while the continuing "Washington consensus" stressed minimal regulation, a growing green movement demanded increased governance for ecological protection.

Market emphases notwithstanding, the new broadly shared conception of sustainable human development was reflected by the UNDP and its *Human Development Report*.[35] Started in 1990 by a prominent Pakistani economist, Muhbub ul-Haq, then carried on by Richard Jolly of the United Kingdom, the annual reports analyzed international cooperation for development in a broad, multifaceted way. The annual report sometimes stressed human rights, sometimes women, sometimes ecology. It ranked countries not just by GNP per capita, but by a more complex formula attempting to measure quality of life. Wealth and prosperity loomed large, of course, but so did education and medical care. Various indices sought to measure discrimination against women, not only legally and politically but also in terms of basic health and education. In its approach to development, the UNDP dovetailed with the Overseas Development Council (ODC), a private group based in the United States, that had pioneered in the creation of the Physical Quality of Life Index, which sought to measure the quality of all countries according to wealth, medical care, and education.

The UN *Human Development Report* and the ODC Physical Quality of Life Index both treated development in the broad fashion intended by the UN's approach to development in the fourth phase. The controversial nature of the UN report stemmed from several factors. First, a United Nations agency "rated" countries according to subjective criteria—and states on the bottom disliked the publicity, while states not quite at the top, including the United States, grumbled. Second, many governments resented the fact that poorer neighbors got higher ratings because they were better at making decisions about priorities, having devoted more of their limited resources to education and health instead of spending them on weapons.

So it was generally clear that by 2003 the UN, in a long and torturous process, had evolved a broad notion of development. In some ways the United States, the most powerful state, had finally been brought into the global consensus. Washington agreed that it and the other developed countries had an obligation to assist poorer countries, and that thus there was a role for assistance and beneficial regulation. U.S. development policy under George W. Bush, however, emphasized bilateral rather than multilateral arrangements. Moreover, U.S. leadership still had not been brought to bear to link the WTO to broader concerns, or to give priority attention to global warming. But at least a core consensus was emerging.

To return for a moment to the debates about the possible links between development and violent conflict, it is hardly surprising that such connections should attract attention. That the poverty and human rights abuses in Afghanistan seemed to permit the growth of Al Qaeda appears plausible if not proved. As Nobel Laureate Amartya Sen stated: "Even though definitive empirical work on the causal linkages between political turmoil and economic deprivations may be rare, the basic presumption that the two phenomena have firm causal links is widespread . . . of course, avoidance of war and eradication of destitution are both important ends, and it is quite plausible that each feeds the other."[36]

With UNDP and ILO support, the Rural Artisan Training Centre in Dakar instructs rural artisans, such as this potter.
(UN/DPI Photo/Y. Nagata)

With this overview of changing development thinking in mind, we now turn to the UN and international cooperation for development at a more specific level. What is the record of such bodies as the World Bank in advancing development? What is the "value added" of the UNDP? What is the track record of the GEF? What can UNEP be expected to do in reality? To what extent do development efforts respect a right of participation by the stakeholders of the process? How does agreement on a theory of development play out in the real world of national interests, humanitarian crises, and environmental degradation?

Notes

1. For an analysis of the entire period, see Louis Emmerij, Richard Jolly, and Thomas G. Weiss, *Ahead of the Curve? UN Ideas and Global Challenges* (Bloomington: Indiana University Press, 2001). For a treatment of the primary documents, see Mahfuzur Rahman, *World Economic Issues at the United Nations: Half a Century of Debate* (Dordrecht: Kluwer, 2002)

2. See World Bank, *World Development Report 1990* (Oxford: Oxford University Press, 1990).

3. Food and Agricultural Organization, *State of Food Insecurity in the World 1999* (Rome: FAO, 1999); and UN Development Programme, *Human Development Report 2002* (New York: Oxford University Press, 2002), Table 3.

4. Deaths from wars and governmental repression have been enormous. See R. J. Rummel, *Death by Government: Genocide and Mass Murder since 1900* (New Brunswick, N.J.: Transaction Publishers, 1994).

5. Boutros Boutros-Ghali, *An Agenda for Peace: Preventive Diplomacy, Peacemaking and Peace-keeping* (New York: UN, 1992), para. 15.

6. UNDP, *Human Development Report 1993* (New York: Oxford University Press, 1993), p. 5.

7. Commission on Human Security, *Human Security Now* (New York: Commission on Human Security, 2003), p. iv.

8. UN Document A/AC.257/12, December 18, 2000.

9. On the democratic peace, which overlaps with the notion of peace via economic integration, in addition to the literature cited in Part Two, see Bruce Russet, *Grasping the Democratic Peace: Principles for a Post-Cold War World* (Princeton: Princeton University Press, 1994); Michael W. Doyle, "Kant, Liberal Legacies and Foreign Affairs," *Philosophy and Public Affairs* 12, Part 1 (Summer 1983) and Part 2 (Fall 1983), pp. 205–235 and pp. 323–353; Doyle, "Liberalism and World Politics," *American Political Science Review,* 80 (December 1980), pp. 1151–1169; and John M. Owen, "How Liberalism Produces Democratic Peace," *International Security* 19 (Fall 1994), pp. 87–125. In a lighter vein, *New York Times* journalist and columnist writer Thomas Friedman developed the "McDonald's thesis of international peace and security," namely that no two countries that manifested McDonald's restaurants had ever gone to war with each other. This thesis was apparently falsified when nineteen NATO countries bombed Serbia in 1999.

10. Kenneth Dadzie, "The UN and the Problem of Economic Development," in Adam Roberts and Benedict Kingsbury, eds., *United Nations, Divided World: The UN's Roles in International Relations,* second edition (Oxford: Clarendon Publishers, 1995), pp. 297–326.

11. See Olav Stokke, *International Development Assistance: The UN Contribution* (Bloomington: Indiana University Press, forthcoming 2004).

12. Craig N. Murphy, *International Organization and Industrial Change: Global Governance since 1850* (Oxford: Oxford University Press, 1994).

13. The Clinton administration angered the Europeans by vetoing their preferred choice for head of the IMF. From the European view, such a decision was theirs alone. But as a reflection of U.S. hyperpower after the Cold War, the Clinton team felt that the German national nominated was not an appropriate choice. The Europeans then proceeded to their second preference, with considerable hard feelings toward the United States. The rest of the world had no say in such matters.

14. For a discussion, see Yves Berthelot, ed., *Unity and Diversity in Development: The Regional Commissions' Experience* (Bloomington: Indiana University Press, 2004).

15. See Erskine Childers with Brian Urquhart, *Renewing the United Nations System* (Uppsala, Sweden: Dag Hammarskjöld Foundation, 1994).

16. David Mitrany, *A Working Peace System* (Chicago: Quadrangle Books, 1966) and *The Progress of International Government* (New Haven, Conn.: Yale University Press, 1933). Later, a "neo-functionalist" school formed around such ideas linked to European integration, including Ernst B. Haas, *Beyond the Nation State* (Stanford: Stanford University Press, 1964).

17. For an overview of much of the functionalist and neo-functionalist literature applied to Europe, see Robert O. Keohane and Stanley Hoffmann, eds., *The New European Community: Decisionmaking and Institutional Change* (Boulder: Westview Press, 1991). Certainly in the North Atlantic area, various functionalist theories have faded with time.

18. For a fuller discussion of approaches to development, see Richard Jolly, Louis Emmerij, Dharam Ghai, and Frédéric Lapeyre, *UN Development Theory and Practice* (Bloomington: Indiana University Press, 2004).

19. See Neta C. Crawford, *Argument and Change in World Politics: Ethics, Decolonization, and Humanitarian Intervention* (Cambridge: Cambridge University Press, 2002).

20. See Thomas G. Weiss, *Multilateral Development Diplomacy in UNCTAD, 1964–84* (London: Macmillan, 1986).

21. The two main schools were a more radical version proposed by André Gunnar Frank in *Development and Underdevelopment in Latin America* (New York: Monthly Review Press, 1967), and a subtler version by Fernando Henrique Cardoso, *Dependency and Development in Latin America* (Los Angeles: University of California Press, 1979).

22. See John and Richard Toye, *The North-South Encounter: Trade, Finance, and Development* (Bloomington: Indiana University Press, 2004).

23. See Robert S. Jordan, "Why an NIEO? The View from the Third World," in Harold K. Jacobson and Dusam Aidjanski, eds., *The Emerging International Economic Order: Dynamic Processes, Constraints and Opportunities* (Beverly Hills, Calif.: Sage, 1982), pp. 59-80.

24. See Thomas G. Weiss and Robert S. Jordan, *The World Food Conference and Global Problem Solving* (New York: Praeger, 1976). For an overview, see Michael Schecter, ed., *United Nations-sponsored World Conferences* (Tokyo: UN University Press, 2001).

25. See Robert S. Jordan, op. cit. at n. 23, pp. 59-80.

26. *A Study of the Capacity of the United Nations Development System* (Geneva: UN, 1969), document DP/5.

27. Richard Benedick, *Ozone Diplomacy: New Directions in Safeguarding the Planet* (Cambridge, Mass.: Harvard University Press, 1998, second edition). This is the definitive if overly detailed account of how developing countries were enticed into concrete measures to protect the ozone. It is also an account of how pragmatic diplomats and business leaders were able to get the Reagan administration, with its free market and anti-regulation ideology, to support international law to protect the environment.

28. See Devesh Kapur, John P. Lewis, and Richard Webb, *The World Bank: Its First Half-Century* (Washington, D.C.: Brookings Institution, 1997); and Norman K. Humphreys, ed., *Historical Dictionary of the IMF* (Washington, D.C.: IMF, 2000).

29. John Williamson, "The Washington Consensus Revisited," in Louis Emmerij, ed., *Economic and Social Development in the 21ˢᵗ Century* (Baltimore: Johns Hopkins University Press, 1997), pp. 48–61.

30. Robert L. Ayres, "Breaking the Bank," *Foreign Policy* No. 43 (Summer 1981), pp. 104–120. At the same time, the Reagan administration reversed bipartisan support for the emerging Law of the Sea Treaty. One of the Reagan critiques was that there was too much public regulation for the deep seabed area, thought to have commercial potential for the mining of

metallic nodules. At that time Washington was not interested in an equitable sharing of the potential economic benefits of the deep seabed area, but preferred traditional economic competition, which was of course to the detriment of the poor countries that lacked the necessary technology to compete. In this sense the Reagan team was far less concerned with equitable global bargains than the Nixon-Kissinger team of traditional realists. Nixon-Kissinger had supported earlier drafts of the LOS treaty. The Reagan team was far more ideologically opposed to international legal regulation of commerce.

31. See Richard Jolly, *Adjustments with a Human Face: Country Case Studies* (Oxford: Oxford University Press, 1992).

32. Dadzie, "The UN and the Problem of Economic Development," p. 307.

33. World Commission on Environment and Development, *Our Common Future* (Oxford: Oxford University Press, 1987).

34. For an overview, see Michael Schecter, ed., *United Nations-sponsored World Conferences* (Tokyo: UN University Press, 2001).

35. These reports are published annually by Oxford University Press. A CD-ROM is also available for the entire series.

36. Amartya Sen, "Global Inequality and Persistent Conflicts," paper presented at the Nobel Awards Conference 2002, reprinted in Commission on Human Security, *Human Security Now* (New York: Commission on Human Security, 2003), p. 132.

9 Sustainable Development as Process: UN Organizations and Norms

As is apparent from Chapter 8, the United Nations' work in the development field was born decentralized, with little coherence until recently. Over the decades, scores of development-related agencies, funds, programs, commissions, and committees have sprung up creating a complex institutional web (see Appendix A). In "unpacking" the complex structure of UN development activities, several main aspects need to be clarified. First, there are several main clusters of somewhat autonomous activity: 1) the United Nations proper—that is, the relevant principal organs and the permanent regional and functional commissions, which at least sometimes operate more or less in tandem with the specialized agencies; and 2) the Bretton Woods institutions; and 3) more recently the World Trade Organization (WTO). Second, within each agency it is important to differentiate between their governing bodies and the secretariats. In development as in other fields, again we meet the two United Nations—one of states and one of international civil servants. Third, it is also important to understand how all these UN elements relate to international relations more broadly defined to include the private for-profit sector as well as nonprofit non-governmental organizations (NGOs), not to mention regional inter-governmental organizations (IGOs) like the European Union (EU).

We start by reviewing some recent efforts at improved coordination. Then we address particular agencies and programs in order to address the question of what these UN elements contribute to sustainable human development. Of course we cannot be comprehensive in this regard, but we can use a representative sample to give an introduction. Next, and most importantly, we suggest that beyond the particular contributions of particular parts of the UN system, the UN system in development is most important for nurturing agreement about ideas for sustainable human development—also known as human security. Former Secretary-General Boutros Boutros-Ghali wrote in 1998, "The United Nations is the mechanism in place and is best prepared to facilitate the work of achieving a new development rationale."[1] So he stressed ideas and not field operations. Particularly in a world in which states and their preferred organizations beyond the UN (narrowly defined) still control many of the resources that contribute to development, like money and terms of trade, we should not overlook the important role of ideas—development rationales—that shape how resources are employed. After all, much of international relations is about ideas and changing ideas.[2] Our hope is that by the end of the chapter the reader will be familiar in some detail with the various moving parts of the UN and how they contribute to sustainable development.

Unpacking the Organogram: Coordination, Again

By now it should be clear that the UN is an alphabet-soup of semi-autonomous programs, funds, committees, commissions, and agencies. At the core of this system is the General Assembly (GA). Most development issues are dealt with in the assembly's Second Committee (Economic and Financial), which is comprised of representatives of all member states (in UN parlance, "a committee of the whole"). It was the General Assembly, for example, that voted in 1983 to create what came to be called the Bruntland Commission, which was an important milestone in changing ideas about development, managing to merge pursuit of economic growth with environmental protection. (We provide more on this later in the chapter.) Over the years, however, the most important work of the assembly in the development field generally has taken place in special sessions or in the calling of global, ad hoc conferences convened to consider specific issues or topics, such as women, population, development financing, and HIV/AIDS. Normally the assembly deals with substantive ideas rather than the details of management, administration, and coordination.

The assembly elects fifty-four of its member states to sit on the Economic and Social Council (ECOSOC), which under Article 55 of the Charter is the main UN organ mandated with the responsibility for promoting development and coordinating UN activities. It is important to understand in this regard that ECOSOC is not independently staffed, as is, for example, the committee structure of the U.S. Congress. The General Assembly, ECOSOC, and other UN governing bodies are comprised of states but reliant on the UN's administrative branch—the secretariat—for staffing and support. This fact becomes especially important when we discuss coordination issues below.

ECOSOC is comprised of five regional and ten functional commissions that cover the gambit of development issues and concerns. It also receives reports from and thus officially coordinates the work of fourteen specialized agencies and eleven UN funds and programs. Some of the regional economic commissions, such as the ones for Asia and the Pacific (ESCAP) and Latin America and the Caribbean (ECLAC), have over the years been instrumental in establishing international development financial institutions and other development infrastructures within their respective regions. As we saw in the previous chapter, prominent people and ideas from ECLAC also served as the catalyst for the creation of the UN Conference on Trade and Development (UNCTAD) and many of the ideas that became manifest in the call for the establishment of a New International Economic Order (NIEO). As discussed in Chapter 6 with respect to the Commission on Human Rights (CHR), many of the functional commissions do very important work. Examples include: the status of women, population and development, social development, science and technology for development, and sustainable development. Of these, the Commission on Sustainable Development (CSD) is of particular importance and will be discussed in more detail later.

Sierra Leonean refugees and Liberian displaced persons construct a new well in Liberia during 1993. (UNHCR Photo/23113/11.1993/L. Taylor)

When one considers the numerous UN development-related bodies for which ECOSOC is to oversee coordination, the alphabet soup thickens. These UN bodies include: the Development Program (UNDP), the Children's Fund (UNICEF), UNCTAD, Population Fund (UNFPA), High Commission for Refugees (UNHCR), High Commissioner for Human Rights (UNHCHR), Environment Programme (UNEP), and the World Food Programme (WFP). The mandates and work programs of these various agencies overlap tremendously, which has made the job of coordination especially daunting. So has the fact that these UN bodies are only part of the much larger UN system for which ECOSOC is responsible for facilitating cooperation and coordination. Before discussing in greater detail what some of these specific agencies actually do, it is helpful to see how the UN has tried to deal recently with the challenges of coordination. The fact is that in reality ECOSOC is something of a mailbox between the General Assembly and the rest of the socio-economic agencies involved in development. Were ECOSOC a true super-coordinator, there would not be a need for the types of supplemental coordinating arrangements discussed next.

When Kofi A. Annan was elected to the office of Secretary-General in December 1996, he was unique in having spent his entire professional career as an international civil servant, inside the system. He had spent nearly three decades working his way up through the ranks and being exposed to the best and the worst of the organizational beast. Upon arriving in office, he committed himself and the world organization to a reform process.[3] This subject was also important in Washington, where the largest donor to both the regular and voluntary UN budgets had long been pressing for administrative reform. According to one of the chief critics of the UN, former U.S. Senator Jesse Helms, the "literally hundreds of UN agencies, commissions, committees, and subcommittees [that] have proliferated" since 1945 is one of the chief problems of the organization. Thus Helms argued that either the Secretary-General should lead a drastic reform effort, or the UN could not be saved.[4] So Annan both knew the organization from the inside, and knew about important pressures for administrative reform from the outside.

At the heart of Annan's reform program lies the reorientation and reorganization of the UN's administration and management. In his effort to bring unity of purpose to the diverse activities of the UN and provide clear lines of responsibility, he created —for the first time in the UN's half-century—a cabinet structure. This Senior Management Group (SMG), as it is called, is comprised of the various Under-Secretaries-General, the heads of UN funds and programs, and the Deputy-Secretary-General (a post created in 1998 and held by Louise Frechette of Canada, who among other things is responsible for overseeing the reform process and the coordination of development activities). Relatedly, four thematic executive committees (Peace and Security, Humanitarian Affairs, Economic and Social Affairs, and United Nations Development Group) were created and charged with overseeing the coordination of policy development, management, and decisionmaking. The convenors of each of these committees sit on the Senior Management Group.

Two of these executive committees are of particular importance for development. The Economic and Social Affairs Executive Committee (EC-ESA) is convened by the Under-Secretary-General for economic and social affairs and comprises representatives from eighteen UN bodies. Like all the other executive committees, the EC-ESA serves as a consultative body for facilitating decisionmaking, policy development and coordination, and better management.

The United Nations Development Group Executive Committee is convened by the administrator of UNDP and includes the UNFPA, UNICEF, and WFP. This body also serves as the secretariat for the United Nations Development Group (UNDG), which was created in 1997 to provide better coordination among the numerous UN funds, programs, and other bodies that have proliferated over the years in the development area. In addition to its own operational activities, the UNDP administers several special-purpose funds and programs, including the UN Capital Development Fund (UNCDF). And in cooperation with the World Bank and UNEP, the UNDP serves as an implementing agency for GEF, which provides concessional funding and grants for certain environmentally sound development projects.

At present, therefore, there is enhanced coordination of UN development activities. It comes via the office of the Secretary-General and via UNDP. Given that states vote to create all sorts of UN development agencies and bodies, it falls to these two parts of the UN system to bring as much order as possible to a multifaceted process.

Particular Contributions to Sustainable Development

As we take a micro approach and look at particular UN agencies and bodies working for sustainable development, it becomes clear that many of them were given unrealistic mandates or obviously overlapped with already existing parts of the UN system. It should be stressed that the responsibility for this state of affairs rests with the states that voted to create these units.

Likewise, the fact that many if not most of these UN units manifest inadequate funding reflects state policy with regard to both the administrative/assessed and supplementary/voluntary budgets of the system. The former budget is for basic administrative costs of the UN proper at headquarters. The latter budget is for other programming. Something in the range of $8 billion to $10 billion annually is spent by the UN system (excluding the World Bank and IMF) on development, broadly defined to include transitions from emergency relief. By comparison, for the Marshall Plan after World War II, the U.S. alone spent the equivalent in 1992 dollars of about $115 billion for the reconstruction of just one region of the world—Europe.[5]

Nevertheless, many of these UN agencies and bodies play important roles in several ways: persistently pushing states to live up to their obligations or develop new ones; participating in joint efforts that do have some discernible impact in advancing development goals; helping to bring a modicum of order to what we have already called a shotgun approach to development.

In what follows we stress primarily the interplay of economics and ecology, for reasons of space.

The UNDP

Aside from its general coordinating duties, the UNDP is the center of the world organization's development work. It is the primary unit devoted to capacity building for social and economic development. As discussed in Chapter 8, the program was created in 1965 to take the lead in providing technical assistance. In this regard, it works with other UN units in a wide variety of thematic contexts. For example, it provides assistance to the Department of Economic and Social Affairs (DESA) in support of the UN's standard-setting and normative work in developing countries and provides integrated follow-up to the UN's global conferences of the 1990s. It works in the security realm to support elections, demobilization and reconciliation initiatives, and human rights and to promote preventive development. In the humanitarian field, the agency provides support for disaster prevention, mitigation, and preparedness; the reintegration into society of refugees, former combatants, and internally displaced people; the implementation of post-disaster national plans for reintegration, reconstruction, and recovery; and similar activities. It is also the administering agency for a number of special development-related funds and programs, such as UNIFEM.[6]

In recent years, the UNDP has reprioritized its program around four interrelated themes: advocacy, advice, pilot projects, and partnerships. UNDP Administrator Mark Malloch Brown, an American, has argued that the program's annual Human Development Report gives the agency a "special voice and pulpit and authority to develop alternative ideas."[7] The advisory function focuses on capacity building in a variety of areas, including legal, political, and regulatory frameworks as well as infrastructure for basic social and economic development. Given the agency's limited budget of $1.850 million for 2002, it concentrates on doing things that can serve as catalysts for mainstreaming particular policy agendas as opposed to taking on expensive large-scale projects. (How can a budget be "limited" when it is over a billion dollars? The U.S. Department of Defense is now spending in the neighborhood of $380 billion annually. In the lifetime of this book's current edition, that number will move to $400 billion.) Long ago, Western donors placed that kind of investment in the World Bank.

UNDP's partnership function is a wide-ranging one that focuses on integrating diverse elements of society and the private sector into development initiatives. The agency is committed to the belief that promoting sustainable development requires new forms of cooperation involving complex interventions from a wide variety of actors—governments at all levels, NGOs, private business enterprises, and local community groups. The focus is on empowering people and creating the conditions necessary for "people-centered" development. The guiding philosophy is that "people should guide both the state and the market, which need to work in tandem, with people sufficiently empowered to exert a more effective influence over both."[8] In brief, the UNDP's underlying theme is getting the product to the poor and empowering them with the capacity for good governance. Priority is placed on democratization and empowerment through participation.

Of course, empowerment, like most development activities, requires resources, especially financial resources. In this regard, the UNDP, working with the UN Capital Development Fund, has undertaken an initiative to provide what is called microfinance—providing financial services to the poor at the local level. Its Special Unit for Microfinance (SUM) is devoted to supporting the creation of start-up micro-financial institutions in rural areas in the poorest countries. The underlying philosophy is simple: "The program is predicated on the concept that most donor support has been so far directed towards large and successful organizations, and that small amounts of capital (up to $150,000) invested primarily in recipient organizations displaying vision, commitment and competence, can help widen tomorrow's market of successful microfinancial institutions."[9]

At the end of Chapter 8, we asked, "What is the value added of the UNDP?" The answer to this question, of course, needs to be viewed in the context of the shrinking financial resource base for multilateral development assistance over the last decade or so. In the past few years, the UNDP's core operating budget has been greatly diminished and the size of the headquarters staff cut by a quarter. When viewed in this context, the self-assessment offered recently by Malloch Brown seems on target:

> When I took office the agenda was clear: Reform of UNDP. Indeed, I do not think I dramatise it when I say the message was close to reform or die. Some were beginning to conclude that the world was carrying one multilateral development agency too many . . . . That notion is now banished, as the organization that is spearhead-

ing the Millennium Development Goals from global conferences to the poorest neighbourhoods of the poorest countries; that is making global and local waves with Human Development Reports dealing with issues ranging from technology to democracy to the crisis of the Arab region; that is addressing down-to-earth development challenges in some 140 countries with our National Human Development Reports; that is innovating new approaches to technical cooperation and capacity-building across all our practice areas, proves that we are once more part of the conversation because we are part of the solution.[10]

But as Malloch Brown went on to acknowledge, "in the final analysis, we cannot judge our reform by its impact on UNDP alone, but rather on how we help strengthen the critical role of the United Nations system as a whole in all aspects of development cooperation."[11] In this regard, the jury is still out.

UNCTAD

This institution began as a debating forum and think tank for disgruntled developing countries and their advocates who sought a counter-forum to the General Agreement on Tariffs and Trade (GATT). For most of its existence, it largely served that function. The conference itself meets in formal session every four years, but its Trade and Development Board (TDB) meets annually, and the secretariat in Geneva operates continuously. As mentioned in Chapter 8, UNCTAD served as the focal point for the formulation and articulation of NIEO ideas. However, the end of the Cold War brought with it hard times for the agency. Then, after the creation of the WTO, UNCTAD adopted a more conciliatory tone.

More recently, UNCTAD has come full step into Kofi Annan's initiative to forge new and innovative partnerships with other international organizations, local governments, NGOs, the private sector, and civil society. UNCTAD's role has taken a wide variety of forms and complexions. In 1999, for example, UNCTAD, along with UNDP and HABITAT, initiated a global partnership—World Alliance of Cities Against Poverty (WACAP)—with civil society, the private sector, and local governments to carry out the goal of the 1995 Social Summit in Copenhagen. This new alliance quickly became formalized and has grown substantially. Its primary goal is to strengthen the network and partnership between cities around the world. During the recent Third UN Conference on Least Developed Countries (LDCs) in Brussels, WACAP organized a parallel "Mayors Meeting," bringing together representatives from 216 cities around the world. The primary purpose of this conference was action, not talk. A "city-to-city solidarity market" was held in which demands of assistance were matched with offers. On the spot, twelve formal agreements of cooperation were concluded between cities in Belgium and cities in Africa, Asia, and Latin America. The requests of another 120 cities from developing regions were tendered and are currently either under consideration or being related to cities throughout the world through the numerous global, regional, and national city networks that also participated at the meeting.[12]

UNICEF

The UN Children's Fund is almost always called by its acronym and is involved in a wide variety of development-related activities around the world. Its work ranges from child and maternal health care and basic education to water and sanitation.[13] It has special initiatives dealing with HIV/AIDS, participation and rights of adolescent girls, tobacco-free youth, adolescent health and development, and school health, hygiene and nutrition. The agency's basic budget for 2002 was $1.454 million. Beyond this, it initiates specific appeals to meet challenging crises. In 2003, for example, UNICEF undertook an appeal to deal with a series of overlapping and overwhelming crises in six southern African countries. Extreme poverty, a severe drought, HIV/AIDS, and an educational crisis have put more than 2.4 million children under the age of five and their more than 10 million family members in imminent risk of dying.

Reference to "family members" should be understood to mean that UNICEF focuses as much on women and mothers as on children, which is logical. Underdevelopment is greatly gendered, which means that women and girls bear the brunt of much poverty, denial of adequate education and health care, and other forms of discrimination. In the same way that refugees are mostly women, children, and the aged, so underdevelopment is especially harsh on women, children, and the aged. It is not too strong to say that women in underdeveloped countries constitute a "new global underclass."[14] Among several other UN agencies, UNICEF is confronting and trying to change this reality.

UNICEF is a full and active participant in the UN's sustainable human development partnership. A key focus in this regard is girls' education in the context of "education for every child." Education is seen as the path to empowerment. The agency's executive director has argued forcefully that "there can be no significant or sustainable transformation in societies and no significant reduction in poverty until girls receive the quality basic education they need to take their rightful place as equal partners in development."[15]

UNICEF led preparations for the 2002 UN General Assembly Special Session on Children, where member states adopted the Declaration and Plan of Action, *A World Fit for Children*. This action plan was intended to commit governments to a specific set of goals for youth and an associated timetable for achieving them. In May 2003, UNICEF issued its first report card on the attainment of those commitments. In the report, *The United Nations Special Session on Children: A First Anniversary Report on Follow-up*, the authors bemoaned that "the world's attention and resources have been diverted to crises and war while pressing yet hidden challenges facing humankind— fighting HIV/AIDS, child illness and malnutrition, illiteracy and child abuse—have been sidelined." In 2003 when much of the world was focused on "regime change" in Iraq, the UNICEF Executive Director Carol Bellamy voiced this criticism:

> The children of Iraq are important, but there are 2.1 billion children in this world, half of them living in abject poverty, 150 million who are malnourished, 120 million who never go to school, and 11 million who die from totally preventable causes every year. These are the things that governments must focus on with consistency and rigor.[16]

In the domain of children, once again we see that states endorse worthy goals, and reiterate them, but do not always follow up on the ground. As Bellamy also said in 2003, "the global follow-up to last year's commitments has gone forward."[17] Yet, UNICEF reported that "most countries have barely begun to implement the targets, with only half of the world's governments even taking the first step of developing an action plan."[18]

Commission on Sustainable Development

Growing out of the Earth Summit in Rio de Janeiro in 1992, the CSD was given the dual responsibilities of overseeing the implementation of the provisions of Agenda 21, which was a policy blueprint for the ecological domain, and coordinating the sustainable development activities of the various organizations within the UN system—and even beyond the boundaries of that system. Agreement did not readily follow, however, over many important details about how this new commission was to be empowered to fulfill its mandate effectively. Although CSD was assigned the role of being the primary mechanism within the UN system for coordinating sustainable development, its relationship to UNEP, the World Bank, the Committee of International Development Institutions on the Environment, and other intergovernmental entities was not clearly defined.

An important mandate for the CSD was to strengthen the role of major societal groups as effective participants in sustainable development decisionmaking at all levels. This "mainstreaming" (that is, integration) of civic-based actors as participants in governance processes was underscored in the Rio Declaration. Moreover, the text of Agenda 21 specifically addressed the roles of eight major groups: NGOs, indigenous peoples, local governments, workers, businesses, scientific communities, farmers, and women, children, and youth. Exactly how this mandate for mainstreaming was to be institutionalized in practice, however, had been left ambiguous. Although only eighteen NGOs were represented at the first CSD meeting, ECOSOC had authorized the CSD to consider including in the work of the new body all 1,400 NGOs that had been represented at the Earth Summit. In addition, the UN Secretary-General was to appoint a high-level advisory panel to the CSD, consisting of between fifteen and twenty-five eminent persons. As recognized in both Agenda 21 and the Rio Declaration, fulfilling this mandate effectively is the fundamental cornerstone for successful implementation of sustainable development programs and practices. Therefore the mandate poses a tremendous challenge for CSD, as well as for the UN system and multilateral organizations more generally. Establishing an effective relationship between the sovereignty-based world of inter-governmental organizations and the global civil society within which that interstate order exists was an elusive quest during the first half century of the UN's existence.[19]

In recent years, the CSD has served as a focal point for reviewing and assessing progress toward the fulfillment of Agenda 21 goals and objectives. During its tenth session beginning in 2001, the CSD functioned as the Preparatory Committee (Prep-Com) for the Agenda 21 ten-year review process, holding four PrepCom sessions in preparation for the World Summit on Sustainable Development in fall 2002. Then, at its eleventh session in May 2003, the CSD decided to organize its multi-year program of work around two-year "implementation cycles," beginning in 2004–2005 and running to 2016–2017. Each work cycle is to focus on a specific thematic cluster of topics and cross-cutting issues. For 2004–2005, for example, the thematic cluster includes water, sanitation, and human settlements with a dozen cross-cutting issues: poverty eradication, changing unsustainable patterns of production and consumption, protecting and managing the natural resource base of economic and social development, sustainable development in a globalizing world, health and sustainable development, sustainable development of small island developing states (SIDS), sustainable development of Africa, other regional initiatives, means of implementation, institutional framework for sustainable development, gender equality, and education. The second two-year cycle will focus on energy, industrial development, air pollution and climate change, with the same cross-cutting issues. Each two-year implementation cycle will include a "Review Year," during which time progress toward implementing sustainable development goals will be assessed, and a "Policy Year," in which decisions will be taken about how to speed up implementation and mobilize additional support.

UNEP

Underlying our discussion in Chapter 8 was a question: "What can UNEP be expected to do in reality?" The answer is more ambiguous here and will take some time to explain. The UN Environment Program was created in 1973 to serve as the UN's main mechanism for "policy review and coordination" on environmental issues, including those associated with development. Its Governing Council consists of fifty-eight members elected by the General Assembly. It meets biennially and reports to the GA through ECOSOC. Its main mandate is to encourage and coordinate environmental activities within the UN system. The work of the program is carried out through a modest secretariat headed by an executive director. The agency is based in Nairobi, Kenya, and is financed through the UN regular budget.

The UNEP, like the CSD which came later, was assigned the function of forging interagency cooperation throughout the UN system to promote environmental protection. Since environmental concerns cut across almost every conceivable area of human activity, this was indeed a broad mandate. The problem was, however, that neither UNEP nor CSD was given primary responsibility to take on operational functions that might interfere with the work of others.

At the same time, both UNEP and CSD were superimposed on existing interorganizational systems. When UNEP was created, a number of UN agencies—including UNESCO, FAO, WHO, and WMO—were already engaged in environmental work. In addition, several UNESCO-related scientific programs—including the International Oceanographic Commission, the International Hydrological Program, and the intergovernmental Man and the Biosphere project—either were functioning or were in some stage of development. The Commission on Sustainable Development was dropped into an even more complex and somewhat chaotic multiorganizational system. Although CSD possessed the potential to serve as a complement to the coordination work of UNEP, the history of international organizations would seem to suggest that CSD was just as likely to act as a fierce competitor.

The process of system-wide interagency coordination in ecodevelopment evolved slowly through trial and error. In UNEP's early years, a comprehensive procedure for systemwide review, called joint programming, was adopted. Interagency discussions focused on selected environmental topics. The objective of these discussions was to identify gaps in existing knowledge and practices and to design strategies to fill them. Over the years, these exercises expanded from bilateral to multilateral thematic programming.

If we place these coordination activities in clearer perspective, the precise nature of UNEP's mandate as it relates to other UN agencies needs to be understood. UNEP's most important role is generating international norms and setting standards to protect the human environment rather than concrete projects to help improve air quality or protect forests. The agency has played an instrumental role in the negotiations and adoption of a number of major international environmental conventions, including the Vienna Convention for the Protection of the Ozone Layer, the Convention on Climate Change, and the Convention on Biodiversity. Although UNEP does administer certain environmental projects, it is not primarily a project-executing agency in the sense that most specialized agencies are. Also, UNEP is not primarily a source of financing, unlike UNDP, the World Bank group, and other multilateral funding agencies. It does, however, disperse modest funds through its Environment Fund. The result has been a somewhat confused mandate, which has been muddied further by the creation of the Commission on Sustainable Development with its overlapping functions.

Effective project implementation most often requires coordination at the operational level in the field. Although UNEP is not involved in executing program actions at the country level, it is involved with scores of other organizations in overseeing the implementation of projects that are supported through resources from the UNEP Environment Fund. A great many of these projects are executed by "cooperating agencies" (that is, UN system agencies and bodies), primarily FAO, UNESCO, WHO, WMO, and UNCHS (UN Center for Human Settlements, or Habitat). Other resources from this fund go to support project implementation by other intergovernmental organizations, NGOs, research institutions, and other civic-based bodies (referred to in UNEP as supporting organizations). When projects also include UNDP sources, the resident coordinator in the country in which the project is located serves as the primary point person for coordination activities in the field.

This overlapping jurisdiction on coordination adds a significant degree of complexity and ambiguity to UNEP's function, as have certain of the major changes within the UN system over the past decade. There has been a definite trend toward greater decentralization, regionalism, and involvement of civic-based entities in global governance, which has complicated the already problematic task of making the UN function coherently. In addition to dwindling funds, another important reason for UNEP's failure to serve as an effective systemwide coordinating mechanism was that a number of major donor governments, most notably the United States, preferred to bypass UNEP regarding financial matters. In such a position, UNEP remains a technical agency concentrating largely on environmental monitoring and assessment. This is an important role. With regard to the 1987 Montreal Protocol on protecting the ozone, UNEP coordinated scientific information about both the problem and alternative solutions, becoming an expert lobby backing up diplomatic efforts to produce broad and binding agreement.[20]

So what can UNEP be expected to do in reality? The short answer is "very little." The task of coordinating the environmental activities of the diverse array of institutional actors and arrangements is massive. These bodies are legally and practically autonomous; many of them were actively engaged in environmental work before the formation of UNEP and have access to far more significant technical and financial resources. Once again, the UN appears as the logical choice for coordination, but UNEP has neither the authority nor the organizational wherewithal to coordinate the globe's network of institutions.

Other Development Agencies

UNESCO began in the 1960s a wide variety of other environmental concerns that cut across its main areas of competence—science, education, culture, and communications. Of course science, education, and communications are very much key to development, however defined. In 1965, a ten-year program, the International Hydrological Decade, was launched to promote the study of hydrological resources, including water pollution. This early environmental focus was strengthened with the hosting of the Biosphere Conference, the 1970 Helsinki Interdisciplinary Symposium on Man's Role in Changing His Environment, and the 1972 Convention for the Protection of the World Cultural and Natural Heritage. UNESCO has been responsible for the creation of a number of affiliated bodies, such as the International Oceanographic Commission (IOC). This particular body, for example, has been important in promoting international marine scientific research with special emphasis on pollution prevention. Since the late 1980s, the UNESCO secretariat in Paris has emphasized proper coordination of the environmentally related activities and programs within its various divisions. It has been actively involved in follow-up activities to the 1992 United Nations Conference on Environment and Development (UNCED) and the implementation of a variety of related agreements.

For many years, UNESCO has had a special relationship with the International Council of Scientific Unions (ICSU) and with its member unions in the environmental area. The ICSU is an NGO comprising scientific academies, research councils, and scientific unions. It facilitates and coordinates the work of large international research programs, such as the International Biological Programme (IBP) and the International Geosphere-Biosphere Programme (IGBP). In 1969 the Scientific Committee on Problems of the Environment (SCOPE) was established within ICSU. This committee has been responsible for reviewing information on the implications of human-induced environmental change. Two decades later, in 1989, the Advisory Committee on the Environment was created to provide counsel to the ICSU Executive Board on all ICSU activities related to the environment and global change and to provide a link with external bodies in this regard.

In addition to UNESCO, most other agencies within the UN system have operational mandates linked to ecodevelopment. The environmental relationships of some of these bodies are more obvious and more direct than others. Most, if not all, of the work of the World Meteorological Organization (WMO) focuses on ecodevelopment concerns. Its broad, heavily scientific mandate includes atmospheric pollution, meteorological aspects of water pollution, climate change, the effects of pollution on climate change and vegetation, and the relationship between climate, weather, and agricultural practices. Along with the IOC and ICSU, the WMO cosponsors the World Climate Research Programme (WCRP). This joint initiative examines the dynamic aspects of the earth's climate system and stands as a counterpart to the IGBP, which studies biological and chemical aspects of global change.

The work of the World Health Organization, at its Geneva headquarters and in the field, focuses broadly on the relationship between human beings and their environments. Its basic or minimal or floor budget for 2002–2003 was $47.8 million. This institution is concerned with controlling environmental pollution in all forms and modes of transmission as well as all other environmental factors that affect health. The agency undertakes pollution surveys and initiates programs for improving methods for measuring pollution and for designing programs for pollution abatement and control. Just as UNICEF has taken more of a human rights approach to its concern for children around the world, so the WHO has been trying to get states to view adequate health as a human right. Recently the WHO undertook a major effort to reduce the use of tobacco in its various forms. Here again we see part of the UN system collecting and disseminating scientific information, then trying to advance ideas based on that knowledge—in this case to improve health. The general process was similar to what the UNEP did in advancing the Montreal Protocol to protect the ozone. (There is more on the WHO and health in the next chapter.)

The FAO has an array of activities on ecodevelopment based both at its headquarters in Rome and in its operational projects in the field. They include sustainable water management through water harvesting, agriculture investment, radioactive contamination, contamination of food by pesticides, and marine pollution related to fisheries. The agency works to establish criteria for water quality management, soil and water resource management, pesticide control, fisheries management, and general control of pollution. Several important environmental conventions fall under FAO auspices, including the International Convention for the Conservation of Atlantic Tunas (ICCAT), the FAO International Code of Conduct on the Distribution and Use of Pesticides, and the Code of Conduct for Responsible Fisheries.

Marine pollution is important to the work of the International Maritime Organization (IMO), established in 1948 as the Intergovernmental Maritime Consultative Organization. At the heart of this agency's work in London are concerns about legal liability and the rights of parties to seek redress from pollution by ships and equipment operating in marine areas, as well as how to prevent such pollution. Over the years, the agency has promoted more than two dozen international conventions and protocols, ranging from the International Convention for the Prevention of Pollution at Sea by Oil (OILPOL) in 1959 to the International Convention on Oil Pollution Preparedness Response and Cooperation (OPPRC) in 1990. In fulfilling its environment-related mandate, the IMO has maintained close working relations with UNEP, FAO, ILO, the United Nations Commission on International Trade Law (UNCITRAL), UNCTAD, and WHO, as well as IUCN, the International Chamber of Shipping, and various other nongovernmental organizations.

The ecodevelopment work of some UN agencies often is not so obvious. The International Civil Aviation Organization (ICAO), for example, deals with aircraft noise pollution from its headquarters in Montreal. The ILO has an interest in the impact of various forms of pollution on the working environment. Of course the ILO, as noted in Chapter 6, tries to ensure that the pursuit of economic growth is accompanied by attention to labor rights. Environmental concerns related to the peaceful uses of nuclear energy, such as radioactive waste management, fall within the realm of the International Atomic Energy Agency (IAEA).

One of the most important international environmental organizations is the hybrid International Union for the Conservation of Nature and National Resources (also known as the World Conservation Union). It comprises states, governmental agencies, and international and national NGOs. Although possessing only a small secretariat, it conducts a remarkably wide range of activities through numerous standing commissions and committees. The IUCN helped forge the conceptual link between development and environment. With the World Wide Fund for Nature (WWF) and UNEP, and in association with FAO and UNESCO, the IUCN launched the World Conservation Strategy in 1980. As a precursor to sustainable development, this initiative set forth principles promoting the sustainable use of the earth's living resources.

Global environmental norms have spread through international conventions and declarations.[21] An extensive codification of international environmental law dealing with marine pollution, for example, has come about in this way since the late 1960s. As discussed, the IMO has played an instrumental role in developing an international maritime pollution regime, with important contributions also coming from UNEP and the multiyear negotiations of the Third United Nations Conference on the Law of the Sea (UNCLOS III).

Additionally, the Global Environmental Facility provides grants to developing countries for environment-related projects and facilitates networking and cooperation among donors. It operates in four main issue areas—protection of the ozone layer, international waters, biodiversity, and climate change—and is charged with working with other UN agencies, regional development banks, and bilateral donors in integrated technical assistance and investment projects. This limited coordination role has been complemented in recent years by the work of the Joint Consultative Group on Policy (JCGP). This body has organized collaborative efforts among five other UN agencies: UNDP, the United Nations Fund for Population Activities (UNFPA), UNICEF, the World Food Programme (WFP), and the International Fund for Agricultural Development (IFAD). Despite such attempts to engender cooperation and undertake coordination within and among the very diverse field of actors in this issue arena, fragmentation abounds.

Although the activities discussed above are often associated with specific UN agencies or UN-sponsored conferences, they normally transcend the formal structures of these organizations. It makes sense to think in terms of broad norms and policymaking processes that regulate an issue, rather than just in terms of this or that particular organization. Social scientists use the notion of an "international regime" to refer to this management of an issue involving principles and rules, and various public and private actors. They also use the notion of "governance" to refer to the same thing. Thus even when trying a micro approach to development, a proper evaluation of particular UN actors requires that we broaden our focus to acknowledge a cumulative impact through joint undertakings. As a leading scholar has concluded, it is very difficult to say with precision why any particular international organization succeeds or fails.[22]

The UN and the Bretton Woods Institutions

As discussed in Chapter 8, for most of the UN system's existence the Washington-based international financial institutions (IFIs) functioned almost completely autonomously from the UN proper. In many depictions of the so-called UN system, dotted lines connected to the World Bank and International Monetary Fund (IMF) suggesting their de facto if not de jure independent status. Part of Kofi Annan's "Quiet Revolution"[23] has sought to redress this situation and bring the UN and the international financial institutions into closer working relations.

The subject is immensely important, starting with budgets and finances. The UN system is chronically starved for adequate financial support. The regular budget amounts to a little over $1 billion each year, with total spending through the entire UN system of core and specialized bodies—excluding enforcement and peacekeeping operations—at about $10 billion per year. This may seem like a large sum of money, but it is not given certain public and private spending in comparison. According to one author, "It is a scandal that each year the managers of the United Nations should have to beg for enough funds to pay staff salaries . . . . But this is only the visible tip of a mass of financial difficulties faced by our most important global enterprise. The entire U.N. system expenditure in 1992 . . . is a trivial amount of money relative to the sums spent annually in some countries on alcohol consumption or weapons procurement. Worldwide, the U.N. cost less than $2 per capita annual in 1992 versus approximately $150 per capita spent on weapons."[24] By comparison, the World Bank dispenses about $40 billion each year. By comparison, the U.S. is estimated to have spent about $20 billion in preparing for and fighting the 2003 war in Iraq.

Beyond finances, a greater integration of Bretton Woods and UN institutions is needed for policy coherence in the development field. We do not lack for criticisms of the World Bank, especially in regard to a very narrow and technical approach to economic growth that leaves out many important aspects of the development process.[25] It is precisely the UN system that increasingly manifests a broader and coherent development rationale through the Millennium Development Goals.

Several steps have been taken to improve linkage for development. One important initiative has been to revitalize the Administrative Committee on Coordination and transform it into a Chief Executive Board for Coordination (CEB). It is chaired by the Secretary-General and is comprised of the executive heads of UN organizations and fourteen specialized agencies, plus the World Bank and IMF.

Annan also appointed an assistant secretary-general for policy coordination and inter-agency affairs who was given the responsibility of identifying ways to strengthen support for the ECOSOC and its coordinating role and to unify the work of the various autonomous UN-related agencies. For two consecutive years (April 1998 and April 1999), a joint high-level meeting was hosted in New York between ECOSOC and officials of the Bretton Woods institutions. General Assembly Resolution 53/169, for example, asked the 1999 session to focus on the "functioning of international financial markets and stability in financing for development."

Although the structural differences and distinct financing remained separate, these meetings were noteworthy in that they represented a different spirit of cooperation between the UN and the Bretton Woods institutions. It would be naïve to overlook history, politics, and the well-known human and bureaucratic tendency to place a huge value on autonomy. Yet as Michel Camdessus, the former managing director of the IMF, declared during the 1999 meeting, better integration of the UN and Bretton Woods institutions is needed to lay the foundation for a more stable global economic order.[26]

That spirit of cooperation had been present in August 1998 when Secretary-General Annan and World Bank President James Wolfensohn held a retreat. As a result, the UNDP and the World Bank initiated a pilot program at the country level to explore the interface between certain programs of the two organizations. Personal chemistry and contacts play a role as well. This spirit of cooperation may strengthen as UNDP Administrator Malloch Brown settles into his job—before assuming this role in 1999, he had served since 1996 as vice president for external affairs and vice president for UN affairs at the World Bank.

These initiatives came at a time when finance flows—both public and private—to developing countries had significantly declined. Official overseas development assistance (ODA) reached an all-time low (0.22 percent of GDP) in 1997 as the world continued to reel from the effects of a global economic crisis. And the least generous country, in terms of the percentage of GNP devoted to ODA, was the United States.[27] But the "ODA crunch" began long before the global financial crisis of the late 1990s. ODA and other kinds of development assistance have declined significantly since the early 1990s, with bilateral assistance flows accounting for most of that decline. In contrast to previous dramatic expansion, private finance flows also fell as international bank lending dropped dramatically.[28] Creating stability for development financing is of particular concern for the least-developed countries (LDCs), which rely heavily on ODA as the main source of their external resource flows and which are extremely vulnerable to such shifts.

To keep things moving forward, the Fifty-Seventh General Assembly decided to host a special high-level meeting among the Bretton Woods institutions, WTO, and representatives of civil society to evaluate progress made since the Monterey Conference.[29] In April 2003, ECOSOC convened a high-level meeting with the Bretton Woods institutions and WTO to discuss policy coherence in implementing the Monterrey Commitments. What is notable in these new initiatives is that for the first time WTO is participating as an active partner.

In this context, the director of the WTO, managing director of the IMF, and president of the World Bank made a joint plea to the Group of 8 (G–8, or the G–7 of richest seven industrialized countries joined by Russia as of mid–2003) to provide the political guidance and follow-through on commitments that is needed to move trade negotiations and the development agenda forward. Their statement reasoned:

> The WTO, the IMF and the World Bank are cooperating to support the full engagement of developing countries in global trade negotiations to produce an outcome that favours the expansion of their trade. Better market access for developing countries' exports is essential for raising and sustaining their economic growth and reducing poverty. At the same time, developing countries need to place trade integration as a central plank of their development and poverty-reduction strategies. These efforts must be backed up by more focused and generous technical and financial support particularly for the poorest countries to help them build the human, institutional and physical capital needed to improve trade opportunities and to integrate the poorest countries successfully into the world economy."[30]

So far, however, the G-8 has demonstrated little collective leadership and guidance in this regard. And voices have been raised in some important circles arguing that the Bank now has such a broad agenda that its programs are unwieldy; consequently, so the argument runs, the Bank should get back to basics.[31]

Norm Creation and Coherence: History of Ideas

We have argued that a more or less coherent framework has emerged at the UN both regarding the fight against poverty and the promotion of human development. Development strategies, the framework suggests, should focus on the eradication of extreme poverty and on sustainability. Capacity building, good governance, and popular participation are all essential ingredients for promoting sustainability. "The primary resource for development is the great untapped reservoir of human creativity and talent of the people of the developing countries themselves; the release of this human potential requires investment in education, infrastructure, public health and other basic social services, as well as in production for the market."[32] According to this new framework, development needs to be people-centered, not state-centered. Good governance, however, is considered to be essential for successful development. This new people-centered development agenda focuses heavily on integrating and empowering relevant stakeholders, especially diverse elements of civil society including the for-profit private sector.

This consensual framework was articulated clearly at the Millennium Summit in September 2000, the largest gathering of heads of state and government in history. The Millennium Declaration expressed a shared commitment to a number of lofty objectives: eradicate extreme poverty; reduce hunger; improve human health and the human environment; create enabling environments at the national and international levels conducive to development; promote good governance both domestically and internationally; mobilize financial resources required for development; and deal comprehensively and effectively with debt problems. In line with the evolving global development framework, the assembled world leaders resolved to: promote gender equality and the empowerment of women; develop and implement strategies to increase employment opportunities; encourage the pharmaceutical industry to make essential drugs more widely available in developing countries; develop strong partnerships with civil society; and ensure that the benefits of new technologies, especially information and communication technologies, are available to all.[33]

Although one is tempted to dismiss such jamborees, the change in discourse and objectives is an important first step in altering policy reality. And the Millennium Summit built upon a number of specific goals and associated targets and quantitative indicators growing out of the extensive series of global conferences in the 1990s.[34] Each target has a time frame and targeted amount and one or more indicators to be monitored to assess movement toward achieving the target. These Millennium Development Goals (MDGs) have been commonly accepted throughout the UN system as a framework for guiding development policies and assessing progress. They are viewed as being mutually reinforcing with the overarching objective being reduction of poverty.

Taken as a whole, the MDGs provide a "framework of accountability for national governments, bilateral and multilateral donors, and many other actors that have a role in development."[35] In the words of UNDP Administrator Malloch Brown, "The MDGs are a very simple but powerful idea whose time has come. They are in effect the international community's effort to set the terms of a globalization not solely driven by the interests of the strong, but managed in the interests of the poor." In brief, the MDGs serve as a mechanism for framing development thinking and the UN's human development agenda. But what does it mean to say "their time has come"? From where and how did these consensual goals and norms emerge? How did the international community of states get from the contentious debates of the 1970s to consensus? Is this consensus genuine? And, perhaps most importantly, does it make a difference?

An important part of the answer to these questions can be found in the multilateral development diplomacy and related institutional processes of recent decades and especially the global, ad hoc conferences of the 1990s that are chronicled in Table 9.1. Building on the activities of the UN's first three development decades (1960–1989),[36] international conversations since the end of the Cold War have transformed the global development debate and UN discourse in general. The Millennium Summit and Millennium Assembly represent just two—albeit two very important—links in a growing chain of multilateral global conferences and activities focusing on development-related issues and problems.

One of the most striking outcomes to emerge from these conferences was that the development debate took on a new character as the concepts of human development and sustainable development became fused in "sustainable human development," which in turn became further entwined with the concept of human security. In many ways the pursuit of international peace and security, the UN's primary raison d'être, has come to be synonymous with promoting and sustaining "human security."

TABLE 9.1 Chronology of Selected Development-Related Conferences, 1990–2003

1990	World Summit for Children (WSC)
	Second World Climate Conference
	World Conference on Education for All
1992	UN Conference on Environment and Development (UNCED)
1993	UNCTAD VIII- Eighth Session of the Conference on Trade and Development
1994	Global Conference on Sustainable Development of Small Island Developing States
	International Conference on Population and Development (ICPD)
1995	Fourth World Conference on Women
	World Summit for Social Development
1996	Second United Nations Conference on Human Settlements (HABITAT II)
	World Food Summit
	UNCTAD IX- Ninth Session of the Conference on Trade and Development
1997	Special Session of UN General Assembly on Sustainable Development
1999	Special Session of UN General Assembly on Small Island Developing States
	Special Session of UN General Assembly on Population and Development
2000	UNCTAD X- Tenth Session of the Conference on Trade and Development
	Special Session of the UN General Assembly on World Summit for Social Development and Beyond: Achieving Social Development for All in a Globalised World
2001	Third United Nations Conference on the Least Developed Countries
	Special Session of UN General Assembly on the Problem of Human Immunodeficiency Virus/Acquired Immunodeficiency Syndrome (HIV/AIDS) in All its Aspects
	International Conference on Fresh Water
2002	International Conference of Financing for Development
	Special Session of UN General Assembly on Children
	World Food Summit: Five Years Later
	World Summit on Sustainable Development
2003	World Summit on the Information Society

From Stockholm, 1972

To understand fully the nature of this synthesis, however, one must look back to a conference held three decades ago in Stockholm—the United Nations Conference on the Human Environment (UNCHE). It was during the preparations for this conference that development and environment became integrated. More specifically, at a meeting of experts in Founex, Switzerland, UNCHE Secretary-General Maurice Strong probed the concept of "ecodevelopment" that would serve as a foundation on which the sustainable development dialogue would be built. Of course, the Club of Rome and others had put forward similar notions. Yet these largely intellectual exercises did not carry the same force or impact as the Founex report.[37] Under the leadership of Strong, the participants were able to bridge some important political divides, in particular the clash of priorities between developing countries in pursuit of economic growth and developed countries concerned about conservation of natural resources. The clash was captured by India's Prime Minister Indira Gandhi, who opened the Stockholm Conference by arguing that in developing countries "poverty is the greatest polluter."[38] By arguing that long-term development was necessary to combat the poverty that contributed to pollution but that such growth also depended on dealing with shorter-term environmental problems, he was able to bridge divergent North-South divide. He also suggested that the governments of industrialized countries help defray the costs of environmental protection that developing countries would be forced to bear. The concept of "additionality," meaning to increase resources in order to apply them to a new problem rather than to subtract them from another use, helped overcome skepticism in the South over global economic inequities.[39]

During the 1970s the environmental debate and the work of UNEP, which grew out of the conference, got caught up in the NIEO debate. The work of the program continued to center on ecodevelopment, including the interrelationships among environment, development, population, and natural resources. But over the next decade, UNEP's agenda expanded incrementally to include a number of additional concerns, including appropriate technology.[40]

UNEP seemed to be caught between the proverbial rock and a hard place. To appease the Group of 77 developing countries, or G-77, the new agency had been located in Nairobi, Kenya. All other UN cities at the time were in the North (New York, Geneva, Paris, Rome, and Vienna). However, UNEP's location there, although a symbolic victory for the South, served to marginalize access to the organization by many developed and developing countries. The G-77 had no permanent presence in Nairobi. Furthermore, few governments of developing countries had any permanent representation in UNEP. Northern governments preferred that the organization deal primarily with monitoring, assessment, and other technical and scientific endeavors; they were able to ensure the implementation of this preference through the power of the purse.

Donor governments and the international agencies through which they preferred to operate began to include environmental considerations in decisionmaking, yet they tended to operate quite independently of UNEP. Meeting in Paris in September 1979, representatives of nine multilateral development banks and other inter-governmental institutions adopted the Declaration of Environmental Policies and Procedures Relating to Economic Development. This declaration was formally issued in New York the following February with the simultaneous announcement of the creation of the Committee of International Development Institutions on the Environment (CIDIE), which has now expanded to sixteen inter-governmental organizations with twenty bilateral donor governments participating as observers.[41] This body was given the tasks of hosting consultations, facilitating joint activities, and promoting the sharing of information among members in order to fully integrate environmental considerations into their development activities. Members also affirmed their commitment to the Stockholm principles and recommendations.

Adoption of the declaration and the creation of CIDIE demonstrated the growing marginalization of UNEP, the UN's principal agency charged with global ecodevelopment discourse and practice. Peter Haas saw UNEP's inability to lead as due to both internal and systemic factors.

While UNEP attempted to ensure that "environment" became a cross-cutting element in the various development-related activities of the UN system, it lacked institutional leverage to effectively influence programmatic efforts by other agencies. Moreover, UNEP suffered throughout the 1980s from internal organizational difficulties that inhibited organizational autonomy. It lacked organizational clout and sufficient money to compel other agencies to change their actions, and was well outside the mainstream of UN diplomacy because of its Nairobi headquarters.[42]

Despite UNEP's marginalization from the overall development picture, other forces pressed the sustainable development agenda forward. The controversy during the 1970s over the role of satisfying basic human needs within development projects became an important element of the global debate. Many Southern governments complained that a basic human-needs approach served to distract attention and divert action from redressing global inequalities; some important Northern donors argued that the approach would divert scarce resources from economic growth. There was a need for a new concept that could play the kind of synthesizing role that ecodevelopment had played in the UNCHE process. But clearly "basic human needs" was not that concept, especially since there was no consensus definition of that term.

A catalyzing idea, however, was emerging within the context of the basic human needs debate. In 1980, the General Assembly approved the World Conservation Strategy, which placed importance on the *sustainability* of natural life-support systems as they relate to satisfying human needs. This strategy, designed by the IUCN in conjunction with UNEP and WWF, facilitated the process of refocusing the global debate on the issue of sustainability in the development process.

The process of building a consensus around this notion of sustainable development was not without obstacles, however. The environmental aspects of this concept remained a high priority for both governments and NGOs in the North but were viewed by many in the South as a potential new form of conditionality, or yet another way that Western donors could make new demands on recipient countries. Indeed, the coincidental formation of CIDIE fueled such speculation.

To sort out these considerations, the General Assembly in 1983 created a special commission, the World Commission on Environment and Development (WCED). Headed by Gro Brundtland, a former prime minister of Norway who became director-general of the WHO in 1999, WCED set about the task of devising a concept of sustainable development. This body, like many others composed of eminent persons to study global issues, became popularly known by the chairman's family name, thus becoming the "Brundtland Commission." Its findings and recommendations were published four years later in *Our Common Future*.[43] Environmental protection, economic equity, and economic growth were brought together.

The Brundtland Commission's formula proved to be very politically attractive. Dealing with environmental problems was seen as being ineffectual unless these actions simultaneously addressed poverty and inequities in the world economy.

Building on this foundation, the UNEP Governing Council defined sustainable development as "development that meets the needs of the present without compromising the ability of future generations to meet their own needs and does not imply in any way encroachment upon national sovereignty."[44] Purely state-based solutions to ecological and economic problems were clearly inadequate and declining in salience among both scholars and many officials. But as we noted in the security and human rights parts of this volume, developing countries were hardly eager to abandon the traditional concept of state sovereignty, which they had gained through independence so recently.

Although the World Bank at the time operated mostly independently from the rest of the UN system, its changing policies were symptomatic of the enhanced status of ecological issues in development policy. Often skeptics wonder about the impact of UN conferences, resolutions, expert groups, and reports. However, at least partly in response to the well-coordinated NGO Multilateral Development Bank Campaign and a host of efforts since the Stockholm Conference in 1972, the World Bank rapidly expanded its environmental profile in the late 1980s.[45] The creation of the Environment Department and the adoption of the Environmental Assessment Operations Directive in 1989 represented major elements in this regard. Environmental assessments were required of all new projects that would have a significant environmental impact. That directive was revised three years later to provide potentially affected people with access to the information contained in those assessments.

This ongoing process of conference diplomacy helped to build a certain degree of mutual understanding and a common, or at least compatible, orientation toward North-South issues within the Group of 77. At the same time, it also tended to foster disenchantment in some major Western governments and led to a heightened degree of mutual mistrust and a deterioration of relations between the North and South.

From the mid-1980s onward, ecodevelopment, particularly as translated into sustainable development, provided a focal point for development dialogue. The convergence around sustainable development as a theme in international development debate and practice was facilitated by the coincidence of a number of factors over the decade of the 1990s. As discussed in Chapter 8, the demands for the establishment of the NIEO had stalled, and the viability of the G-77 as a cohesive mobilizing and caucusing force had become doubtful. Past approaches to development were seen as having done little to reduce the poverty, squalor, and other symptoms of underdevelopment, with a few notable exceptions—for example, the so-called Tigers of Southeast Asia like Taiwan, Singapore, and South Korea.

The ideas associated with sustainable development seemed to fit well with the more pragmatic attitudes prevailing since the late 1980s. The NIEO and its radical and confrontational tone was a dusty memory, and market liberalization and political democratization had replaced redistribution as the battle cry. Further, some Northern donors had grown weary of the constant demands to increase official development assistance. Seeing little evidence that past assistance had made any appreciable difference in alleviating poverty, "donor fatigue" became a prevalent explanation for diminished overseas development assistance (ODA). There was little indication that the quality of life of the average person in developing countries had improved. The message inherent in sustainable development was that development assistance needed to get to the people. This sentiment generally struck a positive chord in the North.

As we argued earlier, the end of the Cold War, the collapse of communist control in Central Europe, and the breakup of the former Soviet Union distracted attention in the North from the development concerns of the Third World. This was especially true in Washington, where the South had suddenly become strategically much less important. Those calling for greater attention to development were searching for a way to capture the attention of donors. Sustainable development provided a potential means to recapture some of the lost focus and garner Northern support for Third World development—that is, there was some leverage in that industrialized countries were at least interested in the adjectival portion of "sustainable development."

Heightened concern in the North during the 1980s over the depletion of the ozone layer, climate change, and the loss of diversity of biological species helped to focus attention on environmental issues and raise their visibility on national and global policy agendas. Growing scientific evidence supported the observation that environmental degradation and poverty were dynamically linked. Projections for undesirable global changes suggested that developing countries would need to understand the wisdom of environmental protection in order to avoid undesirable future degradations in the global physical environment. The more cooperative atmosphere of North-South relations made such a change plausible.

From the mid-1980s onward, the concerns for ecodevelopment, especially after it became sustainable development, provided a focal point for the development dialogue. The crest of the second major surge of global environmental diplomacy was marked by a series of events, negotiations, and other activities during 1991–1992 in connection with the United Nations Conference on Environment and Development (UNCED) held in Rio de Janeiro in June 1992. These diverse activities have come collectively to be referred to as the "Rio process."

To Rio, 1992

The preparations for and activities surrounding what also was known as the "Earth Summit" far exceeded almost all normal conceptions of a conference, as did the extensive documentation.[46] The Rio process was massive. In addition to the inter-governmental conference, which incorporated a summit meeting of heads of state or government during its final days, the Rio gathering included a series of related events, unparalleled in scope and sponsored by civic-based entities that together were referred to as the Global Forum. These parallel activities drew tens of thousands of participants and an estimated 200,000 onlookers. A record number of national governmental delegations attended the Earth Summit, and some 1,400 NGOs with approximately 18,000 participants were at the parallel Global Forum.

Movement among the respective sites for activities, however, was severely restricted by logistics. The inter-governmental conference, UNCED, was held at the Rio-Centro at the edge of the sprawling and populous city; the non-governmental activities in

Brazilian president Collor de Mello acknowledges the applause of world leaders after he formally closes the UN Conference on Environment and Development in June 1992. (UN Photo 180108/T. Prendergast)

the Global Forum were held around Rio's Flamingo Park, some thirty miles away. Moreover, the Global Forum was more of a "happening" or cluster of events than a centralized and well-focused conference. Various activities were held at several dozen sites around the city. The scope of the two conferences was so overwhelming and the general scale of associated activities was so great that meaningful participation in both the inter-governmental and nongovernmental events was impossible, even for fleet-of-foot journalists.

UNCED produced two environmental conventions, a global action plan now known as "Agenda 21" and a general agreement over the text of two declarations. Yet the Rio process itself was perhaps the most significant product and began long before the summer of 1992. In response to the Brundtland Commission's report, the General Assembly adopted Resolution 44/228 in December 1989 to sponsor a conference for the purpose of developing strategies to "halt and reverse the effects of environmental degradation in the context of increased national and international efforts to promote sustainable and environmentally sound development in all countries."

Over the next eighteen months a concerted effort was launched to produce a package of agreements that could be finalized ceremoniously by heads of government at the Earth Summit. A set of negotiations conducted by the PrepCom focused on drafting a comprehensive development and environment agenda for action (Agenda 21), a declaration on environmental principles (the Rio Declaration on Environment and Development, or the Rio Declaration), and a statement on forest principles. The evolving agenda came to center on nine main environmental issues and nearly two dozen related development concerns. The environmental side of the deliberations focused on issues related to the atmosphere, biotechnology, the diversity of biological species (biodiversity), fresh water, hazardous wastes, human health, human habitats, oceans, and land resources. The development-related issues were equally, if not more, wide-ranging. The negotiation process was further complicated by the need to hammer out many institutional and financial issues in keeping with the broad concept of sustainable development.

The "road to Rio,"[47] then, was long and arduous. Participants were engaged in the preparatory process almost continuously for three years. Maurice Strong, who after twenty years was selected to serve again as secretary-general of the conference secretariat, had said in reference to UNCHE nearly twenty years earlier that in many important respects "the process was the policy."[48] The process of building consensus was regarded by many participants as being just as important an outcome of UNCED as any set of declarations, treaties, or other specific products. However, that process was not always an easy one, and the end products were not satisfactory to a majority of the participants. After three years of laborious and often tedious negotiations, for example, the specification of timetables, qualitative and quantitative targets, and acceptable limits still eluded negotiators as they rushed to finalize agreement on the conventions, statements of principles, and plan of action.

Basic North-South tensions that underpinned multilateral politics in general surfaced during the political process of negotiating consensus around the massive conference agenda. As at Stockholm, Southern governments were skeptical of the Northern push to impose ecological imperatives on the global development agenda. This reluctance should not imply that the dynamic relationships between poverty and other aspects of underdevelopment and environmental degradation were not perceived or taken seriously in the South. A great many environmental concerns, including depletion of freshwater and other resources, deforestation, and atmospheric pollution, were seen as serious threats to improving the overall quality of life. Yet other issues stressed in the North, such as ozone depletion, hazardous waste pollution, and global warming, were seen by many Southern participants as being historical products of industrialization and overconsumption in the North; thus, it was incumbent upon the North to pay the bill.

If Northern governments now wanted the active partnership of the South in redressing these problems, that participation should not come, the South argued, at the expense of its development. In exchange for Southern participation, Northern donor governments should make available additional financial and technical resources. There was ample incentive for such sacrifice, the South argued, because as deforestation, industrial pollution, desertification, and other environmentally degrading conditions continued to intensify within Southern societies, they loomed as ominous threats to overall global security.

These North-South tensions were brought into particularly sharp focus during the debate over forest principles. Southern negotiators, led by the Brazilians, Indians, and Malaysians—many of the same countries that reacted similarly when sovereignty was under siege in the security and human rights arenas—forcefully resisted any incursion into the principle of sovereignty over natural resources. Similarly, tensions prevailed in drafting the Rio Declaration, which was to guide governments and nongovernmental actors in implementing the many provisions of Agenda 21. With its unmistakable flavor of compromise between negotiators from industrialized countries and developing ones, this declaration integrated many of the most important elements of the development and environment perspectives of both sides. Even as the rights to exploit resources within a state's geographical boundaries were reaffirmed, the responsibility of states to exercise control over environmentally damaging activities within their boundaries also was proclaimed. In addition, among the twenty-seven principles embodied in the declaration was one stating that the cost of pollution should be borne at the source and should be reflected in product cost at all stages of production.

In addition to the PrepCom negotiations, two legally binding international conventions—on biodiversity and on climate change—were incorporated as part of the larger Rio process. The Convention on Biodiversity requires signatories to pursue economic development in such a way as to preserve existing species and ecosystems. The Convention on Climate Change embodies a general set of principles and obligations aimed at reducing greenhouse gases. Due largely to the intransigent position of the first Bush administration during the negotiation process, formal intergovernmental negotiations over the creation of these two legal conventions proved to be difficult to finalize. The final documents emerging from the Earth Summit represented "framework conventions." Although these conventions designated general principles and obligations, specific timetables and targets were left unspecified and subject to future negotiations over protocols—that is, additional treaties.

At center stage in the Rio process was Agenda 21. In its final form this document comprised over 600 pages and covered an enormous array of issues. Although the vast majority of this text was agreed to before UNCED, a number of contentious items were carried to the Earth Summit itself. In keeping with the general tenor of debates, problems included issues related to biodiversity, biotechnology, deforestation, and institutional and procedural issues involving financing, technology transfer, and institutional arrangements for carrying out the elements of the action agenda.

A number of these issues, including certain details about institutional arrangements to carry out the action program, proved to be intractable and remained unresolved at the close of UNCED. Foremost among them was how to generate the financial resources needed to implement the program of action and associated activities. Estimates varied; the calculations made by the UNCED secretariat put the price tag at well over $100 billion per year for the first decade alone. These huge figures reflected the massive scope of the components inherent in the marriage between development and environment as they had come together within the Rio process.

Linked to the issue of financing was governance. At the core is the question: Who decides when and how such resources are to be spent? As the negotiations during the Rio process clearly revealed, some minimal basic agreement about governance is a prerequisite for agreement over financing. Again, North-South tensions fueled the debate.

The issue of multilateral development financing was, of course, not specific to this particular social setting. In keeping with practice, the Northern negotiators, led by the

United States, pressed to have all such financing channeled through the World Bank group. In that setting, the locus of control would be well established, with the G-7's largest industrialized countries possessing effective veto power. The Global Environmental Facility (GEF) was in place and might be expanded to encompass a broader mandate.

This proposed solution, however, was not acceptable to most Southern participants, who preferred what they called a "more democratic" arrangement. These governments proposed the creation of a new "green fund," which would operate on more egalitarian voting principles. Most major Northern donors found this proposal wholly unacceptable. For them to commit significant levels of funding, some guarantee of control was required. A compromise was achieved to enhance the South's participation while retaining for donor states elements of control. Interim financing for Agenda 21 implementation would be provided under the aegis of the World Bank group. The Global Environmental Facility would be expanded and its rules altered to provide for decisionmaking by consensus among equally represented groupings of donors and recipients. Although the governance issue has, at least temporarily, been put to rest, the matter of securing the requisite financial resources remains problematic, with only a very small fraction of the resources actually committed to date.

Beyond Rio

In the years immediately following the Earth Summit, two overriding challenges arose to making the post-Rio process succeed. The first was how to generate and sustain effective cooperation. This problem had both horizontal and vertical dimensions. Effective cooperation would be required horizontally across different autonomous organizational domains, legal jurisdictions, and sectors of society as well as vertically across different levels of social aggregation, from individuals in their roles in groups and communities to representative governance in international forums.

The second challenge was how to reorient UN discourse and practice to overcome the constraints inherent in the organization's legal foundations in state sovereignty. The immediately preceding discussion of the UN's involvement in ecodevelopment rejoins our earlier treatment of its activities in international peace and security and human rights matters. They all highlight the limits of working with a system so circumscribed by the concept of sovereignty. The foundations of the UN Charter, especially Article 2 (7), and the institutional structures and practices of multilateral diplomacy, constrain attempts to incorporate non-state and market actors into a full partnership in global policy processes.

These challenges seem forbidding, but as the heads of government at Rio pointed out, the costs of not rising to the challenge could be perilous. As they warned in the preamble of Agenda 21, "Humanity stands at a defining moment in history. We are confronted with a perpetuation of disparities between and within nations, a worsening of poverty, hunger, ill health and illiteracy, and the continuing deterioration of the ecosystems on which we depend for our well-being." The Agenda 21 text argues that only by creating global partnerships and involving all sectors of world society can the world's peoples expect "the fulfillment of basic needs, improved living standards for all, better-protected and better-managed ecosystems and a safer, more prosperous future." Creating the necessary global partnerships on an unprecedented scale will, in turn, require meeting the twin challenges of cooperating effectively and moving beyond the confines of sovereignty. Before exploring the nature and scope of those challenges, however, we need a better understanding of the dynamic interplay of the forces and tensions that have given shape to the contemporary discourse and practice of sustainable development.

The debate over sustainable development places people-centered development at the core of the UN's development work. This was also the case in respect to issues such as population, human settlements, health, food, and women. This shifting focus was captured in the names of special organizational campaigns, programmatic slogans, and conference titles reflected in Table 9.1. This evolving emphasis on people-centered development was given enhanced visibility through the reports of a series of special high-level, independent global commissions comprising eminent persons, which had begun with the Pearson Commission in 1969 but shifted away from governments and economic development with the three most prominent recent ones on global governance (1995), intervention and state sovereignty (2001), and human security (2003).[49]

The important point here is that there was a growing awareness that dealing with global issues required a perspective and responses that were simultaneously holistic, historical, interdisciplinary, and structural. It was not helpful and actually harmful to view the world as being divided into discrete spheres of reality. Narrowly conceived functionalist thinking and logic slowly gave ground to more dynamic and synthetic approaches.

The role that sustainable development has played in traversing the turf and ideological divide that otherwise separates actors in the global arena provides a key for speculating about the future of the UN's development work. In the Rio process and beyond, sustainability has served as an important bridge in institutional bargaining. The associated political process has been characterized by bargaining among autonomous and self-interested participants striving for consensus. Operating under a veil of uncertainty about the likely effects of their alternative choices, participants engage in transnational alliance formation and politics that link issues. Many may be associated with specific communities of knowledge, but the political process is a pluralistic one in which groups of participants perceive and act on differing conceptions of problems, values, interests, and stakes.

Despite numerous difficulties, the general ideas articulated at Rio in behalf of sustainable development increasingly took hold. In the mid-1990s the UNDP/UNFPA Executive Board decision 94/14 adopted "sustainable human development" as a new mission for technical assistance. Like other development concepts before it, sustainable human development was viewed as a key requisite for creating and maintaining a secure and peaceful world order. The barrage of political discourse over development in the 1990s led most member states to expect the UN to play a meaningful role in bringing about such a goal.

The decade of the 1990s witnessed an almost continuous negotiating process. As is obvious from Table 9.1, member states were constantly involved in or preparing for

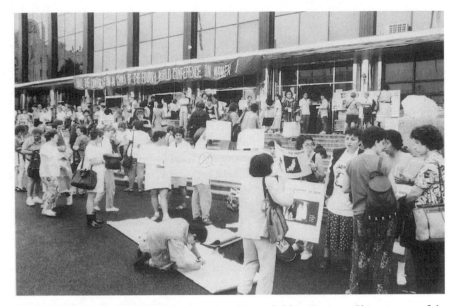

Scene at the Non-Governmental Organizations Forum held in Huairou, China, as part of the UN Fourth World Conference on Women held in Beijing, China, September 4–15, 1995. (UN/DPI Photo/M. Grant)

or actually attending a major international social-economic gathering. And this became especially the case when many of them began to have planned follow-up sessions at five-and ten-year intervals. But conferencing was not the only significant process. In the early years of his administration, former Secretary-General Boutros Boutros-Ghali and his top staff argued that the UN should concentrate on issues in which it had the comparative advantage. That is, the world body should focus on providing assistance in situations where conditions are critical or deteriorating. From this perspective, development assistance, which is much broader than critical-aid programs and which substitutes environmentally degrading practices for sustainable ones, should be left to the multilateral development banks and other funding institutions that are presumably far better endowed and equipped for such activities.

In May 1994, Boutros-Ghali presented the General Assembly with his *An Agenda for Development*,[50] a companion volume to his *An Agenda for Peace* that figured so prominently in our discussions in Chapters 3 and 4. Declaring development to be a fundamental human right, he presented a general framework within which he highlighted the interdependent nature of peace, economy, civil society, democracy, social justice, and environment as indispensable components of the development process. In the context of all of these activities, a general agreement was emerging, at least at the level of principle, that "development" means something much broader than simply economic growth. Development increasingly came to be viewed in human, as opposed to exclusively national economic, terms. Reality always lags rhetoric, but UN documents now clearly indicate that "development" signifies not only improved material welfare with adequate attention to sustainability but also improved human rights and social justice.

In a related fashion, the concept of "good governance" came into common use within UN developmental circles in the 1980s and 1990s although it is as old as human history. The emergence of the idea of good governance can be traced to international concern with state-dominated models of economic and social development so prevalent throughout the socialist bloc and much of the Third World in the 1950s, 1960s, and 1970s. International efforts, especially since the early 1980s, have emphasized support for political democratization (including elections, accountability, and human rights) and economic liberalization. In short, "good" governance consists of applying the liberal capitalist model that we encountered in Chapter 8 rather than the "bad" governance that had characterized the development models in vogue in the heyday of UNCTAD and the NIEO.

In its *Human Development Report 1993,* the UNDP provided a basic framework for focusing subsequent discourse. It suggested that the UN's development work needed to be based on at least five "new pillars": new concepts of human security, new models of sustainable human development, new partnerships between states and markets, new patterns of national and global governance, and new forms of international cooperation. Each subsequent *Human Development Report* has served to elaborate, extend, and clarify various aspects of the development-human security nexus.

Without denying the benefits of growth, the reports and the Copenhagen conference insist on cataloging the aggravation of poverty and the growing divides between rich and poor, within societies and among them; increasing unemployment; a disintegrating social fabric and exclusion; and environmental damage. In addition to an overall analysis, each of the successive reports has emphasized a specific theme: funding priorities (1991); global markets (1992); democracy (1993); environment (1994); gender (1995); growth (1996); poverty (1997); consumption patterns (1998); globalization (1999); human rights (2000); sustainable livelihoods (2001); democracy (2002); and millennium development goals (2003).

Participation and empowerment have been two of the priority themes running throughout annual *Human Development Reports.* A new people-centered development agenda places a premium on enhancing the participation of all relevant stakeholders, including especially women, youth, the poor, and other marginalized elements of society, as well as civil society and the private sector. The way to eradicate poverty, the UNDP reports have argued, is to empower the poor and marginalized elements of society to provide for the satisfaction of their own basic needs and values. The notion of popular sovereignty has come to eclipse older conceptions of state sovereignty (that is, sovereignty of the people not of the sovereign).

In attempting to correct the euphoria that had surrounded the so-called Washington consensus of the early 1990s, arguments within the UN often have sought to counterbalance or dilute the approaches in vogue since the Reagan and Thatcher administrations—namely, that anything the government can do, the private sector can do better; and that more open markets, free trade, and capital flows are necessarily beneficial to everyone, everywhere.

Refugees returning to Cambodia in 1992 under the oversight of the UN Transitional Authority in Cambodia were offered different forms of UNHCR assistance, including a house plot and house kit. This man assembles a home in Battambang Province. (UNHCR Photo/K. Gooi)

In a departure from its previous orthodoxy and as a sign of the pendulum's swing, the World Bank's *World Development Report 1997* emphasized that the state is capable of, and should perform the role of, producing welfare-enhancing outcomes.[51] The report's subtitle, *The State in a Changing World*, was indicative of a reversal led by Joseph Stiglitz, the controversial chief economist and senior vice-president of the Bank.[52] Essentially, in contrast to the wave of economic liberalization programs of the 1980s, the political liberalization programs of the 1990s gradually came to place a greater emphasis on substantive democracy, human rights, the role of law and individual access to justice, and basic freedoms. Stiglitz won the Nobel Prize for Economic Science after his resignation from the World Bank over substantive differences.

Reflections and Recent Developments

The UN's primary contribution to development over time has been to alter the emphasis in the good governance debate that originally had been cast as the mirror image of the state-dominated model of economic and social development of previous decades. Today's debate about good governance stresses improving the leadership and management of democracies, including the "deepening" of democracy and more active roles for nonstate actors.

Yet these new patterns of governance remained rather vague and unspecified. Decentralization of power is lauded as one of the best ways to bring about the empowerment of people, but decentralization at whatever level—local, state, national, and global—can result in empowering elites even more, rather than empowering people in the sense of popular participation. New participants may lack the time, motivation, and skills to participate, leaving entrenched elites with unchallenged power. This point is important because sustainable growth and development require the active participation of people at all levels of governance.

With regard to UN structure, the most difficult choice may be between the traditional focus on the specialized agencies and the growing need to raise environmental concerns in broader, cross-cutting arenas. In the post-UNCED era, the discourse of environmentalism is clearly moving in the direction of cross-cutting themes. The traditional ecosystemic focus on air, land, water, and species is giving way to a social-systems focus on international trade, global finance, sovereignty, development, and other key processes and institutions. The old focus was consistent with the functional organization of the United Nations into specialized agencies; the emerging focus demands a new forum.[53]

In this regard, the special initiatives with system-wide coordination and partnership building discussed above have tended to reinforce the evolving consensus over the UN system development strategy. At both the Ministerial Conference of the WTO held in Doha, Qatar, in September 2001 and the summit-level UN-sponsored Conference on Financing for Development in Monterrey, Mexico, in March 2002, for example, donor countries expressed an increased commitment to fight poverty. In addition to the new spirit of cooperation between UN and the Bretton Woods institutions noted earlier, the Monterrey gathering for the first time brought together stakeholders representing governments, business, civil society, and international institutions for a formal exchange of views. The "Monterrey Consensus," as that conference's outcome document was called, recognized the need to increase ODA significantly in order to meet the MDGs.

The World Summit on Sustainable Development followed from August 26 to September 4. Coming ten years after the 1992 Earth Summit in Rio, the "Johannesburg Summit 2002" represented an attempt to reinvigorate the sustainable development activities in the wake of deepening poverty and environmental degradation. New targets were set, timetables established, and commitments agreed. Yet, as the UN website for Johannesburg Summit 2002 made clear, "there were no silver bullet solutions . . . no magic and no miracle—only the realization that practical and sustained steps were needed to address many of the world's most pressing problems." The summit reflected a new approach to conferencing and to sustainable development more generally. It was a dialogue among major stakeholders from governments, civil society, and the private sector. Instead of concentrating primarily on the production of treaties and other outcome documents, participants focused on the creation of new partnerships to bring additional resources to bear for sustainable development initiatives.

Also, as discussed earlier, Secretary-General Annan and his core administrative staff in the UNDP and elsewhere have aggressively been building an array of partnerships with civil society and the private sector. Predictably, these activities—most especially

A visiting foreign official inspects a solar cooker at a research facility in Gansu Province. The Natural Energy Research Institute focuses on new forms of energy-producing products. (UN Photo 150767/D. Lovejoy)

through the "Global Compact" with business—have bought with them another dimension of the challenge to sovereignty debate.[54] The notion of the Global Compact is predicated on the assumption that development, especially for the lesser developed countries (LDCs), cannot occur through governmental or inter-governmental means alone, even with the kind assistance of the multitude of nongovernmental development assistance organizations. Neither can it occur through unbridled market forces alone. Creating local, national, and international enabling environments is essential, and a broad-based partnership involving all relevant "stakeholders" is required.

Of course, this may be deemed inappropriate or unacceptable from some—often of quite diverse and even opposing ideological perspectives—that see various particular types of stakeholders as being unacceptable or illegitimate partners.[55] Nonetheless, the Global Compact has been steadily expanding. As of mid–2003, more than 700 corporate partners had joined the agreement. One of the principles that underpins the Global Compact is that UN organizations should "undertake a deeper examination of issues related to corporate governance" in the context of developing countries' specific legal, social, and cultural environments in order "to develop and implement international accounting, reporting and auditing standards." While encouraging information sharing about potential investment opportunities, the UN development framework cautions that "international institutions involved in supporting FDI flows should evaluate the development impact of investment flows in recipient countries, including social development concerns."[56]

The Global Compact represents only one dimension of the UN system's evolving partnership with the private sector. As noted previously, under Administrator Malloch Brown, the UNDP has reprioritized its functions around four themes: advocacy, advice, pilot projects, and partnerships. The partnership function is wide-ranging. It begins with the UN and the Bretton Woods institutions and expands. It entails building and expanding constructive partnerships with civil society, the private sector, and local authorities. Underpinning this strategy is the belief that "people should guide both the state and the market, which need to work together in tandem, with people sufficiently empowered to exert a more effective influence over both."[57] Critical to this endeavor is creating in these varied constituencies an identity of being "stakeholders."

Within the developing world this initiative to forge new partnerships has taken a variety of complexions. In general there has been a move to strengthen the UNDP and other UN agencies' direct involvement with diverse elements of society, including NGOs, the private sector, and civil society organizations. Similar efforts have also been made in the Bretton Woods institutions. While active engagement with NGOs has been widely recognized for some time, cooperation with private sector entities at the country level has been less widely publicized. However, these measures are not without controversy. Yet, in a world with scarce and dwindling financial resources and limited access to technology, the prospects of gaining greater access is difficult to resist, despite many potential stumbling blocks and drawbacks.

The UN's Sustainable Human Development Model

Sustainable human development is part of an overall human security framework that has been in the making since at least the early 1990s if not the 1970s. In this regard, the UNDP's *Human Development Report 1993* provides a useful point of departure. The report proposed "five new pillars of a people-centered world order: new concepts of human security, new models of sustainable human development, new partnerships between state and markets, new patterns of national and global governance, and new forms of international cooperation."[58]

Making human beings secure, the approach argues, means more than protecting them from armed violence and alleviating their suffering. If international organizations are to contribute meaningfully to the promotion of *human* security, security needs to be defined in much broader terms than protection from threats to physical well-being from military violence. It is worth noting, as we did in the first two parts of this volume, that protecting civilians in war zones or from thuggish repression is itself far from guaranteed. Doing both simultaneously, as the human security concept proposes, is logical but hardly easy. The *1993 Human Development Report* was a precursor to the 2003 one from the Commission on Human Security in that this concept "must stress the security of people, not only of nations. . . . The concept of security must change—from an exclusive stress on national security to a much greater stress on people's security, from security through armaments to security through human development, from territorial security to food, employment, and environ-

A water pump powered by solar energy at Thies, Senegal.
(UN Photo 150182/S. Sprague)

mental security."[59] Thus sustainable human development can be viewed as a process of improving and sustaining human security.

Sustainable development, like human security, is a qualitative condition that entails individual and collective perceptions of low threats to physical and psychological well-being from all agents and forces that could degrade lives, values, and property. At a minimum, people may be considered secure if they are protected from the threat of the physical destruction of their lives or property as a result of assault from others. At the opposite extreme, maximum human security can be imagined in a totally threat-free environment where human beings are protected against all threats to their lives, values, and property. Various qualities of human security can be imagined depending on the relative ordering of the priorities that people place on the satisfaction of various needs, values, and interests.

Human security bridges the traditional divisions of international organizational agendas, where questions of "war and peace" have been strictly separated from "economic and social" ones. According to this new conceptualization, peace as the lack of direct violence is only one attribute of a secure environment, and international organizational action is the means of establishing this peace. Further, the notion of human security focuses the attention of international organizations directly on individuals and their circumstances, thereby constituting a subtle challenge to state sovereignty. Making people psychologically secure may, under some circumstances, be the antithesis of making the governments of states and their territorial boundaries physically secure, especially when states themselves are the perpetrators of individual insecurities. Pressing international organizations into the service of individually focused human security could therefore constitute an incremental step toward circumventing or marginalizing states and legitimizing supranational governance.

Most important, conceptualizing the mission of multilateral organizations as one of comprehensively promoting human security rather than separately promoting economic and social development, sustainable development, military security, human rights, and a variety of other goals frees the policy imagination to contemplate holistically the nature and variety of threats to individual environments. Although critics also point out that such a blanket concept can lead to fuzzy thinking and unrealistic policy prescriptions,[60] human security can free the policy imagination to consider how such threats may be removed and to wonder how international organizations might contribute to removing them. Because the sources of human insecurity vary from region to region, so, too, will the definition of human security and the missions of international organizations. It may be that in many, if not most, cases multilateral agencies are not very appropriate, efficient, or effective mechanisms for transferring material development assistance. They appear to be relatively better suited to promoting and enhancing human security via policies, programs, and activities that focus on nonmaterial resource transfers and exchanges, including training and the exchange of ideas and information. But such a shift of institutional focus requires rethinking the nature and meaning of sustainable human development.

Creating the foundation for sustainable human development entails empowering individuals, groups, and communities to become engaged constructively and effectively in satisfying their own needs, values, and interests, thereby providing them with a genuine sense of control over their own futures. Simply stated:

Human development is development *of* the people *for* the people *by* the people. Development *of* the people means investing in human capabilities, whether in education or health or skills, so that they can work productively and creatively. Development *for* the people means ensuring that the economic growth they generate is distributed widely and fairly. . . . [D]evelopment *by* the people [means] giving everyone a chance to participate.[61]

As the 1993 UNDP report argued, "People's participation is becoming the central issue of our time," and it is inextricably linked with and is an inherent component, if not a requisite, of both sustainable human development and larger notions of sustainable human security. Yet the concept of participation has proven to be woolly and the debate about its meaning, unfocused. In the World Bank, for example, popular participation has at various times and in various contexts been articulated as and associated with the "empowerment" of NGOs and the enhancement of their involvement in making bank policy; increased bank accountability and control of the bank's programs, projects, and activities by "domestic" actors; and the active engagement in project planning of previously excluded individuals and groups with an emphasis on the importance of local knowledge and the satisfaction of local needs. These aspects of participation are important, but this discourse has so far done little to change the course of the Bank's policy so as to enhance its role in promoting human security or to construct new models of development focusing on the satisfaction of basic human needs and values. Debate has not even succeeded in integrating in any creative and constructive way various elements of society into the Bank's work. Development models and institutional policies that fail to take adequate account of human needs may actually work to erode human security and inhibit sustainable human development.

The last three elements—new partnerships between state and markets, new patterns of national and global governance, and new forms of international cooperation—build on this basic conceptual foundation. They are treated in the next chapter in the context of new threats in the form of globalization. It is important to stress here in closing this chapter that the UN's development agenda is an ever-evolving process. There is a definite new unity of purpose as most world leaders acknowledge that "security" in the twenty-first century means "human security," and that the UN's development agenda is a necessary component. However, will there be sufficient international political will to move fast enough to balance the various forces and tensions inherent in the processes of globalization, HIV/AIDS, extreme poverty, terrorism, and other social maladies? It is to these forces and tensions and the global response to them that we now turn.

Notes

1. Boutros Boutros-Ghali, "A New Departure on Development," *Foreign Policy* no. 98 (Spring 1995), p. 47.

2. See especially John Mueller, *Quiet Cataclysm: Reflections on the Recent Transformation of World Politics* (New York: Harper Collins, 1995).

3. Kofi A. Annan, *Renewing the United Nations: A Programme for Reform* (New York: UN, 1997).

4. Jesse Helms, "Saving the U.N.: A Challenge to the Next Secretary General," *Foreign Affairs* 75, 5 (Fall 1996), pp. 2–7, at 5.

5. Gerald B. Helman and Steven R. Ratner, "Saving Failed States," *Foreign Policy*, no. 89 (Winter 1992–1993), pp. 3–20, at p. 6.

6. UNDP, *UNDP Today: Introducing the Organization,* 1999.

7. UNDP, *Annual Report of the Administrator,* June 19, 2003.

8. UNDP, *Human Development Report 1993.*

9. www.uncdf.org/sum/index.html.

10. Mark Malloch Brown, Opening Statement at the UNDP/UNFPA Executive Board, New York, June 10, 2003, p. 1.

11. Ibid., p. 11.

12. UNCTAD-UNDP-HABITAT Press Release, May 16, 2001.

13. See Yves Beigbeder, *New Challenges for UNICEF: Children, Women, and Human Rights,* (New York: Palgrave for Macmillan, 2001).

14. See further Mayra Buvnic, "Women in Poverty: A New Global Underclass," *Foreign Policy* no. 108 (Fall 1997), pp. 38–54.

15. www.unicef.org/programme/girlseducation/25_2005/index.htm.

16. UNICEF Press Release, May 8, 2003.

17. UNICEF, *The United Nations Special Session on Children: A First Anniversary Report on Follow-up,* May 8, 2003.

18. UN News Centre, "Countries slow to act on 2002 summit goals to better children's lives—UNICEF," May 27, 2003.

19. For an overview, see Helmut Anheier, Marlies Glasius, and Mark Kaldor, *Global Civil Society 2001* (Oxford: Oxford University Press, 2001).

20. See further Richard Benedick, *Ozone Diplomacy: New Directions in Safeguarding the Planet* (Cambridge, Mass.: Harvard University Press, 1998 enlarged edition). Benedick shows that UNEP, especially through the activity of its executive director, Mostafa Tolba, was an important player in diplomatic proceedings.

21. See, for example, Norman J. Vig and Regina S. Axelrod, eds., *The Global Environment: Institutions, Law, and Policy* (Washington: CQ Press, 1999).

22. Robert O. Keohane, "International Institutions: Can Interdependence Work?" *Foreign Policy,* Special Edition (Spring 1998), pp. 82–96.

23. Kofi Annan, "The Quiet Revolution," *Global Governance* 4, 2 (April–June 1998), pp. 123–138.

24. Ingvar Carlsson, "The U.N. at 50: A Time to Reform," *Foreign Policy no. 109* (Fall 1995), 16.

25. See, for example, Jonathan Pincus, et al., *Reinventing the World Bank* (Ithaca, N.Y.: Cornell University Press, 2002); and John P. Lewis et al., *The World Bank: Its First Half Century* (Washington, D.C.: Brookings Institution, 1997). As for the IMF, see Devesh Kapur, "The IMF: A Cure or a Curse?," *Foreign Policy* No. 111 (Summer 1998), pp. 114–131. In general see Graham Bird and Joseph P. Joyce, "Remodeling the Multilateral Financial Institutions," *Global Governance* 7, 1 (January–March 2001), pp. 75–94.

26. Press Release ECOSOC/5818, April 29, 1999.

27. Organization for Economic Cooperation and Development, *1998 Development Cooperation Report, Efforts and Policies of the Members* (Paris: OECD, 1998)

28. UN, *Development Update,* no. 27, March 1999.

29. United Nations Chronicle (on line edition), Issue 1, 2003.

30. IMF Press Release No. 03/68.

31. Jessica Einhorn, "The World Bank's Mission Creep," *Foreign Affairs* 80, 5 (Fall 2001), pp. 22–35.

32. A/AC.257/12, December 18, 2000.

33. A/RES/55/2, September 18, 2000.

34. For a discussion, see Louis Emmerij, Richard Jolly, and Thomas G. Weiss, *Ahead of the Curve? UN Ideas and Global Challenges* (Bloomington: Indiana University Press, 2001), pp. 80–119; and Jacques Fomerand, "UN Conferences: Media Events or Genuine Diplomacy," *Global Governance* 2, no. 3 (September–December 1996), pp. 361–375.

35. A/RES/55/2, September 18, 2000.

36. See Richard Jolly, Louis Emmerij, Dharam Ghai, and Frédéric Lapeyre, *UN Contributions to Development Theory and Practice* (Bloomington: Indiana University Press, 2004).

37. UNEP, "Development and Environment: The Founex Report: In Defense of the Earth," *The Basic Texts on Environment*, UNEP Executive Series 1, Nairobi, 1981.

38. Quoted by Maurice Strong, "Policy Lessons Learned in a Thirty Years' Perspective," Ministry of the Environment, Stockholm Thirty Years On (Stockholm: Ministry of the Environment, 2002), p. 18. The essays in this volume provide an interesting historical overview.

39. Branislav Gosovic, *The Quest for World Environmental Cooperation: The Case of the UN Global Environment Monitoring System* (London: Routledge, 1992).

40. Peter M. Haas, "From Theory to Practice: Ecological Ideas and Development Policy," Working Paper Series, no. 92–2, Center for International Affairs (Cambridge, Mass.: Harvard University Press, 1992), pp. 31–34.

41. Union of International Associations, *Yearbook of International Organizations 1992/1993* (Brussels: Union of International Associations, 1993), pp. 280–281.

42. Haas, "From Theory to Practice," p. 34.

43. World Commission on Environment and Development, *Our Common Future* (New York: Oxford University Press, 1987).

44. UNEP Governing Council Decision 15, Annex II, May 1989.

45. Robert Wade, "Greening the Bank: The Struggle over the Environment, 1970–1995," in Lewis et al., *The World Bank,* vol. 2, pp. 611–734; Richard Haeuber, "The World Bank and Environmental Assessment: The Role of Nongovernmental Organizations," *Environmental Impact Assessment Review* 1 (1992), pp. 1–17; World Bank, *Funding Ecological and Social Destruction: The World Bank and the International Monetary Fund* (Washington, D.C.: Bank Information Center, 1990); and Sierra Club, *Bankrolling Disasters: International Development Banks and the Global Environment* (San Francisco: Sierra Club, 1986).

46. For a review of the documentation see Shanna Halpren, *The United Nations Conference on Environment and Development: Process and Documentation* (Providence, R.I.: Academic Council on the United Nations System, 1992).

47. For a discussion, see Michael McCoy and Patrick McCully, *The Road from Rio: An NGO Guide to Environment and Development* (Amsterdam: International Books, 1993).

48. For this and other stories, see Maurice Strong, *Where on Earth Are We Going* (New York: Norton, 2001).

49. Commission on International Development, *Partners in Development* (New York: Praeger, 1969); Commission on Global Governance, *Our Global Neighbourhood* (Oxford: Oxford University Press, 1995); International Commission on Intervention and State Sovereignty, *The Responsibility to Protect* (Ottawa: ICISS, 2001); and Commission on Human Security, *Human Security Now* (New York: Commission on Human Security, 2003).

50. Boutros Boutros-Ghali, *An Agenda for Development* (New York: UN, 1995).

51. World Bank, *World Development Report 1997: The State in a Changing World* (New York: Oxford University Press, 1997).

52. See, for example, Joseph Stiglitz, "Redefining the Role of the State: What Should It Do? How Should It Do It? And How Should These Decisions Be Made?" http://www.worldbank.org.

53. Craig Murphy, "Global Institutions and the Pursuit of Human Needs," in Roger A. Coate and Jerel A. Rosati, eds., *The Power of Human Needs in World Society* (Boulder: Lynne Rienner, 1988), p. 217.

54. For a short treatment of the topic, see John Gerard Ruggie, "global_governance.net: The Global Compact as Learning Network," *Global Governance* 7, no. 4 (October–December 2001), pp. 371–378.

55. Ellen Paine, "The Road to the Global Compact: Corporate Power and the Battle Over Global Public Policy at the United Nations," http://www.globqalpolicy.org/reform/papers/2000/road.htm.

56. UN document A/AC.257/12.

57. UNDP, *Human Development Report 1993.*

58. Ken Conca, "Greening the UN: Environmental Organizations and the UN System," in Thomas G. Weiss and Leon Gordenker, eds., *NGOs, the UN, and Global Governance* (Boulder: Lynne Rienner, 1996), pp. 114–115.

59. UNDP, *Human Development Report 1993* (New York: Oxford University Press, 1993), p. 2.

60. See S. Neil MacFarlane and Yuen Foong-Khong, *A Critical History of Human Security* (Bloomington: Indiana University Press, 2004); and Roland Paris, "Peacebuilding and the Limits of International Liberalism," *International Security* 22 (Fall 1997), pp. 54–89.

61. UNDP, *Human Development Report 1993.*

10 The UN, Development, and Globalization

The United Nations Millennium Declaration, adopted by the General Assembly at the close of the Millennium Summit in 2002, identified challenges related to globalization as the key issue confronting the international community of states.[1] In particular, states in the assembly endorsed this language:

> We believe that the central challenge we face today is to ensure that globalization becomes a positive force for all the world's people. For while globalization offers great opportunities, at present its benefits are very unevenly shared, while its costs are unevenly distributed. We recognize that developing countries and countries with economies in transition face special difficulties in responding to this central challenge.[2]

In short, while globalization yields many benefits, especially to those of us located in wealthier countries, it has brought with it a scale of inequality unprecedented in human history.

Secretary-General Kofi Annan had already reflected on this problem in his own report, *"We the Peoples": The Role of the United Nations in the 21st Century*, which he presented to the assembly in 2000. He wrote: "The benefits of globalization are plain to see: faster economic growth, higher living standards, accelerated innovation and diffusion of technology and management skills, new economic opportunities for individuals and countries alike." Yet these benefits are distributed very unequally and inequitably. They are "highly concentrated among a relatively small number of countries and are spread unevenly within them."[3]

The impact of globalization varies dramatically from region to region and case to case. As underscored in an earlier report by the Secretary-General, the "actual experience of globalization, to a great degree, varied with the level of development at which a country experienced it."[4] In some cases, where national economies were well positioned in terms of capacity and economic orientation, rapid economic growth has ensued. Elsewhere the result has been much less positive, contributing to increased poverty, inequality, marginalization, and human insecurity. It is therefore quite possible that in some places globalization may undermine many of the development efforts by UN agencies noted in the previous two chapters.

But what is this "thing" called globalization? What is the relationship between globalization processes and global governance? How should we assess the UN system's responses to it? These and other questions are explored in this chapter in the context of the recently developed consensual framework—the Millennium Development Goal framework—to promote sustainable human development and security.

Globalization and Global Governance

"Globalization" has become the topic of the day. Scores of books dealing with the topic are continually being written, especially in combination with the notion of "global governance."[5] Conferences galore are held. Supporters extol its virtues. Anti-globalizationists—certain transnational social movement actors—traverse the planet in protest against it. On one hand, the concept is often viewed as a useful tool for understanding contemporary world affairs. On the other hand, the murkiness of the concept—no widely accepted definition has yet been coined—leads many other scholars to argue that the usefulness of the concept is highly suspect.

At its core, and apart from other implications discussed below, globalization refers to the movement of things and ideas across borders. In this sense it is a synonym for internationalization, interconnectedness, interdependence. At the close of the 1990s, for example, global transactions in foreign exchange markets had reached a level nearly eighty times larger than world trade. The growth in foreign direct investment and portfolio capital flows in developing countries rose during the 1990s and have been far outpacing international trade. In 2000, world-wide foreign direct investment flows exceeded $1.1 trillion dollars—representing a doubling in just four years.[6] Long- and short-term capital movements, however, have been very unevenly distributed—more than four fifths being concentrated in developed countries and much of the remainder highly-concentrated in a relatively small number of developing countries. In 1998, ten countries accounted for 70 percent of all foreign direct investment flows to the developing world.[7] While total foreign direct investment to developing countries in 2000 remained at the same level as in 1999, the developing world's share in the global total declined from 19.3 to 17 percent.[8]

The expansion of global markets and production and other aspects of the world-wide diffusion of capitalism, however, is only one dimension of the social transformations involved in globalization. Ngaire Woods, for example, suggests that there exist three core elements of globalization: the expansion of markets, challenges to the state and institutions, and the rise of new social and political movements.[9] While the economic core entails the proliferation of production, trade, and financial activity spurred by technological change and governmental deregulation, the second core element focuses on the emergence of a new form of global politics enabled and necessitated by the first. Also, Woods argues that society and culture themselves are being transformed, which bring reactions, resistance, and even rebellions.

Jan Aart Scholte, a keen British observer of global social transformation, identifies production, governance, and culture as main areas underlying the globalization debates. To these, he adds a fourth: modernity and post-modernity. He goes further to suggest that there are at least five broad definitions of the globalization concept.[10] First, globalization is often treated as being synonymous with internationalization—the spread of cross-border relations and activities—and growing interdependence. Second, the concept is frequently used to imply the opening up or liberalization of inter-societal relations. In this context, the removal of governmental restrictions on trade and other social exchanges is seen to be yielding a more borderless world. Writers from this orientation often talk of the decline of the state and the rise to predominance of civil society and the private corporate world. As portrayed in Table 10.1, they point to the differential in shear size and hence the inferred influence and power of most national governments that are dwarfed by private firms. Clearly, the size of markets and financial enterprises mean that some states are more equal than others.

The impacts of globalization processes, it is argued by proponents of this third view, are profoundly changing the face of world politics and the nature of human social interaction and existence. The nature, structure, geographical pattern, and magnitude of world trade and investment, for example, are in transformation, and these changes impact especially hard on poor developing countries in terms of growth, poverty, and income inequality. Economic liberalization has fostered the diffusion of multinational production networks, capital mobility, and new technologies, which has tended in many cases to place downward pressures on wages and working conditions and otherwise make labor in developing societies increasingly susceptible to global forces. The development of financial markets and institutions, along with the tremendous growth in foreign direct investment, short-term portfolio investment, and other transnational capital flows in developing regions, have dramatically transformed the political economic climate there.[11]

Yet another take on globalization concentrates on the universalization or worldwide syntheses of values and cultures. The fourth derivation is less neutral. It equates globalization with the Westernization or even Americanization of the world's cultures. "Following this idea globalization is a dynamic whereby the social structures of modernity (capitalism, rationalism, industrialism, bureaucratism, etc,) are spread the world over, normally destroying preexisting cultures and local self-determination in the process."[12] Scholte refers to these conceptualizations as "redundant" concepts.

He prefers a fifth conceptualization, the idea that globalization focuses on the reconfiguration of social space beyond traditional conceptions of territorial boundaries. Like David Held and collaborators,[13] Scholte structures his interpretations and understandings of processes of globalization on the basis of this fifth conceptualization.[14] We too concentrate here on those processes that reconfigure and transform the organization of social relations and transactions in social space and in the minds of social actors.

When social scientists talk and write about this reconfiguration—not just shrinking or contraction—of social space and time, they tend to find current concepts and conventional language insufficient to portray their intended meanings. So they have turned to a vocabulary than the average student finds stultifying. Words like "globality," "teterritorialization," "supraterritorial relations,"[15] "unbundled territoriality,"[16] and "hyperglobalism"[17] are offered as central organizing concepts. Turgid language or not, the intent is to portray a set or sets of social processes that are transforming both the world and how human beings think about it and behave within it. As stressed by Manuel Castells, Ankie Hoogvelt, and others, at the core of this transformation is the ascendancy of "real time virtual reality" over physical time and space.[18] They argue that the distinguishing characteristic of contemporary globalization is not to be found

TABLE 10.1   Economic Comparison of National Governmental Expenditures and Selected Corporate Earnings

Company /Country	Revenues ($ millions)/ Budget Expenditures		Company /Country	Revenues ($ millions)/ Budget Expenditures
1	United States	1,703,000	41 Altria Group	72,944.0
2	Germany	825,000	42 Marubeni	71,756.6
3	Japan	718,000	43 Turkey	69,100
4	United Kingdom	540,000	44 Verizon	67,190.0
5	Italy	517,000	Communications	
6	France	240,000	45 Deutsche Bank	66,839.9
7	Wal-Mart Stores	219,812.0	46 E. ON	66,453.0
8	China	191,800	47 U.S. Postal Service	65,834.0
9	Exxon Mobil	191,581.0	48 AXA	65,579.9
10	General Motors	177,260.0	49 Credit Suisse	64,204.5
11	BP	174,218.0	50 Hitachi	63,931.2
12	Ford Motor	162,412.0	51 Nippon Life Insurance	63,827.2
13	Canada	161,400	52 American Intl. Group	62,402.0
14	Mexico	140,000	53 Carrefour	62,224.6
15	Enron	138,718.0	54 American Electric	61,257.0
16	Daimler Chrysler	136,897.3	Power	
17	Royal Dutch/	135,211.0	55 Sony	60,608.0
	Shell Group		56 Royal Ahold	59,633.9
18	Netherlands	134,000	57 Duke Energy	59,503.0
19	General Electric	125,913.0	58 AT&T	59,142.0
20	Toyota Motor	120,814.4	59 Honda Motor	58,882.0
21	Citigroup	112,022.0	60 Boeing	58,198.0
22	Sweden	110,000	61 Norway	57,600
23	Spain	109,000	62 El Paso	57,475.0
24	Belgium	106,000	63 BNP Paribas	55,044.4
25	Mitsubishi	105,813.9	64 Matsushita Electric	54,997.1
26	Mitsui	101,205.6	Industrial	
27	ChevronTexaco	99,699.0	65 Austria	54,000
28	Korea, South	95,700	66 Saudi Arabia	54,000
29	Total Fina Elf	94,311.9	67 Home Depot	53,553.0
30	Nippon Telegraph &	93,424.8	68 Bank of America Corp.	52,641.0
	Telephone		69 Aviva	52,317.6
31	Brazil	91,600	70 Poland	52,300
32	Itochu	91,176.6	71 Fiat	51,944.2
33	Allianz	85,929.2	72 Assicurazioni Generali	51,394.3
34	Intl. Business	85,866.0	73 Vivendi Universal	51,365.7
	Machines		74 Denmark	51,300
35	Australia	84,100	75 Fannie Mae	50,803.0
36	ING Group	82,999.1	76 Rwe	50,663.8
37	Volkswagen	79,287.3	77 J.P. Morgan Chase	50,429.0
38	India	78,200	78 Nestlé	50,192.4
39	Siemens	77,358.9	79 Kroger	50,098.0
40	Sumitomo	77,140.1	80 McKesson	50,006.0

	Company /Country	Revenues ($ millions)/ Budget Expenditures		Company /Country	Revenues ($ millions)/ Budget Expenditures
81	Nissan Motor	49,555.2	92	PDVSA	46,250.0
82	UBS	48,503.4	93	CenterPoint Energy	46,225.8
83	State Power	48,374.5	94	Unilever	46,130.6
84	Argentina	48,000	95	SBC Communications	45,908.0
85	Portugal	48,000	96	Hewlett-Packard	45,226.0
86	Cardinal Health	47,947.6	97	ENI	44,636.9
87	Merck	47,715.7	98	Metro	44,346.8
88	Greece	47,600	99	Morgan Stanley	43,727
89	State Farm Insurance	46,705.2	100	Nisho Iwai	43,703
90	HSBC Holding PLC	46,424.0			
91	Peugeot	46,264.1			

in the widening—that is the global geographic spread—of human social relations of production, consumption, and so on, but in the deepening and intensification of "capitalist integration" and global consciousness.[19] Some talk of global villages, others about the emergence of global civil society, and still others about a global informational network society.[20]

Very little of this theorizing provides much guidance for restructuring global governance and the work of international institutions to fulfill their mandates in promoting human security and sustainable human development in the face of all these oftentimes seemingly overwhelming changes. Perhaps more than any other analyst, James Mittelman provides concrete insight in this regard. In his discussion of "captors" and "captives" of globalization, he discusses the dialectic of inclusion and exclusion that results from the complex forces and tensions at play.[21] Further, he suggests that to create adequate governance responses, three very "vexing" aspects must be dealt with: control, autonomy, and agency. In other words, we need not only to understand globalization processes themselves, but also how different communities respond to them and benefit or suffer deprivations from them. Globalization is a contested process. In this contested process there is no predetermined outcome. At the same time, however, control and power structures are very uneven, and that fact greatly influences outcomes. Participants' needs, values, and interests all play critical roles.

As Kofi Annan indicated in the report cited at the start of this chapter, the central challenge facing the UN is to find ways to use the tremendous opportunities inherent in globalization to help people everywhere better cope with globalization's nondesirable effects and side effects. The opportunities he listed are especially those related to increased access to new-age information and communications technology, greater public exposure to and awareness of their interdependence and vulnerabilities, and "real-time" social exchanges. Could it be that this is what the UN's MDG process is all about? If so, what should we make of it and how should we evaluate it? Before addressing these and other questions, a better understanding of the process for implementing the MDGs is needed. Although we mentioned these briefly in both Chapters 8 and 9, they merit brief review here.

The Millennium Goal Strategy

As discussed in Chapter 9, international gatherings beginning in the 1990s have resulted in a largely consensual strategy for assessing progress toward dealing with the negative impacts of globalization and eradicating poverty. This strategy is organized around eight main development goals and eighteen related targets. Each target has a specific time frame and targeted amount and one or more indicators to be monitored to assess movement toward achieving the target. These Millennium Development Goals, spelled out in Table 10.2, have been commonly accepted throughout the UN system as a framework for guiding development policies and assessing progress. They are viewed as being mutually reinforcing with the overarching objective being poverty reduction as the world organization's highest priority. Seven of the eight main goals focus on substantive objectives. The eighth MDG deals with creating the capacity to achieve the other seven.

Cumulatively, these goals can be seen as both mutually reinforcing and intertwined. Eradicating extreme poverty, for example, would most likely drastically reduce infant mortality, improve maternal health, and better ensure environmental sustainability. Similarly, achieving universal primary education, promoting gender equality, empowering women, and combating HIV/AIDS, malaria, and other diseases would undoubtedly move forward progress toward eradicating poverty. Moreover, as suggested on the UNAIDS website, "There is a close link between the HIV/AIDS epidemic and the Millennium Development Goals . . . , in that the achievement of the MDGs by the target date of 2015 will depend on progress in turning around the HIV/AIDS epidemic and, conversely, success in the response to the epidemic will not be possible without achievement of the MDGs."[22]

A UN system-wide strategy has been designed for mobilizing support and monitoring progress toward achieving the MDGs. As the first chair of the United Nations Development Group (UNDG) and head of the UN Development Programme (UNDP), Malloch Brown served as coordinator of the UN's overall effort. The strategy has four main components: Millennium Project, Millennium Campaign, Millennium Reports, and country-level monitoring and operational country-level activities. The Millennium Project seeks to mobilize scholars from around the world and focus their collective wisdom and research efforts on achieving the MDGs. The purpose of this three-year initiative is to help member states and agencies develop implementation strategies for accomplishing the MDGs. "The Millennium Project's research focuses on identifying the operational priorities, organizational means of implementation, and financing structures necessary to achieve the MDGs."[23] The project is directed by Columbia University professor Jeffrey Sachs, who serves as special adviser to the Secretary-General. Ten expert task forces have been set up to carry out the needed research and report their findings to the Secretary-General and the UNDP Administrator. Each task force focuses on a specific set of MGD targets. Drawing on

Table 10.2   Millennium Development Goals and Targets

Goal 1:   ***Eradicate extreme poverty and hunger***

Target 1   Halve, between 1990 and 2015, the proportion of people whose income is less than one dollar a day

Target 2   Halve, between 1990 and 2015, the proportion of people who suffer from hunger

Goal 2:   ***Achieve universal primary education***

Target 3   Ensure that, by 2015, children everywhere, boys and girls alike, will be able to complete a full course of primary schooling

Goal 3:   ***Promote gender equality and empower women***

Target 4   Eliminate gender disparity in primary and secondary education, preferably by 2005, and to all levels of education no later than 2015

Goal 4:   ***Reduce child mortality***

Target 5   Reduce by two-thirds, between 1990 and 2015, the under-five mortality rate

Goal 5:   ***Improve maternal health***

Target 6   Reduce by three-quarters, between 1990 and 2015, the maternal mortality ratio

Goal 6:   ***Combat HIV/AIDS, malaria and other diseases***

Target 7   Have halted by 2015 and begun to reverse the spread of HIV/AIDS

Target 8   Have halted by 2015 and begun to reverse the incidence of malaria and other major diseases

Goal 7:   ***Ensure environmental sustainability***

Target 9   Integrate the principles of sustainable development into country policies and programs and reverse the loss of environmental resources

Target 10   Halve, by 2015, the proportion of people without sustainable access to safe drinking water

Target 11   By 2020, to have achieved a significant improvement in the lives of at least 100 million slum dwellers

Goal 8:   ***Develop a global partnership for development***

Target 12   Develop further an open, rule-based, predictable, non-discriminatory trading and financial system [Includes a commitment to good governance, development, and poverty reduction—both nationally and internationally]

Target 13   Address the Special Needs of the Least Developed Countries [Includes: tariff and quota free access for LDC exports; enhanced program of debt relief for HIPC and cancellation of official bilateral debt; and more generous ODA for countries committed to poverty reduction]

Target 14   Address the Special Needs of landlocked countries and small island developing States (through the Program of Action for the Sustainable Development of Small Island Developing States and the outcome of the 22nd special session of the General Assembly)

Target 15   Deal comprehensively with the debt problems of developing countries through
             national and international measures in order to make debt sustainable in the
             long term
Target 16   In co-operation with developing countries, develop, and implement strategies for
             decent and productive work for youth
Target 17   In co-operation with pharmaceutical companies, provide access to affordable,
             essential drugs in developing countries
Target 18   In co-operation with the private sector, make available the benefits of new
             technologies, especially information and communications

SOURCE: http://www.milleniumproject.org/html/dev_goals.shtm.

the work of these task forces, the 2003 UNDP *Human Development Report* focuses on
the MDGs and their attainment.[24] Also, the campaign seeks to promote and reinforce
cooperation among UN agencies, Bretton Woods institutions, and the WTO. An
interim report is scheduled for mid-2004, and the final report is due on June 30,
2005.

Two advisory groups have been established to assist in implementing the project.
The first is the UN Experts Group, consisting of senior representatives from UN
agencies whose role is to ensure that the ten task forces have access to and fully utilize
the relevant knowledge, experience, and capacities of the UN system. The second is
an International Advisory Panel of experts in the respective areas of concern. The project is scheduled to issue an Interim Report to the UN Secretary-General and the
UNDP Administrator in mid-2004. Then, final recommendations by the Millennium Project are to be submitted to the UN Secretary-General on June 30, 2005.

The Millennium Campaign was designed to mobilize support for the MDGs. It
was first directed by Evelyn Herfkens, former minister for development cooperation
of the Netherlands, and was mandated the task of mobilizing support for the MDGs
among member states. This task entails coaching member states to comply with the
commitments already made and convincing them that greater consistency across
trade, finance, education, health, development, and other ministries is crucial to
MDG success.

Millennium Reports (MDGRs) constitute the third pillar of the strategy. The
reports are in essence individual country report cards. Country-level monitoring
entails collecting and analyzing data on progress toward achieving individual MDGs.
UN Country Teams assist countries in designing and implementing policies necessary
for successful progress. As of December 2002, seventeen countries had completed
MDGRs.

The MDG concept appears to have been an idea whose time has come. As the UN
Non-governmental Liaison Service has put it, "The Millennium Development Goals,
over a relatively short period of time, have gained tremendous currency, primarily in
development circles but increasingly in related trade and finance circles. Many actors
are now counting on the goals . . . to galvanize disparate and sometimes competing
development agendas and are imagining how they might become a powerful political

A "booby trap" mine. Returning Kosovars in 1999 had to live in fear of being injured or killed by land mines as they worked in the fields and collected firewood for winter. (UN/UNHCR Photo/R. Chalasani)

tool to hold governments and international institutions accountable."[25] For our purposes in this book, the MDGs provide a unique framework for examining the work of the UN system in response to globalization. In the following section, we give concrete examples of implementing each goal by focusing on UN agencies' attempts to do so.

Implementing the MDGs

Rather than discussing goals in the abstract, we should illustrate the relevance of such efforts under a number of specific topics of interest to many readers: education, women, and transnational public health. These issue-areas help set the stage for the following discussion of a wider global partnership. It will become increasingly obvious in the following discussions how efforts to address discrete problems are interrelated.

Eradicating Poverty and Hunger Through Education

In proclaiming 1996 to be the International Year for, and 1997–2006 as the First United Nations Decade for, the Eradication of Poverty, the General Assembly acknowledged that "poverty is a complex and multi-dimensional problem with origins in both the national and international domains, and that its eradication in all countries, in particular in developing countries, has become one of the priority development objectives for the 1990s."[26] Member States at the 1995 World Summit for Social Development in Copenhagen described the goal of eradicating poverty "as an ethical, social, political and economic imperative of humankind."[27]

Poverty rates declined in most regions between 1990 and 1999, with the notable exceptions of Europe and Central Asia and Sub-Saharan Africa. China is distinctive in having made tremendous strides during the 1990s in reducing the number of extremely poor. This Chinese success correlates highly with its unprecedented economic growth during the same time period. A number of other East Asian and Pacific countries made impressive gains too—cutting by half the number of extremely poor in the region as a whole.[28] With China excluded, however, the absolute number of people in the developing world living on less than $1 a day has increased, not decreased, over this same period. South Asia and Sub-Saharan Africa share the dubious distinction of being home to the absolute largest number of poor. The greatest concern is Sub-Saharan Africa, where HIV/AIDS, armed conflict and domestic unrest, malnutrition, and slow economic growth inhibit almost any meaningful progress.

Hunger and malnutrition are, of course, highly correlated with poverty. Over the last several decades, most regions of the world have experienced significant reductions in the proportion of underweight children. However, over 150 million children in developing regions remain malnourished. Sub-Saharan Africa is particularly hard hit. Current trend rates are not sufficient for meeting the MDG target for 2015. In articulating the MDGs, the eradication of extreme poverty and hunger was placed at the top of the list, and achieving universal primary education was placed second as it represents a most instrumental means to achieve Goal No. 1.

A major initiative was launched in Jomtien, Thailand, in 1990 at the UNESCO-sponsored Conference on Education for All. During the decade of the 1990s, literacy rates of those aged fifteen to twenty-four years increased in all regions of the developing world. Data from UNESCO indicate that developing country rates overall improved from 81 to 84 percent. In the least developed countries, the progress was more dramatic—increasing from 57 to 65 percent. Yet since 1990, many developing and least developed countries—seventeen middle-income and twenty-one low-income countries—have suffered reversals or further declines toward the education-for-all goal.[29] At the World Education Forum in Dakar in 2000, over 1,000 participants, including over 100 ministers of education and development and representatives of international agencies, civil society, and the private sector came together and adopted a Framework for Action. The declaration reiterated the international commitment to achieve education for all. Governments were called on to make quality education a priority item in their development planning and financing.[30]

In its *2002 Education for All Global Monitoring Report: Is the World On Track?* UNESCO reported that eighty-three countries were on track to achieve the World Education Forum's education for all goals. However, seventy other countries were not on target, and some countries were even moving backward.[31] Progress varied dramatically from region to region. Sub-Saharan Africa and South Asia, for example, were lagging significantly behind the rest of the world. In fact, 74 percent of the 120 million primary-school-age children that remained out of school lived in these two regions.[32]

Population growth plays a major role in facilitating or constraining a country's ability to make progress. In certain regions, such as East Asia and the Pacific, where the school-age population is projected to decline by over 22 million in the next dozen years, providing universal education is not as daunting as in other developing regions. On the other hand, in Sub-Saharan Africa the primary-school-age population is projected to grow by over 34 million, adding yet additional stress to already over-burdened educational infrastructures.[33] Accordingly, Sub-Saharan Africa lags well behind the other regions. A large part of that region is unlikely to reach the MDG education goal.

To spearhead the drive for universal literacy, the General Assembly has declared the decade 2003–2012 as The UN Literacy Decade. This UN-system-wide effort, coordinated by UNESCO, focuses on extending literacy to all who are not currently literate—children and adults alike. Thus, the poorest and marginalized population segments are key targets for the campaign, which is being conducted under the banner of "Literacy for All: Voice for All, Learning for All."

A primary objective of the initiative is to create sustainable local "literacy environments." "These environments will give people opportunities to express their ideas and views, engage in effective learning, participate in the written communication which characterizes democratic societies, and exchange knowledge with others. This will include increasingly the use of electronic media and information technologies, both as a means of self-expression and for accessing and assessing the vast stores or knowledge available today."[34]

The International Plan of Action for the Literacy Decade outlines six primary avenues of effort. First, policy change is required in most countries to provide a framework for increased local participation in literacy programs. Second, literacy programs need to be flexible, use appropriate and culturally relevant materials, respect the needs of learners, and use appropriate languages. Third, due attention needs to be paid to capacity building and training literacy facilitators. Fourth, policies and policy actions need to be grounded in sound empirical research. Fifth, broad-based community participation is required to build a sense of community "ownership" over the literacy programs. Finally, effective indicators of progress are needed, as are enhanced systems for monitoring and evaluation.

Women in Development

Among the most marginalized social groups who do not benefit from globalization are poor women. MDG # 3 focuses on gender inequality and empowering women for development. While promoting gender equality may be conceived as an important objective in itself, enhancing the status of women in society is also important for a variety of reasons. Reducing gender differences in education may lead to other positive effects, such as increased creation of sustainable livelihoods and increases in productivity, improved maternal health, reduced fertility rates, and higher primary school retention. As Malloch Brown has argued, which we noted in Chapter 9:

> Empowering women is not just one of the goals; it plays a critical role in the achievement of the other seven as well. All over the world, where UNDP works, women are the poorest of the poor: disproportionately, women lack access to land, water, and sources of energy; women lack access to education and other social services; and too often women are absent from decision-making, not only at the national, regional, or local level, but even within their own families.[35]

The main target specified for this goal is to eliminate gender disparity in primary and secondary education, preferably by 2005 and in all levels of education by no later than 2015. A large number of countries for which there is reliable data appear to be on track. However, the current rate of increase is not sufficient to reach the overall 2005 preferred target date. Gender inequality in school enrollment continues to be especially problematic in parts of Sub-Saharan Africa and South Asia. The World Bank's Millennium Goal website points out that "differences persist everywhere in legal rights, labor market opportunities, and the ability to participate in public life and decision making."[36]

However, a May 2003 UNIFEM report, *Progress of the World's Women 2002: Gender Equality and the Millennium Development Goals,* discloses that "although women have progressed relatively slowly in the last two years in the areas of education, literacy and employment, there have been encouraging signs of improvement in women's legislative representation." The report points out that this MDG indicator is the only gender inequality indicator that is not linked to poverty and disparities between rich and poor countries. "The United States, France and Japan, where women's share of parliamentary seats are 12 per cent, 11.8 per cent and 10 per cent respectively, lag behind 13 developing countries in sub-Saharan Africa, which is experiencing the greatest regional poverty in the world. In South Africa and Mozambique, women's share of seats is 30 per cent, while Rwanda and Uganda have 25.7 per cent and 24.7 per cent respectively."[37]

Underlying the UN's work in this area for the past two and a half decades has been the Convention on the Elimination of All Forms of Discrimination against Women (CEDAW), introduced in this volume's Chapters 5–6. The convention binds acceding states to several important obligations. State parties agree to: incorporate the principles of equality of men and women in their legal system, abolish all discriminatory laws, and adopt appropriate ones prohibiting discrimination against women; establish tribunals and other public institutions to ensure the effective protection of women against discrimination; and ensure elimination of all acts of discrimination against women by persons, organizations, or enterprises.[38] It should be noted that, although the United States is a signatory to the convention, it has never ratified it. Some 170 other countries have ratified CEDAW.

UN member states' collective commitment to the rights of women was reinforced at the Fourth World Conference on Women in Beijing in 1995, twenty years after the issue was officially flagged for the international agenda at a first global conference on women in Mexico City. The UN Commission on Human Rights, treated in Part 2 of this volume, has been another important forum for promoting women's rights. A focal point of the 2003 Commission proceedings was an open debate on "integration of the human rights of women and a gender perspective." Commission members addressed a number of critical issues, including eradicating violence against women.[39]

UNIFEM plays a key advocacy role in promoting women's rights and CEDAW implementation. UNIFEM is committed to working to eliminate violence against women and girls. One such form of violence is "trafficking in persons." Here women and girls are most vulnerable to systematic exploitation. Article 3, paragraph (a) of the Protocol to Prevent, Suppress and Punish Trafficking in Persons defines the legal concept as follows:

> . . . the recruitment, transportation, transfer, harbouring or receipt of persons, by means of the threat or use of force or other forms of coercion, of abduction, of fraud, of deception, of the abuse of power or of a position of vulnerability or of the giving or receiving of payments or benefits to achieve the consent of a person having control over another person, for the purpose of exploitation. Exploitation shall include, at a minimum, the exploitation of the prostitution of others or other forms of sexual exploitation, forced labour or services, slavery or practices similar to slavery, servitude or the removal of organs.[40]

While trafficking in persons is not new, trafficking especially in women and girls is the fastest-growing area of organized crime.[41] In 2000, the UN General Assembly adopted the UN Convention against Transnational Organized Crime and the associated Protocol against the Smuggling of Migrants by Land, Sea or Air and the Protocol to Prevent, Suppress and Punish Trafficking in Persons, especially Women and Children. As of November 2002, 143 member states had signed the convention and nineteen had ratified the Protocol.[42] In 2002 the CHR announced the "establishment of the Intergovernmental Organization Contact Group on Trafficking and Migrant Smuggling, under the coordination of the Office of the High Commissioner for Human Rights (UNHCHR) and co-chaired by the Office of the United Nations High Commissioner for Refugees (UNHCR) and the International Labour Organization (ILO). This brings together representatives of the major Geneva-based intergovernmental organizations working on trafficking, as well as relevant non-governmental organizations, for collaboration and cooperation on the issue of trafficking.[43] The issue was also the focal point of the UN Commission on Crime Prevention and Criminal Justice in Vienna in May 2003.

Beyond legal norms and diplomatic statements, however, the UN has had to confront this issue of trafficking in its own field operations. Some personnel in UN peacekeeping and other missions related to conflict (for example, civilian police forces) have been involved in certain aspects of the organized traffic in women, as in the Balkans. The UN has moved to deal with the issue in the context of negative publicity.

Transnational Public Health

Three Millennium Development Goals deal with various health-related topics: reducing child mortality; improving maternal health; and combating HIV/AIDS, malaria, and other diseases. In addition, one of the targets for the eighth MDG calls for a global partnership with pharmaceutical companies to provide access to affordable, essential drugs in developing countries. All of these health-related goals are mutually reinforcing and are highly associated with the overall goal of poverty reduction. Disease and poor health provide a drag on economic growth and development. HIV/AIDS is particularly acute in this regard and threatens to undermine the development efforts of the entire Sub-Saharan African region.

The issue of the role of child mortality in development is a complex one, as the World Health Organization (WHO) has recently explained:

> The feasibility of meeting the MDGs in the low-income countries is widely debated. On the one side of the debate are those who believe that the health goals will take care of themselves, as a fairly automatic by-product of economic growth. With the mortality rates of children under 5 in the least-developed countries standing at 159 per 1,000 births, compared with 6 per 1,000 births in high-income countries. They take the view that it's just a matter of time before the mortality rates in the low-income world will converge with those of the rich countries. This is false for two reasons . . . . First, the disease burden itself will slow the economic growth that is presumed to solve the health problems; second, economic growth is indeed important, but is very far from enough.[44]

Many things stand in the way of reducing infant and child mortality: lack of adequate medical treatment and immunization, unsafe drinking water, poor sanitation, civil strife, endemic disease, and malnutrition. Approximately 70 percent of child deaths are associated with some combination of disease and/or malnutrition. "Rapid improvements before 1990 gave hope that mortality rates of children under five could be cut by two-thirds in the following 25 years. But progress slowed almost everywhere in the 1990s, and in parts of Africa infant mortality rates increased."[45]

The situation with regard to progress toward achieving the MDG child mortality goal is bleak. It is estimated that only thirty-six developing countries are on target for reducing under-five child mortality to a third of its 1990 level by 2015.[46] In 2002, more children died from disease and malnutrition than the total number of adults who died from the three great endemic killer diseases: HIV/AIDS, malaria, and tuberculosis. Moreover, funding for child health care has declined in recent years.

At its May 2003 annual meeting, the World Health Assembly of the WHO adopted a new strategic initiative to deal with child and youth health care. It identifies and targets seven priority areas for the future: maternal health, nutrition, prevention of communicable diseases, injuries, physical environment, psychosocial development and mental health and children in difficult circumstances. In the context of this new strategy, WHO Family and Community Health Executive Director Tomris Turmen offers that "The improvement of child and adolescent health should be the easiest of the Millennium Development Goals to achieve . . . . The strategy shows the way."[47] However, fulfilling the strategy and achieving the goal requires enhanced resources and commitment.

Goal #5 is improving maternal health care. The target set for this goals is to reduce by three-quarters, between 1990 and 2015, the maternal mortality ratio. Nearly all maternal-related deaths occur in developing countries. Most such deaths are preventable. Inadequate delivery services and prenatal and postnatal care as well as unsafe abortions account for a large number of such deaths. In the context of high-income countries the answer seems simple: adequate pre- and postnatal maternal health care, family planning, skilled birth attendants, clean birthing facilities with adequate and safe blood supplies, and prevention of unsafe abortions. Unfortunately, in poor countries such luxuries simply are often not available, especially to the poor. Progress toward achieving the MDG target for maternal health is mixed and in parts of Asia and nearly all of Sub-Saharan Africa very disappointing.

It should be noted that adequately measuring and assessing maternal mortality is exceedingly difficult. Most countries do not have good vital registration systems and there is much underreporting. Underreporting is especially acute in situations where there is not a skilled health attendant present. An important reason why the proportion of births attended by skilled health personnel is used as a basic indicator is the high correlation between maternal mortality and the absence of such skilled personnel. Also, in Sub-Saharan Africa, maternal mortality is, of course, linked in important ways to HIV/AIDS, malaria, and other endemic diseases—or Goal #6.

HIV/AIDS is one of the most devastating health pandemics of our time—or, for that matter, any time in history—that challenges international cooperation.[48] In fact, HIV/AIDS has become the fourth-largest cause of death in the world. The MDG target related to AIDS is to have halted and begun to reverse the spread of HIV/AIDS by 2015. Yet this task seems daunting, especially in Africa and other low-income countries.

Sub-Saharan Africa continues to suffer the most. In 2002, 3.5 million newly infected persons brought the region's total population living with HIV/AIDS to 29.4 million. At the same time, approximately 2.4 million persons died of AIDS-related causes. The economic impact of AIDS in Africa has been profound, as the UN secretariat reports:

> It is estimated that the annual per capita growth in half the countries of sub-Saharan Africa is falling by 0.5–1.2% as a direct result of AIDS. By 2010, per capita GDP in some of the hardest hit countries may drop by 8% and per capita consumption may fall even farther. Calculations show that heavily affected countries could lose more than 20% of GDP by 2020. . . . An index of existing social and economic injustices, the epidemic is driving a ruthless cycle of impoverishment. People at all income levels are vulnerable to the economic impact of HIV/AIDS, but the poor suffer most acutely. One quarter of households in Botswana, where adult HIV prevalence is over 35%, can expect to lose an income earner within the next 10 years. A rapid increase in the number of very poor and destitute families is

anticipated. Per capita household income for the poorest quarter of households is expected to fall by 13%, while every income earner in this category can expect to take on four more dependents as a result of HIV/AIDS.[49]

Another document reported that "[i]n four southern African countries, national adult HIV prevalence has risen higher than thought possible, exceeding 30%: Botswana (38.8%), Lesotho (31%), Swaziland (33.4%) and Zimbabwe (33.7%)."[50] As might be expected, Sub-Saharan Africa has suffered significant setbacks in life expectancy. In nearly two dozen countries, life expectancy has fallen over the last decade and a half. In six—Botswana, Burundi, Namibia, Rwanda, Zambia, and Zimbabwe—the decline has been more than seven years. In Botswana, Malawi, Mozambique and Swaziland life expectancy is now less than forty years. Overall in sub-Saharan Africa, instead of an average life expectancy of sixty-two years, which is estimated in the absence of HIV/AIDS, it is only forty-seven years.[51] In the face of this overwhelming health crisis, Africa is experiencing a profound shortage of personnel in the health-care sector.[52]

As illustrated in Table 10.3, the impact of the pandemic varies dramatically from region to region with the worst horror based in developing regions and transitional societies. The fastest-growing AIDS epidemic continues to be in Eastern Europe—especially the Russian Federation, Estonia, Ukraine, and Latvia—and Central Asia. Of the estimated 1.2 million people in the region living with HIV, 250,000 persons were newly infected during 2002. In Russia, new infections have been almost doubling every year since 1998. The Caribbean is the second-most affected area of the world. Asia and the Pacific are estimated to now have 7.2 million people living with HIV/AIDS, and 485,000 people died of the disease in 2002.[53] In the last few years, the HIV-prevalence rate in India has risen to the point where India now records the second largest HIV-infected population in the world—3.97 million persons living with HIV/AIDS.

The relationship between HIV/AIDS and humanitarian crises is a matter of much concern. Particularly acute has been the situation in southern Africa where extremely high levels of HIV coexist with a severe food crisis. At the end of 2002, over 14 million persons were at the verge of starvation in six southern African countries, including Lesotho, Swaziland, and Zimbabwe, where adult HIV prevalence exceeds 30 percent. "Longstanding, severe epidemics are plunging millions of people deeper into destitution and desperation as their labour power weakens, incomes dwindle, assets shrink and households disintegrate."[54]

The implications of AIDS for development go way beyond economic factors. One of the most significant impacts has been on educational systems. In the most highly infected countries, "HIV/AIDS kills teachers faster than they can be trained, makes orphans of students, and threatens to derail efforts . . . to get all boys and girls into primary school by 2015." HIV prevalence among teachers, for example, is 30 percent in Malawi, 20 percent in Zambia, and 12 percent in South Africa. Moreover, AIDS has resulted in a widening gender gap. In addition to being more susceptible to infection than boys, girls are more prone to dropping out of school to care for sick family members.[55]

TABLE 10.3   Regional HIV/AIDS Statistics, end of 2002

Region	Epidemic started	Adults & children living with HIV/AIDS	Adults & children newly infected with HIV
Sub-Saharan Africa	late 70s/ early 80s	29.4 million	3.5 million
North Africa & Middle East	late 80s	550,000	83,000
South and South-East Asia	late 80s	6 million	700, 000
East Asia & Pacific	late 80s	1.2 million	270,000
Latin America	late 70s/ early 80s	1.5 million	150,000
Caribbean	early 90s	440,000	60,000
Eastern Europe & Central Asia	late 70s early 80s	1.2 million	250,000
Western Europe	late 70s/ early 80s	570,000	30,000
North America	late 70s/ early 80s	980,000	45,000
Australia & New Zealand	late 70s/ early 80s	15,000	500
TOTAL		42 million	5 million

SOURCE: UNAIDS, AIDS epidemic update: December 2002; http://www.unaids.org/worldaids-day/2002/press/update/epiupdate2002_en.doc

There is some reason for optimism. A recent report by the Global HIV Prevention Working Group, *Access to HIV Prevention: Closing the Gap*, suggests that 29 million of the 45 million persons who are expected to be newly infected between now and 2010 could be saved if adequate preventive strategies were increased dramatically.[56] The group is calling for a "combination prevention approach" that is using a variety of proven strategies.

Among other things, the report details the substantial HIV-funding gap in the context of future needs. Its sets the worldwide funding need for 2005 at $5.7 billion. With the 2002 actual funding level of $1.9 billion that means there is a gap of $3.8 billion annually. One hopeful sign is that in May 2003, President Bush signed into law the U.S. Leadership against HIV/AIDS, Tuberculosis and Malaria Act of 2003, proving an expenditure of $3 billion a year for five years to help stop the spread of HIV/AIDS. The optimism must be tempered because the funds have, thus far, only been authorized and not appropriated for expenditure.[57] Nonetheless, the culture of indifference in Washington and elsewhere appears to be giving way to the need for action.

The second target set for Goal #6 is to have halted by 2015 and begun to reverse the incidence of malaria and other major diseases. Although malaria is found in over 100 countries, approximately 90 percent of the cases are located in Sub-Saharan Africa with other pockets of prevalence in tropical climates. The death rate from malaria in Sub-Saharan Africa is truly staggering and stands at nearly 800 per 100,000 children. Northern Africa has the second-highest death rate, at forty-seven, followed by Western Asia at twenty-six per 100,000.[58] But again, the core of the disease resides in Sub-Saharan Africa, where malaria accounts for over one-fifth of all child deaths and places a tremendous strain on health-care facilities and systems.[59]

In terms of impact, tuberculosis is the single most devastating disease among adults in the developing world, and Sub-Saharan Africa and southern Asia are the most affected regions. On the other hand, one of the success stories in international health has been the battle against polio. Only a few small pockets of the disease persist. Ninety-nine percent of all remaining cases are located in three countries—India, Nigeria, and Pakistan—with most of the remaining 1 percent of cases located in just four additional countries. WHO, UNICEF, the U.S. Centers for Disease Control, and Rotary International announced a new Global Polio Eradication Initiative in May 2003. This program will focus its efforts in these seven most affected countries and in six others where there exists significant risk of reinfection.[60]

New on the scene is SARS (Severe Acute Respiratory Syndrome), a powerful reminder, if one was needed, how globalization can spread disease as easily as tourists and financial flows. In fact, SARS is the first new major communicable disease to emerge in the twenty-first century. Although one might get the sense that SARS has been around for some time now, the first SARS case was identified in February 2003 in Hanoi, Vietnam. There had been previous occurrences of the disease and there was much concern in Guandong Province and other parts of China about an unidentified atypical respiratory disease. Yet the virus had not yet been isolated. The WHO was quick to act and mid-March issued a global alert about mysterious cases of a severe atypical pneumonia with unknown etiology. Two days later, Canadian health authorities reported two deaths from a similar phenomenon. The following day, WHO elevated its alert as cases were being reported in Singapore and elsewhere. Within weeks the situation worsened in Hong Kong, Beijing, and Guangdong and had spread to Taiwan. WHO took the unprecedented step of quickly issuing travel advisories for Beijing, Hong Kong, Guangdong Province, Shanxi Province, and Toronto. The international health agency later, on April 29, lifted the advisory against Toronto after the situation there had seemed to improve. But then, less than a month later, Toronto and SARS were back in the news.

The global response to SARS illustrates how effective international cooperation can be in response to a crisis when there is widespread commitment to respond with a sense of urgency. It also demonstrated how important international organizations and their leadership can be. In this case, the WHO under the leadership of Gro Harlem Brundtland did not hesitate to confront both a great power (China) and a traditional organizational supporter (Canada). The level of cooperation has been unprecedented. While not yet fully contained everywhere, the potential rapid spread of the lethal disease (an estimated 8–10 percent of cases) does appear to have been checked.[61]

A Global Partnership for Development

As argued consistently throughout this volume, new forms of cooperation and partnerships are needed among states, markets, the private sector, voluntary and civic organizations, local communities, and other stakeholders. This was noted especially regarding human rights and humanitarian affairs, where the role of NGOs and multinational corporations (MNCs) was discussed. The effort to forge new partnerships for sustainable human development or human security has taken a variety of forms and complexions. In general there has been a move to strengthen UN agencies' direct involvement with diverse elements of society, including NGOs, the private sector, and many other types of civil society organizations. Similar efforts have also been made in the Bretton Woods institutions. UN cooperation with other actors varies from issue to issue, with some examples of close cooperation and some examples of lack of same.

Business in General

UN partnership activities with private for-profit actors—most especially through the "Global Compact" that was discussed briefly in Chapter 9—have involved innovative thinking and actions. The compact brings together the Executive Office of the Secretary-General in collaboration with the International Labor Organization, the Office of the High Commissioner for Human Rights, UNEP, UNDP, and the Fund for International Partnerships (UNFIP). It seeks to engage the private sector constructively in helping to make globalization work for all the world's peoples. Partners to the compact are asked to embrace nine principles drawn from the Universal Declaration of Human Rights, the ILO's Fundamental Principles on Rights at Work, and the Rio Principles on Environment and Development. It engages a wide diversity of partners, including: international inter-sectoral business associations; international, sectoral business associations; national business associations; workers' organizations; and NGOs.

The main assumption underlying the Global Compact is that development cannot occur through governmental, inter-governmental, and nongovernmental organizations, nor can it occur through unbridled market forces alone. Creating local, national, and international enabling environments is essential, and a broad-based partnership involving all relevant "stakeholders" is required.

However, bringing the private sector into the United Nations has brought with it some concerns and opposition. Many governments, for example, still hang tenaciously to the tenets of sovereignty and resent actions by multilateral agencies that do not respect the sanctity of that norm. Other governments, including China as a notable example, have come to embrace this notion of multi-stakeholder partnerships. In his statement before the Second Preparatory Session of the Preparatory Committee for the World Summit on Sustainable Development, for example, Chinese Ambas-

Squamish Nation canoe at the Qatuwas Festival, a gathering of Pacific Rim indigenous people. (UN/DPI Photo 186590/J. Isaac)

sador Shen Guofang said that China believes "that governments, NGOs and business have enormous potentials for cooperation. We support the establishment of partnerships among governments, businesses and other major groups so as to make use of the creativity and initiative of all sides and enable them to contribute to sustainable development."[62] On another occasion, he went even further to argue that China hopes "that in the future, more heavy-weight and influential transnational corporations could participate" in the development work of the United Nations.[63]

Trade and Finance

Cooperation by the UN narrowly defined has not been so impressive in the domain of trade and finance, although the Bretton Woods institutions may themselves be reaching out to more actors from civil society. The same is not true for the WTO.

The first target under MDG #8 is to "develop further an open, rule-based, predictable, non-discriminatory trading and financial system." This goal inherently includes a commitment to good governance, development, and poverty reduction—both nationally and internationally. However, one of the major problems confronting the United Nations system almost since its inception has been that the management of trade and finance has seldom, if ever, functioned as the broad and coherent system that appears on paper. We should recall the argument in Chapter 8 that the United Nations is but one of a group of interrelated international institutions that was created by the Allied Powers during World War II to build a post-war world order based on liberal ideological principles. This series of institutions was designed to work toward achieving a set of common ends related to promoting and ensuring international peace, security, and human well-being. The United Nations narrowly defined was not the first but rather the *fourth* of the international organizations created during and at the close of the war. It followed on the Food and Agricultural Organization, the World Bank, and the International Monetary Fund. UNESCO was created simultaneously with the UN and also came into being in 1945. The role of each organization, including the UN, was to complement the others and in combination form a coherent whole.

In short, the UN system was designed to function as a norm- and rule-based system of institutions. A liberal, open, rule-based, predictable, non-discriminatory trading and financial system was to be very much part of this new order. In fact, it was to serve as its foundation. As we have seen, the Cold War and other factors, such as rich-country distrust of majority voting, intervened to frustrate the grand design. As the Cold War wound down and liberal economic ideas prevailed, political space opened for the further globalization of the capitalist world economy. Yet old habits persisted, affected by the North-South conflict. For half a century, trade and financial liberalization had been primarily a matter reserved to governments of advanced market economies. Now, pressure for change arose as global inequalities grew and extreme poverty persisted in large pockets around the globe. The story of the evolving focus on sustainable human development was rehearsed above and need not be repeated here. But the North and South at least professed that time had come to move toward a more equitable capitalist world order.

Chapter 9 detailed some of the steps—in terms of pronouncements, styles, and policies—taken in the last few years to bring closer together the Bretton Woods institutions, the WTO, and the UN system. Progress could hardly be made in meeting such goals as Target #12 on trade and finance without such collaboration. What has happened? The Millennium Project reports that:

> Tariffs have been falling. After the Uruguay Round of trade negotiations concluded in 1994, average tariffs on agricultural products and textiles and clothing–two important categories of developing country exports–fell in most rich countries . . . . Even if the use of tariffs and quotas is further reduced, many developing countries will not benefit much, especially in Africa. One estimate, based on reducing trade protection by half, shows that developing countries would gain about $200 billion by 2015. But only $2.4 billion of this would go to Sub-Saharan Africa, and only another $3.3 billion to South Asia outside of India. To make trade an effective source of growth, developing countries need to increase the efficiency of their producers, shippers, freight handlers, and customs services–their capacity to trade. Rich countries can help by providing "aid for trade" and sharing knowledge needed to establish competitive export industries.[64]

Moreover, the UNDP and World Bank, for example, have initiated a pilot program at the country level to explore the interface between UNDAF and the World

Bank's Country Assistance Strategy. Another collaborative effort has been the "Money Matters: Private Finance for Development" initiative. It is aimed at assisting emerging market economies to mobilize and attract private finance for sustainable human development. It gave rise to the creation in 1995 of the Money Matters Institute (MMI), a forum for exchange of experience and ideas among leaders in financial services, international organizations, and policy makers in developing countries about the role of private members of MMI and have included the private companies Arthur Andersen, Concord International Investments, Fidelity Investments, LIA Worldwide, MFS Investment Management, Prudential Securities, State Street Corporation, and United Gulf Management.[65]

Debt Relief

More concrete action, however, is to be found in the area of debt relief. The importance of the subject merits special focus, though it is an aspect of finance. In 1996 the World Bank and IMF launched a plan to provide debt relief for the world's poorest, most heavily indebted countries. Under this Heavily Indebted Poor Countries initiative, creditors collectively move to provide exceptional assistance aimed at bringing the debtor country into a position of debt sustainability. Here is how HIPC works:

> All countries requesting HIPC Initiative assistance must have (i) adopted a Poverty Reduction Strategy Paper . . . through a broad-based participatory process, by the *decision point* . . . ; and (ii) have made progress in implementing this strategy for at least one year by the *completion point* . . . . To qualify for assistance, the country must adopt adjustment and reform programs supported by the IMF and the World Bank and establish a satisfactory track record. During that time, it will continue to receive traditional concessional assistance from all the relevant donors and multilateral institutions, as well as debt relief from bilateral creditors (including the Paris Club) . . . . At the end of the first phase, a debt sustainability analysis will be carried out to determine the current external debt situation of the country. If the external debt ratio for that country after traditional debt relief mechanisms is above 150 percent for the net present value of debt to exports, it qualifies for assistance under the Initiative . . . . At the decision point, the Executive Boards of the IMF and World Bank will formally decide on a country's eligibility, and the international community will commit to provide sufficient assistance by the completion point (see below) for the country to achieve debt sustainability calculated at the decision point. The delivery of assistance committed by the Fund and Bank will depend on satisfactory assurances of action by other creditors . . . . Once eligible for support under the Initiative, the country must establish a further track record of good performance under IMF/World Bank-supported programs. The length of this second period under the enhanced framework is not time bound, but depends on the satisfactory implementation of key structural policy reforms agreed at the decision point, the maintenance of macroeconomic stability, and the adoption and implementation of a poverty reduction strategy developed through a broad-based participatory process . . . . During this second phase, bilateral and commercial creditors

are generally expected to reschedule obligations coming due, with a 90 percent reduction in net present value. Both the World Bank and the IMF are expecting to provide "interim relief" between the decision and completion points, and other multilateral creditors are considering also to advance some of the assistance from the completion point . . . . Remaining assistance will be provided at this [completion] point.[66]

A vexing issue for many developing countries is making their debt burden sustainable. Over the past half decade years, the IMF and World Bank have moved to revise their lending approaches to integrate poverty reduction with macroeconomic policies. Since 1999, for example, the IMF and the International Development Association (IDA) of the World Bank Group support strategies and programs that emerge directly from the borrowing country's Poverty Reduction Strategy Paper (PRSP). These PRSPs reflect each country's own strategy which is to be prepared in consultation with the poor and other elements of civil society as well as other development partners. A new facility, the Poverty Reduction Growth Facility (PRGF), was created to replace the Enhanced Structural Adjustment Facility. The main difference between the older facility and the new one is the integration of poverty reduction into macroeconomic policymaking and an additional emphasis on good governance.[67]

In addition, a more open and flexible approach to dealing with debt seems to be emerging. In their meeting in Deauville, France, in May 2003, for example, the G–8 finance ministers issued a communiqué calling for the Paris Club of official creditors to take a more flexible approach and work with the IMF to help debtor countries achieve sustainability. Although it is not clear whether official creditors will respond with more openness and flexibility, it is clear that something more than what has been done in the past is necessary to achieve the MDG target set.

Good Governance

Improving trade and finance alone, even with special attention to debt relief, is insufficient. As the UNDP's *Poverty Report 2000* argued, "if poverty reduction programmes are to succeed, local government must be strengthened," as must popular participation and the role of civil society in governance processes.[68] The UNDP has placed special emphasis on governance and has dubbed good governance as the "missing link" between anti-poverty efforts and poverty reduction. "Poverty eradication and good governance are inseparable. Good governance brings about a proper balance among state action, the private sector, civil society, and the communities themselves."[69] Well-functioning, effective, and accountable public and private institutions that are viewed as legitimate in the eyes of those being governed are required to mobilize the social capital required for sustaining development.[70]

UN agencies like the UNDP, however, find it easier to focus on what might be termed micro-democracy—the participation of stakeholders in UNDP projects—than in traditional macro-democracy—national election campaigns. The same is true, to slightly lesser extent, at the World Bank. Whereas public commentary by these international agencies on national election personalities and issues runs the risk of being characterized as unacceptable interference with state sovereignty and domestic affairs, involving persons in international development projects is often pictured as less intrusive once the national government has agreed to the project in the first place.

Poorest of the Poor

Another main MDG target related to building a global partnership for development focuses on addressing the special needs of the least developed countries. Most of the very poor countries have been especially hard pressed to deal with globalization processes no matter how one defines them. Although African countries and indeed all of the least developed have experienced significant improvements in the rates of growth of their gross domestic products (GDP) since 1995 compared with the previous decade, that rate of growth has declined from its peak of 4.6 percent in 1996 to an estimated 3.0 percent for 1999. According to the World Bank's *African Development Indicators 2001*, the average gross domestic product in the region declined nearly 1 percent in 1998–1999.[71] The record has been similar for the poorest as a whole. "Recent economic growth has not been strong or sustained enough to increase per capita income or make an impact on the levels of poverty in the sub-Saharan region. It has been estimated that 44 percent of Africans as a whole and 51 percent of those in sub-Saharan Africa live in absolute poverty."[72] The Secretary-General's report goes on to detail three main impediments to sustaining development in Africa and the poorest countries in general: poor governance, low productivity, and difficulties in mobilizing resources for development, in addition to protracted social conflicts in many countries. A key factor in this regard is the lack of capacity and the inability to sustain capacity building, which, in turn, is dependent on education, health, nutrition, sanitation, population dynamics, and various other human development factors. Of the thirty-five countries that scored "low" in the human development category in the UNDP's *Human Development Report 1999*, thirty were from Africa and thirty-one were among the least developed.[73]

This situation is complicated, especially in the long term, by the impact of diseases, such as HIV/AIDS. Of the thirty-four countries most affected by HIV/AIDS, nearly all (thirty-one) are either African or among the poorest countries. AIDS is now the leading cause of death in Africa, and it hits especially hard among the professional class. However, the largest single number of HIV cases is in India, and HIV infections in Asia increased by 70 percent between 1996 and 1998. Nor is HIV/AIDS the only significant health problem. Other core diseases still plaguing poor regions include: polio, diphtheria, tuberculosis, measles, tetanus, and whooping cough–for all of which there exist vaccinations, yet a significant proportion of the world's children remain unprotected.

In brief, most very poor countries lack sufficient capacity to integrate productively into the global economy. Many suffer from weak and unpredictable political and economic institutions. Their economies tend to be based on low productivity traditional sectors. Many of these countries are extremely disadvantaged with respect to such essential development elements as education, sanitation, transportation, communication, clean water, adequate development financing, electrical power and energy resources, and political stability. Globalization, it can be noted, has hardly made a dent in these problems.

The Third UN Conference on poor countries summarized the situation succinctly:

> Ten years after the adoption of the Paris Programme of Action . . . , the objectives and goals set out therein have not been achieved. LDCs (Lesser Developed Countries) are being bypassed by the process of globalization, leading to their further marginalization. For their part, most LDCs have pursued economic reform programmes set out in the previous Programme of Action, including elimination or substantially reducing tariffs and other trade barriers, liberalizing currency regimes, privatizing public enterprises, establishing and strengthening institutional and regulatory frameworks and adopting liberal investment policies. The results of these reform efforts have been below expectations. Declining availability of financial resources, domestic and external, including ODA, a heavy and unsustainable debt burden, falling or volatile commodity prices, complex trade barriers, lack of economic and export diversification and market access for key products which LDCs benefit from, as well as supply-side constraints, have seriously affected the growth and development prospects for LDCs.[74]

Since the late 1960s, the United Nations has paid special attention to those developing countries that are in the worst economic condition. Beginning in 1981, the UN has held three high-level conferences exclusively devoted to LDC concerns. Each conference has issued a new program of action to guide the UN's efforts for the subsequent decade. The Third United Nations Conference on the Least Developing Countries, hosted by the EU in Brussels in May 2001 was no exception. The Brussels Programme of Action specified seven specific commitments centered around fostering a people-centered policy framework, good governance, human and institutional capacity building, making globalization work for LDCs, enhancing the role of trade in development, environmental protection, and mobilizing financial resources for development. This program of action was subsequently endorsed by the General Assembly along with a work plan for the 2001–2010 decade in Resolutions 55/279 and 56/227.

As originally envisioned, creditors were to share the cost of HIPC assistance on the basis of equitable burden sharing and provide relief on a basis that is proportional to their share of the debt after the full application of traditional forms of debt relief. Debtor countries must agree to undertake sustained implementation of integrated poverty reduction and economic reform programs.

Over the last several years, the G-8 and other countries have taken additional initiatives to enhance HIPC. In 1999, the HIPC initiative was enhanced and the number of eligible countries was expanded. In addition, the absolute amount of debt relief that any one country could receive was increased and delivery of the relief was speeded up. The enhanced HIPC also permitted governments to use freed resources to support poverty reduction strategies.

Thirty-eight countries currently qualify for assistance under the enhanced HIPC program. Twenty-six countries now have debt relief. The average debt service due in

2001–2003 was about 30 percent less than that paid before relief began in 1998–1999. In 2001–2002 social spending in HIPC countries was "about $6.5 billion–45 percent higher than in 1999 and about three times the level of debt service."[75] Of these twenty-six countries, eight have now reached their completion points. The last two countries to have achieved this status at the time of this writing were Mali and Benin, which reached their final points on March 7 and March 25, 2003, respectively.

Geographically Challenged

The MDG strategy also places special emphasis on the situation of landlocked (LLDCs) and small island developing states (SIDS). These two groups of states challenged by their geographical situation increasingly have drawn international attention especially since the early 1990s. Although these two groups of states hold many things in common, each has its own set of particular constraints and problems. The United Nations has summarized the special situation of land-locked countries concisely:

> Lack of territorial access to the sea, remoteness and isolation from world markets and high transit costs continue to impose serious constraints on the overall socio-economic development of landlocked developing countries. The economic performance of landlocked developing countries reflects the direct and indirect impact of geographical situation on key-economic variables. Landlocked developing countries are generally among the poorest of the developing countries, with the weakest growth rates, and are typically heavily dependent on a very limited number of commodities for their export earnings. Moreover, of thirty landlocked developing countries sixteen are classified as least developed. The lack of territorial access to the sea, remoteness and isolation from world markets, appear to be the primary cause of their relative poverty. Their sea borne trade unavoidably depends on transit through other countries. Additional border crossings and long distance from the market substantially increase the total expenses for the transport services.[76]

A few statistics will provide some perspective on the nature of the situation. The distance to seaports and world trade routes is in many cases extreme. Six LLDCs, for example, are located more than 2,000 kilometers from the nearest sea, with Kazakhstan being situated 3,750 kilometers from the sea.[77] Also, over half of the LLDCs are least developed countries and this adds a further dimension to the plight of these countries as discussed earlier.

At its session in 2001 the General Assembly decided by Resolution 56/180 to convene an International Ministerial Conference of Landlocked and Transit Developing States. The Government of Kazakhstan offered to host this special conference in Almaty in August 2003. In preparation for this conference, the Secretary-General issued a report in August 2002 to the General Assembly. He summarized six objectives of the LLDCs with respect to their transit needs: secure unfettered access to the sea, reduce transportation costs and improve services to increase competitiveness, reduce delivery costs of imports, clear trade routes from delays, lessen deterioration and loss of goods during transit, and provide mechanisms for expanding trade.[78]

In comparison, small island developing states tend to have small resources bases, be highly subject to climatic conditions and natural and environmental disasters and deterioration, have limited fresh water resources, be dependent on conventional energy resources, and have small domestic markets and small populations with rapid growth rates. The situation confronting SIDS was addressed at the Earth Summit in Rio in 1992 and has been an issue before the Commission on Sustainable Development (CSD) since its creation in the aftermath of the summit—being addressed at the CSD's fourth, sixth, seventh and eleventh sessions in 1996, 1998, 1999, and 2003.

The big push for an international agenda for dealing with SIDS, however, was the Global Conference on the Sustainable Development of Small Island Developing States, held in Bridgetown, Barbados, in April–May 1994. The conference adopted the Barbados Programme of Action which set forth specific recommendations and actions for promoting the sustainable development of SIDS.[79] Five years later, at the Twenty-Second Special Session of the General Assembly, the member states of the UN carried out an assessment of the implementation of the action program and called for more concerted action to carry it out.[80]

This call was reinforced in the Johannesburg Plan of Action, adopted at the World Summit on Sustainable Development in September 2002.[81] Immediately after the summit, the General Assembly decided to convene a ten-year review of the Barbados Programme of Action. This review will be the focus of a high-level conference to be held in Mauritius in 2004.

To mobilize support and oversee the implementation of plans for dealing with these specially situated states, as well as dealing with LDCs in general, in 2001 the General Assembly created the Office of the High Representative for the Least Developed Countries, Landlocked Developing Countries and Small Island States (OHRLLS). The purpose is to ensure that the special problems and challenges of these disadvantaged countries are not forgotten by donor countries, the members of the UN system, civil society, the media, academia, and foundations.[82]

TRIPS

A key to dealing with endemic diseases like HIV/AIDS is providing affordable access to medicines and treatments. Although the situation in the developed world is far from perfect, access to affordable drugs on a sustainable basis is not available to over one third of the developing world's population. In both Sub-Saharan Africa and South-central Asia less than 50 percent have such access. Of course, the situation is far worse for the extremely poor and marginalized parts of the populations.

Solving this problem is not a simple task because it is bundled up with a variety of economic, politic, legal, and moral issues. Access to medicines to treat those afflicted with HIV/AIDS has sparked a heated debate between developing and the most developed counties. As discussed above, over 90 percent of the 42 million persons currently living with HIV/AIDS live in the developing world. Yet nearly all the drugs that have been developed to treat the disease and its symptoms are produced and controlled under license by pharmaceutical companies in the developed world.

At the center of the controversy over the access issue in recent years has been the Agreement on Trade-Related Aspects of Intellectual Property Rights (TRIPS). Negotiated in the context of WTO, the TRIPS agreement represented an attempt to strike a balance between protecting the property rights of the inventory and providing access to the consumer. Article 7 of the TRIPS agreement

> recognizes that the protection of intellectual property should contribute to the promotion of technological innovation and to the transfer and dissemination of technology, to the mutual advantage of users and producers of technological knowledge and in a manner conducive to social and economic welfare and to a balance of rights and obligations. It is not an Agreement about simply maximizing the level of protection for intellectual property; rather, it emerged from a genuine negotiating process where the need for balance was very much to the fore.[83]

There are three main aspects of the TRIPS agreement. First, the agreement sets minimum standards of protection and obligations for each member country. Second, TRIPS specifies general principles that must be followed in all intellectual property rights enforcement procedures. Finally, all disputes under TRIPS are subject to WTO dispute settlement procedures.

In the context of international health, TRIPS has meant trying to find a balance between the interests of pharmaceutical companies and their home states, and non-technologically advanced countries who desire greater access to drugs that are essential for public health reasons. Under Article 31 of the TRIPS agreement, members are allowed to exercise "compulsory licensing" without the authorization of the property right holder under certain conditions, such as public health necessities. However, the nature of this right is quite ambiguous and subject to dispute. Moreover, many developing countries do not have adequate enough manufacturing capabilities in pharmaceuticals to enable them even to make effective use of compulsory licensing.

At the WTO Ministerial Conference in Doha in November 2001, this issue came to a head. Developing country governments, seeking greater access to drugs for treating HIV/AIDS, tuberculosis, and other endemic diseases, were able to get member states to agree to a compromise. In adopting the Doha Declaration on the TRIPS Agreement and Public Health, the member states affirmed that

> the TRIPS Agreement does not and should not prevent members from taking measures to protect public health. Accordingly, while reiterating our commitment to the TRIPS Agreement, we affirm that the Agreement can and should be interpreted and implemented in a manner supportive of WTO members' right to protect public health and, in particular, to promote access to medicines for all.[84]

The declaration specified that the least-developed countries would be given until January 2016 before being required to implement or enforce the TRIPS agreement with regard to pharmaceutical products. The declaration, however, still left unresolved the issue of how to deal with those countries that do not have sufficient manufacturing capabilities in pharmaceuticals to enable them even to make effective use of compulsory licensing.

This issue remains a contested one, with the WTO Council on TRIPS attempting to forge a compromise between the United States and other technologically advanced countries and those less technologically advanced member states that are demanding more flexible patent rules in cases where there exist national public health exigencies. Clearly, the jury is still out.

Information/Communication Technology

The TRIPS debate, of course, lies at the heart of the globalization debate, as does the related issue of making the benefits of new technologies, especially information and communications technologies (ICTs), available to all. Information and communications technology (ICT) is the primary enabling agent for the pervasive and invasive globalization processes that underpin the new information age. If development is to occur, it must take place in the context of this globalization and its many faces. As the *United Nations Millennium Declaration* observed in Resolution 55/2:

> We believe that the central challenge we face today is to ensure that globalizaiton becomes a positive force for all the world's people. For while globalization offers great opportunities, at present its benefits are very unevenly shared, while its costs are unevenly distributed. We recognize that developing countries and countries with economies in transition face special difficulties in responding to this central challenge.

While there is nearly universal telephone and cellular phone usage in developed countries, less than one-fifth of people in the developing world are subscribers to either. In 2001, access to a personal computer (PC) remained a very exclusive luxury available for less than 3 percent of the population in the Global South, while in the North PCs were rapidly entering most households. Far more telling, however, is the growing gap that has developed over the last decade in this regard. In 1990, relatively few persons had their own PCs. The tremendous gap that has developed has grown up in those few short years. The critical question is how to make the information revolution work for all peoples in all regions of the world.

Reflecting on the Millennium Declaration, it would seem in retrospect that the declaration greatly understated the issue, especially in the context of the global information and communications revolution. The tremendous inequalities inherent in the present information order—the so-called digital divide—present an awesome challenge for the international community:

> The scale of the ICT challenge is immense. Despite the forces of market liberalization and globalization and efforts at public policy reform, the goal of achieving universal access to ICT and the Global Information Infrastructure has remained elusive, and the disparity in access to ICT is growing. Today 96 percent of Internet

host computers reside in the highest income nations with only 16 percent of the world's population. There are more Internet hosts in Finland than the whole of Latin America and the Caribbean, more in New York City than on the entire continent of Africa.[85]

The challenge is not only that of coping with and overcoming poverty, hunger, and other aspects of underdevelopment. The tremendous imbalance inherent in the current information order also challenges cultural norms, linguistic diversity, local governance capacity and numerous other dimensions of basic human security.

With regard to promoting human development, it is important to put ICT in a larger context. The final report of the UNDP's Digital Opportunity Initiative has attempted to do just that:

> Numerous factors influence the extent and speed of social and economic development—not least political stability, physical infrastructure, basic literacy and basic health care. There is no suggestion that ICT can eliminate the need for these or offer a panacea for all development problems. But detailed analysis of experience around the world reveals ample evidence that, used in the right way and for the right purposes, ICT can have a dramatic impact on achieving specific social and economic development goals as well as play a key role in broader national development strategies. The real benefits lie not in the provision of technology per se, but rather in its application to create powerful social and economic networks by dramatically improving communication and the exchange of information.[86]

Indeed, "ICT provides developing nations with an unprecedented opportunity to meet vital development goals such as poverty reduction, basic healthcare, and education far more effectively than before."[87] In the highly globalized information age, it is hard to envision how development can occur without such social and economic networks.

These concerns have not been lost in idle words. The UN system has in many ways been energized by the possibilities ICT presents for promoting human development and achieving the MDGs. For some years now, the UNDP has been working with member states and other agencies to make ICT an integral part of development strategies and policies. Much of this work has focused on assisting countries integrate and prioritize ICT planning in their policy frameworks and Poverty Reduction Strategy Papers (PRSPs). Also, UNDP places emphasis on using ICT to improve governance and the capacity of government to more effectively achieve the MDGs and to foster greater participation of civil society and the private sector in governance.

In this area, creating effective partnerships among international institutions, governments, civil society and the private sector for promoting human development have grown. While some of these partnerships have been initiated by UN agencies, others have had their genesis outside the UN system. The Digital Opportunities Task Force (DOT Force), for example, was the initiative of the G-8 summit in Okinawa in July 2000. This initiative integrated the resources and talents of a variety of other partners, including the EU, a number of developing countries, the UNDP, World Bank, ITU, OECD, ECOSOC, UNESCO, and various private sector associations and NGOs. In the Okinawa Charter, the DOT Force focused on creating national "e-strategies," improving access and connectivity, human capacity building and promoting participation in e-commerce and enhancing entrepreneurship.[88] The task force presented its recommendations at the G-8 summit meeting in Genoa in 2001 and an implementation strategy was adopted for carrying out the "Genoa Plan of Action."

Another important initiative has been the United Nations Information and Communications Task Force (ICT Task Force), established by the Secretary-General in response to a March 2001 request from ECOSOC. The UN ICT Task Force was given the task of providing overall leadership to the UN and forge strategic partnership with private industry, foundations, donors, and other relevant stakeholders.[89] The ICT Task Force works in close cooperation with a growing number of other UN-system networking and capacity-building ICT initiatives, including the Digital Opportunity Initiative (launched by the UNDP, World Bank, Anderson Consulting and Markle Foundation), the Network Readiness and Resource Initiative (UN Foundation, IBM, Markle Foundation, World Economic Forum, Harvard University and other partners), the UN Volunteers (UNV) program's United Nations Information Technology Service (UNITS), WHO's Health InterNetwork, and Netaid.org. The list alone connotes how wide a net must be cast routinely even to form a task force with relevant expertise. As with other issues on the globalization agenda, the solutions must be found across disciplines and across countries and across institutions. That is what the "global" part of "globalization" means.

These efforts and others are being brought together in the planning and preparatory work for the World Summit on the Information Society. Resolution 56/183 states the purpose of the summit as developing "a common vision and understanding" of the information society and to adopt a declaration and plan of action for bridging the digital divide. The summit is unusual in that it is scheduled in two phases. The first is in Geneva in December 2003, and the second in Tunis in 2005. A Plan of Action to provide access to use ICTs effectively as tools for sustainable development is to be adopted at the 2003 meeting. Then, in 2005, the focus will be on assessing progress toward meeting those goals. The agenda is ambitious, and the stakes are high. As witnessed with the conferencing frenzy of the 1990s, the process is a large part of the outcome—building a consensus and a sense of shared commitment and determination.

Sum: Globalization, MDGs, Partnerships

Where does all this lead us? Depending on who is asked, the answer is likely to be quite different.

It seems clear enough that globalization is not a panacea. To say that it is a "golden straightjacket" that restricts choice but definitely leads to good things is far too simple a summary judgment.[90] There can be negatives, as noted: diseases may move faster and more broadly; wages and other benefits won by labor in one country or region may be undercut by capital moving to exploit cheap and unsophisticated labor elsewhere; and so forth. Trading and investment may be computerized, but that does little good to those beyond the communications revolution.

It also seems clear enough that a formal consensus exists over the Millennium Development Goals. Of course, the consensus is not universal. But, nonetheless, a generally shared orientation, underpinned by shared meanings and shared values, appears to be present. The primary element of disagreement is on the sacrifice that is necessary to make the development strategy work. Governments in Zimbabwe or Liberia, to take but two prominent examples, may vote for the MDGs in New York. But their policies on the ground at home reflect anything but a deep commitment to doing what is necessary to enhance human security there. Governments in Washington and Bern may also vote for the MDGs, but whether they are prepared to renegotiate debt relief and enhanced trade arrangements for the developing countries remains to be seen. The European Union continues to protect European agriculture to the detriment of the poor countries' sales to Europe.

UN agencies and Bretton Woods institutions have formed interesting and valuable partnerships in an effort to do something concrete about sustainable human development. Some results are impressive, but unfortunately not often in Sub-Sahara Africa or parts of South Asia. But international arrangements, whether called partnerships or international regimes, can do only so much in the context of war, failed states, and chronic thievery by ruling elites.

Our specific analysis above indicates that progress thus far toward achieving the Millennium Development Goals has been very mixed. In poverty-ridden Sub-Saharan Africa and least developed countries the situation is particularly bleak, as noted. In this context, Kofi Annan, speaking before the 2002 World Economic Forum in New York, designated poverty as a major threat to global security. As reflected on earlier, the Secretary-General, in his first annual report on how member states have followed up the Millennium Declaration, reflected disappointingly that "the world is falling short. If we carry on the way we are, most of the pledges are not going to be fulfilled." He referred to progress toward achieving the MDGs as being a mixed record, with significant differences across the world's regions.[91]

Without doubt there can be better movement toward achieving the Millennium Development Goals. Targets are set. Indicators have been specified. Results now need to be forthcoming. The specificity of the MDG process has played a major role in securing general widespread consensus. In the future, however, it may well be that same specificity that provides the greatest challenge to moving the UN's development agenda forward.

UN agencies and the Bretton Woods institutions have clearly made changes in behalf of the MDGs. But states need to do their part regarding creation and maintenance of political stability, reduction of corruption and crony capitalism, and reduction of military spending for the sake of socio-economic investments. States should also do more in the areas of trade and finance, particularly through reduction of trade barriers for the benefit of developing countries.

What is equally clear is that the Millennium Development Goals, even if they are achieved, in and of themselves are not a panacea for bringing about sustainable human development and human security. They do, however, serve to focus governments and peoples on the plight of the world's poor and marginalized peoples. The MDGs provide a prioritized focus for development assistance activities and give clear benchmarks against which to measure success and failure. And, most importantly, states and the inter-governmental institutions created by them are making concrete steps in the right direction.

Explaining Change

As a concept for guiding thinking and policy changes, sustainable human development may fade. But the social forces and global changes that underlie thinking on sustainability are unlikely to go away. Thus, students of international organization should struggle to understand why processes and structures in the UN have evolved as they have with regard to sustainable development, and consider what directions development activities might take in the future. It is in this context that a dispassionate assessment can be made of what the world organization can and cannot reasonably be expected to accomplish to promote sustainable development.

A traditional starting point for such an assessment is to examine these sustainable development activities in the context of functionalism. Functionalists argue that "growth of technology and spread and intensification of the desire for higher standards of material welfare" lead to greater international cooperation in search of expanded political authority.[92] A functionalist perspective suggests that popular interest in sustainable development results from expanded technical cooperation in developmental and environmental concerns. Accordingly, technical cooperation for development has spilled over into the environmental area, and technical cooperation on ecological concerns has come to encompass development issues. The interplay between the two has thus become so pervasive that environment and development are no longer separate concepts.

Proponents of this thesis point to the evolving process, beginning around the time of the Stockholm Conference, whereby the concept of ecodevelopment came onto the global agenda. In attempting to lay the foundations of a global plan of action for dealing with environmental issues, Maurice Strong and other UN planners quickly came to perceive the inseparability of the two previously separate issues. This orientation evolved over later decades as the environmental science community, development assistance practitioners and scholars, international financiers, government officials, and many others came to see their own work to be achievable only in the context of a more holistic ecodevelopment worldview.

The two explanations examined in Chapter 7 for the spread of cooperation in the human rights area—that is, consensual-knowledge communities and social learning—grow out of this more general functionalist perspective. The first explanation suggests that the convergence of development and environment into sustainable development and the subsequent convergence of sustainable development and human development/security into sustainable human development on the global public policy agenda grows from consensual agreement over ecodevelopment in private communities of knowledge. The second explanation emphasizes the importance of institutional learning and argues that the convergence is a product of a learning process in which state actors have recognized the inherent inseparability of the two issues.

Proponents of the consensual-knowledge approach point to the tremendous growth and involvement, at least of Northern civic actors, in sustainable development politics at the global intergovernmental level. They also point to the evolution of the role of NGOs since Stockholm, to the activities of NGOs in the Rio and subsequent conference processes, and to the influence of knowledge communities on issues such as protection of the ozone layer, as evidence that this approach is valid.[93]

The nature of the evolution of NGO involvement in the sustainable human development area, however, casts doubt on the validity of this view. There are hundreds of opinion communities concerned with sustainable development. Yet the diversity and often outright antagonisms among these communities challenge the notion that some dominant consensual body of knowledge underlies events within global sustainable development processes. The windows broken and the stores looted in Seattle, plus Genoa, Montreal, and Evian (the sites of G-8 summits) attest to this reality.[94]

This is not to suggest that at a general level there has not been a convergence of interests over sustainability issues. Indeed, the concept has come to dominate much of the debate over both development and environment. For example, there was a substantial increase in the number of articles about sustainable development in scientific journals in the years immediately before the Rio conference. These figures, however, can be misleading.

Although growing consensus can be observed within specific areas of environmental concern, that consensus has yet to be translated into a coherent global scientific consensus about sustainable development. Moreover, a large gulf still separates basic and applied scientists over many ecodevelopment issues.

The notion that some coherent and identifiable social learning process underpins global sustainable development activities is suspect, yet may hold somewhat more promise. On one hand, for example, it was not until after the election of Barber Conable as World Bank president in 1986 and the application of concerted pressure by NGOs that the World Bank showed any serious signs of becoming environmentally concerned. Before this time, Bank staff demonstrated little, if any, willingness to cooperate with UNEP or nonbusiness civic-based actors. As argued above, the idea of sustainable development has served as a common denominator bridging the turf and ideological divide that otherwise separates the financial and monetary institutions from other members of the UN family.[95]

Furthermore, there is no universal consensus about definitions. In global debates, Northern delegates continue to tend to define sustainability rather narrowly as environmental protection and resource conservation. Southerners normally define the concept with specific reference to meeting basic human needs and reducing poverty. The focus here is on people, on promoting economic growth that produces employment and encourages the wider participation of people in economic processes.[96] Economists have their own definition. They say sustainable development is "an economic process in which the quantity and quality of our stocks of natural resources (like forests) and the integrity of biogeochemical cycles (like climate) are sustained and passed on to the future generations unimpaired."[97]

On the other hand, the feedback from seemingly endless conferencing processes and the ever-evolving closer relationship among previously discordant agencies—especially the Bretton Woods institutions and UN organizations—may have well served to create a genuine learning environment. Equally important, the Global Compact was from its origins a normative exercise designed to create social learning. One of its architects, John Ruggie, pointed out: "Companies submit case studies of what they have done to translate their commitment to the GC principles into concrete corporate practices. This occasions a dialogue among GC participants from all sectors—the UN, labor, and civil society organizations . . . . A research network, led by the Corporate Citizenship Unit of Warick University, facilitates the dialogue. Its aim is to reach broader consensus-based definitions of what constitutes good practices than any of the parties could achieve alone. Those definitions, together with illustrative case studies, are then publicized in an on-line learning bank, which will become a standard reference source for corporate social responsibility."[98]

Of course, these examples do not provide concrete proof of an effective learning process. However, they do point to the possibility that organizational learning may well be occurring and helps to explain the growing convergence around the MDG consensual framework.

Notes

1. Portions of this chapter draw on Roger A. Coate and Gail Karlsson, "Mobilizing Support for the Millennium Development Goals," *A Global Agenda: Issues before the 58th General Assembly* (New York: Rowman & Littlefield, 2003), chapter 5. This annual publication is a good source for "what's new?"

2. UN document A/RES/55/2, September 18, 2000.

3. Kofi A. Annan, *"We the Peoples": The Role of the United Nations in the 21st Century* (New York: UN, 2000), pp. 9–10. Also available at www.un.org/millennium/sg/report/.

4. UN document A.AC.253/25, March 22, 2000.

5. For a recent selection, see Rorden Wilkinson and Steve Hughes, eds., *Global Governance: Critical Perspectives* (London: Routledge, 2002); Esref Aksu and Joseph A. Camilleri, eds., *Democratizing Global Governance* (New York: Palgrave, 2002); Robert O'Brien, Ann Marie Goetz, Jan Aaart Scholte, and Marc Williams, *Contesting Global Governance: Multilateral Economic Institutions and Global Social Movements* (Cambridge: Cambridge University Press, 2000); Paul Kennedy, Dirk Messner, and Franz Nuscheler, *Global Trends and Global Governance* (London: Pluto, 2002); Andrew F. Cooper, John English, and Ramesh Thakur, eds., *Enhancing Global Governance: Towards a New Diplomacy* (Tokyo: UN University Press, 2002); and Anthony Giddens, *Runaway World: How Globalization Is Reshaping Our Lives* (New York: Routledge, 2000).

6. UNCTAD Press Release, "World FDI Flows Exceed U.S. $1.1 Trillion in 2000," TAD/INF/PR/075, July 12, 2000.

7. Ibid.

8. Ibid.

9. Nagire Woods, "The Political Economy of Globalization," in Nagire Woods, *The Political Economy of Globalization* (New York: St. Martin's Press, 2000), pp. 1–19.

10. Jan Aart Scholte, *Globalization: A Critical Introduction* (New York: St. Martin's Press, 2000), pp. 13–40.

11. "Impact of Globalization on Social Development," UN document A.AC.253/25, March 12, 2000, pp. 3–8.

12. Jan Aart Scholte, "Globalization: Governance and Corporate Citizenship," Remarks to the Third Annual Warwick Corporate Citizenship Unit Conference, Searman House, Warwick, July 10, 2000, p. 4.

13. David Held and Anthony McGrew, David Goldblatt, and Jonathan Perraton, *Global Transformations: Politics, Economics and Culture* (Cambridge: Polity Press, 1999).

14. Ibid., p. 5.

15. Jan Aart Scholte, *Globalization: A Critical Introduction* (New York: St. Martin's Press, 2000).

16. John Gerard Ruggie, "Territoriality and Beyond: Problematizing Modernity in International Relations," *International Organization* 47, no. 1 (Winter 1993), pp. 139–174.

17. For an examination of these issues, see Held et al., *Global Transformations*.

18. Ankie Hoogvelt, *Globalization and the Postcolonial World*, second edition (Baltimore: Johns Hopkins University Press, 2001); and Manuel Castells, *The Rise of the Network Society* (Cambridge: Oxford University Press, 1996).

19. Hoogvelt, *Globalization*, p. 121.

20. See Hoogvelt's review of the writings of Roland Robertson, David Harvey, Anthony Giddens, and Manuel Castells in this regard in ibid., pp. 120–143.

21. James H. Mittelman and Norani Othman, *Capturing Globalization* (London: Routledge, 2001).

22. Available at http://elink.unaids.org/menew/MDG/MDG.asp.

23. Available at http://www.unmillenniumproject.org/html/about.shtm.

24. UNDP, *Human Development Report 2003* (New York: Oxford University Press, 2003).

25. NGLS Roundup, "MDGs: Moving Forward the Millennium Development Goals," November 2002.

26. UN document A/48/183, 1993.

27. UN Department for Policy Coordination and Sustainable Development, *Bulletin on the Eradication of Poverty*, No. 1 (1996).

28. Available at www.developmentgoals.org/Poverty.htm.

29. Available at http://millenniumindicators.un.org/unsd/mi/mi_worldregn.asp.

30. "Education for All: Meeting Our Collective Commitments," World Economic Forum, Dakar, Senegal, April 26–28, 2000.

31. Available at www.unesco.org/bpi/eng/unescopress/2002/02–93e.shtml.

32. Available at www.developmentgoals.org/Education.htm.

33. Available at www.paris21.org/betterworld/education.htm.

34. Available at http://potyal.unesco.org/education/ev.php?URL_ID=5000&URL_DO=DO_TOPIC&URL.

35. Mark Malloch Brown, "World's Top Goals Require Women's Empowerment," March 8, 2003.

36. Available at www.developmentgoals.org/Gender_Equality.htm.

37. UNIFEM Press Release, May 1, 2003.

38. Available at www.un.org/womenwatch/daw/cedaw/.

39. UN Commission on Human Rights Press Release, April 9, 2003.

40. Available at www.unodc.org/unodc/en/trafficking_human_beings.html.

41. Available at www.odccp.org/odccp/trafficking_human_beings.html.

42. UN document EGM/TRAF/2002/WP.2, November 8, 2002.

43. UN document E/CN.4/2002/L.63, paragraph 19.

44. See further www.who.int/mdg/en/.

45. See www.developmentgoals.org/Child_Mortality.htm.

46. http://www.developmentgoals.org/Child_Mortality.htm.

47. WHO Press Relase, May 26, 2003.

48. See Leon Gordenker, Roger A. Coate, Christer Jönsson, and Peter Söderholm, *International Cooperation in Response to AIDS* (London: Pinter, 1995); and Peter Söderholm, *Global Governance of AIDS: Partnerships with Civil Society* (Lund: Lund University Press, 1997).

49. UNAIDS, AIDS Epidemic Update December 2001.

50. UNAIDS, AIDS Epidemic Update December 2002.

51. UNAIDS, AIDS Epidemic Update December 2001.

52. WHO Press Release/ReliefWeb, February 1, 2002.

53. UNAIDS, AIDS Epidemic Update December 2002, p. 30.

54. Ibid.

55. World Bank, *Education and HIV/AIDS: A Window of Hope*, available at www.worldbank.org/developmentnews/stories/html/050802a.htm.

56. Global HIV Prevention Working Group, *Access to HIV Prevention: Closing the Gap*, UNAIDS, May 2003.

57. World Bank Press Release, May 27, 2003.

58. Available at http://millenniumindicators.un.org/unsd/mi/mi_worldregn.asp.

59. WHO, Africa Malaria Report 2003, available at www.rbm.who.int/amd2003/amr2003/.

60. UNICEF Press Release, May 13, 2003.

61. WHO Press Release, May 22, 2003.

62. Available at http://china-un.org/eng/24581.html.

63. Available at http://china-un.org/eng/20234.html.

64. Available at www.developmentgoals.org/Partnership.htm.

65. Available at http://www.worldpartner.com/ MMI.html.

66. Available at www.imf.org/external/np/exr/facts/hipc.htm.

67. Available at www.imf.org/external/np/exr/facts/prgf.htm.

68. UNDP, *Overcoming Human Poverty: UNDP Poverty Report 2000* (New York: UN, 2000), chapter 5.

69. UNDP, *UNDP Today: Fighting Poverty* (New York: UN, 1999).

70. UNDP, *Overcoming Human Poverty*.

71. World Bank Press Release, February 14, 2001.

72. Report by the Secretary-General, "Acceleration of Development in Africa and the Least Developed Countries," UN document A/AC.253/22, February 24, 2000, p. 2.

73. UNDP, *Human Development Report 1999* (New York: Oxford University Press, 1999).

74. UN document A/CONF.191/11, 8 June 2001.

75. Available at www.developmentgoals.org/Partnership.htm.

76. Available at www.un.org/special-rep/ohrlls/lldc/default.htm.

77. UN document A/57/340, August 23, 2002.

78. UN document A/57/340, August 23, 2002.

79. UN document A/CONF.167/9, part I, Annex I (1994).

80. UN document A/S–22/9/Rev.1 and Supplement No. 3(A/S–22/9/Rev.1).

81. Available at www.un.org/esa/sustdev/documents/WSSD_POI_PD/English/POI Chapter7.htm.

82. Available at www.un.org/special-rep/ohrlls/ohrlls/aboutus.htm.

83. Available at http://www.wto.org/english/tratop_e/trips_e/pharma_ato186_e.htm.

84. Available at www.wto.org/wto/english/thewto_e/minist_e/min01_e/mindecl_trips_e.htm.

85. UNDP Fast Facts: "Driving Information and Communications Technology for Development, A UNDP Agenda for Action 2000–2001," October 2000.

86. Available at www.opt-init.org/framework/pages/es.html.

87. UNDP Fast Facts: "Driving Information."

88. Available at http://usembassy.state.gov/tokyo/wwwhg063.htm.

89. Available at www.unicttaskforce.org/about/principal.asp.

90. Thomas Friedman, *The Lexus and the Olive Tree* (New York: HarperCollins, 1999).

91. Available at www.in.org/News/briefings/docs/2002/mdgpc.doc.htm.

92. Harold Jacobson, *Networks of Interdependence* (New York: Alfred A. Knopf, 1984), pp. 62–63.

93. See, for example, Peter Haas, "Banning Chlorofluorocarbons: Epistemic Community Efforts to Protect Stratospheric Ozone," *International Organization* 46, no. 1 (Winter 1992), pp. 187–224.

94. For a more optimistic view, see Michael Edwards, *Future Positive: International Cooperation in the 21ˢᵗ Century* (London: Earthscan, 2000); and *NGO Rights and Responsibilities: A New Deal for Global Governance* (London: Foreign Policy Centre, 2000).

95. For an overview of the evolution of ecodevelopment politics, see Lynton K. Caldwell, *International Environmental Policy: Emergence and Dimensions*, second edition (Durham, N.C.: Duke University Press, 1991), p. 81.

96. Alvao Soto, "The Global Environment: A Southern Perspective," *International Journal* 15, no. 8 (Autumn 1992), pp. 679–705; and UNDP, *Human Development Report 1993* (New York: Oxford University Press, 1993). This theme reappears in all subsequent annual reports.

97. Anil Agarwal, "What Is Sustainable Development?" *Concordare* no. 4 (Spring 1993), p. 2.

98. John Gerard Ruggie, "Global_governance.net The Global Compact as Learning Network," *Global Governance* 7, no. 4 (2001), pp. 372–373.

Conclusion

Learning from Change

> In a time when winds of change are blowing very strong, we must rest content with knowing that foresight is always imperfect and that choices must always be made in ignorance of their full consequences. That is the price we pay for being able to make the world over by changing our own behavior, individually and collectively, in response to cherished hopes and shared purposes, framed in words. Our capacity to err is our capacity to learn and thereby achieve partial and imperfect, but real, improvement in the conditions of human life.
>
> —William H. McNeill, "Winds of Change,"
> *Foreign Affairs* 69, no. 4 (May-June 1995)

From the outset of this book, we have portrayed the United Nations and the broader system of UN-related autonomous organizations as highly interdependent with their political context. We have shown the dynamic interplay of interstate politics as the primary force determining the evolution of the UN system. With the blinders of Cold War views removed, even in a world of clear United States military primacy, it is becoming clearer that global organizations can influence the course of world politics—especially when viewed from a longer-run perspective. For the United Nations to become the centerpiece of global governance, as envisioned by some of its proponents, however, states would need to transfer much more loyalty, power, and authority to the world body so that it could control its surroundings rather than the reverse. But such a radical change is still distant. Yet world politics continues to evolve and change, and there is a pressing need to manage transnational problems.[1]

It would help us analyze the UN and chart its future if we had a sure grasp of the nature of world politics after the Cold War. In William McNeill's words, it would certainly be nice to know in which direction the winds of change are blowing. Alas, this is not easy. The initial euphoria about the end of the Cold War and optimism about possibilities for democratization have given way to a more realistic, and perhaps normal, caution. The winds seem to be swirling in no discernible direction. As we have portrayed in the previous chapters, UN security operations increased rapidly beginning in 1988, then declined, then underwent renewed attention. The notion of security has been broadened incrementally and inconsistently to encompass the idea of human security—a still evolving concept. The requirements for global action in the humanitarian affairs and human rights arenas have been expanding. Discourse certainly has changed, and advances in humanitarian delivery and prevention have been very much in evidence, yet the world organization's capacity to respond has not kept pace with demands; budgetary shortfalls hinder effective responses. Moreover, some challenges to the predominance of liberal democracy seem to be gaining strength, as we see especially in fundamental political Islamic circles. On the human development front, the world is becoming ever more polarized between the rich and poor, with some of the poorest—in Sub-Sahara Africa especially—losing absolute as well as relative ground. Yet we have also seen growing consensus, in the form of the UN Millennium Development Goals, about what should be done to advance sustainable human development.

James Rosenau tells us that world politics is characterized by "turbulence" in which basic patterns are not clear.[2] In this view, world politics can be conceptualized as having "macro" and "micro" dimensions, with "macro" covering the world of states and IGOs and "micro" covering the world of individuals, local communities, and other elements of civil society. Both are in such turmoil at the beginning of the twenty-first century that one can only project alternative scenarios for the future, not specifically describe the likely structure or basic features of world politics.

Our readers may have noted also that during the United Nations' first half-century, the density of UN politics covering individuals and NGOs was quite different in the three parts of the book. In the security arena, where states historically have presumably had a monopoly on force—except over insurgents and terrorists—considerably fewer non-governmental organizations have dealt with large-scale force than with human rights or sustainable development. In the human rights and sustainable development arenas, NGOs are active in analysis, lobbying, and operations to such a degree that students may be blinded by the number of acronyms that appear in this text. Yet in today's turbulent world political climate and the increasingly nonstate character of threats to global, regional, and local peace, there are mounting pressures to think in terms of human security—as opposed to state security—and a need to integrate elements and dimensions of civil society into the security sphere.

Some scholars attempt to deal with such turbulence by focusing on the importance of competing forces in shaping world politics and international organization. Some frame their analyses in terms of simultaneous forces of integration and disintegration. For example, West European states formed the European Community (now European Union), which transcends the territorial state in some ways, creating a supranational authority for some issues. In some of these very same states, political movements—such as the Basque movement in Spain—are seeking smaller political-legal units. For an example of competing forces within a single country, some circles of opinion in the United States want more multilateral diplomacy; others insist that the United States should withdraw from most IGOs and pursue a unilateral foreign policy that is driven strictly by narrow American interests and that is unaffected by the interests of the larger community of states. In yet another contrast, the United States, Canada, and Mexico negotiated a free trade agreement (the North American Free Trade Agreement, or NAFTA) directed at the larger collective good while former federal

Yugoslavia disintegrated into a bloody conflict of smaller nationalisms. Competing centripetal and centrifugal forces are integral to the clash between globalism and localism highlighted in the preceding pages and will remain so in the foreseeable future.[3]

In world politics after the Cold War the United Nations is caught in a political transition. The old patterns of interaction have broken down or changed significantly, but new patterns have not yet crystallized. Many old norms—like non-intervention in domestic affairs—are under challenge, but new ones—like humanitarian intervention—have not yet been codified. Old ways of doing things may prove insufficient for new problems, yet new ways may be characterized by mistakes. States may be dissatisfied with the record of the old United Nations, but they may not yet have reached the point of providing the political will and material resources necessary for a new UN to manage world politics after the Cold War.

Even in more stable times, it is not easy to agree on the principal lessons to be learned from history. History has been as much misused as well used in guiding foreign policy.[4] Many U.S. policymakers misused the "lesson of Munich" in fashioning policy for Southeast Asia in the 1960s and 1970s. Believing that in 1938 the Western states whetted the aggressive appetite of Hitler by appeasing him through the "give-away" of Czechoslovakia in negotiations at Munich, these policymakers were determined not to "give away" South Vietnam to the communists. This, it was thought, would only whet the aggressive appetite of other communist leaders in Hanoi, Beijing, and Moscow. Yet the eventual creation of a communist Vietnam in 1975 did not lead to falling dominoes throughout Asia and the world. Indeed, by the 1990s communism itself was retreating virtually everywhere. Even governments that called themselves "communist," as in China and Vietnam, used increasingly capitalist policies in their pursuit of economic growth. The United States lost more than 55,000 of its own military personnel in Southeast Asia and killed a much larger number of Asians by using a myth as a guide. The intentions may have been noble to the extent that U.S. policymakers believed that they were fighting for freedom, but the results were disastrous for almost everyone involved.

One can try to be careful and systematic in wrestling with the lessons of history.[5] One can try to separate what is known from what is unknown or just presumed. In using historical analogies, one can try to be precise about the similarities to, or differences from, a current situation. One can delve into the details of history, clarify current options, guard against presumptions, avoid stereotypes. But in the final analysis, there is much room for debate about the pertinence of particular historical lessons.

Nevertheless, when many policymakers look at a contemporary problem, they draw on historical evidence. The ones who do not even try are justly criticized for this deficiency. In the 1990s the UN secretariat was fairly criticized for not having a policy-planning group able to draw historical lessons from past use of UN force. Certain state bureaucracies, and many academics, were prepared to evaluate UN peacekeeping against the historical background of what had gone wrong with ONUC in the Belgian Congo in 1960 to 1964, or what had gone right in Central America regarding ONUSAL and ONUCA.

The next time there is a UN enforcement action inside a country, whether to deliver humanitarian relief or to disarm fighting parties, it will be only natural to try to draw historical lessons from events in northern Iraq, Somalia, Bosnia, Rwanda, Haiti, or Kosovo in the 1990s. The next time the UN Security Council authorizes the use of force in response to aggression, many policymakers will draw comparisons with the historical lessons from events of 1990–1991 in Iraq and Kuwait. The fact that there was a decline in UN peacekeeping operations after the mid-1990s does not lessen the need for organizational learning. Experience in Kosovo and Timor indicated that there would be cases in which peacekeeping and enforcement actions would be deemed necessary in the twenty-first century—in the Democratic Republic of the Congo, for example. The lessons, such as they are, from Afghanistan and the war in Iraq are simply unknown as we face challenges of terrorism and weapons of mass destruction (WMD).

One factor that complicates the task of learning is the pace of change in the 1990s; the other is the culture of the UN bureaucracy. An examination of UN military operations is illustrative of a more general problem of learning within the world organization. We noted at the outset of this book the dramatic acceleration in the number and variety of UN military missions—the Security Council approved over twice as many operations from 1989 to 1996 as during the previous forty years. There also has been a proliferation of analyses about multilateral military operations from a variety of perspectives since 1990, mostly in journals rather than books.[6] The so-called War on Terrorism adds yet more uncertainty. As one outspoken UN official wrote, we "too often find ourselves steering a rattling vehicle that is moving at breakneck speed, without an up-to-date roadmap, while trying to fix the engine at the same time."[7]

Learning lessons is different from adapting, because adapting is more reactive and less comprehensive and is represented by incremental and often ambiguous institutional change. As two of the foremost analysts of institutional learning, Peter and Ernst Haas, have written, "Organizations characterized by irreconcilable disagreements over desirable world orders or ineptitude may not even be made capable of learning to manage interdependence rather than merely adapting to it."[8]

The United Nations still has to make a substantial effort to digest the lessons from the recent past in order to formulate a workable strategy for future military operations. The mere establishment of the Lessons-Learned Unit in the Department of Peace-keeping Operations (DPKO), along with similarly labeled units in the Department of Political Affairs (DPA) and Office for the Coordination of Humanitarian Affairs (OCHA), is not necessarily evidence of progress. These units were established in the 1990s but are largely bureaucratic responses by both of the "two United Nations"—the first, where governments meet and make decisions, and the second, comprising the various secretariats, officials, and soldiers who implement these decisions.

In drawing historical lessons, it is important to consider closely three fundamental political tasks that are characteristic of policymaking and problem solving: articulating interests and consolidating interest groups, making rules, and applying those rules.[9] We conclude this analysis of the first fifty years of the United Nations with our evaluation of what has been learned along these lines. We chart change at the UN before and after the Cold War, and we suggest what these changes portend for the immediate future.

Articulation and Aggregation of Interests

It is important, albeit elementary, that governments of states have learned that they need the United Nations. After the Cold War many new states wanted to join the UN; none of the old members wanted to get out. Since 1945 only one state, Indonesia, has withdrawn even temporarily from the world organization, and its quixotic attempt to create a rival organization soon collapsed. The delegation from South Africa was barred for a time, during part of the apartheid era, from participating in the General Assembly, but the state was still a member of the organization. All states recognize that they need the UN to build diplomatic coalitions, make rules, and monitor adherence to and enforce those rules. The cliché happens to be true: If the UN did not exist, it would have to be invented. This is as true in Washington as elsewhere.

In our preface and introduction we noted the importance of how states defined their national interests, and how these definitions affect the UN's evolution. We noted the crucial nature of short-term and narrow interests. As a general rule, "the United Nations is successful over the long haul only if it helps to uncover or develop genuinely shared interests."[10] A dominant state or coalition can control policy for a time, but the United Nations is likely to be more effective if it is used in pursuit of widely shared interests.

After the Cold War, the United States was the most important state in the UN. It was the only state capable of projecting military power everywhere in the world, it had the world's largest economy, and at least since 1941 it had periodically played a leadership role in world politics. In fact, the United States had always been the UN's most important member state. The UN had never undertaken the use of force, for either peacekeeping or enforcement, without genuine U.S. support. The UN had attempted human rights and economic programs in opposition to U.S. policy, but these programs had not achieved much. The rejection of SUNFED is a good example of the futility of attempting a major program without Washington's support. One should also recall the fate of demands for the NIEO, which floundered largely because of adamant U.S. opposition.

To be sure, many UN members were not altogether happy with U.S. domination of the UN in the early twenty-first century. At one point the General Assembly passed a resolution criticizing the United States for continuing its economic pressures against Cuba; and in 2002 the United States failed to be given a seat on the Human Rights Commission (HRC) for the first time since its creation. This was a viable manifestation in UN proceedings of resentment against U.S. power. The lack of support from Washington for the Convention on the Rights of the Child, the treaty to ban land mines, the Kyoto Protocol to slow global warming, the diplomacy to restrict the introduction of light arms into conflict zones, and the International Criminal Court (ICC) led to much criticism of U.S. unilateralism.[11] This international criticism of U.S. unilateralism became a torrent after the United States led an invasion of Iraq in 2003 without Security Council authorization. Of course a number of governments supported the Bush administration's position about the need to remove the Saddam Hussein regime, and there was more general deference to Washington's hegemonic position. While noting U.S. unilateralism, we can recall that there were indeed a number of issues at the UN on which there was genuine shared interest among UN members. Most states were opposed to Iraqi aggression in 1991. Most states were appalled at human suffering in Somalia about 1992. Most states were in favor of at least diplomatic support for human rights. Most states recognized the need to promote sustainable development.

It is helpful to think of world politics as a multi-level game. On the military level, or chessboard, the United States clearly has primacy. But on the economic level, the expanding European Union and the cumulative weight of Asia means that the United States, while very important, is not clearly primary in power. The UNDP *Human Development Report 1996* argued that if the past quarter century of economic growth rates is any indication of things to come, the next century may be an Asian one, not an American- or Euro-centered one: "The more than 7% average annual per capita income growth rate of East Asia in the 1970s and 1980s is the most sustained and widespread development miracle of the twentieth century, perhaps all history."[12] Beyond the military and economic levels of world politics, the more general diplomatic level manifests much more multilateral elements. The United States was not able to block the landmine treaty or the treaty creating an International Criminal Court.

The complexity of world politics and the difficulty of extracting precise lessons of history—in general the challenge of knowing which way the winds of change are blowing—serves as appropriate background for a final review of our three main issue areas.

Security Issues

In the 1990s the United States was the primary player or moving force in the UN campaign to repel Iraqi aggression against Kuwait, to pressure Iraq to comply with various UN resolutions after Desert Storm, to deliver humanitarian relief in Somalia, and to make other UN security operations succeed. In a continuation of past patterns, no UN security operation was undertaken against the wishes of Washington. When the UN was less than fully effective in some security matters, as early on in Bosnia or Haiti, it was largely a reflection of the unwillingness of the United States to engage fully.

This is not to say that other states were unimportant after the Cold War in UN security affairs. Japan played a very large role in UNTAC's efforts to stabilize and democratize Cambodia. The British and French deployed relatively large numbers of peacekeeping troops in the Balkans. Canada and Norway and some other states continued to be stalwart supporters of UN peacekeeping. The French mounted an operation in Rwanda and Congo, the Russians in Georgia, and the Nigerians in Liberia. And indeed, it should be recalled that all the permanent members of the Security Council have to at least avoid using the veto for UN decisions in peace and security matters to be made. Apart from Security Council members, numerous states have supported UN peace and security efforts. For example, Costa Rica and other Spanish-speaking states played important roles in supporting mediation by the UN Secretary-General in Central America in the 1980s.

The first Reagan administration aside, in general it is usually the case that the United States wants at least the UN's collective approval, and sometimes the UN's more direct help, in managing security issues. It is still not clear at the time of writing, however, how the George W. Bush administration saw the UN in this regard. It took its concerns about Iraq to the Security Council in 2002, but it attacked Iraq in 2003 without a UN blessing. However, after the brief combat, the Bush administration went back to the council for approval of its plans for occupation and reconstruction of Iraq. True, early occupation was directed by Washington. But as difficulties mounted, it seemed the Bush team was more amenable to UN involvement.

Despite U.S. unilateral use of force in places such as Grenada and Panama and its almost total exclusion of the UN from the negotiations leading to the Dayton peace accords for the former Yugoslavia, the dominant trend among all states, including the United States, is to involve the UN in managing military security problems. Logically, if emotional unilateralism does not interfere, there should be a desire by all to share responsibility and costs. As explained in Part One, one of the reasons for relying on the UN for the collective management of security issues is that most other collective options, aside from NATO, offer so little prospect of success; at a minimum, the world organization is required to be associated with security efforts to make subcontracted states and coalitions of the willing more accountable for actions undertaken in the name of the larger community of states. For instance, when Nigeria became bogged down in trying to pacify Liberia and Sierra Leone through the use of ECOWAS, this had the effect of increasing, not lessening, demands that the UN become more involved, which in fact actually transpired.

It is too soon to know at the time of writing, but Iraq may come to look similar to Kosovo, which provided a model for a kind of division of labor. The United States led in military action without UN authorization, but the UN came to be deeply involved in post-combat transitions. It may even be the case that in Afghanistan, Washington may wish that it had involved the UN more in various post-combat operations, given that reconstruction under U.S. and NATO influence was floundering.

Overall, both great and small powers have sought to confer on the UN an enhanced security role after the Cold War. The articulation of interests and aggregation of interest groups have varied from issue to issue. And states have not always provided sufficient political and material support to enable UN forces and representatives to succeed. Nevertheless, most states seem to have learned that major problems can be entailed in pursuing unilateral action. Apart from direct threats to a state's existence, multilateral security diplomacy has been the preferable option. For example, no state wanted to intervene unilaterally in what was then eastern Zaire in 1996 to guarantee refugee security; Canada was willing to lead a multilateral effort via the UN but was slower than the rebels, who took matters into their own hands and liberated Hutus held hostage in camps. And by 2003, after what may have been the death of 3.3 million people, the UN was once again seized of trying to stabilize what had become known, once again, as the Congo.

There is no doubt but that the basically U.S. and British attack on Iraq in 2003 greatly damaged the UN. From 1919, there had been a major international effort to restrict the first use of force; U.S. policy undermined this historic effort—in a bold and brazen way.[13] Council debates were well publicized. There was no ambiguity in the fact that the United States was resorting to first use of force when a majority in the council, not just a few dissidents, did not believe the use of force was then justified or that diplomacy had been exhausted. Yet many observers thought it was highly premature to dismiss the role of the council in the future.[14] We share this view. We have already indicated above the reasons why multilateral management of security issues is the dominant long-term trend, and why the George W. Bush administration has not been totally dismissive of UN involvement in conflict situations (although there are some strong unilateralists in that administration). First use of force without council authorization cannot be ruled out, witness Kosovo and the 2003 Iraq war, but the historical trend to try to greatly restrict that first use of force will continue. The UN will be a central forum in that regard.

Human Rights Interests

As explained in Chapter 5, the United States has been much less of a dominant or hegemonic leader in human rights than in security and economic affairs.[15] The articulation of human rights interests and the aggregation of human rights interest groups, principally through the UN Human Rights Commission, has come about less because of the United States and more because of a series of compromises among a large number of states. Nevertheless, at the 1993 Vienna World Conference on Human Rights, U.S. delegates played the leading role in pushing for reaffirmation of universal human rights. At one point they circulated an informal list of the states that were dragging their diplomatic feet. And when it came to the matter of delivering humanitarian assistance in situations of armed conflict, the UN took the most decisive steps in northern Iraq and Somalia, precisely where the United States displayed the most interest and commitment.

Whatever the U.S. role, just as most states sought to involve the UN in the management of security issues, so most states sought to use the world organization to promote human rights through international standards and to give at least some attention to their implementation—mostly by diplomacy. Particularly after the Cold War, human rights were vigorously articulated by many democratic governments that had succeeded authoritarian ones—whether communist or otherwise. The Czech Republic and Uruguay are just two examples of governments that sought extensive UN action on human rights as a result of their own previous and traumatic experience with the denial of most internationally recognized rights.

Certainly there were states—for example, China, Cuba, Iraq, Syria, Vietnam, and Malaysia—that resisted this dominant trend. Others, such as Saudi Arabia, Algeria, and various states throughout the Middle East, also opposed UN action on human rights, but they found it politically prudent to keep a low profile.

But it remains true that most governmental officials have articulated either a moral or an expediential interest in internationally recognized human rights. They have learned that the advancement of such rights is conducive to human dignity or that such rights have politically desirable consequences—for example, international peace, domestic tranquility, and uninterrupted foreign assistance. There has been little alternative for states but to use the United Nations for the articulation and aggregation of universal human rights interests. One can in theory develop universal human rights standards outside the UN. International humanitarian law was developed in this way for human rights in armed conflicts, but this is the major exception that proves the general rule that international society needs the United Nations for the articulation and aggregation of global human rights rules. The UN has been the scene of debates about the wisdom of various types of international criminal courts.

It is a very important question whether most states have now learned the wisdom of developing international courts so as to move the protection of human rights (including international humanitarian law in armed conflict) from the diplomatic to the judicial realm. Whether the community of states can move from the two primary ad hoc courts for former Yugoslavia and Rwanda to an important ICC, is a major question. Whether other partially international courts, as for Cambodia under the Khmer Rouge or for Sierra Leone, can advance the role of international courts in international human rights and humanitarian matters bears close scrutiny.[16]

Ironically, the U.S., which leads a determined opposition to the ICC, is the locus of much litigation over internationally recognized human rights in its own courts. Under national legislation dating from the eighteenth century, private parties can bring legal claims against other private parties for violating international law. There have been many court cases in the U.S. dealing with such internationally recognized human rights violations as torture, forced labor, and rape. Private individuals and corporations, of various nationalities, have been defendants. So while the United States bitterly opposes a Belgian law leading to legal charges against various national leaders, including some Americans, U.S. law itself shows that individuals and human rights NGOs are pushing for more judicial protection of human rights and humanitarian standards, whether in international or national courts.[17] Clearly, UN norms on human rights can be adjudicated in national courts.

Sustainable Development

In Chapters 8–10, we have shown how the UN has been a central forum for the articulation and aggregation of interests regarding sustainable human development—a.k.a. "human security." We pointed out how the adoption of the Millennium Development Goals (MDGs) represents a culmination of this long process, which has taken some five decades.

The UN network used to be used mostly by developing countries to articulate, as an aggregate, their views of what should be done about poverty in particular and underdevelopment in general. Some of their demands, such as for SUNFED and the NIEO, did not lead to "planetary bargains" between North and South, but now major compromises have been struck, with various UN agencies and personalities playing important roles in facilitating that agreement. Over time the rich countries have come around to the view that UN agencies have important roles to play in bridging the

North-South divide and that private markets alone cannot provide all that is necessary to overcome underdevelopment in all its forms.

It is now clear in the MDGs that ecological protection is very much part of the quest for sustainable human development. The 1992 Rio Conference, where the lengthy Agenda 21 was hammered out and articulated as a policy guideline for the twenty-first century, and where treaties on biodiversity and rain forests were negotiated, remains part of the basic road map in this regard. The processes of negotiation represent important steps in interest-group aggregation and articulation in the ecodevelopment arena. Therefore Agenda 21 and various conventions and declarations that emerged from the Rio process are perhaps best seen as snapshots of an evolving political process, not as static political outcomes. The Commission on Sustainable Development, like the United Nations Environment Program (UNEP) itself twenty years earlier, was the result of a compromise among states about what the United Nations could do to interject environmental protection into efforts to produce economic growth.

The United Nations has not exercised a monopoly over efforts to articulate interests related to sustainable development. All developed countries, and many developing ones as well, have their individual programs for environmental protection. Regional organizations such as the European Union also have environmental programs that, when added to efforts to ensure economic growth, produce a combined policy on sustainable development. But as with security and human rights issues, the UN has been used by various actors to articulate a vision of how economic growth can be combined with protection of the environment.

Naturally on such a complex matter as ecodevelopment or sustainable human development or human security, different views persist. Should UN agencies and the World Bank continue to support massive dam projects that displace many? Should the Kyoto Protocol be central to efforts to combat global warming? What is a reasonable economic cost to pay for enhanced ecological measures? We noted with regard to security issues that there were long-term trends toward multilateral management of many particular issues in that domain. The same seems to be true for development, with general agreement often accompanied by particular disagreement.

Rule-Making

Every society requires a collective procedure to establish rules that differentiate permissible from impermissible behavior. The United Nations plays a central role in this essential rule-making for international society—largely through the Security Council, General Assembly, and associated world conferences—but other mechanisms in international society also create rules. Some treaties are made outside the UN system, and some regional organizations make rules. The murky institution of customary international law, which is greatly affected by the behavior of powerful states, also plays a role. But in the final analysis, the UN has a major role in rule-making for world politics regarding all three of our issues, to which we now turn in an attempt to appreciate what has been learned about rule-making in the past five decades.

Security Rules

Many security rules for world politics have been vague. Neither the International Court of Justice (ICJ) nor the Security Council has specified the distinction between a breach of the peace and outright aggression. Moreover, the term "intervention" has never been authoritatively specified; despite a 1974 General Assembly attempt to define aggression, many ambiguities remain. The 1998 Rome Statute for the International Criminal Court recognizes this problem, indicating that no charges can be brought against individuals for aggression until that concept is better specified in international law. Moreover, are reprisals legal in peacetime given that the UN Charter has outlawed the threat or use of force in the absence of an armed attack? Can force be used to implement legal rights? Can a regional organization employ force without prior authorization from the Security Council? These and other questions about security rules could benefit from clearer answers.

Since the end of the Cold War, the Security Council in particular has made a number of decisions that clarify at least some questions about security rule-making. The council is sharpening security rules far more than the World Court. The latter does not normally get the opportunity to pronounce on legal issues related to armed conflict. Most states have regarded security rules as too important to be turned over to fifteen jurists. Therefore, they have not given consent to the court to rule on these matters. The case of *Nicaragua vs. the United States* (1986) is an exception that proves the general rule (and the wisdom of that judgment was extensively debated—especially by the United States, which, having lost the case, refused to implement the judgment). If international security law is to be clarified, it is primarily the Security Council that will do it.

The Security Council in the 1990s gave a very broad interpretation to the scope of Chapter VII of the Charter pertaining to enforcement action in response to threats to and breaches of the peace and acts of aggression. It has said that peace and security issues may arise from human-rights, economic, and ecological situations—and even from HIV/AIDS in Africa—not just from the use of force across borders by states. It has even said that humanitarian conditions within a state, even those that do not seem to generate external material effects, may constitute a threat to international peace and security and merit an enforcement action under Chapter VII of the Charter.[18] It has decided to authorize such action to restore an elected government overthrown by military force. Along the way, the Security Council has specified that individuals in zones of armed conflict have a right to humanitarian assistance, and that to interfere with that right is a war crime for which there can be individual prosecution. The council has also authorized member states to seize the property of a state (Iraq) in order to assist in the implementation of binding sanctions. Under Chapter VII the council has created a war-crimes tribunal for the former Yugoslavia and for Rwanda. These are just a few of the decisions about security rules made by the council under Chapter VII.

If this trend, which is based on agreement among the permanent members, continues, international security rules will be expanded as well as specified. This will be a remarkable and important change, especially given the conventional wisdom that much international security law is likely to remain vague because the competing claims of states are rarely authoritatively reviewed by the Security Council or the World Court. In the 1990s the council was clearly doing what it had not been able to do since June 1950, namely, distinguish aggression from self-defense and make use of Chapter VII to organize a legally binding response to threats to and breaches of the peace.

Human Rights Rules

The UN has been codifying rules on internationally recognized human rights since 1948, when the General Assembly adopted the Universal Declaration of Human Rights and also approved the treaty on genocide. Since then, there has been sufficient formal or informal consensus (reflecting an aggregation of interests) to produce numerous treaties, declarations, and resolutions.

Several new developments have happened within the United Nations regarding human rights rules since the end of the Cold War. The Security Council has merged human rights and security rules to a great extent, making decisions under Chapter VII pertaining to peace and security that involved such fundamental rights as the one to adequate nutrition (for example, in Somalia) and freedom from repression (for example, in Iraq). In fact, Stanley Hoffmann has described "international peace and security" as an "all-purpose parachute" (remarks made at a symposium on collective responses to common threats, Oslo, Norway, June 22–23, 1993). In Haiti, the council voted a binding and comprehensive economic embargo on the country during summer 1993 after military elements deposed an elected civilian president. Moreover, the UN Human Rights Commission expanded its rule-making even beyond the several dozen treaties and declarations already adopted. The commission took on the complex subjects of the rights of minorities and indigenous peoples.

The 1993 Vienna conference made clear that there was tremendous NGO pressure on all states to continue with UN rule-making on human rights. At Vienna there was especially strong demand for further attention to rules on women's rights. Even states not genuinely committed to personal rights found it difficult to withstand combined NGO and state pressure in support of expanded UN rule-making. The political situation was such that it was easier for these dissenting states to formally accept rules that they did not really support than to stand up and try to oppose them directly. The Vienna process also indicated clearly that established principles of human rights might not be as universally accepted as many UN and human rights observers had previously thought. The debates in Vienna brought out significant challenges to what in some corners are perceived to be Anglo-Saxon-dominated international norms. Although these challenges were kept at bay in Vienna, they have persisted and are not likely to go away given the turbulent nature of the post–Cold War world order.

Since Vienna there is ample evidence that the plethora of UN rules on human rights are marked also by great state hypocrisy about those rules. The UN treaty monitoring system is plagued by late and superficial reports, not to mention lack of adequate funding to ensure the timely review of the reports. The systematic election of rights-violating states to the UNHRC indicates that many states still give preference to traditional bargaining and geographical considerations, rather than to serious respect for the rules. So while the human rights domain at the UN is characterized by extensive codification and other norm development, reflecting a formal statement of interests, there is much concern by human rights NGOs about state sincerity of purpose.

Rules for Sustainable Development

The Millennium Assembly has clearly identified some basic principles now supported by consensus, which we summarized in Table 10.2 and which comprise more or less the equivalent of the Universal Declaration of Human Rights for the development domain. These core principles include a focus on poverty and hunger, on education, on gender equality, on children's and maternal welfare, on good health and especially the threat of HIV/AIDS, and on such general matters as sustainable ecology and broad partnership for development. The MDGs also contain relatively specific targets for advancement toward human security.

These MDGs do not compose a treaty, and in some respects the new rules for development are general. This is especially true regarding the statements on ecology and partnerships. So it remains to be seen whether the MDGs constitute a real road map for development, or just another set of pious statements that states do not take seriously. The history of human rights treaties indicates the gap that can exist between normative theory and behavorial reality.

UN agencies and personalities, however, will be pressing states to take the MDGs seriously. Just as human rights NGOs lobby for attention to the international rules in the domain of human rights and humanitarian affairs, so there will be non-state actors of various types seeking to follow up on the new rules for development.

Rule Enforcement

What is perhaps most striking about the UN in the 1990s is the extent to which its bodies are passing judgment about the behavior of states under UN-sponsored rules, which themselves are a reflection of interests articulated and aggregated through UN channels. The past fifty years reveal important lessons for UN rule enforcement within our three thematic areas.

Enforcing Security Rules

The UN Security Council has clearly eclipsed the General Assembly in the security area, as the Charter originally intended. In the 1990s the locus of supervisory activity concerning state use of force and other security policies was in the council. In one respect matters have not changed since 1945. The Security Council cannot be expected to supervise the permanent members in any vigorous or rigorous way. Each still possesses the veto, which guarantees council impotence when a permanent member's policy is challenged. This is not the result of poor drafting by the Charter's framers but of recognition of the realities of power. No coalition of states could hope militarily to coerce the United States into changing its policies; it is doubtful that any coalition could do likewise against Britain, France, Russia, or China without enormous disruption to world politics. Certainly force could not be used without overwhelming destruction out of proportion to the offense, possibly triggering violations of international law.

What one saw in spring 2003 was most of the members of the council trying to offset U.S. military power, then focused on Iraq, with diplomatic and legal arguments. In a sense this was classical balance-of-power politics, in that France, Russia, Germany, China, and others tried to restrain the United States (and Britain and Spain) with diplomatic and legal measures. This balancing failed, in the sense that the U.S. was not deterred in its first use of force against Iraq. Indeed, given the preponderance of American power, it is difficult to see how such a diplomatic démarche could effectively constitute a real balance.

The U.S. aside, never before in world history has an IGO sought to pass judgment on states' security policies to the extent that the UN Security Council did in the early 1990s. In historical perspective, this was a major experiment. The outcomes constituted a mixed record.

Working closely with the Secretary-General, the Security Council could count a number of successes in supervising various policies in places such as Southwest Africa/Namibia and Central America in the late 1980s and early 1990s. The result was both independence for Namibia and significant steps toward regional peace and national reconciliation in El Salvador and Nicaragua.

From August 1990 the council successfully countered various Iraqi policies that violated international law, primarily because the United States took a very strong interest in resisting aggression against Kuwait and in seeing that council follow-up resolutions were enforced. The council was also successful in ameliorating disorder and starvation in Somalia in 1992 and early 1993, again because the United States decided, for whatever reason, that the situation was intolerable.

At the same time, the Security Council passed numerous resolutions pertaining to the former Yugoslavia that were not implemented. The state members of the council were diplomatically engaged in supervising the policies of the various parties engaged in armed conflict—Serbians, Croats, Bosnians, Bosnian Serbs, Bosnian Croats, and Bosnian Muslims. Those same council members, however, lacked the will to see that the necessary political and material resources were made available to UN forces and representatives in the field. Multilateral diplomacy was divorced from threat or effective use of power, with predictably disappointing results. Serbia's original war aims ended up being the negotiated final solution. Nevertheless, the UN did commendable work in trying circumstances by providing humanitarian relief to many thousands of persons through the activities of the UNHCR, UNICEF, and UNPROFOR.

In Somalia from May 1993, the council and its field representatives through UNOSOM II tried to accomplish what U.S. forces had been unwilling to do under UNOSOM I or UNITAF—namely, to disarm the internal factions that had been threatening civilian life and to protect relief officials. But this task proved difficult given the inadequate training, coordination, equipment, and overall force levels of UN military contingents. Calling the effort an enforcement operation under Chapter

VII did not resolve problems in the field, and it was evident that the UN had difficulty in suppressing factions that had long used force to gain their political objectives.

The situation was similar for UNTAC in Cambodia. General elections were supervised in May 1993, but the Security Council found it difficult to fashion a policy that would control the Khmer Rouge while helping competing domestic factions that supported national reconciliation. The United Nations also found itself only nominally in control of key departments in the central government, with much power being exercised apart from UN supervision. The four leading Cambodian factions found it difficult to proceed without UN approval, but the world organization found itself facing great difficulties in making its supervision effective. But even those critical of the UN in Cambodia did not seem to have other viable options, and the largest UN operation to date completed its withdrawal in November 1993 without full peace for Cambodia.

The delayed reactions to genocide in Rwanda and to the ouster of the elected government in Haiti also tarnished the UN's reputation. But in these and other security situations, there was a tendency for the state members of the council to pass resolutions that they were not committed to implementing unless the costs were deemed to be reasonable and the length of the time of an operation short. This attitude damaged the UN's reputation. For example, the credibility of the council was damaged when it declared "safe areas" for civilians in the former Yugoslavia only to have the fighting parties attack them with impunity. It hurt the UN for the council to create a war-crimes tribunal for the former Yugoslavia but then not to provide adequate staffing for the preliminary investigations or urge IFOR to pursue indicted criminals. The world organization got the criticism, but the real problem was state foreign policy channeled through the United Nations.

Nevertheless, a state that was not a permanent member but that was contemplating action that might be found to be a threat to or breach of the peace had to deal with the possibility that the UN Security Council would find its action in violation of international law and therefore launch some coercive response. The UN's probability of firm reaction was in almost direct proportion to the interest that the United States took in the situation and Washington's willingness to act. This state of affairs was markedly different from the Cold War period, when great-power disagreement guaranteed the lack of a firm council response to peace and security issues, with the partial exception of white-minority rule in Africa (Rhodesia and South Africa).

To be effective, peacekeeping and enforcement operations should be based on unambiguous operational guidelines and procedures. In this regard, the Security Council moved in 1994 to articulate criteria for a variety of important aspects of operational activities, including the initial deployment of forces, ongoing operational reviews, training, command and control, and financing. In addition, effective rule enforcement entails an adequate capacity to act. In the context of the multitude of security-related activities in which the organization is engaged, the United Nations quite simply does not possess this capacity. The world organization is perpetually drained and strained financially to the limits, as new tasks are added without the requisite addition of new financial and other resources. In the late 1990s, cumulative debts and arrears hovered around $3.5 billion, or about three times the regular annual budget. As demonstrated clearly in the case of dealing with the crisis in the former Yugoslavia, U.S. officials have shown increasing willingness to "let the UN do it" or to "do it in the name of the UN," but there has not been an equally determined commitment to make certain that the required funds are also forthcoming. In his 1993 address to the General Assembly, President Clinton cautioned that the UN must know when to say "no." At that time as well as during the second Clinton administration, this implies that the United States must know when to say "yes." Despite a "deal" to pay U.S. arrears in December 1999 that narrowly avoided the loss of the U.S. vote in the General Assembly and a much-publicized visit by the Senate's Foreign Relations Committee to the United Nations in January 2000, the future of the UN's capacity to enforce security rules is far from certain.

This uncertainty is reflected in two events that occurred in 1999 and 2000. The crisis in Kosovo was the first, and it showed the old problem that when the Permanent Five members are divided, the Security Council cannot be directly or explicitly involved in security operations. Thus the United States led NATO to use military force in modern Yugoslavia outside the council, because Russia and China were not prepared to support such action against Serbia's persecution of Albanian Kosovars. Russia saw itself as the historical protector of the Serbs, and China was worried about UN approval of strong action against a government's treatment of its own citizens. In the second crisis, however, that pertaining to East Timor and Indonesia, the council was able to authorize a deployment of force to ease the transition problems as East Timor moved from unstable internal status to national independence. Russia expressed no opposition, China was willing to defer, and the United States was content with developments since Australia agreed to take the lead on the ground. Facilitating the entire process was political change in Indonesia, which finally (after much destruction and many deaths) led to considerable cooperation between Jakarta and the UN-approved military force. So in the first instance, there was not Permanent Five agreement, and in the second, there was. In the first, the target government (Belgrade) did not give its consent to what was being discussed in the council, and in the second, Jakarta finally did.

Enforcing Human Rights Rules

Since about 1970 the United Nations, principally via the Human Rights Commission, has been more-or-less systematically using embarrassment to pressure states violating UN human rights rules, but it has employed double standards. Before 1970 there was some sporadic UN supervision of rights performance, but only after 1970 did the world organization make this supervision a regular feature of its actions. The realm of domestic jurisdiction has shrunk progressively, and the realm of international supervision has expanded.

Small and weak developing countries were the most likely targets of UN human rights supervision, but no state could be guaranteed immunity from diplomatic pressure. It was true that the Expert Committee supervising the UN Covenant on Economic, Social, and Cultural Rights took on the Dominican Republic; the UN Committee on Human Rights supervising the UN Covenant on Civil and Political Rights confronted Uruguay; and the UN Human Rights Commission broke some new diplomatic ground in supervising Guinea-Bissau. But it was also true that more important states such as China, Iran, and Iraq, not to mention Israel, were sometimes targeted for diplomatic supervision. Russia has been the only permanent member of the council officially condemned by the HRC; that occurred because of Moscow's heavy-handed policies in the break-away republic of Chechnya. China has avoided censure in that commission by the narrowest of votes.

By the 1990s many states could not be sure that the Security Council would not declare a particular human rights situation a threat to international peace and engage in some type of enforcement. Iraq, Somalia, and Haiti had been so targeted. Bosnia was a case where human rights violations were intertwined with aggression, in the view of the council, and Chapter VII was invoked to deal with both types of issues.

Power still greatly affects human rights issues at the United Nations. The U.S. and Japan were not as likely as Israel to be pressured about "racial discrimination." Haiti was more likely to be coercively pressured about the denial of political rights than Myanmar (formerly Burma). China could avoid the issue of suppression of Tibetan rights at the Vienna conference, whereas Israel could not so easily avoid the issue of Palestinian rights to self-determination. Various double standards had impaired the reputation of the UN Human Rights Commission over time, not to mention the election to that commission of states known for the systematic violation of important human rights, or even the election of Libya as chair in 2003.

Nevertheless, as a historical trend, the United Nations is supervising more rights in more states through more intrusive measures than ever before. Although the world organization's record on supervising human rights paled in comparison with the Council of Europe's, the UN might in some respects approximate the Organization of American States; and the UN did not fare so badly in comparisons with the former Organization of African Unity and the Arab League. Many, if not most, states had apparently learned the necessity, if not the benefit, of having the United Nations pass judgment about their human rights performances. During the 1990s, an International Criminal Court was finally approved by UN member states, and special tribunals were created to deal with genocide and other human rights atrocities in Rwanda and Yugoslavia. There remained, however, considerable disagreement about enforcing some human rights via international criminal courts.

Enforcing Rules on Sustainable Development

In this issue area the UN's record on supervision is not only exceedingly complex but also affected by the fact that until the Millennium Assembly there had been few generally agreed rules. Even with the MDGs, one still found rather general policy statements, not precise rules enforceable in a judicial sense. True, the ILO monitored labor conditions (usually treated as a human rights question), WHO monitored health conditions (also treated by some as a human rights issue), and UNESCO kept an eye on educational issues.

But on many core issues of sustainable development, the basic rules, as well as the very meaning of the concept, have only recently met with consensus. Moreover, some sustainable development concerns are treated outside the official framework of the United Nations. For example, the Montreal Protocol on the ozone and related agreements have been negotiated outside the UN, but with some participation by UNEP.

The United Nations has never played as definitive and large a role in monitoring state economic and ecological policies as it has in supervising security and human rights policies. International supervision of economics has been performed more by the World Bank and the International Monetary Fund. Since 1995, the World Trade Organization, of course, handles disputes about trading rules. It is likely that in the future, given the MDGs, various UN agencies will engage in "naming and shaming" in an effort to prod states into meeting stated targets. But the more persistent role for these UN agencies will be in positive assistance to help states meet the targets.

Just how the Security Council, the General Assembly, or some other centralized UN body, such as a proposed Economic Security Council, could impose itself on a fragmented UN system, and how such a centralized entity would link to the World Bank and its billions in loan funds, is unclear. Furthermore, there is growing recognition that sustainable development, as indicated by the Millennium Assembly, entails processes and conditions that lie well outside the scope and domain of interstate relations. It calls for popular participation in decisionmaking processes and project implementation. Sustainable development reaches to the lowest level of social aggregation—local communities, social groups, and individuals. These are elements of sustainable human development and of human security that do not fit well with intergovernmentalism, UN style, and associated assumptions of national state sovereignty and noninterference in "domestic affairs." Indeed, in many ways the worldviews underlying interstate relations, on the one hand, and sustainable development, on the other, do not portray the real world at all. The turbulence that characterizes post–Cold War world politics in this regard will need to be addressed if the CSD is to effectively carry out its various mandates. This task and the way it is handled will foretell much about the future of the United Nations in social and economic areas. Bridging the gap between micro- and macrophenomena is a key to coping with turbulence and for promoting human as well as global security.

Some Final Thoughts

Earlier we discussed the appearance of "good governance" as a topic at the national level for the UN system. At the international level, another concept has emerged, "global governance," whose origins can be traced to a growing dissatisfaction among students of international relations with the realist and liberal-institutionalist theories that had dominated the study of international organization since World War II. In particular, these traditional perspectives failed to capture adequately the vast increase, in both numbers and influence, of nonstate actors and the implications of technology in an age of globalization. We have emphasized in previous chapters the growing network of actors circumscribing the UN's role in all major activities. Thus we would like to conclude with the significance of global governance for the twenty-first century, a subject of growing interest among scholars and practitioners.[19]

The journey to explore the concept has barely begun, and so readers will not be surprised to learn that the nature of global governance is more inchoate than the nature of governance within countries. At the same time that part of Europe adopts a common currency and tries to move toward a common defense and security policy, how can the former Yugoslavia implode? James Rosenau, the American academic most closely associated with the notion of global governance, invented the term "fragmegration"[20] to capture the simultaneous integration and fragmentation of societal interactions and authority patterns. Moreover, burgeoning information, communication, market, finance, networking, and business activities are producing a world in which patterns are difficult to discern.

Larry Finkelstein has gone so far as to quip that "we say 'governance' because we don't really know what to call what is going on."[21] In short, analysts are understandably uncomfortable with the traditional frameworks and vocabulary used to describe international relations. However, the nomenclature of "global governance" is akin to "Cold War," which signifies that one period has ended but that we do not as yet have an accurate shorthand to depict the essential dynamics of the new epoch.

In spite of vagueness in ongoing scholarly and policy debates, the application of the notion of governance to the globe was the natural result of mounting evidence that the international system was no longer composed simply of states, but that the world was undergoing fundamental change. Although such actors as the Catholic Church, General Motors, and the International Committee of the Red Cross (ICRC) are hardly new to the Westphalian system, it should be clear to readers by now that the proliferation of nonstate actors and their growing importance and power are a distinctive feature of contemporary world affairs.[22]

Global governance invokes the shifting location of authority. The implications for international action jump from the title of Rosenau's edited volume, with Ernst-Otto Czempiel, *Governance Without Government*. Mobilizing support from the bottom up involves increasing the skills and capacities of individuals and altering the horizons of identification in patterns of global life. Elsewhere, Rosenau characterizes global governance as "systems of rule at all levels of human activity—from the family to the international organization—in which the pursuit of goals through the exercise of control has transnational repercussions."[23]

Globalization is neither uniform nor homogeneous, but it is indisputably accelerating the pace and intensity of economic and social interactions at all levels. Although the history is long,[24] its present manifestation is fundamentally different in scale, intensity, and form from what preceded. As David Held and others have put it, "Contemporary globalization represents the beginning of a new epoch in human affairs [causing] as profound an impact as the Industrial Revolution and the global empires of the nineteenth century."[25] Students and professors, policy analysts and practitioners should not feel uncomfortable about admitting their uneasiness and ignorance about understanding the details of the contemporary political economy, and especially about not knowing the best way to address a bewildering array of global problems.

The logical link between the patterns of governance at the national and global levels lies in solving the collective action puzzle in order to provide public goods. "In both modern domestic political systems and the modern international system, the state has been the key structural arena within which collective action has been situated and undertaken," observes Philip Cerny. And as a result of a multiplicity of interactions, "the authority, legitimacy, policymaking capacity, and policy-implementing effectiveness of the state will be eroded and undermined both within and without."[26] Mark Zacher has summarized the nature of the modest order in today's international economic system in the following way: "In short, without these and other regimes and public goods generated by the UN system, it would truly be 'a jungle out there.'"[27]

But governments and their intergovernmental creations are inadequate. Cerny argues that, as market activity intensifies and economic organization becomes increasingly complex, the institutional scale of political structures is no longer capable of providing a suitable range of public goods. In effect, economic globalization is undermining the effectiveness of state-based collective action. Although the state remains a cultural force, its effectiveness as a civil association has declined significantly. The result may be a crisis of legitimacy. This is not to say that state-based collective action has reached its end, but it is significantly different from what it was in the past.

And at the global level, collective action is still more evasive. Although realists and idealists who analyze international organizations disagree about many issues, they agree that the state system is "anarchic." Whatever the framers of the UN Charter had in mind and whatever John Maynard Keynes and his colleagues imagined at Bretton Woods, nothing like an overarching authority for either the high politics of international peace and security or the low politics of economic and social development has emerged.

In one crucial aspect then, "global governance" is distinct from good or bad governance at the national level. At the country level, a "good" (that is, accountable, efficient, lawful, representative, and transparent) government usually leads to good governance, whereas bad governance is correlated with conspicuously bad government. Although the merits of more-or-less interventionist stances by states can be debated, there is a primary and identifiable sovereign agent at the helm. Prescriptions to improve policy- and decisionmaking flow naturally, albeit controversially, from adjusting the potential contribution of the state as agent.

At the global level, in contrast, we need a term to signify the reality that there has never been a world government, and there undoubtedly will not be one during our lifetime. Finkelstein, for instance, sees global governance as "doing internationally what governments do at home."[28] But his formulation fails to specify the agencies that are supposed to accomplish globally the numerous tasks that governments do nationally. Thus, at both the country and the global levels, governance encompasses more than government. But as there is no government at the global level, of what utility is the notion of global governance? Is it, as Brian Urquhart once quipped, like the grinning but bodiless Cheshire cat in *Alice in Wonderland*, an agreeable notion because it is without substance?

The United Nations Millennium Summit, the largest gathering in history of world leaders, brought together 149 heads of state and government and high-ranking officials from more than forty countries. (UN Photo/T. Deglau)

For us, global governance is most usefully seen as a heuristic device to capture and describe the seemingly ever-accelerating transformation of the international system within which the United Nations operates. States are central to it, but their authority is eroding in important ways. Their creations, intergovernmental organizations, are no more in control than they ever were. Local and international NGOs are proliferating and gaining authority and resources. And technological developments are increasing the wherewithal of corporations and criminal groups. Within this context, collective action problems associated with the provision of global public goods have become still more intractable than is their provision in the national setting.[29]

The subtext, here and in the analyses of most proponents, is that multilateral institutions, both universal and regional, should be strengthened. The longing for a monolithic and top-down view of governance for the globe is understandable but seems misplaced in an increasingly decentralized world. At a time when both problems and solutions transcend national borders and there is no likelihood of a central sovereign, the visceral calls from internationalists to strengthen intergovernmental institutions are comprehensible but appear wistful. It would be better to think creatively about ways to pool the collective strengths and avoid the collective weaknesses of governments, intergovernmental organizations, NGOs, and global civil society. Ironically, this is the conceptual and operational challenge for supporters of the United Nations in the face of changing world politics.

Indeed, this was the organizing principle behind the September 2000 Millennium Summit, which Singapore's ambassador to the UN Kishore Mahbubani called "the mother of all summits." Some 150 heads of government participated in an intense series of private and public sessions. But New York's traffic was congested by more than government limousines because of Secretary-General Kofi Annan's effort to reflect the diverse reality of problem-solving in the contemporary world with a "global compact" between the United Nations and representatives of NGOs and business as well as of governments.[30]

In conclusion, we need to reflect again on the primary raison d'être of the United Nations, which is the promotion and maintenance of peace and security and—most especially concerning the movement into the new millennium—human security. In this regard, we need to stress the inherent and inextricably linked nature of human security, democratization and human rights, and sustainable human development. The latter is aimed at cumulatively improving and sustaining human security and reducing perceived and actual threats to physical and psychological well-being from all manner of agents and forces that could degrade lives, values, and property. Both sustainable human security and sustainable human development require democracy and the protection of fundamental human rights. In short, enhancing human security is what both development and democracy are about.

The United Nations has always been a blend of ideals and reality.[31] Its Charter represents the ideal goals of international society, a world of peace and justice. Its operation represents the reality of state foreign policies mediated by the views of nonstate parties such as NGOs and independent international civil servants. The UN thus represents both the striving for a better world—more peaceful, with more human dignity and equitable and sustainable prosperity—and the failure to achieve those goals, largely because of shortsighted and self-serving national preoccupations.

After the Cold War there is an opportunity for states to cooperate more through the United Nations. The debilitating competition between Washington and Moscow, between NATO and the Warsaw Pact, between capitalist democracies and authoritarian or socialist states, has been reduced. States have indeed learned to profit from this post–Cold War opportunity, cooperating within the security realm (for instance, in the Persian Gulf and Somalia), the human rights arena (for instance, in Haiti and El Salvador), and the field of sustainable development (for instance, in the Commission on Sustainable Development).

But interstate cooperation via the United Nations clearly has its limits. States learned conflicting things about the wisdom of projecting the UN into armed conflict in places like the former Yugoslavia, into the human rights situation in places like China, and how to handle sustainable development in both the North and the South. How effective UN efforts will be in helping to reconstitute Afghanistan and Iraq are clearly as unknown as the effectivenesss of the U.S.-led War on Terrorism and regime change in Iraq.

In evaluating the successes and failures attributed to the United Nations, we can take a maximalist or minimalist position. If we compare the real record of achievement to the lofty goals stated in the Charter, the UN record is bound to be the subject of criticism or even of derision. If we recognize that UN actions depend heavily on state foreign policy, which is ever sensitive to national interests, and that much of the time the UN is given the difficult problems that states have not been able to solve on their own, then criticism is moderated. In this respect we may do well to conclude with words attributed to Secretary-General Dag Hammarskjöld: "The purpose of the

UN is not to get us to heaven but to save us from hell." As Secretary-General Kofi Annan suggested in his inaugural remarks, modesty is undoubtedly a helpful approach in this post–post–Cold War era.

Notes

1. See further J. Martin Rochester, *Waiting for the Millennium: The United Nations and the Future of World Order* (Columbia: University of South Carolina Press, 1993).

2. James N. Rosenau, *Turbulence in World Politics: A Theory of Change and Continuity* (Princeton: Princeton University Press, 1990). The implications of this view for the United Nations are found in his *The United Nations in a Turbulent World* (Boulder: Lynne Rienner, 1992).

3. The clash between the new global forces and the traditional local forces has been popularly treated by Thomas L. Friedman, *The Lexus and the Olive Tree* (New York: HarperCollins, 1999); and by Benjamin R. Barber, *Jihad vs. McWorld* (New York: Ballantine Books, 1995).

4. Ernest R. May, *"Lessons" of the Past: The Use and Misuse of History in American Foreign Policy* (New York: Oxford University Press, 1975).

5. See further Richard E. Neustadt and Ernest R. May, *Thinking in Time: The Uses of History for Decision Makers* (New York: Free Press, 1986).

6. See Cindy Collins and Thomas G. Weiss, *Review of the Peacekeeping Literature, 1990–1996* (Providence, R.I.: Watson Institute, 1997).

7. Shashi Tharoor, "Forward," in Donald C. F. Daniel and Bradd C. Hayes, eds., *Beyond Traditional Peacekeeping* (London: Macmillan, 1995), p. xviii.

8. Peter M. Haas and Ernst B. Haas, "Learning to Learn: Improving International Governance," *Global Governance* 1, no. 3 (September–December 1995), pp. 255–285, quote at p. 278.

9. For an example of this approach applied to international organizations, see Harold K. Jacobson, *Networks of Interdependence: International Organizations and the Global Political System* (New York: Knopf, 1979).

10. Robert E. Riggs, *US/UN: Foreign Policy and International Organization* (New York: Appleton-Century-Crofts, 1971), p. 298.

11. From a wealth of sources see Clyde Prestowitz, *Rouge Nation: American Unilateralism and the Failure of Good Intentions* (New York: Basic Books, 2003); and David M. Malone and Yuen Foong Khong, eds., *Unilateralism and U.S. Foreign Policy: International Perspectives* (Boulder: Lynne Rienner, 2003).

12. UNDP, *Human Development Report 1996* (New York: UN, 1996), p. 12.

13. See especially Michael J. Glennon, "Why the Security Council Failed," *Foreign Affairs,* 82, 3 (May–June 2003), pp. 16–35.

14. See the views of Joseph P. Nye, Edward C. Luck, Anne-Marie Slaughter, and Ian Hurd in *Foreign Affairs,* 82, 3 (Summer 2003). See also Mats Berdal, "The UN Security Council: Ineffective but Indispensable," *Survival,* 45, 2 (Summer 2003), pp. 7–30. These views were representative of a larger slice of expert commentary.

15. See especially Tony Evans, *US Hegemony and the Project of Universal Human Rights* (New York: St. Martin's Press 1996); and David P. Forsythe, *Human Rights in International Relations* (Cambridge: Cambridge University Press, 2000).

16. From many sources see Sarah B. Sewall and Carl Kaysen, eds., *The United States and the International Criminal Court* (Lanham, Md.: Rowman and Littlefield, 2000).

17. See further Aryeh Neier, *War Crimes: Brutality, Genocide, Terror, and the Struggle for Justice* (New York: Times Books, 1998); and Steven R. Ratner and Jason S. Abrams, *Accountabil-*

ity for Human Rights Atrocities in International Law: Beyond the Nuremberg Legacy (Oxford: Clarendon Press, 1997).

18. See further International Commission on Intervention and State Sovereignty, *The Responsibility to Protect* (Ottaw: ICISS, 2001).

19. Since 1995 Lynne Rienner Publishers has, in cooperation with the Academic Council on the United Nations System and the UN University, published the journal *Global Governance*. The Commission on Global Governance was chaired by Sonny Ramphal and Ingmar Carlsson and published the views of the eminent practitioners in *Our Global Neighbourhood* (Oxford: Oxford University Press, 1995). In addition, there is a voluminous and growing literature. See James N. Rosenau and Ernst-Otto Czempiel, eds., *Governance Without Government: Order and Change in World Politics* (Cambridge, U.K. Cambridge University Press, 1992); Jan Kooiman, ed., *Modern Governance: New Government-Society Interactions* (London: Sage, 1993); Mihaly Simai, *The Future of Global Governance: Managing Risk and Change in the International System* (Washington, D.C.: U.S. Institute of Peace, 1994); Meghnad Desai and Paul Redfern, eds., *Global Governance: Ethics and Economics of the World Order* (London: Pinter, 1995); Richard Falk, O*n Humane Governance* (University Park: Pennsylvania State Press, 1995); Paul F. Diehl, ed., *The Politics of Global Governance: International Organizations in an Interdependent World* (Boulder: Lynne Rienner, 1997); Martin Hewson and Timothy J. Sinclair, eds., *Approaches to Global Governance Theory* (Albany: State University of New York Press, 1999); and Errol E. Harris and James A. Yunker, eds., *Toward Genuine Global Governance: Critical Reflection to Our Global Neighbourhood* (Westport, Conn.: Praeger, 1999). In addition, numerous publications from international agencies have used the concept in their titles and analyses. See, for example, World Bank, *Governance and Development* (Washington, D.C.: World Bank, 1992); UN Development Programme, *The Shrinking State: Governance and Human Development in Eastern Europe and the Commonwealth of Independent States* (New York: UNDP, 1997); Andrew F. Cooper, John English, and Ramesh Thakur, eds., *Enhancing Global Governance: Towards a New Diplomacy?* (Tokyo: UN University Press, 2002); Robert O'Brien, Anne Marie Goetz, Jan Aart Scholte, and Marc Williams, *Contesting Global Governance: Multilateral Economic Institutions and Global Social Movements* (Cambridge: Cambridge University Press, 2000); Rorden Wilkinson and Steve Hughes, eds., *Global Governance: Critical Perspectives* (London: Routledge, 2002); and Esref Aksu and Joseph A. Camilleri, eds., *Democratizing Global Governance* (London: Palgrave, 2002).

20. James N. Rosenau, "'Fragmegrative' Challenges to National Security," in Terry Hens, ed., *Understanding US Strategy: A Reader* (Washington, D.C.: National Defense University, 1983), pp. 65–82.

21. Lawrence S. Finkelstein, "What Is Global Governance?" *Global Governance* 1, no. 3 (September–December 1995), p. 368.

22. For a persuasive discussion, see David Held and Anthony McGrew, with David Goldblatt and Jonathan Peraton, *Global Transformations: Politics, Economics, and Culture* (Stanford: Stanford University Press, 1999).

23. James N. Rosenau, "Governance in the Twenty-first Century," *Global Governance* 1, no. 1 (May–August 1995), p. 13.

24. Emma Rothschild, "Globalization and the Return of History," *Foreign Policy* no. 115 (Summer 1999), pp. 106–116.

25. David Held and Anthony McGrew, with David Goldblatt and Jonathan Peraton, "Globalization," *Global Governance* 5, no. 4 (October–December 1999), p. 494.

26. Philip G. Cerny, "Globalization and the Changing Logic of Collective Action," *International Organization* 49, no. 4 (Autumn 1995), pp. 595, 621.

27. Mark W. Zacher, *The United Nations and Global Commerce* (New York: UN, 1999), p. 5.

28. Finkelstein, "What Is Global Governance?" p. 369.

29. Inge Kaul, Isabelle Grunberg, and Marc A. Stern, *Global Public Goods: International Cooperation in the 21st Century* (New York: Oxford University Press, 1999).

30. Kofi, Annan, *"We the Peoples": The United Nations in the 21st Century* (New York: United Nations, 2000).

31. See further Peter R. Baehr and Leon Gordenker, *The United Nations. Reality and Ideal* (New York: Praeger, 1984; rev. ed., Macmillan and St. Martin's Press, 1991).

Appendix A
The United Nations System

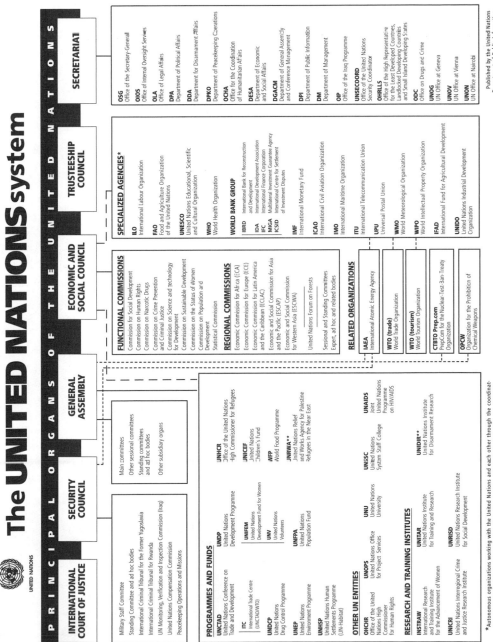

The UNITED NATIONS system

PRINCIPAL ORGANS OF THE UNITED NATIONS

INTERNATIONAL COURT OF JUSTICE | **SECURITY COUNCIL** | **GENERAL ASSEMBLY** | **ECONOMIC AND SOCIAL COUNCIL** | **TRUSTEESHIP COUNCIL** | **SECRETARIAT**

SECURITY COUNCIL
Military Staff Committee
Standing Committee and ad hoc bodies
International Criminal Tribunal for the Former Yugoslavia
International Criminal Tribunal for Rwanda
UN Monitoring, Verification and Inspection Commission (Iraq)
United Nations Compensation Commission
Peacekeeping Operations and Missions

GENERAL ASSEMBLY
Main committees
Other sessional committees
Standing committees and ad hoc bodies
Other subsidiary organs

PROGRAMMES AND FUNDS

UNCTAD United Nations Conference on Trade and Development
  ITC International Trade Centre (UNCTAD/WTO)
UNDCP United Nations Drug Control Programme
UNEP United Nations Environment Programme
UNHSP United Nations Human Settlements Programme (UN-Habitat)

UNDP United Nations Development Programme
  UNIFEM United Nations Development Fund for Women
  UNV United Nations Volunteers
UNFPA United Nations Population Fund

UNHCR Office of the United Nations High Commissioner for Refugees
UNICEF United Nations Children's Fund
WFP World Food Programme
UNRWA** United Nations Relief and Works Agency for Palestine Refugees in the Near East

UNAIDS Joint United Nations Programme on HIV/AIDS

OTHER UN ENTITIES
OHCHR Office of the United Nations High Commissioner for Human Rights

UNOPS United Nations Office for Project Services
UNU United Nations University
UNSSC United Nations System Staff College
UNIDIR** United Nations Institute for Disarmament Research

RESEARCH AND TRAINING INSTITUTES
INSTRAW International Research and Training Institute for the Advancement of Women
UNICRI United Nations Interregional Crime and Justice Research Institute
UNITAR United Nations Institute for Training and Research
UNRISD United Nations Research Institute for Social Development

FUNCTIONAL COMMISSIONS
Commission for Social Development
Commission on Human Rights
Commission on Narcotic Drugs
Commission on Crime Prevention and Criminal Justice
Commission on Science and Technology for Development
Commission on Sustainable Development
Commission on the Status of Women
Commission on Population and Development
Statistical Commission

REGIONAL COMMISSIONS
Economic Commission for Africa (ECA)
Economic Commission for Europe (ECE)
Economic Commission for Latin America and the Caribbean (ECLAC)
Economic and Social Commission for Asia and the Pacific (ESCAP)
Economic and Social Commission for Western Asia (ESCWA)

United Nations Forum on Forests

Sessional and Standing Committees
Expert, ad hoc and related bodies

RELATED ORGANIZATIONS
IAEA International Atomic Energy Agency
WTO (trade) World Trade Organization
WTO (tourism) World Tourism Organization
CTBTO Prep.com PrepCom for the Nuclear-Test-Ban-Treaty Organization
OPCW Organization for the Prohibition of Chemical Weapons

SPECIALIZED AGENCIES*
ILO International Labour Organization
FAO Food and Agriculture Organization of the United Nations
UNESCO United Nations Educational, Scientific and Cultural Organization
WHO World Health Organization
WORLD BANK GROUP
  IBRD International Bank for Reconstruction and Development
  IDA International Development Association
  IFC International Finance Corporation
  MIGA Multilateral Investment Guarantee Agency
  ICSID International Centre for Settlement of Investment Disputes
IMF International Monetary Fund
ICAO International Civil Aviation Organization
IMO International Maritime Organization
ITU International Telecommunication Union
UPU Universal Postal Union
WMO World Meteorological Organization
WIPO World Intellectual Property Organization
IFAD International Fund for Agricultural Development
UNIDO United Nations Industrial Development Organization

SECRETARIAT
OSG Office of the Secretary-General
OIOS Office of Internal Oversight Services
OLA Office of Legal Affairs
DPA Department of Political Affairs
DDA Department for Disarmament Affairs
DPKO Department of Peacekeeping Operations
OCHA Office for the Coordination of Humanitarian Affairs
DESA Department of Economic and Social Affairs
DGACM Department of General Assembly and Conference Management
DPI Department of Public Information
DM Department of Management
OIP Office of the Iraq Programme
UNSECOORD Office of the United Nations Security Coordinator
OHRLLS Office of the High Representative for the Least Developed Countries, Landlocked Developing Countries and Small Island Developing States
ODC Office on Drugs and Crime
UNOG UN Office at Geneva
UNOV UN Office at Vienna
UNON UN Office at Nairobi

*Autonomous organizations working with the United Nations and each other through the coordinating machinery of the Economic and Social Council.
**Report only to the General Assembly.

Published by the United Nations
Department of Public Information
DPI/2299 - February 2003

Appendix B
Concise List of Internet Sites
Relevant to the United Nations

General Information on International Relations with Frequent Attention to the UN

Council on Foreign Relations and *Foreign Affairs* magazine: www.cfr.org

Carnegie Council on Ethics: www.carnegiecouncil.org

Foreign Policy Magazine: www.foreignpolicy.com

International Crisis Group: www.intl-crisis-grp.org

General Information on the UN and the UN System

The United Nations Homepage*: www.un.org

The United Nations University: www.unu.edu

UN Wire: www.unwire.org

Academic Council on the UN System (ACUNS): www.yale.edu/acuns/

UN Association of the USA: www.unausa.org

UN Chronicle magazine: www.un.org/Pubs/chronicle

Security Issues

International Security Magazine: www.harvard.edu/publications/cfm

International Institute for Strategic Studies and *Survival* Magazine: www.iiss.org

Center for Strategic and International Studies: www.csis.org

Women in International Security: www.wiis.org

Human Rights and Humanitarian Affairs

International Committee of the Red Cross: www.icrc.org

Amnesty International: www.amnesty.org

Human Rights Watch: www.hrw.org

Coalition for International Justice: www.cij.org

Freedom House: www.freedomhouse.org

Sustainable Human Development

World Bank: www.worldbank.org

Overseas Development Council: www.odc.org

Organization for Economic Cooperation and Development: www.oecd.org

US Agency for International Development: www.usaid.gov

Center for International Development: www.cid.harvard.edu

---

*All of the websites of the agencies, bodies, programs, and funds of the UN system can be accessed through this site. They are not repeated under substantive headings.

Appendix C
Charter of the United Nations

Preamble

We the Peoples of the United Nations Determined

to save succeeding generations from the scourge of war, which twice in our lifetime has brought untold sorrow to mankind, and

to reaffirm faith in fundamental human rights, in the dignity and worth of the human person, in the equal rights of men and women and of nations large and small, and

to establish conditions under which justice and respect for the obligations arising from treaties and other sources of international law can be maintained, and

to promote social progress and better standards of life in larger freedom,

And for these Ends

to practice tolerance and live together in peace with one another as good neighbors, and

to unite our strength to maintain international peace and security, and

to ensure by the acceptance of principles and the institution of methods, that armed force shall not be used, save in the common interest, and

to employ international machinery for the promotion of the economic and social advancement of all peoples,

Have Resolved to Combine our Efforts to Accomplish these Aims

Accordingly, our respective Governments, through representatives assembled in the city of San Francisco, who have exhibited their full powers found to be in good and due form, have agreed to the present Charter of the United Nations and do hereby establish an international organization to be known as the United Nations.

CHAPTER I   PURPOSES AND PRINCIPLES

Article 1

The Purposes of the United Nations are:

1. To maintain international peace and security, and to that end: to take effective collective measures for the prevention and removal of threats to the peace, and for the suppression of acts of aggression or other breaches of the peace, and to bring about by peaceful means, and in conformity with the principles of justice and international law, adjustment or settlement of international disputes or situations which might lead to a breach of the peace;
2. To develop friendly relations among nations based on respect for the principle of equal rights and self-determination of peoples, and to take other appropriate measures to strengthen universal peace;

3. To achieve international cooperation in solving international problems of an economic, social, cultural, or humanitarian character, and in promoting and encouraging respect for human rights and for fundamental freedoms for all without distinction as to race, sex, language, or religion; and
4. To be a center for harmonizing the actions of nations in the attainment of these common ends.

Article 2

The Organization and its Members, in pursuit of the Purposes stated in Article 1, shall act in accordance with the following Principles.

1. The Organization is based on the principle of the sovereign equality of all its Members.
2. All Members, in order to ensure to all of them the rights and benefits resulting from membership, shall fulfill in good faith the obligations assumed by them in accordance with the present Charter.
3. All Members shall settle their international disputes by peaceful means in such a manner that international peace and security, and justice, are not endangered.
4. All Members shall refrain in their international relations from the threat or use of force against the territorial integrity or political independence of any state, or in any other manner inconsistent with the Purposes of the United Nations.
5. All Members shall give the United Nations every assistance in any action it takes in accordance with the present Charter, and shall refrain from giving assistance to any state against which the United Nations is taking preventive or enforcement action.
6. The Organization shall ensure that states which are not Members of the United Nations act in accordance with these Principles so far as may be necessary for the maintenance of international peace and security.
7. Nothing contained in the present Charter shall authorize the United Nations to intervene in matters which are essentially within the domestic jurisdiction of any state or shall require the Members to submit such matters to settlement under the present Charter; but this principle shall not prejudice the application of enforcement measures under Chapter VII.

CHAPTER II MEMBERSHIP

Article 3

The original Members of the United Nations shall be the states which, having participated in the United Nations Conference on International Organization at San Francisco, or having previously signed the Declaration by United Nations of January 1, 1942, sign the present Charter and ratify it in accordance with Article 110.

Article 4

1. Membership in the United Nations is open to all other peace-loving states which accept the obligations contained in the present Charter and, in the judgment of the Organization, are able and willing to carry out these obligations.
2. The admission of any such state to membership in the United Nations will be effected by a decision of the General Assembly upon the recommendation of the Security Council.

Article 5

A member of the United Nations against which preventive or enforcement action has been taken by the Security Council may be suspended from the exercise of the rights and privileges of membership by the General Assembly upon the recommendation of the Security Council. The exercise of these rights and privileges may be restored by the Security Council.

Article 6

A Member of the United Nations which has persistently violated the Principles contained in the present Charter may be expelled from the Organization by the General Assembly upon the recommendation of the Security Council.

CHAPTER III   ORGANS

Article 7

1. There are established as the principal organs of the United Nations: a General Assembly, a Security Council, an Economic and Social Council, a Trusteeship Council, an International Court of Justice, and a Secretariat.
2. Such subsidiary organs as may be found necessary may be established in accordance with the present Charter.

Article 8

The United Nations shall place no restrictions on the eligibility of men and women to participate in any capacity and under conditions of equality in its principal and subsidiary organs.

CHAPTER IV   THE GENERAL ASSEMBLY

Composition

Article 9

1. The General Assembly shall consist of all the Members of the United Nations.
2. Each member shall have not more than five representatives in the General Assembly.

Functions and Powers

Article 10b

The General Assembly may discuss any questions or any matters within the scope of the present Charter or relating to the powers and functions of any organs provided for in the present Charter, and, except as provided in Article 12, may make recommendations to the Members of the United Nations or to the Security Council or to both on any such questions or matters.

Article 11

1. The General Assembly may consider the general principles of cooperation in the maintenance of international peace and security, including the principles governing disarmament and the regulation of armaments, and may make recommendations with regard to such principles to the Members or to the Security Council or to both.

2. The General Assembly may discuss any questions relating to the maintenance of international peace and security brought before it by any Member of the United Nations, or by the Security Council, or by a state which is not a Member of the United Nations in accordance with Article 35, paragraph 2, and, except as provided in Article 12, may make recommendations with regard to any such questions to the state or states concerned or to the Security Council or to both. Any such question on which action is necessary shall be referred to the Security Council by the General Assembly either before or after discussion.
3. The General Assembly may call the attention of the Security Council to situations which are likely to endanger international peace and security.
4. The powers of the General Assembly set forth in this Article shall not limit the general scope of Article 10.

Article 12

1. While the Security Council is exercising in respect of any dispute or situation the functions assigned to it in the present Charter, the General Assembly shall not make any recommendation with regard to that dispute or situation unless the Security Council so requests.
2. The Secretary-General, with the consent of the Security Council, shall notify the General Assembly at each session of any matters relative to the maintenance of international peace and security which are being dealt with by the Security Council and shall similarly notify the General Assembly, or the Members of the United Nations if the General Assembly is not in session, immediately the Security Council ceases to deal with such matters.

Article 13

1. 1. The General Assembly shall initiate studies and make recommendations for the purpose of:
    A. promoting international cooperation in the political field and encouraging the progressive development of international law and its codification;
    B. promoting international cooperation in the economic, social, cultural, educational, and health fields, and assisting in the realization of human rights and fundamental freedoms for all without distinction as to race, sex, language, or religion.
2. The further responsibilities, functions and powers of the General Assembly with respect to matters mentioned in paragraph 1(b) above are set forth in Chapters IX and X.

Article 14

Subject to the provisions of Article 12, the General Assembly may recommend measures for the peaceful adjustment of any situation, regardless of origin, which it deems likely to impair the general welfare or friendly relations among nations, including situations resulting from a violation of the provisions of the present Charter setting forth the Purposes and Principles of the United Nations.

Article 15

1. The General Assembly shall receive and consider annual and special reports from the Security Council; these reports shall include an account of the measures that the Security Council has decided upon or taken to maintain international peace and security.
2. The General Assembly shall receive and consider reports from the other organs of the United Nations.

Article 16

The General Assembly shall perform such functions with respect to the international trusteeship system as are assigned to it under Chapters XII and XIII, including the approval of the trusteeship agreements for areas not designated as strategic.

Article 17

1. The General Assembly shall consider and approve the budget of the Organization.
2. The expenses of the Organization shall be borne by the Members as apportioned by the General Assembly.
3. The General Assembly shall consider and approve any financial and budgetary arrangements with specialized agencies referred to in Article 57 and shall examine the administrative budgets of such specialized agencies with a view to making recommendations to the agencies concerned.

Voting

Article 18

1. Each member of the General Assembly shall have one vote.
2. Decisions of the General Assembly on important questions shall be made by a two-thirds majority of the members present and voting. These questions shall include: recommendations with respect to the maintenance of international peace and security, the election of the non-permanent members of the Security Council, the election of the members of the Economic and Social Council, the election of members of the Trusteeship Council in accordance with paragraph 1(c) of Article 86, the admission of new Members to the United Nations, the suspension of the rights and privileges of membership, the expulsion of Members, questions relating to the operation of the trusteeship system, and budgetary questions.
3. Decisions on other questions, including the determination of additional categories of questions to be decided by a two-thirds majority, shall be made by a majority of the members present and voting.

Article 19

A Member of the United Nations which is in arrears in the payment of its financial contributions to the Organization shall have no vote in the General Assembly if the amount of its arrears equals or exceeds the amount of the contributions due from it for the preceding two full years. The General Assembly may, nevertheless, permit such a Member to vote if it is satisfied that the failure to pay is due to conditions beyond the control of the Member.

Procedure

Article 20

The General Assembly shall meet in regular annual sessions and in such special sessions as occasion may require. Special sessions shall be convoked by the Secretary-General at the request of the Security Council or of a majority of the Members of the United Nations.

Article 21

The General Assembly shall adopt its own rules of procedure. It shall elect its President for each session.

Article 22

The General Assembly may establish such subsidiary organs as it deems necessary for the performance of its functions.

CHAPTER V   THE SECURITY COUNCIL

Article 23

1. The Security Council shall consist of fifteen Members of the United Nations. The Republic of China, France, the Union of Soviet Socialist Republics, the United Kingdom of Great Britain and Northern Ireland, and the United States of America shall be permanent members of the Security Council. The General Assembly shall elect ten other Members of the United Nations to be non-permanent members of the Security Council, due regard being specially paid, in the first instance to the contribution of Members of the United Nations to the maintenance of international peace and security and to the other purposes of the Organization, and also to equitable geographical distribution.
2. The non-permanent members of the Security Council shall be elected for a term of two years. In the first election of the non-permanent members after the increase of the membership of the Security Council from eleven to fifteen, two of the four additional members shall be chosen for a term of one year. A retiring member shall not be eligible for immediate re-election.
3. Each member of the Security Council shall have one representative.

Functions and Powers

Article 24

1. In order to ensure prompt and effective action by the United Nations, its Members confer on the Security Council primary responsibility for the maintenance of international peace and security, and agree that in carrying out its duties under this responsibility the Security Council acts on their behalf.
2. In discharging these duties the Security Council shall act in accordance with the Purposes and Principles of the United Nations. The specific powers granted to the Security Council for the discharge of these duties are laid down in Chapters VI, VII, VIII, and XII.
3. The Security Council shall submit annual and, when necessary, special reports to the General Assembly for its consideration.

Article 25

The Members of the United Nations agree to accept and carry out the decisions of the Security Council in accordance with the present Charter.

Article 26

In order to promote the establishment and maintenance of international peace and security with the least diversion for armaments of the world's human and economic resources, the Security Council shall be responsible for formulating, with the assistance of the Military Staff Committee referred to in Article 47, plans to be submitted to the Members of the United Nations for the establishment of a system for the regulation of armaments.

Voting

Article 27

1. Each member of the Security Council shall have one vote.
2. Decisions of the Security Council on procedural matters shall be made by an affirmative vote of nine members.
3. Decisions of the Security Council on all other matters shall be made by an affirmative vote of nine members including the concurring votes of the permanent members; provided that, in decisions under Chapter VI, and under paragraph 3 of Article 52, a party to a dispute shall abstain from voting.

Procedure

Article 28

1. The Security Council shall be so organized as to be able to function continuously. Each member of the Security Council shall for this purpose be represented at all times at the seat of the Organization.
2. The Security Council shall hold periodic meetings at which each of its members may, if it so desires, be represented by a member of the government or by some other specially designated representative.
3. The Security Council may hold meetings at such places other than the seat of the Organization as in its judgment will best facilitate its work.

Article 29

The Security Council may establish such subsidiary organs as it deems necessary for the performance of its functions.

Article 30

The Security Council shall adopt its own rules of procedure, including the method of selecting its President.

Article 31

Any Member of the United Nations which is not a member of the Security Council may participate, without vote, in the discussion of any question brought before the Security Council whenever the latter considers that the interests of that Member are specially affected.

Article 32

Any Member of the United Nations which is not a member of the Security Council or any state which is not a Member of the United Nations, if it is a party to a dispute under consideration by the Security Council, shall be invited to participate, without vote, in the discussion relating to the dispute. The Security Council shall lay down such conditions as it deems just for the participation of a state which is not a Member of the United Nations.

CHAPTER VI   PACIFIC SETTLEMENT OF DISPUTES

Article 33

1. The parties to any dispute, the continuance of which is likely to endanger the maintenance of international peace and security, shall, first of all, seek a solution by negotiation, enquiry, mediation, conciliation, arbitration, judicial settlement, resort to regional agencies or arrangements, or other peaceful means of their own choice.
2. The Security Council shall, when it deems necessary, call upon the parties to settle their dispute by such means.

Article 34

The Security Council may investigate any dispute, or any situation which might lead to international friction or give rise to a dispute, in order to determine whether the continuance of the dispute or situation is likely to endanger the maintenance of international peace and security.

Article 35

1. Any Member of the United Nations may bring any dispute, or any situation of the nature referred to in Article 34, to the attention of the Security Council or of the General Assembly.
2. A state which is not a Member of the United Nations may bring to the attention of the Security Council or of the General Assembly any dispute to which it is a party if it accepts in advance, for the purposes of the dispute, the obligations of pacific settlement provided in the present Charter.
3. The proceedings of the General Assembly in respect of matters brought to its attention under this Article will be subject to the provisions of Articles 11 and 12.

Article 36

1. The Security Council may, at any stage of a dispute of the nature referred to in Article 33 or of a situation of like nature, recommend appropriate procedures or methods of adjustment.
2. The Security Council should take into consideration any procedures for the settlement of the dispute which have already been adopted by the parties.
3. In making recommendations under this Article the Security Council should also take into consideration that legal disputes should as a general rule be referred by the parties to the International Court of Justice in accordance with the provisions of the Statute of the Court.

Article 37

1. Should the parties to a dispute of the nature referred to in Article 33 fail to settle it by the means indicated in that Article, they shall refer it to the Security Council.
2. If the Security Council deems that the continuance of the dispute is in fact likely to endanger the maintenance of international peace and security, it shall decide whether to take action under Article 36 or to recommend such terms of settlement as it may consider appropriate.

Article 38

Without prejudice to the provisions of Articles 33 to 37, the Security Council may, if all the parties to any dispute so request, make recommendations to the parties with a view to a pacific settlement of the dispute.

CHAPTER VII
ACTION WITH RESPECT TO THREATS TO THE PEACE, BREACHES OF THE PEACE, AND ACTS OF AGGRESSION

Article 39

The Security Council shall determine the existence of any threat to the peace, breach of the peace, or act of aggression and shall make recommendations, or decide what measures shall be taken in accordance with Articles 41 and 42, to maintain or restore international peace and security.

Article 40

In order to prevent an aggravation of the situation, the Security Council may, before making the recommendations or deciding upon the measures provided for in Article 39, call upon the parties concerned to comply with such provisional measures as it deems necessary or desirable. Such provisional measures shall be without prejudice to the rights, claims, or position of the parties concerned. The Security Council shall duly take account of failure to comply with such provisional measures.

Article 41

The Security Council may decide what measures not involving the use of armed force are to be employed to give effect to its decisions, and it may call upon the Members of the United Nations to apply such measures. These may include complete or partial interruption of economic relations and of rail, sea, air, postal, telegraphic, radio, and other means of communication, and the severance of diplomatic relations.

Article 42

Should the Security Council consider that measures provided for in Article 41 would be inadequate or have proved to be inadequate, it may take such action by air, sea, or land forces as may be necessary to maintain or restore international peace and security. Such action may include demonstrations, blockade, and other operations by air, sea, or land forces of Members of the United Nations.

Article 43

1. All Members of the United Nations, in order to contribute to the maintenance of international peace and security, undertake to make available to the Security Council, on its call and in accordance with a special agreement or agreements, armed forces, assistance, and facilities, including rights of passage, necessary for the purpose of maintaining international peace and security.
2. Such agreement or agreements shall govern the numbers and types of forces. their degree of readiness and general location, and the nature of the facilities and assistance to be provided.
3. The agreement or agreements shall be negotiated as soon as possible on the initiative of the Security Council. They shall be concluded between the Security Council and Members or between the Security Council and groups of Members and shall be subject to ratification by the signatory states in accordance with their respective constitutional processes.

Article 44

When the Security Council has decided to use force it shall, before calling upon a Member not represented on it to provide armed forces in fulfillment of the obligations assumed under Article 43, invite that Member, if the Member so desires, to participate in the decisions of the Security Council concerning the employment of contingents of that Member's armed forces.

Article 45

In order to enable the United Nations to take urgent military measures Members shall hold immediately available national air-force contingents for combined international enforcement action. The strength and degree of readiness of these contingents and plans for their combined action shall be determined, within the limits laid down in the special agreement or agreements referred to in Article 43, by the Security Council with the assistance of the Military Staff Committee.

Article 46

Plans for the application of armed force shall be made by the Security Council with the assistance of the Military Staff Committee.

Article 47

1. There shall be established a Military Staff Committee to advise and assist the Security Council on all questions relating to the Security Council's military requirements for the maintenance of international peace and security, the employment and command of forces placed at its disposal, the regulation of armaments, and possible disarmament.
2. The Military Staff Committee shall consist of the Chiefs of Staff of the permanent members of the Security Council or their representatives. Any Member of the United Nations not permanently represented on the Committee shall be invited by the Committee to be associated with it when the efficient discharge of the Committee's responsibilities requires the participation of that Member in its work.
3. The Military Staff Committee shall be responsible under the Security Council for the strategic direction of any armed forces placed at the disposal of the Security Council. Questions relating to the command of such forces shall be worked out subsequently.

4. The Military Staff Committee, with the authorization of the Security Council and after consultation with appropriate regional agencies, may establish regional subcommittees.

Article 48

1. The action required to carry out the decisions of the Security Council for the maintenance of international peace and security shall be taken by all the Members of the United Nations or by some of them, as the Security Council may determine.
2. Such decisions shall be carried out by the Members of the United Nations directly and through their action in the appropriate international agencies of which they are members.

Article 49

The Members of the United Nations shall join in affording mutual assistance in carrying out the measures decided upon by the Security Council.

Article 50

If preventive or enforcement measures against any state are taken by the Security Council, any other state, whether a Member of the United Nations or not, which finds itself confronted with special economic problems arising from the carrying out of those measures shall have the right to consult the Security Council with regard to a solution of those problems.

Article 51

Nothing in the present Charter shall impair the inherent right of individual or collective self-defense if an armed attack occurs against a Member of the United Nations, until the Security Council has taken measures necessary to maintain international peace and security. Measures taken by Members in the exercise of this right of self-defense shall be immediately reported to the Security Council and shall not in any way affect the authority and responsibility of the Security Council under the present Charter to take at any time such action as it deems necessary in order to maintain or restore international peace and security.

CHAPTER VIII   REGIONAL ARRANGEMENTS

Article 52

1. Nothing in the present Charter precludes the existence of regional arrangements or agencies for dealing with such matters relating to the maintenance of international peace and security as are appropriate for regional action, provided that such arrangements or agencies and their activities are consistent with the Purposes and Principles of the United Nations.
2. The Members of the United Nations entering into such arrangements or constituting such agencies shall make every effort to achieve pacific settlement of local disputes through such regional arrangements or by such regional agencies before referring them to the Security Council.
3. The Security Council shall encourage the development of pacific settlement of local disputes through such regional arrangements or by such regional agencies either on the initiative of the states concerned or by reference from the Security Council.
4. This Article in no way impairs the application of Articles 34 and 35.

Article 53

1. The Security Council shall, where appropriate, utilize such regional arrangements or agencies for enforcement action under its authority. But no enforcement action shall be taken under regional arrangements or by regional agencies without the authorization of the Security Council, with the exception of measures against any enemy state, as defined in paragraph 2 of this Article, provided for pursuant to Article 107 or in regional arrangements directed against renewal of aggressive policy on the part of any such state, until such time as the Organization may, on request of the Governments concerned, be charged with the responsibility for preventing further aggression by such a state.

2. The term enemy state as used in paragraph 1 of this Article applies to any state which during the Second World War has been an enemy of any signatory of the present Charter.

Article 54

The Security Council shall at all times be kept fully informed of activities undertaken or in contemplation under regional arrangements or by regional agencies for the maintenance of international peace and security.

CHAPTER IX INTERNATIONAL ECONOMIC AND SOCIAL CO-OPERATION

Article 55

With a view to the creation of conditions of stability and well-being which are necessary for peaceful and friendly relations among nations based on respect for the principle of equal rights and self-determination of peoples, the United Nations shall promote:

A. higher standards of living, full employment, and conditions of economic and social progress and development;
B. solutions of international economic, social, health, and related problems; and international cultural and educational co-operation; and
C. universal respect for, and observance of, human rights and fundamental freedoms for all without distinction as to race, sex, language, or religion.

Article 56

All Members pledge themselves to take joint and separate action in cooperation with the Organization for the achievement of the purposes set forth in Article 55.

Article 57

1. The various specialized agencies, established by intergovernmental agreement and having wide international responsibilities, as defined in their basic instruments, in economic, social, cultural, educational, health, and related fields, shall be brought into relationship with the United Nations in accordance with the provisions of Article 63.

2. Such agencies thus brought into relationship with the United Nations are hereinafter referred to as specialized agencies.

Article 58

The Organization shall make recommendations for the coordination of the policies and activities of the specialized agencies.

Article 59

The Organization shall, where appropriate, initiate negotiations among the states concerned for the creation of any new specialized agencies required for the accomplishment of the purposes set forth in Article 55.

Article 60

Responsibility for the discharge of the functions of the Organization set forth in this Chapter shall be vested in the General Assembly and, under the authority of the General Assembly, in the Economic and Social Council, which shall have for this purpose the powers set forth in Chapter X.

CHAPTER X
THE ECONOMIC AND SOCIAL COUNCIL

Composition

Article 61

1. The Economic and Social Council shall consist of fifty-four Members of the United Nations elected by the General Assembly.
2. Subject to the provisions of paragraph 3, eighteen members of the Economic and Social Council shall be elected each year for a term of three years. A retiring member shall be eligible for immediate re-election.
3. At the first election after the increase in the membership of the Economic and Social Council from twenty-seven to fifty-four members, in addition to the members elected in place of the nine members whose term of office expires at the end of that year, twenty-seven additional members shall be elected. Of these twenty-seven additional members, the term of office of nine members so elected shall expire at the end of one year, and of nine other members at the end of two years, in accordance with arrangements made by the General Assembly.
4. Each member of the Economic and Social Council shall have one representative.

Functions and Powers

Article 62

1. The Economic and Social Council may make or initiate studies and reports with respect to international economic, social, cultural, educational, health, and related matters and may make recommendations with respect to any such matters to the General Assembly, to the Members of the United Nations, and to the specialized agencies concerned.
2. It may make recommendations for the purpose of promoting respect for, and observance of, human rights and fundamental freedoms for all.
3. It may prepare draft conventions for submission to the General Assembly, with respect to matters falling within its competence.

4. It may call, in accordance with the rules prescribed by the United Nations, international conferences on matters falling within its competence.

Article 63

1. The Economic and Social Council may enter into agreements with any of the agencies referred to in Article 57, defining the terms on which the agency concerned shall be brought into relationship with the United Nations. Such agreements shall be subject to approval by the General Assembly.
2. It may coordinate the activities of the specialized agencies through consultation with and recommendations to such agencies and through recommendations to the General Assembly and to the Members of the United Nations.

Article 64

1. The Economic and Social Council may take appropriate steps to obtain regular reports from the specialized agencies. It may make arrangements with the Members of the United Nations and with the specialized agencies to obtain reports on the steps taken to give effect to its own recommendations and to recommendations on matters falling within its competence made by the General Assembly.
2. It may communicate its observations on these reports to the General Assembly.

Article 65

The Economic and Social Council may furnish information to the Security Council and shall assist the Security Council upon its request.

Article 66

1. The Economic and Social Council shall perform such functions as fall within its competence in connection with the carrying out of the recommendations of the General Assembly.
2. It may, with the approval of the General Assembly, perform services at the request of Members of the United Nations and at the request of specialized agencies.
3. It shall perform such other functions as are specified elsewhere in the present Charter or as may be assigned to it by the General Assembly.

Article 67

1. Each member of the Economic and Social Council shall have one vote.
2. Decisions of the Economic and Social Council shall be made by a majority of the members present and voting.

Procedure
Article 68

The Economic and Social Council shall set up commissions in economic and social fields and for the promotion of human rights, and such other commissions as may be required for the performance of its functions.

Article 69

The Economic and Social Council shall invite any Member of the United Nations to participate, without vote, in its deliberations on any matter of particular concern to that Member.

Article 70

The Economic and Social Council may make arrangements for representatives of the specialized agencies to participate, without vote, in its deliberations and in those of the commissions established by it, and for its representatives to participate in the deliberations of the specialized agencies.

Article 71

The Economic and Social Council may make suitable arrangements for consultation with nongovernmental organizations which are concerned with matters within its competence. Such arrangements may be made with international organizations and, where appropriate, with national organizations after consultation with the Member of the United Nations concerned.

Article 72

1. The Economic and Social Council shall adopt its own rules of procedure, including the method of selecting its President.
2. The Economic and Social Council shall meet as required in accordance with its rules, which shall include provision for the convening of meetings on the request of a majority of its members.

CHAPTER XI
DECLARATION REGARDING NON-SELF-GOVERNING TERRITORIES

Article 73

Members of the United Nations which have or assume responsibilities for the administration of territories whose peoples have not yet attained a full measure of self-government recognize the principle that the interests of the inhabitants of these territories are paramount, and accept as a sacred trust the obligation to promote to the utmost, within the system of international peace and security established by the present Charter, the well-being of the inhabitants of these territories, and, to this end:

A. to ensure, with due respect for the culture of the peoples concerned, their political, economic, social, and educational advancement, their just treatment, and their protection against abuses;
B. to develop self-government, to take due account of the political aspirations of the peoples, and to assist them in the progressive development of their free political institutions, according to the particular circumstances of each territory and its peoples and their varying stages of advancement;
C. to further international peace and security;
D. to promote constructive measures of development, to encourage research, and to cooperate with one another and, when and where appropriate, with specialized interna-

tional bodies with a view to the practical achievement of the social, economic, and scientific purposes set forth in this Article; and

E. to transmit regularly to the Secretary-General for information purposes, subject to such limitation as security and constitutional considerations may require, statistical and other information of a technical nature relating to economic, social, and educational conditions in the territories for which they are respectively responsible other than those territories to which Chapters XII and XIII apply.

Article 74

Members of the United Nations also agree that their policy in respect of the territories to which this Chapter applies, no less than in respect of their metropolitan areas, must be based on the general principle of good-neighborliness, due account being taken of the interests and well-being of the rest of the world, in social, economic, and commercial matters.

CHAPTER XII   INTERNATIONAL TRUSTEESHIP SYSTEM

Article 75

The United Nations shall establish under its authority an international trusteeship system for the administration and supervision of such territories as may be placed thereunder by subsequent individual agreements. These territories are hereinafter referred to as trust territories.

Article 76

The basic objectives of the trusteeship system, in accordance with the Purposes of the United Nations laid down in Article 1 of the present Charter, shall be:

A. to further international peace and security;
B. to promote the political, economic, social, and educational advancement of the inhabitants of the trust territories, and their progressive development towards self-government or independence as may be appropriate to the particular circumstances of each territory and its peoples and the freely expressed wishes of the peoples concerned, and as may be provided by the terms of each trusteeship agreement;
C. to encourage respect for human rights and for fundamental freedoms for all without distinction as to race, sex, language, or religion, and to encourage recognition of the interdependence of the peoples of the world; and
D. to ensure equal treatment in social, economic, and commercial matters for all Members of the United Nations and their nationals and also equal treatment for the latter in the administration of justice without prejudice to the attainment of the foregoing objectives and subject to the provisions of Article 80.

Article 77

1. The trusteeship system shall apply to such territories in the following categories as may be placed thereunder by means of trusteeship agreements:
    A. territories now held under mandate;
    B. territories which may be detached from enemy states as a result of the Second World War, and
    C. territories voluntarily placed under the system by states responsible for their administration.

2. It will be a matter for subsequent agreement as to which territories in the foregoing categories will be brought under the trusteeship system and upon what terms.

Article 78

The trusteeship system shall not apply to territories which have become Members of the United Nations, relationship among which shall be based on respect for the principle of sovereign equality.

Article 79

The terms of trusteeship for each territory to be placed under the trusteeship system, including any alteration or amendment, shall be agreed upon by the states directly concerned, including the mandatory power in the case of territories held under mandate by a Member of the United Nations, and shall be approved as provided for in Articles 83 and 85.

Article 80

1. Except as may be agreed upon in individual trusteeship agreements, made under Articles 77, 79, and 81, placing each territory under the trusteeship system, and until such agreements have been concluded, nothing in this Chapter shall be construed in or of itself to alter in any manner the rights whatsoever of any states or any peoples or the terms of existing international instruments to which Members of the United Nations may respectively be parties.
2. Paragraph 1 of this Article shall not be interpreted as giving grounds for delay or post-ponement of the negotiation and conclusion of agreements for placing mandated and other territories under the trusteeship system as provided for in Article 77.

Article 81

The trusteeship agreement shall in each case include the terms under which the trust territory will be administered and designate the authority which will exercise the administration of the trust territory. Such authority, hereinafter called the administering authority, may be one or more states or the Organization itself.

Article 82

There may be designated, in any trusteeship agreement, a strategic area or areas which may include part or all of the trust territory to which the agreement applies, without prejudice to any special agreement or agreements made under Article 43.

Article 83

1. All functions of the United Nations relating to strategic areas, including the approval of the terms of the trusteeship agreements and of their alteration or amendment, shall be exercised by the Security Council.
2. The basic objectives set forth in Article 76 shall be applicable to the people of each strategic area.
3. The Security Council shall, subject to the provisions of the trusteeship agreements and without prejudice to security considerations, avail itself of the assistance of the Trusteeship Council to perform those functions of the United Nations under the trusteeship system relating to political. economic, social, and educational matters in the strategic areas.

Article 84

It shall be the duty of the administering authority to ensure that the trust territory shall play its part in the maintenance of international peace and security. To this end the administering authority may make use of volunteer forces, facilities, and assistance from the trust territory in carrying out the obligations towards the Security Council undertaken in this regard by the administering authority, as well as for local defense and the maintenance of law and order within the trust territory.

Article 85

1. The functions of the United Nations with regard to trusteeship agreements for all areas not designated as strategic, including the approval of the terms of the trusteeship agreements and of their alteration or amendment, shall be exercised by the General Assembly.
2. The Trusteeship Council, operating under the authority of the General Assembly, shall assist the General Assembly in carrying out these functions.

CHAPTER XIII   THE TRUSTEESHIP COUNCIL

Composition

Article 86

1. The Trusteeship Council shall consist of the following Members of the United Nations:
   A. those Members administering trust territories;
   B. such of those Members mentioned by name in Article 23 as are not administering trust territories; and
   C. as many other Members elected for three-year terms by the General Assembly as may be necessary to ensure that the total number of members of the Trusteeship Council is equally divided between those Members of the United Nations which administer trust territories and those which do not.
2. Each member of the Trusteeship Council shall designate one specially qualified person to represent it therein.

Functions and Powers

Article 87

The General Assembly and, under its authority, the Trusteeship Council, in carrying out their functions, may:

A. consider reports submitted by the administering authority;
B. accept petitions and examine them in consultation with the administering authority;
C. provide for periodic visits to the respective trust territories at times agreed upon with the administering authority; and
D. take these and other actions in conformity with the terms of the trusteeship agreements.

Article 88

The Trusteeship Council shall formulate a questionnaire on the political, economic, social, and educational advancement of the inhabitants of each trust territory, and the administering authority for each trust territory within the competence of the General Assembly shall make an annual report to the General Assembly upon the basis of such questionnaire.

Voting
Article 89

1. Each member of the Trusteeship Council shall have one vote.
2. Decisions of the Trusteeship Council shall be made by a majority of the members present and voting.

Procedure
Article 90

1. The Trusteeship Council shall adopt its own rules of procedure, including the method of selecting its President.
2. The Trusteeship Council shall meet as required in accordance with its rules, which shall include provision for the convening of meetings on the request of a majority of its members.

Article 91

The Trusteeship Council shall, when appropriate, avail itself of the assistance of the Economic and Social Council and of the specialized agencies in regard to matters with which they are respectively concerned.

CHAPTER XIV   THE INTERNATIONAL COURT OF JUSTICE

Article 92

The International Court of Justice shall be the principal judicial organ of the United Nations. It shall function in accordance with the annexed Statute which is based upon the Statute of the Permanent Court of International Justice and forms an integral part of the present Charter.

Article 93

1. All Members of the United Nations are ipso facto parties to the Statute of the International Court of Justice.
2. A state which is not a Member of the United Nations may become a party to the Statute of the International Court of Justice on conditions to be determined in each case by the General Assembly upon the recommendation of the Security Council.

Article 94

1. Each Member of the United Nations undertakes to comply with the decision of the International Court of Justice in any case to which it is a party.
2. If any party to a case fails to perform the obligations incumbent upon it under a judgment rendered by the Court, the other party may have recourse to the Security Council, which may, if it deems necessary, make recommendations or decide upon measures to be taken to give effect to the judgment.

Article 95

Nothing in the present Charter shall prevent Members of the United Nations from entrusting the solution of their differences to other tribunals by virtue of agreements already in existence or which may be concluded in the future.

Article 96

1. The General Assembly or the Security Council may request the International Court of Justice to give an advisory opinion on any legal question.
2. Other organs of the United Nations and specialized agencies, which may at any time be so authorized by the General Assembly, may also request advisory opinions of the Court on legal questions arising within the scope of their activities.

CHAPTER XV   THE SECRETARIAT

Article 97

The Secretariat shall comprise a Secretary-General and such staff as the Organization may require. The Secretary-General shall be appointed by the General Assembly upon the recommendation of the Security Council. He shall be the chief administrative officer of the Organization.

Article 98

The Secretary-General shall act in that capacity in all meetings of the General Assembly, of the Security Council, of the Economic and Social Council, and of the Trusteeship Council, and shall perform such other functions as are entrusted to him by these organs. The Secretary-General shall make an annual report to the General Assembly on the work of the Organization.

Article 99

The Secretary-General may bring to the attention of the Security Council any matter which in his opinion may threaten the maintenance of international peace and security.

Article 100

1. In the performance of their duties the Secretary-General and the staff shall not seek or receive instructions from any government or from any other authority external to the Organization. They shall refrain from any action which might reflect on their position as international officials responsible only to the Organization.
2. Each Member of the United Nations undertakes to respect the exclusively international character of the responsibilities of the Secretary-General and the staff and not to seek to influence them in the discharge of their responsibilities.

Article 101

1. The staff shall be appointed by the Secretary-General under regulations established by the General Assembly.
2. Appropriate staffs shall be permanently assigned to the Economic and Social Council, the Trusteeship Council, and, as required, to other organs of the United Nations. These staffs shall form a part of the Secretariat.

3. The paramount consideration in the employment of the staff and in the determination of the conditions of service shall be the necessity of securing the highest standards of efficiency, competence, and integrity. Due regard shall be paid to the importance of recruiting the staff on as wide a geographical basis as possible.

CHAPTER XVI   MISCELLANEOUS PROVISIONS

Article 102

1. Every treaty and every international agreement entered into by any Member of the United Nations after the present Charter comes into force shall as soon as possible be registered with the Secretariat and published by it.
2. No party to any such treaty or international agreement which has not been registered in accordance with the provisions of paragraph I of this Article may invoke that treaty or agreement before any organ of the United Nations.

Article 103

In the event of a conflict between the obligations of the Members of the United Nations under the present Charter and their obligations under any other international agreement, their obligations under the present Charter shall prevail.

Article 104

The Organization shall enjoy in the territory of each of its Members such legal capacity as may be necessary for the exercise of its functions and the fulfillment of its purposes.

Article 105

1. The Organization shall enjoy in the territory of each of its Members such privileges and immunities as are necessary for the fulfillment of its purposes.
2. Representatives of the Members of the United Nations and officials of the Organization shall similarly enjoy such privileges and immunities as are necessary for the independent exercise of their functions in connection with the Organization.
3. The General Assembly may make recommendations with a view to determining the details of the application of paragraphs 1 and 2 of this Article or may propose conventions to the Members of the United Nations for this purpose.

CHAPTER XVII   TRANSITIONAL SECURITY ARRANGEMENTS

Article 106

Pending the coming into force of such special agreements referred to in Article 43 as in the opinion of the Security Council enable it to begin the exercise of its responsibilities under Article 42, the parties to the Four-Nation Declaration, signed at Moscow October 30, 1943, and France, shall, in accordance with the provisions of paragraph 5 of that Declaration, consult with one another and as occasion requires with other Members of the United Nations with a view to such joint action on behalf of the Organization as may be necessary for the purpose of maintaining international peace and security.

Article 107

Nothing in the present Charter shall invalidate or preclude action, in relation to any state which during the Second World War has been an enemy of any signatory to the present Charter, taken or authorized as a result of that war by the Governments having responsibility for such action.

CHAPTER XVIII   AMENDMENTS

Article 108

Amendments to the present Charter shall come into force for all Members of the United Nations when they have been adopted by a vote of two thirds of the members of the General Assembly and ratified in accordance with their respective constitutional processes by two thirds of the Members of the United Nations, including all the permanent members of the Security Council.

Article 109

1. A General Conference of the Members of the United Nations for the purpose of reviewing the present Charter may be held at a date and place to be fixed by a two-thirds vote of the members of the General Assembly and by a vote of any seven members of the Security Council. Each Member of the United Nations shall have one vote in the conference.
2. Any alteration of the present Charter recommended by a two-thirds vote of the conference shall take effect when ratified in accordance with their respective constitutional processes by two thirds of the Members of the United Nations including all the permanent members of the Security Council.
3. If such a conference has not been held before the tenth annual session of the General Assembly following the coming into force of the present Charter, the proposal to call such a conference shall be placed on the agenda of that session of the General Assembly, and the conference shall be held if so decided by a majority vote of the members of the General Assembly and by a vote of any seven members of the Security Council.

CHAPTER XIX   RATIFICATION AND SIGNATURE

Article 110

1. The present Charter shall be ratified by the signatory states in accordance with their respective constitutional processes.
2. The ratifications shall be deposited with the Government of the United States of America, which shall notify all the signatory states of each deposit as well as the Secretary-General of the Organization when he has been appointed.
3. The present Charter shall come into force upon the deposit of ratifications by the Republic of China, France, the Union of Soviet Socialist Republics, the United Kingdom of Great Britain and Northern Ireland, and the United States of America, and by a majority of the other signatory states. A protocol of the ratifications deposited shall thereupon be drawn up by the Government of the United States of America which shall communicate copies thereof to all the signatory states.

4. The states signatory to the present Charter which ratify it after it has come into force will become original Members of the United Nations on the date of the deposit of their respective ratifications.

Article 111

The present Charter, of which the Chinese, French, Russian, English, and Spanish texts are equally authentic, shall remain deposited in the archives of the Government of the United States of America. Duly certified copies thereof shall be transmitted by that Government to the Governments of the other signatory states.

IN FAITH WHEREOF the representatives of the Governments of the United Nations have signed the present Charter.

DONE at the city of San Francisco the twenty-sixth day of June, one thousand nine hundred and forty-five.

Index

About the Book and Authors

Well-covered debates on Iraq in the Security Council. Resolutions on terrorism. New peace-keeping in the Congo. Gulf War coalition-building. Humanitarian intervention in Somalia, Kosovo, and East Timor. War-crimes tribunals in the former Yugoslavia and Rwanda. International Criminal Court. A Nobel Peace Prize for the Secretary-General and the world organization. Development debates in Beijing, Cairo, and beyond. Environmental regime-building in and after Rio. New attention to women in development. After decades of neglect—and at times ridicule—the United Nations is back, pressing a multilateral agenda in the wake of a new unilateral moment, which is remarkably akin to the bipolar "bad old days" of the Cold War.

In this nicely thematic and synthetic text, the authors bring to life the alphabet soup of the United Nations, moving from its historical foundations to its day-to-day expanding role in an as-yet-unconsolidated new world order. Students of all levels will learn what the UN is, how it operates, and what its relationships are with the universe of external actors and institutions, from sovereign states to the plethora of nongovernmental and intergovernmental organizations now playing important roles in world politics.

The authors, all of whom have practical as well as academic experience with the UN, show how it has exerted operational and normative influence on issues in three key areas—security, human rights, and sustainable development—even as they make recommendations for improved UN performance in the future.

Well documented and well illustrated, this substantially revised and updated edition includes the UN Charter and organizational schema, extensive suggested readings through expanded reference notes, and photos of UN activities. *The United Nations and Changing World Politics* is essential to a comprehensive and contemporary understanding of the world's leading intergovernmental organization—one that, in the words of Dag Hammarskjöld, may not get us to heaven but could save us from hell.

Thomas G. Weiss is Presidential Professor and Director of the Ralph Bunche Institute for International Studies at The Graduate Center of The City University of New York, where he is co-director of the UN Intellectual History Project and one of the editors of the journal *Global Governance*. Previously, he was research professor and director of the Global Security Program at Brown University's Watson Institute for International Studies. He has also held a number of UN posts (at UNCTAD, the UN Commission for Namibia, UNITAR, and ILO) and served as executive director of both the International Peace Academy and the Academic Council on the United Nations System. He has written or edited some thirty books about international organization related to North-South relations, peacekeeping, economic and social development, and humanitarian action.

David P. Forsythe is University Professor and Charles J. Mach Distinguished Professor of Political Science at the University of Nebraska–Lincoln. His research interests include international law, organization, and human rights. His research in those areas led to the 2003 Quincy

Wright Distinguished Scholar Award given by the Midwest Section of the International Studies Association. He is the author or editor of numerous publications including recently *Human Rights and Diversity* (with Patrice C. McMahon), *Human Rights in International Relations, Human Rights and Comparative Foreign Policy,* and *The US and Human Rights*. A former consultant to the International Red Cross and Red Crescent movement, he is now a consultant to the Office of the United Nations High Commissioner for Refugees.

Roger A. Coate is a professor of international organization at the University of South Carolina and has taught at Arizona State University. He has worked in the UN Centre for Human Rights, as a consultant to the U.S. National Commission for UNESCO and the Bureau of International Organization Affairs of the U.S. Department of State, as a member of the HABITAT II Secretary-General's Advisory Panel on Housing Rights, and as head of the International Organization Section of the International Studies Association. His most recent books include *International Cooperation in Response to AIDS* (with Leon Gordenker, Christer Jönsson, and Peter Söderholm) and *United States Policy and the Future of the United Nations*. He was founding coeditor of the journal *Global Governance: A Review of Multilateralism and International Organizations*. He currently directs a large transnational collaborative research and professional development program in partnership with the Executive Office of the UN Secretary-General and the United National University.